A HISTORY OF
FUNDAMENTALISM
IN AMERICA

A HISTORY OF

BOB JONES UNIVERSITY PRESS • UNUSUAL PUBLICATIONS

FUNDAMENTALISM
IN AMERICA

By George W. Dollar

Professor of Church History
Bob Jones University

 GREENVILLE, SOUTH CAROLINA 29614

A History of Fundamentalism in America
by George W. Dollar

© 1973 Bob Jones University Press,
Greenville, South Carolina

Printed in the United States of America

To
Dorothy Lee, Marcia Karen, and George William, Jr.,
my family in the Lord

FOREWORD

No responsible and comprehensive history of Fundamentalism has hitherto appeared, although the subject has been discussed by Liberals and secular writers, often superficially and, many times, with abuse or ridicule. Few historical facts about the movement have been made available to the general public. It is high time, therefore, that the history of this very important religious movement should appear.

Dr. George W. Dollar is respected in Christian circles and regarded with some trepidation in various liberal ones as an outspoken defender of the Faith, a distinguished theologian, and a knowledgeable authority in the field of church history. The preparation that went into this study consisted not only of a historian's wide and scholarly research but also of a personal knowledge of the movement itself and a personal acquaintance with many of the leaders of the movement over the last thirty years. Though he might differ with some of the conclusions and evaluations of Dr. Dollar, no critic can honestly question his presentation of the facts; and all sincere and thorough students of American religious history will welcome this volume as a valuable aid and source for further study.

The author draws definite lines of separation between fundamentalism as a Biblical, theological position and Fundamentalism as an organized movement. Going even further, he differentiates between Biblical orthodoxy and Fundamentalism, pointing out that the former gives assent to the infallibility of the Scripture while the latter is armed and active in the defense of Scriptural Truth; and

Dr. Dollar incorporates this principle into his definition of Fundamentalism and Fundamentalists.

As a young man of nineteen, when a graduate student in history at the University of Pittsburgh, I traveled one summer weekend to Columbus, Ohio, to address the World's Christian Fundamentals Association when it was headed by Dr. Paul Rood. Although I had been brought up by a father who was active in the organization and himself a strong and outspoken foe of theological liberalism and infidelity in all of its guises, this was my own first contact with organized Fundamentalism. At that time I was writing a graduate thesis on the history of the professional evangelist in America during the period between the end of the Civil War and the First World War, and I was struck with the strong tie-ins between Scriptural evangelism as practiced by the great late-nineteenth and early-twentieth-century evangelists and the Fundamentalist cause. My own life has been given to the defense of the Scriptures and to a strong Fundamentalist stand. As an institution, Bob Jones University has never swerved from such a course. I am especially happy, therefore, that this first comprehensive history of American Fundamentalism should have been written by a professor of the Bob Jones University School of Religion and published by its press.

BOB JONES

PREFACE

Of the issues that have unsettled American Christianity one has provoked an especially vitriolic criticism. This is the issue posed by the convictions and contentions known collectively as Fundamentalism. As a movement it is distinctly American, raising standards and affirming dogmas that oppose the drift of American Christianity. Whereas other countries have seen a sporadic appearance of outstanding individuals of Fundamental convictions, only the United States has knows a *movement* so distinct and so dynamic as to command the attention of critics and raise a formidable protest against the prevailing decline and decay.

In Colonial Christianity, a virile orthodoxy, grounded in Reformation tenets, appeared. Whether Congregational, Presbyterian, or Anglican, each group claimed that its creed and organization were of Reformation descent. Little attack on the unique character of the Word of God appeared, and the little that did appear within churches had small influence on the masses of Christians. The century following the Declaration of Independence saw the rise of many types of dissent from the forms and truths of the established church. Among the dissenting groups were the Unitarians, the Universalists, the followers of New England theology, the frontier revivalists with their emphasis on emotional experience, and various new groups such as Christians and Disciples. But the major denominations—the Baptists, Methodists, Presbyterians, Congregationalists, and Anglicans—maintained an orthodox stance. It is true that in the early part of the century Unitarianism and Transcendentalism attracted some notice, but both remained small and affected only Congregationalism to any extent. At the time of the Civil War, American Christianity was still orthodox and traditional in belief and practice.

The course of American Christianity in the century since the Civil War, however, has been a different story. No large denomination has escaped the ravages of Liberalism and radicalism. Each has embraced rationalism, the social gospel, and Neo-Orthodoxy. New movements have appeared and continue to appear, offering new ways to adapt Christian ideas and ideals to the changing times. No period of American Christianity has seen so much disruption and decay. It has been in the midst of this vast wilderness of departures from everything Christian that Fundamentalism has arisen and grown, lifting up its voice against all forms of apostasy. It has undergone merciless attacks from all sides but, amazingly, has managed to survive.

No comprehensive history of Fundamentalism has been available to students of the movement, although accounts of particular periods or of special aspects of Fundamentalism have appeared. Stewart Cole's *History of Fundamentalism* is weak in factual material and gives little more than a one-sided criticism of the movement. Norman Furniss thoroughly researched his history of *The Fundamentalist-Modernist Controversy in the Northern Baptist Convention, 1918 to 1932,* and his study is still a valuable aid to an understanding of the period. Edwin H. Rian, in *The Presbyterian Conflict,* provided an objective study of the titanic struggle of the Princeton scholars to preserve Orthodoxy as Northern Presbyterianism drifted shamefully into the shoals of liberal thought. Louis Gaspar is concerned with Fundamentalist organizations since 1930 in *The Fundamentalist Movement.* A recent study by Ernest Sandeen, *The Origins of Fundamentalism,* is a fair and factual study of the movement from 1870 to 1920, and Sandeen provides many helpful insights. None of these writers except Sandeen include the first period of Fundamentalism, which spanned the last quarter of the last century. Furthermore, neither Sandeen nor any other writer has credited the preaching ministries of those who erected great centers of Bible preaching and inspired many young men to preach. These were the architects of Fundamentalism.

To provide a complete history of this movement is difficult. Since American Fundamentalism has been ruggedly individualistic, biographical details are necessary to a complete understanding of the movement; but few men have had an interest in writing their histories or seeing them in print. Another problem is how to balance the strong with the weak points of the heroes of Fundamentalism so as to be fair to the men and to the truth at the same time. Finally, much of American Fundamentalism has been a series of unconnected islands of protest, evangelistic effort, and educational adventures, very often without regard for systematic procedure and established standards. Nevertheless, it has been the conviction of the author that the attempt ought to be made. Although the discovery of new and important materials will make revisions necessary for years to come, it is apparent that the main structure of American Fundamentalism is before us now. Moreover, dangerous currents swirl around Fundamentalism in these days, and it is important for those who call themselves Fundamentalists to be informed.

Many friends and associates have contributed long hours of their time to the work of this book. Assisting with the preparation of the manuscript were Mrs. Edna Boschen, Richard Horner, and Dale Stanley. The Glossary was prepared by Elmer Jantz. Many hundreds of people have cooperated in gathering the information for the Biographical Index, and to them, young readers who desire to know their fathers in the Fundamentalist faith owe a great debt. To Bob Jones, Jr., a special word of appreciation is due. His close observation of Fundamentalism for four decades has borne fruit in many constructive suggestions, and several parts of the work reflect his precise and accurate judgments.

Finally, a debt must be acknowledged to the many students, pastors, and Christian friends whose encouragement has enabled the author to pursue a difficult work to the finish. The book is offered with the hope that students of American church history will honestly face the facts of Fundamentalism before engaging in caricature and rejection. It is the firm conviction of the author that the God of the Bible has been the God of American Fundamentalism, whatever its failings and its faults. May He enlighten all Christians to the great and lasting contributions of Fundamentalism, and by His grace may Fundamentalism and Fundamentalists increase.

Greenville, South Carolina   George W. Dollar

CONTENTS

Historic Fundamentalism is the literal exposition of all the affirmations and attitudes of the Bible and the militant exposure of all non-Biblical affirmations and attitudes.

INTRODUCTION

The War Between the States was over; weary and wounded soldiers of both sides returned to shattered homes and farms. Their heroism has been amply recorded by historians, and none would deny their valor. Respect for high and noble principles had brought about the bloodiest civil strife on the North American continent. Decades would ensue before wounds would heal, prejudices be overcome, and both sections be reunited, and before the American Ship of State would once again sail proudly and smoothly.

But another war broke out on the heels of the Civil War, the War against the Word, the Battle over the Book. This new war was destined to do more damage, wreck more churches, erode more theological centers, and confuse more people than any other struggle in our history. Traditionally, religious institutions in general had respected and revered the Bible with an attitude akin to veneration. Its pages had been the object of national obedience and study. In the last quarter of the nineteenth century, a massive attack was raised against the Bible and against its time-honored place as the verbally inspired and absolutely authoritative Word of God. Slowly but surely, that veneration was crumbling as scholars, teachers, denominational leaders, and educators within and without the Christian body joined to reject or redefine the historic truths of Christianity. It was a war without a formal declaration of hostilities, without the marching of armies and the firing of guns; but it was more deadly than military warfare, for·it swept away the spiritual foundations of our churches, our nation, and our heritage. In their place has come a new set of values, more scientific than Scriptural, more man-centered than God-centered, more accommodating to the culture and political climate than the sound doctrine demanded by the Apostle Paul when he wrote Timothy that the time would come when they would not endure sound doctrine (II Tim. 4:3).

It was in the midst of a widespread turning away from the faith of our fathers that a valiant few arose to defend the complete trustworthiness of the Scriptures; without regard for personal costs they alerted their disciples to the perils of the times and sounded bugle calls to join the battle to preserve the faith once and for all delivered to the saints. These were the pioneer Fundamentalists, and like the early Christians at Antioch, they and their cause existed for a considerable time before the name Fundamentalist was applied. So complete was the attack of the enemies of the Bible—or, as they preferred to be known, the liberal scholars of the times—that according to the conclusions of a careful student of this period, the faith that had dominated the nation for a century and a half perished from the earth in one short night.[1] Orthodoxy collapsed in the last quarter of the nineteenth century. Most of the religious strife, divisions, and defections since that time can be traced to the mighty forces of Liberalism released during that period. The tracing of these lines of liberal thought and a fair and factual study of the brave men and forces that opposed them and raised new movements and churches has been presented in only a few classrooms by a small number of teachers. Indeed, this was a century of controversy, confusion, charges, and countercharges in the vast areas of Liberalism, Orthodoxy, and Fundamentalism. To analyze and assess it is the purpose of this study; and I believe the laws of scholarship and Scriptural loyalties demand a look at the facts.

Liberalism deserves a Scriptural and historical study, and the latter has been done by a few in the liberal camp. Fundamentalism is even more deserving of a factual and Scriptural analysis in order that its history can be known, its claims examined, its leaders given proper recognition, and its results assessed. This analysis has not previously been done, although a few studies of some aspects have appeared, such as the works of Furniss, Cole, Gasper, and Sandeen.[2] These have suffered in that they confined themselves to small sections of the movement. A definitive history has been in demand but has not been supplied. Several reasons for this are apparent. Fundamentalists have included few first-rate historians, and therefore, the number of men capable of the research and writing has been, and still is, surprisingly small. It is hoped that this group will

---

[1]Frank H. Foster, *A Genetic History of New England Theology* (New York: Russell and Russell, 1963). All too few are acquainted with this worthwhile examination of the general collapse of Christian beliefs.

[2]Norman Furniss, *The Fundamentalist-Modernist Controversy* (New Haven: Yale University Press, 1954). Stewart Cole, *A History of Fundamentalism* (New York: R. R. Smith, 1931). Louis Gasper, *The Fundamentalist Movement* (Paris: Mouton, 1963). Ernest Sandeen, *The Roots of Fundamentalism* (Chicago: Univ. of Chicago Press, 1970).

increase. Further, few Fundamentalists have been convinced that their history was worth knowing or telling. Each generation has had its own battles and problems, and this has seemed to demand too much effort. After all, what could the methods and men in past battles contribute to present-day issues and conflicts? Again, the general downgrading of quality education and institutions by so many Fundamentalists has led many to believe, if not to state, that one's general ignorance of all but the Bible is a sure guarantee of spirituality. It is superfluous to examine this mood, its influence has been so obvious. Moreover, the very institutions generated by this Biblical movement have failed to value their roots and heritage, and a new generation has arisen that, seemingly, is indifferent to its Fundamentalist heritage. So widespread is this attitude that the future frightens those who know this history and fear that its best aspects will die for want of support. Other factors contribute to this depressing spectacle. Perhaps the Lord will be pleased to use this account to arouse a sleeping Fundamentalism. It needs to be aroused to its present dangers and alerted to its heritage. Thus aroused, men would strive to safeguard the sound affirmations and attitudes of the Bible in order that these might be passed on to future generations.

An Introduction ought to set the stage for the study to follow. I would follow this dictum by asserting that American Fundamentalism—and there is no other as an organized and continuing movement in any other country—has had its fathers, its faith, its fights, its failures, and its founding of institutions and fellowships. It challenges us to analyze its century of existence. The author admits to a continuing fascination with this movement, one with which he is identified by convictions as abiding as life itself. He has found in the fathers and the faith of Fundamentalism an example of unmatched fidelity to all that the Bible teaches and a willingness to pay dearly for that loyalty. Furthermore, the author sees the movement in weakened and sickly form at present and in jeopardy from the inroads of a serious cancer. This has caused him again and again to ask the hymn writer's question, "Who follows in their train?"

The last century has been one of open assault by many against the affirmations, authority, and attitudes of the Bible. In a time of war there are three possible alternatives: retreat in defeat, surrender, or fight because essential truths and precious life-giving ideas are at stake. In England, Liberalism was met by the reaffirmation of major evangelical positions, by the Spurgeonic position of more open exposure of Liberalism (the so-called downgrade controversy), and with the vibrant and vital preaching of the Word. One result of this reaction in England was the rise of the Keswick movement in the

1870's, which has spread to America and is on the increase today under the labels of "Deeper Life" or "Victorious Life." But one fact ought to be kept in mind—the English reaction differed essentially from the American in that the British and Scottish evangelicals said little about ecclesiology and eschatology. Very little attention was ever given to future things. American reaction centered in prophecy—its literal acceptance and its prominent place in preaching and teaching. In this major area American Fundamentalists have created their own distinct image and formulated a very different answer to Liberalism. American Fundamentalists have never felt that they had a special obligation to continue the truths and the traditions of the Reformation, but have put foremost their purpose to restore every truth and discipline of the apostles. In this they agreed with a statement attributed to the great Spurgeon that he liked the fathers (Church Fathers) but he loved the grandfathers (apostles).

Secular students of this period, such as Henry Steele Commager, insisted that the 1890's constituted a watershed in American history with regard to the influence of the Christian faith on the nation. To put the case more bluntly, since the 1890's America has been less conservative, less orthodox, and less Fundamental than ever in its history. Pastors, students, teachers, and Christian workers have virtually ignored this. Citing a few blessings, these have sought to avoid the inevitable conclusion that our nation is in a godless era. One possible conclusion is that the true Christian witness is becoming less and less effective, and this decline will continue until the Lord returns and takes His own to be with Him. Conversions and "revivals" do rescue a few, but the masses remain untouched and degeneracy increases.

The deterioration of the true Christian witness, which began during the last quarter of the nineteenth century, is accelerating rapidly. Fundamentalists for their part are fighting this alarming trend. This analysis will examine in detail both camps in their continuing battle.

REACTION AND RESTORATION
1875-1900

1
The Attack on the Bible

Humanly speaking, Orthodoxy and Fundamentalism might have survived the nineteenth century with very little weakening had it not been for one major attack. This was the attack of new thought and Liberal attitudes, which was a part of a many-sided declaration of war on the Word. Many sources of opposition to well-established beliefs and spiritual disciplines were then evident, which formed such an attack against the Word of God that Orthodoxy collapsed and Fundamentalism, as it emerged, became a minority movement. American Christianity was so vitiated that it would never again dominate the American thinking.

Several able thinkers and writers provided the intellectual stimulus to an academic renaissance in the last half of the nineteenth century. Among them were Immanuel Kant, G. F. Hegel, F. C. Baur, Albrecht Ritschl, and G. F. Schleiermacher. All five catapulted German philosophy and theology onto the American scene, philosophizing its theology, providing sharp tools to destroy the historic faith, and bringing into slavery the minds of the intelligentsia and the prospective leaders of the denominations.

In the system of Immanuel Kant, reason was given supreme place, and it has been central in theological circles ever since. In his book *Religion Within the Bounds of Reason* (1793), he applied the critical rules for general and particular knowledge to the realm of the spiritual. This was a fatal mistake, though one devotedly followed by Liberals. Kant held that duty provided a basic obligation, leading one to a religious faith in God and His forgiveness for our sins; but he did not clearly define sin as did the Apostle Paul in Romans 3. To need grace meant little more to Kant than to need added strength from God. Therefore, what he thought he ought to do was the imperative from God. To him, ethics were nothing more than those moral precepts dictated by conscience; these would show themselves in loyalty to country, army, school, and family, and in obedience to the courts of the land.

To things religious and Christian Kant contributed five things. First of all, he held that a special history of redemption was not needed. There can then be a great indifference to the doctrines of the pre-existence of Christ and the Trinity. Secondly, he maintained that God speaks through the conscience (this in turn pointing to a moral law). Because one would, therefore, not need a church, Kant stayed away from church all his adult life. In this respect he turned away from the example of his mother, who was a Pietist. Again, he saw sin as the conflict between good and bad principles in man. Original sin was denied, and he said that man could resist the inclination to evil. In the fourth place, Christ was held to be a great example, but the historical facts about Him were unimportant. There was no vicarious atonement for sin, and the truly supernatural in Christ was either ignored or downgraded. Last of all, he saw the church as merely a society interested in moral laws.

Hegel (1770-1831), a professor at Berlin, tried to reconcile reason and religion. He identified the human spirit with thinking and God with Absolute Mind. It is the essence of religion to see Absolute Mind in symbols, and the field of philosophy helps by giving the rational formulas for these. Christianity was held to be the highest religion, for in it we have the clearest expression of Absolute Mind in the God-Man, and the deepest thoughts of Christ's self-consciousness. In reality it was a philosophy; and to Hegel, a Christian is primarily a philosopher exploring this consciousness of Christ. One of his disciples was David Strauss (1808-1874), who in 1835 braved the anger of sound orthodox people with his *Life of Jesus*, in which he denied the miracles and pictured Jesus as solely a human being; in addition, he raised questions as to how much truth there was in the Gospels, claiming they contained many legends that grew out of the strong enthusiasm of Jesus' followers. He allowed that some of the God-consciousness is to be found in Christ but insisted that much of it is distributed over all humanity.

F. C. Baur (1792-1862) at Tübingen followed Hegel much of the way with a special interest in the history of dogma and the early centuries of church history. He had a great mind, as far as natural capacities are concerned, and his learning became a model in his day both in breadth and depth. He saw Christianity as one chapter in the history of the progress of revelation. This basic premise, he maintained, had been covered and obscured by the claims of the supernatural, myth, and irrational dogmas. He liked Peter, who saw and taught the Messianic ideas of the Old Testament as fulfilled in Jesus, but he found Paul to have a new message altogether. He thus created a false contest and conflict between Peter and Paul. In addition, Baur claimed that the Gospels were written after the first century, and seriously questioned their reliability.

Another great figure in German Liberalism was Frederick Schleiermacher (1768-1834), who came from a Reformed background. He studied under Kant and at Halle University, and held a lifelong interest in and fascination with philosophy. In 1799 he published his *Discourses on Religion,* in which he defined religion not as truth or doctrine but as an intuition or feeling for the universe, often defined as an awareness of God. One's religion is "to have life and know life in immediate feeling, only as such an existence in the Infinite and Eternal."[1] Doctrines and creeds are valuable only as they express these feelings or intuitions. He found God in man, nature, and history. In his book *The Christian Faith,* he held that in all religions, one's consciousness of his reliance on the Infinite is basic. Religion shows itself in a dependent feeling or general reverence for the unseen. The Infinite is revealed to the soul in natural events.

Schleiermacher held that all central truths of historic Christianity ought to be reinterpreted to express the deepest roots of Christian experiences. We are Christian to the extent that God impresses us in all our experiences, not as we study and believe the events or dogmas of the life of Christ. We should know the latter only as they are valid expressions of the lives of Christians. Thus the gate is wide open for many an interpretation of everything Christian. So widespread has this become in Liberal thought that Schleiermacher has been commonly named the Father of Modern Theology. (Equally so would be warranted the title of the Hitler of Christian Empiricism and the Kaiser of true German faith.) Few men have done so much harm to the faith of young men anxious to serve in the Christian ministry. Schleiermacher's wicked attacks continue today with many modifications and, sad to say, many disciples.

Also sharing the spotlight of German criticism was Albrecht Ritschl, who taught at Goettingen till his death in 1889. He did his best to eliminate from Christianity its intellectual elements, its emotional parts, and its mysticism. He saw true Christian faith from the standpoint of the will and ethics. Salvation seemed little more than a discovery and dedication to ethics. As for the New Testament books, those closest to the apostles were more reliable and important. The place of Christ was based on the revelation He made

[1] Frederich Schleiermacher, *Speeches on Religion* (New York: Harper, 1958), p. 14.

of divine love but not on any ministry to establish a special relationship between man and God. Trust in God was included, but reconciliation was more of an accord than a deliverance of a terrible sinner from the consequences of his sin. Therefore, man should seek for experiences with Christ and not spend time making assertions about Him. Thus, religion is a day-by-day uprightness in character; salvation is essentially man's deliverance from bondage to nature so that he enjoys dominion over nature.

Ritschl saw the Kingdom of God as the total company of all who act on the inspiration of love. Thus, we have a grand concourse of unsaved men acting according to their own self-established, highest ethical purposes; the Kingdom would be that concourse, and to many Liberals today it is little more. This has become evident in the Social Gospel, which aims to improve or even to save society. It is little more than ordinary socialism with a religious label on it. Ritschl emphasized that God is love, with the concept of holiness set aside and that of judgment completely ignored. Thus, judgment and condemnation of men by God is unthinkable. Liberals have followed this concept and abhor any hint that millions of people will suffer eternally because of their sins.

— Another keen mind that greatly influenced Liberalism was Ernst Troeltsch (1865-1923), truly a philosopher of history, knowing religions as few men have. As a professor at Heidelberg and Berlin, he impressed on his students a basic premise—that the best of the New Testament could be found in other religions and that the study of these gave a deep insight into the Christian faith, thereby creating a science of religions which led to the denial of Christian distinctives. A study of men's desires and aspirations, especially in times of great ecstasy, should be pursued by Christian students. Troeltsch said he found God active in the "world process," and on this false premise he based the main ideas of religion and culture. He accepted Kant's view that religion is "a priori" and followed Hegel and Schleiermacher in finding great relativism in doctrines. Two major premises dominated his thinking: man's freedom to believe and the presence of God in the rational process of all laws. By asserting that religion should use scientific law, he renounced the distinctive tenets of Christianity. God is not sovereign but immanent in the world around us. Scholars should seek to discover the "integral continuity" in that world. Three laws would assist them: criticism, relativity, and analogy. Such religious views would come to the following conclusions:

(1) All religions are inside the development of basic interests.
(2) Religion is that contact with the supersensible.
(3) Christianity is a syncretism, though unique.
(4) Missions should educate, not try to convert.

(5) Evolution is the unfolding of new out of the old.
(6) We cannot know the secret of any religion.
(7) Christ is the symbol for knowing the highest truth.
(8) The future was a Neo-Platonic Nirvana.
(9) Our religion helps us as others help other people. Thus all religions are beneficial.

This able-minded philosopher left no single New Testament truth untouched. To Fundamentalists he was an enemy of the Faith and a thinker who ignored the wisdom of God, though skilled in man's wisdom.

~ Still another source of attack on the Bible was the theory and premises of evolution. The basic views of this false position were forcibly presented by Charles Darwin in 1859 in his *Origin of Species,* which brought sharp discussion and disagreement in scientific circles but a world of upheaval in Christian circles. Darwin argued for organic evolution in biological life with a planned development by natural selection from lower to higher form. The survival of forms of life depended on their responses to environment with this process accounting for new species. Even man was said to have evolved from a lower form of life. This was in open conflict with the Genesis account, and the great many plausible rationalizations which followed could not erase this plain fact. Did man come directly from the hand of God as Genesis 1 states, or did he evolve from an ape or monkey? Some sought to soften the controversy by holding that true science and the Bible could never be at odds. Others sought to up-date their thinking and attitude by propounding a theory of theistic evolution, which meant that God had used the evolutionary process as His means of creation. To thousands of believers in the Bible as the verbally inspired Word of God, this was a vicious, unfounded attack on the divine origin of man as recorded in the first book of the bible. True Christians could not accept this new theory; after all, it was simply a hypothesis, and the Genesis account was the very Word of God. This anti-evolutionary stand by Fundamentalists has continued in spite of the modifications in evolutionary thinking and the passionate efforts of evangelicals to get Moses and Darwin to agree for the sake of a peaceful relationship between science and the Scriptures. Since Darwin's day, scientists have contended that man is millions of years old in his history; this seems logical to them in order to account for the long process of vast changes in the natural world. Liberals were all too anxious to accept the claims of the proponents of evolution and place a religious label on them by seeking to place God in the middle of the process, honoring Him as the Main One in creation and change. Thus began a battle royal over the reliability of the Bible in the areas of science, history, and other disciplines. To Fundamentalists the Bible must be accepted as verbally given by God and trustworthy in all that it says;

to ignore it in any of its statements is to cast critical doubts on its authority and inspiration. The applications of evolutionary ideas to theological education has been devastating. To survey this story is to conclude that most theological education has become non-theological, non-Biblical, and anti-salvation, since without the infallible Word the ministry has been robbed of its message, the churches of their purpose for existence, and the common people their right to hear the truth of God. This theological piracy has been committed in the name of Christianity. Since the advent of the theory of evolution, all religious life has been pictured as an upward and elevating story with spiritual realities and morals on the ascendancy, and therefore, with no future cataclysm or judgment to be contemplated. A grand scheme of man's improvement through resident forces is inevitable; grace as man's hope is certainly a minor thing and the wrath of God on unbelievers too incongruous to bring anything but smiles of incredulity.

We shall not continue the story of German and European criticism as it forged nineteenth-century Liberalism but turn to the American scene to understand how these liberal principles have eroded American sound doctrine and caused a theological collapse and apostasy. Many men were engaged in bringing the principles of European Liberalism to this country, and they will be discussed in succeeding chapters. To three men go the discredit of planting liberal ideas in the soil of American churches: William Rainey Harper, founder of the University of Chicago; William Newton Clarke, professor of theology at Hamilton Institute (now Colgate Rochester Divinity School) with his very influential book *Outline of Christian Theology;* and William Adams Brown of Union Seminary in New York and his textbook *Christian Theology in Outline.* All three men joined in enunciating fifteen principles of theological Liberalism in America, and these principles continued to characterize this movement for a century. We shall list them for the sake of brevity as an introduction to American Liberalism:

(1) We must promote adjustment to new ideas in science, philosophy, economics, and politics.

(2) There must be a tolerance of true liberal type toward any devotion to truth as men find it anywhere.

(3) We must be sympathetic to all views within the religious community and actively engage in pooling all these ideas as valuable and worthwhile.

(4) Christians should be skeptical about reaching ultimate truth in any field and always be mindful of the glory of searching though not finding certain results.

(5) Scholars should put the emphasis on continuity and concern for harmony and not on conflict between Christianity and other religions and between God and men.

(6)   Man deserves to be optimistic concerning his powers, future, and ability to conquer nature and human ills.

(7)   Our emphasis should be on human experiences and not on doctrines such as the Authority of the Bible, Redemption, and Revelation.

(8)   The Person of Christ ought to be accorded great honor, although there have been concepts added to this through the centuries such as His Deity, the two natures of His Person, and His imminent bodily Return.

(9)   A new interest is needed in social reform, and we are to rebuild society into the Kingdom of God.

(10)   God must be taught as immanent in the world because of a basic unity between God and the world. God does not break into this process with miracles and the supernatural, but He has been and always is within the grand order we call Nature.

(11)   The humanity of Jesus must be rediscovered. In our search for the human Jesus we ought to admit that he made mistakes as did his countrymen and, indeed, that he accepted many of their ideas and prejudices.

(12)   True scholarship will repudiate the deity of Christ as taught traditionally in the historic faith and will redefine it as his "consciousness of God," his desire to serve God completely, and his purpose to identify with the purposes of God. We must see him as our brother, example, leader, teacher of ideals, one morally unique among men. An effect of this was to drive a sharp wedge between the Christ of the Gospels and the Christ of the creeds, the Gospel of Jesus and the Gospel of Paul. Many held that we are supposed not to have any beliefs about Jesus but only to obey his teachings.

(13)   New stress should be put on the dignity and divinity of man. No longer should he be thought of as a worm but as a worthy, no more a thing of degradation but one of nobility of character and great potential. Man's personality is of highest value, even as Henry Drummond spoke of the ascent of man. Man is free and able to cooperate with God. His future life was downgraded while life here and now was most important. In essence, eternity was denied.

(14)   The true and basic authority is no longer the Church of the Romanist nor the Bible of the Protestant, but the inward experiences springing from reason and intuition. It was an open revolt against the Scriptures, and so complete that it was openly confessed by such a thinker as R. H. Niebuhr that we have a God without wrath, a man without sin, and a Christ without a Cross.

(15)   There emerged the social gospel. Should the Christian do anything about the open sores of society? Horace Bushnell had stressed the deep and abiding influence of one's environment upon character. Basically, it was contended that sin is essentially social and one should be saved socially, and a salvation would happen only when society is Christianized. The father of the social gospel, Washington Gladden, wrote in 1876 that "now that slavery is out of the way, the questions that concern our free laborers are coming forward . . . intelligent men need to be admonished of their urgency . . . they are in a large sense moral questions, nay they touch the very marrow of that religion of goodwill of which Christ was the founder.

It is plain the the pulpit must have something to say about them."[2] Several hymns to express social salvation arose, such as F. M. North's "Where Cross the Crowded Ways of Life," Gladden's "O Master, Let Me Walk With Thee," and Ernest W. Shurtleff's "Lead On, O King Eternal." It was highly popularized by Charles M. Sheldon's *In His Steps,* which sold over twenty million copies and alerted people within the churches and outside to great social questions and needs.

[2]Washington Gladden, cited in C. H. Hopkıns, *The Rise of the Social Gospel in American Protestantism* (New Haven: Yale Univ. Press, 1940), p. 24.

2
A Leading Liberal and a Fundamentalist Figure

The most influential Liberal in the early period was William Newton Clarke, who taught Christian theology at Colgate in Hamilton, New York, the forerunner of the present Colgate Rochester Divinity School in Rochester, New York. His major book was *An Outline of Christian Theology,* published in 1894 by Charles Scribner's Sons in New York. A well-written volume, it included most of the liberal tenets commonly held during the last century. We turn to it to find the grass-roots thinking of the early Liberals.

Verbal inspiration and the full trustworthiness of the Bible were denied by Clarke. It was his teaching that turned a young man, Harry Fosdick, from his evangelical background to Modernism in its popular form. Clarke wrote that "the Old Testament gives evidence of a gradual discovery of God on the part of man .... it can be best explained by a deliberate, gracious self-revealing on the part of God."[1] The second half of this concept is sound doctrine to all Bible believers, while the first is decidedly man-centered and dangerous. In fact, Clarke contended that "Christianity is not a book but a life-religion and Christ gave us the Bible."[2] His radical thought is clearly seen in his declaration that the Bible did "not bring us the entire revelation of God or even the entire Christian revelation."[3] Where else would we seek it? The revelation would probably be in the vast

[1]William Newton Clarke, *An Outline of Christian Theology* (New York: Scribner's, 1894), p. 10.
[2]Ibid., p. 21.
[3]Ibid., p. 23.

volume called Christian experience, though unwritten. In the Bible itself, "the selection of a collection of sacred books," it was "not done by the direct command or authority of God."[4] Rather it was the "outcome of the religious life that sprang from the divine revelation. .. formed by the religious judgment of believing people."[5] He claimed that "one half of the pages of the Old Testament are of unknown or uncertain scholarship."[6] In Clarke's view, the Bible "itself releases us from the obligation to maintain its complete inerrancy."[7] He stated that the writers of the Bible "never claim accuracy for all its statements."[8] He pointed to the two records of the Sermon on the Mount and said that both could not be accurate, for, observed this Liberal, "Christianity is grounded not in the inspiration of its documents but in the reality of its facts."[9] Fundamentalists have always charged that one without the other is an orphan. Again, the Colgate teacher wrote, "Nor does any theory of verbal inspiration holding that God gave the writers the very words accord with the facts."[10] He wrote, "There are no verbally inspired scriptures and we have no evidence that there ever were any."[11] (In this regard, Fundamentalists still ask what the Son of God possibly could have meant when He stated without reservation in Matthew 4:4 that man should live "by every word that proceedeth out of the mouth of God.") To Clarke, inspiration was "an awakening or creation of thought, quickening of ability ... enlargement of capacity for perception."[12] Furthermore, he defined God as "the Personal Spirit, perfectly good, Who in holy love creates, sustains, and orders all."[13]

Clarke gave the primary emphasis to God's fatherhood, although listing His attributes. He rejected the idea of three Persons in the Trinity and explained this doctrine as three modes of being, stating such to be "God as original and unuttered ... God uttered and going forth ... God in whom the first and second are united;"[14] however, "there are not three personalities but they are separate aspects of one personality."[15] It is noteworthy that from the beginning, American Liberalism has been unitarian in its concept of the Trinity. This was a rash departure from both Orthodoxy and historic American faith.

[4]Ibid., p. 24.
[5]Ibid.
[6]Ibid.
[7]Ibid., p. 35.
[8]Ibid., p. 38.
[9]Ibid.
[10]Ibid., p. 40.
[11]Ibid.
[12]Ibid., p. 41.
[13]Ibid., p. 66.
[14]Ibid., p. 174.
[15]Ibid., p. 175.

⤙Clarke saw man as one who "finds his own mind a counterpart of the Creator's . . . experimentally found to be of kindred nature with God the Spirit";[16] "the natural relation between God and man is essentially that of parent and child."[17] Of the origin of man, he wrote, we must "remand the question of the origin of the world . . . to the appropriate sciences of astronomy and geology."[18] To him it is no longer tenable that the world was created in six days, and he was happy that theology could now agree with science in whatever science says about the world. As to the origin of man, "we remand that to the science of anthropology,"[19] and he knew and admitted that from this source, theology "would receive an evolutionary answer"[20] and "the special creation of man may come to appear improbable."[21] Clarke held that the second chapter of Genesis was "a human tradition, a commonly accepted concept of beginnings," and not "a literal narrative of occurrences."[22]

He redefined sin as a "departure from duty,"[23] claiming basis for this in Romans 2. It could be seen as the "placing of self-will or selfishness above the claims of love and duty or opposition to God's moral government."[24] Such vagueness could elicit only Fundamentalist scorn and utter rejection. Another of Clarke's concepts was that Genesis 3 gave a "true insight regarding the meaning and relations of sin."[25] Its influence on man since then must be seen in the context of a "double flow of good and evil in the common stream of life."[26] But Clarke's position included the idea that there is no "inheriting of guilt before God from the first sinner or from any other ancestor."[27]

That Christ was born of a virgin is allowed by Clarke, who, nevertheless, did not condemn those who accept an ancient tradition that He had a human father. To Clarke, Christ was most conscious of the "fatherhood of God," which He proclaimed, and no student "should fail to study the fatherhood of God in the Sermon on the Mount."[28] Miracles in His life may be evidences of His divine mission but should be seen, primarily, as "works of love." The disregard of His atoning death is obvious in Clarke, a liberal defect

[16]Ibid., p. 192.
[17]Ibid.
[18]Ibid., p. 222.
[19]Ibid., p. 223.
[20]Ibid., p. 224.
[21]Ibid., p. 225.
[22]Ibid.
[23]Ibid., p. 234.
[24]Ibid., p. 237.
[25]Ibid., p. 241.
[26]Ibid., p. 242.
[27]Ibid., p. 244.
[28]Ibid., p. 268.

truly tragic. The resurrection is not dealt with in any detail; Clarke did not believe that it was "a return to bodily life" but rather "a rising from death into glorious spiritual life."[29] The vagueness of this concept inflamed Fundamentalist scholars to charge that the professor had ignored Paul's teaching in I Corinthians 15. Clarke concluded this section of his study by remarking that the "mode of His rising is not vital to Christianity."[30] In I Corinthians 15 Paul makes it central and vital; otherwise, Christian faith and preaching are vain.

In the crucial area of eschatology (future things), Clarke insisted that "God has not given us a map of coming time."[31] When we read the prophecies and predictions of the prophets, we ought to admit that their main object was "instruction and inspiration for the time then present . . . . the event was not always as the prophet had conceived it."[32] Even prophecies of Messiah were claimed to be more ideal than specific, and "no one beforehand could have pictured Jesus as time revealed Him from the materials that prophecy provided."[33] Thus he concluded that the "Bible does not contain the materials for a clear and consistent outline of things to come."[34] Thus both premillennial and postmillennial views were impossible. To Clarke, neither did justice to the whole Bible. He saw the central passage of Revelation 20:1-10 as part of a book of symbols; "every literal thing stands as illustrative of some spiritual reality."[35] This passage "does not promise a period of Christian victory yet to come."[36] The words of the Revelation were intended "for immediate cheer in the midst of trials"; they were "neither intended for exact fulfillment nor capable of receiving it."[37] On this flimsy contention the professor held that there is "no ground for a premillennial or postmillennial advent . . . . the language of future events is language that ought never to have been taken literally."[38] "Even in the Gospels we have language borrowed from the prophets of the Old Testament who applied it to events on the earth, in which, of course, it could not be literally fulfilled."[39] Of such major passages as Daniel 7:13, 27; Matthew 24:29; Isaiah 13:10; and Ezekiel 32:7, he declares, "Upon such symbolic pictures it is impossible to build definite

---

[29]Ibid., p. 273.
[30]Ibid., p. 362.
[31]Ibid., p. 430.
[32]Ibid.
[33]Ibid., p. 431.
[34]Ibid., p. 432.
[35]Ibid., p. 433.
[36]Ibid.
[37]Ibid., p. 434.
[38]Ibid.
[39]Ibid., p. 438.

expectations of future events."[40] Fundamentalists asserted, Biblically, that Christ would come in the clouds of heaven; Clarke counterasserted that "the Biblical usage does not warrant a literal interpretation."[41] A. J. Gordon would often remind the readers of his paper, *The Watchword,* that one must take the Bible literally or liberally. Surely, Clarke and the Liberals lived up to their name and took it liberally, while the Fundamentalists took their stand on literalism.

On the live issue of the return of the Lord, Clarke admitted that "some look for an event that literally corresponds to Christ's predictions of His coming."[42] But he contended that what He meant was His spiritual presence, which was "free from the narrow and carnal character of the Jewish hope."[43] All the predictions of Christ and others in the Bible ought to be "interpreted in the light of current thought of the age . . . for critical knowledge of the literal quality of the ancient prophecies had then no existence."[44] To Clarke, Christ has been King throughout the centuries of church history. The abiding presence of the Holy Spirit fulfills all prophecies of the coming of Christ. This would necessarily mean a process, not an event, and Christ has been coming more and more into the life of the world. The New Jerusalem at the end of the Book of Revelation has for Clarke one significant meaning: it "is the ideal church of Christ in this world."[45] This interpretation led Clarke to conclude that "no visible return of Christ to the earth is to be expected but rather the long and steady advance of his spiritual kingdom."[46] To believe in a single event as climactic would be "Jewish but not Christian."[47] Clarke also gave an altogether new interpretation of the resurrection of the body. He stated that the Pharisees taught a resurrection of the flesh, but "Paul's doctrine was distinctly opposite . . . . that there will be a resurrection of flesh and blood . . . he strenuously denies."[48]

➤ Very prominent in this period of reaction and restoration was Adoniram Judson Gordon of Boston, Massachusetts. Two works have been written on the life of this noble warrior for the Faith—one by his evangelical son, Ernest Gordon, author of the more widely known and used work on the inroads of Modernism, *The Leaven of the Sadducees,* and the other an unpublished doctoral dissertation by a member of the faculty of Dallas Seminary, George G. Houghton.

[40]Ibid., p. 435.
[41]Ibid.
[42]Ibid., p. 437.
[43]Ibid., p. 440.
[44]Ibid., p. 441.
[45]Ibid., p. 444.
[46]Ibid.
[47]Ibid.
[48]Ibid., p. 455.

The first is a brief biographical sketch, whereas the second plots Gordon's place within, and contributions to, American Fundamentalism.

The souls of evangelical Christians were being sorely tried in the last quarter of the nineteenth century. The need for courageous leaders and men of deepest convictions and consecration was monumental. One man who stood in the gap was Gordon. Born in New Hampton, New Hampshire, in 1836 and named after the first American missionary, Adoniram Judson, he was saved at the age of sixteen and joined a local Baptist Church, where his father was a deacon. He was educated at New London Academy in New Hampshire, Brown University, and Newton Theological Institution, from which he graduated in 1863. He began his ministry at the Baptist Church in Jamaica Plain, a suburb of Boston, Massachusetts. In 1869 he began his great work as pastor of Clarendon Street Baptist Church in Boston, where he remained until his death, February 2, 1895.

Gordon was destined of God to live in a period of many changes in American life, particularly in its churches and schools that were dedicated to the Christian faith. The critical affirmations and attitudes soon became a vast menacing danger to everything he believed in. Too many teachers adopted the evolutionary theories as basic truth, even in their presentation of Christian doctrines. Raised up of God and highly trained, Gordon was irrevocably committed to the Word of God and regarded the evolutionary teaching as deadly.

Gordon was not an outstanding theologian but withal a keen thinker. His keenness is abundantly clear in his many books and in his own paper, *The Watchword*, which he edited from its beginning in 1878 until his death. The stated purpose of the paper was to restore the primitive *faith, hope,* and *charity.* He contributed many articles to *The Christian Herald, The Signs of Our Times,* and *The Missionary Review of the World.* His books dealt with music and worship, the person and work of Christ, prophecy (the best known one was *Ecce Venit*), the Person and work of the Holy Spirit, and many others. *How Christ Came to Church* was widely used, but *The Ministry of the Holy Spirit* continues to have an even greater reading and influence.

A thorough-going Biblicist, Gordon contended for the Faith once and for all delivered to the saints. He believed that the Bible was verbally inspired and without error or lack; he tended toward the dictation theory, believing that the very words were specified by the Holy Spirit. Committed to taking the Scriptures literally, he wrote, "We must take the Word of God literally unless there is something in the context explicitly indicating that it was intended to be taken figuratively."[49] To him, literalism was the best ally and friend of sound doctrine.

The drift of men into Liberalism was easily understood by Gordon. He knew that when men "get careless and easygoing in their opinions, they drift into what is called Liberalism."[50] Again, he severely condemned Liberalism for its lack of power to transform sinners. Some men were openly avowing Orthodoxy and yet recommending men of critical works and views; Gordon openly condemned even a respected scholar as Marcus Dods of Edinburgh.

Gordon placed high the ministry of the Holy Spirit in his day, calling our present era "the dispensation of the Holy Spirit,"[51] for He became "embodied in the Church on the Day of Pentecost"[52] and this was the baptism of the Spirit taking place once and for all on that Day. On this point he taught that this baptism was a gift but that it was possible for a Christian not to accept this gift. It seemed to Gordon that it was one thing to be renewed by the Spirit and another (sealing, filling, anointing) to be endowed for ministry by the Spirit. The latter showed itself in victory over sin, and power to have a Spirit-honoring ministry. In this regard, Gordon was greatly interested in the early issues which English Keswick has continued to raise. One was the power to live above *known* sin. It was basically a British reaction to the Liberalism which had swept the Isles; its counterpart in America had been Fundamentalism, although English Keswick has never had the same interest in prophecy or in erecting schools for preaching and teaching the Word. Later, Keswick made more of an impact on American evangelicals and influenced some schools to follow its basic concerns and answers, notably Columbia Bible College in Columbia, South Carolina and Prairie Bible Institute in Three Hills, Alberta, to which many American students have gone for training. England reacted to outright Liberalism with three movements: (1) the most vocal opposition came from the great preacher, C.H. Spurgeon, who left the Baptist Union in the so-called Downgrade controversy, (2) a soft-spoken Evangelicalism, which has tended to survive in middle-of-the-road Orthodoxy, sometimes called Fundamentalism (as seen in such a work as *Fundamentalism and the Church* by Gabriel Hebert), and (3) the continuing Keswick movement starting in the 1870's, described in *So Great Salvation* by Steven Barabas and later brought to America by such men as Alan Redpath and W. Ian Thomas. Its strength is now on the rise as more and more

---

[49]A. J. Gordon, *The Watchword*, Oct., 1878.
[50]Ibid., May, 1880.
[51]A. J. Gordon, *The Ministry of the Spirit* (New York: Revell, 1894), pp. 15f.
[52]Ibid., p. 21.

conferences are held at churches and conference centers and advertised as "Deeper Life" or "Victorious Life" meetings.

Gordon allowed for present-day miracles of healing and described his insights in *The Ministry of Healing,* published in 1882. His main proof texts were Matthew 8:17, Mark 16:17-18, and James 5:14-15. B. B. Warfield commended Gordon's work as "the most rational presentation of the views of the Faith-healers."[53]

It was his contribution in prophecy that made Gordon so important to early Fundamentalism; for his image as pastor, Bible student, cogent and persuasive writer was most helpful. His major work was *Ecce Venit* (Behold He Cometh). He recognized the *main* dispensations without stressing the seven eras. Among them were the Fall of Adam, the Jewish Period, the Present One, the Millennium, and the Eternal Ages To Come. On one thing he was most insistent: the clear-cut distinction between Israel and the Church. Between Israel's ancient past and its prophesied future stood the present Ecclesia or Church. To Gordon, Romans 9-11 was the most central prophecy. Israel is now in blindness but a Great Day is coming. He saw ahead the regathering of Israel in unbelief (this has started since Gordon's day), the sure wrath of God on her, and the coming of Messiah to redeem Israel and restore to her all the blessings of ancient covenants. Gordon believed firmly in the bodily resurrection of the saints at the rapture, not at the death of the believers. The rapture he believed to be the "any-moment" return of Christ. In *The Watchword* he wrote that "we ought to be always waiting and expecting our Master's return . . . . such we believe to have been the constant attitude of the primitive church."[54] Gordon also wrote the following concerning His coming:

> His faithful and expectant saints will be caught up to meet Him in the air. They will be His escort as He afterward descends to the earth to take unto Him His great power and reign.
>
> At the sound of the last trumpet, the Lord will gather His church and save it from consuming fires of that great Day.[55]

Earlier he had said:

> The Lord's coming FOR us may be at any moment. The Lord's appearance WITH us and with all His saints cannot be for some time—until the expiration of Daniel's seventieth week. This is a period of seven years. In the midst of the seven years Revelation 6-18 will be fulfilled.
>
> Are there two comings?—this quibble comes badly from those who generally make several comings—who will tell that death is a second

[53]B. B. Warfield, *Miracles: Yesterday and Today* (Grand Rapids: Eerdmans, 1965). A reprint of a study of the subject of miracles.

[54]*The Watchword,* June, 1881.

[55]Ibid., Aug., 1879.

coming and the destruction of Jerusalem a second coming. His first coming was in two stages (Bethlehem and Calvary) and the second will be in two stages. If a Queen visited a city and as she approached the nobles and chieftains met her and formed an escort to return with her, does this make her visit a double one?[56]

To the first disciples the event was imminent and inspiring. Literalism is the best friend to sound doctrine. If Isaiah 53 is literal then also is Isaiah 11 literal.[57]

In 1891 Gordon wrote, "The church is to be caught up to be with the Lord in the air before the Lawless One is enthroned, before the Great Tribulation."[58] This will be followed by the Marriage Supper, and then He will be escorted by His saints to return to the earth to set up His kingdom. He said:

I hold to the view that the Church will be caught up to be with the Lord in the air before the Lawless One is enthroned and worshipped by all who dwell upon the earth before the Great Tribulation.[59]

By this time *The Watchword* of Gordon and *The Truth* of James H. Brookes had joined, with Robert Cameron as editor. Cameron later became a post-tribulationist. Gordon held that II Thessalonians 2:7-8 meant that "when the hidden mystery (the Church) is removed, then the mystery of iniquity (already at work) will spring into exaltation and enthronement."[60] These words of Gordon's should erase the false notion that Gordon was a post-tribulationist. As a true Fundamentalist Gordon believed in a literal thousand years—even in a literal throne with "His glorified Bride sitting by Him on His Throne, Queen consort with her enthroned Lord."[61] In 1889 he established the Boston Missionary Training School, later renamed Gordon Bible College, and now known as Gordon College in Wenham, Massachusetts. Gordon had as his first teacher in theology, Reverend F. H. Chapell, a Baptist pastor from Flemington, New Jersey.[62] Chapell held to the futurist school of interpretation of the Book of Revelation, which among other things sees most of the Revelation as future—the main part taking place during the first and second phases of His coming, or during the Great Tribulation period of seven years. A third school, then called the Comprehensive or Harmonic School, held that both of these were correct on the basis that the main prophecies have an immediate and a far-reaching application, commonly known as the principle of

---

[56]Ibid., 4 (1878).
[57]Ibid., Oct., 1878.
[58]Ibid., Aug., 1891.
[59]*The Watchword and Truth,* Aug., 1891. Robert Cameron, editor.
[60]Ibid., Aug., 1891.
[61]A. J. Gordon, *Ecce Venit* (New York: Revell, 1889), p. 295.
[62]See the author's "The Reverend F. L. Chapell, Early American Dispensationalist," *Bibliotheca Sacra,* 120 (April-June, 1961), 126-36.

double application. James H. Brookes inclined to this, as did Gordon on some prophecies. Surprisingly, Gordon held that most of the Revelation has taken place during the Church Age or will take place in that time gap. For instance, the Man of Sin was to Gordon the papacy in its historical development during church history. In this viewpoint Gordon followed his great English friend H. Grattan Guinness. Again, he may have been drawn to this position by the terrible history of Romanism with its tragic history as far as human souls and human progress are concerned. As to human influences on Gordon, it would be disrespectful to leave out the name of "Uncle" John Vassar, a devoted soulwinner of Clarendon Street Baptist Church; to Vassar the imminent return of the Lord was a great incentive to soulwinning. Gordon and others were indebted to many of the Plymouth Brethren movement, but this debt must be recognized as limited, since they differed greatly when it came to the doctrine of the Church.

Some have questioned whether Gordon should be called a dispensationalist. If making a clear-cut line between Israel and the Church classifies one as such, then indeed Gordon must be included. If it includes a seven-dispensation interpretation of all Scripture and slavish application of Matthew 24-25 to Israel in the future, then he would not qualify. The fairest assessment would seem to be that he was an early mild dispensationalist before the ramifications and details of modern Dispensationalism had been enunciated. Doubtless, if he were living today he would not fit too well with the thorough-going dispensationalists. In this regard he has blazed such a path for Fundamentalists, for most of them have held to a general type of dispensationalism but not to the well-worked systems of Scofield or L. S. Chafer, founder of Dallas Theological Seminary.

It was in the realm of the practical that Gordon did an outstanding work and must be listed as a giant among Fundamentalists. This work is recorded here, for it is abundantly clear that at the heart of Fundamentalism has been the ministry of the local church and all else must flow out from that New Testament unit. The work at Clarendon Street over twenty-five years shows an outstanding record of souls saved, converts baptized, spiritual growth, and cooperation with D. L. Moody in the great campaign in 1877. A strong and forthright stand was taken on several issues, such as unsaved paid musicians, the use of entertainment to attract the unchurched, and the stand, rather unusual for that day, against the theater. He held firmly that the Holy Spirit was the God-appointed administrator of the local church and must be so recognized for spiritual power and blessing. The church membership grew from 358 in 1869 to over one thousand in 1895; for that day it was considered a large church in America. When Gordon came, the church supported one evangelist and one foreign missionary; at his death there were twelve evangelists supported and an equal number of missionaries. Many missions and benevolent agencies for both whites and blacks were started or supported. (One has been very active, the Boston Industrial Home for the men of the street, one of the buildings to be demolished as part of Boston's Urban Renewal program.) Works among Chinese and Jews were started. In a wider outreach, Gordon served as chairman of the Evangelistic Association of New England. Many of his summer vacations in the 1880's were profitably used at Northfield in loving ministry at Moody's summer Bible conferences.

Gordon was interested in anything even remotely connected with social reform. He sought to reach and help alcoholics, aiding in the Boston Industrial Home and in *The Watchword* carrying on a Prohibition crusade almost constantly. Also he allowed his church to be used for meetings of Temperance Unions.

Gordon was a preacher and pulpit figure—this has all too often been ignored. He is called "an orator with commanding speech and presence, speaking without notes."[63] There was a spiritual punch without offense, a ruggedness of Bible convictions without nastiness in attitude. He laid aside any earlier desire for a literary style, though he read widely, and aimed at a direct, simple presentation of Bible truth. In this he followed a great Puritan divine of New England, the Reverend John Cotton, who shelved any attempt at literary excellence for the straightforward, simple presentation of Bible truth. In this, Fundamentalism owes much to Gordon and his example. He had a Scriptural flavor, lovingly but firmly communicating essential Bible truths. He refused to use his pulpit for discussion of political or social issues.

The wife of Gordon was born Maria Hale in Providence, Rhode Island, August 19, 1842, of both Congregational and Baptist backgrounds. Her mother held that she was converted at the age of four. She married Gordon about the time he went to pastor in Jamaica Plain, Massachusetts. A daughter, Haley, married Edwin Poteat, who later became president of Furman University in Greenville, South Carolina; the second child, Ernest, knew thirteen languages and for years wrote for the *Sunday School Times*. He also wrote a life of his father and *The Leaven of the Sadducees*, which told how Andover and other seminaries were captured by Liberals. A son, Arthur, was a Baptist minister, and a daughter, Helen, married

[63]George G. Houghton, "The Contributions of Adoniram Judson Gordon to American Christianity," (unpublished Th.D. dissertation, Dallas Theological Seminary, 1970), p. 108.

[64]Ernest B. Gordon, *A. J. Gordon: A Biography* (New York: Revell, 1896), p. 301.

lawyer Robert Hall (they are now living on Cape Cod). Mrs. Gordon died in 1921. On her stone was inscribed, "I shall be satisfied when I awake in His likeness."[64]

Testimonies to the greatness of Gordon were numerous. It was stated at the 1895 meeting of the Massachusetts Baptist Convention that this man was fully committed not only to the Word of God but also to the very words of God. This was an anchor in days of storm, criticism, and theological drift. In his war against the critics, Gordon did not forget that we must watch ourselves. To him the Word of God must be the sole staple of both preaching and living. Two doctrines were especially attractive: the imminent return of the Lord and the present ministry of the Holy Spirit. On this last truth, A. T. Pierson held that Gordon made his greatest contribution in that he made "the Holy Spirit the active, invisible, present Administrator of a spiritual body of disciples."[65] His mild dispensationalism opened up to him, for preaching and understanding, large portions of closed Scriptures. James M. Gray of Moody Bible Institute fame believed that faith was the greatest mark of Gordon's life. A. T. Pierson wondered if he had ever known a more Spirit-filled man.

Concerning the Brethren, Gordon very honestly doubted if any body of Christians ever set forth such a variety of Biblical literature in the same period of time. He believed they demonstrated the virtues of asceticism, high Calvinism, free grace, Biblical baptism, and apostolic fervor.

Gordon's contacts were widespread. He spoke on many campuses in the days when more college chapels were open to such men. His ministry extended to Brown, Princeton, Newton, and Moody Bible Institute. He was a man of action, and yet with such endeavor his spiritual life seemed to deepen. Not a perfectionist, he did live out a life of trust and victory over sin. His was not a defeated life here and now as he waited for His Lord, but one of victory after victory as that blessed hope continued to inspire and direct his steps.

[65]*The Watchword*, Feb. and March, 1895.

3
Affirmations Asserted

C. E. Harrington contended that early Fundamentalists were disturbed by the presence of vast neglected fields, neglected forces, and neglected truth.[1] These areas of neglected truth now became, and have remained, areas of close study, explanation, and defense. The method of interpretation (hermeneutics) had to be determined, and it was settled as a strict literalism. The Bible was given and must be taken either literally or liberally. In it were major neglected truths: the promises to Israel; the any-moment return of Christ for the Church; the rapture as the next important event; the certainty of the thousand-year reign of Christ; the separation of Christians from worldly things; and worldwide evangelism before Christ comes. In conferences, pulpits, and religious periodicals, these truths came to occupy a central place in the thinking of the Fundamentalists—so much so that they became the distinctives of the movement. They were "restored" since they had had a spotty existence in church history and had never been great cardinal tenets of a main body of Christians (with the possible exception of small dissenting groups). While these were theological characteristics, there was a reaffirmation of historic doctrines such as the virgin birth, man's depravity, the substitutionary atonement of Christ, the bodily resurrection, and the sure destiny of all men in Heaven or Hell.

The first gathering of men in this interest was at Swampscott, Massachusetts, in July, 1876. A small group met annually for the

[1]C. E. Harrington, "The Fundamentalist Movement in America" (unpublished Ph.D. dissertation, Univ. of California, 1959).

next twenty-five years with the exception of 1884. In 1890 this group became known as the Niagara Bible Conference, for they met at Niagara, New York from 1883 until 1898. They met again at Asbury Park, New Jersey in 1900, and in Philadelphia in 1901 for the last time because of dwindling attendance. At the early gathering at Swampscott were such men as L.W. Munhall, James H. Brookes, W.J. Erdman, H.M. Parsons, D.W. Whittle, and George C. Needham. Usually, conferences lasted ten days with three sessions a day. In 1877 the Conference met at Watkins Cove, New York, for the next three years at Clifton Springs, New York, and in 1881 at Old Orchard, Maine. The first conference at Swampscott was the father of a brood of Bible conferences, and the major theme of them all was the Second Coming. But annual summer Bible conferences would have had a small effect indeed on national Christian thinking if they had not spawned two larger conferences at which definitive tenets were enunciated—the conference of 1878 in New York, and in Chicago in 1886. With them the Fundamentalists' die was cast; indeed, these cities deserve to be hailed as the birthplace of American Fundamentalism.

The first important conference of Fundamentalism was held October 30 to November 1, 1878, at the Church of the Holy Trinity in New York. The *New York Tribune* published an extra edition of fifty thousand copies containing the addresses of that conference. We are indebted to the F. H. Revell Company of New York for the publication of the addresses. It was rightfully entitled *Premillennial Essays of the Prophetic Conference* and was edited by Nathaniel West, whose book on the thousand-year reign of Christ was one of the earliest millennial studies. The book was published in 1879. In his Introduction, West attests to the millennial flavor of the Conference by writing that "the prophetic words of both the Old Testament and New Testament concerning His second coming will be literally fulfilled," and added that, "this second coming of the Lord Jesus is everywhere revealed in the Scriptures as imminent and it may occur at any moment; yet the precise day and hour thereof is unknown to man and known only to God."[2] This truth was further held to be "one of the mightiest incentives to earnestness in preaching the Gospel to every creature."

Outstanding men from various Christian groups issued the call for the Conference. Their names deserve at least a word, for they were the pioneers of the Bible conference movement, and through it they became pioneers of historic Fundamentalism. Members of the committee were James H. Brookes, A. J. Gordon, S. H. Tyng, Jr., W. R. Nicholson, Maurice Baldwin, W. G. Moorehead, H. M. Parsons,

---

[2]Nathaniel W. West, *Premillennial Essays* (Chicago: Revell, 1879).

and R. W. Clarke. One hundred and nineteen other names are listed as joining in issuing the call for the conference. Some of these men had unusual ministries in pulpit or page, and several of them should at least be listed. Among them were George C. Lorimer of Tremont Temple in Boston, then an outstanding center of evangelism; Joseph A. Seiss, a Lutheran pastor in Philadelphia, who later wrote two volumes on the Book of Revelation; John Wanamaker, Presbyterian layman and merchant of Philadelphia (Wanamaker stores were founded by him); John Duffield of Princeton College; W. E. Blackstone, a Methodist pastor in Oak Park, Illinois, whose little book, entitled *Jesus Is Coming,* has had such a wide distribution and influence, J. D. Herr of Central Baptist in New York; and F. L. Chapell of Evanston, Illinois, later to be first Professor of Theology at A. J. Gordon's school in Boston, forerunner of Gordon College.

These men rejected the allegorical method of interpretation of Old Testament prophecies and agreed with Canon Ryle, Anglican exegete, that

the literal sense of the Old Testament prophecies has been far too much neglected by the churches and is far too much neglected in this present day and that, under the mistaken system of spiritualizing and accommodating Bible language, Christians have too often completely missed its meaning.[3]

A resolution was passed by the conference using Ryle's exact words:

The prophetic words of both the Old Testament and New Testament concerning His second coming will be literally fulfilled in His visible bodily return to this earth in like manner as He went up into Heaven: and this glorious Epiphany of the Great God, our Saviour Jesus Christ, is the blessed hope of the believer and of the Church during this entire dispensation.[4]

The committee issuing the Call wrote:

When from any cause some vital doctrine of God's word has fallen into neglect or suffered contradiction and reproach, it becomes the serious duty of those who hold it, not only strongly and constantly to reaffirm it, but to seek by all means in their power to bring back the Lord's people to its apprehension and acceptance. The precious doctrine of Christ's personal appearing has, we are constrained to believe, long lain under such neglect and misapprehension.[5]

So vital indeed is this truth represented to be that the denial of it is pointed out as one of the conspicuous signs of the apostasy of the last days . . . after the long sleep of the church, the wise are at long last rising up and trimming their lamps in preparation for the coming of the Bridegroom.[6]

Many references were made to the Fathers, it being held that the

[3]Ibid., p. 7.
[4]Ibid., p. 8.
[5]Ibid., p. 11.
[6]Ibid.

Fathers, before the time of Origen (185-254), taught the personal and visible return of the Lord. The speakers pointed out that the first departure from this was by Origen with his method of allegorizing the Scripture. An open attack was launched on "the mystical, spiritualizing school of exposition."[7] Christians ought to follow the law of Bishop Newton that "a literal rendering is always to be given in the reading of the Scripture unless the context makes it absurd."[8] Groups such as "the Socinian, Calvinist, Arminian, Swedenborgian and every other school of theological thought will spiritualize in opposite ways to suit their several schemes."[9] Also indicted were German rationalists who did it to naturalize church history, the theologians of Romanism, and the American revivalists. The doctrine of His literal return was important, for one verse in twenty-five in the New Testament speaks of this event—in all, three hundred verses. So, concluded the conference speakers, "this assertion of the personal and visible return is fundamental to all."[10] Attempts to interpret His coming as the fall of Jerusalem, the progress of the Gospel, or the spiritual presence of Christ in believers today were analyzed and found unacceptable. Although some have held it meant the death of each one, the Conference rightly observed that death is always seen as an enemy and that not a single passage could be found "which associates death with the Coming of the Lord."[11] Three Greek words used for "coming" were discussed briefly—*apokalupsis* (19 passages) *epiphaneia* (10 passages) and *parousia* (24 times).

S. H. Kellogg of the Allegheny Presbyterian Seminary answered some charges made against the millenarians, such as the one that after the resurrection, Christians would need a physical body in order to carry on earthly life in reigning with Christ over the earth for one thousand years. Thus it was claimed that millennialism taught that saints would need to rise in a body of flesh and blood in order to have an earthly ministry in the millennium. Professor Kellogg refuted this. While accepting that their bodies will be spiritual, he contended that the "Lord Himself during the forty days after His resurrection appeared in a body of flesh and bones upon this earth [which implies] . . . his life was a life in the flesh."[12] The professor brought up the question of a worldwide conversion before the Lord's return and questioned if this is sound doctrine. He concluded, "This is not to be expected before the Lord Jesus shall

---

[7]Ibid., p. 25.
[8]Ibid., p. 26.
[9]Ibid., p. 27.
[10]Ibid., p. 28.
[11]Ibid., p. 36.
[12]Ibid., p. 50.

return."[13] The Gospel shall spread, but "the Word of God gives us no reason to look for any radical and real spiritual change in the condition of the world till the glorious appearing of the Lord."[14] He stated that Paul did not expect worldwide conversion (see II Cor. 5:11, 14; II Tim. 1:10; I Cor. 9:23; II Tim. 3:1). Passages elsewhere point to the exact opposite of worldwide conversion (Acts 15:14 and Matt. 24:14) where the Gospel is a witness but no general conversion is alluded to. Otherwise, the admonition to "watch" of Matthew 24:42 is meaningless; but the plain teaching is that "the Lord intended that we should think of His Advent as always possible and forbids us to interpose any such fixed period of time between us and His coming."[15] Kellogg further stated that the times before the second coming will not be good times but evil times, thus wrecking the illusionary dreams of the postmillennialists, and he found support in such passages as I Timothy 4; II Timothy 3:1, 5; II Peter 3:2, 5; I John 2:18; I Thessalonians 5:3; II Thessalonians 2:1-8.

A. J. Gordon of Clarendon Street Baptist Church in Boston, Massachusetts, took a prominent part in this conference and the much more important one in 1886. In the 1878 conference he spoke on the controversial passage in Revelation 20:4-6. He admitted that a large class of interpreters deny that the passage teaches two distinct resurrections with a thousand years between. Gordon stated the case for all when he said that it was "purely a question of interpretation."[16] He held the first resurrection must be literal and corporeal and not spiritual, for the word translated "beheaded" (Greek, *pepelekismenon*) cannot be spiritualized; "the condition of literal death has been so unmistakably pointed to . . . the quickening is a literal and corporeal quickening."[17] Again, it is stated that disembodied spirits "lived" and the word (Greek, *ezesan*) in the New Testament is "constantly used to describe that reanimation by which the soul is united again to its tabernacle of flesh."[18] It is called the first resurrection (Greek, *anastasis*), which occurs forty-two times in the New Testament, and with one exception (Luke 2:34) "it always signifies the resurrection of the body."[19] Since the second resurrection in the Revelation passage is obviously a literal one, the meaning of this resurrection would fix the meaning of the other resurrection. To Gordon there were two distinct classes and two literal resurrections—there "are the dead who live and those who do

[13]Ibid., p. 52.
[14]Ibid.
[15]Ibid., p. 59.
[16]Ibid., p. 78.
[17]Ibid., p. 80.
[18]Ibid., p. 81.
[19]Ibid., p. 82.

not live till a thousand years later .... there are those who reign with Christ and those who stand before the Throne to be judged."[20] He turned next to I Corinthians 15:21-25, and in addition to classes involved in resurrection and also in the words "afterward" (Greek, *epeita*) and "then" (Greek, *eita*) he found "considerable spaces of time between the respective divisions."[21] "Afterward" has marked a period of at least two thousand years, and so its correlative "then" marks a considerable period. The Revelation 20 passage "gives us the time marked by 'then' of I Corinthians 15 or the space between the second and third divisions of the resurrection host."[22] Then, Gordon turned to Luke 20:35 and Philippians 3:11 to emphasize the resurrection "out of" the dead, "a separation and quickening to life out from among the dead,"[23] and this resurrection "out of" the dead is the invariable usage throughout the New Testament. Some have quoted II Timothy 4:1 in order to deny the two resurrections, but he used Tischendorf and Alford to give a better rendering, namely, "I charge thee before God and Jesus Christ who is about to judge the quick and the dead, and by His appearing and His kingdom."[24] He referred to another text often used to deny two literal resurrections, namely, John 5:28-29, where it is taught that all in the graves shall come forth, but asked if this necessarily taught a simultaneous resurrection. He says that "hour" (Greek, *hora*) refers to an era (see Rom. 13:11 and I John 2:18), and in the context verse 25 must cover the whole Gospel age. The passage itself sets two periods in contrast—one hour that now is and the second hour that is coming. Thus in the period yet to come, all the dead shall be raised, the righteous at its beginning and the rest at the end of it.

The regeneration yet ahead was discussed at this conference by Charles K. Imbrie of Jersey City as he looked forward to the "blissful change to come," the coming Millennium. It will be a regeneration of this earth and the race upon it, and such truth cannot be put aside by "spiritual significations."[25] Biblical passages used were Romans 8:21; Acts 3:21; Isaiah 65:17; II Peter 3:13; Revelation 21:1; and Matthew 19:28. Differing views were noted, such as the amillennial, the Reformed, and the "spiritual view," which inevitably leads to the postmillennial position. All three ignore the laws of language and substitute for the plain teaching the idea of a "protracted state of blessed rest and holiness in the Church universal between the present time and the return of the Lord of which the Scripture says

[20]Ibid., p. 85.
[21]Ibid., p. 87.
[22]Ibid., p. 88.
[23]Ibid., p. 90.
[24]Ibid., p. 94.
[25]Ibid., p. 109.

not one word."[26] The correct view is the premillennial one, which was held by the Early Church for three centuries and "has had ever since a great many adherents among the most learned and faithful of the Christian Church."[27] Imbrie's discourse must have taxed the patience of the many hearers, for in the Revell edition it covers sixty-five pages. At least one obvious fact must be recognized and it is that a great amount of study in the prophecies of the Bible had taken place and a determined effort had been made to find their plain grammatical meaning.

Professor H. Lummis, a Methodist from Monson, Massachusetts, dealt with "The Kingdom and the Church." The respected president of Boston University, a Methodist center then as now, Dr. William F. Warren, had written that the Christian Church was the Kingdom of God. Lummis stated that John the Baptist, Joseph of Arimathea, the robber on the cross, and Paul disagreed with Warren and also with the Presbyterian theologian, Charles Hodge, who held that the Kingdom was as old as human history (even as the Church) and, therefore, that the terms are relatively synonymous, a claim that Lummis rightly admits was the popular and prevalent one.

The Lummis study revealed that the word for "building" in Matthew 16 was not once used of the Kingdom, either Kingdom of Heaven or Kingdom of God. The expressions of "advancing the Kingdom" and the "extension of the Kingdom" are unscriptural. We are "heirs" of the Kingdom but never called heirs of the Church. In the Gospels, to "enter the Kingdom" is found ten times, one-half of them being future and the rest indefinite, with "not one case occurring in which any one is mentioned as having entered into the Kingdom of God."[28] Moreover, the Kingdom is a unit, while the Church is an aggregate of churches. The professor quoted approvingly an English brother who prayed, "I mean by the grace of God to find a home in the Kingdom."[29] He also pointed out that no reference is made to the Lutheran Kingdom or the Methodist Kingdom. And why not, if the terms mean the same thing? Much clarity would result if one prayed that the Kingdom WOULD come and the will of God be done on the EARTH. A question was raised by John's declaration that the kingdom "draweth near" or "is approaching"; Paul spoke of the Day being at hand but two millennia have already passed. Lummis concluded that true believers should expect the Kingdom and their constant word should be "watch."

H. M. Parsons of Buffalo analyzed the program of Antichrist in

[26]Ibid., p. 114.
[27]Ibid.
[28]Ibid., p. 191.
[29]Ibid., p. 193.

this present age. He found that Matthew 13 "contains the history of the Kingdom of Heaven in mystery during this present age."[30] The parable of the leaven illustrates the results of corruptions during the age "introduced by those who are within the church."[31] He concluded that universal corruption will prevail at the end of the age rather than universal conversion. If the mission of the Holy Spirit had been to convert all in this age, then we have a "marvelous impeachment of the power and love of the Holy Spirit."[32] With each age since the Church began have come increasing numbers saved, and in parallel fashion a "similar rapid growth in the elements and forces of evil opposed to the Kingdom of God."[33] He referred to increasing culture and civilization but questioned their final benefit without God and Christ. A keen analysis was made of the titles given in the Bible to Antichrist, each one significantly revealing some trait of character or activity. A good column of contrasts between Christ and Antichrist is given on page 217 of this volume of *Premillennial Essays of the Prophetic Conference*. Like Christ, Antichrist must be a real person. Parsons saw several forces recruiting for Antichrist in his own day, and he named these forces as atheism, pantheism, skepticism, rationalism, "and all the forces and phases of intellectual speculation which deny the word of the living God today."[34]

Bishop W. R. Nicholson of the Reformed Episcopal Seminary in Philadelphia brought an incisive discourse on the Gathering of Israel, using such passages as Ezekiel 36:22-28 and 37:15-22, saying these "can possibly refer only to the literal Israel and to their restoration to Palestine."[35] He stated bluntly that "references to literal Israel could not be more demonstrated nor the fact of their restoration to Palestine more positively stated."[36] He found in Amos 9:9-14 a "vigorous description of their divinely inflicted dispersion" which "has continued to the present, their divinely wrought preservation . . . literally a land" and "literally the tribes of Jacob gathered back to where they had nationally dwelt long centuries before."[37] In such passages as Romans 9 and 11, the "literal national Israel is God's ancient people; and as such He has not cast them away."[38] So the future restoration of national Israel is prophesied in two installments—(1) at the end of the Great Tribulation period of

[30]Ibid., p. 209.
[31]Ibid.
[32]Ibid., p. 210.
[33]Ibid., p. 211.
[34]Ibid., p. 218.
[35]Ibid., p. 223.
[36]Ibid., p. 224.
[37]Ibid., p. 226.
[38]Ibid., p. 227.

seven years (Zech. 14) and (2) at a subsequent time after the
millennial coming of the Lord Jesus (Isa. 11:11-16). These have
nothing to do with the Babylonian Captivity. Jews will go back in
their unconverted state; they will reestablish their temple services,
and then they will be chastised before being converted. Only one
third will survive that Day of Jacob's Trouble. The bishop identified
them with the 144,000 of Revelation 7. The remnant shall have a
"great and exalted position in the Millennium."[39]

J. T. Cooper of Allegheny Presbyterian Seminary (later
Pittsburgh) spoke on the Judgments. To him the "whole of the
millennial dispensation has been represented as the last day, the
day of the Lord, and the day of judgement."[40] He spoke of the
judgment of Christians as found in II Corinthians 5:10 and Romans
14:10 and pointed out that "this is a judgment of believers in relation
to their faithfulness."[41] There is also a judgment of both houses of
Israel: Hosea 3:4-5; Jeremiah 30:7; Zechariah 12:8-9; Isaiah 4:3-4;
Zechariah 14:1-4; 12:9-12; Ezekiel 20:32-38. Again, there will be a
judgment of the nations, spoken of by the Lord in Matthew 25:31-
46—"to set before us the solemn fact that there is a day of reckoning
before the nations of the earth and that day is the time of our Lord's
glorious advent."[42] This scene does not include any in the
resurrection, for the passage does not mention a resurrection and the
use of the words must point to the living (*ethnos* is used 150 times in
the New Testament but never once in relation to the dead). This
agrees with other testimony of Scripture, such as Isaiah 34:2; Joel
3:2, 11-12, 21; and Zechariah 14:1-2. All passages refer to a judgment
of the living. The basis of judgment could not apply to millions of
infants who had died and the "multitudes who have passed away
who never heard of the name of Jesus or His brethren."[43] This
judgment is wholly distinct from that in Revelation 20:11-15.
"Nations" probably refers to the Gentiles and their treatment of the
brethren of Christ. There is, in addition, a judgment of the dead as
seen in Revelation 20. This is not on earth, for the heavens and earth
have dissolved. Here Cooper was against the idea of believers' being
in this assize. These judgments reminded Cooper of the sweeping
statement of a professor of theology of Utrecht, who said that "while
the path of eschatology is traced over the highest mountain height,
the loftiest peaks are bordered by the deepest chasms."[44]

A central figure in the Fundamentalist movement of this era was

[39]Ibid., p. 236.
[40]Ibid., p. 249.
[41]Ibid., p. 249.
[42]Ibid., p. 252.
[43]Ibid., p. 255.
[44]Ibid., p. 263.

James H. Brookes of the Washington and Compton Avenue Presbyterian Church of St. Louis. A militant premillennialist, Brookes was commended as an able Bible student by C. I. Scofield of Scofield Reference Bible fame. Only one life of Brookes has been written, and that is by David R. Williams, published in 1898 by the Presbyterian Board of Publications. Brookes edited *The Truth* for many years, a paper which joined with *The Watchword* (founded and published by A. J. Gordon till his death in 1895) as *The Watchword and The Truth*. At the 1878 conference, Brookes spoke on the Coming of the Lord in its Relation to Christian Doctrine. He began by quoting an ardent postmillenarian, David Brown, who contended that millennial truth pervaded the entire system of theology, calling attention to the central place this truth has in the Word. To Brown this truth was the "very pole star of the Church,"[45] and to this Brookes agreed. The latter added that in the Old Testament more "than one hundred verses announce His Second Coming to every one verse that proclaims His First Coming."[46] Because of this truth, warnings are issued; hypocrisy is seen in blackest hue; servants are put on their guard; disciples are enlivened by true hopes; nations are told of sure judgment; high honors are promised to those watching; universal worldliness is prophesied, and universal apostasy is foretold. Brookes listed in all one hundred benefits, each with Scripture, arising from this truth so that it is "a golden cord through the entire New Testament ... touching every doctrine, binding every duty, arousing, consoling, directing, guarding, inspiring the believer at every step of his pilgrimage."[47] In succeeding paragraphs he showed the relation of this doctrine to the Unity of the Church, the Divine Purpose, the Curse, Justification, Sanctification, Inspiration, and the Resurrection.

Nathaniel West of Cincinnati, Ohio, traced the history of premillennialism, beginning with the visions of Daniel and John, which were contrasted in detailed fashion. The Apostolic Fathers quoted or referred to included Clement of Rome, Polycarp, Ignatius, Papias, and Irenaeus. Premillennial views were seen in the Apologists such as Tatian, Justin Martyr, Melito of Sardis, Tertullian, and many more. West pictured premillennialism as a tenet of the faith commonly held by the fathers until the time of Origen, who was the first to break with it. Origen held that "matter was bad, the earth must be annihilated, and the future glory of the saints is not connected with the glorification of their earthly bodies interpenetrated by the resurrection life of Christ."[48] The teachers of

---

[45]Ibid., p. 271.
[46]Ibid., p. 273.
[47]Ibid., p. 293.
[48]Ibid., p. 345.

the Alexandrine school asserted that "the divine promises pertain to nothing earthly."[49]

West claimed that the men of the Nicene Age were chiliastic, and took the Greek historian Gelasius Cyzicus of the fifth century as his authority who "with meticulous care" collected the testimonies of Nicene writers, but his work was "buried out of sight . . . by the advancing papacy under the plea that the Chiliastic doctrine of a kingdom, different from the Christian empire was offensive to the national feelings of Greeks and Romans."[50] The Dark Ages buried many truths, and a "new generation . . . [was] intoxicated with the Christian conquest of heathenism, the careening splendor of a church and state establishment, and whirling a mystic dance around the tranquility of the empire."[51] According to church historian Kurtz, the "State Church of that time forgot the millennial glory of the future."[52] Jamieson and Faussett stated that "Christians began looking at its existing temporal prosperity as fulfilling the prophecies, and ceased to look for Christ's promised reign on earth."[53] As the power of the papacy advanced, chiliasm declined. The Church gradually became a Harlot and correspondingly ceased to be a Bride of Christ. The visible state, now claiming to be Christian, became the Kingdom. The visions of Daniel and John were now referred to the first advent rather than the second. The cross, once a symbol of ignominy, now was one of honor, and with this vast transformation came the doctrines of baptismal regeneration and other complicated ceremonial acts. Martyrs were forgotten, and saints and intercessors were created. New Jerusalem was given second place and Rome in all splendor took primacy, and the one thousand years of its reign was falsely dated from the birth of Christ. The binding of Satan was the wickedness still continuing in the hearts of the wicked. The great name in the formation of this colossal dream was Augustine, and sound teaching in prophecy was lost in veneration for him. Martyr faith was condemned and a new day dawned, the day of "the presence of their images, the sanctity of their tombs and their ghostly intercession."[54] Now a "carnal caricature of the Millennial Kingdom of Christ was laid in the Empire."[55] The Church thus created a counterfeit Millennium, "one sunk in the gross

[49]Ibid., p. 346.
[50]Ibid., p. 347.
[51]Ibid., p. 348.
[52]Ibid.
[53]Ibid., p. 349.
[54]Ibid., p. 351.
[55]Ibid., p. 352.

materialism and idolatry of medieval, political, and military Christianity."[56]

When the thousand years ended about A.D. 1000 and no Last Trump sounded and no Great White Throne appeared, why did not men cast away their theorizing? A new date was set as the beginning—that of the great Emperor Constantine and the date of A.D. 312, and another lease of over three centuries ensued. By that time the commanding place of the Papacy and the identification of Antichrist with such people as the Ottoman Turks seemed enough for minds so drugged with superstition.

With the Reformation, glimmers of light appeared. The Pope was openly labeled Antichrist and Rome labeled as Babylon either in embryo or actual reality. This was not new for the Waldenses, Wycliffe, and even some men within Rome itself. Wycliffe had railed against "that proud priest of Rome—that open Antichrist," and Huss joined in calling him "The Vicar of Judas Iscariot."[57] But a larger problem remained—where to put the thousand-year reign—and here the Reformers disagreed. Was the Reformation itself the period of the First Resurrection? When was the Beast destroyed? Was this the breaking of the yoke of Rome? One sure result of the Reformation was that "Chiliasm obtained an almost universal diffusion through the Church."[58] But with it came the uncertainties of preterism, which put much of Daniel and the Revelation in the past. One good result of the Reformed position was to reassert the surety of the coming of Christ, and the parousia of the New Testament could not be interpreted as death or spiritual presence or conversion of the world. But preterism did grow and this "gave the Romanists every advantage."[59] And preterism led to antichiliasm, as seen in the Westminster Standards.

West brought to light a central claim of both Orthodoxy and Fundamentalism ever since his day. And that claim was that the emphasis of the Reformers was in the area of salvation, justification by faith, and in other great doctrines of grace. Doing such valiant service, they could not give the proper time and study to the vast area of eschatology. Many followed the Reformers on great doctrines on grace and by inference accepted their eschatology and became amillennial. They looked for the speedy return of Christ and the judgment of the vile system of Romanism; but they accounted Gog and Magog to be the Ottoman Turks and so their refrain, proverbially sung, was "from the Pope, the Turk, and the Devil,

[56]Ibid.
[57]Ibid., p. 355.
[58]Ibid., p. 359.
[59]Ibid., p. 361.

Good Lord, deliver us."[60] Again, they reacted to the counterfeit
kingdom of Munster and the prophets of Zwickau, which in all,
brought reproach to even the serious study of prophetic truths, let
alone their literal understanding and acceptance. Calvin thought
the thousand years started with Constantine and rejected a future
reign of a literal one thousand years, as seen in his *Institutes,* III, 25,
Section 5. The Augsburg Confession struck at Jewish opinions
(millennialism) and included a barbed attack on the Anabaptists,
who were the premillenarians of the times. West contended that
Reformed statements of faith did not condemn premillennialism
but only the false chiliasm of their periods.

To West the seventeenth century was a time of the "advance of
Chiliasm."[61] A long list of premillennial men is given, including the
more commonly known ones such as Lange, Spener, Milton, and
Francke. Principal Baillie of the General Presbyterian Assembly of
Scotland complained that there were too many who held to
premillennial truth and even published a *Dissuasive* to convert
them. In England they were called "Brownists," which was a
general catchall for all dissenters who in any way would not
conform to the Church of England. But among so many the Man of
Sin and Babylon were identified in public and in private with Rome.
Many thought of the thousand years as a period, but had their
problems in dating its beginning. Many did think the coming of the
Kingdom to be future as well as the times of refreshing and the
binding of Satan. The dealings of God with Israel as a nation was
the subject of some study by the Puritans, both English and
Colonial.

In the eighteenth century the theory of Whitby, in which he
identified the Millennium with the Church, and the conversion of the
world to Christ before He comes as the fulfillment of Revelation 20,
was popular because of the Great Awakening and the ministry of
such men as Edwards and Fairbairn. Revelation 20 was seen as the
grand revival movements, including concerts of prayer for
worldwide missions and conversion. A righteous optimism pervaded
their minds and hopefully they looked for the overthrow of Islam, the
Papacy, false science, and rationalism. So hopeful but so wrong! Yet
a vigorous protest ensued against the Whitby thesis. Foremost in
this was the German scholar, Bengel, who took a mild premillennial
position, writing that "the time will come when a pure Chiliasm will
be thought an integral part of Orthodoxy."[62]

West found a galaxy of able nineteenth-century Bible students of
the premillennial persuasion. Exegesis had been emancipated from

[60]Ibid., p. 362.
[61]Ibid., p. 367.
[62]Ibid., p. 385.

"the fetters of a lingering medievalism."[63] The indissoluble connection of Revelation 19 and Revelation 20 had "wrecked all anti-chiliastic expositions."[64] The Beast must be judged before the Millennium begins. Dean Alford was one of the ablest exegetes and scholars, and his dictum was that "the majority, both in number, learning, and research adopt the premillennial advent, following the plain and undeniable sense of the sacred text."[65] There is a long list of names given by West of the millennial stalwarts in the theological world. Most of the men are Americans and represent the large "communions," but many of the best-known scholars of Britain and Germany are included. Lange called this truth the "pearl of truth," and Schaff, the church historian, spoke of it as "this precious hope."[66]

Professor John T. Duffield of Princeton College spoke of the arguments in defense of premillennialism. To him the major problem was whether the millennial era would come before or after the second coming. If the Millennium came during this dispensation, then we should see this truth taught in the New Testament, but "it is not expressly and unequivocally taught in a single passage."[67] It was strange to the professor that supporters of amillennialism "do not pretend to find a single passage in its favor in Acts or the Apostolic Epistles."[68] Until we come to the last of the Revelation, the Church is presented as "the church militant not the church triumphant."[69] The Church is called out and as such is to have a witness, with the Christian life "a warfare in the world and Satan and the flesh as enemies."[70] In II Thessalonians 2 Paul wrote of the Apostasy, and not the Millennium, as coming before the advent. To Duffield it was central to maintain that "the Advent was ever present as an event ever imminent."[71] And no truth "of our holy religion is more frequently urged as an incentive to holiness, to patience under suffering, to steadfastness in faith, to vigilance and fidelity in Christ's service."[72] Again, he asserted that "the Apostolic Church understood the Apostles to teach that the Second Coming of the Lord was an event ever imminent."[73] Testimonies to support this position came from Dr. Hodge, Barnes on Romans, Lange on I

[63]Ibid., p. 386.
[64]Ibid.
[65]Ibid., p. 387.
[66]Ibid., p. 403.
[67]Ibid., p. 408.
[68]Ibid., p. 409.
[69]Ibid., p. 410.
[70]Ibid., p. 411.
[71]Ibid., p. 412.
[72]Ibid., p. 413.
[73]Ibid., p. 419.

Corinthians, and the *Life of Paul* by Conybeare and Howson. And this truth, Duffield recognized, continued until the time of Origen as the accepted view of the Fathers. In support of his position he quoted the Westminster Confession, Luther, Calvin, Knox, and Bishop Henshaw of Rhode Island.

At the close of this volume including the addresses at this all-important conference, were forty-two pages of appendices with extracts from many works such as the *Berlerberg Bible, Richter's Bible,* Starke's *Synopsis of the New Testament,* Theueer, Pfleiderer, Ebrard's *Christian Dogma,* Schenkel's *Christian Dogma,* Van-Oosterzee's *Christian Dogma,* Dormer's *Person of Christ* and other authors such as Lange, Auberlen, Rothe, Roos, Schmidt, Kock, and Stephan. From this first conference, the birthplace of theological Fundamentalism, came the following conclusions:

(1) All prophecies are to be taken literally.
(2) The second coming is imminent.
(3) Romanism is the Babylon of Revelation.
(4) Prophecy must be given a central place in theology, evangelism, missions, and personal living.

4
Affirmations Amplified

The prophetic conference of 1886 was a Plymouth Rock in the history of Fundamentalism; a Magna Charta of its doctrinal insights; a Valley Forge in facing the onslaught of liberal theology; a Waterloo in the emergence of a victorious confidence in its rightness of interpretation, and a D-Day for embattled pastors and professors who had been sickened and saddened by the liberal debacle. Furthermore, it was a birthday for Biblical truths, an exposure of God's enemies, and a determined and valiant answer that the war was on and Fundamentalists would fight.

The 1878 conference speakers had rapidly surveyed the scene of liberal premises, and, with their almost complete attention to prophecy, had awakened a wide constituency to the dangers at hand. A literalism in prophecy had been propounded, but many prophecies had been left untouched. Crucial issues had been joined, but a full-fledged Fundamentalism had not yet been created to answer all Liberals and liberal positions. The 1886 conference was to complete a work nobly begun by the meeting of 1878. Clearer positions were enunciated, more exacting exegesis was developed, and a much larger picture of God's unchanging plans for the present and future was unfolded. More solid prophetic truth was presented at that conference than has been taught in most Bible schools and seminaries established at that time or since. Difficult questions were honestly faced, and often this was done with very little literature to help. Indeed, the literature on prophecy was exceedingly meager. These brave soldiers had to go to the Book to find out what was going on, where to go from there, and what to expect in the future.

It is simply a matter of historical fact that these men in 1886 did not have a system of theology. Many had Reformed backgrounds in their theological training but this system helped them very little in matters of prophecy, since it had left out any serious study of things to come. It would be appropriate to call them early dispensationalists in that they held to three distinct eras or economies in God's work: Old Testament, New Testament or Church Age, and the Coming Kingdom. A few of them went beyond this to hold to more than three eras, some even seven, but there is no evidence that all subscribed to more than three and it is fanciful to so assume. Again, these early dispensationalists did not have a Scofield Reference Bible, for their meeting took place thirty years before the Scofield Reference Bible was published. Modern dispensationalists might like to think that these early Fundamentalists accepted all that is in the Scofield notes, but in reality Scofield and his fellow editors drew on the vast store of research materials from these and succeeding conferences. Usually no mention is made of this; perhaps because some feel that everything fundamental or dispensational began with C. I. Scofield. Indeed, it was his spiritual teacher, James H. Brookes, whom Scofield revered and esteemed to be the greatest Bible teacher he had known and who had exercised a great influence on him.

It should be noted that this conference was interdenominational, and no denominational distinctives were in evidence. In fact, no references to denominational positions appeared in the conference, possibly because denominations had been so enamored with their own progress that God's program had been ignored or given secondary consideration. Also we must remember that the 1880's preceded the creation of unified budgets and cooperative programs, which were to arise and abound in the twentieth century. In the 1886 prophecy conference, Baptists, Presbyterians, Methodists, Congregationalists, and Lutherans carefully scrutinized the Book to discover God's prophetic timetable and signs of their own times. They were discouraged at what they saw about them but encouraged by what they found in the Word.

We turn to a detailed study of the 1886 conference, and the reasons listed should be sufficient to interest students in this period and the movement called Fundamentalism. The theological positions and interests have continued in Fundamentalism, differing only because of the unusual ministries of the successors of the early giants and because the American religious scene has changed. The continuing witness of Fundamentalism will not be obvious unless the earliest affirmations and attitudes are accurately understood and seen in the context of the great fight against Satanic enemies, both in the churches and the educational institutions.

In the 1886 prophetic conference the following main truths and theological positions were presented:

(1) A strict literalism in interpreting the Bible, particularly its prophecies.

(2) An all-consuming interest in the coming of the Lord and His Kingdom to be established on the earth.

(3) A clear-cut picture of the enemies of prophecy in schools of spiritualizers, postmillenarians, and figurative interpreters.

(4) A continuing exposure of Romanism as the great enemy of the Truth and the true Church, setting the stage for the coming of Babylon the Great.

(5) The central place of Israel in the future Kingdom.

(6) Increasing wickededness, with all the world heading toward the period of the Great Tribulation.

(7) Judgments and rewards awaiting Christians.

(8) A special study of the activities of Antichrist.

(9) The peculiar delusions of the present day.

(10) A constant rejection of men's opinions in all matters of truth and practice and constant reliance on plain scriptures.

The members of the committee arranging the Conference, together with the speakers on the program, formed a Who's Who of first-generation Fundamentalism. Their names should be household words among their successors today, but, alas, they are mostly unknown men. The times and the issues are so much with us that a knowledge of our history, our heritage, and our heroes has been completely lost. The committee included the leaders of the 1878 conference: A. J. Gordon (Baptist) of Boston; James H. Brookes (Presbyterian) of St. Louis; Nathaniel West (Presbyterian) of Minneapolis; George C. Needham (Baptist) of Boston; W. R. Nicholson (Reformed Episcopal) of Philadelphia; L. W. Munhall (Methodist) of Germantown, Pennsylvania; W. G. Moorehead (Presbyterian) of Xenia, Ohio; A. J. Frost (Baptist) of Sacramento, California; W. J. Erdman (Congregational) of Boston; and D. W. Whittle (Congregational) of Chicago. Anglicans were not taking the part they had in the 1878 meeting. On the program were such men as E. P. Goodwin (Congregational) of Chicago; E. T. Stroeter (Wesleyan) of Warrenton, Maryland; F. L. Chapell (Baptist) of Flemington, New Jersey; A. T. Pierson (a Presbyterian who turned Baptist) of Philadelphia; Professor Lummis of Lawrence University, Appelton, Wisconsin; George S. Bishop (Reformed) of Orange, New Jersey; H. M. Parsons (Presbyterian) of Toronto, Canada; D. C. Marquis of McCormick Theological Seminary in Chicago (Presbyterian); G. N. H. Peters (Lutheran) of Springfield, Ohio; Professor J. T. Duffield (Presbyterian) of Princeton, New Jersey; W. E. Blackstone (Methodist) of Oak Park, Illinois; and Bishop Baldwin (Anglican) of Ontario, Canada. Letters were received from such well-known leaders as D. L. Moody, Professor Godet, and Profes sor Delitzsch, who congratulated the men on the new interest in prophetic studies and agreed with their premillennial approach to the Bible.

The committee made it clear that the speakers at the Conference were "neither idle star-gazers, erratic timesetters, nor theological adventurers."[1] On the positive side, these speakers were known for "their ecclesiastical standing, their spirituality of heart, their scholarship, their eloquence."[2]

The secretary of the Conference was Evangelist George C. Needham, who was a member of Gordon's church, the Clarendon Street Baptist in Boston. To him must go the credit for organizing the Conference, but we are at a loss to know anything more about him, for the published works on the conferences make only passing reference to him, and his name appears only rarely in the records of the times. Gordon and Brookes were the most prominent names. Evidently, Needham was willing to use his gift for organizing and then left the scene. But his name deserves recognition among early Fundamentalists.

On the last day of the Conference a set of resolutions was passed, and they were identical to the affirmations of the 1878 conference; in brief, their message was as follows:

(1) Absolute authority of the Word on doctrine and duty.
(2) The literal fulfillment of the prophetic words about His second coming.
(3) The second coming is "everywhere in the Scriptures represented as imminent and may occur at any moment."[3]
(4) The world will not be converted nor become a reign of peace before His coming but "only at and by His Coming in power and glory will the prophecies concerning the progress of evil and the development of Antichrist, the times of the Gentiles, the ingathering of Israel, the resurrection of the dead in Christ, and the transfiguration of His living saints, receive their fulfillment, and the period of millennial blessedness its inauguration."[4]
(5) The duty of the church is to watch and pray, work and wait, to go into all the world and preach the Gospel to every creature and thus hasten the coming of the day of God.
(6) "The doctrine of our Lord's premillennial advent, instead of paralyzing evangelistic and missionary effort, is one of the mightiest incentives to earnestness in preaching the Gospel to every creature, until He comes."[5]

The Conference met in Farwell Hall, Chicago, from November 16 through November 21. Presiding was the secretary, George C.

[1] *Prophetic Studies of the International Prophetic Conference.* (New York: Revell, 1886), Preface.
[2] Ibid.
[3] Ibid.
[4] Ibid.
[5] Ibid.

Needham, who had been pastor at Moody Church and was now in evangelistic work and living at Manchester-On-The-Sea, Massachusetts. Its interdenominational character was evident, for on the committee and the program were men from Baptist, Congregational, Methodist, Lutheran, Presbyterian, and Anglican churches. For reasons not given, the Brethren, Adventist, and Holiness groups were not represented. Possibly, their size and lack of outstanding and well-known Bible expositors was a factor.

Since the 1886 conference reaffirmed the resolutions and doctrines and emphases of 1878, and in more detail, an examination of the 1886 meeting will prove helpful. The depth of Biblical perception, lucidity of language, profound range of prophetic perspective, and sharp knowledge of key passages in the matters of prophecy are noteworthy. Their exposure of prevailing conditions and defections was unusually outspoken and unrestrained. These men were so bent on telling the prophetic truth and exposing the savage enemies of the Word that they were most refreshingly bold. They spoke all the truths in love but were unusually outspoken about the things that were and things that were to come. The summations of their papers and addresses reveal these great traits. There was a wise combination of pastors, professors, and evangelists, but by far the largest number were pastors. This has been a continuing point of strength of Fundamentalism, namely, that pastors stationed in the front line trenches have felt most keenly the full impact of unbiblical attacks on people and have been motivated to meet that attack with an all-out defense of all the Bible. All too often professors have been content to enunciate the truth but reticent to take up the cudgels when the attacks are most severe and use them where they will be most effective. But there has been a remnant of pastors whose hearts have been most deeply stirred by the Grand Erosion evident everywhere, who have been bold, by grace, to do all to defend the Faith both in principle and practice. A matter of deep discouragement to many faithful pastors, laboring in a most difficult field, has been the lack of support from college and seminary professors, who have spent too much time with theory and too little in the active use of the whole armor of God in the present struggle.

We turn to an examination of the Conference sessions, truths, dogmas, observations, and positions concerning prophecy and prevailing theological views and drifts.

The 1886 conference grew out of the 1878 meeting in New York. A Committee of twenty-one had been named, and several of these were the main voices for early Fundamentalism—men such as Gordon, Brookes, Needham, Nicholson, Frost, Kellogg, and West. Of the twenty-one, four were from Boston, one from St. Louis, two from

Chicago, three from Canada, two from Pennsylvania, two from Ohio, and one each from New York, Wisconsin, Kansas, Minnesota, Virginia, California, and Indiana. Only one was from the South; it was not till the next generation of Fundamentalists that the South took millennialism seriously and men arose to oppose creeping Liberalism and postmillennialism. But in this period the Southern churches, ordinarily conservative and Gospel preaching, were recovering from the horrible devastations of the Civil War. It was a generation later that the more serious trends of Modernism and Liberalism were to do their hatchet jobs on Southern colleges and seminaries. Thus Northern churchmen were to lead in the first generation of Fundamentalist protest and dissent. In fact, too many in the South have been satisfied with a conservative position and have failed to see all the attacks and issues and recognize the necessity of a Fundamentalist position. For this reason, Fundamentalism has remained a minority movement in the South; for while the South today has many hard-working and faithful Fundamentalists in its pulpits, these are greatly outnumbered by the conservative, orthodox, middle-of-the-road men who will not take a clean-cut separatist position.

We have already listed the main truths enunciated in the sessions. On the negative side, other things were discussed with genuine conviction and urgency. The following are the main ones:

(1) The present time is marked by increasing hardness and blindness. The Gospel is not winning, for the present time is marked by the darkest combinations of organized wickedness and godlessness ... most fiendish cruelties and tortures ... most grievous and sickening moral leprosy" (E. F. Stroeter, a Wesleyan of Warrenton, Mo.). Even elements of progress in religion, education and politics form a "lever of perdition."

(2) There ought to be more separation from the world in order to have service, suffering, and sacrifice.

(3) The second coming is separate from the fall of Jerusalem or the death of any individual. The second coming involves the Man in the Glory Who will come visibly, and there is no reference to the death of individuals in passages on the coming.

(4) It is not true that the Spirit will leave the earth at the coming. In fact during the Great Tribulation the world will be baptized or flooded with the Spirit (Rev. F. H. Chapell of Flemington, N. J.). In 1889 Gordon named Chapell the first professor of theology in the newly organized Boston Missionary Training School, which later was renamed as Gordon College to honor the founder.[6]

(5) A. T. Pierson of Philadelphia stressed the imminency of His Com-

---

[6]For a study of the Fundamentalism of Chapell see George W. Dollar, "The Reverend Frank L. Chapell," *Bibliotheca Sacra*, 120 (1963), 126-36.

ing and saw in it two aspects, namely, its certainty (assurance that He will come) and uncertainty (we do not know the time of His coming). The Early Church held to imminency, and because it did it was permeated and penetrated by missionary enthusiasm. When imminency has not been taught or believed, then believers have drifted into self-indulgence and controversy on minor issues.

(6)   There is a woeful lack of general dispensational teaching. All dispensations have had the following features:

advance in revelation
gradual declension
conformity to the world
emerging large civilization (larger but more godless)
parallel development of evil and good
apostasy
catastrophe

(7)   The present times reveal a ripening bordering on rottenness, said Pierson, even an awful anarchy resulting from atheism.

(8)   The Millennium is not to be an outgrowth of human development, achievement, or progress. Daniel saw the rise of the Stone Who would crush human governments.

(9)   The defection in the theological schools is due to a progressive orthodoxy of a new theology that insinuates its subtle coils into theological seminaries. Now an ethical conscience takes the place of the Cross of Christ, and "millions of believers are swept away by mighty tidal waves of error."[7] The landmarks of the Fathers are removed, and "we expect to see the evil come to its awful ripeness."[8]

J. M. Orrock of Boston drew attention to the Revelation 20 passage which has been a favorite of Fundamentalists since and which galls spiritualizers and Liberals with the pointedness of its teachings on Satan, the saints, and the earth under future control. Many lessons should be learned from this passage, and Orrock, a student of Adventist ideas for forty years, pointed out the errors of Millerites, who had set 1843 and 1846 as the dates for His coming but were, of course, disappointed. Yet Orrock frontally denies many charges made against Adventists, such as wearing ascension robes in 1843 and being characterized by extreme excitement. Scholarship was against all Adventist views, but this pastor said, if a man has good common sense, has a fair English education, and is taught by the Spirit in the Word, he will "know more of the mind of the Lord than college professors and doctors of divinity who are not humble enough to hear and take God at His Word."[9]

Another charge against Fundamentalists was that they contended for bloody sacrifices after the coming and all the temple sacrifices' being reestablished according to Ezekiel 40-48. Orrock

[7]*Prophetic Studies,* p. 36.
[8]Ibid.
[9]Ibid., p. 44.

stated very bluntly that many premillennials did not believe that, and here again is a feature that distinguishes early Fundamentalists from modern dispensationalists, who are insistent on this point. Orrock pointed to the extended work of G. N. H. Peters, who in his massive work, *Theocratic Kingdom,* does not sustain such a view.

Professor Henry Lummis of Lawrence University in Appleton, Wisconsin, studied the predictions of Christ of things to come, and he did so "by the common sense of the common people."[10] It was just as easy to understand the predictive words of Christ about the future as it was to grasp what He meant when He predicted the denials of Peter, for "the latter requires the adoption of no mystical sense to harmonize His words with the facts."[11] In His prophetic statement on Lazarus He used a figurative word, "sleep"; and this the literalist admits and recognizes, for "to reach that actual sense is to reach the literal meaning."[12]

A Reformed pastor from Orange, New Jersey, George S. Bishop, addressed himself to the phrase "times of the Gentiles," which he applied to the Church dispensation, but added, "the phrase does not include the church, which, looked upon as heavenly, is outside the scene altogether and, incognito, waits for her rapture."[13] These times are to ripen into the time of the Antichrist, and he showed that the Book of Daniel gave a telescopic panorama in the Great Image and the Four Empires (Babylon, Persia, Greece, and Rome) and pointed out that "the world of the present is Rome."[14] The same subject is presented from God's view in the Beast, and God reveals that the trend of human development is not up but down. A beast has intelligence and strength, but no higher nature. These times show "progressive deterioration . . . metallic values of image decline . . . scripture teaches that the world . . . grows worse and worse."[15] The speaker pointed to the false system on earth, namely Rome. This descent is from "God's will to man's will"[16] and "all refinements of civilization are always in direct relation with the forgetfulness of God."[17] Humanity is described as being self-deifying and self-exalting.

A Congregational pastor from Boston, W. J. Erdman, studied the fulness of the Gentiles of Romans 11:25-27. To understand and believe what is taught is to have the proper antidote to the self-

[10]Ibid., p. 46.
[11]Ibid.
[12]Ibid., p. 48.
[13]Ibid., p. 49.
[14]Ibid., p. 51.
[15]Ibid., p. 52.
[16]Ibid., p. 54.
[17]Ibid.

complacency of believers who think there is no future for Israel. Does "fulness" refer to the full number as nations or as persons? Is "all Israel" to be spiritualized (as by Calvin) in order to include all the redeemed of all the ages? It clearly means the natural, national Israel. There are several reasons given why "fulness" refers to individuals and not nations. It is noted that until Israel shall be saved, the nations of the earth will not be converted. The work of God is to reach a peak when national conversion of Israel takes place.

The Abraham of American Fundamentalism, A. J. Gordon, made one of the outstanding addresses of the Conference when he dealt with latter-day delusions. At the 1878 conference, this noted expositor and spiritual leader had contributed a most significant exegesis of Revelation 20 and had proved, conclusively, that the two resurrections of that passage must be physical resurrections and that one may not be spiritualized to mean the new birth of believers, a favorite claim of those who rejected the millennial position. He realized that it was possible to exaggerate the successes or evils of the present time, but the believer must face up to the present-day schemes of the Evil One in the deluding of the saints. Gordon was, by any standards, one of the outstanding orators of the period. He contended eloquently that Satan was masquerading "in the symbols and sacraments of the church, to manipulate the machinery of miracles, and by supernatural signs and wonders to accredit the doctrine of demons."[18]

One needs only to look to I Timothy 4 and Revelation 13 to be instructed in the work of demons and thereby to see the appalling characteristics of the 1880's as "seducing spirits, doctrines of demons, and Satanic miracles."[19] Gordon found the superstitions of his day to be of three types:

(1) Spiritualism proceeding from the pit.
(2) Ritualism proceeding from the papacy.
(3) Theosophy proceeding from paganism.

Under the first form of superstition, he discovered this practice of demonology to have twenty million followers, although condemned in Exodus 7:2 and 22:18. Too many people deny the existence of demons and have become the easiest prey to their seductions. Thousands of Christians are now in the coils of this delusion. When many claim "to talk to departed friends they are really talking to fallen spirits. Every preceding dispensation closed with an outbreak of demoniacal manifestation."[20] If Gordon were on the scene today he would, doubtlessly, point to the celebrated Bishop Pike case as an

18Ibid., p. 63.
19Ibid.
20Ibid., p. 65.

evidence of speaking to evil spirits, although Pike claimed he spoke to his dead son. This is hair-raising even to consider, let alone believe!

Gordon referred to the famous John Henry Newman, who left the Anglican Church to go into the Church of Rome while admitting that holy water and other elements in Romish worship were "very instruments and appendages of demon worship now sanctified by adoption into the church."[21] It is in the Book of Ezekiel that God denounces such heathen practices as weeping for Tammuz (identical with the pagan god Osiris) as part of Babylonianism. The initial letter of Tammuz is now seen in the cross; for Tau, the nineteenth letter of the Greek alphabet, was used in Babylonian worship as early as 1500 B.C. Gordon drew upon the useful research of Hislop's good work, *The Two Babylons*. The Book of Baruch in the Apocrypha has a detailed description of Babylonian rituals including processions of priests, candles, images, and the confessional. Rather than the church's sanctifying them, as Newman claimed, "the Church," Gordon declared, "has been unsanctified by their adoption."[22] Two of the greatest errors coming from this verse are baptismal regeneration and transubstantiation, the latter being "the center and sum of the mystery of lawlessness."[23]

In Psalm 96:5 and I Corinthians 10:20 these false gods of men are plainly identified as demons directed by Satan; Roman apostasy has been "that career of blood and blasphemy unmatched by anything in human history."[24] Gordon stated that in the Roman system "Satan is the real Pope (and) . . . demons the real cardinals."[25] Few churchmen of our day would be so outspoken, no matter how vile a system had become. Gordon named two scholars of the Roman system, Manning and Newman, both of whom were prostrating themselves on their faces before a deified man, Manning writing that "in the person of Pius IX, Jesus reigns on earth and He must reign till He hath put all enemies under His feet."[26] Such blasphemy stirred the Fundamentalists of that day to their depths and aroused their undying hatred for a system that promotes such theological delusions. According to Gordon, "Rome is so drunk with the blood of the martyrs that she does not even know that she has been drinking."[27] He concluded that the return of any Protestant nation to Rome would put that nation under the sway of demons.

[21]Ibid.
[22]Ibid., p. 66.
[23]Ibid.
[24]Ibid., p. 67.
[25]Ibid.
[26]Ibid.
[27]Ibid.

In addition, Gordon contended that another delusion was "the cooking stove apostasy," which saw many church basements turned into "places of feasting."[28] He deplored this practice and said, we "lift up our warning against them as another device of the enemy for corrupting and enervating the Church of God."[29] When he spoke these solemn words of warning, those on the platform and in the congregation arose and voiced their sentiments with a great amen. This was a historic moment for Fundamentalism, when one of its revered leaders solemnly charged the church with delusion in having feasts in church basements. (Not many have followed this leader's serious warning.) He finished his message on delusions with more scathing words on the Roman pontiff. They bear full repetition lest any charge that Fundamentalists did not realize the real enemies of the Word and say so. To them, Romanism was no theological theory but a great and brash Satanic conspiracy which ought to be unmasked and carefully described. Gordon said:

> I speak rather of the Book than of any human books and avow my conviction that the Papal Man of Sin was accurately photographed on the camera of prophecy thousands of years ago; that no detective searching for him today would need any other description of him than that found on the pages of the Bible. Taking these photographs of Daniel and John and Paul and searching the world upside down for their originals, I am confident that this same detective would stop at the Vatican, and after gazing a few moments at the Pontiff, who sits there gnawing the bone of infallibility, which he acquired in 1870, and clutching for that other bone of temporal sovereignty which he lost the very same year, he would lay his hand on him and say 'you are wanted in the court of the Most High to answer to the indictment of certain souls beneath the altar who were slain for the Word of God and for the testimony which they bore and who are crying 'How long, O Lord holy and true, dost Thou not judge and avenge our blood on them that dwell upon the earth.' My brethren, let us search the Scriptures anew and be sure that they do not require it of us before we silence our testimony against the Man of Rome as Antichrist.[30]

A Methodist pastor from Abingdon, Virginia, J. S. Kennedy, spoke on "the practical influence and power of Christ's second coming" and in so doing pointed out some twelve lessons to be remembered:

(1) The regeneration of the cosmos is to take place.
(2) All stand face to face with a world crisis.
(3) His coming is at the end of times of Gentiles.
(4) Before the Coming will be "religious formalism, adulterous friendships with the world, waning of faith, tyranny, anarchy, general revolution"[31]

[28]Ibid., p. 68.
[29]Ibid.
[30]Ibid., p. 71.
[31]Ibid., p. 74.

(5)   The Church will be raptured (I Thess. 4).

(6)   It is a motive to mortification of earthly lusts (Col. 3:4-6; Titus 2:11-13; and John 3:2-3).

(7)   It is an incentive to heavenly mindedness.

(8)   It is an incentive to works of mercy (Mat. 25:31-40).

(9)   It is an incentive to pastoral diligence (I Pet. 5:2-4).

(10)   It is an incentive to greater watchfulness (Luke 12:35-37). (Mat. 25 and Luke 12 apply to Gentile Christians, as well as to Jews.)

(11)   It enhances our faith (I Cor. 1:4-8).

(12)   It elevates the affections and emotions.

H. M. Parsons of Toronto, Canada, spoke on the subject of judgments and rewards and turned to three judgments. First of all, there was the Judgment for Christians, on "their motive character" (II Corinthians 5:10; also I Corinthians 9:27, when they are "unable to stand the test"). "It will be an inspection of deeds."[32] There will be a proportionate reward or rejection and "these rewards or losses bear upon the position of believers in the coming Kingdom of Glory."[33] Again, this marks a distinct difference of viewpoint from many Fundamentalists of this day, who slavishly follow the Scofield system and apply all of Matthew 24 and 25 to Jews. Early Fundamentalists did not have a system to straitjacket them. Parsons further declared that the test of the Bema Seat will be conducted on the basis of the glory of God (I Cor. 3:13, 15 and Revelation 4:10). Secondly, there will be a Judgment of the Living Nations (Matt. 25:33). There is a co-partnership on this throne with that innumerable company in this dispensation as predicted in Isaiah 53:11. For admission of the nations to the kingdom of priests we have the wedding garment of Matthew 24:11-12, the oil of Matthew 26:3-4, and the faithful use of the talents of Matthew 25:2-30. Here again we pause to note that early Fundamentalists did not restrict Matthew 24 and 25 to Israel. This has been vigorously denied by dispensationalists of our day, but in that time dispensationalists differed among themselves on this. Those exegetes—and that they were in the highest and truest sense of the word—held that the words "sheep" and "goats" imply "an organized state of Christianity."[34] This judgment may include the millennial age, Parsons concluded, for everlasting punishment has the element of eternity and a final settlement with the nations. Thirdly, there was the Last Judgment as given in Revelation 20:11-15. The place of it is "some point in space apart from our globe."[35] The sentencing then will be on the basis of character as revealed by the books; and no mistake is made, for "The Lamb's Book of Life is searched for the name of every one

[32]Ibid., p. 79.
[33]Ibid.
[34]Ibid., p. 81.
[35]Ibid., p. 82.

condemned by his works."[36] Also, there will be a purgation of the earth as revealed in II Peter 3.

One of the more searching discussions of the entire conference was given by Professor D. C. Marquis of McCormick Theological Seminary in Chicago. His subject was "Eschatology as Taught by Christ." It was a most carefully worded study of Luke 21 and Matthew 24-25. He noted the marked similarity of Luke 21:8-11 and Matthew 24:4-6 and of Luke 21:29-33 and Matthew 24:32-35. These are almost word for word. To Professor Marquis it was a basic premise that Luke 21:12 goes forward and "predicts a history that shall follow events predicted."[37] Matthew deals with the end *(telos),* while Luke does not. Luke is more detailed on the destruction of Jerusalem, and Matthew's signs (24:15) are not for the same event as that of Luke 21:20. It is impossible to harmonize the two as two accounts of the same event. So we have two periods of woe in two different periods of the world's history, although they overlap. In the account by Luke we have (1) warning against deception (vv. 8-9); (2) many natural upheavals in world history (the present age in rapid survey) (vv. 10-11); (3) a turning back to Church troubles and woes to the fall of Jerusalem (v. 12); and (4) persecutions to be faced by the disciples (vv. 12-19). Then the destruction of Jerusalem shall come (vv. 22-24) with the escape of Christians to Pella at the invasion of Titus. Then follows Gentile domination until the times of the Gentiles are fulfilled and "reaches now the very point indicated at the close of v. 11." Then will come (5) the opening of a Great Tribulation (v. 26) and (6) the glorious appearing (v. 27), for the "separation of the saints from the world shall take place at the beginning of the Tribulation."[38] So this is strictly a pre-tribulation truth. The only sign of the start of the great tribulation (v. 29) is the budding of leaves (troubles), though "we can predict nothing as to time but with the fulfillment, times are to fall within the limits of a single generation, 'this generation.' "[39]

As to the Matthew account, Professor Marquis started with the premise that Matthew was keenly aware of the future of Israel. Jesus was asked for a sign of the *parousia* ("coming" or "presence") and the consummation of the age; and these were probably suggested to the disciples by their previous hearing of the Lukan discourse. Jesus began his answer with a repetition of the previous discourse (almost word for word) (vv. 4-7), speaking of Church trials (vv. 4-6), and an epitome of the world's history (v. 7). But Matthew's account goes not back but forward to sketch the history of the Jews during the

[36]Ibid.
[37]Ibid., p. 84.
[38]Ibid., p. 85.
[39]Ibid.

tribulation of the end time, and six characteristics of that time appear:

(1) A peculiar enmity by the nations of earth.
(2) Defection and betrayals among themselves.
(3) False prophets deceiving many.
(4) Faithful being discouraged.
(5) Those abiding faithful through apostasy to be saved.
(6) The testifying to the Gospel of the Kingdom.

He pointed to the "abomination of desolation" and rejected the theory that it took place at the destruction of Jerusalem in 70 A.D. because the sign was asked about His *parousia* and not about any destruction. He tried to understand the Greek preposition *oun* ("therefore"). The abomination had to refer to something dealing with restored Israel. (It could be the Man of Lawlessness of II Thess. 2.) When he does appear, then the saints are to leave (vv. 17-18), due distress is to come (vv. 19-21), and the period is to be shortened (v. 22) for the sake of the elect. Then (v. 23) would follow the Great Tribulation, which is the reign of the coming false messiah or Antichrist. Just as corruption is everywhere visible, so shall be the coming of the true Messiah (vv. 23-28). This will be immediately succeeded by the throes of dissolution in nature (v. 29), the loosing of laws over solar bodies, and the appearing of Christ in His glory. Angels will gather (v. 31) from earth and heaven those saved before the Tribulation and during it. The Tribulation will fall within one generation (v. 34), and people will not be expecting it any more than they expected the judgment in Noah's day (vv. 37-39). This is illustrated in the two farmers and the two women, of which one of each pair is taken to meet the Lord and the other left (vv. 40-41). Modern dispensationalists take the opposite view, saying that those taken are for judgment and those left are to enter the millennial reign. The command to watch is annulled if we are to watch and then see some taken for judgment.

Then Marquis gave a Fundamentalist position on the parables of the ten virgins, saying they "illustrate the reception He will have from the Church at the Parousia," and of the talents, which show "the principle on which awards will be distributed at the Parousia or judgment." It follows that "the Bible teaches a dual Parousia of grace and judgment and a dual dispensation of Gentile and Jew as constituting the age."[40] Dispensationalists following Scofield have restricted Matthew 24 and 25 to Israel, for the virgins and talents must be so interpreted. This interpretation has found a large following, but there are still many (including the writer) who apply it to the Church.

Also on the program, but unable to attend, was J. R. Graves of

[40]Ibid., p. 89.

Memphis, Tennessee, a famed pastor of deep Scriptural insights and writer of the Landmark persuasion. The well-known Robert G. Lee described him as the greatest orator Southern Baptists ever produced. This recognition from such a prominent Baptist leader is high praise indeed. Many books by Graves are today still available from the headquarters of the American Baptist Association in Texarkana, Texas. Graves believed Jesus began a Baptist church, and fellowship with, or immersion by, one other than one in a line of succession from John the Baptist would be error in thought and practice. Graves held it was not an organic line but a line of sound New Testament principle and polity. He was a foe of the "invisible church" theory, believing, as did B. H. Carroll, in the local church as the New Testament church, since ecclesia must mean an assembly. For a full understanding of this position, see B. H. Carroll's *Ecclesia.*[41] A strong segment of Baptist Fundamentalism has followed the Graves position and certainly that of Carroll, but a large number follow Scofield in holding to an "invisible church," of which the local church is only a manifestation. The latter position owes its widespread popularity to the Scofield Reference Bible and the writings of many Brethren authors and Bible teachers such as J. N. Darby. A head count today of Independent Baptists would give the local church group the majority, but there is a strong minority for the invisible church-view because of their training in the Bible institutes, colleges, and seminaries.

Albert Erdman of Morristown, New Jersey, read a paper on Jude and its emphasis on the "once-for-all" faith, concluding "that no other faith will ever be given. In Jude there is a reference to every Fundamental doctrine which in our day is assaulted, disputed, and denied."[42] One such doctrine is "grace," and for it there is substituted looseness, excesses, or church ordinances. There are denials of the vicarious sacrifice of Christ, the Trinity, a personal devil, the bodily resurrection, future eternal punishment, and the doctrine of the second coming. All these are vital doctrines of the Faith; these are facts and sublime realities of the Christian faith. The primitive faith produced those who believed it and therefore were "ready to contend for it, defend it, testify to it, and die for it."[43]

At one session, a letter was read from Canon Faussett (of the widely used Jamieson, Faussett, and Brown commentary), who wrote that "my own plan has been to investigate the literal and grammatical sense of each passage."[44] Then the context and the circumstances of time and place were examined by the great canon.

[41]This can be ordered from the press of the *Baptist Examiner* in Ashland, Kentucky.
[42]*Prophetic Studies*, p. 91.
[43]Ibid., p. 93.
[44]Ibid.

He quoted with approval Augustine, who said that "the literal sense of Scripture is the basis of the Scripture, else the latter would be a building resting on air."[45]

A learned Presbyterian, Professor W. G. Moorehead of Xenia, Ohio, spoke on Antichrist. He started with Daniel 7:7-11 and used II Thessalonians 2 and Revelation 13 in dealing with three schools of interpretation—the preterist, the present, and the futurist. He found the word Antichrist used four times in the New Testament—I John 2:18-22; 4:3; and II John 7. He understood Antichrist as another Christ, a pretender to the name of Christ, one counterfeiting Christ and who fights against Christ. Daniel pictured him as a beast and a representation of political power. He has eyes like a man (Dan. 7), which points to "predominant intellect, dazzling intelligence, power to know men and to sway them."[46] His success is pointed out in Daniel 8:23-25 and Revelation 13:13-14. He is the supreme blasphemer (II Thess. 2:9-10). He sets aside all authority, human and divine, and then wars against the saints. All three pictures point to an apostasy, and in Daniel 8:23 we are told that it will occur when transgressors are come to the full. In II Thessalonians 2 it is given as coming at the time when the falling away is at its flood, and in Revelation 13, when men worship the Beast. So the willful king of David, the Lawless One of Paul, and the Beast of John are one, the Antichrist. Some have tried to identify Nero as Antichrist, but Nero died by his own hand in a villa four miles from Rome. The Antichrist will be destroyed by the coming of the Lord. The prevailing Fundamentalist view is that popery is the Beast, and there are remarkable similarities as "related to the Old Roman Empire, wide departure from the truth, idolatry, persecuting spirit, daring assumptions, blasphemous pretensions."[47] But they differ in the following:

(1) Antichrist is atheistic (I John 2:22 and Dan. 11:36-37). The papacy has never been atheistic.
(2) Antichrist is the blasphemous head of civil power. The papacy has only a very petty rule.
(3) Antichrist has universal sway.
(4) Antichrist gives two alternatives—worship or die (Rev. 13:15).
(5) The apostate church has some saints in it, but there is not a single saint among the Beast-worshippers.
(6) The Beast is distinct from the Harlot (Rev. 17).

The woman "represents the false apostate church."[48] She is seated on the Beast and "compels him to support her, guides, and uses him

[45]Ibid., p. 95.
[46]Ibid., p. 99.
[47]Ibid., p. 101.
[48]Ibid., p. 102.

for the accomplishment of her purposes."[49] But the Beast and ten Kings will hate and "tear her bedizened rags from her loathsome body, her polluted flesh from her putrid bones."[50] The Antichrist is characterized by the Scriptures as follows:

(1) He is a person. All actions are those of a personality. Paul calls him a Man of Sin.
(2) He is the supreme head of world power in final and diabolical form.
(3) He is of supernatural origin (Rev. 11:7 and 17:8), for he comes out of the bottomless pit and Satan gives him his powers. He has a parousia (II Thess. 2).
(4) He will appear when the person or something which is restraining is removed. Professor Morehead held it was "the moral civil order of society."[51]

There has been a check on the flood of lawlessness, but the world of civilization and progress will end in revolt against God.

During one session of the Conference a letter was received from D. L. Moody, who believed that "the coming of the Lord was a most precious truth and constant inspiration to work." Another letter came from A. G. Brown, Baptist leader in England, who regretted that dispensational truth had been ignored, said that Christianity was apostate, and stated that he held "the Lord's Return, my brightest hope and my most powerful inspiration for unwearied service."[52] A. A. Bonar also wrote that the Blessed Hope was an awakening doctrine and that he was "stimulated greater to do my utmost through the Grace of God to gather in souls at home and abroad."[53]

Another letter came from Professor Godet who did not defend

the spiritualizer who reduces the prophetic pictures to facts already accomplished or daily occurring, or interprets the prophecies in a merely ethical manner ... Jesus has not thus intended ... neither did the Apostles of Jesus so interpret them and the Apostles of Jesus are not false prophets.[54]

This learned European scholar said that he divided things to come into three categories, namely, things preceding the coming, the coming itself, and the things following the coming. About things before His coming, there will be little or no faith on the earth (Luke 18:8). Days will be like those of Noah and "among the Jews there will be a condition of Gentile infidelity."[55] There will be apostasy, and from a bosom of apostasy will arise the Man of Sin as a "false Jewish

---

[49]Ibid.
[50]Ibid.
[51]Ibid., p. 106.
[52]Ibid., p. 41.
[53]Ibid., p. 42.
[54]Ibid., p. 120.
[55]Ibid.

Messiah."[56] In the area of coming events, Godet rapidly surveyed more general material already mentioned in this study.

Nathaniel W. West, of the First Presbyterian Church in Minneapolis, delivered a long discourse on prophecy and Israel. He started by claiming that all the past and future of Israel has been ordained by God, since "the fortunes of Israel are, have been, and will be precisely what God intends."[57] Salvation is from the Jews, "by the free grace and compassion of God."[58] He listed many things about the past and the future of Israel, for it is Israel who is "to form the outward visible glory at the end of the present age."[59] In prophecy Israel is the elect agent of salvation, and Israel and Messiah are "indissolubly united as mediators and bringers of salvation to the world, one nationally, the other personally."[60] Jesus spoke of one generation that would not pass away, and He was speaking of one race, the Jews. In the future Israel shall shine again as the national leader and light of the world. The "first made last by unbelief shall yet become the last made first by faith."[61] There is a law that governs the unveiling of all divine plans, and Christians should see the near and far horizons with Israel as the central figure. The events are far apart but look close together; when we understand this we come to apprehend the law that governs. Much that seems to point to the first coming will be found to belong to the second coming and "much of what seems to belong to the Second Coming belongs to an epoch or age later on."[62] Sometimes a partial fulfillment is necessary together with a future event, such as the Day of Pentecost, for Joel's prophecy was not exhausted at Pentecost nor at the fall of Jerusalem; the predictions of Christ for "prophecy has a precursive fulfillment in history ... looking to the ultimate and covering all intermediate fulfillments."[63] Thus we can see both the Now (times of the Gentiles) and the Beyond (the times of the Jews). But we can never see the basileia (Kingdom) come, apart from Israel's national conversion.

West rejected the spiritualizing of "Old Testament prophecy to see the church as taking Israel's place."[64] In the place of this theory he accepted the "realistic" interpretation, which "takes predictions and promises in a literal sense and not as abstract spiritual truths clothed in perishable literary envelopes of Oriental imagery or

[56]Ibid.
[57]Ibid., p. 122.
[58]Ibid.
[59]Ibid.
[60]Ibid., p. 123.
[61]Ibid.
[62]Ibid.
[63]Ibid., p. 124.
[64]Ibid.

Jewish drapery."[65] This literal interpretation was that of the Early Church for three hundred years. But in the fourth century the church-state alliance arose, and a false interpretation of Revelation resulted. Alexandrine philosophy arose; the pride of the Roman hierarchy and contempt of the Jews increased, and as a result "the present heretical faith of the State Church became orthodox."[66] In this change the Jew was ousted from his central place, and the content of prophecy was changed. The line between Israel and the Church was obliterated. All promised blessings to Israel were now applied to the Church, while the curses on Israel were left out in their literal sense. This is, at best, an extremely arbitrary exegesis. "Israel was spoiled and robbed in the name of hermeneutics, under the delusion of a fourth-century millennium with an unbaptized heathen [Constantine] on the throne."[67] The dining room of a Roman emperor was identified as the New Jerusalem of the Book of Revelation!

To offset this perversion, Paul wrote Romans 9-11, which is a philosophy of history of both Jew and Gentile. Was the covenant of God to Israel conditional or unconditional? Israel was set aside but only temporarily, for Israel is still "His people." Its historic mission is now in abeyance, all "Israel in solidarity and acting nationally as one shall be saved."[68] To be ignorant of this breeds conceit in the Church, conceit begotten of false wisdom, pride, and Gentile boasting. The odor of this conceit

> was already in the air when Paul wrote to seven-hilled Rome his celebrated Three Chapters. Its beginning already floated in those classic Gentile Cities of the Roman world where the church had been planted, omen of that spreading darkness of understanding whereby soon all Christendom would appropriate to itself the prophecies concerning Israel's distinctive future and tell the world that these are now accomplished in the Christian Church.[69]

Israel alone "is the bringer of salvation to the world."[70] Citing Romans 11:15 West said that "just as Christ's resurrection brought new life to the nations, so Israel's resurrection shall bring a new life to the nations of the world."[71] Peter referred to this in Acts 3:19-21. This will be preceded by a tribulation, unparalleled since the world began. There will be "new life out of the dead," and this "new life" has at least a dozen characteristics:

(1) Outbursting power careening through a millennial age.

[65]Ibid.
[66]Ibid., p. 125.
[67]Ibid.
[68]Ibid., p. 126.
[69]Ibid., pp. 126-27
[70]Ibid., p. 127.
[71]Ibid., p. 128.

(2) Life in a national sense (Israel).
(3) Life in a literal sense.
(4) Life for the sleeping saints of God in both dispensations and re-
      stored Israel in front of all.
(5) The resurrection of Israel (Ez. 37:7-9; Dan. 12:1-3; Isa. 26:10).
(6) The sunrise of the Jews (Rev. 20:9; Isa. 60:1).
(7) A deluge of salvation (Heb. 7:14; Isa. 11:9 and 66:19).
(8) The passing of spiritual death from the earth.
(9) The appearance and rule of Israel's king as King of Kings.

Franz Delitzsch wrote to the Conference in a letter dated October
14, 1886, that "in predictions of Last Things spiritual interpretation
would be a distortion of their original meaning, a flat negation of
what is said."[72] The well-known Bible exegete stated that the Book of
Revelation represents the *eschata* ("last things") in their future
chronology. Delitzsch added, "I believe in the literal reality of the
apocalyptic picture without pressing slavishly the letter."[73] He did
sound a note out of temper with others on the program in rejecting
the idea of Christ, reigning on a throne in Jerusalem, and termed
this "crass Chiliasm."[74]

Bishop W. R. Nicholson of the Reformed Episcopal Church of
Philadelphia spoke on the kingly glory of Messiah and made some
ten main points in his discourse:

(1) Jesus' reign as Messiah.
(2) Jesus' reign on an earthly throne.
(3) The preaching of a Gospel of the Kingdom.
(4) The identity of the Kingdom of Heaven as the Kingdom of God.
(5) The reestablishment of the Throne of David.
(6) The rebuilding of tabernacle of David.
(7) The rehabilitation of Israel in its own country.
(8) The innovation of physical nature.
(9) The health of all humans.
(10) The establishment of one grand, perfect government over all.

J. D. Herr, a Baptist pastor of Milwaukee, set forth three major
reasons for studying prophecy:

(1) To see the emphases which the Bible itself makes. "The prophetic
      writings of the Bible constitute the major portion of the Bible,"[75]
      yet too many have been timid or silent on these.
(2) To know and follow the teachings of Christ about the future.
(3) To "learn the true destiny of the world"[76] History is the dial-plate
      upon which "the finger of God indicates the epochs of prophecy."[77]

The author of the widely used *Theocratic Kingdom,* G. N. H.
Peters, a Lutheran from Springfield, Ohio, spoke on the subject of

---

[72]Ibid., p. 137.
[73]Ibid., p. 138.
[74]Ibid.
[75]Ibid., p. 154
[76]Ibid.
[77]Ibid., p. 155.

the covenants and the Kingdom. At this session prayer was offered by President Charles Blanchard of Wheaton College.[78] Peters asked how believers should relate the promises made to Abraham, Isaac, and Jacob to the coming Kingdom. These covenants were confirmed by oath and no matter how long the period of time, there is absolute assurance they will be verified. Peters observed that most Christians reject the entire Davidic Covenant—it is "utterly ignored."[79] Are we to take these promises in "their plain grammatical meaning?"[80] His answer was a dogmatic "yes."

> Is it in the nature of a covenant that embraces the vital interests of the Messiah, of believers, of the race, of the world that it should be so constructed that, instead of conveying a decisive meaning clearly expressed in its wording, it presents a hidden or typical one which requires the revolution of centuries to develop through such men as Origen, Augustine, Swedenborg and others? Would God who said (Matt. 7:9) 'what man is there of you whom, if his son ask bread, will he give him a stone?' give a grammatical signification, accessible to all who read, that is deceptive and misleading that fosters a faith which can never be attained, and that leads to hopes which can never be realized?[81]

Peters noted that some have unfairly criticized our faith as "fanatical" and extravagant in this age "that abounds in unbelief."[82] The believer should follow the example of Abraham, who believed the promises of God. The covenant with Abraham had to do with the earth, that it will be delivered from the curse and renewed under the all-providing creative hand of Him Who will make all things new. From the time these covenants were made by the Lord there "must be a direct and special intervention of a power exerted by the supernatural."[83] Because of these promises there will be:

(1) Inheritance of a renewed earth.
(2) Effectual removal of the curse.
(3) Glorious theocratic reign of His co-heirs.
(4) Perpetual deliverance from suffering, sickness, tears, sorrow, and death.
(5) Removal of the bondage of nature.
(6) Restoration of all forfeited blessings.[84]

If this covenant fails, then the blood of Jesus has lost its power, "its sealing efficaciousness."[85] But we have faith in that precious blood. The death of Christ is a "requisite to a restoring to us once forfeited

---

[78]See George W. Dollar, "Dr. Charles A. Blanchard and the Book of the Revelation," *Bibliotheca Sacra,* 120 (July-Sept., 1963), 243-50.
[79]*Prophetic Essays,* p. 158.
[80]Ibid.
[81]Ibid., p. 159.
[82]Ibid., p. 160.
[83]Ibid., p. 161.
[84]Ibid.
[85]Ibid., p. 163.

but now covenanted blessings of an Edenic state."[86] It is error to "limit a portion as demanded by so-called progress to modify or change the plain grammatical sense."[87]

A. J. Frost of Sacramento, California, read a paper on the conditions prevailing at the time of the second advent. He believed things will grow morally worse both in the Church and the state and that this dispensation will end in diabolical wickedness; there will come the downfall of all human institutions and the complete overthrow of the great world powers. It will close in the utter failure of man's hopes. From the past dispensations we learn the age-old story of man's faithlessness and lack of responsibility. Frost took a close look at four dispensations—the paradisical, the antediluvian, the patriarchal, and the Mosaic. Of the first one he said, "Never did one start with better opportunities and more favorable prospects," but "it ended in universal apostasy."[88] In the second period there was good and evil in worship (Cain and Abel), in alliances as well as in judgments. In the patriarchal age, Noah and his family stood at the head of a new dispensation, and there was a new trial of good and evil; "it closed with the world lying in wickedness and God's chosen people in bondage."[89]

To Frost, no method of exegesis could overthrow the fact that our Lord, in speaking of the condition of the world at His second coming, purposely selected the "darkest period in both the antediluvian and patriarchal dispensations to represent the coming apostasy and retributive judgments of God."[90] In the Mosaic period one nation [the Hebrews] "so exalted to Heaven in privilege . . . [yet displayed] idolatry and spiritual whoredom."[91] In the vision of Daniel, there were four kingdoms in world power, and all four were to deteriorate to the end. He pointed out that in the parables of Christ the tares outgrew the wheat and that the treasure will be taken out and not the whole field taken. In all the prophecies of Christ and the apostles there is not one that tells of the rise of universal reception of the Gospel. Shall He find faith on the earth? In I Timothy 4 and II Timothy 3 are pictures of departure from the faith. In Matthew 24:30 all nations will mourn, but not one will be converted. As in the days of Belshazzar, these are the days of the world's feasting and merriment, and the captivity of God's people has been forgotten. Now "men are so filled with themselves, their ease, their comforts

---

[86]Ibid., p. 164.
[87]Ibid.
[88]Ibid., pp. 166-67.
[89]Ibid., p. 167.
[90]Ibid.
[91]Ibid.

(this was said in 1886!) that sudden destruction will overtake them."[92]

Frost was the first speaker in the Conference to make reference to the seven churches of Revelation 2-3. He held that they "represent seven successive pages of church history, and that the Laodicean accurately portrays the condition of nominal Christendom at the end of this dispensation."[93] This dispensation will end in the "most fearful apostasy this world has ever known."[94] All believers should heed the clear predictions of Christ, Paul, and Peter as recorded in Matthew 24:11-12, II Timothy 4, and II Peter 3:3-4. The nominal Christian world will be "one vast mass of baptized professions ... a spiritual malformation, a masterpiece of Satan, the corruption of the truth of God ... the darkest moral blot in the universe of God."[95] If one wishes to know the true condition of the nominal church he should "read with blanched cheek and bated breath from the fifth chapter of Revelation to chapter twenty."[96] The postmillennialists are mistaken in quoting from Isaiah 35 and Isaiah 11, for in each passage there is an announcement of judgment or vengeance from God before great blessings. In reality, there is not a passage in the Bible which teaches that the nations are to be converted during the present dispensation. We should look in briefest form at the signs of the times, and among them are the following:

(1) Millions more unconverted people than ever before.
(2) Hypocrisy, impiety, and hollow-heartedness in church and state.
(3) Shameless worldliness of professing Christians.
(4) Insubordination running riot in Christian homes.
(5) Four-fifths of population avoiding the house of God.
(6) Drinking upheld by Catholic and Protestant churches.
(7) Opening of thousands of houses of ill repute by Christian votes.
(8) Increase of unconsecrated wealth in the churches.
(9) Two-thirds of Christendom under one vast overshadowing hierarchy.
(10) Other one-third compromised by rationalism.
(11) Thousands under theological dry rot.
(12) Confulsions within society.[97]

At the end of the volume of these prophetic studies, Needham enunciated the reasons for the conferences. There are six main ones as he gave them and these form a basic part of the reasons for Fundamentalism, for they have characterized the movement. They are the following:

(1) To give prominence to neglected truth. The main truth in mind

[92]Ibid., p. 169.
[93]Ibid.
[94]Ibid.
[95]Ibid., p. 170.
[96]Ibid., p. 171.
[97]Ibid., pp. 173-74.

was unfulfilled prophecy. Before, it had been claimed that prophecy "bred fanaticism" and that it is both "unpractical and non-essential." To these men it showed how far a heart was from God "for any to dare affirm there is anything non-essential in the Bible."[98]

(2) To emphasize the true principles of Scripture interpretation. It lifted up the flag against figurizing. Figurizing or spiritualizing is inconsistent, for it is stated in Zechariah 9 that the Lord should come riding on an ass and in chapter 14 that His feet shall stand on the Mount of Olives. Those who figurize say the first means an ass but the second means the broken heart of the penitent sinner. The conferences insisted that "where no figure is intended the Word of God is to be interpreted in its plain literal and grammatical sense."[99]

(3) To awaken Christians from slumber, since the Hour is near and the saints need to arouse themselves. They need to be awake because of "the present intensity of sin and philosophical forms of wickedness, the unregenerate state of our neighbors, our sons and our daughters, our husbands and our wives; of the drunken state of society, and the benumbed and paralyzed condition of Christendom."[100]

(4) To produce the most majestic motives for world-wide evangelism.

(5) To call attention to the doctrine of last things, which is a bulwark against the skepticism of modern theology, for "premillenarianism, pure and simple, forms a breakwater against every advancing tide which would throw upon the clean beach of a God-given theology the jelly-fish theories, evolved out of man's erratic consciousness, pride, and self-will ... waiting for the Son from heaven is an antidote against the feverishness of the age, as shown in its excited race after theological novelties."[101]

(6) To strengthen greatly the Christian fellowship, for "oneness in Christ is made more real and precious because of this present communion." But it is no special clique—no exclusive company of self-admiring Pharisees, "The memory, so precious of hallowed delight Shall strengthen our faith and equip for the fight When severed in presence there still doth remain, Our oneness in hope of His coming again."[102]

[98]Ibid., p. 215.
[99]Ibid.
[100]Ibid., p. 216.
[101]Ibid.
[102]Ibid.

5
New Winds Blowing

The generation prior to 1900 witnessed the blowing of new winds across the horizon of American Christianity; some were drastically to change religious life, and others were to increase the attacks on the historic faith. These we must recognize, although it is always difficult to assess accurately their total effect for good or evil.

Immigration brought relief to thousands of oppressed Europeans, many of whom had lived in want and poverty. Despair and hopelessness had dogged their steps. Now the Statue of Liberty in New York harbor bade them welcome to a new land, even as it appealed to other countries to send their homeless and their poor. They came and brought with them a rugged allegiance to the traditions and customs of their homelands, as well as a hard and fast loyalty to their religious backgrounds, predominantly Roman Catholicism. Thus America turned from being a predominantly Protestant land to one on which Romanism made increasingly fierce demands. This change has awed politicians and churchmen alike, and the Protestant churches, by and large, have yielded to the influence of Rome, accompanied by invitations to return to this ancient church. The modern ecumenical movement is proof of the success of this strategy of Rome.

Romanism issued new dogmas, such as the famous Syllabus of Errors of Pope Pius X in 1864, which openly condemned protestantism, Bible societies, and the separation of church and state. The doctrine of the Immaculate Conception had been promulgated ten years before. Then, in 1870, the decree of papal infallibility was issued; in essence, it stated that when the Pope spoke ex cathedra, he could make no mistake in matters of faith and practice. Not all Catholics went along with this, and some Old Catholic groups emerged. By 1950 these groups (American Catholic, North American Catholic, and the Old Catholic Church in America) numbered about 90,000. Resentment of Romanist influence in American politics showed in the 1884 presidential campaign when the Reverend S. D. Burchard told some clergy in New York that the antecedents of the Democratic Party were "rum, Romanism, and rebellion." This angered Catholics and probably swung enough votes against the Republican ticket in New York State to send Grover Cleveland to the White House.

New orators appeared among the Liberals to enhance the prestige of anti-orthodox thinking. Foremost among them were Henry Ward Beecher of Brooklyn and Phillips Brooks of Boston. On the evangelical side, the only man of such eminence was T. DeWitt Talmadge of Brooklyn. It is claimed that D. L. Moody had him in mind when he said that he was sick of windmills and tired of essay preaching. Somewhat along the same line of flowery oratory was the eloquence of Russell Conwell of Philadelphia, founder of Temple University.

Still another developing pressure on Bible believers was that of the new "Gospel of Gold." This period was called the Gilded Age, a time when fiscal greatness dawned on the United States and people began to look to money as the road to human happiness and blessing. It was believed that some people became wealthy because America was moral, intelligent, and industrious, and these characteristics were held up as Christian virtues. It was claimed by the industrial giants and captains of capitalism that God had given them large gifts to use for human good as they decided; and this was a religious duty. Thus, many notable financiers gave handsomely to found and maintain such Christian schools as Vanderbilt, Colgate, Crozer, the University of Chicago, and McCormick Seminary. One donation alone, that of John D. Rockefeller, amounting to seventy-five million, was given to build the University of Chicago. Churches received the donations of the czars of industry with gratitude, thus appearing to approve the entire capitalistic system as good and helpful.

When this giving was at a peak, a reaction set in, and its influence has continued and increased. This was the idealistic desire to reform the whole system in the face of great injustices and inequalities within it. The new movement produced the "Social Gospel." It began in this period under such leaders as Washington Gladden, Francis Peabody, Richard T. Ely, and Josiah Strong. Strong's book *Our Country* (1885) contended that greed for money had ruined this land and that it was a national curse that so few owned so much and so many had so little. The issue was popularized by Charles M. Sheldon's *In His Steps,* published in 1897. It was fictional and was read by this Congregational pastor, chapter by chapter each Sunday night, to his congregation in Topeka, Kansas. Its sales ran into the millions, surpassing for a time the sale of any printed work other than the Bible. It asked church members to be guided by the simple question "What Would Jesus Do?" in all their decisions in the everyday practical events of their lives. Many charged that it taught a works salvation, implying that people would go to Heaven if they followed the ethics of Jesus. Others held that it was a good guide for believers as far as normal Christian testimony is involved. It is certain that it made millions of people aware that every job and relationship ought to be examined and tested to see if they were right. Gladden's books *Applied Christianity* (1887) and *Social Salvation* (1902) claimed that *laissez faire* society is unchristian and that a new power of love should take over and cleanse it. Thus, Christians should work together to Christianize society. This claim came at a time when Fundamentalists saw society as doomed and were busy in the task of winning individual souls out of the wickedness around them. So the Fundamentalists and Liberals had two different attitudes toward society then, and these have increased the gap between the two groups.

Other winds were blowing in this turbulent period. One was the issue of temperance and drinking. The liquor industry increased its investments from 29 million in 1860 to 190 million in 1880. More and more city corners were occupied by saloons with their reeking atmosphere, increasing human dissipation from year to year. The churches met this problem by taking pledges of total abstinence, but the people most affected by the bottle were not in the churches. Some towns refused to grant liquor licenses, and by 1898 five states—Maine, New Hampshire, Vermont, Kansas, and North Dakota had passed legislation prohibiting the manufacture and sale of liquor. Women took an active role in the movements against "booze," especially through the formation of the Women's Christian Temperance Union under the gifted leadership of Miss Frances Willard. The churches rallied behind this organization as a most effective weapon. Another force was the Anti-Saloon League organized by W. B. Wheeler. Its work was directed toward getting legislation against the hated traffic, and it had a large part to play in the ground swell which finally brought about the passage of the Eighteenth Amendment in 1919, followed the next year by the Volstead Act, which prohibited the sale of intoxicating liquor, namely, beverages containing more than one-half of one percent alcohol.

Other issues arose to plague the souls of Bible believers, among them the bitterness resulting from the War Between the States, the drift toward internationalism, and the decline of moral standards.

It was a period that witnessed various reactions to the sweep of Liberalism. One was the rise and growth of the Bible conference movement, led by such figures as A. J. Gordon, James H. Brookes, George C. Needham, N. W. West, and W. R. Nicholson. In addition, there were many men with Reformed doctrine, Orthodox convictions, and Conservative views who held tenaciously to the essential truths of Reformation Christianity. These truths were held as a sacred trust at such rock-ribbed institutions as Princeton Seminary and Southern Baptist Seminary. These men appreciated the outcries of the Fundamentalists, but they were never part of their protest. The former were more intellectual and more insistent on strict adherence to Reformation views, and had little interest in evangelism and eschatology. Orthodoxy resisted the demands of the Liberals, but their set of answers was different from that of the Fundamentalists. They did their best to preserve the Reformed faith, while the Fundamentalists somewhat bypassed the Reformation and went farther back in their appeals to restore the apostolic principles and practices. But Fundamentalists appreciated the solid contributions to apologetic literature that came from such theological giants as Charles Hodge, E. Y. Mullins, B. B. Warfield, and J. R. Sampey.

Another wind counteracting increasing Liberalism was the Bible school movement. It has played a large part in the rise of Fundamentalism and deserves to be so recognized. It is now decreasing in its role in militant Fundamentalism, but its history is noteworthy. Some have contended that the Bible-school concept was at the root of our colonial colleges, which made the Bible and Christian standards central. This was the thesis of S. A. Witmer in his work *Education with Dimension,* by far the best history of the Bible schools. The colonial colleges had some similarities to the modern Bible schools but were basically centers of liberal arts training, while the Bible schools have not been such and cannot be while maintaining a Bible-centered curriculum. Some inspiration for the Bible schools may have come from Spurgeon's college in London, which had a long line of evangelical graduates in many parts of the world. H. Grattan Guinness organized the East London Institute for Home and Foreign Missions in 1872 for the purpose of bypassing university training for those called to the mission fields. This institute majored in the knowledge of the Bible and practical experience. In the first five years over seven hundred applied for training. This work had a great effect on A. B. Simpson, who wrote an article in the March 1880 issue of *The Gospel in All Lands* calling for the erection of a missionary training college. One did open under his leadership in October, 1883, in the rear of the Christian and Missionary Alliance Tabernacle, then meeting in the Twenty-Third Street Theater in New York. It was patterned after Guinness' school and opened as a three-year training course with forty students and two teachers. In 1879 D. L. Moody had opened Northfield Seminary, a high school for the training of young women, later adding a similar school for boys. In 1886 Moody had a leading part in the genesis of the Chicago Evangelistic Society, the forerunner of Moody Bible Institute. Its purpose was to fill in the "gap" between the number of graduates from the schools and the great needs of a lost world. In the three decades following 1882, a score of Bible schools of various types were founded, some being evening schools with a few classes. These were hardly of collegiate standing but did not claim to be so. Principal ones to be opened were the Boston Missionary Training School started by A. J. Gordon in 1889 and later renamed Gordon College, and the Northwestern Schools founded by W. B. Riley in Minneapolis. The latter was providentially raised up to have a far-reaching influence in the great Northwest until the 1950's. More schools continued to spring up until by 1940 some 167 had been started with 140 still functioning, 91 of which were operating day classes and offering degree programs.[1] In 1947 the Accrediting Association of Bible Colleges (AABC) was launched for the expressed purpose of standardizing and improving programs and giving them recognized status, including listing in government publications. Witmer's account is a full and factual discussion of this agency. Not included in this study nor in any material issued by the AABC office in Wheaton, Illinois, is there any mention of the recent inroads of new evangelical moods and alliances, the lowering of disciplinary standards, or weaknesses in academics. Also lacking is any reference to the place of the movement in present-day Fundamentalism. However, it should be remembered that this failure is a common weakness of most so-called fundamental institutions of our day, be they Bible schools, colleges, or seminaries.

The output of liberal and mildly evangelical writers was very influential in this period and a constant aggravation to militant Fundamentalists. Among the most widely used authors and books were George A. Gordon, *The Church of Today* (1895); O. B. Frothingham, *Religion of Humanity* (1873), E. C. Smyth, *Progressive Orthodoxy* (1886); C. A. Briggs, *The Authority of Holy Scripture* (1891); Newman Smyth, *Old Faith in New Light* (1897); and J. H. Allen, *Our Liberal Movement in Theology* (1892).

[1]Harold W. Boon, *History of Bible Colleges and Institutes* (unpublished Ph.D. dissertation, New York Univ., 1950).

The Fundamentalists did not respond with an equal number of talented writers and well-polished works but rather with outstanding pastorates and Bible conferences. The early history of the conferences on prophecy may go back to the 1860's, to some small meetings for prayer and Bible study. A few men met in 1875 near Chicago, including N. W. West, J. H. Brookes, F. H. Revell, and P. P. Bliss. In the meeting held the next year, A. J. Gordon, H. M. Parsons and W. J. Erdman were added when this group met at Swampscott, Massachusetts, under the name of the Believers' Meeting. In 1877 it met at Watkins Cove, New York, and then for three years at Clifton Springs, New York, moving to Old Orchard, Maine, and Mackinac Island, before settling permanently at Niagara-on-the-Lake, a few miles from the world-famous falls; there it was known as the Niagara Bible Conference. In a fourteen-year span at Niagara, great speakers graced the platforms. It is indeed a pity that tape recorders were not there to record for posterity those auspicious hours, for thousands of great addresses by Fundamentalists were lost forever. What a loss that was! Among the giants at Niagara were Gordon, Brookes, A. C. Dixon, L. W. Munhall, Hudson Taylor, A. T. Pierson, H. M. Parsons, and Robert Cameron. After 1897, with both Brookes and Gordon gone, the Conference declined, due mainly to growing internal dissensions among the brethren as to whether or not the rapture was pretribulational; the strong advocates of pretribulationism, led by A. C. Gaebelein, left the old site and started another conference at Sandy Cove, New York. The Niagara Conference vanished from the Fundamentalist sky, and we might add here that all too many great centers, schools, seminaries, and churches have left the movement because of weaknesses in eschatology. In itself, this has been a story of decline and death. Part of that story, perhaps the first chapter of it, would be the death of Niagara. But in the 1880's it was hailed as "the greatest gathering of the saints of God on the continent."[2] This article said these were great gatherings because of the quality of the teachers and the motives behind them. It listed the names of Gordon, West, Brookes, Erdman, Nicholson, Parsons, and Needham. W. J. Erdman was the secretary for many years. In 1895 they issued a Statement of Belief to spread essential truths. These have been commonly listed as the Five Fundamentals of Niagara: the inspiration of the Bible, the depravity of man, redemption through Christ's blood, the true church made up of all believers, and the coming of the Lord to set up His reign.

Much has been made of these Articles or Statements of Niagara, but a serious injustice has been done to the Conference and its

---

[2]"The Fundamentals of the Faith," *Christian Workers' Magazine,* Dec., 1913.

speakers and to Fundamentalism in general. Writers and teachers have repeated the Famous Five, in some form, and held them to be the Magna Charta of Fundamentalism. Actually, the Statement of Belief listed fourteen articles; in addition to those there were the Trinity, the fall of Adam, the need of the new birth, full deliverance from guilt at salvation, the assurance of salvation, the centrality of Christ in the Bible, the walk after the Spirit, the resurrection of both believers and unbelievers, and the ripening of the present age for judgment. On the matter of eschatology, two things about Niagara bear mention. One was the fixed position as to the conditions at the end of the present age, for a fearful apostasy was foreseen within the professing Christian body. The second conviction was that the premillennial coming of the Lord is the only hope of man. It might be noted, also, that the imminent return of the Lord is omitted from the Statement of Belief. By this time this truth had become the subject of debate, with Gordon and Brookes holding to the "any-moment" or imminent coming, and others such as Cameron holding to a post-tribulation rapture. While this debate mounted, A. C. Gaebelein moved into the scene and started the conference at Sandy Cove with openly avowed pretribulational teaching. By 1900, Niagara was a thing of the past.

Two small items in this period of Fundamentalism deserve brief mention. Often it has been asserted that early Fundamentalists leaned wholly on the views of the Plymouth Brethren and, therefore, insisted on the truths of imminency and any-moment rapture. It is true that Brethren teachers such as J. N. Darby and B. W. Newton were known in America. What is not commonly known is that there was a serious breach between the Brethren and Spurgeon. A. J. Gordon knew of this rift and he was not silent on the matter. Writing in his own paper, *The Watchword,* he noted the deaths of E. B. Pusey and J. N. Darby in 1882 and said of the Brethren:

> the bane and the torment of the Dissenting Churches [is] the robbing their flocks of their best and most spiritual members, while the Brethren movement itself has presented a most unseemly exhibition of narrow and disorganizing sectarianism.[3]

In the next issue of the paper he quoted from the great Spurgeon who had written:

> The Brethren was a movement almost ultra-Biblical, a body of men almost ultra-apostolic in their style of life and service. No people ever began with higher aims or nobler purposes and none has more utterly disappointed this early promise by the spectacle of unseemly narrowness and strife which it [Brethren] has displayed.[4]

[3] *The Watchword,* May, 1883.
[4] *The Watchword,* June, 1883.

It is only fair to note that not all members of Brethren groups or those akin to them in doctrine and church organization have had the same narrowness. It might be helpful to add that Brethren did not participate in the prophetic conferences of 1878 and 1886. Perhaps this could be accounted for by the fact that most of the leaders were pastors, and they could hardly be expected to appreciate or want on their programs men who denied the office of pastor.

Another volume of this period setting forth prophetic truth was entitled *The Second Coming of Christ* (1873), written by R. C. Shimeall of the Presbytery of New York. It was a scholarly attempt to answer the amillennial views of Shedd. Shimeall said that the Lord's Coming was imminent; he held to the literal interpretation of prophecy and rejected the use of spiritual (so-called) and allegorical rules. In addition, he rejected Millerism, that is, the teachings of William Miller and the Adventist movement of the 1840's, which alleged "the fulfillment of all prophecies . . . of the conversion of Israel by the return of the Jews from Babylonian captivity."[5] He castigated Miller for saying that the Millennium started with the Emperor Constantine, saying such was "pure fiction."[6] Shimeall also rejected the writings of Bishop Pierce, Adam Clarke, and Albert Barnes, who took a figurative interpretation, "which is a violation of all the laws of prophetic interpretation."[7] This New York Presbyterian denied the teaching of a general resurrection, holding to two resurrections, a thousand years apart. He also believed, "the times of the Gentiles and the millennial period are two separate dispensations."[8] Shimeall saw five conditions existing at the coming of the Lord: (1) ignorance of divine things (2) general apostasy (3) religious formalism (4) inquiry about the truth of the second coming and (5) dominance of the superstitions of the papacy. This Presbyterian divine saw Origen and Augustine as joint sources of the allegorizing of prophecy. He said that from the time of Origen to the Reformation there had existed the "loss of the only true law of scriptural hermeneutics."[9] Dr. Milner had written in his *Ecclesiastical History* that "no one had injured the church more than Origen."[10] The author did give credit to the Anabaptists who were millenarians. Among the modern millenarians listed were Bonar, Delitzsch, Increase Mather, Cotton Mather, John Wesley, A. M. Toplady, and many of the westminster divines. He noted some periodicals of his time which presented millennial truth as *The*

[5]R. C. Shimeall, *The Second Coming of Christ* (New York: Goodspeed, 1873), p. 98.
[6]Ibid., p. 107.
[7]Ibid., p. 127.
[8]Ibid.
[9]Ibid., p. 14.
[10]Ibid., p. 15.

Israelite Indeed, edited by G. R. Lederer of New York, and the *Prophetical Times,* edited by J. A. Seiss, Newton, and Duffield.

There is an outstanding academic institution located at Wheaton, Illinois, called Wheaton College, which was at one time led by Jonathan Blanchard and his son, Charles. It was commonly referred to as "a Fundamentalist island in a sea of unbelief." But Wheaton has gone through many changes since the days of Blanchard and today is a leading outpost for new-evangelical moods and alliances. Surely no one would call it a Fundamentalist island today.

Did the Fundamentalists of the 1870's lean heavily on millenarians prior to their own day? It is the conviction of Sandeen, who has carefully studied this aspect of the subject, that "not till the Prophetic Conferences of the 1870's did there emerge in the United States a millenarian movement that is a group with identifiable membership, recognized leaders, and clearly defined but not necessarily static beliefs."[11] Quite correctly, he dismisses William Miller of the 1840's, since the latter did not believe that Christ would reign for one thousand years after He returned. More influential was James Inglis of Scottish Presbyterian background, who came to the United States, became a Baptist, served the First Baptist Church in Detroit, and then moved to New York. There he ran a bookstore and published a paper *Waymarks in the Wilderness.* No great leader of millenarians appeared until A. J. Gordon arrived on the scene. Others whose names appear from time to time were James M. Stifler, who helped in the Niagara Conference and served in the Chair of New Testament at Crozer Seminary; A. J. Frost, a Baptist pastor in New York, Michigan, and California, who later served as Dean of the Bible Training School in Minneapolis; and A. T. Pierson of Presbyterian background, who learned millennial truths from George Müller in 1878 and became a close friend of Gordon.

A small air mass in the winds of the days was the Baptist Society for Bible Study which was organized in Brooklyn in 1890, meeting on November 18-21 of that year in Centennial Baptist Church. Gordon was president, and on the executive committee were F. H. Chapell, G. C. Needham, G. W. Folwell, and Samuel McBride, with J. D. Herr as secretary. On the program were such men as T. G. Field of the American Baptist Missionary Union and Professor J. H. Gilmore of Rochester Seminary. In his paper Gordon wrote that "the meetings were serious, instructive, and deeply spiritual."[12] He added that they were not confined to Baptists, for the executive committee "invited evangelicals of every school ... and the official paper would

[11]Ernest R. Sandeen, *Foundations* (Baptist Church History Society), Jan.-March, 1970, p. 21.
[12]*The Watchword,* 12 (1890), 309.

not be denominational but strictly spiritual, not sectarian but scriptural."[13]

Another voice for Fundamentalism was the widely known and beloved Northfield Conferences, begun in 1880 by D. L. Moody, a year after he opened Northfield Seminary, a preparatory school for girls, and a year before he started Mount Hermon School for boys. The Conferences were well attended and they continued until 1902 as among the largest of gatherings because of the stature and name of Moody. From the first, there was an emphasis on the need for the full power of the Holy Spirit. Powerful heart-searching messages were heard and whole conferences seemed bathed with the keen sense of the Spirit's presence and blessing. Great men wept as they spoke; many hearts were "melted" and "broken." In 1881 Bonar of Scotland was the main speaker and was at his peak in spiritual power. No conferences were held from 1882 to 1885 because Moody was in England. Among the speakers for the 1885 conference were Gordon, G. F. Pentecost, A. T. Pierson, L. W. Munhall, and Needham. One conference saw over one hundred volunteers come forward for foreign missionary service, a prelude to the Student Volunteer Movement. In Moody's absence in 1887, Gordon chaired the summer meetings, as he did again in 1892. Gordon's sermons at the 1894 Conference were unusually blessed; and they were his last, for he had gone to his eternal rest before the summer of 1895. He had founded the Boston Missionary Training School in 1889; in the same year, schools with similar purposes had been started by Mabie in Minneapolis and by Needham in Kansas City. Brookes did not start a school but later a school was organized in St. Louis, which carries his name to this day, Brookes Bible Institute. All of these aimed to train lay workers for missionary service at home and abroad. Some fields needed older men with limited training and some practical aptitudes, together with a basic knowledge of the Bible; these have continued to be the main qualities of the Bible-college type of training. Spiritual culture was given first place and was stressed above mental development. Gordon insisted that his school stress the imminent coming of Christ and named as first teacher in theology, the Reverend F. H. Chapell of Flemington, New Jersey. Chapell's classroom notes form a valuable part of the Vining Collection of the Gordon College Library at Wenham, Massachusetts. The early days of the school saw an emphasis on dispensational truth of the Gordon type, but in 1911 this emphasis

[13]Ibid.

was changed to a "Christocentric point of view as the doctrinal policy of the School."[14]

The last century has seen the rise of modern evangelism with the same old-fashioned Gospel message of past evangelists. But new faces and methods have come upon the stage of Christianity, and even newer methods are now projected. Many adaptations to American conditions have been made. Rugged individuals, some caustic and others with charming Christian sweetness, have created a varied picture. All evangelists have been the enemies of hardcore Liberalism, and all have aided both Fundamentalist pastors and churches until the present day, in which the evangelists favoring New Evangelicalism and cooperative evangelism have departed from Fundamentalism. Since the 1950's two types of evangelists have worked within evangelical circles, namely, those of hard-line Fundamentalist convictions and those of the persuasions and affiliations of New Evangelicalism. (These developments will be discussed in a later section.)

In the period from 1875 to 1900, four men led large evangelistic campaigns in which thousands heard the Gospel for the first time with countless thousands converted by the saving grace of God. These four were Dwight L. Moody, B. Fay Mills, Samuel Paul Jones, and Rodney "Gipsy" Smith.

That these four could dent the American scene with such success is a remarkable achievement, particularly when great national changes were taking place, as recorded in secular history books. Big business was getting its first great start; corruption in politics was becoming widespread; cities were growing rapidly; fortunes were being made by business tycoons; people were moving into the Great West; machinery was helping the farmer, and new sports and games were being played. Indeed, a new order was emerging and keen students of the *times* were convinced that the times were out of joint. Because of the great changes a new result appeared in the aftermath of great evangelistic efforts, namely, the effort to rid society of some of its ugly sins and depressing social conditions. The evangelists of that period did not aim to save society; they aimed to rescue souls. But the number of their converts did change the face of society for the better.

By 1875 Moody was the central figure in evangelism, having shaken England from 1873 to 1875 "as nothing had done since the time of Whitefield and the Wesleys."[15] In the mid-summer of 1875 a

---

[14]Nathan R. Wood, *A School of Christ* (Boston: Gordon College of Theology and Missions, 1953), p. 55. Since the publication of this history of the school, it has moved to Wenham, Mass.

[15]Bob Jones, "American Evangelism" (unpublished M.A. thesis, Univ. of Pittsburgh, 1933), p. 20.

month of meetings was held in Brooklyn, followed by a two months' campaign in Philadelphia with audiences totalling 700,000 and over 4,000 making professions of faith in the Saviour. Meetings followed in Boston, New York, Baltimore, and Chicago. The scene of Mr. Moody's largest audiences and converts was in Chicago.

Moody was the creator of many innovations in evangelism, such as the effective use of publicity, organization, and advertising, and in so doing he "completed the reduction of evangelism to a matter of technique and personality."[16] Moody was unlike his predecessors in his lack of education and his brusqueness of speech with his many "Dan'ls" and "Sam'ls." He once told a group, "I wunt leave myself in the hands of no committee." Nevertheless, his utter sincerity and New Testament simplicity were more than enough to cause his hearers to overlook crudities and errors in speech. He was most happy to receive the support of the well-to-do, even millionaires such as John Wanamaker and John Keene in Philadelphia and Morris J. Jessup in New York. Some have even charged that "revivalism has rested squarely, at least, on the support of the new class of postwar millionaires."[17] In eight years he effected a "rejuvenation of evangelism." Moody reached millions that the new science and knowledge had not reached. One reason was that the middle-class man was still a village boy in his heart, and Moody spoke to his deepest feelings and desires. Moody's main emphasis was the love of God for the sinner and not the judgments of God. His most compelling appeals were to receive the love of Christ and resist the Devil, who wants us to spurn that love. Moody's theology, if he even had one, was simple Gospel truth, simple enough to embrace any evangelical viewpoint, "deftly avoiding any entanglements in creeds and platforms."[18] Factually, D. L. Moody was a quick-thinking businessman in the business of saving souls. He attracted men to Christ because of Christ's love and sacrificial death for them. After his death, both Liberals and Fundamentalists claimed him as one of their own. His son, Paul, thought that his father would not have been in sympathy with the hard-line Fundamentalist of the 1920's. R. A. Torrey took issue with this misrepresentation and defended Moody's position against the statements of his son.[19] By the 1920's a galaxy of men were trying to perpetuate two aspects of the Moody revivalism, namely, the use of new methods to increase results and an area-wide revivalistic spirit in small towns and small churches.

[16]Bernard Weisberger, *They Gathered at the River* (Boston: Little, Brown, 1958), p. 177.
[17]Ibid., p. 205.
[18]Ibid., p. 209.
[19]See *Moody Monthly,* 24 (1923-24), 173-74, 235-36.

Another evangelist was B. Fay Mills, who was born in Rahway, New Jersey, in 1857. Leaving the pastorate, he entered evangelism in 1886 with a major stress on preparations for meetings, demanding efficiency even before the meetings began. Cities were divided into districts with prayer meetings arranged in all of them. In a Cincinnati campaign in 1886, some seventy churches were enlisted with a combined membership of 20,000. Women took a major role in the prayer meetings. The meetings went on for six weeks with over 8,000 professions, most of them Presbyterians by preference. Following the example of Moody, who had Ira Sankey as soloist, Mills had Lawrence B. Greenwood as musician, a man with a beautiful voice and an unusual ability to train a choir of one thousand. Assisting Mills was a Presbyterian minister, J. Wilbur Chapman, pastor of Wanamaker's church, Bethany Presbyterian, in Philadelphia. Also helping in the campaign was George C. Stebbins who wrote many hymns and was outstanding in his later work with Chapman in large meetings. Then tragedy struck, as it has too many times in evangelistic circles, namely, in that Mills turned away from sound doctrine to "deism and pantheism."[20] He organized the Los Angeles Fellowship. He was not the first nor will he be the last to exemplify the truth of the prediction of the Apostle Paul that many would turn from the Faith to the doctrines of demons (I Tim. 4:1).

Samuel Paul Jones, known only as Sam Jones throughout his career, was converted from a life of drink in 1872, shortly before his father's death, and "became the most unique and original evangelist that America has ever known."[21] He was a Methodist and was sent to North Georgia to preach on a circuit, but left it in 1880 to go into evangelistic work. His first major meeting was in Memphis, and his largest one was held in Nashville in 1885. He was a fiery preacher in the fullest sense of that word, and was most outspoken in his denunciation of the sins of that hour: the theater, dancing, and card playing. His language was unusually sharp and folksy. He was hardhitting, and in this he antedated the equally expressive Billy Sunday. Large crowds gathered to hear him in St. Louis, Chicago, and Boston. His musician was E. O. Excell who composed many hymns. Jones dropped dead near Little Rock, Arkansas, in 1906. The name of Sam Jones remains unique among the long list of Methodist evangelists—sound, fiery, clean-cut, and pleasant in memory.

The last evangelist of that period was the unusual and very colorful Rodney "Gipsy" Smith, born in 1860 in Wanstead, England, of genuine gypsy parents. He made seventy crossings of the Atlantic

[20]Jones, p. 31.
[21]Ibid.

in his lifetime, the first one in 1889. Without the benefits of a formal education but given to disciplined self-study, the famous Gipsy sang with great acceptance though he knew little music. Thousands wept as he sang "Jesus Revealed in Me" and "This Wonderful Saviour Is Mine." Like Moody, he preached often on the love of Christ for the sinner, the need of repentance on the part of the sinner, and the special sweetness of the Lord Jesus, which should characterize the lives of true Christians. He cherished his connections with old-time Methodism and demonstrated that warmheartedness which had characterized the solid heart of Wesleyan Methodist preaching and singing throughout its history. What a sharp contrast this is to the cold, formal, lifeless religion now parading as Methodism. With true love and feeling Gipsy Smith would ask people to raise one hand for Jesus since he raised two hands for them. A few of his sermons were preached around the world to thrilled audiences. A well-known one entitled "Stripe Washing," was based on the conversion of the Philippian jailer, and one of this writer's fondest memories is of hearing the Gipsy preach this message in Chicago shortly before he died in 1947.

How did these four evangelists help Fundamentalism? First of all, they were sharp instruments in the hands of the Lord for the salvation of thousands, and Fundamentalists honored and promoted soulwinning efforts. Again, they affirmed the hardcore truths of old-fashioned Bible religion, and Fundamentalists always applauded that. In the third place, they raised a standard against the Liberalism and radicalism then sweeping the college and seminary campuses. Few faculty members and students would listen to them, but the common people heard them gladly. Again, Moody was very close to A. J. Gordon and his group of Fundamentalists and upheld their meetings and convictions. These men did not knowingly sympathize with, nor support, Liberals in what they were teaching or doing to the Christian faith. Often it has been stated that Moody invited Henry Drummond of Scotland, an evolutionist, to speak at Bible conferences at Northfield. In the earlier days he did have him, but later he refused to have him back. Although Moody was not a theologian, he respected those who were and was not ashamed to take a stand for theological truth. Drummond was one of the most effective public speakers of the era, and to cancel him from the Northfield program took genuine courage. Moody erected several schools as training centers for Christian young people. In this he was doing what C. H. Spurgeon had done in London; what Gordon did in Boston; what Riley was to do in Minneapolis; Norris, in Fort Worth; Shields, in Toronto; and John Brown and Bob Jones, Sr., in the South. Others who followed their example are Lee Roberson in Chattanooga; Tom Malone in

Pontiac, Michigan; T. C. Horton in Los Angeles; Lewis Sperry Chafer in Dallas; and Richard V. Clearwaters in Minneapolis. The list is long and impressive.

REVULSION AND REVOLT
1900-1935

Introduction

While the winds of Liberalism and reaction blew steadily during the last quarter of the nineteenth century and the early years of the twentieth, they became full-force gales, even tornadoes, that swept through American Christianity. The results, good and bad, are still with us. Liberalism produced its most appealing personalities in Fosdick, Matthews, and Rauschenbusch, even as Fundamentalism produced its most inspiring, though erratic, giants in the persons of Shields, Riley, Straton, and Norris. Those were days as never before, and probably never again, when giants strode across the land, locked in fiercest debates, none giving quarter, and all dedicated to their positions until the death.

Churches shook under the mighty hammering of pulpit princes. Christians listened in awe and amazement as great debaters and mighty opponents hurled verbal brickbats, each one designed to bring blood. Conventions and other associations of Christians rocked and reeled under the charges and countercharges leveled and releveled by the knowledgeable and strong in persuasion; each debater plumbed the depths of history, Bible, and human experiences in order to reinforce his dogmas and hurl back his foes. The weak withdrew from the arena, unable to stand the sight of blood and the sound of abuse. The soft-hearted wished for quiet days (like our own) and believed very little except that war between Christians was wrong and that debates were divisive. Middle-of-the-roaders refused to listen to arguments while the great mass of convention disciples blithely looked upon the whole affair as a clash of personalities.

The 1920's placed a high-water mark on the nationwide battle between Fundamentalists and Modernists. Norris, Shields, Riley, and Straton were then in the peak of their pulpit effectiveness. The Liberals were in such control of denominational machinery and institutions that they could almost count the votes before issues were raised. As clever churchmen, they (the Liberals) knew the rank and file would never be interested in the details of heresy, false doctrine, and defection from ancient landmarks. They would never take very seriously the predictions of the prophets of doom and gloom that terrible judgments would come on the churches and conventions if men deserted ancient truths. Brave and courageous Fundamentalists knew the grass-roots Christians were sound and Biblical as far as they went, but by this time the grass-roots people had very little say in determining the direction of the major bodies of Christians in America. This lesson was painfully learned by the Fundamentalists.

It was a period of a countdown—of how much time the Fundamentalists would have to charge and accuse within the bounds of major religious bodies. The twenties marked the end of Fundamentalist protest within the bodies, and it has not, and will not, ever resume. Here and there an individual Fundamentalist within the denomination raises a voice, but it is politely tolerated and ignored as far as doctrinal direction is concerned. Thus the Fundamentalists lost the battles but not the Book; they left the religious structures but not the Scriptures, for no man could take these from them. They attempted to cleanse their groups and failed. Now they turned to new fellowships and new schools, thereby becoming isolated from the mainstream of American religious life. This separation is part of the story of this period of rebellion. This civil war on a theological plane resulted in a numerical victory for the Liberals, and it was followed, as was the political severance of the 1860's, by a period of reconstruction in things spiritual. The latter dates from 1935 to the present, and its end is at our doors.

No period of American Fundamentalism has seen such violent reaction to all phases of Liberalism or such a courageous struggle to maintain the Faith as this one. It saw the rise on the American scene of the prima donnas of the movement—a tremendous trio without equal in their type of leadership and inspiration. These thrilling and yet disappointing men were J. Frank Norris, William B. Riley and Thomas T. Shields. Fundamentalism had produced its giants; kings they were of Fundamentalist empires, Shields in Canada, Riley in the North, and Norris in the South. These men were very different and yet each was talented and gifted in fighting the battles of the hour. Their contributions were monumental, their energies Niagara-like, and their influence on their generation of young preachers, and on their successors in our generation, was without equal. They were men of rugged, Alpine-like convictions, willing to do battle with great ecclesiastical machines and leaders. Their hold on their congregations and followers was prolonged and marked by devotion. On the platform they had charisma or pulpit presence, which made them superior speakers, debaters, and exponents of the great truths of the Bible. Shields had an English approach, always dignified in appearance and diction and masterful in knowledge and perception. Riley stood tall and straight in preaching power, and in debate stood with the finest across the continent. Norris was truly "the Texas Tornado" who, with a rhetorical edge and persuasion that was the envy of friend and foe, attacked the giant Southern Baptist colossus and spawned a Southern Fundamentalism that is very much alive today in hundreds of independent Baptist churches across the nation. The story of these three is, in itself, a saga of Fundamentalism.

It was a day when Liberalism consolidated its forces and gathered enough strength to flex its muscles in public and to ride roughshod over opposition. Seminaries and colleges became the hotbeds of evolution and Modernism. Peace at any price was the goal of denominational executives in order to continue the growth of the convention structure. The Northern Baptists, still very young as a denomination, officially organized as late as 1907, drove forward at a relentless pace in their unity programs. They became the great protector of the inclusive policy, which meant that all shades of theological opinion and activity would not only be welcomed under the denominational umbrella but must also receive from all sides a cordial sanction and friendly smiling approval. Thus, Northern Baptists became so broad that Fundamentalists were faced with one of three choices: (1) fight for the Faith, which would eventually lead to separation; (2) remain sound in doctrine within the Convention but not fight for the Faith; (3) accommodate with the new theology while still seeking to maintain the best of the historic position. This study will seek to recapture the highlights of all three moods and movements within this group. Southern Baptists moved much more slowly toward outright Liberalism in this period. They confined themselves to denominational growth, with colleges and seminaries drifting more and more into evolutionary thinking and postmillennial programs and hopes, while their faculties toyed more and more with Neo-Orthodox views. The vast evangelistic efforts glossed over the theological shifts and trends. The Norris movement hammered away at these Southern Baptist trends, not being able to seriously divide the Convention but drawing hundreds of young men to the banner of Fundamentalism and inspiring these to go out to build churches and Sunday Schools, at which Norris was a master. His students today are carrying this out in such groups as the Baptist Bible Fellowship and World Baptist Fellowship. Canadian Baptists fell into modernistic ways early, especially at such schools as McMaster University and Brandon College. Liberal thinking was slowly but surely eating away at the vitals of this group and T. T. Shields, in raising the banner, saw himself politely pushed out into the cold. This brought about his association with Fundamentalists in the United States, with whom he fought side by side during this period.

The Methodists never had a serious threat from Fundamentalists within. Methodist schools had adopted the principles and philosophies of Liberalism early in the century, and such schools as Boston University, Duke University, and Garrett Biblical Institute had embraced the New Learning and were training their young men in these tenets. There were some stalwart Methodist figures of the old school of Wesley and Asbury, and these as individuals refused to accept the new ideas. Among them were men like L. W. Munhall, H. C. Morrison, Bob Jones, Sr., and Bob Shuler. They had special gifts as preachers and evangelists but they belonged to a small, yet noble, minority crying out in the wilderness of Methodism, warning and winning souls but failing to impede the downward slide of a great denomination and body of Christians. Eventually they had to admit that their efforts on the inside could not salvage the group, but their main purpose was to remain true individually, no matter what others did.

Presbyterians saw the greatest of their internal convulsions in this period when the able and courageous J. Gresham Machen, Robert Dick Wilson, and others made a last-ditch fight for the Reformed faith at Princeton Seminary, the West Point of Orthodoxy. Their noble stand for the historic creeds and dogmas of the Reformation soon succeeded not only in producing open debate but also in the founding of a new seminary (Westminster Theological Seminary) and the Independent Board for Presbyterian Foreign Missions (1933). Finally, in 1936 Machen, Charles Woodbridge, and Carl McIntire were tried by the Northern Presbyterians and "unfrocked." Out of the split came the Orthodox Presbyterian group, the Bible Presbyterians, and such schools as Shelton College, Covenant College, Covenant Seminary, and Faith Seminary. Leading figures in these groups have been McIntire, Allan MacRae, J. Oliver Buswell, Laird Harris, and Robert Rayburn. A second outcropping among Presbyterians and some Congregationalists resulted in the formation of Bible churches and the creation of the Independent Fundamental Churches of America (IFCA), centering at first in the St. Louis and Chicago areas. The earliest leader of the IFCA was William McCarrell of Cicero, Illinois. The IFCA continues today with the same allegiance to historic Fundamental doctrine, but it has been under severe pressure to tone down and soften its militant attitude, and in many cases it has done this, to the chagrin of some of its best members.

Not all dissent at this time took an organized form. Many Bible-believing men and churches looked with continuing distrust at church fights, convention harangues, and their like. An uncounted number of these continued to hold their faith but refused to fight, take a stand, and vote on issues. Thus, there continued a "middle-of-the-road" group basically holding a moderate fundamentalist position. Many later left that for a modified position and thus accepted most of the affinities and some tenets of the New Evangelicals. Thus the jungle structure not only continued but grew.

One important footnote to this period is the rise of new schools and the growth of some great churches. The rise of new schools will be noted through discussion of such institutions as Dallas Theological Seminary, Columbia Bible College, and Bob Jones University, to name only a few. A number of faith missions were begun. Many churches showed great growth due to Fundamentalist influence, such as First Baptist in Fort Worth (reaching upwards of ten thousand members), First Baptist in Minneapolis, The Church of the Open Door in Los Angeles, Tremont Temple in Boston, Calvary Baptist and First Baptist in New York City, Moody Memorial in Chicago, and First Presbyterian in Seattle. The age of greatest growth in numbers came after 1935, but there were great churches in the land in this earlier period. There was a slow change coming in the rank and file of the churches, in that new and more modern men were coming out of the schools and seminaries and up-dating the pulpits and minds of the hearers.

Lesser lights also appeared in the Fundamentalist sky. While their convictions were no less adamant and constant, their ministries were restricted and their brilliance in debate, preaching, and crowd-gathering was far below that of the prima donnas. Among these lesser lights were Oliver W. Van Osdel, pastor of Wealthy Street Baptist in Grand Rapids from 1909 until his retirement in 1934. Another was Courtland Myers, the able and flamboyant pastor of Tremont Temple in Boston in the early twenties. Still another was Jasper C. Massee of the Baptist Temple in Brooklyn and later of Tremont Temple. Also among less prominent Fundamentalists was R. E. Neighbour of Ohio, pastor and early pioneer in the founding of the Baptist Bible Union. Gifted in preaching and debate was Harry G. Hamilton of First Baptist in Buffalo, New York, later associated with J. Frank Norris in his Fort Worth empire. Younger but taking a strong Fundamentalist position was Robert T. Ketcham, who later became a pastor in Pennsylvania and Iowa, and has been for many years the elder statesman of the GARB. In the Bible-teaching field was Harry A. Ironside of Moody Memorial Church in Chicago and Will H. Houghton of Calvary Baptist in New York and Moody Bible Institute. Among other figures were such young men as Bob Jones, Sr., and Bob Shuler in evangelism. One ought not to leave out Peter W. Philpott of Philpott Tabernacle in Hamilton, Ontario, Moody Memorial, and the Church of the Open Door in Los Angeles, along with such men as Louis T. Talbot and A. Z. Conrad. Paul W. Rood helped in Fundamentalist organizations, as did Harry Rimmer, J. W. Porter, and T. T. Martin. Among the educators was Asbury's staunch Fundamentalist, Henry C. Morrison. And none living in those days could ever forget the great revival fires started in tents, tabernacles, and great outdoor meetings by Billy Sunday in his heyday. Of lesser note was Paul Rader of Chicago, of Moody Church and Tabernacle, preaching with tremendous zeal and drawing thousands to hear him. R. A. Torrey, the founder of Montrose Bible Conference, made great contributions to education both at Moody Bible Institute and the Bible Institute of Los Angeles, in addition to taking many world trips as an evangelist. W. E. Biederwolf kindled many hearts with his soul-searching Bible messages and left behind him many fragrant memories. Indeed, the second period of Fundamentalism had an abundance of able exegetes, teachers, pastors, and preachers. It was one of the most fruitful eras of American Christianity.

6
A Liberal and the Language of the Liberals

One careful student of this period has expressed clearly the spirit of Liberalism as

> a certain attitude toward all of life and the world as one great process with God at work in it to give purpose with man at the center in the image of God. This divine deposit is to be developed to the highest extent through the rule of love. When it is widespread we will have a world brotherhood living up to the highest ideal even as Jesus did. We discover God in the vast evolutionary process and to contemplate this is to show man his deepest aspirations and religious experiences. Men will respond to these innate ideas even as the Hebrews did (Old Testament in a nutshell) and Jesus as prime example. Truth changes with each and every generation with present religious experiences clarifying Biblical truths more than those of a past did. There is an added impulse through the impact of the historical Jesus for spiritual impulses and more inspiration still flow from Him. In truth, He is the Incarnation not of a person of a heavenly group but incarnation of the human personality. As such he shows us God as he shows us the best of mankind. In his word of instruction he pictured the Kingdom of God which is the goal of good men to be gained by service and love such as he had.[1]

Two leading students of the entire scope of liberal thought, Dillenberger and Welch, have pointed out the heart of the movement for us in writing:

> Central among the presuppositions, or informing principles, of liberal Protestantism was the liberal spirit—the spirit of open-mindedness, of tolerance and humility, of devotion to truth wherever it might be found.

[1]Kenneth Cauthen, *The Impact of American Religious Liberalism* (New York: Harper, 1962), pp. 209f.

Often . . . it was held that theological differences were insignificant. Four other themes were . . . respect for science and the scientific method . . . scepticism as to the possibility of achieving certain knowledge of ultimate reality . . . concern for similarity and likeness rather than difference and opposition . . . confidence in man and his future. . . . In the place of an infallible Bible . . . liberalism put the living witness of the religious life.[2]

In contrast to this prevailing thought, there was Fundamentalism, which was "distinguished from other forms of conservatism by its self-conscious and inflexible resistance to the entire liberal development."[3]

Liberals abounded in this period in places of leadership in churches, colleges, and denominational executive offices. Many were gifted in writing, and the period verily swarmed with liberal literature. Only a brief introduction to this vast library is possible here.

No one can realize the sheer desperation of the fight on the hands of the Fundamentalists without some look at these writers and their books, pamphlets, magazines, and articles in leading journals. These demand attention, for they influenced millions of people away from the truths of the Word of God. They taught young men who were anxious to serve the Lord the "modern" approach to the needs of people in what they regard as a vastly different world from that of the twenties and thirties. In this way, a whole generation of prospects for the ministry came under the sway of radical teachers and interpretations. In turn, these molded the minds of their congregations, especially the young people who took their counsel on what colleges to attend that would open doors to ministry. In such a cycle there was spawned a whole generation of liberal thinkers and leaders among the young, and these would continue the job of tearing down the faith, which was already in weakened condition. Thus, the image of America thirty years later is that of a great land which has left the old paths and turned to the vagaries and the uncertainties of a new theology and a new type of Christianity and church. Tragedy is written all across the scene.

The names of the Liberals of this period are legion. So many arose to defend the new ideas and their many attractive elements that more than one book would be needed to record their names, analyze the sermons, scan the prolific literature, and even introduce students to the great variety of affirmations and attitudes. Wilbur M. Smith's *Therefore Stand* is very helpful for understanding the scope of

---

[2]John Dillenberger and Claude Welch, *Protestant Christianity* (New York: Scribner's, 1954), pp. 211-16.
[3]Ibid., p. 227.

liberal ideas and leading voices, and it deserves concentrated study.[4] One conclusion from this research work is that most statements of leading Liberals were at once bizarre and blasphemous.

Universities and seminaries took the lead in introducing young men and women to Liberalism in all its varied concepts and opinions. Some of these institutions of learning actually became the headquarters of the New Thought and liberal theology. The main ones deserve mention and take the discredit they deserve for the corruption and confusion they produced in the minds of hundreds of students. This criminal activity reached its zenith as prospects for the ministry were brainwashed and misdirected from the truths of the Word of God to the uncertain labyrinth of human speculations, concepts, philosophy, and social-reform programs. Leading the Liberals in their apostasy from the truth were the theological faculties of the University of Chicago, Union Seminary in New York, Rochester Theological Seminary, Boston University, Duke Divinity School, Harvard Divinity School, Yale Divinity School, Garrett Biblical Institute, Crozer Theological Seminary, Hartford Theological Seminary, Oberlin College, and Western Theological Seminary. Several men were prominent leaders in special positions: among them were Harry Emerson Fosdick of Riverside Church in New York and Professor at Union Seminary; Walter Rauschenbusch, a church history teacher at Rochester and author of major works on the social gospel; and Shailer Matthews of the University of Chicago, to whom Baptists should give the credit of liberalizing the Northern Baptist Convention to the apostate status it now occupies under the name of the American Baptist Convention. Fundamentalists would do well to know Matthews, Fosdick, and Rauschenbusch.

A LEADING LIBERAL

The most popular figure in Liberalism in this period was Harry Emerson Fosdick. He was born near Buffalo, New York, on May 24, 1878, year of the first prophetic conference. His parents were of Baptist connections but they were open-minded to liberal ideas. With his family he attended Prospect Avenue Baptist Church in the city and at the age of seven joined a nearby church, Westfield Baptist. Early in life he had "religious fears," especially torments over the thought of a Hell. He was rebellious against the "religious taboos" such as cards, the dance, and the theatre. He heard D. L. Moody when young and was impressed by him.

His education set his sail in things religious. From 1896 to 1900 he

4Wilbur M. Smith, *Therefore Stand* (Boston: Wilde, 1945).

attended Colgate, where he accepted the theory of evolution, doubted
the authenticity of the Bible, and revolted against orthodox views.
He began his theological training at the divinity school at Colgate
and came under the strong influence of the leading liberal scholar of
that period, William Newton Clarke. He accepted the new idea that
much of Hebrew history was no more than folklore. His teacher
helped him forge a new direction in his thinking, one of open
criticism of all dogma, even of the Trinity. His teacher motivated his
mind to think independently of theologians and Bible writers. He
reacted to some of the conservative teachers at Colgate by
transferring to Union Seminary and Columbia University in New
York, where he took his B.D. in 1904 and M.A. in 1908. He had been
ordained as a Baptist in 1903 with Clarke preaching the ordination
sermon and in the next fifty years received some seventeen honorary
degrees. At Columbia he took philosophy under Nicholas Murray
Butler, and at Union he studied theology under A. C. McGiffert, who
had broad modernist sympathies. Union Seminary had earlier
separated from the Presbyterian Church when the latter had taken
action and unfrocked C. A. Briggs on charges of heresy in 1892. Ever
since that episode it has rivaled the University of Chicago Divinity
School and Harvard Divinity School for radicalism. One major
influence on Fosdick at Union was the stress on the social
application of Christian principles. He found the social gospel of
Rauschenbusch of Rochester Seminary profound and challenging.
While a student at Union, Fosdick worked in the well-known "Hell's
Kitchen" in the city and at the mission at Mariners' Temple in the
Bowery. At Madison Avenue Baptist he assisted George C. Lorimer,
who later pastored the famed Tremont Temple in Boston with an
effective evangelical and evangelistic ministry and for whom a large
hall in the Temple has been named. Others making a mark on his
mind were Frame of the New Testament department at Union and
Knox in the department of Philosophy of Religion.

From 1904 to 1915 he was pastor of the Baptist church at
Montclair, New Jersey, and was an instructor in Practical Theology
at Union. He continued to teach at Union until 1946, when he retired.
His sermons reflected more and more interest in social issues and in
their analysis and solution through religious dedication. In many
ways he found the cry of Rauschenbusch to be his own, namely, the
establishment of the Kingdom of God as that order of social justice
and humanitarian improvement which, he claimed, was the aim of
Old Testament prophets and of Jesus Himself.[5] While at Montclair
he decided against expository preaching, for he believed

[5]For a study of the social gospel see Walter Rauschenbusch, *The Theology of the
Social Gospel* (New York: Macmillan, 1917).

congregations were not interested in the meaning of texts; his sermons became more and more like lectures on problem-solving techniques and attitudes. Their themes were items of personal and current interest, and he drew from the accumulated wisdom of the past, within the Bible and outside, for his answers. In this way he offered solutions to the common problems of disillusionment, defeat, and despair. He used modern psychology as a valued ally, thus antedating Norman Vincent Peale and his success with "Positive Thinking," most of which is non-Biblical. Another influence on Fosdick's thinking was the Quaker, Rufus Jones, whom he greatly admired, a fact he demonstrated by publishing an anthology from his fifty-seven books under the title *Rufus Jones Speaks to Our Time*—an outline of religious insights based on so-called spiritual inwardness. Fosdick once was reported to have said that had he not stayed at Riverside Church in New York, he would have joined the Quakers.

He left Montclair in 1915 to join the faculty of Union Seminary as Professor of Practical Theology, also assisting in the area of homiletics. Now he gave himself to study modern situations and their meanings in human experience and to clothe them in Biblical language. Another interest was in finding the development or evolution of religious ideas within the Bible itself and their natural development since Bible times. This he put in print in one of the most misleading books circulated among American churches—*The Modern Use of the Bible*. It might have been more appropriately entitled "The Modern Disuse of the Bible." Few books have led so many thousands of sincere people away from the Bible.

From 1919 to 1925 he supplied the pulpit of First Presbyterian Church in New York, the church which had recently merged with University Place Presbyterian and Madison Square Presbyterian. Congregations increased, for his lectures had great personal appeal and his delivery had an important element which he taught in his classes, namely "drive." His popularity grew rapidly and, although he was not himself a Presbyterian, he brought the crowds to a Presbyterian Church. There seemed no great storm ahead, but one came which shook the church and Baptist and Presbyterian circles to their very foundations. In May, 1922, he preached a sermon entitled "Shall the Fundamentalists Win?" To this question his answer was that the churches should include both those of strict Biblical belief and those of liberal persuasion. It was a plea for toleration and a charge that Fundamentalists were cantankerous and unloving. Fosdick did not intend to publish it, but a layman in his church, Mr. Ivy Lee, did publish it under the title "The New Knowledge and the Christian Faith." It was widely distributed and both the Orthodox and the Fundamentalists read it as a call to battle. A grand furor was on. Lee's purpose was to alert churchgoing people to the Fundamentalist threat, and certainly he could not have imagined the national reaction. It was published to label Fundamentalists as opposed to science, to modern culture, and to all who did not interpret the Scriptures exactly as they did. To Fosdick, cantankerousness was worse than heterodoxy. By this time it was evident from his sermons that he rejected the historic doctrines of the virgin birth, the inerrancy of the Bible and its literal interpretation, and the second coming of Christ. His lectures at Yale Divinity School in 1923 gave the substance of his *The Modern Use of the Bible* and exposed his full departure from Biblical faith.

Both the Orthodox and the Fundamentalists rose up in arms. The former were led by Clarence E. Macartney of Philadelphia, who affirmed that Fosdick denied the very basic foundational truths of Presbyterianism and that he was doing this in a Presbyterian church.[6] Macartney's presbytery in Philadelphia made the proper request (overture) to the New York Presbytery and the General Assembly, which directed the New York Presbytery to correct the situation, but it refused to see anything heretical in Fosdick's actions. Another possibility for resolution of the problem was to get Fosdick to place his ordination within the Presbyterian Church and then to be put on trial on charges of heresy as had C. A. Briggs before him. It would be well to remember at this point that historic Presbyterianism had stressed five main doctrines: the miracles in the Bible, the virgin birth, the inerrancy of the Bible, the substitutionary death of Christ, and the bodily resurrection of Christ. Fosdick did not accept a single one of the "Famous Five" while occupying a Presbyterian pulpit, and his congregation and its presbytery were either too weak or too spiritually anemic to do anything about it. In fact, on a vote, the church stood behind Fosdick. Bewilderment followed—how could a Christian church rally around a man who denied everything Christian in doctrine? The General Assembly of 1924 invited Fosdick to join the Presbyterian Church, it being a known fact that Mark Matthews of the First Presbyterian Church in Seattle, Washington, the largest in the denomination, was ready to press charges against him when he joined. But Fosdick did not join, and no trial could be held. He resigned from First Presbyterian Church in October, 1924, effective as of March of 1925. In his letter of resignation he accused the General Assembly of applying the principle of "the closed shop." Macartney questioned his good taste, since he was only a guest in the pulpit each Sunday, but saw as even worse "his frank assault

[6]The full story of this and other struggles of Presbyterians against heresy is told by E. H. Rian, *The Presbyterian Conflict* (Grand Rapids: Eerdmans, 1940).

upon creeds, not the Presbyterian Creed in particular, but all creeds
. . . raising in the minds of others as to whether or not he himself
receives these great New Testament facts."[7] Professor J. G. Machen
of Princeton was bolder and obviously on the attack when he wrote
that Fosdick's resignation,

> like all his utterance, is the expression of a thorough-going skepticism
> . . . he rejects all doctrine . . . the truth is that two mutually exclusive re-
> ligions are struggling for the control of the Presbyterian Church . . . one
> is Christianity with its appeal to faces: the other is the naturalistic or
> agnostic modernism which is represented by Dr. Fosdick and hundreds
> of ministers in the Presbyterian Church. The separation of the two is
> demanded not only by the interests of the Christian faith but by simple
> honesty.[8]

W. L. Pettingill wrote the following in the same issue of *Serving and
Waiting,*

> The fight is on and it grows hotter. Let us praise God for that. A fight is
> much better than a disgraceful surrender and a fight is necessary just
> now that the truth of the Gospel may continue with us.[9]

From 1925 to 1930 Fosdick served the Park Avenue Baptist, the
church of Cornelius Woelfkin—noted Liberal within Northern
Baptists—and John D. Rockefeller. The latter showed his generosity
by supporting a call to Fosdick to Park Avenue on the terms that
immersion be dropped as a requirement for membership and plans
be started for a new church, even though Park Avenue had been built
as recently as 1922. This church had known a great evangelical as
pastor, Thomas B. Armitage, and later a Liberal, W. H. P. Faunce,
who went from this pulpit to the presidency of Brown University.

Rockefeller was willing to give a large sum for the erection of a
new edifice, and by 1930 the very beautiful Riverside Church was
ready. It was a gem of Gothic beauty overlooking the Hudson River
from Morningside Heights in Manhattan. Again the Rockefeller
millions were thrown to the side of Liberalism. Riverside was a
cathedral of Liberalism, one of non-sectarian inclusive fellowship.
But the beauty of the ten-million-dollar structure should not blind us
to the facts that it has never had a Bible-preaching pastor in its
history and that for such an expensive building its auditorium is on
a small scale. Riverside provided a pulpit for Harry Emerson
Fosdick to keep on solving personal problems and attacking social
ills. The National Broadcasting Company was so impressed by his
stature that it gave him free time on Sunday afternoon for "National
Vespers." His talks on this program were stimulating to the
intellectual and comforting to the religious, always with the

---

[7] *Serving and Waiting* (Philadelphia School of the Bible), Jan., 1925, p. 420.
[8] Ibid.
[9] Ibid.

assumption of man's brotherhood under the fatherhood of God. He would upbraid Liberals at times for being too optimistic about man's goodness. He saw the rising theology of Neo-Orthodoxy as a thing of disillusionment unless men came to it through Liberalism, as did Reinhold Niebuhr. He believed Karl Barth brought some refinements because he did recognize man as a needy creature.

He felt Barth was right in charging that Liberalism was too blind toward human sin. With the coming of World War II, men needed convictions as well as toleration, and Fosdick saw Barth and Brunner as making significant contributions toward the filling of this vacuum, for very clearly they were dissatisfied with the Liberalism of the early years of this century, with its unhealthy optimism. They went to the extreme of strong pessimism with God as the wholly Other, as an alternative to the demoralizing ideas of his immanence within the world process and human story. Now Barth and Brunner turned thousands of intelligent Christians to God's self-revelation. Both reason and faith needed each other. Liberalism had pioneered the inclusive spirit, which tolerated too much and believed too little. Now followed a wholesale confession that. Modernism had little in common with Christianity except a few terms. Liberals had preserved a general revelation in everything, but Neo-Orthodoxy turned to the Revelation in Christ, and so was Christocentric, although omitting much of the Bible picture of Christ. Fosdick was within the mainstream of this thinking and suggested a Christian realism because of the disillusionment from two world wars. Because of this disillusionment Fosdick turned more and more to the Quaker position of pacifism and became, as the cliché has it, "wrong-headed in the right direction."

He retired from Union Seminary and Riverside Church in 1946. Until his death a few years ago he continued to maintain his liberal stance, although today one seldom hears his name mentioned or reference made to him in liberal periodicals. Until the end of his life he walked an individualistic road between old-time Liberalism and the more popular Neo-Orthodoxy.

THE LANGUAGE OF THE LIBERALS

Union Seminary in New York was the hotbed of infidel teaching on all sides. Indeed, at times it seemed as if there existed an ambition among faculty members to outdo one another in extreme radicalism. Union owed its origin to godly men of the 1830's who built this Presbyterian school on sound Reformed doctrine, and for seventy years it was required that each faculty member take the oath to uphold and teach the Westminster Confession of Faith. But in 1905, at the beginning of this period of Fundamentalism, the Board of

Trustees revoked this and in its place substituted the nebulous requirement that all members of the faculty should satisfy the board of their Christian life and faith. In the light of how little a board usually knows of the facts of a faculty member's faith and of his life, this is license of the strongest sort. This was the time when Union severed all relationships with the Presbyterian Church, U.S.A., after one of its professors, C. A. Briggs, had been tried and found guilty of heresy and unfrocked. But Briggs sought and received Episcopal ordination and continued to teach at Union. This severance of Union was not the great blessing it might be supposed, since Presbyterian pulpits were still supplied by its graduates. One of Union's important faculty figures was William Adams Brown. Writing in the *Harvard Theological Review* in 1911, he stated that salvation was not an act but "a process going on through the ages and rooted as truly as sin itself in the nature of men."[10] Another faculty member, A. C. McGiffert, stated in lectures at Yale in 1922 that "early Gentile converts may well have taken Christ as their Lord and Saviour without taking his God and Father as their God." Another, G. A. J. Ross, returned from a trip to the Orient in 1921 and said, "I believe that long ago Christ and Buddha have met in that large world of the spirit and I cannot but believe that it was a meeting marked by mutual love and veneration." Certainly Fundamentalist blood boiled and still boils at such imaginative and blasphemous attacks on the deity of Christ. Serving on Union's faculty in the field of Religious Education was G. A. Coe, who accepted the premise that man's highest destiny was to be his whole self. He spoke of "twice-born men as probably determined by some persistent, though not yet defined, physiological depression . . . I worship God . . . I bow my spirit before the spirit of world democracy, that is to be."[11] Furthermore, he believed that the "thought of God may indeed undergo yet many transformations . . . it will continually be renewed as the expression of the depth and height of social experience and social aspiration."[12] A colleague of Coe on the faculty was the popular radio preacher Harry E. Fosdick, who wrote that the "substitutionary atonement, where one suffers in the place of others . . . is in the view of modern ideas of justice an immoral outrage."[13] Few men have written books which have so kept the masses from the Bible or crushed the faith of those who had believed the Bible. In one of his works, Fosdick declared that "a storm god, dwelling on a mountain, whose major activity was war . . . was the beginning of the

[10]*Harvard Theological Review*, No. 4, 1911.
[11]Quoted in Smith, p. 39.
[12]Ibid.
[13]Harry E. Fosdick, *A Guide to the Understanding of the Bible* (New York: Harper, 1938), p. 50.

development of the Jewish ideas of God."[14] A. C. McGiffert also held that "Christ is essentially no more divine than we are or nature is."[15]

Another liberal spokesman was Gerald B. Smith of the University of Chicago, who said:

> May we not demand that God shall be required to receive the moral approval of man . . . it has been assumed that a study of the Bible would adequately prepare one to have a moral life. Nothing is farther from the truth.[16]

Equally blasphemous was E. A. Burtt of Cornell, who said that "God is no longer the central fact in religion. . . . His place is taken by man's religious experience."[17] J. W. Bowman of Western Seminary (Presbyterian) in Pittsburgh wrote:

> If Jesus knew of the tradition of his virgin birth, he never pressed it. After all, who should have decided between him and any number of demigods and heroes for whom such a birth was claimed. It was the Church that added these mundane traditions to its Gospels.[18]

E. E. Aubrey of the faculty of the University of Chicago said that "Jesus . . . is not the Creator who made heaven and earth, nor is he all of God."[19] He was joined by H. P. Van Dusen of Union Seminary in attacking the deity of Christ. Van Dusen wrote that "it is mistaken to claim that in Jesus, the whole Being of God was present, that God's purpose was fully expressed through Him."[20] Hornell Hart of Duke Divinity School joined the attack by writing that "to pretend that the historic Nazarene was perfect is to deny the Christ in order to glorify Jesus."[21] Fosdick agreed with these scholars, as is witnessed by his sermon entitled "The Peril of Worshipping Jesus." The Baptist historian, H. C. Vedder, added to the attack by writing:

> of all the slanders men have perpetrated against the Most High [the substitutionary atonement] . . . is the most insulting. No sin cannot be escaped by a bloody sacrifice. Jesus never taught and never authorized anybody to teach in his name that he suffered in our stead and bore the penalty of our sins.[22]

An imposing figure in Liberalism was E. S. Brightman of Boston University. His was an important post, since it was in Methodism's largest institution. In one of his many books, Brightman stated:

[14]Ibid., p. 6.
[15]A. C. McGiffert, *The Rise of the Modern Religious Ideas* (New York: Harper, 1915), p. 208.
[16]Quoted by Ernest Gordon, *The Leaven of the Sadducees* (Chicago: Bible Institute Association, 1926), p. 178.
[17]Quoted in Smith, p. 40.
[18]Ibid., p. 45.
[19]Ibid., p. 52.
[20]Ibid.
[21]Ibid., p. 57.
[22]Gordon, p. 219. This is a quotation of some sermons published in the Chester *News*, Chester, Pa.

The Christian Church will come to recognize in Buddhism, Confucianism, and Modernism other roads to God. The Christian will treat representatives of these religions as brothers and not as heathen enemies of the faith.[23]

One of the schools to be founded after the Great Awakening under George Whitefield was Dartmouth College at Hanover, New Hampshire. It had as a founding purpose the training of missionaries to go to the frontiers to win converts, including those of Indian backgrounds. But with the times Dartmouth also has changed. In a student paper published in 1927 it was brazenly announced that the College had a large percentage of atheists and agnostics and boasted that "Dartmouth is proud of her disbelievers."[24]

One commonly used quotation from Fosdick declared that he did "not believe in the Virgin Birth or in that old-fashioned doctrine of the atonement and I do not know of any intelligent person who does."[25] Dan Gilbert of the World's Christian Fundamentals Association spent considerable time in collecting the more common statements of the Modernists. He pointed out that W. M. Horton of Oberlin had written that "God is my own better self... God is all that is best in our human heritage."[26] Another figure among the radicals was Sherwood Eddy who wrote in his book, *Religion and Social Justice,* that experience has shown that immorality is the inevitable accompaniment of marriage that is fixed and indissolute."[27] A college president added to the confusion by writing that "the man who does not know the Bible or whose acquaintance with it has begun in an unimpressionable age will probably never know that he is missing anything."[28] H. N. Wieman of the University of Chicago admitted that "I fear my religion has never been religious . . . whatever God is, he is not a personality."[29]

The place of Karl Barth in the modern theological jungle can possibly be gleaned from the work of Van Til, although the latter's cumbersome and heavy style will discourage most readers.[30] Barth's entry into theological status came with his *Commentary on Romans*

---

[23]Quoted in Smith, p. 94.

[24]Ibid., p. 118.

[25]Quoted in R. T. Ketcham, *The Answer* (Des Plaines, Illinois: General Association of Baptist Churches, 1965), pp. 27-28.

[26]Quoted in Dan Gilbert, *Our Retreat from Modernism* (San Diego: Danielle Press, 1939), p. 39.

[27]Ibid., p. 106.

[28]James Bissett Pratt, "Religion and the Young Generation," *Yale Review,* 12 (April, 1923), 602.

[29]Quoted in Smith, pp. 127f.

[30]Cornelius Van Til, *The New Modernism,* (Philadelphia: Presbyterian and Reformed Publishing Company, 1947).

in 1919. World War I saw the optimistic dream of the do-gooders, hopeful Liberals, and social Kingdom builders collapse. Barth called thinkers back to some Reformation concepts, and one was that God has revealed Himself in acts, especially in Christ and the Bible. He did emphasize the word of God but that was not to be identified with the written Word. Also in the camp of Neo-Orthodoxy was Emil Brunner, who helped to undercut historic doctrines; he was a strong critic of the "paper-pope," drawing a clear line between revelation and the Scriptures. Upholding them in America was Reinhold Niebuhr, who put the stress on the individual self-hood, which he claimed he got from the Bible, and this gave him the proper sense of meaning, namely history. The vagueness of his philosophy was seen very clearly when he called Jesus the "Image-Point."[31] Sin was undue self-concern, though he would make a large place for human freedom and believed that education would increase man's opportunities for good and evil. He declared that the Biblical "Christ and . . . Anti-Christ are symbols of the fact that good and evil grow in history. . . . a greater evil is always a corruption of the greater good."[32]

Since the days of those named above, other liberal thinkers, writers, and pulpiteers have come on the scene to further attract thinking young Turks in theological circles and to add to the problems of thinking Fundamentalists, who must needs analyze and expose their unbiblical concepts. Liberals of popular appeal have included E. Stanley Jones, Ralph Sockman, Elton Trueblood, John Haynes Holmes, W. E. Garrison, and James A. Pike. Among the intellectuals have appeared such radicals as Paul Tillich, Reinhold and H. R. Niebuhr, Shailer Matthews, Karl Jaspers, Heidegger, Berdyaev, Bultman, Marcel, Sartre, and Rufus Jones. Some figures have become well-known because of specialized ministries or appeals, and representatives of this type would be Martin Luther King, Jr., Joseph Fletcher, Norman Vincent Peale, T. J. J. Altizer, Harvey Cox, W. M. Horton, C. C. Morrison, E. S. Ames, W. L. Stidger, Roy L. Smith, Preston Bradley, and G. A. Buttrick. Faculty members of wide audience would include A. W. Palmer, H. P. Van Dusen, E. F. Scott, Georgia Harkness, Liston Pope, S. J. Case, and E. S. Brightman. Better-known churchmen should be noted such as B. I. Bell, H. S. Leiper, George A. Gordon, F. J. McConnell, and E. F. Tittle. Each one has played a significant role in the creation of ecumenical theology—one utterly devoid of Bible truth but Satan-inspired to blind millions to the saving grace of God and the need

---

[31]The interested reader of Niebuhr will find this and other equally vague expressions in his book *The Nature and Destiny of Man* (New York: Scribner's, 1964).
[32]Ibid., p. ix.

of the new birth which our Saviour told Nicodemus was necessary for entrance into the Kingdom of God. These men have prepared a rotting American Protestantism for the erection, worldwide, of the One Church which will rule the hearts of most men during the Great Tribulation. God will destroy it, for its character, its name, and its destruction, as Babylon the Great, Mother of Harlots and abominations of the earth, are clearly designated in Revelation 17-18.

7
The Prima Donnas of Fundamentalism

Four men were sensations in this period among Fundamentalists. Friends and foes loved or attacked them, and today they are remembered with the deepest religious nostalgia. Their great moments are remembered with keenest emotions and deepest respect. Their feats of manhood in the midst of titanic struggles still remain beacon lights of testimony. They differed greatly among themselves, but each in his amazing array of gifts took on the whole conspiracy of Modernism, apostasy, Liberalism, and evolution-peddlers on faculties, and were writers of finest scholastic background and acumen. These four were warriors in the forefront of the fight for Fundamentalism, giants in the proclamation of the Gospel of grace. They were Thomas Todhunter Shields of Toronto, Canada; William Bell Riley of Minneapolis, Minnesota; John Roach Straton of New York City; and John Frank Norris of Fort Worth, Texas. This generation knows little of the herculean battles these men endured while pastoring large and growing churches. Their example to young men was overwhelming, and most Fundamentalists on the scene today are directly or indirectly indebted to their loyal stand and their magnificent defense of the Faith when schools, seminaries, and denominations came under the spell of Satan in the acceptance of false doctrine. Our study demands that we not only notice them but plot their place in the movement called Fundamentalism.

T. T. SHIELDS (1873-1955)

Although a Canadian, Shields of Toronto exercised a mighty influence on the course of Fundamentalism in the United States. He was a "man of special gifts, a mountain peak without peer as preacher, teacher, writer—a veritable genius, the Canadian Spurgeon, a battling Baptist, and a devoted pastor."[1] Of solid British stock, he was born in England in 1873 into a family of preachers. His parents are buried in Hamilton, Ontario. He was converted in 1891 under his father's ministry at Leamington, Ontario, where his father died in 1902. Young T. T. (a Jr. and affectionately called Tod by his father) preached his first sermon at Tiverton, Ontario, in 1894. He had no formal college or seminary training. His honorary degrees (two D.D.'s) were from McMaster and Temple Universities. He was pastor at Florence from 1894-1895, then Dutton, 1895-1897, Delhi 1897-1900, Wentworth Street in Hamilton 1900-1904, Adelaide Street in London 1904-1910, and then held his longest and most outstanding pastorate at Jarvis Street in Toronto from 1910 till his death in 1955.[2] He was always loyal to England and its institutions; his knowledge of English leaders and history was most unusual for a Baptist preacher. Although he began his ministry with no formal college or seminary training, he—like the great C. H. Spurgeon, who was his ideal—was self-taught to a remarkable extent. At Jarvis Street Baptist, the "Cathedral" Baptist Church of Canada, Shields exercised a mighty ministry. Jarvis Street had had noble pastors but not outstanding throughout the Empire or the continent, and none involved in the American scene and certainly not in Fundamentalism. But T. T. Shields was destined to move as a massive figure in the theological battles of both Canada and the United States from 1920 until his death. Jarvis Street was a metropolitan or premier church of the Dominion—in church affairs and particularly in those of Baptist life. It was the leading church in the Ontario and Quebec Convention, which had as a training school, McMaster University in Hamilton, Ontario —formerly Toronto Baptist College but later heavily endowed by Senator McMaster and renamed after him. This is now a typical liberal arts university with a small divinity house connected with it. Today the University has no connection with the Ontario and Quebec Convention. Large in stature and commanding in appearance and ways, T. T. Shields was aptly dubbed the Spurgeon of Canada—indeed Charles Haddon Spurgeon was his favorite of all

[1]Leslie Tarr, *Shields of Canada* (Toronto, Canada: Jarvis Street Baptist Church, 1967), from the Foreword, written by H. C. Slade, Shields' successor.
[2]Ibid., pp. 47-149.

preachers, and he never tired of referring to him. As early as 1908 Elmore Harris (1854-1910) charged that I. G. Matthews of McMaster University was unsound in doctrine but the convention of 1910 openly endorsed the University, and Shields went along with the decision.

He was first noticed by the American Fundamentalists in his attempt to prevent Modernism from taking over McMaster, the official school of his convention. His ministry at Jarvis Street for the first ten years saw growth and honors for its pastor, with the conferral of the D. D. by both Russell H. Conwell on behalf of Temple University in Philadelphia and McMaster University, of which he was a trustee. By 1919 Jarvis Street had a membership of seven hundred, which was large in Canadian Baptist circles. His first open protest came that year over a liberal professor at McMaster, I. G. Matthews, but the latter left that year. Then the *Canadian Baptist,* the Convention paper, published an editorial attacking the inspiration of the Scriptures; the leaven of McMaster had started to "leaven the whole lump." Shields was greatly alarmed over this editorial and held that it took a vague view of Scripture. He took his protest to the floor of the 1919 Convention of the Ontario and Quebec Baptists and had the editorial officially condemned. This was a Pyrrhic victory, for the Liberals would be back as usual, and the next time it would be a different story. In 1921 Shields spoke openly against the damage being done by worldly amusements, preaching on Sunday February 13, 1921, on "The Christian Attitude Toward Amusements." By Fundamentalist standards, this was rather mild, but an upheaval took place that was not mild.[3] Several votes were taken by the church, with charges leveled against him of being a dictator and unethical in the debates. The major item being lost, the McMaster supporters wanted him out of the church because of his protest against the school. When votes were taken he was sustained by a vote of 284 to 199 and again on September 21 by a vote of 351 to 310. Three hundred and forty-one left the church, with many joining Yorkminster Baptist in Toronto, which then and now has taken a very liberal attitude on matters Biblical. Others organized Park Road Baptist. In May, 1922, Shields started the *Gospel Witness,* intending to expose Romanism and Modernism and to publish his sermons. It became well-known among preachers and was one of the most powerful organs of the Fundamentalist Movement in the 1920's and 1930's.[4]

An uncertain calm settled over the relationship of Shields to McMaster and the Convention, which calm ensued from 1921 to

[3]Shields himself has related the whole story of this in *The Plot That Failed* (Toronto, Canada: *The Gospel Witness,* 1937).
[4]Tarr, p. 110.

1927. But in this period he became deeply involved in the affairs of American Fundamentalism, for in 1923 he helped to start the Baptist Bible Union and was its president for its entire life of seven years. In 1923, taking a cue from Norris himself, Shields changed his Sunday School from the afternoon, a common time in Canada, to the morning just before the worship service, and his attendance went to 1,000, the largest in the Dominion. But his fears for the future of his convention were largely gone, for in the *Gospel Witness* of September, 1922, he avowed that most men in the Convention were Fundamentalists. Here we ought to insert a word of explanation. The word "Fundamentalism" has never had the same meaning in Canada as in the United States. In the Dominion it is synonymous with orthodox or evangelical and refers to, or includes, any person who rejects the tenets of the Modernists or the Liberals. Shields was against the Liberalism of schools in Canada like Brandon College, the divinity houses at Toronto University, and McMaster. Probably he was right in 1922 that most of the preachers in the Convention and their members were against Modernism. But this had not convinced Liberals that they had lost. Indeed, they made their very clever plans to win in spite of this, and their plan was to infiltrate the schools of training and preparation for the ministry. Neither Shields nor anyone else in the Dominion was alert to this, although later they saw it and the terrible damage that ensued. In 1924 he had Norris come for a month, and using Massey Hall had audiences totaling 50,000. In the *Gospel Witness* of June 26, 1924, Shields wrote that the trust of Senator McMaster had been betrayed by the trustees. It had been a slow process, starting with Professor George Cross (by 1924 at Rochester) and I. G. Matthews (by now at Crozer). Another symptom was the appointment of H. P. Whidden as Chancellor, although he had led Brandon College in Manitoba into ruin. Another proof of apostasy was the granting of a D.D. to W. H. P. Faunce of Brown University. Accordingly, the Jarvis Street leader wrote:

> For fifteen years the University has followed a policy of drift. It has been a ship without a captain and one needs no telescope to discern the breakers ahead .... [it is a question] whether a policy more deplorably weak, characterized by vacillation, compromise and expediency could be immagined than the McMaster policy.[5]

But the calm in the Canadian Baptist situation was suddenly shattered by the appointment of Professor L. H. Marshall to the faculty of McMaster in 1925; to Shields this was an open declaration of war. So Shields answered the open challenge at once and wrote that he took a firm stand because there was a principle at stake. At

[5] *The Gospel Witness,* June 26, 1924, p. 10.

the 1926 convention Shields and Marshall faced each other, and the results were published in 176 pages of the *Gospel Witness.* The Convention sided with the school—after all, it was the Convention's school, and how could it do otherwise? What has happened to this convention since is a matter of history. McMaster has led it farther down the road of liberal thought. One result is seen in the fact that in 1920 it had 492 churches with 350 pastors and 61,000 members; in 1960 it had only 442 churches with 373 pastors and but 50,535 members. It has joined other Baptists in supporting the ecumenical movement. A Baptist writer in Canada has acknowledged, "Baptists apparently are not quite sure what the battle is all about and to date, we appear to be waiting for the certain sound of the trumpet, although perhaps we are not quite sure of its source or nature."[6] Had the writer read the history of Baptists in Canada he would have known that trumpeter Shields blew the certain sound on the trumpet in the 1920's, but Baptists, so called, turned away and have gone into those murky depths of Modernism, compromise, and unbelief; drugged by the disease of deterioration, they have failed to hear or even recognize that a clear trumpet was blown. They have turned from the Faith and the faithful men of the faith in the 1920's, and their sons and daughters have built a Baptist kingdom devoid of Bible truth and insight. Many men have led in this apostasy, men such as F. W. Patterson, W. C. Smiley, T. B. MacDormand, Simeon Spidle, J. B. McLaurin, Watson Kirkconnell, and H. P. Whidden. On October 14, 1927, Jarvis Street Church was officially voted out of the Ontario and Quebec Convention. So in 1927 a new group was established—the Union of Regular Baptist Churches, meeting to organize at Jarvis Street on October 19, 1927.

During these years the schedule of this giant of Jarvis Street was seemingly more than full. At Kansas City in 1923 he helped with the founding of the Baptist Bible Union and was its first president. Over three thousand attended the first meetings held in a tent borrowed from Walter L. Wilson. Other leaders there were Norris, R. E. Neighbour, Riley, and W. L. Pettingill; and, according to Shields, "the express purpose was to declare and wage relentless and uncompromising war on Modernism on all fronts."[7] Meetings of this organization will be discussed later, but Shields was a key figure in the BBU as long as it lasted. In 1922 he opened Toronto Baptist Seminary with eighteen day students and twenty-eight in evening classes. Riley came for the opening exercises.

The *Gospel Witness* presented some of the issues which were being debated and fought. There were open charges against the

[6]Neil G. Price in *The Baptist Advance,* ed. D. C. Wooley (Nashville, Tenn.: Broadman Press, 1964), p. 176.
[7]*The Gospel Witness,* Feb. 3, 1927.

Foreign Mission Board of the Northern Baptist Convention and hostile antichristian teaching on the mission fields in China. The article named C. G. Fiedler as the main heretic, charging as unitarian his statement that "he accepted evolution, utterly repudiated the atonement, and claimed that neither the Old Testament nor the New Testament was infallible."[8] The Body of Managers of the Foreign Mission Board decided to give this man a year of study at Andover Newton. Shields saw little hope for anyone going to Andover Newton to regain orthodoxy and added, "when a patient is in ill-health, it is not usual for the physician to send the patient to a place where the disease from which the patient is suffering is already rampant."[9] To sum it up, Shields felt that the Foreign Mission enterprise was reeking with Modernism, and "whoever supports such a Board is in danger of contributing to another thirty pieces of silver to pay some modern Judas to betray the Lord Jesus to be crucified afresh."[10] An article in 1926 stated that the supreme issue at the Northern Baptist Convention was the admission of representatives of Park Avenue Baptist in New York City (of which Fosdick was the pastor), which had unimmersed members. The article charged Shailer Matthews with duplicity of belief in claiming that the NBC did not have the right to define a Baptist Church solely as one having immersed members. The University of Chicago was doing everything it could to destroy the independence of a local church. To Shields, Matthews was an example of Modern thinking that "so warps the mind that it becomes impossible for its devotees to either speak or write the truth."[11] Jarvis Street Church at the annual meeting of 1926 had a membership of 2,012, with additions of 380 during the year.

In 1927 he took over the leadership of Des Moines University in Des Moines, Iowa, and this will be considered in connection with the BBU, which controlled it. But Shields was the leading figure in its takeover and management for the two years it lasted. He was keenly disappointed when a student riot in the spring of 1929 forced the closing of the school and brought the BBU to its lowest point of strength. Shields was accused of gross indiscretion, among other things, and he and the official BBU representative there, Miss Edith Rebman, left the American scene. His part in American Fundamentalism was over except for a few times after 1929 when he came to speak in American churches. This was not the only reason for his withdrawal. American Fundamentalists were making much of the subject of prophecy, speaking forthrightly for

[8]Ibid.
[9]Ibid.
[10]Ibid., April 22, 1926.
[11]Ibid.

premillennialism, with most of them using the Scofield Reference Bible. In the 1930's it was noticeable that Shields was more and more taking an amillennial stand and pushing it in the *Gospel Witness.* His attacks on the Scofield Bible were more frequent, and while a large number of American Fundamentalists were willing to admit some errors and questionable notes, they could not sanction such open attacks. In 1935 he suffered a serious heart attack, but lived a most active life for twenty years more. Tarr relates that in later life Shields regarded the Des Moines University episode as "an adventure that he regretted undertaking."[12] At another time he dubbed it "a colossal headache."

Jarvis Street Church was destroyed by fire on March 4, 1938, "by an enemy's hand," but a handsome new building (with plans drawn in detail by Shields) was erected. By January 28, 1947, it was joyfully announced that "our Holy and Beautiful House" was free of debt; it had cost, with additions, about half a million dollars. It should be noted that much of this was during the strain of the war years. The auditorium with all the halls would accommodate 3,500. A special issue of the *Gospel Witness,* dated January 30, 1947, gave details with pictures of the very commodious and exquisitely beautiful furniture and the heading of the front page was "Our Zion Now Entirely Free of Debt," with a quotation from Psalm 48:12-13 in large letters.[13]

Few men living in Shields' day knew as much about the doctrines and practices of Romanism as he did. No one in Canada raised such an effective voice against the domination of Rome in the arena of politics. He resented and exposed its tyranny in no uncertain language. Reading the *Gospel Witness* for this period would be an education in all phases of the history of that church. Shields saw the growing power of Catholic Quebec as a huge cloud of darkness over the Canadian scene. He initiated the Canadian Protestant League to rally the people and alert them to the dangers. Even the Prime Minister did not escape his charges of cowardice, and W. L. Mackenzie King said openly that he had contempt for Shields. Thus he was recognized as the most loved, feared, and hated pulpiteer in all of Canada.

In 1948 he joined the International Council of Christian Churches and he and Carl McIntire became fast friends. He preached his last sermon at Jarvis Street on May 30, 1954, thus ending a pastorate of forty-four years. Early in 1955 he indicated H. C. Slade as his choice as successor, and the church followed its beloved leader's choice in this important post of leadership. A few years before, he had gone through the agony of open rifts with two of his closest workers and

[12]Tarr, p. 105.
[13]*The Gospel Witness,* March 4, 1938.

associates, W. G. Brown and W. S. Whitcombe. Brown had been Dean of Toronto Baptist Seminary but was dismissed in 1948 and took most of the students with him to organize Central Baptist Seminary of Toronto, where he still leads. Whitcombe broke later and joined the faculty of Central, where he still teaches and pastors a church in Toronto. Both cases greatly weakened Toronto Baptist Seminary, and today it is a small seminary housed in properties at Jarvis Street Church. Shields died on April 4, 1955. His funeral services were conducted by Slade and by his comrades in arms for the Lord, Robert McCaul of Brooklyn, New York, and C. J. Loney of Hamilton, with Carl McIntire preaching the funeral sermon. A memorial was published by Jarvis Street as a special issue of the *Gospel Witness,* complete with pictures of the "great Doctor's" life. Of his life Shields once wrote:

> I had a stormy life . . . . I have been zealous for the Gospel . . . . I regret nothing of my contention for the faith, save that I have not striven more heroically and continuously for the glory of the Gospel . . . . Preaching is the biggest business I know . . . . I am a soldier in the field . . . . I will have no compromise with the enemy.[14]

He had to fight Modernists, for they were wrong; they were poisonous; they did not build churches but rather stole those already built.

W. B. RILEY (1861-1947)

William Bell Riley was born in 1861 in Green County, Indiana, and went to be with his Lord in December of 1947.[15] He attended Hanover College, where he majored in the classics and took an active part in debating. From 1885 to 1888 he attended Southern Baptist Seminary, and he always remembered with gratitude the professors at the Seminary—Whitsitt, Manly, Kerfoot, Sampey, and Broadus. These he held to be thoroughly sound in doctrine except in prophetic teachings, for they were not premillennial. While at the Seminary he heard D. L. Moody and desired for himself a soulwinning ministry, and that he did have. After having pastorates in Bloomington and Chicago (Calvary Baptist), he was called to First Baptist in Minneapolis in 1897. This was the first part of a dream, for he had cherished the hope of a great downtown preaching center. His ideal in this was the famed Tremont Temple in Boston, which Moody had designated the greatest soulwinning church in the world. In Riley's lifetime, Tremont boasted such outstanding

---

[14]Tarr, pp. 145-58.

[15]There are two unpublished dissertations on Riley. One is by Lloyd B. Hull, "A Rhetorical Study of the Preaching of William Bell Riley" (Wayne State Univ., 1960). Another, by Robert S. McBirnie, is "Basic Issues in the Fundamentalism of W. B. Riley " (State Univ. of Iowa, 1952).

pulpiteers as George C. Lorimer, Courtland Myers, and Jasper C. Massee. Riley served First Baptist in Minneapolis for forty-five years. In 1902 he founded the Northwestern Bible School, where hundreds would be trained. A seminary program was added in 1935 and a college of liberal arts in 1944. The three together were known as Northwestern Schools.

From the early days of his Minneapolis pastorate, Riley sensed the creeping dangers of Modernism and "fought to maintain the *status quo* against the New Theology."[16] As such he has been hailed as "Fundamentalism's most energetic organizer and leader."[17] He excelled as a preacher and public debater, and was a feared opponent of evolution and Modernism, as well as a warm-hearted and faithful pastor. Fundamentalists all over the nation looked to this skilled analyst and leader as their champion.[18] Tall and rugged in manly physique, he was equally imposing in pulpit and platform. Riley was located during this time in a very strong Swedish and Lutheran territory, but he was able to fill the large auditorium of First Baptist which had 2,640 seats. Prominent in his sermons were the great truths of Fundamentalism, namely, the verbally inspired Word, sin, the Person and work of Christ, and His second coming. This last truth he saw as and believed to be the imminent, any-moment return of the Lord to rapture the Church. About the Church and the Kingdom, Riley wrote, "Are the church and the Kingdom the same?—NEVER. The kingdom is a future thing and the church is a present thing. The church is not to go through the Tribulation."[19] Riley wrote over ninety volumes, had seventy-five scrapbooks, and had a personal library of three thousand volumes.

Early in his pastorate at Minneapolis he noticed the drift in Baptist circles toward Higher Criticism and the more and more open avowal of evolutionary and modernistic ideas. To him it was crystal clear that "the heresies which have afflicted the church have, almost without exception, been invented by learned scholars and the speculations which have blighted the faith of the believers have generally been hatched and brooded in theological schools."[20] These he vigorously opposed and exposed—indeed much of his public ministry would be to this end.[21] To him Modernism was a theology based on the concept that the Bible was of human origin and that

[16]McBirnie, p. 2.

[17]Marie Acomb Riley, *The Dynamic of a Dream* (Grand Rapids, Mich.: W. B. Eerdmans, 1938), p. 3.

[18]Ibid.

[19]W. B. Riley, *The Menace of Modernism* (New York: Christian Alliance, 1917), p. 349.

[20]Ibid., p. 136.

[21]A good analysis can be found in George H. Moulds, "The Conflict Between the Fundamentalists and the Modernists in the Northern Baptist Convention" (unpublished M.A. thesis, State University of Iowa, 1940).

"its inspiration exists only in its ability to inspire . . . . its interpretation is a matter of mental conscience."[22] Riley's answer was that "(1) the Bible was finished in heaven and handed down, (2) the King James Version was absolutely inerrant, and (3) its literal acceptance was alone correct."[23] His book *The Menace of Modernism* charges Liberalism with holding that the wisdom of man should be substituted for the Word of God, and it expresses his deep-seated contempt for university professors who criticize and slander the Bible without knowing that Book and hide their ignorance by excessive gloating. Riley concluded that by World War I there was not one of the great denominations of the North that had not been infected with infidelity. Here he quoted L. W. Munhall, who named three Methodist schools into which infidelity had already come: Boston University, Wesleyan University, and Syracuse University . By lip and pen Modernists had rejected the Lord Jesus and had repudiated the Bible.[24] At times Riley would lash out at Modernists with such powerful and incisive attacks as:

> Any Jesus, not begotten by the Holy Ghost, born of Mary, crucified on Calvary, raised the third day, ascended to the right hand of God and destined to descend to the earth and reign from sea to sea is as much a figment of a distempered imagination as are the diseases resulting from an overdose of meat.[25]

In 1919 he took the leading part in organizing the World's Christian Fundamentals Association, giving the keynote address and leading it for eleven years. In the keynote message Riley said, "The hour has struck for the rise of a new Protestantism . . . . this organization is of more importance than the nailing of the 95 Theses."[26] The WCFA was to "war on Modernism," and this was Riley's forte for two decades. Soon the organization would seize on one important issue and make it a great symbol of Fundamentalism versus Modernism. That issue was evolution, and for some seven years after the inception of the WCFA its platform would resound with all the arguments and invectives against those who held to any form of the Darwinian evolutionary hypothesis. Riley was second to none in this fierce and crucial debate. He would meet with able debaters on the stage of many forums and colleges and hold his own with the very best. Among his opponents were Metcalf of the State College of North Carolina, Burts of Chicago, Maynard Shipley of the Science League of America, and Lindsley of California. A debate was scheduled with Clarence Darrow but, for reasons never made

[22]Riley, *The Menace of Modernism,* p. 11.
[23]Ibid., p. 9.
[24]Ibid., p. 35.
[25]Ibid., p. 39.
[26]W. B. Riley, ed., *The School and Church* (official organ of WCFA), July, 1919, p. 183.

public, Darrow withdrew. Professor Henry Smith of Chicago rightly contended that all such debates were part of the fight between a stiff thoroughgoing orthodoxy and a stiff thoroughgoing infidelity. Riley rejected evolution because it was contrary to the facts and because it was the philosophy of skeptics. Often he referred to the fact that Darwin himself had left his early allegiance to the sound doctrine of the Bible and toward the close of his life had said that he deserved to be called an atheist. This cause and effect was sure proof to the Minneapolis Fundamentalist that evolution was of Satanic origin.

Riley took a commanding position as a defender of sound Baptist doctrine while the schools and agencies of Northern Baptists drifted more and more completely into Modernism. While he had issued warning after warning, nothing of an organizational threat within the Northern Baptist Convention was launched until 1920.[27] His part in this conflict will emerge in the chapter dealing with the Northern Baptist crisis. Concerning the social gospel, Riley wrote the following:

> For 25 years I have listened to a never ending refrain in favor of the Social Gospel and have given hours of fleshly weariness and mental disgust to famed orators who repudiated the shed blood while they pleaded for service of man to man, finer education, fewer tenement houses, flowers in the front yard . . . . I should count myself a sacred fool to suppose that they could ever be made a substitute for the Gospel of Grace.[28]

Riley joined with J. Frank Norris and T. T. Shields in the formation of the Baptist Bible Union in 1923 and was a featured speaker at Union rallies and meetings for the next seven years of its existence. His relationship with Norris cooled after the Chipps shooting case in 1926, even though the courts found Norris innocent, exonerating him on the basis of self-defense. Riley's relation with Shields cooled when Shields, in the name of the Union, took over Des Moines University in 1927, assuming a large debt accumulated under Northern Baptist leadership. Riley could hardly be enthusiastic over the proposition when he had a school of his own, although he did not as yet have a liberal arts program.

At a mass meeting held at Calvary Baptist in New York on December 27, 1923, he charged the denominational leaders with having "an autocracy intolerable to Baptists."[29] He recognized that ecclesiasticism was the spirit of the times, but he could not excuse Baptists for imbibing it. He saw Romanism as a prime example of it, but found the same thing among Protestants, for "the Methodist

[27]A careful analysis of the two opposing forces in this greatest of all struggles is given by Norman Furniss in *The Fundamentalist-Modernist Controversy in the Northern Baptist Convention 1918-1933* (1954; rpt. Hamden, Conn.: Archon Books, 1963).

[28]Riley, *The Menace of Modernism*, p. 337.

[29]*The Faith-Fundamentalist* (Calvary Baptist Church, N. Y.), Dec. 27, 1923.

episcopacy increases its papal tendencies . . . . the Methodist bishops impose on ministerial novices the rationalistic literature condemned in the last representative gathering of that church."[30] He found that Baptists and Congregationalists were clamoring for kings and rulers. Referring to the Board of Promotion of Northern Baptists, he labeled it as pronounced a hierarchy as is known to ecclesiasticism. Riley charged that these executives had declared brutal war on all opponents, so-called reactionaries, separatists, and denominational splitters (in fact, anyone who opposed Board policies and programs). One special target was Professor H. C. Vedder, Baptist historian of Crozer, "whose sad theological drift has occasioned no little sorrow in the denomination."[31] Then Riley buttressed his case by citing outstanding Baptists who had opposed ecclesiastic overlords, and in the list were Spurgeon, Gordon, and A. H. Newman. Riley prophesied denominational death if this aristocracy were allowed to continue. Northern Baptists have gone into both theological drift and ecclesiastical overlordship, but one of their saddest weaknesses is their failure to see their plight.

In the midst of denominational and interdenominational wars Riley continued his work as pastor in Minneapolis. This factor in Fundamentalism has all too often been ignored. While church overlords planned, plotted, and carried out the programs for denominational liberalizing, Fundamentalists were preaching in their own pulpits and in special meetings, winning the lost and teaching the saints the Word of God. Their time was taken up in evangelism and Bible teaching, and it was most difficult for such men to believe that others claiming to be in the ministry and doing the Lord's work would not be active in the same. Herein lies a naiveté that has been a hallmark of Fundamentalism. During this time Riley was training young men for the ministry, and many of them are in that great work today because of his life and example. More and more of them took a separatist and independent course and helped promote an anti-convention independency, and this prepared the way for the Minnesota Convention to leave the Northern Baptists; it took an independent course as did the State Convention of Arizona. One enigma of the situation was the fact that First Baptist in Minneapolis never did leave the Northern Baptist Convention, and it still maintains that affiliation. An irony of the story is that in his last year Riley, as an individual, did leave the Northern Baptist Convention.[32]

One reason for the establishment of the Northwestern Bible and

---

[30]Ibid.
[31]Ibid.
[32]Joseph M. Stowell, *Background and History of the General Association of Reg ular Baptist Churches* (Hayward, Calif.: Gospel Tracts Unlimited, 1949).

Missionary Training School (its full name) in 1902 was that "Eastern Seminaries were largely Modernistic."[33] It began with seven students but fifty years later enrolled about one thousand.

Riley often called himself a Fundamentalist without apology and without compromise. He held that there is no higher goal for a man of God, and with this high ideal he set himself to defend the Faith when the wars against it were hottest. Riley claimed there had been a drift in the wrong direction for twenty-five years. He blamed Nietzsche and Darwin, identifying the former as "the one European thinker who had carried the evolutionary principle and ethics to their logical conclusion."[34] From Germany had come both militarism and Modernism, and they have "combined to strike the most deadly blow [in the Church] since the days of Augustine when he united a sick church with a stinking State;"[35] "It strikes truth to the ground, exiles righteousness from civilization . . . [it is] the damnable dastardly deed of German Culture . . . it is a doctrine of devils."[36] Germany had paid for it in that

> Her people are well cared for . . . but their leaders have denied the deity of Christianity, they have disputed the authority of the Bible; they have dethroned God and put the spirit of Germany in His seat; and while doing it they have lifted the lid off hell and permitted that evil cauldron of the universe to pour its fumes of living death and its lava streams of destruction.[37]

Middle-of-the-roaders and moderates were also dangerous, although Riley was slow to see their weaknesses. One whose friendship he had, but who deserted him, was J. Whitcomb Brougher, Sr., successor to J. C. Massee at Tremont Temple. Many men played the coward when it became a life-and-death struggle within the ranks of Northern Baptists. Riley was troubled that Conservatives who had been within the Fundamentalist ranks yielded many times on key issues. Of Brougher, Riley said, "I love Jim and enjoy his companionship but I cannot share his compromises."[38] He also included Brougher's son, J. W., Jr., in his indictment, and criticized his part in organizing the Baptist Ministers' Covenant in Southern California (one method to unite Baptists behind the Northern Baptist program), saying that his organization was "as destitute of Biblical truth as a newborn babe [is] of clothes."[39]

Baptist Liberals were using one tactic consistently, and that was a cry for religious and academic freedom in both schools and

[33]*The Pilot*, Jan., 1943.
[34]Riley, *The Menace of Modernism*, p. 333.
[35]Ibid., p. 337.
[36]Ibid.
[37]Ibid.
[38]*The Pilot*, April, 1945.
[39]Ibid.

churches; this was a deadly weapon and most effective, for it sounded so Christian. Should a Christian be allowed private judgment in doctrinal matters? A denominational paper, *The Baptist* argued constantly for private judgment as a Baptist tenet. To Riley this was a "pillar-laster," for "it has nothing in common with marble, with granite, or even with sandstone. In fact, it utterly lacks solidarity and is therefore the plaster-product for the express purpose of sustaining a theological fabric that sadly needs support."[40] In the place of this straw doctrine Riley proposed that all Baptists express their allegiance to the Word of God. His expectation was that a solid majority would do this very thing. He was terribly frustrated as he saw that fewer and fewer of the total membership of Northern Baptist churches would follow him. He had to admit with dismay and great sorrow that,

> that primary and important article in all Baptist Confessions provided a hurdle too high for the galloping steeds of Modernism and so they have sought to stealthily remove it and create for themselves only the low and well-trimmed hedges of independent free expression, private judgment and separation of Church and State.[41]

That college professors would hide their unbelief behind such a mask was detestable to Riley. It was understood that these professors would be acquainted with German thought (as Riley was himself), but to accept it and impart it to young men training for the ministry was the blackest crime of all; to pass on theological trash as the truth was the crime of all crimes, the most despicable of all deeds of any men claiming to be in the Baptist ministry.

He made a strong case that Modernism was intellectually inferior to Fundamentalism, and this sounded strange indeed. Liberals had had the accredited schools and required their men to take so many courses in so many fields, supposedly under the most competent professors and research specialists. Riley contended that Fundamentalists, to reach any defensible position, had to think for themselves; others could not do it for them. The latter came to their own convictions through hard study while Modernists followed their leaders and mouthed their clichés, modernistic mottoes, and pronouncements clothed in liberal polish. As for Riley, he "would rather cast his lot with the Conservatives who did their own thinking than with the crowd that accepts, and blindly, for the sake of the loaves and fishes follows leadership."[42] Even such a man as Fosdick did not awe Riley, for the latter answered his famous sermon "Shall the Fundamentalists Win?" with a sermon entitled "Fundamentalism vs. the New Faith or Riley vs. Fosdick."[43] Riley

[40]*The Pilot*, April, 1940.
[41]Ibid.
[42]*The Pilot*, June, 1945.
[43]McBirnie, p. 27.

maintained, as many men admitted, that the God of the Modernists was very different indeed from the God of the Fundamentalists. Indeed, the Christianity of the Federal Council of Churches was a different brand from his. Thus he wrote:

Modernism has a different God, a different Christ, a different Bible from the God, the Christ, and the Bible of the Fundamentalists. If Fundamentalism is not to oppose the Federal Council, the fight should be declared over, the war in the churches at an end, the compromise regarded as a conquest for the Federal Council.[44]

It took time for Riley to understand how far Modernism had progressed, for he found it hard to believe that men falsely claiming to be saved and serving the Lord could monopolize the leadership posts. Again, it was heartbreaking to recognize that the schools to which so much of the Lord's money had gone and in which so many of the Lord's people had participated were now apostate. But he had to recognize it or close his eyes to the facts. He saw and he recognized, and so he wrote that "Modernism started in to capture the schools. It didn't leave a single one to the Fundamentalists, a commentary on the openmindedness claim always made by Liberals . . . [they] went after the Seminaries, Rochester, Newton, Crozer, Berkeley . . . a new trick by which to bar sound men from being acceptable to the ministry."[45] Even good schools had gone into liberal orbits. He pointed to Northfield Conference, once a well-known center for bible teaching under D. L. Moody. Riley stated that Paul Moody, son of D. L. Moody, was a Modernist and "Modernism will kill any Bible Conference" and "Paul Moody never invites a Fundamentalist to the Northfield Conference."[46]

Because of denominational defection he advocated that Baptists withhold their monies from convention programs, and this did give anxious hours to college administrators. In promoting this withholding Riley stated that, "I would far rather give my money to a school that was not labeled Baptist but was devoted to the Bible and to Christ than to one that was labeled Baptist but was known to deny the inspiration of the first and the deity of the latter."[47] The following appeared in an editorial:

Sometimes we hear of GARB and Independent Baptists quitting the Convention. The Southern Baptists in their separation didn't quit. The GARB are the true defenders of the Convention . . . . in fact these rebels vs. the Denomination are the conservators of the denomination. They resent Unitarian leadership [who] name them as dissenters from the liberal control of the Northern Convention.[48]

Very close to Riley in his work at First Baptist and Northwestern

[44]*The Pilot,* Nov., 1942.
[45]Riley, *The Menace of Modernism,* p. 290.
[46]*The Pilot,* July, 1944.
[47]Ibid.
[48]*The Pilot,* Aug., 1945.

Schools was Robert L. Moyer (1886-1944), who had been saved in a J. Wilbur Chapman meeting in Williamsport, Pennsylvania. Moyer went to Moody Bible Institute and then served for six years as pastor of the United Brethren Church in Minneapolis, teaching part-time at Northwestern. Then he became a full-time teacher and finally assistant to Riley. After Riley's resignation in March, 1942, he was called as successor in 1943, but died of diabetes eighteen months later. Moyer was Riley's right arm; to students he was a superb teacher and to pastors an exemplary Christian. What a different course that institution might have taken under his leadership had he lived. Later the seminary part was dropped (1956) but it continued at Fourth Baptist Church under Richard V. Clearwaters and still operates as the Central Baptist Seminary of Minneapolis. Minneapolis.

Riley resigned as pastor of First Baptist in March of 1942, having served in that post for forty-five years. Moyer's short ministry of eighteen months followed; and in 1944 an assistant pastor of First Baptist, Curtis B. Akenson, was chosen as pastor, and he still serves in that office. After resigning his pastorate in 1942, Riley intended to give his full time to the Bible School and Seminary, the latter having been added to the work in 1935. In 1943 the College of Liberal Arts was added, so that by 1943 Northwestern Schools had three major schools under its name.

William Bell Riley died in December of 1947, and a memorial issue of *The Pilot* was published the following month. Tributes to his greatness were contributed by many Fundamentalists, eminent pastors, and evangelists. W. L. Pettingill, an old warrior of the Faith himself, spoke of Riley's fearlessness and faithfulness as a mighty warrior for the faith. Billy Graham was listed as editor of *The Pilot,* and he preached the funeral sermon. In 1949 he became the president of Northwestern Schools. *The Pilot* stated that it had been militant in its stand against Modernism throughout its history of twenty-five years. Pastor Akenson of First Baptist said Riley was the ablest defender of the Faith that this generation had seen. H. H. Savage, of Pontiac, Michigan, said that Riley had denounced fearlessly the growing apostasy within Baptist ranks. He added that the eloquence and platform (of Riley) were "a consternation to his enemies but a constant encouragement to those of like precious faith."[49] John R. Rice said he "was a colorful and charming speaker . . . . he won enough people to build the largest Baptist church in the Northern Baptist Convention . . . . he will be classed with the great evangelists."[50]

Rice remembered that Bryan had called Riley the first statesman

[49]*The Pilot,* Jan., 1948.
[50]Ibid.

of the American pulpit. The Southern Baptist orator, Robert G. Lee, said that Riley was potent in personality, potent in the pulpit, and potent with the pen, and he fought against the teachings of the modernistic theologians and theologians rightly classed as middle-of-the-roaders. In typical Lee fashion he stated in a telegram at the time of the death that Riley weighed sixteen ounces to the pound, measured twelve inches to the foot, and always struck twelve for God. A close associate of Riley was Richard V. Clearwaters of Fourth Baptist in Minneapolis, Dean of Northwestern Seminary. He called Riley a second Martin Luther with the "fearless fire of Luther, the organizing genius of Wesley, and natural eloquence of Savonarola."[51] "His books have left a deposit as an antidote for Modernism in every denomination that all the deceivers cannot destroy; his students from these three Northwestern schools with the same Gospel are girdling the globe under the banner of almost every denomination."[52] Clearwaters wrote of the last hours spent with his dear friend, who was upset with the "deepening gloom of the apostasy, blighting effects of Unitarianism, Humanism, Nationalism, and Communism . . . . this can be nothing but the last days."[53] Clearwaters has carried on much of the Riley heritage in the two schools he has guided, Pillsbury Baptist Bible College in Owatonna, Minnesota, and Central Baptist Seminary of Minneapolis. Northwestern Schools abandoned first the Bible College and Seminary and later the Liberal Arts College. Recently the property has been sold to the state of Minnesota and a new property bought from the Roman Catholics some five miles north of St. Paul. The former business manager, William Berntsen, led in opening a college in the fall of 1972. Support for the new venture is expected from Conservative Baptist churches both within and beyond Minnesota, while the Clearwaters forces control the state convention and their college and seminary. Thus the Riley empire has fallen into several parts, but a great work still goes on through the many graduates of the schools, who have circled the globe with churches, mission stations, and teaching posts.

Both Robert G. Lee and Bob Jones, Sr., focused on the heart of the Riley ministry: Lee wrote that "no greater and more heroic friend did the Bible and Christ's Church and Christian education ever have"[54]; Jones wired that "I have never known a greater or more courageous man."[55] Charles E. Fuller said his passing "was a tremendous loss to the cause of Christ."[56] R. S. Beal, long-time pastor

[51]Ibid.
[52]Ibid.
[53]Ibid.
[54]Ibid.
[55]Ibid.
[56]Ibid.

of the First Baptist Church in Tucson, said he "was a great man of God."[57]

J. FRANK NORRIS (1877-1952)

Few men who knew J. Frank Norris of Fort Worth, Texas, would even attempt to describe in any detail this many-sided, powerful, eccentric, pulpiteering Fundamentalist. One associate saw him as the "most colorful and dramatic personality in the entire Fundamentalist-Modernist controversy, a controversy he himself helped create."[58] As a central figure in the fierce battle, he created a legend in his own lifetime, for he "had an unique ability to assemble and hold a vast crowd of followers through the span of a lifetime."[59] To him preaching came first, and he strove to be a preacher's preacher; and to hundreds of young men in the ministry then and since he was exactly that. Tatum saw him as "a gladiator in a conflict, a spiritual war whose life could know no moderation or compromise, except conquest or failure."[60] Three others have analyzed this phenomenal man, and their works can be used with profit. One revealing work by his close associate, Louis Entzminger, issued in paperback in 1947, is entitled *The J. Frank Norris I Have Known for 34 Years.* A thesis on Norris was written by Henry S. Terre-Blanche at Dallas Seminary in 1965. Norris' successor, Homer Ritchie, wrote an M.A. thesis on him and his church at Texas Christian University in 1966.

Norris was born in 1877 in Alabama of a quite ordinary father but a very godly and inspiring mother. At an early age he moved with the family to Hubbard, Texas. While living there he was converted under "Cat" Smith, and the prayers and example of his mother, Mary Davis Norris, were paramount. He went to Baylor University, where he took a B.A. in 1903, and then received the Th.M. from Southern Baptist Seminary in Louisville, Kentucky, the best-known among all Southern Baptist schools. During these days he came under the great impact of such men as B. H. Carroll, J. A. Broadus, and J. R. Sampey. For three years he pastored the McKinney Avenue Baptist Church of Dallas, which grew from less than one hundred members to over one thousand in attendance. For two years he edited the Baptist paper for Texas, *The Baptist Standard.* As editor, he engaged in his first public fight, and that was over the issue of racetrack gambling at the State Fair in Dallas. With another Dallas pastor he was able to get the matter before the Texas legislature, which showed its appreciation of his fight by outlawing the

[57]Ibid.
[58]Ray Tatum, *J. Frank Norris, Conquest or Failure?* (Dallas: Baptist Foundation, 1966), p. 5.
[59]Ibid., p. 6.
[60]Ibid., p. 7.

gambling. While editor of the paper he cooperated with B. H. Carroll, pastor at Waco and professor at Baylor, in getting a seminary started in Fort Worth, a seminary that has become the largest Protestant seminary in the world—Southwestern Baptist Theological Seminary with some two thousand students.

In 1909 he accepted the call to First Baptist in Fort Worth, Texas, known widely as the Church of the Cattle Kings. It did have in its membership many of the leading citizens and businessmen of the city. It had had a respectable but unspectacular history as a typical First Church. One man with more than usual admiration for Norris in First Baptist at that time was J. T. Pemberton, who became an ardent supporter of Norris but had voted against his coming as pastor. Later he told Norris that it was his conviction that if Norris came, there would be the "all-firedest" explosion any church ever had—and such there was. Pemberton saw First Baptist at peace with the world, the flesh, the devil, and the city, and that Norris with a broad ax would forever end that. And that he did. For the first two years of his pastorate (1909-1911) all went normally with Norris; he was physically well cared for and content. But there was a growing restlessness within. In 1911 he went to Owensboro, Kentucky, to hold a meeting for Carroll's son, feeling depressed and disgusted with himself and his ministry. His meeting in Owensboro was remarkably blessed with souls saved and revival fires lighted among the church members. When he returned to Fort Worth he took an entirely different course in his ministry. This new direction has stamped its particular image on Fundamentalism in the South and in many churches outside the South, especially those of the Baptist Bible Fellowship. His new type of ministry had many unusual and commendable features, and these are most difficult for a historian to factually assess. Great patience and accurate insight are needed in enumerating and explaining these. One was his passion for great pulpit performances, always directed toward the major goal of winning the lost to a saving knowledge of the Lord Jesus Christ. Therefore, he aimed at making his church not a place of ease for respectable church members but a great soulwinning station in the heart of the city with the members working with him for the souls of men. He went beyond his own church building with his message, with campaigns in several parts of the city, and thousands responded. His enemies thundered against him, but none ever questioned his power as a preacher and soulwinner. He spoke against people in prominent places and especially against his own members who were involved in drinking parties. Thus, he turned to sensational preaching and in the process became a sensation himself. Having gained this eminence he refused to depart from it, which meant more sensational issues, more powerful preaching, and more efforts in soulwinning. Of these efforts he made Fort

Worth the center, and that city has not been the same since his hectic and action-filled ministry. As a controversialist he became the number one topic of conversation, and this swelled his congregations in the days before radios and television sets. Powerful public speaking was a crowd-gatherer in any community, and on this Norris capitalized. Truly he was the stormy petrel in his city. His deacons were most upset and met to dismiss him, thinking this would end the problem. But Norris was no regular Baptist preacher —in turn he dismissed them and in old First Baptist of Fort Worth there was an "all-firing time." Perhaps this was the beginning of "Cowtown Christianity"—one molded and stamped by the tactics and passions of Norris. Now he was the voice of First Baptist; for the membership voted with him, and boards, committees, and organizations among ladies and young people ceased. First Baptist became a cathedral of preaching, and all else was shelved in order to support such a ministry. First Baptist was a Norris preaching post and little else.

He developed a preaching style that has never been successfully imitated or analyzed; it defies attempts at either. In fact, no scholarly attempt has yet been made to analyze it or compare it with others' of pulpit fame. To preachers it was a thing of envy and delight. Hundreds of men still preaching came under its spell, and for the rest of their lives their grand goal will be to preach. He had more than pulpit charisma; he had the keenest sense of the thinking and the expectations of his audience. He was able to command attention and to lead great crowds into enthusiastic acceptance of the truths he believed and preached. His voice was not beautiful, as was George W. Truett's, but it was far more heart-rending and convincing. People enjoyed Truett, but they were spiritually upset and inspired by Norris. His courage in exposing sin was transparently clear to all and his fearlessness always appealed to the common people. His ability to make a service a command performance producing spiritual conviction, decisions, and church-wide applause and amens from all corners made him a preachers' preacher without a single parallel. Men of the stature of Shields, Riley, and Pettingill thrilled at his superb mastery of an audience, of which he himself was most conscious. His was an egotism born in the excitement of Bible preaching. Is there a sure way to examine a virtue such as this? Today, thousands would love to hear him just once again, realizing that there will never be another like him. When the multitudes began to beat a path to the door of First Baptist, they came to hear a phenomenal Gospel exhorter. In his own mighty Texas style he made the strongest weep, and his hearers were moved to follow him devotedly or to oppose him vehemently for fear of what he might do to them and their organizations. In the earlier days he did not show those unusual eccentricities and love for hard-boiled personal disputes which marred his later life. W. L. Pettingill summed up Norris correctly when he characterized him as:

the stormy petrel of the turbulent theological sea in the South, and perhaps at once the most cordially hated and loved man below the Mason-Dixon line. Every Modernist hates Norris and every Conservative who really knows him loves him.[61]

To tell all the ups and downs of this Texas Tornado would be, in itself, a mountainous task. We can give only a brief resumé. His church burned on January 11, 1912, and he was charged with arson; and this was the beginning of a long list of public and legal disputes. This could have broken him, for few men can stand the blazing light of public ridicule and attacks. But Norris was something like John Knox, who suffered terribly for eighteen months as a galley slave under the French, conditions under which most men were broken for life. It steeled Knox, as did other adversities. Also, in 1912 Norris' parsonage burned, and rumors spread that the fire was set. Norris moved his congregation to the old Byers Theater in Fort Worth and went to work. In 1913 he called Louis Entzminger from Kentucky to come and build the world's largest Sunday School. This the two men did together, and their friendship continued until death parted them. The Sunday School started with 250 in 1913 but by 1917 it was up to 1,500 and by 1920 it was nearly 3,000. It peaked at 5,000 in 1926. Great crowds came to First Baptist in those days, as seen in a figure released by the church for Sunday, September 13, 1919, when 12,000 attended the Sunday School and two services of the day. Entzminger often remarked that when he came to Fort Worth, razor blades were flying a thousand feet high around Norris. The two men had a few set opinions on Sunday School building, and one was that no literature would be used but the King James Version of the Bible. After thirty-four years with Norris, Entzminger would summarize his work with him as

strenuous, sometimes tragic, sometimes dark, not a star in the sky, sometimes on transfiguration heights, sometimes in the nadir of despair, sometimes and oftentimes in the most glorious soulwinning campaigns I have ever witnessed, and going to this hour and more glorious than ever.[62]

Norris was tried in court more than once. In 1912 he faced the charges of arson but was declared innocent, and a great Baptist statesman of the hour, J. B. Gambrell of the *Baptist Standard,* called the charge "the most colossal frameup of wickedness."[63] It was

[61]W. L. Pettingill, *Serving and Waiting* (Philadelphia Bible College), July, 1923, p. 116.
[62]Louis Entzminger, *The J. Frank Norris I Have Known for 34 Years* (Fort Worth: First Baptist Church, 1947), p. 27.
[63]Ibid., p. 140.

quite well-known that twenty thousand dollars had been raised to get Norris out of Fort Worth, but many of the ringleaders in the plot were converted and later confessed their sin. A great man among liquor interests in the city, Bill Blevins, of the Retail Liquor Association, was challenged by Norris to come and hear him preach, and as a result he was saved.

In 1917, Norris began a paper called *The Fence Rail*, which in 1921 became *The Searchlight* and again changed its name in 1927 to *The Fundamentalist*. Riley would hardly appreciate this name for the paper since his own was called *The Christian Fundamentals*. In pulpit and in his paper Norris would continue his exposé of sin in any and all phases of life, but the big battle began when he started to expose false teaching in his own alma mater, Baylor University. In the March 2, 1917 issue of the *Fence Rail* he devoted four pages to the second coming and announced a Bible conference with Dixon, Riley, W. B. Hinson, A. C. Gaebelein, and R. A. Torrey. By April of that year the Sunday School recorded 1,820, and 40 additions were reported for one Sunday. In an October issue two pages were devoted to praise of Bob Shuler, "fighting Bob," of Trinity Methodist in Los Angeles. In December Norris held a two-week meeting in Moody Church in Chicago. The first attack on Baylor came in 1919 when denominational officials became alarmed when Norris refused to use the regular Sunday School literature and would not cooperate in the Seventy-Five Million Dollar Campaign, put on by Baptists in the South, as a way to support their schools and mission projects. At the same time he accused Baylor professors of teaching evolution. On these two items Southern Baptist pastors and officials now became infuriated, for their own beloved school was attacked and their own financial setup was endangered. On these issues, Norris held it was the sole and sovereign right of First Baptist of Fort Worth to decide without influence or attack from without. Leading the fight against Norris were George W. Truett of Dallas, Lee R. Scarborough of Southwestern Baptist Seminary, and President S. P. Brooks of Baylor University. Rather than turning full attention to the specifics of Norris' charges and criticisms, they turned on the man himself with full intention to ruin him and, if possible, to drive him from his church. Southern Baptists have produced many fine preachers and people, but by the early 1920's their executives had set up a cooperative way to support their interests, and no criticism of a serious nature would be tolerated. Non-support of programs has become more important than sound doctrine. Norris held firmly, without backing up a single inch, that his church had the right to use solely the Bible and to give or not to give to denominational programs as it decided. For the 1919 campaign he was asked for $100,000, and this he refused, although some $20,000 was given by

First Baptist. It was the first serious threat Southern Baptists had ever faced, and single-handedly Norris faced the entire denominational structure and, on conviction, would not bow. Later, in 1925, the Cooperative Program was established to further cement the project of 1919, but by then Norris had been sluiced out of the Texas Baptist circles. Baptist leaders questioned the right of Norris and First Baptist to call themselves Southern Baptists and not work with other pastors and Baptist officials. The Rubicon was crossed and J. Frank Norris would not cross with the leaders. He would pursue his type of evangelism, run his church as he wanted to, and give to what he chose, and that procedure must remain his own business. Southern Baptists would not allow him so to do and stay within. Here he forged one strong link of the Fundamentalist chain, namely, that the local pastor and church should be completely and sovereignly self-determining and autonomous in every item and that its link to outside organizations is its sole right and privilege to determine. Fundamentalists have followed Norris on this and held to it as a sacred New Testament right. The denominations, North and South, could not allow this much freedom, and in this respect Baptist Convention churches have surrendered part of their Baptist liberty and heritage. Norris was most outspoken on this issue and cried aloud in pulpit and paper that "this ecclesiastical machine wants money, money, money."[64] By September, 1921, the *Searchlight* reported that the membership of First Baptist stood at 5,100 and that in September the Sunday School had 5,263 present —an all-time record for any church in history. In 1922, Norris was expelled from the Tarrant County Baptist Association, and L. R. Scarborough led the attack with a vicious smear tract called "The Fruits of Norrisism", the heart of which was that Norris was not cooperating with other Baptist brethren and that he was disagreeing with men and naming them. This writer has a copy of this vitriolic tract by Scarborough in which J. Frank is accused of lying about Baptist officials and of starting "a New Cult," and his ways are likened to Bolshevism. In the tract Norris is accused of creating a storm center of a ceaseless and vicious attack upon the boards, with officers and prominent men under fire. This was Baptist balderdash unless the tract had printed the lies and proved them to be such. None of this was ever done. Another outcome of the explosive situation was the radio hatefest in Fort Worth, in which Scarborough and J. L. Ward of Decatur Baptist College broadcast their attacks on Norris, with Ward claiming that he "would look over the parapets of heaven and see Frank Norris frying in the pits of hell."[65] Epithets used against Norris on the radio were "liar,"

[64]J. F. Norris, *The Searchlight,* Sept. 29, 1922.
[65]Entzminger, p. 164.

"diabolical," "thief," "devilish," "dastardly," "corrupt"," perjurer," and "reprobate." If Norris were guilty of only some of these, he still must be regarded as a novel Baptist preacher, to say the least. But out of these bloodletting battles came at least two good results, one of which was that both the State Baptist Convention of Texas and the Southern Baptist Convention passed anti-evolution resolutions, and the other that at least eight faculty members of Baylor were dismissed. Of course, Norris got no credit for any of this. One New York paper, *The World's Work,* published an article in 1923 on the Fundamentalist war in the churches which said of Norris that though he was "the strongest, shrewdest, most romantically adventuresome prince of crowd gatherers, paragon of advertisers... he is limited by his belief in the personal, imminent, bodily, visible return of the Lord."[66]

Through all of this, the *Searchlight* carried the great struggles within Baptist circles, and its circulation reportedly went up to 70,000, a phenomenal thing in those days. But at the 1922 meeting of the Texas Baptist Convention, officials had firm control, and Baylor was commended and Norris was censored. In the October issue of the *Searchlight,* a call was issued for a Baptist Union, which was later answered by the formation of the Baptist Bible Union in 1923. In this controversy Truett took a commanding part and even helped to encourage the vote against Norris by preaching on "The Enemies of Baylor." Now an all-out fight took place between Norris and the teachers of evolution, supported by the denominational leaders. Many pastors sympathized with Norris but did not join him, for they were wary and hoped for a housecleaning and better conditions in Baptist schools. Hundreds still have this hope, although the course ever since the Norris era has been one of defection, doctrinal disease, and spiritual declension. In 1923 the Texas Convention refused to seat a lone delegate from Norris' church, and the following year it officially expelled him and his church. The Convention was broad enough to allow postmillennialists but not a Fundamentalist who insisted on the full right of his church to choose whether or not to cooperate. Here the Southern Baptist Convention made a turn in the road; and in 1925 it adopted the Cooperative Program, which has been a rallying point ever since. Since then, few exposés by Norris and others have been taken seriously, because the denomination is building a "kingdom." No official action was ever taken against Norris by the Southern Baptist Convention itself. State action was enough. On one occasion Norris told Entzminger privately that three things had made him a preacher: (1) the fight of the devil against him, (2) his courage in defying the Texas Baptist machine, and (3) God's grace in preserving him physically and spiritually. In

[66]Ibid., p. 244.

spite of the denominational battles, First Baptist was prospering with hundreds saved, but it was common knowledge that the converts were not coming from the aristocratic segments of the city's people but from the common people and "the down-and-outers."

His fame as a preacher reached many preachers and churches, and we should mention representative cases. He held a campaign in First Baptist of San Antonio in 1923 with over six hundred professions. The pastor there, I. E. Gates, said after hearing Norris, "I know the fight between Fundamentalism and Modernism and I and the church are lining up with Fundamentalists." This shows the great power of Norris, although the First Church of San Antonio has never been a Fundamentalist church. A month-long meeting was held in First Baptist of Houston with a thousand conversions reported. That such a turbulent figure could be so greatly used was a knotty problem indeed to his enemies.

Was Norris prepared to erect a Fundamentalist organization at this time? The best observation was that he was willing to support fully the Baptist Bible Union, which had started in 1923, and to foster his non-cooperation with Southern Baptist works and to expose them that others might be warned. Few in the 1920's left their own groups to start independent structures; rather they pursued a non-cooperating route which led them in time to out-and-out independency. Norris continued his expose of Southern Baptists until the end of his life just as if he were still a Southern Baptist and exercising his right to criticize from within. In the 1940's he carried on a continuous vendetta against Louie D. Newton, president of the Convention in the late forties and pastor of Druid Hills Baptist Church in Atlanta, Georgia. Norris would publish a tract with the picture of Newton on the front and title him the Modern Jehoshaphat and throw together many disjointed statements charging him with gullibility in visiting Russia and giving a somewhat favorable picture of that country. He held that Newton was saying nice things about Stalin (whose name Norris always insisted on pronouncing as if it were stay-lynn) and suggesting that Russians and Baptists had many things in common. Often Norris would rent halls near the sites of the annual meetings of the Convention and there utter his tirades against liberal leaders, literature, and professors. In the late 1940's he believed there were sympathizers with communism on some faculties of Baptist colleges. At the most, the Norris blasts slowed down the Southern Baptist capitulation to out-and-out Liberalism. Since his passing in 1952, the pace of surrender to liberal thought has accelerated. No other voice had the delaying power of that of J. Frank Norris of Fort Worth.

During the years that followed his ouster from the Tarrant County Association, Norris conducted annual Bible Conferences in his own church, inviting such great speakers as Shields, Torrey, Massee, and Riley; these provided a rich menu in spiritual things for great crowds and Bible-hungry preachers, many of whom had no formal training. Such meetings were really big affairs with the church members providing free rooms and board for visiting preachers. But no permanent organization arose out of these, for Norris continued throughout the twenties to support the Baptist Bible Union and the World's Christian Fundamentals Association. After the collapse of the BBU in 1932 he attended to his own affairs and roped together dissenting preachers and churches into the World Baptist Fellowship. The first name ever attached to the Norris group was "The New Testament World Fundamental Baptist Missionary Fellowship."[67] Some might wonder why it should have the word "World" attached to it when it was quite small. The First Baptist Church of Fort Worth, in the vocabulary of J. Frank Norris, was the greatest church in the world, and he fully expected that soon a worldwide fellowship of great churches would join him in a common front. This never materialized, but Norris was not averse to big dreams. Meanwhile, all the time hundreds more were hearing him and coming under the magnetism of his pulpit power. Tremendous meetings were held in Jarvis Street Baptist in Toronto for Shields and in Calvary Baptist in New York for Straton.

On March 19, 1926, he held a meeting in the First Baptist Church of Lexington, Kentucky, where George Ragland was pastor. The church paper, *The Sling and the Stone,* devoted its entire issue of March 11, 1926, to Norris with the note that First Baptist in Fort Worth then had 8,400 members and that Norris was regarded as "one of the greatest preachers in America." Norris now claimed some 8,000 in Sunday School with the Whole English Bible course being taught as published by Union Gospel Press. In February of 1926 a radio station opened at the church (FFQB). In the same month the *Searchlight* published the funeral sermon preached by Riley for Charles A. Blanchard, a truly Fundamentalist president of Wheaton College, Wheaton, Illinois. In April circulation was claimed to be 55,000, and the May issue answered E. Y. Mullins and L. R. Scarborough on the extent of liberal influence among Southern Baptists. The July 16 issue of the paper reported fifteen thousand total in all three Sunday services with seventy-one additions. It published a message Norris had given to the First Baptist Church in Houston in which he referred to his experiences in the pastorate at Fort Worth. Norris said that after two years he was "the most knocked-down, run-over, chewed-up, 'fried-and-fricasseed' preacher in the world"; for he was preaching in a city of 100,000 and no one

---

[67]Letter from Norris to C. O. Johnson dated April 21, 1947.

was paying any attention to him. Norris told his congregation that it would not be long before every man, woman, and child would know where the church was and that when he exposed the conditions of vice in the city, business would pick up and the old church would no longer be a corpse.

In the late twenties another Norris novelty was unwrapped. The pastor led his church in a very extended house-to-house visitation, a technique copied by friend and foe ever since. It is now a common practice throughout the South and in the North, particularly with Fundamentalists; but Norris has not received credit for it, though he rightly deserves it. No money was raised for the church through suppers, sales, and lotteries. There were no pledges ever taken at First Church in Fort Worth—everything depended on the pastor's power to raise the funds needed. The new church burned in 1929 at a loss of $300,000, and the congregation greatly decreased. Norris took to building a new congregation, but also turned against Gothic architecture as definitely anti-New Testament. He once wrote that "instead of the cloud-reaching spires and churches patterned after cathedrals, we believe that the church building should be a modern lighthouse, a workshop for the Lord, practical and simple."[68] From now on efficiency, practicality, and simplicity of church buildings must be prominent. Anyone who has seen the old building at Fourth and Throckmorton in Fort Worth in the last twenty years of Norris' ministry will attest to the very simple appearance of the building, with no spires and no stained-glass windows. It was simply an overgrown preaching hall with rooms just as simply built for Sunday School classes. One large room in that Sunday School building was the John Birch Hall. It was named after John Birch, a young man, born of missionary parents, who left Mercer University in Macon, Georgia, to attend Norris' school in Fort Worth; later he lost his life at the hands of the communists. This building has now been sold for a parking garage in downtown Fort Worth and a beautiful new two-million-dollar edifice erected some five blocks away. It is a small replica of the great preaching station that was First Baptist from 1909 to 1952.

In 1923 Norris assisted Shields and Riley in the formation of the Baptist Bible Union. This Union did rally Fundamentalist forces in the North for seven years, but it never received much support in the South, for Modernism in its most blatant form came into the Southern Baptist ranks much later. In the 1920's, Southern schools of all major denominations were still conservative, although evolutionary ideas were creeping in. But Norris did play a major role in rallies held throughout the North and South, and his machine-like

[68]Entzminger, p. 61.

oratory was a welcome change, although it was never of the suspense-creating type of William Jennings Bryan.

In 1926 tragedy struck Norris and left a mark on his reputation that remained all his life. Norris had had a running battle with Mayor H. C. Meacham of Fort Worth over the purchase of land from the Catholic Church. In addition, he had exposed bootlegging in the county and attributed part of the increase of this evil to the Catholic Church. The Roman Church sold some property to the city for $152,000, although the Real Estate Board had assessed it for $60,000; and Norris held Meacham largely responsible. These charges were carried in the *Searchlight* and distributed in Meacham's Department Store. As a result, six members of First Baptist were fired from the store. As an outcome of the tense situation, D. E. Chipps, a wealthy lumberman, called Norris at the church on Saturday afternoon, July 17, 1926, and threatened him. Chipps came to the pastor's study and threatened him again. Believing Chipps was about to shoot him, Norris fired first and killed him. Norris was made out to be a gun-totin', hateful man, gunning down a poor innocent man. One main fact stood out, and that was that Norris thought his life was in mortal danger and defended himself. He was, of course, charged with murder, but his church people took up an offering in a galvanized washtub and collected over $16,000 for his defense. That the tragedy gave him and Fundamentalism a black eye is obvious; that he was a killer was not proved by the facts. The jury found him innocent on its first vote, basing their decision on the Texas law of self-defense. One interesting fact in this was that Shields stood beside him and offered to help, while other Fundamentalists avoided him and shied away from his circle of influence. In this circumstance we see a rift between Norris and the main body of Fundamentalists, for Shields deserted the premillennial position and Norris continued as a lonely Fundamentalist. Thereafter, his ministry in the North was limited, while it increased in the great Southland.

There was one exception to this limitation, and that was the city of Detroit, Michigan. Beginning in 1934, Norris held two meetings in Detroit, one in a tent on a lot provided by a Christian layman and a second one in a cinder-block tabernacle on a large lot, owned by General Motors, at the corner of Cass and Amsterdam. Hundreds were saved in the meetings and joined Temple Baptist Church, a member of the Northern Baptist Convention, which had had some evangelical preaching under Albert Johnson. Soon the pressure was on for Norris to become pastor of Temple, which responsibility he assumed along with his pastorate in Fort Worth, although the churches were 1,300 miles apart. This arrangement continued for thirteen years; when Temple Baptist in Detroit left the Northern

Baptist Convention in 1935, Norris was now pastor of two large independent Baptist churches. The reports given about these two churches are simply staggering; for in the period from 1934 to 1947, during which time Norris pastored both of them, there were twenty-four thousand additions, over three million dollars raised for all purposes, and eighteen million copies of *The Fundamentalist* published. Their property was estimated to be worth over three million dollars. In the same period there were some 1,800 students enrolled at the Bible Baptist Seminary, though the peak enrollment was 305 in one year. The churches boasted of having the two largest Sunday Schools in the world. In 1946 Norris claimed that the two churches had a combined membership of 25,000. At Detroit, Norris had the help of G. Beauchamp Vick, whom he named superintendent in 1936 and who succeeded him as pastor of Temple Baptist, where he is still laboring. Vick helped to form a new group in 1950, the Baptist Bible Fellowship, and has been one of its leaders since its inception, also serving as president of the Fellowship school, Baptist Bible College, in Springfield, Missouri.

In 1950 festering resentment within the World Baptist Fellowship broke into the open, the story of the struggle only recently having been set forth by Billy Vick Bartlett in his *A History of Baptist Separatism*. As a result, over a hundred pastors left Norris and organized a new Fellowship. Much of the trouble stemmed from the operation of the Bible Baptist Seminary, which Norris had organized in 1939 in his Fort Worth church. Over part of the building used for classes was a sign "The Only Seminary in the World Teaching the Whole English Bible." It was not a seminary in the traditional sense of the word, for it did not require college work as prerequisite nor did it have the standard courses in languages, theology, and church history. Rather it was of the Bible institute type, specializing in the preaching of the English Bible and the practice of visitation and building Sunday Schools, a rare combination then but used most effectively since. This writer has a copy of the 1945-1946 catalog, and most courses were in English Bible, with a few in music and Sunday School work. The seminary granted the B.D. degree without the college prerequisite. There was no tuition. In 1945 there were 224 enrolled. By 1950 a growing number of men in the World Baptist Fellowship wanted more authority in the management of the Seminary, since they were being asked to support it. Vick had been named president of the Seminary in 1948, but he resigned in 1950; and a battle royal broke out in the May meeting in 1950, with Norris claiming there was a conspiracy against him and Entzminger. Standing against Norris were John Rawlings, Vick, Wendell Zimmerman, and W. E. Dowell. The outcome was a split in which these men and others, a total of 119, left and organized the Baptist Bible Fellowship; in September of 1950 when they organized their own school, Baptist Bible College, in Springfield, Missouri, Norris had some forty pastors still with him. The rest of the story will be told when we consider the BBF in the third period of the history of Fundamentalism. Among those staying with Norris were Earl K. Oldham, president of the old school, now located in Arlington, Texas, and Gerald Fleming, now pastor of Dayton Baptist Temple, Dayton, Ohio. Norris' own son, George L., had left his father five years earlier and organized the Gideon Baptist in Fort Worth, where he was pastor until 1972. After the death of his father, he joined the World Baptist group and for many years taught at their school in Arlington, Texas. There is one sidelight which bears mention in this connection. Norris' city, Fort Worth, has over forty independent Baptist churches with some in the Fellowship and some in the World Baptist group. This makes Fort Worth one of the foremost independent-Baptist cities in the world in the number of churches. The Baptist Bible Fellowship now lists some 2,006 churches fellowshiping with it, and the World Baptist lists about 550. This makes a total of 2,500 churches that directly or indirectly owe their origin or inspiration to J. Frank Norris. Few men in history could claim such an influence. We ought to add to this the untold number of pastors and people who heard him and were determined to preach the Bible, although they would not join his movement or openly align themselves with him. Perhaps we should let his closest associate, Entzminger, summarize this unusually gifted man:

> He was a man who had been hounded by the bloodhounds of hell . . . maligned and slandered by good men . . . . great denominational leaders sought to destroy his life's work . . . . the lowest dives and gangsters of the underworld have been used to malign his character and wreck his ministry.[69]

The dean of his seminary, B. F. Dearmore, once told the writer and his class of students that Norris was the greatest preacher since the Apostle Paul. He must be listed as one of the most scintillating, unpredictable, gifted, charismatic pulpiteers of the western world. We must remember him as the fiery, flamboyant Fundamentalist and eccentric preacher, loved and hated by friend and foe. However, he was one who so exalted preaching that thousands have preached and will continue to preach because of him. Bob Jones, Sr., once wrote that the Lord had raised up Norris as a whip but he wished he would whip the denominational leaders and not the independents so much. In this whipping, he shook leaders, churches, machines, programs and multitudes, who believed that few men have ever preached with such power. He died on August 20, 1952.

[69]Ibid., p. 12.

JOHN ROACH STRATON (1874-1929)

For eleven years (1918-1929) this sensational and extrovert pastor of Calvary Baptist in New York City held a commanding place among Fundamentalists along the East Coast. He was born in Evansville, Indiana, in 1875 in a Baptist preacher's home and attended Mercer University in Macon, Georgia, and Southern Baptist Seminary.[70] He taught briefly at Mercer and at Baylor University in Waco, Texas, and was pastor of Second Baptist in Chicago (1905-1908), Immanuel Baptist in Baltimore (1908-1913), and the First Baptist Church of Norfolk, Virginia (1913-1917). In 1918 he was called to the heart of New York to the eminence of a metropolitan pulpit. Calvary Baptist had been founded in 1847 as the Hope Chapel Baptist Church, incorporated with fourteen people. Its early pastors had been David Bellamy (1847-1850), John Dowling (1850-1852), A. D. Gillette (1852-1863) (during whose time it was renamed Calvary), and R. J. W. Buckland (1864-1869). In 1870 began the longest pastorate of all, that of Robert Stuart MacArthur, who filled this pulpit for forty-one years, resigning in 1911. He was followed by Joseph W. Kemp. Straton was forty-four, in the prime of health and a noble preacher among preachers, when he took the exalted place at Calvary. He was robust in body, spirit, and preaching gifts. But eleven years later he was broken in all three, and died of a stroke in 1929.

Straton saw himself as a modern-day prophet, one called of the Lord to denounce sin and sins while he preached faithfully all the counsel of God. He believed he ought to call a nation to repentance because of its excessive disobedience to God. Many thousands heard his messages, for he lived and preached in the great metropolis in the Roaring Twenties. Straton was a match for all the turbulence of the times and saw many accept his message of salvation. But the Northern Baptist Convention, in which he was a constant aggravation, and his city and nation did not heed his appeals and rushed even more quickly toward greater apostasy and sinfulness. Liberal thought eroded the institutions in which he had believed, and the pleasure craze demoralized the millions swirling around him. Straton was wise in the Word of God, gifted in the use of words with which to clothe his deep-seated convictions, and knowledgeable in the ways of the world, if not always careful in his methods of attack and defense.

He organized a Fundamentalist League of New York, but none of its records and few references to it remain. He published a paper which had various titles, *The Faith-Fundamentalist, The Religious*

[70]To date no biography of this sensational pastor has been written. Our sketch of his ministry must come from sermons, papers, and articles about him.

Searchlight, and *The American Fundamentalist,* and finally *The Calvary Call.*[71] To many he is best known not for the works of his pen but for his dream of demolishing the old church building at 123 West 57th Street in Manhattan and erecting the Salisbury Hotel, a part being used for church purposes and the rest hopefully a profit-making venture in New York's hotel business, providing extra funds for church purposes. But the crash of 1929 dumped into the lap of the church a debt of two millions, and this left to Straton's successors at Calvary a mountain of indebtedness to face. Special efforts to whittle this down were made by two men who followed, namely, Will H. Houghton and William Ward Ayer. But the church still labors under a large debt. H. H. Straton, son of John Roach, kindly sent the author a picture of the old church building, a beautiful one indeed, and with it a newspaper clipping stating that the last services were held in the old building on May 19, 1929. A well-known evangelist, W. E. Biederwolf, was the preacher of the day with a message entitled "Bootleggers, Corkscrews, and Crooks."

Straton had a debate on the theater with William A. Brady, an actor of the 1920's, who debated him on February 12, 1922. It was reported on the front page of the *New York Times* of February 13 that a fighting Irishman called upon the clergymen to preach God and Christ to the actors and actresses rather than slandering them. Straton's ire had been aroused by a play called *The Aphrodite,* which he blistered from the pulpit as a new low in immorality. He was asked for his views and these were published in the February 1920 issue of *Theater,* in which he quoted Rabbi Stephen Wise that "as a business the theater is the dirtiest in America today." Straton deplored the amount of nakedness being exploited in "this degrading bondage to Mammon." He said that the theaters should be boycotted because of the degradation of womanhood. Brady challenged Straton to a debate upon the subject, "Resolved, that present conditions and tendencies on the American stage are a menace to a sound public and private morality." Straton took the affirmative and stated that the evil conditions were evidenced in the attacks on the virtue of womanhood, honor of manhood, sanctity of the marriage vow, virility of the church, integrity of the Sabbath, and the proper rearing of children. He claimed that the theater was ruining Sunday School attendance. Brady denied many of the charges, but called on Straton to preach to them and not to condemn them. Straton wrote later that he was willing to come to Brady's theater, The Playhouse, and preach to the actors, but this never took place. He again debated the issue in 1926 (Nov. 2) in the Brooklyn

[71] I am indebted to his son, H. H. Straton, pastor of First Baptist in Malden, Mass., for a bibliography of 77 entries, sermons, articles, open letters, and books published by his father.

Academy of Music against S. M. Tucker of the Polytechnical Institute of Brooklyn. He referred to Brady, who had admitted by now that he was running a "dirty playhouse."

The controversies of Straton were many. One was a famous debate with a unitarian, Charles F. Potter, in 1924, with the opposing discussions published.[72] The publication of these showed again that there was a battle raging, with two clearly defined sides at war, and that the public was vitally concerned. Four items were debated, namely: Is the Bible the Infallible Word of God?, Did the Earth Come by Evolution?, Is the Virgin Birth Fact or Fiction?, and Was Christ both God and Man? Straton traveled far in many directions to find arguments, aside from copious Biblical references. He used the names of Warren G. Harding and Woodrow Wilson, who "declared themselves as being in sympathy with the Fundamentalists and as opposed to the Modernists in the present religious situation."[73] Straton added that Woodrow Wilson had said that had his father been alive he would have been a Fundamentalist.

Another foe of Straton was the famous Harry Emerson Fosdick, who had come from an evangelical home in western New York State but under the teaching of William Newton Clarke of Hamilton Institute (now Colgate) and the faculty of Union Seminary, had become an open and persuasive Liberal. He supplied the pulpit of First Presbyterian Church of New York in the early twenties and in 1925 took the pastorate of Park Avenue Baptist in Manhattan. From 1930 to 1942 Fosdick served the newly erected Riverside Church on Morningside Heights. The beautiful Gothic structure of Riverside was in large part the gift of John D. Rockefeller. A proverbial story about Fosdick and John D. is that at breakfast one time, Fosdick wondered openly if people would mind the financing of John D., and the latter said that if they could stand Fosdick's theology, surely they could stand John D.'s money. In 1922 Fosdick preached his church-shattering sermon entitled "Shall the Fundamentalists Win?", in which he rejected the vital truths of Fundamentalism and predicted that the latter would not be able to drive non-Fundamentalists out of the American churches. Orthodox Presbyterians were shocked that such preaching would be allowed in a Presbyterian pulpit and, led by such men as Clarence E. Macartney, instituted measures to have the Presbytery of New York prevent such anti-Presbyterian sentiments from being voiced.[74] Straton could not be silent and preached an answer dubbed "Shall

[72]*The Famous New York Fundamentalist-Modernist Debates* (New York: Doran, 1924).
[73]Ibid., p. 129.
[74]A good coverage of this is in E. H. Rian, *The Presbyterian Conflict.*

the Funny Monkeyists Win?" This continued for years as a wrangle between the two men and in 1925 Straton vented his Fundamentalist spleen by writing in his paper:

> tists stand . . . . Dr. Fosdick has made himself nothing other than a Baptist bootlegger . . . . he is also a Presbyterian outlaw . . . . he is the Jesse James of the theological world.[75]

> tists stand . . . Dr. Fosdick has made himself nothing than a Baptist bootlegger . . . he is also a Presbyterian outlaw . . . he is the Jesse James of the theological world.[75]

He was shocked in 1925 when Fosdick, still claiming to be a Baptist, stated he would not only sprinkle but would receive Quakers (upon confession of faith) without any kind of baptism. In spite of this anti-Baptist stand, some forty-one Baptist ministers of New York signed a statement in appreciation of his remarkable ministry at First Presbyterian, his attitude toward the truth of Christ, and his kindly courage. Openly, they expressed the hope he would continue in some pulpit in the city, and Cornelius Woelfkin and J. D. Rockefeller did so arrange, first at Park Avenue and later at Riverside. Straton tried to get the New York Baptist Ministers' Conference to officially condemn Fosdick's view, but that was tabled over strenuous objections, another of the steamroller policies of the Liberals in the name of charity and unity. As Straton wrote afterward, "free speech was throttled and the steamroller is put over anyone who even tries to raise a voice in defense of the old faith, which is still dear to some of our hearts."[76] He wondered whether the Baptist denomination would not be speedily destroyed if such leadership as this was to continue, charged that as a Baptist brotherhood it was driving fast upon the rocks, and asked if the time had not come when there must be a change in the crew of the Baptist ship if it were to be saved.

The Fundamentalist pastor of Calvary Baptist could not contain himself at the Northern Baptist Convention held in Atlantic City in May of 1923 when he noted in the official program that W. H. P. Faunce was to give the keynote address. Straton stood up on a chair on the floor and made his violent protest known publicly, even though he was jeered and hissed. Some thought this was the voice of the pre-convention Fundamentalist meeting, but John Marvin Dean, its spokesman at the time, made it clear that Straton did not speak for the group, for no such action had been planned. Dean also made it clear that Straton did have the right to protest as a private delegate. The Fundamentalist group had severely criticized Faunce for his denial of the virgin birth, along with such men as H. C.

The second paragraph (footnote 75) should read: "Dr. Fosdick has proved himself a lawbreaker, for he still professes to be a Baptist, and yet in his utterances and his conduct he has violated the great Fundamentals and repudiated the elemental truths for which Baptists stand . . . Dr. Fosdick has made himself nothing other than a Baptist bootlegger . . . he is also a Presbyterian outlaw . . . he is the Jesse James of the theological world.[75]"

Vedder of Crozer, George Cross of Rochester, and E. D. Burton of Chicago. It was even suggested that they should leave and join the Unitarians. Of course they did not; why should they when they were liberalizing the Baptist circles to suit their known Modernism?

The Calvary Church Bulletin of July, 1924, rightly commended the pastor as a Fundamentalist, the "Man Who Fights Broadway," adding "a crusader, a two-fisted hard-hitting man of God, always the defendant at the bulwarks of Christianity, he fights with both hands with unmitigated fervor."[77] It noted that "his bitterness against licentious dancing led him on a tour of New York's cabarets which resulted in several arrests" and named him "the most Fundamental of the Fundamentalists."[78] The paper stated that every issue needs a militant and mighty stand for the message of the Lord against all its foes.

His mightiest struggle was against Modernism in all its forms, especially the German scholars who created and promoted it. These he named—Eichhorn, De Wette, Ewald, Vatke, Reuss, Graf, Wellhausen, Pfleiderer, and Ritschl—and commonly referred to them as alien enemies. He railed against them and their whole kind as promoting Germany's false philosophy, calling her destructive criticism of the Bible "as false as hell" because its fruits are just as vile. In a sermon entitled *New York as the Modern Babylon,* he contended that we must either Americanize and Christianize New York or New York will speedily Europeanize and paganize us. In another public utterance on *Religious Democracy* he said there was another battle to win after World War I had ended and that was the defeat of Germany in the realm of the mind and the spirit. He charged that high schools and colleges, along with the seminaries, were full of false philosophy, which had misguided Germany and had plunged the world into awful war. He saw Germany as the source of the skeptical and rationalistic tendencies which were blighting America. The prophet of God could neither blind his eyes to these things nor fail to lift up his voice against them.

He saw these forces destroying his denomination and said so. From the pulpit at 123 West 55th Street in Manhattan he thundered against allowing these tendencies to go on until the denomination died before the eyes of its members. He asked for men to challenge those forces causing the decay. He said that first of all, the Christian brotherhood should cut loose from the skeptical modern philosophy of materialism. He found proof of their deadly effects by stating that in Texas in ten years over 218,000 had been added to Baptist churches while in the Chicago Association, dominated by the University of Chicago, there had been a net loss of 1,000 members in

[77] *The Bulletin* of Calvary Baptist Church, New York, July 20, 1924.
[78] Ibid.

the same period. The lesson was clear to Straton, for he concluded
that when we do anything to discount the Bible, we are cutting from
beneath our feet the only ground on which we have to stand; we are
destroying the very breath of our lives. In a sermon entitled "Can the
Protestant Churches Come Back and All the Christian
Denominations and Sects Be Reunited?" Straton said the trouble
today is that many pulpits are occupied by animated question
marks, the ministry is uncertain, the world is indifferent, and the
church passionless. In a sermon preached October 26, 1926, Straton
went on to say:

> Have we a mere theory which we hope may prove true or have we a
> triumphant certainty? . . . now Protestant Christianity is largely
> paralyzed today because our schools and seminaries are not turning out
> preachers. A false and essentially modernistic philosophy of life and an
> unbelieving view of the Bible . . . dominate for the most part the
> theological seminaries [which] . . . instead of building up the students in
> faith wreck their faith . . . . It is the profound conviction of my soul that
> the only real solution today of the so-called problem of ministerial edu-
> cation is the establishment of schools of the prophets in connection with
> local churches.

The pleasures of the times were, to Straton, Satan's snares for
both sinner and saint. He analyzed a section of his city, an area of
one hundred city blocks from 28th Street to 48th and from Park
Avenue to Eighth and discovered that on one Sunday evening there
were 1,817 in all places of worship and over 75,000 at picture houses.
In a sermon from the Calvary pulpit he exclaimed, "we are on a joy
ride, when we ought to be at a prayer meeting," engaged in "an orgy
of extravagance," and obsessed with luxury. The main menace is
sex. He attacked questionable dances as unquestionably bad. He
described an old man on the dance floor as

> a fossilized octogenerian, self-complacent mollycoddle with ice-water
> in his veins, a dandified dude, a pleasure-cloyed Don Juan, a vitiated
> fop. Can he hold a beautiful young woman with philosophical calm,
> saintly emotions, and Sunday School maxims?[79]

He did not believe that his day was one for soft speech. Rather was
it a day of blood and moral decline. In the above sermon he also
stated that one trouble with us today is that we have all but lost the
capacity for moral indignation. Equally disgusting to Straton was
the growing movement of having dances in the churches with the
introduction of theatrical stars in an effort to attract crowds. The
fashions were bad as well, for he thundered that "when it comes to
women's dress today there is not enough to talk about" (this was in
the twenties, not the seventies!). To him "the true object of dress is
utility and beauty and not sex appeal."[80]

---

[79]Sermon "New York as Modern Babylon," n.p., n.d.
[80]Ibid.

The guns of Straton were leveled often at the seminaries and those professors who were destroying the faith of young men by their liberal attitudes and affirmations. Some, he said, were more than Liberals—they were socialists and even in some cases the stain of Bolshevism was upon them. One of those he especially singled out was the historian H. C. Vedder of Crozer, a Baptist seminary at Chester, Pennsylvania. (Recently it closed its doors and joined with Colgate Rochester, Rochester, N.Y.) To Straton, Vedder was an avowed and open champion of socialism, teaching that we are to look to Jesus Christ and Marx to redeem the world. Others were condemned because there was too much dabbling in the disputes of capitalists and labor.

> If these radical preachers would study their Bibles half as hard as they study socialism, science, and economics and if they devoted one-tenth the time to saving souls both among laborers and capitalists as they devote to dabbling in industrial disputes ... much better conditions would prevail.[81]

He had some choice words for sorry parents who would not bring their children to Sunday School. Some were so weak that they would let the children decide between the picture show and the Sunday School (those were before the talkies and so much cleaner than the movies are now) and the result was

> the cigarette smoking boy who develops into the girl-ogling, sap-headed dude who would not recognize a sound thought or a sound ethical principle if he met it in the street; and the female flapper and flirt who knows more at 16 than her grandmother knew at 60, who hasn't a speaking acquaintance with the art of sweeping a room, sewing a dress, or making a biscuit but is a past mistress with the lip-stick, the powder puff, and the bunny hug.[82]

Straton even took some major swings at Al Smith, Catholic candidate for the presidency in 1928. He held that Smith was a deadly foe of moral progress and further said he was a bluffer, a Tammany trickster, and a coward. The William Allen White investigation of Smith's record proved that the governor of New York had aided prostitution, gambling, and drunkenness, and Straton hailed this as proof of his charges. On August 5, 1928, he preached against Smith, saying he was the deadliest foe of moral progress in public life. Smith suggested they debate this at Calvary Baptist, but Straton suggested the debate be held in Madison Square Garden with 25,000 seats. Smith would not agree to this. On August 5, 1928, Straton aired the whole issue in a sermon entitled:

> The Moral and Religious Stakes in the Present Political Situation—a frank discussion of the dangers of electing as president of the United States any man who advocates the nullification of the moral law and

[81]Ibid.
[82]Ibid.

whose election would give aid and comfort to the forces of lawlessness, immorality, vice, and crime in America.[83]

Again he attacked the wet-partisan press as engaging in a plot to ruin moral forces and bring morals into national contempt. Straton continued to name names, for "we need to remember that much of the talk about not dealing in personalities and much of the sophistry which declares that the exposure of the rotten records of public men is mud slinging is mere twaddle and political claptrap of the most puerile type."[84]

In 1927 Straton tangled with S. Parkes Cadman, popular preacher and president of the Federal Council of Churches (now the National Council). Cadman had preached that there is no Hell. Straton told his hearers that he had the kindest regards for Cadman as a man, but that he was "one of those dear brethren [who] in the pride of the irrationalism and exuberance of their surface optimisms are preaching a milk and water theology . . . who have no theology at all . . . sprinkling cologne upon the putrid iniquities of a rebellious race."[85] To the Calvary pastor it was simply a case of believing Christ or Cadman as to whether the Rich Man lifted up his eyes in Hell or not. Too many were "trying to please everyone and offend none."[86] To Straton, God was "not a mollycoddle . . . and the present wave of crime and vice that is simply devastating America is the direct result of this false and flimsy teaching."[87] It is because of our loyalty to Jesus Christ and our love for lost souls that "the Fundamentalists dare to stand, even in the face of a gainsaying and critical world."[88]

His son, H. H. Straton, has written of his father as a prophet of social righteousness.[89] He bases this on Straton's attacks on economic exploitation, selfish capitalists, apathy in law-making to control the liquor traffic, poor distribution of the fruits of industry, red-light districts, the dance hall, the indecencies of the theater, and the relapse into paganism as displayed in the famous Dempsey-Carpentier prize fight. He also attacked ecclesiastical overlords and said in one sermon that "at least ninety percent of the entire effort of the modern church is devoted merely to keeping the ecclesiastical machine oiled and the wheels turning."[90] On the other side, he stood up for women's rights, separation of church and state, and justice for

[83]Published by the Religious Literature Dept., 123 West 57th Street, New York, n.d., p. 3.
[84]"New York as Modern Babylon."
[85]Published by the Religious Literature Society of Calvary Baptist Church, New York, May 15, 1927.
[86]Ibid.
[87]Ibid.
[88]Ibid.
[89]*Foundations*, 4, No. 1 (Jan., 1962).
[90]Ibid.

the Negro, even to the extent of having some Negro members at Calvary Baptist.

He died at Clifton Springs, New York, at a sanatorium on October 29, 1929, and is buried at Warwick, New York.

8

The Big Baptist Battle

Baptists in the North saw the ranks of their denomination torn by the fiercest of battles.[1] By 1900 Northern Baptists had eight societies active on both home and foreign fields. There were good reasons, as there always are, for consolidation, but in the very process of consolidating and organizing for united efforts, the Liberals saw their opportunity to capture the new consolidated organization. When this organizational dream came true on May 16-17, 1907, with the official recognition of the Northern Baptist Convention, there was no serious protest against centralized authority; when channels were open for the support of good causes, there was not the slightest ripple of protest or even a danger signal to be seen. It was interesting how the Convention directed its course toward Liberalism, for on its first official executive committee was Shailer Matthews of the notoriously modernistic divinity school of the University of Chicago, who by this time was advocating "a social religious attitude."[2] It would be a simple matter to prove that the Convention offices were held by Liberals or those tolerant of Liberalism. In this respect Conservatives were acceptable, just as long as they did not bring up theological differences when it came to appointments to executive positions. Thus, by default, the conservative position was

[1] A full account of this has been provided in detail by Norman Furniss, op. cit.
[2] R. G. Delnay, "Formation of the Northern Baptist Convention," an article in the *Central Conservative Baptist Quarterly* (Central Baptist Seminary of Minneapolis, Minn.), 7, No. 3 (1964).

compromised in the interest of harmony in the Convention. As a matter of fact, the officialdom of the Convention resembled its largest and most flagrantly liberal school, the University of Chicago. It ought to be pointed out that this university *did not go* liberal; when it was founded under William Rainey Harper through the generous donation of John D. Rockefeller in 1892 *it began* liberal and has continued on a liberal course ever since.

As early as 1906 some fears were expressed about drifts among Northern Baptists. Later W. B. Riley would charge that the Northern Baptist Convention was born in the brain of a Chicago theology professor, Shailer Matthews. It was largely framed by him and consequently was planned from the first to turn the denomination into the path of the new theology.[3] A spokesman for this sentiment was A. H. Strong, his concern being the growing number of Liberals in society posts. But, in true tolerant fashion, he was quite active in hiring Liberals for his own faculty at Rochester Theological Seminary. So a protest on his part smacked of naiveté, and his voice of dissent was a hollow one. He retired from his beloved institution in 1912, but blithely announced that his seminary would always be preserved from error. Newton Theological Institution under Alvah Hovey had made the transition with little opposition in spiritually liberal New England. Soon it would receive more Liberals from the wreck of Andover Seminary (becoming Andover-Newton in 1930), and all involved would chant the hymns of progress and unity. Newton entered a new period of growth and continued to send liberal pastors into the churches of New England and the Maritime Provinces of Canada. By 1915 it was clear that Crozer had gone into liberal hands and that there was no hope for any major reversal. The same was true of Colgate, and in 1928 it was joined with Rochester to form the basis of the present Colgate-Rochester-Crozer Seminary at Rochester, New York.

There was one dissenting voice in the early days, that of Oliver W. Van Osdel, who became pastor of Wealthy Street Baptist Church in Grand Rapids, Michigan, in 1909. In the same year he persuaded his church to leave the Northern Baptist Convention, and with others he organized the Michigan Orthodox Baptist Association. By 1925 this Association had twenty-five churches, and one of the prized possessions of this writer is the program of the 1925 annual meeting of this Association. It continued its separate existence until the General Association of Regular Baptist Churches (GARBC) was organized in 1932 and then joined this group. It is a matter of regret that a life of Van Osdel has not been attempted. He retired in 1934 while in his eighties and presided at the installation of his successor,

[3]W. B. Riley, *The Pilot,* May, 1943.

David Otis Fuller, who is still pastor at Wealthy Street. For many years the church published the *Baptist Temple News,* which revealed his views. Van Osdel was a mild Fundamentalist, willing to go the lonely road, but not anxious to stay in the front line when the bloodletting battles took place. He was a Christian gentleman of the mild type without the pugnacity needed for the Fundamentalist fray. Always the Fundamentalists could count on Van Osdel, for he was the elder statesman among them in this period, since he had taken his church out of Northern Baptist circles some ten years before others seriously considered it. In the early days he was joined by Riley, who as early as 1910 admitted that "we have surrendered the denomination into the hands of the Higher Critics."[4] The situation was to get worse, but Riley would be satisfied with protesting until the year of his death (1947), when he took his personal membership out of the NBC. No one could question his insight or his patience, but many will wonder why he had not left as did Van Osdel, at least by the early 1930's. Even as he kept admitting that the seminaries were sending out more and more liberal men he still hoped that this grand drift would change. He has been followed by thousands in both North and South who cling to the elusive dream that denominations will come back. History has shown that they did not and that all hope for such is imaginary religious dreaming. But Van Osdel felt in the early years that fellowship with error was itself an error. This was revealed when the big battle was at its height in 1925. Mrs. Helen Barrett Montgomery contended for the right to support a missionary who held to evolution and Modernism, but also claimed the right to fellowship with the Fundamentalists. Van Osdel wrote an article in his *Temple News* that Modernism was the Devil's substitute for Christianity and that should Modernism and Christianity fellowship, then "unitarianism will reap the harvest."[5] He claimed that the Devil was working hard to get people to think there is no difference between Modernism and Christianity, and he foretold "if real Baptists do not arise speedily and shake off the incubus of Modernism, it will be but a brief period until 'Ichabod' is inscribed above their door."[6]

World War I dampened any efforts to houseclean the schools and denominational posts of liberal office-holders. But during the war, A. H. Strong, formerly of Rochester, expressed alarm over the evident Modernism of missionaries he visited on the fields. His voice went unheard. In 1918 both W. B. Riley and Courtland Myers were asking questions from their pulpits about the teachers and their

[4]Ibid., p. 15.
[5]O. W. Van Osdel, *The Baptist Temple News* (Wealthy Street Baptist Church), March, 1925.
[6]Ibid.

teachings in colleges and seminaries. The answer then was the common one given, namely, that trustees and faculty are capable of handling such vital questions. Thus pastors were politely reminded that their places were in the pulpits and that they should not suspect their brethren. In 1911 the NBC gave the hired servants and executives the vote, and this was to prove the margin of victory when the great battles of the 1920's broke out. But at the time it was adopted on humanitarian and Christian bases. In the same year the M. and M. Fund (for pensions of ministers and missionaries) was started. In a short time it became a most effective tool for the control of preachers, especially young men eager for the ministry and older men with family responsibilities. No Roman Catholic tool of hierarchal lordship was ever more effective. There were many good arguments for it, but through liberal control it ended up as a bludgeon for keeping men in line with programs and promotion. At this time the Rockefeller millions became an important item; in all, the University of Chicago would get thirty-three million and the M. and M. Fund of the Convention seven million.

In 1919 J. C. Massee spoke at the Philadelphia School of the Bible on the second coming, and he added a word for the critics of this tenet. He called the return of Christ the most debated question in the church. He said that he believed in the "doctrine of the physical and imminent return of the Lord."[7] Massee asked the question, "Is being a literalist an intellectual and critical crime?"[8] Concerning the second coming, he believed that it was

> one event in two sections for His saints and with His . . . [there is] no promise of immortality apart from the Coming Again of the Lord Jesus . . .[10] [the] goal of the Gospel . . . is the Second Coming of Christ . . . the ultimate goal of the church itself.[11] The fact of the return is certain;   the time is uncertain, the event imminent.[12]

As to the criticism of the truth of the second coming, Massee held that "at His Coming He will hold us responsible for the false teachings we have permitted and for the false teachers we have countenanced."[13] He expressed his own convictions by saying:

> I am not looking for an immediate residence in heaven. I expect to live there only a little time and then I am coming back with Him to live in a redeemed earth and rule here with Him in the earth. I would regret to believe that I would have to spend my thousand years in heaven. The

---

[7]J. C. Massee, *The Second Coming* (Philadelphia: Philadelphia School of the Bible, 1919), p. 10.
[8]Ibid., p. 12.
[9]Ibid., p. 14.
[10]Ibid., p. 22.
[11]Ibid., p. 44.
[12]Ibid., p. 51.
[13]Ibid., p. 106.

reward of the saints is to have the privilege of coming back with Jesus to reign here over the nations with Him.[14] [He was mindful that] critics not tell us that the ninth and tenth Chapters of Genesis have no historical value . . . away with such piffle.[15] Nothing must take place now before the Rapture.[16]

A fateful year for Northern Baptists was 1919. The annual meeting that year assembled at Denver, Colorado, and created the New World Movement; it was a part of a general Protestant financial drive known more widely as the Interchurch World Movement. The NBC hoped to raise one hundred million dollars over a five-year period. It would be a unified way to support missions at home and abroad, colleges, seminaries, and, lastly, social reform. To promote these interests a new paper, *The Baptist,* was started. The Baptists voted to cooperate with the Interchurch Movement, even though it was dominated by Liberals. John D. Rockefeller offered to donate two million if Baptists would raise six million, and Baptists became very excited, too excited to discuss theology and Liberalism. This was pointed out by Riley, who said that the Interchurch Movement "was without a doctrinal basis."[17] He contended it was the beginning of a superchurch. He noted the leadership exercised by John R. Mott and claimed that "his leadership of the YMCA has resulted in converting that child of the church into the greatest menace to the evangelical faith."[18] One item in the plans of the Interchurch Movement was a program to apportion the world among the various denominations. Northern Baptists endorsed it, but *The Texas Baptist Standard* rejected it, as did Southern Baptists who held that everyone has the right to go into any part of the world. However, the hue and cry of the New World movement was funds, not faith. Fundamentalists and many Conservatives withdrew their support, and the plan fell far short of its goal. In fact, it was such an issue that in 1920 Northern Baptists withdrew from the program altogether. The Convention preacher for 1919 was the Liberal, Harry Emerson Fosdick. Now many men were aroused and looked forward to 1920 as the year of action. Straton organized for the 1920 meetings by creating The Fundamentalist League in the greater New York area.

A pre-convention Conference of Baptists was held at the Delaware Avenue Church in Buffalo, June 21-22, 1920. This must be rated one of the more important meetings in Fundamentalism, although it did not produce the emphasis on prophecy and keen

[14]Ibid., p. 122.
[15]Ibid., p. 201.
[16]Ibid., p. 213.
[17]W. B. Riley, *The Baptist Believer* (New Bethlehem, Pennsylvania), ed. W. H. Houghton, May, 1920, n.p.
[18]Ibid.

exegetical Bible studies which had dominated the 1886 Prophetic Conference. It was not designed as prophetic in nature but as a summation of Baptist doctrines, Baptist dangers, Biblical answers and courses of action to take.[19] The introduction to the collection of addresses was written by Curtis Lee Lawes, editor of the *Watchman-Examiner,* a national Baptist paper, who came home from the 1920 conference in Buffalo and, as he kept thinking of the references to Fundamentals, dubbed the men as "Fundamentalist"—the first recorded use of the name as such. Lawes wrote:

> Not only are we in danger of compromising our distinctive Baptist principles, we are also in danger of compromising our more fundamental Christian principles. The recent Interchurch World Movement emasculated Christianity by eliminating all doctrinal emphasis from its pronouncements and appeals.[20]

A call for the meeting had been sent out in April that included names of both Fundamentalists and Conservatives, both being disturbed by the advances of liberal thought in the schools. Among the Fundamentalists were J. C. Massee, J. R. Straton, W. B. Riley, F. M. Goodchild, Courtland Myers, W. L. Pettingill, Clarence Larkin, and C. S. Thomas. Among the Conservatives in the group were R. H. Conwell, N. E. Wood, C. L. Lawes, J. W. Brougher, and Albert Johnson. The two groups met as one protesting, dissenting conference because of a common enemy. The same make-up could be seen in the World's Christian Fundamentals Association, but the Baptist Bible Union was run by strict Fundamentalists. R. G. Delnay has estimated that of those issuing the call, only a dozen ever left the Convention.

The Conference at Buffalo produced thirteen addresses. Many were reaffirmations of historic principles and practices, such as one by F. L. Anderson of Newton Theological Institution in Newton Center, Massachusetts, which had gone into liberal thought under President Alvah Hovey. Anderson, however, was a showcase Conservative, sound but harmless during Newton's surrender to Modernism. He spoke on the general topic of the spirituality of Christianity and asserted that Baptists had always been evangelicals. He neatly ignored the issue of what to do with all those in the Convention who were not evangelical. F. J. Villers of the First Baptist Church in Detroit spent most of his time on Baptist history, relating how his ancestors had suffered and how they had clung to the sacred truth of the competency of the soul. The Liberals had nothing to fear from such nostalgic reminiscences of the past. F. M. Goodchild of Central Baptist Church in New York City attested to

---

[19]G. N. Brink, *Baptist Fundamentals: Addresses at the Pre-Convention Conference* (Philadelphia: Judson Press, 1920).

[20]Ibid., p. ii.

his faith in the Bible, its authority, and its unity. Here again there was no clarion call to face the real problems and decide, Scripturally, what to do. President E. W. Hunt of Bucknell University affirmed his faith in the Baptist way of using the ordinances, also sounding no note of alarm or showing any sensitivity to what was taking place at the heart of Northern Baptist life. J. M. Dean of Chicago preached on the deity of Christ, and his message was sound and Biblical; but he did not mention the attacks on this truth nor the attackers. S. W. Cummings of Pasadena, California, spoke on the need and the efficacy of prayer. Another message was by W. W. Bustard of Euclid Avenue Baptist Church in Cleveland, who stressed the need of preaching the Gospel and winning souls.

There were four speakers who addressed themselves to the situation facing Northern Baptists. The first was the president of the Conference, who gave the opening address, Jasper C. Massee of the Baptist Temple in Brooklyn. Later Massee was to take the important pulpit of Tremont Temple in Boston, where he would have a strong ministry. Massee held that the men at the meeting were concerned "at the presence in our schools of the radical, scientific attitude of mind toward the Bible, of the materialistic evolutionary theory of life."[21] He contended the Conference was called to discuss "the conservative interpretation of our historic position."[22] The discerning student detects here a weakness on Massee's part in hoping, thereby, to "save our Baptist family from the disastrous results of a departure from the faith."[23] He was man enough to admit that "multitudes can be led astray by false teachers who are willing to maintain the terminology of the orthodox while injecting into it a new content . . . subverting the faith and instituting a final apostasy."[24] He admitted that they were being told to believe that "truth will take care of itself. That is just a new specious phrase of the appeal for personal liberty made by all destroyers of the rights and securities of others."[25] He allowed that some claimed this was not the opportune time to raise these issues, and he asked when that time would come—"when all our schools have been captured by Liberalism . . . when our denominational machinery is under the control of the modernists and when our people generally have been delivered to the teachings of the radical theologians in their pulpits?"[26]

Another note of alarm was sounded by A. C. Dixon of the faculty

[21]Ibid., p. 5.
[22]Ibid., p. 7.
[23]Ibid.
[24]Ibid., p. 8.
[25]Ibid., p. 9.
[26]Ibid., p. 10.

of the Bible Institute of Los Angeles, who denied the theory of organic evolution and even listed six convincing arguments against it. He attributed part of the wrecking of faith to Nietzsche with his pagan brute philosophy, who had called Christianity an immoral blemish. He condemned the Higher Critics, such as Astruc and Eichhorn, who together discredited the Bible and robbed German culture of Christian faith, noting that "these ferocious hordes fled to England to wreck the Christianity founded on the Bible."[27] He added that, as he saw the Baptists and the situation in general, there was needed

> a university with the Bible at its center as the standard of truth, religious, moral, historic and scientific, and the Lord Jesus Christ preeminent in the realm of knowledge as in all other realms.[28]

Courtland Myers of Tremont Temple Baptist Church in Boston gave an address on Things Not Shaken (Hebrews 12:27) and listed those things as the throne of God, the Word of God, and the Church of God. But he did his usual blasting in Baptist style by condemning the Treaty of Versailles, saying:

> No worse failure has ever been put on the table than the Treaty of Versailles . . . . it was a farce from beginning to end . . . because God was utterly ignored. His Name was not mentioned, His blessing not asked. Infidelity wrote that document and then we expect the Good God to see it through . . . a bit of infamy.[29]

Myers had much to say about how rationalism and the philosophy of Nietzsche had led Germany to its disaster. He railed against New Theology, in which

> men lost their authority and depended on their own experiences and this Book was gone . . . . rationalism was the false god that scholars and other people worshipped . . . . we have passed through thirty years of criticism . . . . we have lost the supernatural.[30]

Church leaders came in for his rasping refrain, for he thundered in the Delaware Avenue church,

> Men said if we are going to save the church of Christ, we will save it by having these big things and having big organizations and big money and big machinery . . . . the fact is that nine-tenths of these men are ecclesiastical parasites, they are theological pigmies, they are ministerial traitors . . . telling us how to put it over.[31]

W. B. Riley put his finger on the main issue as he spoke at the Conference on the theme "Modernism in Baptist Schools." His address, analytical and comprehensive, was a highlight of this Conference, verily a call to arms to save Northern Baptists from

[27]Ibid., p. 136.
[28]Ibid., pp. 138-39.
[29]Ibid., p. 153.
[30]Ibid., p. 138.
[31]Ibid., p. 161.

spiritual bankruptcy. He stressed three essential pillars of the Baptist position: an inerrant Book, the deity of Christ, and the need of the new birth. Since these have been believed by Baptists and should be at the present time, he insisted that it would be no sin to enunciate them in a statement of faith, for Baptists have had many such statements.

Riley declared that these essentials of Baptist faith were being denied in Baptist schools. His proofs were the following: the use of the same text teaching evolution as used in state schools and the use of texts in ethics classes that explained our impulses by evolution from ape-like beings ; he asserted many "Baptist seminaries are hotbeds of skepticism."[32] One named was the Divinity House of the University of Chicago, and such prominent Liberals there were named as Powis Smith, E. D. Burton, S. J. Case, and T. G. Soares. He named a book used at Chicago called *A Guide to the Study of the Christian Religion* which made Jehovah of the Old Testament a tribal god, man not the direct creation of God, and the messiahship of Christ traceable to myths. He indicted most Old Testament books as being by several authors, and he made similar criticism of the New Testament texts. The worst example was a book by Casse on Revelation in which "infidelity reached its climax."[33] Riley included Rochester in his scathing denunciation along with Crozer, quoting from a Crozer Bulletin of April, 1919, which openly denied the infallibility of the Scriptures. He also quoted from a Crozer professor, A. S. Hobart, who denied that his guilt had been placed on Christ and that the righteousness of Christ had been imputed to him. He rejected the view of H. C. Vedder of Crozer, who denied the concept of one's vicariously taking the sin of another, noting that Vedder had written in the *Chester Times* of April 10, of "the theory that supposes Christ to have borne our sins and died in our stead": "Of all the slanders men have perpetrated against the Most High, this is positively the grossest, the most impudent, the most insulting."[34] Riley added Berkeley Seminary to the list, but he passed over Northern Baptist Seminary. He summed up the results of these conditions in the seminaries, asserting that "our distinctive doctrines are being denied; our distinctive mission is being disparaged; our distinctive influence is being destroyed."[35] He ended his open charges against the schools and seminaries with a typical Riley blast:

> The Samson of Modernism, blinded by theological fumes from Germany, feels for the pillars of the Christian Temple and would tear the

[32]Ibid., p. 178.
[33]Ibid., p. 181.
[34]Ibid., p. 184.
[35]Ibid., p. 185.

last one away and leave Christianity itself in utter collapse. If in any measure that be accomplished, let it not be said to the shame of Baptists that they were engaged as pipers of peace at the very time when their denomination perished.[36]

When the Fundamentalists came to the Convention sessions they were amazed and shocked to find that their leader, J. C. Massee, had as much clay as he had convictions, for he was willing to refer issues to a committee in order to preserve unity. This became a common device of conventions to take the wind out of Fundamentalist sails and give Liberals time to group, plan their strategy, and plot for the embarrassment and defeat of Fundamentalist forces; in these they succeeded with regularity. The forces for the Bible did present a resolution to houseclean the colleges, but it was lost. It was only the first of a series of defeats; in fact, the Fundamentalists were to lose everything but their faith. In this year the NBC voted officially to join the Federal Council— another step, and a major one, in lining up with the emerging ecumenical movement. Since then, the NBC has remained within this strongly modernist Council.

In 1921 the Convention met at Des Moines, and the Liberals were clever in that they put some Fundamentalists on the program, men like Shields, Massee, J. R. Sampey, L. R. Scarborough, and W. B. Hinson. Fundamentalists met before the regular Convention, calling themselves the Fundamentalist Fellowship. The messages were published by J. C. Massee under the title *Baptist Doctrines*. The report from the committee on the schools was weak; in reality it meant nothing had been done to effect any change and nothing was recommended. This report was accepted, and another die was cast: the schools were safe, and entrenched Liberals on the faculties would not be removed. The Fundamentalists had drawn up a Confession of Faith, *The Goodchild Confession,* but it was not even presented at this conclave. The Fundamentalists were meeting to prepare and then having their protests shelved. Massee and Goodchild as spokesmen were not ready for the fray. The Great Divide had been reached, and all the Fundamentalist oratory, caucuses, plans, and dreams were shattered and whenever Fundamentalists reappeared they never had victory within their grasp. More valiant attempts would be made and brave men would risk their good names by standing to protest, but the fight was over, and only skirmishes would ensue. One such effort was in 1922 at the Indianapolis meeting when an attempt was made to get passage of a doctrinal standard, but Cornelius Woelfkin of New York, as spokesman for the Liberals, moved that the New Testament be the only rule, and this passed by a vote of 1200 to 600. A motion to sell *The Baptist* was also defeated. These defeats had marked the trail of

[36]Ibid., p. 187.

these good men and many now were dissatisfied with Massee's moves. By now it was clear to a growing number that Massee was sound in doctrine but moderate in attitude. A moderate attitude was polite but not the essential ingredient for a battle, and the sound men were in a battle in the North. Dissenters could not but turn in a new direction, for leadership was needed. Thus the Baptist Bible Union was born.

Fundamentalist gatherings took on several names and these should be mentioned. One was the Fundamentalist Fellowship and another was the National Federation of Fundamentalists of Northern Baptists (NFFNB). Later, in the 1940's, the name most often used was The Conservative Baptist Fellowship, for many Fundamentalists had stayed within the Convention, organizing on the inside their own mission boards, and their fellowship was the natural descendant of the old Fundamentalist Fellowship. When the leaders of the Conservative Baptist movement became New Evangelicals or New Evangelical sympathizers, then the old line Fundamentalists (by this time dubbed the "hard-core") continued the witness of the old Fundamentalist Fellowship and renamed their group in 1965 The Fundamentalist Baptist Fellowship.

It still meets annually and publishes *The Information Bulletin.* For years it had an office at 2561 North Clark Street in Chicago, but from 1970 to 1972 its address was 3255 Lowell Blvd. in Denver, Colorado. In the summer of 1972 the office was moved back to Chicago and is now located at Marquette Manor Baptist Church, 6001 South California Avenue in the Windy City. Among its major figures have been G. Archer Weniger, Chester J. McCullough, and M. James Hollowood. Weniger has been a pastor in Oakland, California, for several years; McCullough has pastored in Indiana, Michigan, and Colorado; while Hollowood has been a leader in the Minnesota Baptist Convention, pastor in Buffalo, New York, and is now a faculty member at Maranatha Baptist Bible College in Watertown, Wisconsin.

From 1920 to 1925 the Fundamentalists suffered defeat after defeat on the Convention floor. In 1921 they called for a statement of faith in order to have a check on teachers and missionaries. This was defeated on the flimsy call for adherence to the New Testament as the sole rule of faith and practice by men who were known to have denied the New Testament doctrines, led by Cornelius Woelfkin of New York. At the 1922 convention in Indianapolis, every proposal of the Fundamentalists, aimed at flushing out the Liberals, failed again. Many were plainly disgusted with continuing defeats and began to see that some organization or rallying-center outside the Convention was in order. After all, it was hardly to be expected that strong preachers and dogmatic defenders of the Word, honored in their local churches and areas, would relish going to national gatherings to be defeated on moves to uphold the same precious truth they proclaimed in their own pulpits. Mighty in defense of the Faith, they became mighty in walking outside the narrow confines of a religious body, as they despaired of ever ridding the Convention of the incubus of Liberalism from within. To them it was infuriating that heretics and "softies" had taken control of their beloved denomination, but they were forced to face the facts. Therefore, they began to look to some agency outside the old-line religious circles, and in their dissatisfaction were the seeds of the Baptist Bible Union. The 1923 convention met at Atlantic City, but the Fundamentalists stayed away in large numbers. They gathered instead that year in a large tent in Kansas City and launched the Baptist Bible Union (BBU) with some three thousand five hundred people present at peak attendance. By now Massee had such a blurred vision of what was happening before his eyes that he had persuaded himself that Fundamentalists were making gains among Northern Baptists because (1) they were allowed to designate gifts by official permission, (2) churches had the right to send gifts directly to mission societies, and (3) the Convention budget was divided into three main areas. In addition, he claimed that there was a new interest in doctrine, with more concern shown about the schools and more calls for Baptists to stress preaching. These elements blinded Massee to the liberal strategy of many promises, the bait to quiet conservative protests. Others among Convention Conservatives sided with him and under his leadership went into the backwaters of middle-of-the-roadism. Such men as Russell H. Conwell, J. W. Brougher, Sr., and C. H. Heaton took Massee's compromise position and no longer caused the Liberals any fear. Later Brougher succeeded Massee at Tremont Temple, and with him the Temple began its great slide from a place of world renown as a preaching platform to its present mediocrity. Brougher played too much to the grandstands, and his voice became a hollow one indeed when he performed the wedding ceremony of Mary Pickford of Hollywood and later invited Aimee Semple McPherson of the Four Square Church to speak in his Los Angeles pulpit.

Another middle-of-the-roader was Earle V. Pierce, a close associate of Massee in Convention compromises. For a while, Pierce headed the Fundamentalist Fellowship, but he "studiously avoided bringing pertinent matters before the main body of the Convention for fear of destroying its unity."[37] For his efforts to preserve unity at any price, he was later rewarded by being elected president of the

[37]W. W. Ayer, "Down the Old Apostasy Road," *Christian Crusade Weekly*, Aug. 30, 1971, p. 7.

Convention. Of him, William Ward Ayer, in charity, writes that he was a good man but not a strong man.

At the 1924 convention, Massee was given an important place as the Convention preacher and announced his desire for a moratorium on debate in the interest of soulwinning among Northern Baptists. Thus a good cause, the winning of souls, now became a Convention tool for denominational apostasy, for how could soulwinning be a righteous thing when it was done by men who denied the Bible and its truths? Fundamentalists were doing the soulwinning and would continue to do so; but the hollow front was accepted, and Massee completed his sell-out to the leaders of Conventionism and compromise. He faded from the Fundamentalist picture after this, although he continued to have a strong ministry at Tremont Temple in Boston until the early 1930's. Later he would disavow his views of prophecy as "Jewish notions," and serve within the Conventions, both Northern and Southern, without any further protest.

The 1925 Convention was no better. It was held at Seattle, and delegates from Park Avenue Baptist in New York were received although the church now practiced open membership, that is, the practice of receiving members who had not been immersed. Woelfkin had prepared the way for it, and Fosdick, his successor in 1925, was openly for it. The Fundamentalists still inside the Convention tried to get rid of Modernists serving under the Missions Board, but they failed in this. This was to be expected, for in 1924 the Board issued a statement saying,

Our Board . . . has given to its officials and missionaries a considerable liberty of theological opinion . . . . [our] denomination is made up of men and churches of diverse views . . . [it is] only right that our missionary force should reflect the situation in our churches at home.[38]

A student of this long process of decline in the Northern Baptist ranks has been William Ward Ayer, for fourteen years pastor of Calvary Baptist Church in New York City and now living in St. Petersburg, Florida. He wrote an article for the *Christian Crusade Weekly,* edited by Billy James Hargis, published in the issue of August 30, 1970. It summarized the downward path of Northern Baptists over the past fifty years and pointed out that the same path is being followed by the Southern Baptists. In the case of Northern Baptists it emptied churches, contaminated colleges and seminaries, brought moral lethargy to the pulpits, and created a spiritual impotency. It was Ayer's conclusion that

there is a humanly sentimental weakness among many church leaders. They find it hard to oppose nice, expansive, amiable people who are often the kind that espouse and propagate apostasy. They find these people

[38]*Serving and Waiting,* Feb., 1924, p. 476.

are so likeable, so professedly broad-minded, have so many good traits that it is impossible not to like them. I have discovered over the years that there are hordes of good pastors who do no more than apologize for apostasy.[39]

At the 1926 convention of Northern Baptists, Riley introduced a resolution that immersion be required for membership in Baptist churches; it was a last-ditch attempt to make Park Avenue Baptist and Fosdick leave, but it was defeated two to one. Convention unity was the prime object of the leaders and people attending to make a good religious show. By now it was apparent that there were six issues among Northern Baptists: the schools, soundness of doctrine in preachers, executives, interdenominationalism, missions, and social action.[40]

In recent years, it is the same story among Southern Baptists, who have created a successful method to ignore apostasy. At present, no effective voice can be raised in Southern Baptist meetings against the deepening spiritual decline in schools and churches. Any attempt to correct the deep-rooted sins is met with the enthusiastic claim that the day of arguing over beliefs is over and now is the time to get on with the worldwide task. Two things illustrate this silencing of protest against apostasy. The Sunday School Board still pays some fifteen thousand dollars a year to the National Council for the privilege of using selected portions of Scripture. Again, it was claimed that W. A. Criswell would stem the tides of Liberalism within the Convention, but at the time of the 1970 Convention in Denver, when a split was possible, he completely exonerated all officials of the Convention, the very ones who had presided over the sellout of schools, boards, and literature. This clean bill of health covered the Christian Life Commission, which had the notorious Anglican, Joseph Fletcher, as speaker at an Atlanta program, despite the fact that it was openly known that Fletcher advocated permissiveness in the sex relationships. One denominational figure put the basic problem very well when he told a friend:

> if there wasn't a God it [the program] would work, since Southern Baptist literature is being diverted into non-Biblical channels . . . . you may challenge God's Word but never the program, . . . [it is] a denominational idol.[41]

[39]Ayer, p. 7.
[40]McBirnie, p. 108.
[41]Ayer, p. 7.

9
Fundamentalist Fellowships

The World's Christian Fundamentals Association (WCFA)

A prophecy conference convened in Philadelphia from May 28 to May 30,1918, which was destined to be the forerunner of the WCFA, officially organized the following year. The messages of the 1918 conference were published, and one speaker, Courtland Myers, set the tone for the meeting.[1] Myers was a gifted, fire-eating Fundamentalist pastor of Tremont Temple in Boston, and he announced:

> the abomination of abominations in the modern religious world is that ripe, rank, rampant, rotten new theology made in Germany . . . . [the theologians have] torn it [the Bible] to shreds and trampled it beneath their feet like mere scraps of paper, thus substituting for real Christianity and the principles of the Gospel of the Son of God the law of survival of the fittest with the result now manifest on our world the tidal wave of barbarism, savagery, and immorality.[2]

Like so many Americans, Myers was turning his stern and scornful criticism against German thinking which had brought on World War I. Especially was the preacher solidly and openly against the invasions of the churches and schools by German ideas. He told the hearers at the Philadelphia conclave that

> If the churches of Great Britain, America, and France fifty years ago had fought this iniquity, this infamous thing, there would never have been any war in the world now. . . . the crimson stream had its source in

[1]"Light on Prophecy," *The Christian Herald,* 1918.
[2]Ibid., p. 176.

the rank German theology that has been forcing its way into the veins and arteries of all our religious life.... we ought to fight it to the finish.... by the Grace of God no foreigner can transact this unholy business with me; we will have none of it.[3]

The WCFA organized in Philadelphia in May of 1919 under the leadership of W. B. Riley, J. C. Massee, W. H. Griffith Thomas, P. W. Philpott, A. B. Winchester, R. A. Torrey, L. S. Chafer, W. W. Rugh, G. E. Guille, W. L. Pettingill, L. W. Munhall, I. M. Haldeman, George McNeeley, and J. R. Straton. It was the natural child of the Premillennial Conference held the previous year. The call that had gone out in June of 1918 for the first conference was signed by thirty-seven ministers and laymen, sparked by R. H. Haines, a leading businessman of Philadelphia. The Academy of Music, holding six thousand, was used for the conference. On the committee arranging for the 1919 meeting were three laymen: C. L. Huston, T. E. Rose, and J. D. Adams. These men bore the financial load. Perhaps a few words about some of the leaders will set the stage.

Haldeman was the longtime pastor of First Baptist in New York City and one of the first pulpiteers to make prophecy a regular part of his sermons. He made First Baptist a Fundamentalist stronghold and center of great preaching of the Word. He was followed by men of his strong convictions in the pulpit such as W. L. Pettingill, W. H. Rogers, and A. F. Williams. It is now a GARBC church though greatly weakened in size. But Haldeman was not an organization man, and the WCFA was the only organization he supported strongly. W. H. Griffith Thomas was an Anglican scholar, taking a lonely stand within his church for sound doctrine. Later he assisted L. S. Chafer in the founding of the Evangelical Theological College, to become Dallas Theological Seminary in Dallas, Texas. P. W. Philpott had an outstanding ministry in the Philpott Tabernacle in Hamilton, Ontario; Moody Church in Chicago; and the Church of the Open Door in Los Angeles. Chafer had been associated with C. I. Scofield as a songleader but by 1921 was a Bible teacher of note, and in 1924 he led in the founding of Dallas Seminary, hoping thereby to persuade the Presbyterians to accept his well-defined dispensationalism. Few Presbyterians followed him, but he kept following this goal until his death in 1952. L. W. Munhall was a grand old man in Methodism, an evangelist and editor, one of the few links with the first generation Fundamentalists. Another to grace the program in 1919 was James M. Gray. The Confession of Faith of the WCFA was strongly Fundamental, even stating in Article VII that "we believe in that Blessed Hope, the personal, premillennial, and imminent return of our Lord and Saviour, Jesus

Christ."[5] In 1922 it met in Los Angeles under the sponsorship of the Bible Institute of Los Angeles, led by T. C. Horton.

The WCFA held its fifth Annual Meeting in First Baptist in Fort Worth from April 29 to May 6, 1923. There was a large attendance but this was deceptive, for it did not indicate the size of the group. The great majority of hearers were Norris' followers who came to Fort Worth to hear fervent Baptist preaching and Fundamentalist attacks on Southern Baptists and Modernists of all types. Every time Norris had any meeting, a great rally followed, and the throngs came to hear exciting preaching and uplifting exhortations. At this meeting Pettingill was the Bible teacher, and others on the program were Riley, Munhall, C. G. Trumbull of the *Sunday School Times,* Shields, J. F. Stevenson of Chicago, T. C. Horton of Los Angeles and John Thomas of England. This was the first time the World's Christian Fundamentals Association met in Fort Worth or in the South, and it was something of a novelty. The 1923 meeting saw the endorsement of such papers as *The King's Business* (published by the Bible Institute of Los Angeles), *Moody Monthly, Christian Fundamentals in School and Church, Wonderful Word, Serving and Waiting,* and *Our Hope* (edited by A. C. Gaebelein). This conference recommended a new Sunday School course of study. It also recommended the establishment of a premillennial seminary. It set a goal of 100,000 members for the next year and planned to meet with Riley in Minneapolis in 1924.

Its eighth meeting was held in Jarvis Street Baptist in Toronto in April of 1926, thus showing its international cast. Among the speakers were Roy R. Brown, Clinton Howard, and Riley. The total attendance for the four services held at Jarvis Street and Massey Hall was over seven thousand. A note appeared in the *Gospel Witness* of May 6, 1926, saying all expenses had been met and some funds were left over. The same issue carried a notice that Shields was the commencement speaker that year at Wheaton College, Wheaton, Illinois.

Two men guided the WCFA during its existence of more than thirty years, W. B. Riley and Paul W. Rood, who had been president of Biola from 1935 to 1938. In 1942 Dan Gilbert became its general secretary. In January of 1942 Gilbert estimated there were twenty million Fundamentalists in the country. To be exact, he should have said there were twenty million American Christians who did not agree with the Modernists. During the 1940's the WCFA weakened as the National Association of Evangelicals and the American Council of Christian Churches arose to defend the faith and expose all forms of Modernist unbelief.

[5]W. B. Riley, *The Christian Fundamentals in School and Church,* (Northwestern Schools), 1919, p. 22.

It continued throughout the forties but gradually weakened and finally died. In the 1940's other leaders included J. Harold Smith, Bob Jones, Sr., W. W. Ayer, H. J. Ockenga, John E. Brown, Theodore Epp, Charles E. Fuller, and Paul Rees. In 1942 it reported aiming at getting 100,000 members. Its office was at Glendale, California. In 1942 Bob Jones, Sr., wrote Rood that several representatives of Fundamental groups had been left out, and he asked to be left off the Advisory Committee because of the resentment of some members toward him.[6]

There were other Fundamentalist organizations in the 1920's, such as the Anti-Evolution League started in 1923 by Riley, J. W. Porter of Kentucky, and T. T. Martin of Mississippi. Another group was the Bryan Bible League under Paul Rood of Turlock, California, which later joined with the WCFA. Harry Rimmer of Los Angeles guided the Research Science Bureau. Gerald W. Winrod of Wichita, Kansas, headed the Defenders of the Faith, and on the public platform and by his *Defenders' Magazine* he exposed communist activities along with evolution and anti-Christian teaching in the schools. George W. Washburn of Massachusetts founded the Bible Crusaders in 1925 with a paper called *The Crusaders' Champion*. The paper did not catch on and ceased publication within a year.

The Baptist Bible Union

By 1923 three groups were ready and eager for a new organization, and this led to the formation of the Baptist Bible Union. One group was the disappointed Fundamentalists within the Northern Baptist Convention. They had expected a housecleaning within the schools and the Mission Board of the Convention but had seen their efforts thwarted by the skilled political leaders of the Northern Baptist hierarchy. In their opinion J. C. Massee had adopted a "trundling attitude" which had proved suicidal. Protesters had expected success at the Buffalo convention in 1920; they had continued to hope for a change at Des Moines in 1921; they had seen failure written on the walls of the 1922 conclave at Indianapolis; and they had been soundly defeated and routed at the Atlantic City meeting in 1923. Their fears were well-founded, for in the 1924 convention in Washington, Massee capitulated and called for a moratorium on debate in deference to the greater cause of soulwinning. This moratorium was needed, he claimed, in order that more energies "be dedicated to soulwinning and a rededication of the denominational machinery."[7] This call had a hollow sound, for the greatest soulwinning churches on the continent were those of the

---

[6]A letter dated July 27, 1942, from Bob Jones, Sr., to Paul W. Rood.

[7]R. G. Delnay, *The Central Conservative Baptist Quarterly* (Central Baptist Seminary), Spring, 1965, p. 33.

Fundamentalists, such as Calvary Baptist in New York, First in Fort Worth, and First in Minneapolis. Massee gave himself to the pulpit of Tremont Temple in Boston and later demonstrated his weakening position by admitting that his strong prophetic views had been "Jewish notions." The debacle of the protest was seen in Atlantic City when J. Whitcomb Brougher spoke for the dissenters; he was a Convention Conservative but was unable to see beyond Convention walls for any kind of witness.

A second group ready for a new organization were those men under the influence of J. Frank Norris. These were at the time largely from among the laymen; for although the preachers had heard of him, few were yet following him. But the Flame of Fort Worth was ready for national action, and the BBU would provide a platform for his many gifts. A third force was represented by the redoubtable T. T. Shields of Jarvis Street Baptist in Toronto. He was still within the confines of the Ontario and Quebec Baptist Convention, but the ties were under heavy strain.

The meeting opened in May, 1923, at Kansas City, Missouri, in a tent rented from Walter L. Wilson. It was characterized as having a large attendance with an intensely spiritual atmosphere. One report stated that there were 3,300 present at the first meeting. Men of the Fundamentalist Fellowship were there, such as Riley, O. W. Van Osdel, and W. L. Pettingill. Others were Norris and Shields along with R. E. Neighbour, who had proposed such a movement for some time, as had Norris. It was outside the confines of the conventions and therefore unhampered by caucuses, strategy for floor victories, and mundane convention business. The BBU could be a live-wire affair with great Bible exhortation and great excoriation and exposure of Modernists, evolution, and Baptist apostasy. T. T. Shields was elected the first president, and on the executive committee were Norris, A. C. Dixon, Neighbour, Riley, Pettingill, Van Osdel, and E. C. Miller. It should be pointed out that the BBU did not take a firm separatist stand, for it was resolved that

> We declare our determination not to withdraw from the various conventions but to purge our beloved denominations from such heresies [as those of Cornelius Woelfkin including lack of a creed, toleration for spiritism, weakness on baptism and toleration for Fosdick] . . . and refuse henceforth to contribute funds administered by rationalistic modernist officials.[8]

Riley brought one of the messages at the opening and spoke for the Confession of Faith, which was adopted, and his address was published in tract form.[9] He held that the present apostasy called for organized resistance, claiming that "no apostasy of the past had

[8]*Serving and Waiting,* July, 1923, p. 125.
[9]W. B. Riley, *Why the Baptist Bible Union?,* n.p., n.d., pp. 5-6.

been so worldwide, as doggedly determined against the Faith, ... as surreptitious in methods and adroit in messages as Modernism."[10] The Minneapolis pastor trembled to "see the children of our progenitors playing the coward in the presence of the boastful Goliaths of Modernism."[11] He stormed against the steamroller machines in Baptist circles, especially the change in the church from soulwinning to social improvement. With obvious approval he quoted the widely used dictum of B. H. Carroll:

> Modernism, like another cuckoo, laid its eggs in our schools, deceiving the conservative, not only into incubating for it but feeding its young, fooled by the notion that it was caring for its very own.[12]

To Riley the BBU was a rallying point for all Fundamentalist Baptists, North and South, and even abroad. In fact he expressed the hope publicly that it would unite with the Baptist Bible Union of England and that together they would create a worldwide fellowship of Fundamental Baptists. That never materialized—indeed Riley was to live to see his beloved BBU slide into confusion and death. Perhaps the end of the BBU dissuaded Riley from leaving the Northern Baptist Convention until the year of his death. Perhaps it would not be wrong to wonder if hundreds of Fundamental men had stayed within Convention ranks, North and South, because they saw the frustrating schisms and bloodletting within the groups which had left and taken a separatist stand. Shields put it bluntly but factually when he said that the BBU was organized for "the express purpose of declaring and waging relentless and uncompromised war on modernism on all fronts."[13]

The BBU did take a modified stand on prophecy, although it held to the second coming of Christ. It passed one resolution saying:

> We welcome to its membership all Baptists who sign its confession of faith, whatever variations of interpretation they may hold on the millennial question, consistent with belief in the personal bodily second coming of Christ according to the scriptures.[14]

Perhaps this generalization was designed to accommodate Shields, who would soon take an amillennial position, or it may have indicated a desire not to insist on the strict doctrine of the imminent return before the Great Tribulation but to get enough men to agree on a bodily return of Christ. Actually, it was a revised version of the New Hampshire Confession whose last article was openly premillennial. During the 1920's Fundamental Baptists were mildly dispensational and used the Scofield Reference Bible, but they did

---

[10]Ibid.
[11]Ibid., p. 4.
[12]Ibid., p. 6.
[13]Tarr, p. 103.
[14]*Serving and Waiting,* July, 1923, p. 126.

not preach a series on dispensational truth nor dwell on items in that system. Neighbour, who was there at the start, was not a recognized leader but was a capable platform man, one of the traditional pastor-type, a strategist but not a sensationalist. He was never a noisy man on the pretribulation rapture but used the main ideas of Haldeman, Gray, and Gaebelein, along with Ironside and Pettingill.

Together with Norris from the South were such men as T. T. Martin, who was a firebrand but not a sensationalist like Norris. Scarborough and Carroll were counted Fundamental but not of the militant type. The South was a citadel for postmillennial ideas, along with the preaching of the simple Gospel and church loyalty and heavy reliance on revival meetings. On the doctrine of the second coming, the BBU deserted the hard line of Gordon, Haldeman, and Needham. Too often have Fundamentalists accommodated and failure has resulted. Here may be one element in the debacle of the BBU. Perhaps the BBU hoped to attract a considerable segment of Southern Baptists and felt that their postmillennial leanings might be an obstacle. So the BBU dipped its flag ever so slightly, although the immediate damage was not noticeable since it changed no man's mind. Average Christians, with the exception of Shields, thought of the BBU as premillennial and, felt that since Shields was Canadian, his influence would be small. But his place was to be a large one, for he would lead the BBU for its nine years and take over Des Moines University, only to see it go into shambles.

It might be asked if the BBU was strictly separatist. It was to the point that it was outside denominational bounds and control, but for years many of its speakers and members were inside their respective denominations. Norris was the only one outside in 1923, because he and his church were not acceptable to the Tarrant County Association. But Shields remained in the Ontario and Quebec Convention until 1927 and Riley in the NBC until 1947. However, the BBU did serve to alarm men to the extent that gradually they came to see that the denominations were past salvation in respect to sound doctrine. Although more and more attempts would be made to save them, all were doomed to failure. So many had friends within and investments in pension plans that they carefully considered before deciding on a break. But one great obstacle blocked their separation, the ignorance of the congregations about the real state of affairs and the depths of apostasy. Many pastors in small churches could not risk a rupture. Few, then as now, would admit that a school or denomination was past redemption, even if a mountain of evidence pointed to a number of weaknesses or heresies. There were many Fundamentalists then, as at present, who could not see themselves as responsible for what was going on and so they did their own job where they were and argued their consciences into cooperation.

The call for the formation of the BBU went out over the signatures of Shields, Riley, and A. C. Dixon. The program had as speakers such men as Riley, Shields, Norris, Van Osdel, Straton, R. T. Ketcham, Neighbour, Pettingill, W. H. Rogers, Louis Entzminger, and H. H. Savage. What a gathering of Fundamentalist brains and talent! The Prima Donnas dominated from the beginning; their age, pulpit gifts, and battle scars set them aside on a special pinnacle of eminence. Neighbour took a lowly place and slowly faded out of the picture. Dixon stayed two years and then resigned, believing the work of the BBU was over. He died in 1925. Ketcham stayed till it faltered badly and then out of the ashes helped to erect its successor, the General Association of Regular Baptist Churches. Entzminger stayed in the background but commanded respect for the great Sunday School work done for Norris at Fort Worth and at Detroit. Rogers later had a strong ministry at First Baptist in New York, and Savage pastored at First Baptist in Pontiac, Michigan, each playing a strong role in the Conservative Baptist groups. The BBU was a preachers' movement, a loose fellowship of individuals. At its peak in 1927 it claimed fifty thousand members, but this number is questionable, for such an estimate included many who attended to hear the great preachers and could not themselves be called dissenters. The same is often true of American church rolls.

Shields was president from the beginning and projected the image for the organization. It was militant in its attacks on Liberals and their views, Modernism in the schools, and denominational machines which harbored such enemies. It was, in the main, directed at Baptist groups; few others would pay any attention. The inclusive policy of the Northern Convention was criticized with rising scorn, and there was an increasing dissatisfaction among those staying inside because of a hope of saving their denomination. Many left the NBC havens of comfort to go into BBU circles. This created an ecclesiastical stigma in the eyes of the "Liberal Love Leaders" and brought a black-listing before vacant churches and prospective openings. Because the BBU was formed by preachers it headlined preaching as if it expected the oratorical powers of Riley, Shields, and Norris to save American churches from apostasy. The platform ministry did have one weakness: it attracted thousands who came to hear the giants, and organization, planning, and effective implementation were submerged. Fundamentalism has done this several times, but strong preachers spend their time on censure and ignore other things. What good was done for Fundamentalism by the BBU was done by preaching, in which Fundamentalism had its finest hour. Many still remember with deep nostalgia, wondering if ever again there will be on one platform the equal of Norris, Shields, and Riley. The evidence seems to indicate that such will never happen, and Liberals rejoice that these are out of the way. Bible believers around the world, however, who heard them at their oratorical prime, remember them with emotions close to adoration. Delnay has summed up their feverish activities as that of "constant travel, tremendous pressure, and war being fought on several fronts."[15] J. W. Brougher, a Northern Conservative, made a last-ditch attempt to get the Fundamentalists and the Liberals to make peace. He called a meeting early in 1925 in Chicago, but little came of it.

The Union held its 1926 annual sessions May 19-24 at the Metropolitan Baptist Church in Washington, D.C. It was one of the best-attended and most enthusiastic gatherings of the BBU. At the closing rally at the Washington auditorium both Riley and Norris spoke and scathed the Baptists for their widespread unbelief; indeed it seemed to be the finest hour for both, for a year later Norris would be under the cloud of shooting a man in his study in Fort Worth. The momentum of the Washington meeting gave hope that the Northern Baptists could be redirected. But a main issue raised by Riley on the convention floor of Northern Baptists, calling for the requirement of immersion for church members, was defeated by a two-to-one vote. Straton and Riley still contended they could do more good by continuing to attend the conventions, but Norris was a separatist by now and was out. By this time some wondered why the Liberals could not preach and the Fundamentalists could not count.

What did the BBU accomplish besides providing annual meetings for more preaching, attacks, and fellowship? One accomplishment was its effective exposure of the foreign missions program of the Northern Baptists; another was the constant alarm sounded over the dangers of the teaching of evolution in the schools. In Canada, Shields took up the cudgels against L. H. Marshall on the McMaster faculty at Hamilton, Ontario. Participation in the Federal Council was also attacked as reprehensible, as were the liberal books appearing and being used in Baptist schools. They had to rebuff their former colleague, J. C. Massee, who would stop the fight in the NBC for his good intentions in evangelism, his call for a moratorium showing cowardice and willingness to believe the Liberals in their yearly promises at the conventions. Later J. W. Brougher followed him in his cowardice and naiveté. But separatism continued to be spurned as BBU policy unless the existing conventions forced one out, and soon the conventions, when power was sufficiently in the hands of the Liberals, would do exactly that. A new missions society, The Russian Missionary Society, under William Fetler, attracted

[15]*Central Conservative Baptist Quarterly*, p. 24.

BBU interest, but it proved to be a thorn in the Union side. The BBU also endorsed the Interstate Evangelistic Association under Harold Strathern. In 1932 it voiced support of Baptist Mid-Missions, a board Fundamental Baptists have steadfastly supported. It also gave support to the Association of Baptists for World Evangelism, and this board continues to have Fundamental Baptist support. Many BBU pastors used Union Gospel Press materials for Sunday Schools. These pastors sent young people to Moody Bible Institute and for foreign service through Interdenominational Faith Missions.

The Union's image was tarnished by the tragic shooting of D. E. Chipps by Norris on the afternoon of July 17, 1926, in the pastor's office in Fort Worth. Although Norris was found not guilty by reason of self-defense, yet Shields was the only one of the Union's leaders who stood solidly behind the beleaguered Fort Worth pastor. His church refused to receive his resignation, but the fortunes of the Union in the South evaporated. Norris did have enough sense to disassociate himself from Union meetings for four years. However, this was a serious blow to BBU, for his preaching power was unsurpassed on the continent.

It was announced in 1927 that a series for Sunday Schools on Acts and Romans was planned. It was under the general heading of "A Whole Bible Sunday School Lesson Course." The expositions were by T. T. Shields of Toronto, growing out of some lesson notes he had published in the *Gospel Witness*. Lesson helps were to be purchased from Union Gospel Press in Cleveland. The BBU headquarters were listed as Room 340, Monon Building, 440 South Dearborn Street, Chicago, Illinois. A special appeal came out from the office to help a Baptist Mission in Jamaica, the brochure listing some 210 churches with 32,000 members and 47 missionaries (40 were colored), and an appeal for $10,000 was "being made to the Fundamentalist churches of America to come generously to Jamaica's help." The monies were to be handled by the Reverend T. I. Stockley, Mandeville, Jamaica, B.W.I. A long letter from T. T. Shields (Nov. 10, 1926) spoke of the burning issue before the NBC open membership, named W. E. Atkinson as Field Secretary, and promised support of the Russian Missionary Society under Pastor Fetler and the upkeep of Mrs. W. S. Sweet in Hangchow, China. The letter stressed the need of two thousand dollars at once and the constant need of one thousand dollars per month. It mentioned a special issue of the *Gospel Witness* of 176 pages in order to cover the great debate in the Ontario-Quebec Convention, writing:

> When modernists are driven into a corner, they suddenly develop a passion for evangelism . . . . many of the brethren who accepted the proposal at the NBC [eliminate debates in order to win souls] . . . [were]

being made tools of by the modernists. Whoever heard of a modernist with a zeal for the salvation of souls? . . . Modernism does not recognize any need of salvation.[16]

Years ago I found a letter on BBU stationery signed by Edith Rebman. It listed Shields as president and Norris and Riley as vice-presidents. Listed on the executive committee were A. B. Fowler, W. B. Hinson, John Linton, H. O. Meyer, W. L. Pettingill, and Van Osdel. Its full name was The Baptist Bible Union of North America.

From 1926 to 1930 several things combined to weaken and topple the Union. Massee openly attacked it, and this hurt, for Massee and Riley had been very close. Massee abdicated his place in the Fundamentalist Fellowship, and Frank Goodchild of Central Baptist in New York replaced him. But Goodchild believed the Fundamentalists could recapture the Convention, and Riley still nursed the same hope. Shields saw the fallacy of this type of approach, and to him it was almost laughable that such men should be pawns in the hands of the hierarchy. His own convictions caused him to be ousted from the Ontario Convention in 1927, and in the fall of that year he opened Toronto Baptist Seminary as a protest school with Riley as guest speaker. But Riley was drifting away from the Union, and one more incident would be enough for a serious rift; that came in 1927.

For years, Iowa Baptists had operated Des Moines University, but by 1927 it was bankrupt. Fundamentalists had been withholding support, and this charge was made; but it was their virtue and not their vice so to do. It was a matter of fact that less than half of the Baptist churches in the state did support the school. A trustee of the University, Dr. Frank Foulk, offered the school to the Union if a debt of $75,000 were assumed. Union leadership was divided on the offer and only Shields showed any enthusiasm toward the idea. Riley had his own school to support, while Norris had not yet been sold on the idea of building separate schools. So Shields struck out on his own with the expectation of building a strong Fundamentalist university on the American continent and later adding a seminary to it. The secretary of the Union, Miss Edith Rebman, moved her office to the Des Moines campus. In the fall of 1927 it opened with Shields as President and 367 students and 36 faculty members on hand. Looking back on the situation, one could ask how many of these knew the Union's battle and stand in doctrine and how many would support it if they did know. To say the least, Shields wandered far into the field of assumption, assuming that these 400 people were Fundamentalists. One noteworthy item in the fall term was the appearance of both Norris and Riley on the platform, but their paths

[16]Personal letter from T. T. Shields, dated Nov. 10, 1926.

would diverge after this. Riley was still in the Convention with both Norris and Shields out. Tensions would mount. Van Osdel wanted and asked Riley to lead a separatist group out of the Northern Baptists, but Riley turned him down.

The first year of the operation of DMU under Shields saw a division arise in both faculty and students; it was the common one between the militants and the moderates. Several holdovers from the old administration could work with either modernists, as they had, or with the militants. This infected the students and contaminated campus climate. Dean Bennett of the faculty administration developed hostility to both Shields and Rebman. This situation was greatly aggravated when H. C. Wayman was named president for the school year of 1928-1929. He had been president of William Jewell College in Missouri and, by report, had been ousted because of his strong evangelical views. After he was installed at Des Moines, it was charged that more than one of his degrees had not been earned by proper methods; also, he soon lined up with the anti-Shields faction. The truth was that he was never a Fundamentalist; actually he was less liberal than the controlling group at William Jewell and should have been called an evangelical, but not a Fundamentalist. However, the fall term began well at Des Moines with such men as James M. Gray and O. W. Van Osdel there to receive the LL.D. degree. The guest speaker was J. Gresham Machen, the brilliant orthodox scholar of Princeton. In the running of the University, relations deteriorated between Miss Rebman and Wayman, and his animosity against Shields grew. Miss Rebman, personable and gifted, was Shields' liaison, but the BBU felt the school, though evangelical, was hardly militant in its stand. The alleged bogus degrees of H. C. Wayman was a nightmare to Shields, who had written vehemently against such things in the *Gospel Witness*. Some claimed Miss Rebman was most difficult to get along with. Ugly rumors attempted to incriminate both Shields and her by claiming there were pictures showing Shields and Miss Rebman coming from a hotel in Des Moines. They did leave the hotel, but men on the scene said they saw Shields come on the train, have breakfast with Miss Rebman, and leave. The trustees met on May 10-11, and a student riot broke out with city police standing back and not interrupting. When Shields' life was threatened, he and others beat a hasty retreat out of town because no police protection was granted. The University went under. It finished the spring term but did not reopen. Not a single building of Des Moines University is now in existence. A few days after the riot in 1929 the annual meeting of the Baptist Bible Union was held at the First Baptist Church of Buffalo, New York, with many mixed emotions over DMU, but Shields was reelected as president. Speakers on the program of that year included Shields, H. C. Wayman, O. W. Van Osdel, James McGinlay, Howard C. Fulton, and J. Palmer Muntz. It was noticeable that neither William B. Riley nor J. Frank Norris spoke at or attended that meeting.

Tremendous adverse publicity followed the fall of Des Moines. The average reader of the newspaper accounts knew very little of the true internal situation, but the closing of the school gave all appearance of another Fundamentalist debacle. It gave the Liberals quite an array of facts, for here were Fundamentalists with a school of their own and after only two years it had erupted in rioting (a novel thing for that day) with charges and countercharges. In that same year death claimed John Roach Straton, a leader of the BBU. Several would admit that perhaps Van Osdel had been right, for he had held all along that separation from the denominations should have been the pattern, but now it was very debatable since the confused Des Moines stigma would ensue. Whether Fundamentalists would learn from these mistakes was open to question, but it was clear that many mistakes had been made. The record was long and baffling; and haggling, blundering, and stumbling had tarnished and weakened the Fundamentalist image. Students of this period, the BBU, and the Des Moines situation of 1927-1929 have many questions to research and many knotty problems to unravel.

The 1930 meeting of the BBU was held at Wealthy Street in Grand Rapids, and it was a matter of regret that Riley was not there. It has been surmised that it was now too separatist for him. Miss Rebman was thanked for her services, and Shields continued as the head. One proposal was that the organization become an association of churches under the name of The Missionary Union of Baptist Churches. This stemmed from a general distrust of individual membership. Van Osdel thought a better name would be the Union of Regular Baptists. No meeting was held in 1931, such being the low ebb of interest and activity. The last meeting of the Union was held in 1932 at Belden Avenue Baptist in Chicago with thirty-five delegates present. The call was issued by Shields, but he did not attend because of the illness of his wife. H. C. Fulton of the host church chaired the meeting, and a new name was adopted—the General Association of Regular Baptist Churches (GARBC). With this the old Union ceased and a new organization began.

It is a matter of record that not one of the three Giants was there and not one was ever associated with the new organization. Shields left the American scene and the Union and devoted his great energies to his church, paper, and Toronto Baptist Seminary. He stayed out of organized Fundamentalism in this country until the later 1940's, when he joined Carl McIntire in the American Council of Christian Churches (ACCC). Riley stayed within the ranks of Northern Baptists until the last year of his life, 1947. Norris hammered away at the Southern Baptists, took over the Temple Baptist Church of Detroit, and pastored two churches from 1934 to 1947. Through his churches, his paper, *The Fundamentalist,* and his school at Fort Worth, he sent out young men who would man the churches of the World Baptist Fellowship and the Baptist Bible Fellowship. Fundamentalists need not look for their type again. They mounted the attack, they defended the faith, they fought valiantly, if not always politely, and they set a preaching standard that will not soon be forgotten. Their memory is one of sacred hallowedness to thousands who knew them and sat under their sound and stirring messages. Hundreds of preachers on the American scene owe much of their spiritual vision and vitality to their noble example. It will take years of historical research and study to determine their exact contributions and to evaluate them in their triumphs and tragedies, for they displayed a rare combination of both.

10
Orthodox Allies

Baptist militant Fundamentalists were not alone in their determined stand against Liberalism in any and all forms. Orthodox men of major denominations reaffirmed their statements of faith based on historic creeds and time-honored confessions and decried and denied the anti-Scriptural views of the Modernists and their friends. But many roadblocks faced these valiant orthodox men: roadblocks such as their church polity, which put final power in a few leaders at the top; their eccleciastical structure, which did not allow the common man or pastor any say in the appointment of faculty members in the schools; the widespread insensitivity of their membership to their exposés of liberal encroachments and to their words of warning that the Faith must be defended at all costs.

Many noble men who arose to defend the Faith attempted to take a middle-of-the-road position between the militant Fundamentalists and the Liberals—a road of sound Orthodoxy yet without commitment to the Fundamentalist positions on eschatology, worldliness, and willingness to fight openly for their spiritual freedom. The classic positions of Orthodoxy and their complete contrast with the tenets of the Modernists are found in J. G. Machen's *Christianity and Liberalism.* The Orthodox names shine brightly in the memory of the students and audiences who were privileged to hear these learned expositors of the Scriptures and their well-reasoned, apologetical defenses of the doctrines of the Bible. Their names should still be household words among all those who love the Lord sincerely and seek to honor His Word with truly genuine reverence. Among these were Francis L. Patton, Benjamin Breckenridge Warfield, Robert Dick Wilson, J. Gresham Machen, and Mark Matthews—all these of noble Presbyterian blood. Individuals with more preaching power appeared among the Methodists, such as H. C. Morrison, Sam Jones, Bob Shuler, Bob Jones, Sr., W. A. Candler, and J. Wesley Bready. Here a fact should be added. Several differences ought to be recognized even among these stalwart Fundamental Methodists. Bob Jones, Sr., was not only Fundamental in doctrine but militant in his stand and separatist, as shown later in his withdrawal from the Methodist Church and founding an independent school bearing his name. Shuler was both militant and Fundamental but not a separatist and stayed within the fold of Methodism, always hoping that the denomination would reverse its surrender to Liberalism. As time clearly revealed, his hope was without foundation. Morrison differed in that while Fundamental and a godly man he was not militant or separatist. Candler was a talented preacher and Methodist statesman but stayed with Methodism and started a school (Emory University) which very easily passed into the hands of Modernists. Bready was willing to assert, in writing and public lecturing, the grand old truths of John Wesley, but totally unwilling to pay the price as a militant separatist and leave the apostasy of his church. Among the Baptists were A. T. Robertson, L. R. Scarborough, A. K. DeBlois, John Marvin Dean, Nathan R. Wood, B. H. Carroll, J. W. Brougher, and R. H. Conwell. Among these Baptist men were many stalwart teachers and pastors but not one willing to separate from their denominations, North or South, no matter how firmly entrenched Liberalism had become. Wood, Dean, and DeBlois would issue the warnings in the classrooms and chapels but at the Convention refused to separate from friends and associates as the process of deterioration continued before their very eyes. They would decry the departure of their denomination but would not raise the flag of separate witness. Thus the outright sellout to radicalism increased and the unwillingness to make a stand or become separatists likewise increased. This infuriated the Fundamentalists as they saw their friends sit silently by and watch their beloved schools and agencies rush headlong into liberal hands. But the price of separatism, then as now, seemed too high to many Fundamental men, and their unwillingness to get involved in the fight delivered the denominational leadership and direction to the hands of Bible-denying ecclesiastics. We shall look at the Presbyterian witness to Orthodoxy a little more closely, for the conflict there was more pronounced and open.

It would be improper to omit the fact, often unrecognized or ignored, that many orthodox men saw themselves in a distinctly different line of history, doctrine, and church life from that of the Fundamentalists, and we ought to spell out the contrasts in sharpest detail. The orthodox men affirmed their ancestry from the Protestant Reformation and its widely known and studied confessions and creeds. Most Fundamentalists did not see the Reformation as their spiritual heritage, but rather appealed to the New Testament. Again, the Orthodox had great reverence for the Church Fathers and their syncretism of the many views of their day. The Fundamentalists agreed with Spurgeon's assertion that he liked the fathers but followed the grandfathers.Some orthodox men held to the spiritualizing or allegorical interpretation of the prophecies of the Bible; most Fundamentalists took a literalistic position. For instance, the typical orthodox man applied the covenants to the church, while most Fundamentalists held that these applied to Israel. Most of the Orthodox took an amillennial view of prophecy, holding that the thousand years of the Book of Revelation were not to be taken literally, while a typical Fundamentalist held that they must be taken literally. Many Orthodox did not hold to the imminent coming of the Lord to rapture the Church before the period of the Great Tribulation; Fundamentalist leaders preached the imminent coming. The Orthodox did not contend there were two comings, namely one *for* and one *with* the saints, separated by the seven-year period of the Great Tribulation; Fundamentalists, with few exceptions, did hold this view. The Orthodox put more emphasis in the pulpit on *teaching* sound truth, while the Fundamentalists stressed the *preaching* of the Bible. The Orthodox questioned invitations, evangelistic appeals, and kindred methods; the Fundamentalists used these and increased their devotion to them. The Orthodox would have held tenaciously to "The Fundamentals," so-called, published from 1910 through 1915 (some three million sets of booklets by the same name were sent to all preachers, missionaries, and Christian workers at a cost of about $200,000 by Lyman and Milton Stewart); Fundamentalist fellowships never used this as a complete statement of their faith, since literalism in prophecy, imminency of the Lord's Coming, and a premillennial stand are not found in them. These booklets should be hailed as the Fundamentals of Orthodoxy. Here a word of warning ought to be issued. The more popular use of the word "Fundamentalist" in this period included all those who defended the Bible against the attacks of Liberalism. In particular, the public press saw Machen, Warfield, and their colleagues as belonging to the Fundamentalist group because of their militant stand for sound doctrine. Since that time, the popular use of the word has continued so that even today those believing that Bible is the very Word of God and that it should be taught and defended as such are generally labeled "Fundamental."

A West Point of Orthodoxy was Princeton Seminary in Princeton, New Jersey, which was founded in 1812. It has boasted great names in theology such as A. A. Hodge, Charles Hodge, B. B. Warfield, and Francis L. Patton. This had been a line of honored and gifted theological writers. The story of how Princeton went down has been told factually and forthrightly, although, understandably, there were tears shed as the tragedy unfolded.[1] One stalwart of Orthodoxy, C. E. Macartney, wrote feelingly of Princeton Seminary with its grand and ancient tradition of a stalwart defense of the truth.[2] In 1913 Francis L. Patton resigned from the Seminary (he had been president of both the University and the Seminary) and nominated Woodrow Wilson, earlier of the history faculty, as president of the University. From this position he went on to become Governor of New Jersey in 1910 and President of the United States in 1912. Patton has left a series of lectures on Fundamental Christianity, stating clearly, as was his style, the sound doctrines of Orthodox Presbyterianism. Macartney thought most highly of Patton, who "could rise to greater heights than any preacher I have ever heard."[3] Yet Patton's name is hardly ever mentioned in Presbyterian writings and gatherings. His closing remark to every class was to "pray without ceasing and shave every day."[4]

Macartney was pastor at Paterson, New Jersey, from 1905 to 1913 and then went to Arch Street Presbyterian in Philadelphia. When Fosdick preached against Fundamentalism in 1922, Macartney stated, "It was the first time I had ever seen or heard the word Fundamentalist used in a religious significance."[5] It was "a word tossed about with a great deal of scorn or contempt . . . . the only difference between the Fundamental and evangelical believers . . . [is that] the Fundamentalists hold to a premillennial and imminent coming of Christ."[6] For this he was abused by letters and noted that "so-called Liberals and Modernists did not live up to their vaunted reputation and their claim of sweetness and light."[7] But they have seldom done this. Also standing in the front line of the Presbyterian battle were Machen, Allis, and Wilson. The major highlights of the engineering of this tragedy must be related here, as well as how

---

[1] The full story is told in Rian, op. cit.
[2] C. E. Macartney, *The Making of a Minister* (Great Neck, N.Y.: Channel, 1961)
[3] Ibid., p. 126.
[4] Ibid.
[5] Ibid., p. 184.
[6] Ibid., p. 185.
[7] Ibid., p. 186.

valiant men fought to preserve the grand old Princeton of Hodge and Warfield.

In 1903 the Westminster Confession was altered, and this was the climax of a move which had started as early as 1889, when agitation within the Northern Presbyterian Church forced the naming of a committee to make a report. Such was the first step, though an unnoticed one, toward the toleration of apostasy. Orthodox champions were able to stave off changes then, but a threat was growing. In 1893 C. A. Briggs was suspended from the Presbyterian ministry because of his liberal views of the fallibility of the Scriptures, the sanctification of the soul after death, and the central place of reason and the church in one's salvation. Orthodoxy had enough able spokesmen to flush out a man like Briggs in 1893; today, the views of Briggs are taught at Presbyterian schools.

But in 1903 the Liberals won a victory, for a committee of fifteen was named to recommend changes, and hard-line Calvinism was toned down. In this we see a contrast with Fundamentalism, which had never made Calvinism a test of one's faith or fellowship. The staunch among the Presbyterians, namely the Orthodox, held to the limited atonement of Christ, and this was most seriously rejected by Fundamentalists then and has been since. But the New Theology among Presbyterians came in through the door of a watered-down Calvinism, the system which had been the backbone of this historic denomination. There was a principle at the center of the situation, namely the right of Presbyterians to attack their standards of Faith; whether we agree with those standards or not is beside the vital issue.

Three other things marked the downfall of Orthodoxy within Northern Presbyterianism. One was the naming of J. Ross Stevenson of Baltimore as president of Princeton Seminary in 1914 to succeed a man who had been a Gibraltar of Presbyterian Orthodoxy, Francis L. Patton. Stevenson, a Conservative himself, held to the policy that Princeton should reflect the views of its constituency, keeping up with present-day Presbyterianism, which meant, in simplest terms, modernizing to suit the variety of Presbyterian views. This was disastrous, as future events proved, but the storm flags were not raised then. Presbyterians have regularly had peculiar trouble recognizing storm signals. Within Presbyterianism it has been blandly assumed that any man taking his ordination vows would honor them and uphold the standards of faith and practice of this highly-honored branch of Protestantism. But one central fact has escaped this great group of ministers and elders, and that is that schools, colleges, seminaries, and preachers change, even departing from the Faith and giving heed to seducing spirits (I Tim. 4:1). Even now, great numbers of Presbyterian men in pulpit and pew refuse to face the fact that their brethren, if such many are, have departed; and a fact of history is that they do not return. Brazenly, but often with deepest religious sincerity, these have refused to identify the offenders as false teachers and banish them, as the Bible commands.

The second occurrence in this theological tragedy was the Auburn Affirmation of 1923, when 1,300 ministers, out of a total of 10,000, signed a statement saying that the General Assembly was wrong in 1910 when it required all candidates for ordination to hold to the five doctrines: the virgin birth, inspiration of Scripture, vicarious death of Christ, bodily resurrection, and the miracles. On these five points the infamous Auburn document held that:

(1) no clear statement on inerrancy of Scripture is necessary.
(2) the virgin birth was a theory of the incarnation.
(3) the vicarious aspect of the atonement is also one theory.
(4) the resurrection was not necessarily a bodily one.
(5) miracles were the use of means in works.

Then the Fosdick issue brought the growing trends within Presbyterianism to the surface. Although an ordained Baptist, Harry Emerson Fosdick was supplying the pulpit at First Presbyterian Church in New York City. On May 21, 1922, he preached, attacking Fundamentalism and saying it would not win against Liberalism. It was an attack, not only on Fundamentalism but on old-line Orthodoxy. Both Fundamentalists and Orthodox were anathema to broad-minded Liberals such as Fosdick, and throughout the 1920's the two groups would be attacked as one group because of their unwillingness to adopt the new views, the new theology, and the results of modern science. A layman in the First Presbyterian Church in New York, Mr. Ivy Lee, took it upon himself to have the sermon published, and conservatives reacted quickly and decisively. One of these was the popular Presbyterian pastor, Clarence Macartney, of Philadelphia. He led the Presbytery of Philadelphia into making overtures to the Presbytery of New York to see that the preaching of the First Church was brought into line with standard Presbyterian doctrines. The next year Fosdick lectured at Yale and openly supported Higher Criticism, the very movement which had triggered the Fundamentalist uprising in the 1870's. At the meeting of the General Assembly of the Church, held that year in Indianapolis, the conservative-backed candidate, William Jennings Bryan, was defeated for moderator by a liberal-backed man, C. F. Wishart. It was at this same Assembly that the infamous Auburn Affirmation was tabled, and this became for the Liberals a typical piece of strategy, to stall for time. A tragedy of tragedies then ensued—the conservatives did not protest! With this silence in the name of church unity, all hope for stopping the liberal toboggan slide was gone, and another opportunity would never arise for this once strong, national, Orthodox church. An observation at this point is in order. In this type of dilemma, many Baptists would have started a fight, charging doggedly and valiantly, screaming that silence was cowardice, pleading for men to rise and stand and die for the faith. But Presbyterians, Congregationalists, and Methodists yielded to the temptation to remain silent in the interest of denominational harmony, peace, and progress. In fact, Protestantism of the old-line heritage stood by while the Liberals in the name of love, unity, gentlemanly conduct, and understanding captured the leadership posts, the offices, the schools, the seminaries, and publishing houses. Many Baptists fought with a vitriol and language which raised questions, but at least they fought. With this development in historic Presbyterianism, Orthodoxy passed into the hands of small splinter groups.

Another item in the sad story of the downfall of Presbyterianism was the exodus of Machen, Wilson, and others from the Princeton faculty in 1929 to organize Westminster Seminary in Philadelphia. Although only a small group of fifty students followed, the new school held rigidly to the orthodoxy of the Presbyterian heritage. Machen headed the school and gave the opening address in Witherspoon Hall in Philadelphia on September 25, 1929, on the Westminster Plan and Purpose.[8] The new school was dedicated to the Lord with the Bible at its core. Original languages were to be studied to know the Scriptures, the great Reformation doctrine of the perspicuity of Scripture was to be upheld, Biblical theology was to be taught, and the system of the Reformed Faith was to be taught. He contended that Princeton had been lost to the evangelical cause and that its departure without more uproar was due to the fact that Presbyterian people were too contented and too confident in material resources and that many would not come to his side because they feared the machinery of the church. With the founding of Westminster, according to Machen, Princeton Seminary was dead but the noble Princeton tradition remained alive. However, Westminster was still under Presbyterian auspices and had the support of such church stalwarts Macartney and Mark Matthews of the First Church in Seattle, the largest Presbyterian Church in the world.[9] Thus the new school could counteract the influence of Princeton and of McCormick Seminary in Chicago, which had departed from the faith long before Princeton. This situation might have continued, but in 1933 Machen, Charles Woodbridge, and others led in the formation of the Independent Board of Presbyterian

[8]It was published in full in the Oct. 10, 1929 issue of *The Presbyterian.*
[9]E. P. Giboney and Agnes M. Potter, *The Life of Mark Matthews* (Grand Rapids: Eerdmans, 1948).

Foreign Missions. At this new venture Macartney, Matthews, and many other men withdrew their support of the Machen-led dissent. Woodbridge served as the first secretary of the Independent Board. One of its major figures in later years was J. Gordon Holdcroft, scholarly Presbyterian missionary for many years in Korea and for thirty years the staunch hard-working secretary of the Board. He died in 1972 in his ninety-fifth year.

Machen had evidence of Modernism within the Presbyterian Board, and in 1933 he presented this evidence to the Presbytery of New Brunswick. He revealed that modernistic, even unitarian, literature had been recommended, such as *The Way of Discovery* by Winfred Kirkland, which was used in Riverside Church in New York where Fosdick was pastor. It denied the essential deity of the Lord Jesus Christ and yet was approved by the Presbyterian Board. Another heretical book recommended was *The Never Failing Light* by James H. Franklin. Machen referred to the cooperation of the Board with the National Council of India, which had published a pamphlet denying the inerrancy of the Gospels. In addition, the board had cooperated with the Formosa Christian College in India, which had twenty-nine non-Christians on its faculty, with only thirteen Christians. Again in this same report Machen listed Liberals who had been sent out by the Board, naming A. T. Roy, R. T. Fitch, J. F. Davenport, C. H. Hazlett, P. R. Abbot, M. Allen, L. Bently, R. H. Brown, W. G. Greenslade, G. F. Hood, W. C. Kerr, and G. H. Scherer. Eight of these had signed the heretical Auburn Affirmation of 1923. There were two known Liberals on the Board itself, namely, A. E. Marling and J. M. Speers.

Now the full power of the Church descended on the heads of orthodox men who supported the Independent Board, with charges brought against them, not on the issue of doctrine but on that all-important issue of obeying the church whether or not it obeyed God. Machen's trial was called by a Unitarian writer "the strangest of all church trials" because it involved a "rebel against heresy."[10] The article went on to say the following about the trial of Machen:

> All of the controversy has centered in his theological stand which is fundamental and conservative . . . . there is no question it is a battle of beliefs . . . . his accusers are the ones who should be on trial . . . . in Dr. Machen is centered all the spiritual and intellectual opposition to the heresies within the Presbyterian church . . . . in any case Dr. Machen will not be obedient to the General Assembly and dissolve his new board . . . . to obey God rather than man is an authentic principle as old as the Apostle Paul. It looks to the unprejudiced observer who agrees that truth comes first like a simple case in which Dr. Machen is right . . . . what he has done, according to all the evidence is not enough to bring upon

---

[10]Albert Dieffenbach, *Boston Evening Transcript*, April 6, 1935, p. 5.

him lasting cruel judgment. That would be shameful. . . . one doubts that these elements of Fundamentalism and modernism can ever come together. They have almost nothing intellectual in common. No matter what may be said in slovenly contempt about doctrines—that they do not count—the fact is that they are the only things at last that do count.[11]

Several, including Machen, McIntire, and Woodbridge, were charged and "unfrocked" (their ordination removed), but they had already organized the Orthodox Presbyterian Church, a very small church then and a small one today. It soon divided with McIntire, A. A. MacRae, and J. O. Buswell forming the Bible Presbyterian Church and organizing a new school, Faith Theological Seminary in Philadelphia. At Cape May, New Jersey, McIntire directed a college and the Christian Admiral Hotel for Bible Conference purposes. The college (Shelton) was moved to Florida property on Cape Canaveral, opening there in the fall of 1971. Westminster has continued its solid Orthodox position with such scholars as Cornelius Van Til, E. J. Young, and John Murray. The Bible Presbyterian group has also had its sorrows with several men of the Faith faculty—among them Laird Harris and J. O. Buswell—leaving to organize Covenant College and Seminary in St. Louis; their college division is now located on Lookout Mountain at Chattanooga, Tennessee. The Covenant group has since joined with another small group to form the Reformed Presbyterian Church, Evangelical Synod.

It might be helpful to students of this Orthodox-Modernist conflict to summarize the relation of this struggle to the Fundamentalist-Modernist struggle. Perhaps a listing would clarify the situation.

(1) Many Orthodox scholars did not join the Fundamentalist organizations of the hour: the Baptist Bible Union and the World's Christian Fundamentals Association. No attempt was ever made to organize with Riley, Norris, or Shields.

(2) The Orthodox supplied many outstanding texts for the use of the Fundamentalists, particularly Machen with his masterful works on *The Virgin Birth, The Religion of Paul,* and *Christianity and Liberalism.* No student of this time of struggle should be without these great definitive studies. The Fundamentalists recognized these as truly outstanding, irrefutable, and scholarly, while still sound in the truth.

(3) Orthodox men failed to command the following of large churches and conduct rallies with thousands inspired to follow their lead in joining the battle and fighting the issues to a finish. Norris, Shields, Riley, Van Osdel, and Straton were pastors with large national followings. Machen, Wilson, and Warfield were men of the study and the classroom, and it was simply a fact of life that pastors and elders would determine the issue at the great conclaves.

(4) There was an open sore between the two, the issue of eschatology. Most Orthodox were amillennial, although many who left in the

[11]Ibid.

1936 debacle were premillennial. The Fundamentalists were liter-
alists in prophecy, which made them mildly dispensational and
therefore uninterested in covenant theology. After all, covenant
theology taught that children of Christians were children of the
covenant, and most Fundamentalists questioned this. Fundamentalists held to the imminency of the Lord's coming for His Church,
while the Orthodox did not insist on it.

(5)   The Orthodox taught their students most carefully in the original
languages and the fine points of Reformed Theology. The Fundamentalists did not follow suit here but taught men how to preach,
organize soulwinning campaigns, visit from house to house, and
build large Sunday Schools. It would be interesting to compare two
men such as Machen and Norris. We see Norris with tents, tabernacles, and crowds thronging to hear his attacks on citizens and
religious greats and weeping as hundreds went forward to make
decisions as invitations continued to render results. Then we look
at Machen, scholarly, careful in debate, and most precise in theological expression. It would be interesting to imagine Norris in
Princeton and Machen in First Baptist in Fort Worth.

(6)   Obvious differences arose on matters of personal separation and
ecclesiastical polity. Machen tried against great odds to save the
General Assembly and the Northern Presbyterian Church. Norris
was out to split the Southern Baptists and expose their heretics
as long as he lived. Machen would not call men names but debated
principles on the highest level of accepted Presbyterian custom.
The Fundamentalists engaged in name-calling (e.g. Straton in New
York, who tagged Fosdick as a bootleg Baptist and a Presbyterian
outlaw). Norris paid his respects to Louie D. Newton by calling him
the modern Jehoshaphat. Shields called the Cardinal of Montreal
an unprincipled hypocrite. The enemies of Norris hated and detest-
ed his name while Machen was respected, even by those who led
the church into out-and-out apostasy. Machen left a few churches
and small ones at that, while Norris has left something like 2,500
churches who owe much to his inspiration and his preaching. Machen upheld the cardinal tenets of Reformed Faith in positive,
polished fashion; Norris carried the broad axe, warring on several
fronts, digging out "religious rats" everywhere, castigating and
breathing fire where compromise was even suspected—truly he was
the Texas Tornado. The biographer of Machen wrote that "judged
by various criteria adopted by friend and foe, he was not a fundamentalist at all. His standards of scholarship, his distaste for brief
creeds, his rejection of chiliasm (millennial doctrines), the absence
of pietism from his makeup, and in brief his sense of commitment
to the historic Calvinism of the Westminster Confession of Faith
disqualified him from being classified precisely as a Fundamentalist. And he never thought of himself as a fundamentalist; indeed
he disliked the term."[12] Machen himself dictated this appraisal of
his position by Stonehouse by writing that "the term fundamental-

[12]Ned B. Stonehouse, *J. Gresham Machen: A Biographical Memoir* (Grand
Rapids: Eerdmans, 1955), p. 337.

ism is distasteful to the present writer . . . . I regret being called a fundamentalist . . . but in the presence of the great common foe, I have little time to be attacking my brethren who stand with me in the defense of the Word of God."[13]

[13]Ibid., pp. 337-38.

RECONSTRUCTION, REVIVAL, AND RETREAT
1935-1973

Introduction

In this period Fundamentalism, like ancient Israel, has had many sorrows. The Prima Donnas passed from the scene but not before their empires had crumbled badly and split. The traditional centers of the movement have been under a constant barrage of pressures, both secular and religious, and change and decay have marked the history. New and vigorous defenses of the historic Faith have arisen only in their turn to face unexpected attacks and erosive tendencies which have undermined their testimonies.

Fundamentalism was forced to face a life-and-death struggle for survival. Ancient heresies continued to compete for the minds of the masses and—through clever usage of the printed page, radio, and television—to win over a lion's share of the populace. A new enemy appeared within its own ranks, namely, New Evangelicalism, which eroded Fundamentalist centers of strength to such a degree as to make the student of our time ask seriously whether historic Fundamentalism would survive. Schools, seminaries, mission boards, and publishing houses have capitulated to the deceptions and enormous pressures of New Evangelicalism.

Yet another fact was forced upon the mind of thoughtful Fundamentalists. The second period of their history saw them lose completely their voice of protest within the great denominations. It is true that many Fundamental men stayed within their own groups, hoping for better days, hoping to slow down the apostasy by letting their testimonies count both at headquarters and at home, where they witnessed in their churches. This could not fail to bring a feeling of spiritual nausea to hard-line Fundamentalists, who felt that these men remained within the apostasy for reasons of finances, status, advancement, and a false sense of Christian charity. They saw that this questionable middle-of-the-roadism was leading thousands of earnest Christians to believe that all was well in the religious world and to regard separating Fundamentalists as rancorous people, envious of good men, unstable, and irresponsible. In this way, churches have been sold into the hands of Liberals, neutralists, and compromisers.

Fundamental Baptists have been called upon to play a singular role in this generation. They could move within denominational boundaries and raise an outcry or create a movement to try some housecleaning. No housecleaning has taken place, but the size of the threat has produced many new fellowships and associations. Their answer to their predicament has been manifested in the enthusiasm and excitement of starting new churches and schools. Loyalties to religious bodies, schools, and even friends have had to take second place to the convictions found in the Scriptures. Many faltered under the pressures but many stayed with the battle, even though scarred and forsaken. Out of the Baptist jungle thus created have come such Fundamental groups as the General Association of Regular Baptists, Orthodox Baptists, the American Baptist Association, New Testament Baptists, Baptist Bible Fellowship, the World Baptist Fellowship, the Southwide Baptist Fellowship, and an unlisted number of state and interstate fellowships, besides a host of independent Baptist churches without any solid connections with any group.

Fundamental schools have played a very large part in this era. The movement owes an immeasurable debt to the Bible School movement, for their leaders and teachers have been willing to work and serve at great sacrifice, living out their lives in devoted service to the Lord. Their saga is a noble story which has not yet been told. Most Fundamental pastors and leaders have been affected directly or indirectly by the Bible School movement. It is a matter of keen regret that too many Bible schools have been started without proper staffing and equipment. That accreditation has come in some form by the AABC is a mark of achievement, although at the present time the movement is badly tarnished by the inroads of New Evangelicalism. The future of the Bible School movement is uncertain because of its failure to assess present drifts and trends and to make a stand against the dangers and erosions all around it.

Seminaries have been established in the last forty years to help stem the mighty tides of Liberalism. Many, while having strongly Fundamental men connected with them, have been content with an Orthodox, or even Conservative, stance and have made their peace with denominational leaders and with the present movements of compromise. Some supposedly Fundamentalist institutions have been adamant in holding to dispensationalism but backward in taking a Fundamentalist stand in the present confusion of compromises and drifts. Other seminaries have arisen to take a militant stand on controversial issues and in doing so have stayed true to their Fundamentalist heritage. In these schools there has been an honest attempt to expose the compromise with Liberalism and New Evangelicalism that has swept other institutions from the ranks of Fundamentalism. The fact that these schools have survived and grown without any interest in accreditation shows their vitality.

The empires of Norris, Riley, and Shields have split, although the split in Riley's empire did not come until after his death. But the lives of the Giants did have one great effect. Hundreds of young men had an opportunity to hear these pulpit masters and to forge in their minds an exalted ideal of the nature and grandeur of great preaching. All three were uniquely Churchills of the platform and made thrones out of their pulpits. They were able to inspire young men, for they had been inspired by great rallies, great congregations, and feverish debates. All had gone through tempestuous times in their own denominations. Norris hammered away at fellow Baptists with many listening to him but few following him into a new movement. His empire split, with many leaving to organize the Baptist Bible Fellowship and a new school at Springfield, Missouri. First Baptist in Fort Worth survived, but in weakened form, and Norris' group, the World Baptist Fellowship, continued, although its dramatic days of great battles and victories were past with the passing of the Preachers' Preacher. Shields saw his beloved Toronto Baptist Seminary torn asunder twice by serious dissension and reduced to a small fraction of its size and influence. Jarvis Street continued its defense of the truth but without the aura of his name.

The days of the great battles were over. There would be some skirmishing within Northern Baptist life, some isolated protests among Southern Baptists, and some resolute men within Southern Presbyterianism who would defend their Orthodoxy and delay their denomination's final surrender to Liberalism. Their efforts were praiseworthy but doomed to failure. The swing of the churches was to apostasy and ecumenicalism. Some individuals within the denominations still maintain their doctrinal ideas, but their schools, boards, and publishing centers have crossed the Rubicon, and there will be no re-crossing. The grand exodus out of sound doctrine is about complete and the years ahead look so much like the Wilderness Years.

Presbyterians have suffered greatly in this period. Many

stalwarts of the Reformed faith have left comfortable positions and homes to found such groups as the Orthodox Presbyterian Church, the Bible Presbyterian Church, and the Reformed Presbyterian Church, Evangelical Synod. Others of Presbyterian and Congregational backgrounds have left their old moorings to form Bible Churches, many of them joining the Independent Fundamental Churches of America (IFCA). This group has continued the Presbyterian form of church polity but with a doctrinal dispensationalism. Weak in evangelism, the movement has grown slowly. Of late, New Evangelicalism has entered the ranks and posed the likelihood of present and future dissension. Many Presbyterians of old-line churches have left simple Orthodoxy to take a more Fundamentalist position in doctrinal details, among them such leaders as Carl McIntire, Charles J. Woodbridge, and A. A. MacRae.

Individual Methodists stood by and watched their great testimony go farther and farther down the road of Liberalism. Most were willing to let the churches follow the officials and made few attempts to test the preaching and literature by Biblical standards. But there were a few brave souls in high places who let their voices be heard, and they did what they could to slow down the pace of spiritual decline. Their efforts did not keep the Methodist Church from becoming Modernist, as it is at the present time, but they fought as long as they could.

Among the protesters were Henry C. Morrison, Bob Shuler, Sr., and Bob Jones, Sr. They faced an impossible problem, for their church had lost its schools, and its authority rested in a College of Bishops. Jones had a long career in evangelism and capped it with the building of a school that was, and is, a fortress of Fundamentalism—Bob Jones University in Greenville, South Carolina. Because it was non-denominational in character, it was free to expose heresies and dangers as well, free to teach the truth, and free to fight error. It has created a worldwide image of militant Fundamentalism, although few schools have been so misrepresented and maligned. Shuler was willing to continue his effective ministry at Trinity Methodist in Los Angeles, constantly raising his voice against the swift deterioration in his paper, *The Methodist Challenge,* but Methodists did not heed his challenges. Morrison did a valiant work at Asbury College in keeping it close to the thinking and warmhearted evangelism of John Wesley himself; thereby, he sought to provide a place of training and spiritual exhilaration for Methodists who wanted the truth. That the spiritual image of Asbury has lessened since his days is noticeable, although its alumni, as alumni of most schools, remain unwilling to admit its defections and put their Scriptural convictions first. A host of

Methodist pastors in smaller areas of ministry believed and still believe what Asbury, Wesley, and Morrison held, but their hands are tied, their voices are being stilled, and their testimonies slowly dying.

Many of the grandsons of Methodism have gone to their rewards, and the new ministerial crop has been deeply indoctrinated with New Theology, the Ecumenical Movement, civil rights agitations, and humanitarianism. Thus, the social gospel, human betterment, and cooperation with Rome have become the common diet of Methodist pulpits. Their schools have done a hatchet job on the faith · of Wesley and led a great denomination to the graveyard of social salvation and do-goodism of all kinds. The main centers of the sellout are Boston University, Garrett Biblical Institute, Vanderbilt, Duke Divinity Shool, and the Candler School of Theology of Emory University. Some few have left the grand old Methodist Church and departed for Bible churches or small continuing Methodist fellowships. This has been a trickle indeed; but, though a small line of testimony, it has been a sound one.

In the period after World War II new movements invaded the scene of American Fundamentalism. One was the coming, in force, of the English Keswick movement under such men as W. Ian Thomas, Alan Redpath, and Stephen Olford. This movement started a century ago in the beautiful Lakes region of central England, but has had little impact on American churches till recently. Now Deeper Life conferences stressing and preaching the victorious life and the Lordship of Christ have been widely accepted. The movement has been very influential in such places as Columbia Bible College in Columbia, South Carolina, Moody Church in Chicago, Calvary Baptist Church in New York, and Prairie Bible Institute in Three Hills, Alberta, Canada. Many pastors and churches have resorted to this special brand of spiritual uplift, which offers unusual guidance in the life of the individual Christian. It is experience-centered, and that has a sparkling appeal to emotion hunters and frustrated believers. It is a "honey and sugar" type of sanctification and as such has wide glamor in a day of spiritual breakdowns and tensions.

Fundamentalists found another problem besetting them with increasing aggravation and embarrassment. Although forced to establish new fellowships, they managed to maintain their separate identity as well as continuing to defend the Faith. They had lost great battles but they had not lost their faith. But in the area of education they underwent serious tensions of soul and mind. Many Fundamentalists still went to accredited schools and highly rated universities for their training, but many more stayed away from schools altogether because it was charged that education in general had produced Liberals and ruined young Christians. Others attended regularly accredited colleges and then went on to evangelical seminaries for Bible studies. Many more contented themselves with attending Bible schools and completed their preparation by reading the sermons of others. It was an honest attempt to fill the vacuum without any serious attempt to set patterns or high academic goals. The number of highly qualified teachers and administrators fell far short of the number of schools opened. The Bible schools, in particular, had a large proportion of unqualified faculty members. Seminaries did somewhat better, for their status attracted and held better prepared scholars. The Christian liberal arts colleges pushed hard for well-trained teachers in order to achieve accreditation standards. But in the process they defected almost completely to New Evangelicalism and produced an ever-growing stream of recruits for compromise, middle-of-the-roadism, and new-evangelical organizations.

As if there were not enough headaches for Fundamentalists to endure, a new and powerful movement began in the 1940's. It was carefully defined in the 1950's and then became a national menace in the 1960's, even spilling over onto the mission fields. This was New Evangelicalism, a term coined by Harold John Ockenga of Park Street Church in Boston, Massachusetts—for a time president of Fuller Seminary, and now president of Gordon College and Gordon-Conwell Divinity School in Wenham, Massachusetts. Like a mighty steamroller this new mood or attitude, not basically a theology, has permeated colleges, Bible schools, seminaries, mission boards, youth ministries, and publication companies. Among its best-known advocates and leaders are Campus Crusade, Wheaton College, *Christianity Today,* the National Association of Evangelicals, *Christian Life,* Billy Graham, and Carl F. H. Henry. The movement has spread a permissive attitude on personal and ecclesiastical separation, a new interest in social issues, an openness to worldly standards, and a new toleration of the Ecumenical Movement.

New Evangelicalism has carried on a constant attack on anything Fundamentalist; at times the vehemence of this attack would give the strong impression that New Evangelicals consider only one sin to be serious, namely, being a Fundamentalist. Always New Evangelicals think it proper to be charitable to the left-wingers, the Romanists, the Liberals, and the opponents of Fundamentalists; this charity has not been extended to men of God who have fought the battles of the Faith, nor to the schools that will not bow the knee to modern Baals. In this they have followed their "Liberal" friends who *teach* charity but seldom *exercise* it toward others who disagree with them. Old-line Fundamental establishments such as Conservative Baptists, GARB, Houghton College, Gordon College, and IFCA, as well as many Bible schools, have been invaded by New Evangelicalism. Seriously affected by this philosophy, though not officially endorsing it, are such schools as Moody Bible Institute, Dallas Seminary, Biola College, Trinity College and Seminary, Western Baptist Seminary, and Covenant College. Helping in the spread of this evangelical virus have been the periodicals *Christianity Today* and *Christian Life,* and the program of the mission fields called "Evangelism-in-Depth."

In this period the minds of more and more Americans have turned from things spiritual to religious superficialities, to the making of more and more money, and to self-indulgence through amusements, entertainment, drinking, and drugs. The essence of Fundamentalism is seemingly lost in the maze of modern life and habits. A hardness of attitude toward eternal verities has been noticeable since the second World War. Creature comforts and preparations for the building of the one-world church. He is grieved taken the place of an expectancy of the return of the Lord and His Kingdom. Our problems at home and abroad have mounted, upsetting Americans, both within the church and without. The American is immersed in a mountain of problems in simply trying to make sense out of the grand confusions in our cities, the United Nations, international relations, and in the mounting crimes and crises in every part of the American economy. The rising tides of communism and socialism and the increasing loss of personal liberties have annoyed Bible believers. But the average American has accepted them nonchalantly, assuring himself that none of these things could endanger his country and his personal stake in it. Certainly he will not believe that the divine judgment of Hell preached by the Fundamentalist has any meaning or certainty. The latter is usually ignored; if noticed, he is pitied as one who has sold his soul to pessimism and fatalism, and who is willing to live outside the mainstream of religious life.

The Fundamentalist must reckon with the growing worldwide movement known as the Ecumenical Movement, with its preparations for the building of the one world church. He is grieved that hordes are deceived by this movement, though in other ways they are intelligent, responsible people. His conscience is not only upset but also angered by the success of the deceivers and the peddlers of delusion.

In the area of evangelism the influence of New Evangelicalism has been especially deadly. So vital has been the role of mass and church evangelism in the Fundamentalist movement that its importance cannot be overstated. "It takes evangelistic unction to make orthodoxy function," declared the late Dr. Bob Jones, Sr., a key figure in five decades of American evangelism. At the same time, evangelism uncontrolled, uncircumscribed by the Word of God, can be, and has been, as damaging to the cause of the Lord Jesus Christ as the absence of evangelism. Today's new-evangelical "souls at any cost" philosophy has brought enfeebling alliances to the Church through ecumenical or compromise evangelism. These alliances, the product of spiritually adulterous unions, have so entangled Bible Christianity with those who preach another gospel that the clear line of separation between belief and unbelief, truth and error, righteousness and unrighteousness, has been all but erased. Through this terrible process, the church of Antichrist has been promoted and enlarged, and the Church of the Lord Jesus Christ has been disarrayed and confused and been made indistinguishable and powerless.

Scriptural mass evangelism, so effective in the 1920's and 1930's in America is now all but a thing of the past. The "killing force" in modern evangelism is the spirit of inclusivism as most notably practiced by Billy Graham. Mass evangelism today is characterized by a hyper-promoted entertainment program designed to sell morality and "commitment to Christ." The changing of hearts through repentance and regeneration that produces changed communities is virtually non-existent. In America crowds of great size can no longer be gathered in evangelistic efforts without the magnetism of a "super personality" and the endorsement of ministerial alliances. Preaching on vital Biblical issues is moderated for the sake of maintaining unity. "Inquirers" are channeled to the sponsoring churches, irrespective of their soundness of belief, and the proselytizing of these inquirers by the doctrinally sound participating churches is usually an exercise in futility. When the splash of the gigantic crusade has passed and the excitement of "throng-mania" is over, the respondents settle back into their normal lives of godlessness, unaffected in a permanent way by their "decision."

Although mass evangelism for the most part has been despoiled by Graham and other New Evangelicals, who believe that any methods, any alliances, are holy so long as the holy end of winning lost people is achieved, at the same time local church evangelism continues to flourish. It would seem that the blessing of God now rests upon church-wide evangelistic efforts rather than upon inter-church efforts. Harvest of souls are being reaped, with the churches left strengthened and their members stirred to a sense of their personal responsibility in evangelizing the lost. A large host of uncompromising evangelists, who will go only to separated Fundamental churches, are being greatly used of God through their faithful preaching of His Word.

The Fundamentalists have experienced some successes even in

the midst of a decaying society, marked by more compromises in things religious. A notable one was the building of three large Fundamental schools during this period, schools that promise even greater growth. Bob Jones University in Greenville, South Carolina, with a 180-acre campus worth nearly forty million dollars, enrolled some 4,800 students during the 1972-1973 sessions. This great school is under the leadership of Bob Jones, Jr., as chancellor and Bob Jones, III, as president. Tennessee Temple Schools, of which Lee Roberson is the founder and president, has over 2,200 students. The last of these is Baptist Bible College in Springfield, Missouri, of which G. B. Vick is president, John W. Rawlings vice-president, and W. E. Dowell executive vice-president. Annually, these three schools enroll some 9,000 Christian young people for training. A list of other schools with an out-and-out Fundamentalist testimony would include Maranatha Baptist Bible College in Watertown, Wisconsin, where B. Myron Cedarholm is the president; Pillsbury Bible College in Owatonna, Minnesota, under R. V. Clearwaters; Baptist Bible College in Denver, Colorado, under B. B. Augsburger; and Baptist Midwestern College in Pontiac, Michigan, under Tom Malone.

Some ministries started as Fundamentalist but have veered toward new-evangelical associations and sympathies. Included among these would be Charles E. Fuller's Old-Fashioned Revival Hour and Percy Crawford's ministries among young people, such as King's College. Before his passing, Fuller publicly endorsed new-evangelical efforts such as the Berlin Congress, and Crawford turned against those who would not cooperate with Graham, avowing his distaste for strict Fundamentalists. The largest Gospel radio voice during the time was the Lutheran Hour under Walter A. Maier with over 1,200 stations carrying his pungent Christ-honoring messages.

Arising to offset the forces of the National Association of Evangelicals was the American Council of Christian Churches, led by Carl McIntire for most of its history. Others in its leadership have been R. T. Ketcham, R. F. Hamilton, D. L. Gorham, and L. G. Gordon. The NAE is the larger by far but does not hold the militant position of the ACCC and has become, increasingly, new-evangelical.

Finally, it must be noted that in this period, as in no other, Fundamentalism has been the object of the scorn, ridicule, and caricature of the religious wiseacre and the worldly scoffer. Great preaching centers in large cities have declined, some almost to the vanishing point. Today few American cities can boast of great preachers. More and more denominations have ignored or strangled Fundamentalist voices while pushing, with tremendous enthusiasm and success, programs to build the "Kingdom," cooperating more and more with the movements to build the great world church. Several liberal churchmen have caught the headlines and led the unsuspecting public farther into delusion and confusion. Among these liberal headliners have been such figures as Norman Vincent Peale, James A. Pike, Thomas T. J. Altizer, G. B. Oxnam, John A. Mackay, F. C. Fry, Bishop Sheen, and Preston Bradley. Equally prominent have been the radio voices of heresy and confusion, among them Herbert Armstrong, A. A. Allen, and Oral Roberts.

In addition, Americans in general have had to face new issues and troubles, and Fundamentalists in particular have had to face them too. Among the most aggravating ones are deeper involvements than ever in world crises, more social dissension at home, more divisions over civil rights, racism, slum clearance, crime in cities, and now the problems of ecology. The streets are becoming less and less safe, the business snarls more frequent, with more and more conflicting solutions offered by leaders in politics, business, and sociology. Crises in labor are more vexing and a strange sleep has fallen over the issues of communism and socialism in government. Colorless faces have arisen on the political level with no qualifications but ambition and youthful dash. The masses of the American people have developed a deep suspicion that there are few real solutions on the drawing boards of politicians. Public morality and decency are in a shambles with the road ahead vague and terrifying. Most of our cities are little better than a jungle right now. We spent billions to wage a war we seemed to have no desire to win and billions more to care for a sick society that shows no signs of getting well. The scene itself is one of doom and despair, but Bible-believers are looking for their Saviour to come, to judge, to make war, and then to reign for a thousand years of peace on this earth.

11
The Erosion of the Empires

The empires of Norris, Shields, and Riley continued until the deaths of their founders but began to crumble in their last years, splitting into several groups and becoming mere shadows of their former greatness.

Norris continued at First Baptist in Fort Worth until he passed from the earthly scene in 1952; several men showed some promise of being groomed to succeed him. These included the famous Scottish preacher, Jock Troup, who enjoyed Norris' favor for a short time, but never became pastor in Fort Worth as some had expected. Norris had a major part in the creation, indirectly, of new fellowships while detaching himself from national Fundamentalism in order to promote his work in Fort Worth. In 1934 he took over as pastor of Temple Baptist in Detroit and a year later led it out of the Northern Baptist Convention. He continued to pastor both churches for fourteen years, a man-killing job in itself considering the traveling involved.

In 1939 Norris started the Bible Baptist Institute at his Fort Worth church and later renamed it the Bible Baptist Seminary in order to get government help for veterans. His ministry at both churches and the seminary increased in the 1940's, but by the second half of that decade a restlessness on the part of younger men in both the Detroit church and the Fellowship raised the first major threat. As a result G. B. Vick, who had been superintendent at Detroit, became president of the seminary in 1948, but resigned in 1950 because he did not have a free hand. In the May 1950 meeting of the Fellowship, 119 pastors broke away from Norris and organized the Baptist Bible Fellowship and started the Baptist Bible College in Springfield,

Missouri. The details of this Baptist bloodbath are told, at least from the Fellowship's side, by Billy Vick Bartlett in his *A History of Baptist Separatism*. It was a division marked by strong rancor, vicious charges, and an aftermath of bitterness and personal hatreds.

In twenty years Baptist Bible College has grown to an enrollment of over two thousand students. Vick has headed the College for the entire period in addition to caring for his demanding duties as pastor of the large Temple Baptist in Detroit, now numbering over 14,000 members. Among those leaving to start the new Fellowship were John W. Rawlings, W. E. Dowell, Noel Smith, Art Wilson, and F. D. Donaldson. Some men continued with Norris such as Earl K. Oldham, R. D. Ingle, and Gerald Fleming. Norris' son, George L., had broken from his father some five years before the new Fellowship was started but later rejoined the World Baptist group, in which he has taken an active part in addition to his work as pastor of the Gideon Baptist Church in Fort Worth. First Baptist in Fort Worth called Homer Ritchie as pastor, and for a time the momentum continued from the Norris era and a new church building worth nearly two million dollars was built. But in the last ten years the situation has been rocked with serious disruptions, and the congregation and image of the church are small replicas of their former selves in Fundamentalism. The paper, *The Fundamentalist,* is still issued, but no longer is it read avidly around the world as it was when Norris made and wrote the news. Thus the empire of the Texas Tornado has seriously declined, although the methods he used in drawing crowds and building Sunday Schools are still used in upwards of three thousand churches across America.

The Shields dynasty did not fare as well as that of Norris. "T. T." did continue to exercise a strong ministry at Jarvis Street until his passing in 1955. He gave to his people a strong diet of Biblical principles and exposés of Romanism. He was the guiding spirit in the Canadian Protestant League, which still exists and still sounds a strong witness against the designs and threats of the Catholic Church in Canada. Shields' school, Toronto Baptist Seminary, continued, though small, taking a solid Orthodox stand, though amillennial. His paper, *The Gospel Witness,* had a large reading audience, especially among the preachers of the British Commonwealth. But a serious break came in the work.

W. Gordon Brown, a close associate of Shields in the church and the dean of the seminary, was dismissed in 1948 and took a majority of the students and organized Central Baptist Seminary in Toronto. Both Shields and Brown published their sides of the dispute in lengthy charges and countercharges. This airing of internal wrangles has frequently been a dubious Fundamentalist pastime, both unprincipled and slanted. It was a most upsetting disruption for Shields, for Central Baptist has become the unofficial school of the Fellowship of Evangelical Baptists, the largest evangelical group in the Dominion. Many in this association take a premillennial position while others take an amillennial stand. Both premillennialism and amillennialism are taught. Toronto Baptist Seminary was greatly weakened in numbers by the break. Later, another close associate of Shields, W. S. Whitcombe, severed his connections with Toronto Baptist as a professor. He now pastors in that city and teaches at Central Baptist. Toronto Baptist has never reclaimed its former strength although it has continued in the Shields tradition. H. C. Slade, his successor, has continued the Jarvis Street ministry in spite of the problems incident to a downtown church. But Jarvis Street is practically alone in Canada, and Slade has found his fellowship with McIntire and the International Council of Christian Churches. Many Baptist men who had known and greatly admired Shields have become Independents while others have joined the Fellowship of Evangelical Baptists. The *Gospel Witness* still publishes the sermons of Shields along with others.

The Riley empire's history almost defies accurate description, for many of the details are difficult to ascertain. "W. B." continued a strong and virile ministry at First Baptist in Minneapolis until 1943, when he resigned after forty-five years of service. His close friend and associate Robert L. Moyer was called to succeed him. All looked well for the church and Northwestern Schools, which by 1943 included a Bible School, College, and Seminary. Riley gave his last years to broadening support for his beloved institution. With Moyer at the helm of the church and teaching part-time, the future looked bright indeed. In the early 1940's Richard V. Clearwaters had come to the Fourth Baptist Church in Minneapolis and provided added support for Riley, for Clearwaters took a solid Baptist stand on both doctrine and practice. Later he became dean of the Seminary at Northwestern.

But a series of unexpected events brought the Riley colossus to the shambles it is in today. A key event was the death of Moyer in 1944—in every way a shock and a major setback. The church turned to an assistant, Curtis B. Akenson; for he had come up within the organization, and it was assumed he shared the total convictions of the movement. But he was not an Independent, and as a result First Baptist continued within the fold of the Northern Baptist Convention, now the American Baptist. The leadership position of the church in the state of Minnesota has steadily declined, and it has been shunned by Fundamentalists in the Northwest. Akenson has become a supporter of the Graham movement and New

Evangelicalism, which was just arising in Riley's last days. For president of his Schools, Riley turned to Billy Graham, whose name enhanced the reputation of the institution, and attendance shot up to over a thousand students. But a decline set in, due to a heavy debt, control of New Evangelicalism, and Graham's departure to enter evangelism.

In 1956 the seminary program was discontinued and was taken over by Clearwaters at Fourth Baptist. It continues today as Central Baptist Seminary of Minneapolis. The Bible school program was also phased out, with the hope of enlarging the offerings of the liberal arts college. But the Fundamentalists of the area were turning their money and students to a new school which opened in 1956, Pillsbury Baptist Bible College in Owatonna, Minnesota, controlled by the state convention under the leadership of Clearwaters. By 1968 this new school had grown to an enrollment of over 700 students under the dynamic leadership of Clearwaters, Monroe Parker, and B. Myron Cedarholm. Northwestern so decreased in attendance and support in spite of the aid of Akenson and Mrs. Riley that it was forced to close and sell the property to the state of Minnesota. It was reopened in the fall of 1972 at a new property five miles north of St. Paul, on a site bought from the Roman Catholics. William Berntsen, former business manager of Northwestern, is the main figure in this new venture. It has been assumed by Fundamentalists that it will draw its support from soft-core Conservative Baptists in the Midwest. If this dream is realized, then the Riley line of succession will continue; if not, that noble testimony will fade away. However, it will continue in the ministries and memories of hundreds of pastors, missionaries, and teachers who are convinced Fundamentalists because of the great pulpit ministry of William Bell Riley.

Many lessons are suggested by this decline of Fundamentalist empires. First of all, men of dominating personality and platform power do not gather strong men around them but rather exclude men of genuine potential as recognized and responsible successors. Another lesson is that they do not trust the right men but often put their faith in young men who operate on the basis of connections and not convictions. Gullibility at this point has been most noticeable. A great many men join a movement because of the glamour, scintilating leadership, and power in putting Liberals to flight; too often it has been a way to gain status. Perhaps it is naive to expect that every empire should survive the lifetime of its founder; perhaps his ministry was unique, built on rare qualities and magnetism. The exceptions to this have been very few. A harsh but likely observation is that few great men plan for their succession with proper care and needed safeguards. Several existing Fundamentalist institutions are under the guidance of men who evince little concern for the future. Especially is this true of Bible schools where second generation leaders are enamored with the clothes of office but have started, unwittingly, to sell the schools into compromise and weakness. For this reason alone, it is empty talk to speak of the average Bible school as Fundamentalist. While the fathers of Fundamentalism fought for their Faith, their children do little more than smile.

12
An Enemy Within: New Evangelicalism

No greater enemy to the separatist stand of historic Fundamentalism has emerged in the last twenty years than New Evangelicalism. The term was coined by Harold J. Ockenga in 1947 when he was pastor of Park Street Church in Boston, Massachusetts, and president of the newly established Fuller Seminary in Pasadena, California. He had been a leader in the creation of the NAE and had a strong Orthodox image among Christians, having been trained at Princeton and Westminster Seminary. Over the years he had had a good ministry at historic Park Street. He is now president of Gordon College and Divinity School in Wenham, Massachusetts.

For ten years few saw the importance of the new movement, most thinking it was simply a convenient label for the rising young intellectuals among the Fundamentalists. It was not seen as a serious defection from historic Fundamentalism; many thought of it as an upgrading and a refinement with more scholarly support and interest. It was felt that because Fuller Seminary bore the honored name of Fuller it must be sound, for Charles E. Fuller and his Old-Fashioned Revival Hour had remained true to Gospel preaching and Bible teaching. Such widely recognized scholars of evangelical stance as Wilbur M. Smith, Carl F. H. Henry, and Charles J. Woodbridge graced the faculty, and this seemed to ensure soundness. The scholastic attainments of such a faculty would give the Seminary excellent academic credentials, and the connection with Fuller would produce warmhearted evangelists and pastors. All looked promising indeed, and Fundamentalist eyes saw the Pasadena institution as a life-saving boost for the movement.

By 1957 the picture had changed. One certain proof of change was the press release issued by Ockenga on December 8 that defined accurately and clearly the differences between New Evangelicalism and Fundamentalism. One area was that of social issues and problems which Fundamentalists had avoided; he charged that "Fundamentalism had abdicated leadership and responsibility in the societal realm."[1] New Evangelicals, Ockenga asserted, would handle the social problems and include with personal salvation what he called "a social philosophy." He had just concluded a series of messages from his pulpit in commemoration of his twenty-first anniversary as pastor. He added that the new group would "not delve in personalities which embrace error." He further stated that the Christian should not be "obscurantist in scientific questions as to creation, the age of man, the universality of the flood, and other debatable Biblical questions."[2] It was the contention of the Boston pastor that intellectual questions should be answered within the framework of modern learning and that there should be liberty in minor areas. This meant that such matters as the Lord's imminent return, personal separation, and ecclesiastical separation must be accepted as minor matters. Of course, no Fundamentalist could accept these as minor or agree that Ockenga had the right to downgrade them. The New Evangelicals would be identified with the "Orthodox branch of the historic church . . . with the social emphasis infused."[3] At this time Ockenga made one point very clear, that the new-evangelical strategy must be one of infiltration and not separation. In addition, he named the new-evangelical forces as the NAE, Fuller Seminary, Billy Graham, and *Christianity Today*. He was proud of the new apologetic literature presenting this position, having in mind the works of Carl F. H. Henry, Edward J. Carnell, George Ladd, and himself. In 1960 Ockenga wrote:

> my personal concern as the originator of the New Evangelicalism has been to stir the interest of evangelical Christianity in meeting the societal problems through the content of Biblical Christianity. This is the tradition of Calvin, Luther, and Knox.[4]

Several books, booklets, and articles have appeared exposing the new movement, pointing out its poisons and pressures and clear distinctions from Fundamentalism. One often used is by Charles J.

[1]Harold J. Ockenga, official press release, Dec. 8, 1957, entitled "The New Evangelicalism," and published on the stationery of Park Street Church. This writer has a copy of the original release.
[2]Ibid.
[3]Ibid.
[4]*Bulletin of Wheaton College*, 37(Feb., 1960).

Woodbridge, a pastor, church historian, and former faculty member at Fuller; in fact, he was on the faculty when Ockenga gave his definitive statement and E. J. Carnell was elected president, showing the new direction for the Seminary. He left in protest and has been a major voice raised against its dangerous position. Woodbridge calls the new movement a "theological and moral compromise of the deadliest sort."[5] Such a threat is it that the sharpest language must be used to expose its threat and insidious danger. Therefore he wrote:

> New Evangelicalism advocates toleration of error. It is following the downward path of accommodation to error, cooperation with error, contamination by error, and ultimate capitulation to error.[6]

He indicts it as an unscriptural mood "both toward the Left and the Right in theology."[7] Its method is that of "Jesuit casuistry," that the end justifies the means. It is his conclusion that the new mood and method will be followed by a new theology.

William E. Ashbrook, for many years a faithful pastor in Columbus, Ohio, has applied a fact-gathering approach to the movement in his book, *The New Neutralism*. He lists the schools, mission boards, and youth groups that are the spokesmen for New Evangelicalism, along with prominent Christian leaders who lean to the movement, including such names as Donald Grey Barnhouse, Billy Graham, Paul Rees, Ockenga, Carnell, and Bill Bright. Schools named in the expose include Wheaton College, Gordon College, Fuller Seminary, along with such organizations as Campus Crusade, Young Life, Inter-Varsity, and Youth For Christ.[8] Also identified as New Evangelical are *Christian Life* magazine and the approaches of World Vision and Evangelism-In-Depth among the mission boards. Very approvingly, he quotes Spurgeon, who cut himself "clear of those who err from the faith and even from those who associate with them."[9] His was simply a clear-cut example of Biblical separation without a distinction between first or second degree separation. It is a matter of historical record that Spurgeon's successors at the Metropolitan Tabernacle took the opposite view and reunited with the mixed multitude of the Baptist Union of Great Britain. In the past years a new pastor, Peter Masters, has come to

---

[5]Charles J. Woodbridge, *The New Evangelicalism* (Greenville, S.C.: Bob Jones Univ. Press, 1969), Introduction.
[6]Ibid., p. 15.
[7]Ibid., p. 31.
[8]William E. Ashbrook, *The New Neutralism* (Columbus, Ohio: the author, 1966).
[9]Ibid., p. 43.

the Tabernacle, which he found in a very weak condition, and has led the church to separate from its church affiliation.

Two studies of the theology of New Evangelicals are available. One is by Robert Lightner of Dallas Seminary and the other by Millard Erickson of Wheaton College. The former is not a friend to the movement, while the latter approves of most of it. Lightner starts with the basic concepts of Biblical authority and inerrancy, and progresses through a theological analysis of New Evangelicalism. His work is weak in equating Fundamentalism with the Orthodoxy of *The Fundamentals* of 1909-1912 and the "Five Fundamentals of Niagara" that Sandeen has factually exposed as an error of Stewart Cole. The simple truth is that the New Evangelicals agree with the truths of *The Fundamentals,* since they expressed the truths of Orthodoxy. It would be better history not to say the University of Chicago *went* liberal, for it started that way under William Rainey Harper.[10] His work does point to the basic weakness of New Evangelicals, namely, their vagueness or sin in the area of separation, and he points with pride to the separatist stand of his own beloved GARB. In addition, he upholds the doctrines of Dallas Seminary in sharp contrast with those of the New Evangelicals, as openly stated in the Fuller Seminary Statement of Faith. He does not mention that both the GARB and Dallas Seminary have invited known friends of New Evangelicals to speak on various occasions from public platforms. He seems most sympathetic with many of the charges brought against Fundamentalists by New Evangelicals, but these are beside the main point as to why New Evangelicalism arose and what it has done to muddy the waters of American Christianity.

Erickson's study leans heavily on the books of Carnell, Henry, and Ramm. These men think Fundamentalism too negative, too naive on social needs, and too insistent on literalism in Biblical interpretation. In contrast, the New Evangelicals insist that the Kingdom is here and now and "rather uniformly . . . to reject the pretribulational view."[11] Even Genesis, chapter 1, cannot be taken literally, for we ought to hold to "progressive creationism or threshold creation."[12] Again, according to Erickson, the Fundamentalist has condemned too many things such as wine, dancing, and the movies, and the New Evangelicals think of this as the spirit of legalism. Fundamentalists have not supported and do not even now support the many movements of social reform, such as

[10]Robert P. Lightner, *New Evangelicalism* (Des Plaines, Illinois: Regular Baptist Press, 1965), p. 36.
[11]Millard Erickson, *New Evangelical Theology* (New York and Westwood, N.J.: Revell, 1968), p. 126.
[12]Ibid., p. 160.

those proposed by the National Council of Churches, and have thereby gained "cult status."

Erickson also believes the New Evangelicals have pointed the way to a much-needed unity among Christians, pointing out the existence of over three hundred protestant groups in America. He approves of the NAE as one unifying factor, along with the Berlin Congress on Evangelism of 1966. He endorses evangelicals' staying within such bodies as the National Council for the sake of conversation with the non-evangelicals, and rejects the Fundamentalist position of "separating from those who are not separated."[13] He thinks highly of more recent conversations between Protestants and Catholics. So he rejects Fundamentalism as being too separatist, too demanding of right means to achieve a good goal in Christian service, too critical of Pentecostalism, too sarcastic, and too far away from classical Orthodoxy. It is interesting that he thinks Lightner's book shows a desire "to reconcile the New Evangelicals with the Fundamentalists."[14] In conclusion, Erickson is scholar enough to admit that New Evangelicalism has made "no great thrust in the matter of social welfare."[15] And he admits, probably sadly, that no major indication has arisen to show any shift of the liberal doctrine for the better.

Several articles have appeared on New Evangelicalism. Some have appeared in *The Sword of the Lord,* by editor John R. Rice, G. Archer Weniger, and Monroe Parker. The author of this study wrote in *The Daybreak* in 1962 listing the dangers of the new movement as (1) liberal interpretation of the Scriptures, (2) scholastic mistiness as to what a New Testament church is, and (3) weakness in separatism, with "too much emphasis on degrees and scholastic achievements."[16] The weakness in new-evangelical eschatology was the subject of a paper in which it was discovered that it has no unifying eschatological view, only a general disdain for dispensationalism. Weniger spoke openly of how New Evangelicalism was getting a foothold on college campuses through Campus Crusade, led by its founder, William Bright.[17] He revealed how worldly methods are being used, such as the use of a night club singer (Pat Boone), who endorses the "tongues" movement, and such language as "revolution for Christ," with Bright calling Jesus a revolutionary. He singled out Daniel Fuller of Fuller Seminary, who says that some Scripture is "non-revelatory." Some old-

[13]Ibid., p. 198.
[14]Ibid., p. 225.
[15]Ibid., p. 224.
[16]George W. Dollar, "The Dangers of New Evangelicalism," *Daybreak,* April, 1962.
[17]G. Archer Weniger, "New Evangelicals on the College Campus," *The Sword of the Lord,* Jan. 19, 1971.

fashioned Liberals seem acceptable to this group of the new era of Christian methods. A Canadian pastor, W. T. Adkins, is sure that New Evangelicalism "is a movement born of compromise," and he proves his point with ample documentation.[18] Among his proofs is Billy Graham's prayer for the National Council of Churches in Grace Cathedral in December, 1960. Present were the notorious Liberals James A. Pike and E. T. Dahlberg, president of the Council. He also cites the sending of a check for $65,000 to Vanderbilt University by Billy Graham after the Nashville campaign. Pastor Adkins held that the movement "grows on the appeasement of evil."[19] This was evident at Dallas Seminary by the presence of New Evangelical speakers such as Ted Engstrom of Youth For Christ and Robert Cook of the NAE. Graham himself warned the NAE Convention meeting in Buffalo in 1957 of the danger of "slipping into ultrafundamentalism."

It has become a favorite pastime of new-evangelical writers, who know so little of historic Fundamentalism, to call it offensive names, as if to bury it by opprobrium. The real danger is not strong Fundamentalism but a soft and effeminate Christianity—exotic but cowardly. It is sad that these men would not heed the warning of W. B. Riley about the menace of "middle-of-the-roadism." Should one be suspicious of being suspicious or adopt a soft and unbiblical charity?

On one point all agree, that the successes of the new-evangelical infiltration have been phenomenal. College campuses have received it with open arms or—perhaps we should say "open minds"—this being true of Bible institutes and Bible colleges beyond expectation. Two factors have accounted for this. One has been the large crowds drawn to the Graham crusades and their widespread radio and television appeal. A second factor is that administrators, trustees, and faculty members have failed miserably to alert students to the issues and problems involved and to speak of these from a Biblical viewpoint. Thus have separatism and Fundamentalism gone down by default in these schools. Both teachers and students blindly ignore the vast currents driven by the enemy of men's souls, and, in turn, congregations have gone to sleep. Of the two hundred Bible schools in the United States and Canada hardly more than six have faculty members knowledgeable and courageous enough to present historic Fundamentalism as a movement and warn of its present dangers. Most shy away from any picture of the present maelstrom of apostasy with some excuse that they are not called to such a ministry. As long as some want to obey the Bible and be good soldiers of the Lord they will need to be told of wars for the Faith,

[18]W. T. Adkins, *New Evangelicalism* (Calgary, Alberta, Canada: Westbourne Baptist Church, n.d.), p. 12.
[19]Ibid., Part Two.

their nature, and the need for the flushing out of God's enemies. But each year a new stream of untaught and unwarned graduates sally forth into a world falling apart. Most become content to toy with a few theological concepts and expect congregations to participate in their pious pastime.

It should be part of the record that there are marked exceptions to this wholesale sellout of the schools. There are still some who are militantly Fundamentalist in their attitudes and training, and these will be listed in Chapter 14.

Alumni naturally expect their schools to be regarded as Fundamental. Men of GARB persuasion, expect that Faith Baptist Bible College, Los Angeles Baptist Seminary, and Western Baptist Bible College be included simply because they are connected with the GARB. This would be irresponsible, however, since there is in these schools a pronounced softness toward New Evangelicalism, a lowering of standards, and a disdain for militant Fundamentalists. Some would expect such Christian colleges as King's, Cedarville, and Biola to be added. Their friendliness with New Evangelicals and their silence on the sharp-edged issues of Fundamentalism would disqualify them. At least, many questions would need to be answered before a clean bill of health could be issued. Alumni of Dallas Seminary would raise the old claim that all is sound and Fundamental there, although such known sympathizers with New Evangelicalism as H. G. Hendricks, H. W. Robinson, G. W. Peters, and R. H. Seume serve on the faculty. Each year an array of speakers who travel with the New Evangelicals mold the minds of students to a middle-of-the-road position. These speakers have included R. A. Cook, Arnold T. Olson, H. T. Armerding, Clark Pinnock, F. A. Schaeffer, Carl Henry, Clyde Taylor, and Ted Engstrom. Others would be surprised that Moody Bible Institute would not be listed, but how could it be when its leaders have supported cooperative evangelism, lending their support to the Berlin Congress, the Minneapolis Congress, and the annual Inter-Varsity gatherings at Urbana? Also, it is a fact *Moody Monthly* refused to carry an ad from Bob Jones University that stated the University's stand against New Evangelicalism. In these schools some Fundamentalists do work and teach, but their voices are being muffled or silenced while the platform voices advocating new-evangelical sympathy or support lead the students into compromise. W. L. Pettingill warned many years ago that we should be on the alert and look carefully to the schools, in particular

the Bible Schools. The Bible Schools have for the most part fought a good fight of faith and kept the faith. They are next in line for Satan's onslaughts and they will be attacked without mercy and without quarter. Keep an eye on the Bible Schools and as you love the truth pray mightily for them that they may be kept true in these days of peril.[20]

If the keen-eyed Pettingill were here today he would be shocked and saddened at what has happened at his own school, Philadelphia College of Bible, and other Bible schools across the nation. One of the significant but tragic features of the situation is the fury with which faculty members and trustees deny the existence of these conditions while remaining content to teach pat theological phrases and orthodox clichés. Most dispensationalists are amazingly ignorant of what is happening in Bible schools, colleges, and seminaries, while they spend their time discussing intricately related events within the different periods of the Old Testament. While discernment of the signs of the times has become an academic playtoy, wrapped in theological verbiage, the dispensationalists look incredulously at Fundamentalists who are trying to alert them to the dangers of present conditions. It is a strange phenomenon that militant Fundamentalists are barred from these middle-of-the-road schools while known middle-of-the-roaders and new-evangelical sympathizers are welcomed and praised. The hypocrisy of this compromise seems not to have dawned on the minds of supposedly thoughtful and sincere Christian leaders. They can afford to be friendly with all types and kinds except outspoken Fundamentalists.

There has developed what Ernest Pickering has called "a general doctrinal fuzziness in fellowship with Barthianism . . . a passion to avoid all negativism."[21] Robert O. Ferm of Houghton College tried in 1958 to justify this compromise activity, even claiming that "the Lord Jesus, the Apostles, and the great evangelists in the past followed such a scheme."[22] Ferm believes that as long as the crowds come, we ought to cooperate with all who will cooperate, even if they include the modernistic Protestant Council of New York, Norman Vincent Peale, and Cardinal Cushing of Boston. And the Christian public was led into delusion on these issues because of such respected magazines as *Moody Monthly, Christian Life, Evangelical Christian, King's Business,* and *Christianity Today* gave enthusiastic support to ecumenical evangelism. Another open sign of compromise was the Berlin Congress in November, 1966, led by C. F. H. Henry and Graham, costing half a million dollars. Carl McIntire, with his press credentials, was denied entrance on farcical excuses. But Oral Roberts of the tongues-healing circles was welcomed royally. A Jewish rabbi represented the Jews, and several

---

[20]*Serving and Waiting,* Jan., 1925, p. 421.
[21]Ernest Pickering, *The Present Status of New Evangelicalism* (Minneapolis: Central Baptist Press, n.d., p. 2.
[22]Robert O. Ferm, *Cooperative Evangelism* (Grand Rapids: Zondervan, 1958).

Catholic priests were present as observers; but still the Christian public did not see the weaknesses of it.

There are ample materials available for pastors and students on the issues of New Evangelicalism in general and on the Graham issue in particular. In addition to the authors and works cited above, there is a mimeographed weekly called *The Blu-Print,* published by G. Archer Weniger, pastor of the Foothill Baptist Church in Castro Valley, California. It gathers quotations from all of the anti-Fundamentalist sources and constantly prints the statements of New Evangelicals and their fellow-travelers. Weniger has joined his brother, Arno Q., in the establishment and maintenance of the San Francisco Baptist Seminary and the Lucerne Conference grounds, both bulwarks of hardline Fundamentalism. Weniger has published a list of thirty-six tracts, books, and booklets exposing what is wrong in New Evangelicalism. Among the authors are such keen students of the present scene as W. E. Ashbrook, Bob Jones, Jr., M. H. Reynolds, Noel Smith, Victor Sears, Ford Porter, R. T. Ketcham, R. C. Weeks, and D. A. Waite. This list may be obtained by writing to the San Francisco Baptist Seminary, 1225 Franklin Street, San Francisco, California.

Other materials are available from the Central Baptist Press, Central Baptist Seminary, 2105 North Fremont, Minneapolis, Minnesota. Another good source of information is the Bob Jones University Bookstore in Greenville, South Carolina, which has prepared a packet of documentary materials showing the continuing declension of Billy Graham, in addition to offering a number of other booklets and pamphlets dealing with New Evangelicalism in general and with Campus Crusade specifically.

13
Fellowships of Fundamentalists

Increasingly, independent Baptists have dominated the scene of Fundamentalism from 1935 onward. Their hard-hitting evangelism produced some large churches; their constant emphasis on soulwinning and the erection of independent Baptist schools, with a strong push from interdenominationalism, have given them a commanding place on the American continent. Sometimes bashfully and with understandable envy, other Fundamentalists have befriended these aggressive Baptists and become more and more willing to accept their leadership. One added factor in this new situation has been the deepening apostasy among organized Baptists, Presbyterians, and Methodists. Fundamentalists among the last two groups have had great difficulty in getting many people to leave the old-line denominations. In fact, few Presbyterians and Methodists have been willing to leave at all, even in the face of outrageous apostasy and Liberalism. The few that have left have drifted into the status of an unevangelistic remnant. But Baptists have almost stolen the show—in some places they have so dominated as to cause them to wonder if anyone else believes the truth. When we turn to the Fundamentalist fellowships that have continued to defend the Word in the period of Reconstruction, Revival, and Retreat (1935-1973), there will be a large preponderance of independent Baptists. Although this was not planned, the unwillingness of fellow believers to continue the fight outside denominational walls left them the field by default.

American Baptist Association (ABA)

With headquarters in Texarkana, Texas, the American Baptist Association has some 3,300 churches, and is the largest in number among Fundamental groups in the world. Formerly known as the General Association of Baptist Churches, it began in 1925 through the merger of two groups—one faction leaving Southern Baptist ranks and the other having an independent background. The name was changed to the present one in the year 1924.[1] An official spokesman has clearly described the Association as a

> national group of independent Baptist churches voluntarily associating in their efforts to fulfil the New Testament commission to the churches, maintaining a minimum of organization so designed as to guarantee the complete sovereignty and equal representation of the churches.[2]

It should be noted, lest there be a misuhderstanding due to the similarity of names, that one of the groups coming together in 1924 has been knowu as the Baptist Missionary Association. The literature of the group frankly disavows the convention type of organization and insists strictly on a fellowship of churches. In a prepared statement of faith, some twenty-one articles are listed.[3] The author declares the group to consist of "missionary, Orthodox, Fundamental, Premillennial, and Militant Baptists."[4] The group has maintained a strong adherence to the old Landmark tenets of faith and practice. Since these have marked the thinking and practice of thousands of sound Baptists, we ought to recognize the distinctive ideas of Landmarkism.

In its earliest form, it was associated with two names, J. M. Pendleton and John R. Graves. The former published a tract in 1856 called *An Old Landmark Reset,* while the latter made the concepts more popular in his book, *Landmarkism, What Is It?,* published in 1880. Both men were Southern Baptists, and both claimed to be reasserting historic Baptist principles going back to New Testament times. The prime belief of these men was that there had always been New Testament churches, although designations and names have varied, and that these churches alone are true churches, whether Baptist in name or not. Only these churches had the right to administer the New Testament ordinances, no sacraments being valid. Again, they held that the present-day structures in boards and

---

[1]A. L. Patterson, *The American Baptist Association* (Texarkana: Sunday School Committee of the American Baptist Association, n.d.), p. 3. There is no written history of the Association, and all materials must come from small booklets.

[2]I. K. Cross, *What Is the American Baptist Association?* (Texarkana: Sunday School Committee of the American Baptist Association, n.d.).

[3]See E. C. Gillentine, *What We Believe* (Texarkana: Sunday School Committee of the American Baptist Association, n.d.).

[4]Ibid., p. 3.

conventions have been created by men and are, therefore, not to be found in the New Testament.

These distinctives have separated the ABA, really Landmarkers in the best sense of the word, from all other Christians and from most Baptists. Thousands of other Baptists hold to Landmark tenets but not to the exclusion of other believers who do not agree with them. Perhaps we should list the Landmark teachings arising from the distinctives mentioned above. They are:

(1) John the Baptist's baptism was truly Christian.
(2) Jesus established the Church from John's converts.
(3) Churches of like faith and practice have been existing ever since— so we really have a Baptist perpetuity.
(4) There has been a line (though not necessarily a strict succession) of true churches from the time of Christ to ours.
(5) Jesus gave the two ordinances (Baptism and the Lord's Table) to the Church He founded and to no other. Any other practice is alien.

One essential truth held by the ABA is the importance and the centrality of the local visible church. In fact, the idea of an invisible church is utterly repudiated, such an idea being credited to half-way Protestant theology which took some of the ideas of Romanism. Interdenominationalism is suspect, since it has often blurred so many distinctives, especially under the influence of the Plymouth Brethren and the Scofield Reference Bible with its doctrine of the "invisible church." Cross says succinctly that "it cannot be both" (visible and invisible).[5] He denies that the word "church" is ever used in the New Testament for the total number of believers, saying that the phrase "family of God" (Eph. 3:15) is used for all. This follows exactly the position of the great Southern Baptist scholar and leader B. H. Carroll, set forth in his widely used and very worthwhile booklet *Ecclesia—The Church*.[6] To Cross and other ABA men this is a crucial point, for if one is not right on the doctrine of the church (ecclesiology) and recognizes most of the so-called churches as true churches, then how can he determine true doctrine and practice on other truths that concern true Christians? Cross put the ABA case bluntly when he wrote that "the issue is whether we are going to have Baptist churches in the true Baptist tradition or are we going to settle for some kind of mixture and dilution of interdenominationalism wearing the Baptist tag."[7] The ABA counts as participants in this long line of New Testament churches, such groups as the Montanists, the Novatians, the Donatists, the Paulicians, the Cathari, and the Waldenses. The Anabaptists of the

[5]I. K. Cross, *The Church: Local or Universal?* (Texarkana: Sunday School Committee of the American Baptist Association, n.d.).

[6]This is now published by the press of the *Baptist Examiner* in Ashland, Ky., of which John R. Gilpin is the editor.

[7]Cross, *The Church: Local or Universal?*, p. 23.

sixteenth century were the true spokesmen for what the true fathers (apostles), not the Church Fathers, had believed and stood for. Now, the ABA says flatly, "we stand today, after all the pressures of the centuries, where our fathers stood."[8]

The American Baptist Association numbers about 700,000 members with its major strength in the great Southwest area of the nation. Among the largest churches are Antioch in Little Rock, Arkansas; County Avenue in Texarkana, Texas; Fatherland in Nashville, Tennessee; Bethel in Memphis, Tennessee; First Missionary in Bellflower, California; and Olive Street in Lakeland, Florida. The latest Directory lists 342 churches in Arkansas and 273 in Texas. It states:

> The Scriptures teach there has been a succession of true churches adhering to the doctrines and practices of the New Testament from the time of Christ to this day and that the churches of the American Baptist Association are so identified.[9]

In all, the Directory lists some thirteen Bible institutes the ABA has built and operates, one seminary, and one college. Some of the best known leaders within the group have been A. T. Powers; C. N. Glover, Sheridan, Arkansas; Ben M. Bogard; Albert Garner, Lakeland, Florida; Roy M. Reed, Bellflower, California; Martin Canavan, Long Beach, California; L. D. Forman, Mablevale, Arkansas; James B. Powers, Texarkana Texas; and A. J. Kirkland, who recently died. The strongest churches are in the states of Arkansas, Texas, California, and Florida. It might be noted that Chester E. Tulga served with this group after he had worked for the Fundamentalist wing of the Conservative Baptists and had produced the widely distributed "Case" books.

The ABA published a sharply worded tract by Tulga entitled *Needed: A New Baptist Fundamentalism*. The main part of this booklet was to point out the danger of interdenominational fundamentalism, because it undercut the place and the ministry of the local church; it predicted the drift of interdenominationalism into New Evangelicalism. As a matter of historical fact, this has taken place in most of the interdenominational schools and mission boards. Tulga also made a hard-hitting attack on "jumboism," the trend to make bigness too often the all-important goal of Baptist pastors and groups. This element of bigness has become a most sensitive point with more and more Fundamentalists of Baptist persuasion, and the danger of "numbers neurosis" has increased.

Baptist Bible Fellowship (BBF)

The largest Fundamentalist group in the number of church

---

[8]Cross, *Who Are We?* (Texarkana: Sunday School Committee of the American Baptist Association, n.d.).

[9]*Yearbook* (Texarkana: American Baptist Association, 1970), p. 162.

members is the Baptist Bible Fellowship with headquarters in Springfield, Missouri. It owes its origin to the ministry and inspiration of J. Frank Norris. Many hundreds of its pastors and members in over two thousand churches were converted, inspired toward independency, and led by Norris before his death in 1952. These were privileged to attend great meetings of the World Baptist Fellowship held annually in First Baptist in Fort Worth and there to listen to the Preachers' Preacher, without a peer in pulpit oratory. But in the late 1940's serious tensions arose in the Fellowship, and several of its younger pastors broke away during the May meeting of 1950. Among these were G. Beauchamp Vick, John W. Rawlings, Noel Smith, W. E. Dowell, and Scotty Alexander.

The May meeting of 1950 was most crucial. It started on Monday, May 22, with only a few pastors present. Two factions were active at the time. One, in charge of the Fellowship itself, included Dowell, Wayne Imboden, Alexander, B. H. Hillard, T. W. Hill, C. E. McDowell, and R. D. Ingle. A second group was in charge of the seminary, and in this group were Norris, Vick, Loys Vess, Rawlings, Frank Godsoe, George Crittenden, L. H. Grantham, and Dallas Billington.

The Seminary was nearly $250,000 in debt, and it was generally known that many pastors and churches were not supporting it financially. To gain added finances, Vick had been named president in 1948 while continuing to pastor Temple Baptist. He was able to lower the debt by $114,000 in two years. But veto power in major matters was in the hands of Norris, and at a meeting of students on May 17, 1950, Vick was dismissed even before any action of the trustees was contemplated. On Monday, May 22, the renowned Scottish preacher, Jock Troup, was elected the new president, although the trustees had not yet convened. On May 23 Norris was served an ultimatum by a large group of pastors that these actions must be rescinded or a split would ensue. Now it was discovered that two sets of by-laws were being used, and Norris was charged with using the newer set, which most of the pastors had never even seen. Now the issue was joined, and a large group of dissenters walked out of a public meeting and met in the Texas Hotel to organize the Baptist Bible Fellowship. Norris held another meeting on June 27 of 1950 in order to air his charges that a conspiracy was on foot to oust him and Entzminger from their posts. It was a hectic afternoon session with bouncers present to maintain order. Noel Smith was called a liar by Norris. On June 29 Norris wrote Vick that "if ever a fellow and a bunch of gangsters got annihilated this certainly happened to you and your crowd." But Temple Baptist in Detroit stood by Vick as did the churches of the other dissenters.

Papers to incorporate a new school were taken out on June 29,

1950, and the *Baptist Bible Tribune,* the voice of the BBF, reported that 150 students had applied for admission to the new institution. Operations began on a five-acre lot at Kearney and Summit in Springfield, Missouri. This is the present location, although the school has greatly expanded in its two decades of history, having purchased the properties of High Street Baptist Church of that city. Vick gave his side of the story, writing in the June 23, 1950, issue of the *Tribune* that he could not make his own decisions as head of the seminary, especially in implementing his plans to cut salaries in order to reduce the large indebtedness. Another factor was the expulsion of twenty students (who were from Vick's church) from the Seminary on the basis of the new set of by-laws which Vick had never seen.

Many spiritual and financial blessings rested on the new school from its opening. By 1961 its holdings were worth $750,000, and it had 623 students in its three-year Bible-institute course. By September, 1964, the student body had reached the grand figure of 748. For the academic year 1971-1972 over two thousand were enrolled; this very rapid growth makes it the largest Bible school in the world. Vick has continued as president, and his church is by far the most generous supporter, financially. Rawlings has been vice-president while pastoring his evangelistic empire, Landmark Baptist Temple in Cincinnati, Ohio; W. E. Dowell is the executive vice-president. Several large congregations have helped with money and students, such as Temple in Detroit, Landmark in Cincinnati, High Street in Springfield, Canton Baptist Temple in Canton, Ohio, New Testament Baptist in Miami, and Akron Baptist Temple in Akron, Ohio.

The printed voice of the BBF has been the *Baptist Bible Tribune* with its able and outspoken editor, Noel Smith. He has been especially effective in uncovering unbiblical teachings among Southern Baptists. He has been equally sharp in his criticisms of communism, the National and World Councils of Churches, and Modernism in any form. He has been openly against Billy Graham's evangelism and has charged Southern Baptist Seminary in Louisville with "converting [the Southern Baptist Convention] into a Modernist ecumenical convention from head to foot."[10] In an October issue in 1961 he excoriated Graham's "togetherness" and Norman Vincent Peale's "sugar-teat psychology"—with both being given credit for adding to the apostasy and confusion in the country. Smith charged that Peale's book, *The Power of Positive Thinking,* should have been entitled "The Sorry Confessions of a Flabby, Whitelivered Coward."[11]

[10]*The Baptist Bible Tribune,* Aug. 25, 1961.
[11]Ibid., Oct. 27, 1961.

By 1961 the Fellowship reported 1,200 churches and over one million members. This made it numerically the largest Fundamentalist group in the world, although the ABA had more churches. In the same year the College added a fourth year to its course of study and began to grant a bachelor's degree. But it ought to be noted that no church group in America puts less stock in degrees.

The *Tribune* was not silent when racist charges were leveled against it. Smith wrote that he resented the vilification of the South by a "bellowing bull in New York [Adam Clayton Powell] and a black, pious-talking hypocrite in Atlanta, Georgia [Martin Luther King, Jr.]."[12]

The *Tribune* keeps its readers informed about Fellowship churches and pastors and workers. In the issue of August 7, 1964, many pictures and an excellent write-up told of the expansion of Landmark Baptist Temple in Cincinnati, under John W. Rawlings, in the purchase of 160 acres of land for $365,000 on a major interstate highway going north and south. The church had grown rapidly since Rawlings became its pastor in 1952 with one hundred buses helping to swell the Sunday School to nearly six thousand, while over one hundred radio stations carried the broadcast of the Landmark Hour.

From time to time the *Tribune* has carried articles by such non-Fellowship men as R. A. Torrey, W. M. Smith, and Keith L. Brooks. A series on Baptists in America by the noted historian W. W. Sweet has been included. One issue carried a full-page ad for the Bob Jones University film "Red Runs the River." Smith and other Fellowship leaders have often spoken from the Bob Jones platform. The February 8, 1963, issue carried the account of the dedication of the 1.2-million-dollar Canton Baptist Temple under the leadership of Harold Henniger; the guest speakers were Bob Jones, Jr., and Dallas F. Billington of the famed Akron Baptist Temple in Akron, Ohio.

The 1970-1971 Directory of the Fellowship listed the leaders as Parker Dailey, president; G. B. Vick, president of Baptist Bible College; Jack Bridges, director of missions; and Noel Smith, editor of the *Tribune*. The Fellowship has a missions committee of thirty-two men for the thirty-two countries where it has missionaries. By August, 1971, some 2,006 churches were members of the Fellowship, with Texas leading with 256. Fort Worth alone had 27 with 18 others belonging to the World Baptist Fellowship; it is one of the foremost independent Baptist cities in the world. Ohio has some 101 churches in BBF; Missouri, 105; and Kansas, 99. California reports 88 churches, and Florida, 76. No total membership has been reckoned, but a million and a half would be a conservative estimate.

[12]Ibid.

The BBF is a fellowship of two thousand evangelistic churches, owing much to the impetus and inspiration of J. Frank Norris, with a healthy, growing constituency and the largest Bible college in the world. Some of its churches are sprawling empires in the evangelistic world. Vick's church in Detroit, with a membership of fourteen thousand, has recently built a beautiful new auditorium on West Chicago Avenue in Detroit seating five thousand.

Another mammoth church is the Akron Baptist Temple, founded and pastored by Dallas F. Billington until his passing in August of 1972: it is now headed by his son, Charles F., as pastor. It was established in June of 1934 with thirteen members and has grown to over 20,000 members today with a magnificent church plant. For many years it boasted of having the largest Sunday School in the world with an attendance of six thousand. Landmark Baptist Temple in Cincinnati has been mentioned with its one hundred buses traveling over one-third of a million miles a year to pick up people for its Sunday School. It has a novel setup in that it has no Sunday morning service at all but so arranges its Sunday School program that large classes meet from 9:45 to 11:15, the adult class numbering some 1,700 members.

Other large centers of Fellowship interest include the Thomas Road Baptist Church in Lynchburg, Virginia, where Jerry Falwell is pastor. On June 24, 1972, Sunday School attendance soared to the nineteen thousand mark. The church has twelve associate pastors with a weekly television program in every free country and a Baptist college, which opened in the fall of 1971. A very attractive Christmas 1972 folder disclosed that 450 television stations were carrying "The Old-Fashioned Gospel Hour" and that a Baptist seminary was projected for the fall of 1973. Another thriving Fellowship work is the New Testament Baptist Church in Miami, Florida, of which Al Janney is pastor. He has a large Christian day school (over two thousand were enrolled for the 1971-1972 sessions) and has opened a school offering collegiate work under the name of the Baptist University of America. It should be added that Fellowship pastors in California support the Pacific Baptist Bible College in the southern part of the state. Opening its doors in the fall of 1972, under Harry Vickery, was the Springfield Baptist College in Springfield, Missouri, in a Fellowship church. Only time will reveal whether this will mean a fragmenting of Fellowship pastors, money, and students.

General Association of Regular Baptist Churches (GARBC)

The third largest group within Fundamentalism is the GARB. To this date, regrettably, only one small brief historical sketch of this group has been produced, and this void in history should be filled.[13]

Technically, the GARB is the successor to The Baptist Bible Union, which held its last meeting in Belden Avenue Baptist Church, Chicago, in May, 1932. Only thirty-four delegates attended this meeting, and not one of the giants of the BBU—Norris, Shields, or Riley—was there. But others of the BBU circle were in attendance, including Van Osdel and Harry G. Hamilton. The title of Regular Baptists had been used in Michigan and Ontario, Canada, for those who stood for the Faith and against Modernism in Baptist ranks. From the very first the GARB proposed to be an association of churches, not merely an annual assembly of individuals nor a convention. So many men had suffered already from the hands of the Northern Baptist Convention that conventionism of any type was spurned. Elected as the first president of the new group was Hamilton of First Baptist Church, Buffalo, New York. Later he left the GARB fellowship to work under Norris in Fort Worth.

At the 1933 meeting of the GARB in Buffalo, five objectives were listed:

(1) An association of churches.
(2) Separation from Northern Baptist work of any kind.
(3) Conformity to the London Confession of Faith (1689) and the New Hampshire Confession of Faith.
(4) The promotion of the spirit of missions among pastors.
(5) Helping churches find sound pastors.

It should be noted that among the confessions of faith, the New Hampshire came to be the "standard," except in the area of prophecy, where a strong premillennial position was spelled out; the GARB has held firmly to a premillennial and pretribulational belief in the area of eschatology. The amended statement, some five pages in length, must be subscribed to by each "messenger" to the annual meetings. *The Baptist Bulletin* was created as the official voice of the new movement, and it still remains the written spokesman. Within a year some sixty-eight churches had applied and been accepted for membership. Growth was slow, for it would take many years for pastors and churches to cut all convention ties. By 1934 there were 245 messengers registered at the annual meeting in Gary, Indiana. Soon a Council of Fourteen was set up to carry out the directives of the annual meetings, its members elected by democratic procedure. It has been the responsibility of this committee to recommend certain schools and mission boards to be approved.

Five mission boards have gained acceptance as "approved": Baptist Mid-Missions, The Association of Baptists for World Evangelism, Fellowship of Baptists for Home Missions, Hiawatha

---

[13]Joseph M. Stowell, *A History of the General Association of Regular Baptist Churches* (Hayward, Calif.: Gospel Tracts, 1949).

Independent Baptist Missions, and Evangelical Baptist Missions. Two seminaries are on the "approved" list: Los Angeles Baptist Seminary and Grand Rapids Baptist Seminary. In addition there are six "approved" colleges: Western Baptist Bible College in Salem, Oregon; Faith Baptist Bible College in Ankeny, Iowa; Grand Rapids Baptist Bible College in Grand Rapids, Michigan; Cedarville College in Cedarville, Ohio; Baptist Bible College of Pennsylvania at Clarks Summit, Pennsylvania (formerly Baptist Bible Seminary in Johnson City, New York); and Los Angeles Baptist College, Newhall, California. However, many GARB students have gone to other schools such as Moody Bible Institute, Grace Theological Seminary, Bob Jones University, and Dallas Theological Seminary.

Several facts about the GARB bear mention. First, there has been a rugged consistency in doctrine. No Liberalism at all has been tolerated nor would be tolerated today. The schools and mission agencies supported have been consistently Fundamentalist in matters of belief. Also, it should be noted that a great number of the constituent churches have fought a valiant fight in order to exist in localities where Modernism and Liberalism were deeply entrenched. Northern communities have been gripped by the darkness of Romanism, Christian Science, Unitarianism, Universalism, and hardheaded paganism, in addition to the sellout of thousands of churches to liberal thought and activities. The GARB has tried valiantly to dent these areas, and in most places it has been a very slow process. Thus the evangelistic edge has been dulled, and growth in most churches has been equally slow. To help in spreading the Gospel, the Regular Baptist Press has been the source of sound Sunday School materials and various books. With close to fifteen hundred churches at present, the GARB has shown a rather slow growth in contrast to the BBF. So many Fundamental men have served in the ranks of the group that it might appear partial to mention only a few, but it would be serious bias not to mention any. National representatives of the group have included Robert T. Ketcham, Paul M. Jackson, and the present one, Joseph M. Stowell. Influential pastors, teachers, and executives include H. O. Van Gilder, Sr., Paul Tassell, Carl Elgena, Kenneth Masteller, Howard C. Fulton, John Balyo, James T. Jeremiah, Arthur F. Williams, Merle Hull, W. W. Welch, and Hall Dautel.

Serious tensions have arisen between the GARB and other Fundamental Baptists and Fundamentalists in general. It has seemed to many that there has been a drift, without design, into a type of conventionism, with the Council of Fourteen often thought of as functioning as a convention hierarchy. Again, it has been noted that many men were appointed to academic posts without the proper qualifications; it looked as if loyalty to the GARB was a substitute for even minimal standards in education.

Another source of vexation has been a list of approved schools, seemingly the only acceptable ones for sound Baptists to attend. Some of the pastors of the group have supported the Graham crusades, although the national leadership has not. Still another cause of friction has been the infiltration of new-evangelical moods, through GARB students who have attended Dallas Seminary and reentered the Association as pastors or teachers. They brought with them the open-mindedness of the seminary, which has invited to its platform a long list of New Evangelicals and their fellow-travelers. Thus the sharpness of separatism has been blunted; voices of protest against this trend have been angrily and unfactually denounced with what seems a typical Northern Baptist attitude: "Who are you to speak against *our* schools and *our* men?" Its greatest need, next to outright revival, is a purging from new evangelical sympathies within its ranks, even to the ouster of men of the SSS stamp (silence, sympathy, or support) of New Evangelicalism. At the present moment the power for self-inspection and cleansing is dangerously weak.

For many years the GARBC was the largest single constituent of the American Council of Christian Churches, which started in 1941 as a voice of Fundamentalism under Carl McIntire. But in 1968 GARB men took an active part in the removal of McIntire from leadership and captured the reins of power for themselves. How they will lead this Council without the strong voice and image of McIntire will be an important question facing the ACCC for years to come.

The Independent Fundamental Churches of America (IFCA)

The IFCA traces its history to February of 1930, when a group of thirty-nine men met in the study of William McCarrell, pastor of Cicero Bible Church, Cicero, Illinois. These men were interested in uniting with a small group called the American Conference of Undenominational Churches. It was with the understanding that a new name would be adopted and a stronger doctrinal position be enunciated. Of the men in that first meeting, twelve were Congregationalists, three were Presbyterians, nineteen were Independents, one was Baptist, and four did not have a denominational identification. Prominent in the early years of the movement were such men as McCarrell, M. R. DeHaan, W. P. Loveless, W. E. Pietsch, W. L. Pettingill, L. T. Talbot, M. T. MacPherson, J. F. Walvoord, and J. O. Buswell, Jr.[14]

[14]The history of the movement has been written by William A. Bevier in a Th.D. dissertation at Dallas Theological Seminary, 1957.

For some years its members were allowed membership with another group. This was altered in the 1940's so that dual membership is a rarity, and when allowed, the second membership must be in a Fundamental group. The IFCA grew very slowly. By 1935 it had only 38 churches with a total membership of 550, but in 1940 the number of churches stood at 75. In the latest 1969-1970 Directory there were listed 560 churches with a total membership of 75,000. In addition there are some 340 churches whose pastors are in the IFCA. Adding these to their churches the total would be 900 pastors, and churches with a membership of 122,000. Of the affiliated churches the largest number is in Michigan with 80, followed by Illinois with 78, California with 76, and Pennsylvania with 65. The present leadership includes Lowell Wendt as past president; Robert L. Gray, president; Bryan J. Jones, national executive secretary; and Glen A. Lehman, editor of *The Voice,* published at 145 Washington Avenue, Wheaton, Illinois. Among its best-known leaders today are such men as Charles L. Feinberg, S. H. Sutherland, John F. Walvoord, M. F. Unger, Alden A. Gannett, J. O. Percy, and Frank C. Torrey. Affiliated with it are five Bible schools (eg., the Grand Rapids School of the Bible and Music) and two foreign mission groups, the Fellowship of Independent Missions and the United Missionary Fellowship. Other schools working closely with the IFCA are Calvary Bible College, Dallas Theological Seminary, Biola College, and Talbot Theological Seminary.

Many of its pastors and leaders are from Presbyterian and Congregational backgrounds. Often these practice immersion as their mode of baptism but allow membership to Christians who have been sprinkled. Their Orthodox background has tended to make their churches primarily teaching centers rather than soulwinning stations, and their teaching has tended toward a stagnant dispensationalism. As a consequence, the IFCA has trailed independent Baptist churches in souls saved and in Sunday School growth. New Evangelicalism has made serious inroads into its ranks largely through the strong ministry of Dallas Seminary. This as deen the subject of an analysis by a former member of the IFCA, William E. Ashbrook, in his work *The New Neutralism,* and he has led a group of churches in Ohio to leave the organization. At the present time there is no organized opposition to New Evangelicalism within the IFCA, and therefore it seems likely that this compromise attitude will increase. With continuing weaknesses in evangelism, the prospects for a major growth among the rank and file of the IFCA are very slight.

Another recognizable danger is the infiltration of men without oldline convictions. One member put it succinctly when he wrote:

some of the newer independents are joining the IFCA not because of the grounded conviction regarding our position but because of circumstance or convenience. . . . our position could become vapid and ameliorating due to this influence amongst us of those who are independent because of circumstance. . . . unquestionably much of the difficulty in this area stems from the fact the new generation has only seen the smoke and not been through the fire. . . . [that] the problem is not solved [is] evidenced by the chagrin occasioned by putting members by convenience in places of authority.[15]

Another evidence, small though it is, has been the desire of the *Voice* to hush criticisms of new-evangelical forces. An article in the June 1971 issue tried to defend Scripture Press. The author, Henry Jacobsen, claimed that any charge against this Press was untrue since it stood on the Five Fundamentals. Billy Graham and Harold Ockenga also accept these Fundamentals, though both lead the New Evangelicals. Jacobsen's point was on separation, for he wrote:

we do not find warrant in scripture for separating ourselves from Christians who do not agree with us on such matters as the mode of baptism, versions of scripture, the eschatological timetable, or the practice of separation.[16]

Thus eschatology is downgraded, although the IFCA has stood firmly on dispensationalism. The practice of separation, a main issue in today's religious jungle, is likewise given an insignificant place, although the IFCA was started by separatists. New Evangelicals have done a hatchet job on this good group, and its national *Voice* seems to ignore it. The attempt to whitewash Scripture Press is obviously a sellout by a responsible IFCA agency.

It is interesting that the *Voice* carried an item in the July-August 1970 issue announcing a Scripture Press seminar whose speakers were H. G. Hendricks and G. W. Peters of Dallas Seminary, Herbert Anderson of CBFMS, Walter Frank of Greater Europe Mission, and a speaker from Wheaton College. Would any discerning, honest IFCA member contend that this was a gathering of Fundamentalists? On other pages of the *Voice* are carried news of Campus Crusade, Dallas Bible College, and Christian Service Brigade, with a few references to the coffee-house ministry. How many more new-evangelical groups or fellow-travelers will be endorsed before Fundamentalists recognize that the initials IFCA must now be construed as Independent Front for Christian Activities? More recent issues of the *Voice* do give evidence of a more Fundamentalist position, since many statements have been printed against Key '73. An editorial in the November 1972 issue saw this national ecumenical effort as something to be expected when men turn from Fundamentalism to Evangelicalism. The January 1973

[15]J. A. Paulson, *The Voice*, printed in the 1961 issue and reprinted in the issue of April, 1971, pp. 14-15.
[16]Editorial in *The Voice*, June, 1971, p. 11; Glen Lehman, editor.

issue of the same magazine made too many flattering references to such "soft" mission boards as Far Eastern Gospel Crusade, West Indies Mission, Missionary Aviation, and Conservative Congregational Christian Conference. Thus the paper continues to issue both sweet and sour sounds and edges away too often from a straight-line Fundamentalist separation. A good proof of this was seen in the October 1972 issue of the *Voice,* when the Bible-school movement was praised for holding to its original purpose (which very few have done) and at the same time criticizing both Explo '72 and Key '73.

World Baptist Fellowship (WBF)

Much smaller than the others listed thus far is the WBF with headquarters at 3001 West Division, Arlington, Texas. The office is on a property occupied by the Bible Baptist Seminary, which moved there after a court battle with the First Baptist Church in Fort Worth following the death of J. Frank Norris in 1952. Its interests include the Seminary, the Fellowship Missions, and the paper, *The Fundamentalist.* Among the leaders of the WBF are Earl Oldham, head of the Seminary and pastor of Calvary Baptist Church in Grand Prairie, Texas; T. H. Masters of Wichita, Texas, editor of the paper; Bruce Cummons of Massillon Baptist Temple in Massillon, Ohio; and R. O. Schmidt, Director of Missions. The largest church in the group is the Dayton Baptist Temple, Dayton, Ohio, with nearly two thousand members, pastored by Gerald Fleming.

The latest directory of the Fellowship lists 566 churches, 525 pastors, and 80 missionaries, but about 800 churches support the work of the Fellowship in some way. As would be expected, Texas has the largest number of churches, a total of 177. Other states with Fellowship strength are Ohio with 74, Michigan with 60, and Florida with 58. An interesting statistic from the Directory is that Fort Worth, the center of the Norris empire, has 18 WBF churches, which with other independent Baptist churches makes a total of 45. One is forced to admit that J. Frank Norris left his mark on that Texas community. The seminary in Arlington has undertaken a Junior liberal arts program and changed its name to Arlington Baptist Schools. At present some three hundred students are enrolled at Arlington Baptist.

Conservative Baptists

The size of the Conservative Baptist movement indicates that a full-length study by a competent historian is deserved. So far, the only account has been a small work by Bruce Shelley of the Conservative Baptist Seminary in Denver, Colorado. It does contain helpful material and major excerpts from related documents, but it suffers from a common fallacy among writers in that it lumps together the Fundamentalists, the Orthodox, and many kinds of conservatives. It also uses all three labels without making any distinctions between them. The reader is left confused as to what kind of Baptists started the movement, concluding only that they were Baptists who could not stand the Liberalism of Northern Baptists.

We should not overlook the fact that from its first organizational meetings, CB's consisted of a mixed multitude. How could it be otherwise with their leaders from such a variety of backgrounds as Northwestern Schools, Eastern Baptist Seminary, Moody Bible Institute, Gordon College, and Western Baptist Seminary? This mixture of schools and men has been amply demonstrated by one of its figures, Vernon C. Grounds, in the *Seminary Studies,* published by Conservative Baptist Seminary in Denver, which he heads.

A clearer picture of the variety has been given by R. V. Clearwaters and published by his school, Central Baptist Seminary of Minneapolis. A recent issue by this school lists eight publications which have come from its press, in addition to forty reprints from the *Central Quarterly,* forty-seven monographs, and sixteen tracts. Among the authors have been such well-known Fundamentalists as Clearwaters, Warren Van Hetloo, George J. Carlson, Earle Matteson, Ernest Pickering, G. Archer Weniger, M. J. Hollowood, Monroe Parker, B. Myron Cedarholm, and W. E. Ashbrook.

One of the most prolific writers of the Conservative Baptist Association in the 1940's was Chester E. Tulga. At that time he belonged to the Fundamentalist wing of the movement which took the title of the Conservative Baptist Fellowship. One of his best studies was *The Foreign Missions Controversy in the Northern Baptist Convention,* published in 1950 by the Fellowship. Tulga concluded that the first threat to the soundness of the Convention arose from the Inter-Church Movement, which was proposed at the 1919 meeting of Northern Baptists at Denver. At the same time the Central Board of Promotion, in a move for more power, launched a program to Christianize the world. This venture in the field of social action pointed up the postmillennial thinking of the hour.

In 1920 the first known Modernist among missionary appointees, C. G. Fieldler, was named. A returned missionary, Miss Bertha Henshaw, finding evidence in the Home Office of others who were less than sound in doctrine, left the Foreign Mission Board office in disgust and remorse to publicize her charges. These got into the hands of the Fundamentalist League of New York headed by John Roach Straton. P. J. Lerrigo of the Foreign Board dodged the charges and, as usual, answered in general terms, extolling the high ideals of missions. As the charges gained attention, the Board turned to the well-tested tactics of the Jesuits and editorialized that the Fundamentalists were critical and unchristian in spirit, and that the Board was made up of good men.

In 1923 there was little doubt left about the direction of the Board, for on November 15 of that year it announced its inclusivist policy, according to which its officers and appointees would represent the wide variety of thought in the churches of the Convention. By now these churches were led, in large part, by men of liberal doctrines or liberal spirit who were products of such schools as the University of Chicago, Rochester Seminary, and Crozer. The issue was clear now—the Board would name out-and-out Liberals and out-and-out Fundamentalists. Sound doctrine would not be required.

In 1924 it was discovered that M. R. Hartley had been appointed a missionary, and he was charged with being weak on or uncertain of some major truths. At this point Massee and the Fundamentalists planned to bring this case to the floor of the Convention but were thwarted when the Liberals proposed a full investigation of the Foreign Board. Here the gullibility of Fundamentalists is most apparent. The seminaries were gone or going, the Board had adopted an inclusivist policy—why investigate? But Massee, Brougher, and others believed the myth that the Liberals are sincere and therefore to be trusted to right Convention wrongs, even to the eradication of liberal moods and teachings already a generation old. At this point in Northern Baptist history, sound men had made a horrible blunder; the tides of the Convention had gone too far to be corrected. When the committee named to investigate reported the following year, there was outright endorsement of the Foreign Board; how common this Jesuit practice has become among Convention leaders! A resolution proposed by W. B. Hinson that would have required missionaries to sign a simple statement revealing their evangelical views, was voted down, 742 to 574. Thus ended the attempt of men of sound Biblical doctrines to purge leaven from among Northern Baptist missionaries, and never again has any serious threat been mounted against liberal domination.

Dissent increased among the sound Northern Baptist pastors for the next two decades. Many of the men would attend the rallies of the Baptist Bible Union to be inspired and instructed by its giants—Norris, Shields, and Riley. With few even trying to effect changes for the better, hope to reform the Convention faded. Riley, who would not give up hope that Northern Baptists would return to solid Fundamental Faith, never realized his hope.

The period of dissent was marked by several events. One was the exodus of a few men from convention ranks in 1932 to form the General Association of Regular Baptist Churches (GARBC). Another was the refreshing stream of sound men coming into Baptist churches from such schools as Moody Bible Institute,

Northern Baptist Seminary, Western Baptist Seminary, and Gordon College. A third cause for hope was the publication of the "Case" books by Tulga. Here we provide a list of these helpful exposés of liberal trends on the basis of sound Biblical views that were issued by the Conservative Baptist Fellowship. Thousands of copies are still in the hands of the Fundamental Baptist Fellowship, which has an office at Marquette Manor Baptist Church in Chicago. They provide interesting and factual information. The complete list is as follows:

The Case Against the Social Gospel
The Case Against the National Council of Churches
The Case Against Modernism in Evangelism
The Case for the Virgin Birth
The Case for Jesus the Messiah
The Case for the Atonement
The Case for Dispensationalism
The Case for the Resurrection
The Case for Holiness in These Times
The Case for Separation
The Case for the Independence of the Local Church

In 1943 the patience of sound men in the Northern Baptist ranks was at the breaking point. They had come to a turn in the road that had proved decisive. Since they had smarted so long under the inclusive policy, they felt they could no longer ask their churches to keep on supporting the Convention's missionary efforts. It was crystal clear that Liberals and their fellow-travelers were dominating the boards.

On December 15, 1943, a voice for evangelical missions was organized at Tabernacle Baptist Church in Chicago where George J. Carlson was pastor. It was named the Conservative Baptist Foreign Missions Society (CBFMS) and sought to provide, within the Convention, a route for evangelical missionaries and a door through which monies from evangelical churches could be channeled. It should be made clear that this group included men of unbending Fundamentalist views, men moderately Fundamental in doctrines, and Conservatives who were orthodox but would not continue to support the inclusivist work of the convention. It was a motley group, and the name Conservative was correct—indeed it would have been a misnomer to call it Fundamentalist. Vincent Brushwyler, a pastor from Muscatine, Iowa, was chosen the first director. The Fundamentalist Fellowship had existed for twenty years, and now it helped to mother a missions society. The Northern Baptist leadership had to make the decision as to whether it would recognize a "rump" missions group as a convention agency. Here ought to be considered a major issue which erupted; men who went through those days still remember it.

Pastors with large churches feared action lest splits would follow. Older men in the ministry with lifelong convictions saw over their heads the Damocles sword of pensions, which they might lose if a new missions group was excluded from Convention circles. Again, younger men had smaller churches, and to them the struggle to survive was paramount. Could they be expected to know enough about the liberal erosion to fight factually and persuasively, and ask their people in struggling churches to separate?

In 1944 a committee of nine was named to restore unity; but it met certain death, for any recognition of the new society would be open confession of the truth of charges made against the old board. The Fundamentalist Fellowship now saw itself absorbed into an emerging Conservative movement and in 1946 voted to rename itself the Conservative Baptist Fellowship (CBF). As such it became more vocal and as early as 1945 had started to publish the *Newsletter Information Bulletin*. This bulletin was to make more and more revelations of the apostasy among Northern Baptists, and its overall effect was to hasten a rupture. The "Case" books would make increasing attacks, and Tulga's sharp-edged writing would help to separate the Conservatives from all others in the Convention.

In 1947 another break came with the creation of the Conservative Baptist Association of America (CBA of A) under the enthusiastic leadership of B. Myron Cedarholm. It was launched on May 17 of that year, and although many churches had not yet separated from the convention, the process now got under way. Some would vote out, others would fight their way out, and some would ease out with a minumum of notice until some 1,500 had finally left. How providential, that in the year W. B. Riley passed to his reward (1947), he did see separation; in that same year he asked that his membership be dropped from Northern Baptist rolls although his old church in Minneapolis was to stay in. He had the satisfaction of knowing that he had helped to train hundreds of young men who would leave the old convention and help erect a Fundamentalist empire.

In 1950 the Conservative Baptist Home Mission Society, the last of the three Conservative Baptist groups, was established. In 1953 the three met in Portland, Oregon, to adopt a *manifesto* which would take a separatist stand. But almost immediately, above the clash of strong leaders and conflicting personalities, dissension arose. On paper and in its open pronouncements, the CBA had been premillennial, and to all appearances both the CBFMS and CBHMS were of the same convictions, although this had not been put on paper. An increasing number of vocal pastors within CB circles increased their demands that it be on record. But most of the leaders felt that the issue was not necessary and that disruption would result were it pushed. The issue refused to die, due largely to the constant pressure brought by the CBF. Both Tulga and the CBF came under attacks for forcing the issue, and in 1955 the CBF reaffirmed itself as completely independent, although its men were inside the Conservative movement. By this time other items were added to the controversy plaguing the Conservatives.

It was becoming more apparent that many CB pastors and laymen were unsympathetic toward Fundamentalism with its insistence on the imminency of the Lord's return, literalism in prophecy, and the use of the Scofield Reference Bible. The Conservative leadership, like the Northern Baptist Convention executives, wanted all doctrinal differences toned down in order to get on with the worldwide work of missions. Fundamentalists wanted doctrinal purity as well as a program. The inevitable eruption could hardly be postponed for many years. Conservative pastors from such schools as Wheaton, Gordon, and Eastern felt more and more uncomfortable with those of hard-line Fundamentalism. All three schools producing pastors for Conservative Baptist churches were discrediting a strong premillennial stand, especially that kind of premillennialism that taught the pretribulation rapture and the elements of dispensationalism.[17]

By 1956 Denver Seminary had come to be a focal point of controversy. Under Vernon C. Grounds it represented the middle-of-the-road position of most Conservative Baptists. More and more Fundamentalists were openly attacking the seminary because of its "soft" line and its sympathy for New Evangelicalism, together with its unwillingness to adopt pretribulationism. Several schools now entered the picture to oppose the Denver influence and teaching. One was Central Baptist Seminary of Minneapolis, Minnesota, which began in 1956 as the heir of the seminary program at Northwestern Schools. Clearwaters had headed the seminary work at Northwestern and now led in the formation of the new seminary of which he is still president.

Another of the same Fundamentalist stand was the San Francisco Baptist Seminary, housed in the facilities of the Hamilton Square Baptist Church in San Francisco, Califlfornia, and led by two brothers Arno Q. and G. Archer Weniger, who grew up under the ministry of W. B. Riley. Like Central in Minneapolis, this seminary has been militant in its outspoken Fundamentalism, the only one of its type on the West Coast. Consistent Fundamentalist supporters of this seminary have included such knowledgeable pastors as Roy H.

---

[17]A Fundamentalist analysis of the conflict is found in R. V. Clearwaters, *Forty Years of History Looks Down upon Conservative Baptists* (Minneapolis: Central Baptist Press, n.d.).

Austin, W. Glen Rhoades, Eugene J. Peterson, and Kenneth Smith. During the school year 1970-1971 it enrolled some eighty students. Its ministry and outreach has been enlarged by the operation of the beautiful Lucerne Conference grounds north of San Francisco and by the publication by Archer Weniger of *The Blu-Print,* a weekly mimeographed sheet which has issued a constant exposé of new-evangelical trends, liberal statements, and evidences of apostasy of all kinds. The paper is sent out from Weniger's church, Foothill Baptist in Castro Valley, California, but represents an all-out attack by both the Seminary and Fundamentalists in Northern California.

A third school has been the Baptist Bible College in Denver, which has been a rallying point for Fundamental Baptists in Colorado and the Rockies. Another school, Pillsbury Baptist Bible College in Owatonna, Minnesota, came under the control of the Minnesota Baptist Convention in the 1950's, and under the guiding hands of Clearwaters, Monroe Parker, and B. Myron Cedarholm, it has had a wide ministry in the Northwest. During the past year it enrolled five hundred students. Parker gave outstanding service in the growth of the school, drawing upon his experience in evangelism, the pastorate, and executive ministry at Bob Jones University. He is now in wide demand as an evangelist and, in addition, heads the World Baptist Mission. Another Fundamentalist school fostering strong militant positions is Maranatha Baptist Bible College in Watertown, Wisconson, which was organized in 1968. Its founder and president is B. Myron Cedarholm, who had been director of the CBA of A for seventeen years, and later became president of Pillsbury. In 1968 he led in the purchase of a fine piece of property from the Roman Catholic Church, and over 450 students were in attendance for the 1972-1973 session. Assisting him at Watertown are such seasoned and well-trained Fundamentalists as Richard C. Weeks and M. James Hollowood.

Most Conservative Baptist churches in Wisconsin have left the national Conservative movement to form independent fellowships and are supporters of the Watertown school. Cedarholm's wide contacts throughout Conservative territory will make Maranatha a school of rich Fundamentalist promise. Many Fundamentalists of Conservative backgrounds support other schools and recommend them to young people. Thus more and more young people are going to Bob Jones University, Tennessee Temple Schools, Midwestern Baptist College, and evening Bible schools conducted by local churches for laymen wanting some Bible teaching and practical help for service.

The Conservative movement now reports some seventeen hundred churches in its constituency. Of this total, possibly four hundred could be called Fundamentalist. The CBFMS reports over five hundred missionaries with an annual budget of nearly three million dollars. Probably most of the missionaries would think of themselves as Fundamentalists, being unfamiliar with the Baptist jungle which has grown up in America in the last thirty years. The general director of the CBFMS is Warren Webster, and heading the CBHMS is Rufus Jones, one of the leaders of the National Association of Evangelicals. Because of complete capitulation to new-evangelical attitudes and methods, no serious dissension affects the Conservative Baptists now, and they openly support the strong voices of New Evangelicalism such as Graham, Campus Crusade, Evangelism-in-Depth, and such new-evangelical schools as Denver Seminary, Fuller Seminary,. Wheaton College, Gordon College, and Barrington College.

National Association of Evangelicals (NAE)

The National Association of Evangelicals is today a national voice and spokesman for New Evangelicalism; but in its earlier days it attracted to its membership many Fundamentalists, who thought of it as an updated and more intellectual revision of the old WCFA. It is now thirty-two years old, having organized on October 27-28, 1941 at Moody Bible Institute in Chicago. It was separatist in that it did not sanction apostasy, but it openly avowed that it was not as negative as the American Council, which had been organized a month before under the leadership of Carl McIntire. The latter was shunned because of its announced strategy of attacks on all forms of denominational and organizational defection from the truth; since the early days, the NAE has accused the ACCC of intolerance and bigotry.

Pioneer leaders in the formation of the NAE were J. Elwin Wright of the New England Fellowship of Evangelicals and Harold John Ockenga of Park Street Church in Boston. With them in the leadership of the 1940's were such respected leaders as Will H. Houghton, Herbert Mekeel, V. R. Edman, James D. Murch, and Bob Jones, Sr.

There was one warning flag hoisted by Riley, who claimed that the aims of the NAE were admirable but that its expectation was an illusion. He saw its inherent weaknesses, for they were those of the WCFA. One was the shielding of the apostate movements and the lack of a more open stand against them. He foresaw its defeat, for

its defeat has been accomplished by men who professed allegiance but who betrayed the cause when a showdown came .... Fundamentalism has failed, though accepted by the overwhelming majority of the people, because certain of its members in places of power have been willing to give comfort to the enemy: yea, on occasion to draw the sword against their own brethren in the enemy's behalf .... the request that Fundamentalists lock hands with rejectors of the Blessed Hope in order to join the non-millennialist in the separation of Church and State is to ask too great a sacrifice to gain a desirable end.[18]

The NAE grew rapidly. By the time of the second Annual Convention in Chicago in 1943 some one thousand were in attendance, representing, it was claimed, some fifteen million as a constituency. Clear lines of differentiation from Liberalism were proclaimed, and the main points of the Fundamentals of Orthodoxy of 1909-1912 were reiterated. Here the clear-cut distinction must be made lest it be overlooked: the NAE was taking an Orthodox stand on doctrine but not a Fundamentalist stand because it ignored completely the tenet of the imminent coming of the Lord. Many within it did hold to the imminent coming, but others would not affirm it. In this respect it failed to link itself firmly with historic Fundamentalism. Fundamentalists in the movement were willing to shelve this issue temporarily and in so doing paved the way for the surrender of the movement into new-evangelical hands. Fundamentalists cannot afford to treat their doctrines lightly; to do so is to invite modification of the general position they have held. The NAE showed greater laxity and broad-mindedness in welcoming Pentecostals and holiness groups into its membership, and Fundamentalists were increasingly disturbed about this. The Pentecostal membership is the largest within the NAE; it has kept the movement from outrightly examining and condemning the charismatic trends (emphasis on gifts in tongues and healings) of the last few years. As a case in point, Oral Roberts has been a symbol of the charismatic interests and public activities. In 1966 he was welcomed by Billy Graham to the Berlin Congress and opened his school in Tulsa with Graham as guest speaker. But still Fundamentalists within the NAE would keep hoping that Fundamentalism's influence would grow stronger inside the movement in spite of these drifts.

By 1956 James D. Murch listed some forty-eight groups as members with a total of one and a half million. Among the groups were the Assemblies of God numbering 400,000; the Church of God of Cleveland, Tennessee, 200,000; the Foursquare Gospel Church, 88,000; the Pentecostal Church of America, 45,000; and the Pentecostal Holiness Church, 45,000. The largest single group has been the Freewill Baptists.[19] Due mainly to the leadership of Harold Ockenga, Carl F. H. Henry, and Clyde Taylor; the influence of Fuller Seminary and Wheaton College; and the "success-drome" of Billy

[18]W. B. Riley, *The Pilot*, Nov., 1942, p. 54.
[19]A good survey of the movement may be found in James Deforest Murch, *Cooperation Without Compromise* (Grand Rapids: Eerdmans, 1956).

Graham, the NAE became a mouthpiece of New Evangelicalism and was so identified by Ockenga in his 1957 press release defining New Evangelicalism. Since 1947 there has been a constant pull on NAE members to espouse or keep their silence on the steamroller tactics and attitudes of the New Evangelicals and especially on their open endorsement of Billy Graham.

As New Evangelicalism has developed, the NAE has attacked more and more those who would not travel that route. Among the leaders of the last decade have been Rufus M. Jones, Roswell Flower, and its present president, Hudson T. Armerding, who is also president of Wheaton College. The NAE has been effective in its Washington Office in getting visas for missionaries, representation before the proper authorities for chaplains, and radio time, and in lobbying against Roman Catholic demands. But its history, for the last fifteen years, has not been a part of Fundamentalism, although many of its members would think of themselves as Fundamentalists in spite of their affiliation with a new-evangelical organization.

Brethren Groups

Since these groups have never had a denominational ecclesiastical organization and there is no listing of their "assemblies," a historian must resort to general terms and statistics. There have been two studies of note, one by Andrew Miller and an earlier one by the well-known Bible teacher H. A. Ironside, who belonged to the largest of the groups, the Plymouth Brethren, for thirty years.[20] The latter wrote, "The Brethren . . . in an essential way have contributed to the Fundamentalism of the present day. . . . the Brethren as a whole are Fundamentalists."[21] There has never been a question of their doctrinal soundness, and following an early leader, J. N. Darby, they have been careful students of prophecy. They have differed from mainstream Fundamentalists because they have not recognized the office of pastor and have exercised their right to have the Lord's Supper each Lord's Day. Many Fundamentalist leaders who disagree on these points have been proud to acknowledge their indebtedness to such able Bible teachers among the Brethren as J. N. Darby, B. W. Newton, William R. Newell, and Ironside. One of their ablest Bible expositors at the present time is S. Lewis Johnson of the Dallas Seminary faculty.

They have built one school, Emmaus Bible Institute at Oak Park, Illinois, and have a missions and literature center at Prospect

[20]Andrew Miller, *The Brethren: Their Origin, Progress and Testimony*-(Hong Kong: Empire, 1963) and H. A. Ironside, *A Historical Sketch of the Brethren Movement* (Grand Rapids: Zondervan, 1942).

[21]Ironside, p. 11.

Heights, Illinois. They have hewn quite closely to the lines of dispensationalism in their teaching and shunned the evangelism and evangelistic invitations and revival meetings which have characterized most independent Fundamentalists, especially those of Baptist convictions. They have always been set against Liberalism and Modernism and have been able to avoid ecumenical entanglements. One detriment has been their exclusiveness from all Christian groups, liberal and fundamentalist. As to the recent scourge of New Evangelicalism, most have been willing to watch it and willing to take a "wait-and-see" attitude. Many have cooperated with the Graham meetings while others have continued on their own course. That many local "chapels" may tend to lean toward new-evangelical movements is a distinct danger. Very little is said to warn present-day believers; they have been content to expound the Scriptures and have ignored applications to issues of the hour. A very rough estimate is that there are some 1,600 chapels or local assemblies of various kinds of Brethren in this country at the present time.

Associated Gospel Churches (AGC)

This is primarily a service agency, baptistic in polity and belief, under the dynamic leadership of W. O. H. Garman of Pittsburgh, Pennsylvania. It claims a clientele of over three million, these not being members of the AGC but of the groups served by it. It was able to break the monopoly on the chaplaincy held by the National Council of Churches, and now it has over thirty active chaplains. The two largest groups served by the AGC are the American Baptist Association and the Baptist Bible Fellowship, which total over two million. It represents the groups affiliated with it only on things designated by the groups themselves.

Besides the ones already mentioned, also represented are the Associated Gospel Mission, the Anglican Orthodox Church, Associates in Evangelism, Christian Crusade, Christians for Action, Christian Youth Crusade, Committee for the Prevention of Communist Speakers, Gospel Fellowship Association, Independent Baptist Churches, Independent Lutheran Churches, Southwide Baptist Fellowship, various independent churches, and the Missionary Letter Service. Its purpose is simply stated as that of helping "many dissatisfied, disillusioned, conservative Christian Americans which have been looking for a church fellowship which stands true to the historic faith."[22]

[22]W. O. H. Garman, *Where Does Your Church Stand?* (Pittsburgh: Associated Gospel Churches, n.d.).

Fundamental Presbyterians

The last two generations of sound, Bible-believing Presbyterians have been assaulted by the rampaging forces of Liberalism, Neo-Orthodoxy, ecumenical movements, social-action emphasis, and internal dissensions. Their forces, therefore, have been fragmented; their nationwide ministry has been shattered; and the few sound churches left have been unable to launch expanding evangelistic campaigns to replenish their empty ranks.

The Machen stand in the late twenties and early thirties failed to attract many to its standards. A very small minority left the comfortable manses and beautiful church buildings. These took the names of Orthodox Presbyterian and Bible Presbyterian, their differences being in the area of eschatology and Christian liberty. Associated with the Orthodox group were such men as Cornelius Van Til, John Murray, Oswald T. Allis, and the faculty of Westminster Seminary in Philadelphia. Connected with the Bible Presbyterians have been such leaders as Carl McIntire, A. A. MacRae, J. Oliver Buswell, and Laird Harris. The early death of Machen in 1937 was indeed a great loss. Charles J. Woodbridge, who had been in the midst of the Presbyterian split in the early thirties, separated from both groups to serve in the Southern Presbyterian Church, at Fuller Seminary, and since 1957 as a free-lance Bible conference teacher and writer, an open foe of New Evangelicals.

Since 1940 Fundamental Presbyterians have been through some stormy times. In September of 1940 Bible Presbyterians joined another independent group—the Bible Protestant Church—in planning for a larger national organization. The two groups drew up a constitution by September of 1941 as the American Council of Christian Churches. This new organization was stated to be "militantly pro-Gospel and anti-Modernist."[23] It would oppose Modernism, compromise, and apostasy. Very definitely it was separatistic although majoring on the sound doctrine of the Reformation position with some members of premillennial persuasion. The ACCC was under the strong hand of a strong man indeed, Carl McIntire. He had been ordained into the Presbyterian ministry in 1931, had served for two years at Chelsea Presbyterian Church in Atlantic City, New Jersey, and then had gone to Collingswood Presbyterian Church in Collingswood, New Jersey. He organized a Bible Presbyterian Church at Collingswood in 1938 by leading most of the 1,600 members out of the old church to start a new one in a tabernacle. Rugged in convictions and gifted as a speaker, he has continued as one of the best-known men among

[23]Carl McIntire, *Twentieth Century Reformation* (Collingswood, N. J.: Christian Beacon, 1946), p. 181.

Fundamental Presbyterians.[24] He was a natural to lead the American Council of Christian Churches (ACCC) when it was formed in 1941. He started the *Christian Beacon* and Faith Theological Seminary in Philadelphia, and gained control of National Bible Institute (now Shelton College) of New York, later at Ringwood, New Jersey, Cape May, New Jersey, and now at Cape Canaveral, Florida. In addition, his great energies have carried him to many parts of the world to organize believers against the World Council. In 1948 he founded the International Council of Christian Churches (ICCC) to offset the influence and work of the World Council of Churches. It still continues this offensive, though weakened in strength.

McIntire had the strong support of the GARB and the IFCA in the formation of both the ICC and the ACCC, but both have now rejected his leadership. A major eruption took place in 1954 when a group inside the Bible Presbyterian movement, led by Robert Rayburn of Highland College in California, revolted because it claimed that McIntire's separatism was too extreme and that it did not represent the position of many in the group. Also, several times questions had been raised as to the accuracy of the figures used by McIntire, for by 1954 he claimed to represent over one million people while only some 200,000 constituent members could be counted. The break was complete in 1955 when the majority of the Bible Presbyterian Synod voted to put all agencies under the Synod; so McIntire and a few withdrew, although he continued to use the name of Bible Presbyterian.

To the outsider it was a little confusing to have two Bible Presbyterian Churches, one the Collingswood Synod and one the Columbus Synod. The latter took the name of The Bible Presbyterian Synod, Inc., until 1961 when it took the name of The Evangelical Presbyterian Church in order not to be confused with McIntire's group. By this time it had established Covenant College and Seminary in St. Louis with Rayburn as president and Laird Harris and J. O. Buswell, Jr., on the faculty. In 1965 it united with a much smaller group known as The Reformed Presbyterian Church of North America, forming a new denomination, the Reformed Presbyterian Church, Evangelical Synod. At the time of union it counted 120 ministers and 31 elders. Its 1971 directory has over 14,000 communicant members with a total of 136 churches. Its official mission work is the World Presbyterian Mission, but its churches support missionaries serving many boards. The group claims to be Fundamentalist, although amillennialism is tolerated

[24]See Margaret G. Harden, *A Brief History of the Bible Presbyterian Church* (Collingswood: Christian Beacon, 1968).

and some would be open-minded toward New Evangelicalism.

Covenant College is now located on Lookout Mountain, Chattanooga, Tennessee, with Marion D. Barnes as president. The stated clerk is Paul Gilchrist of Covenant College. The Synod counts itself the inheritor of the Orthodoxy of strong and rugged Presbyterians of the stamp of J. G. Machen, Harold S. Laird, and M. T. MacPherson and acclaims as its scholarly leaders such men as Laird Harris, Peter Stam, J. Oliver Buswell, Jr., and Robert Rayburn.

The break did not keep the courageous McIntire from his energetic campaign of exposing and condemning apostasy in all forms. He had a strong home base at the Bible Presbyterian Church in Collingswood, New Jersey, where he was pastor, an effective weapon in his *Christian Beacon,* and both the ACCC and the ICCC as platforms from which to condemn and expose Modernism on the national and international scenes. He had Faith Theological Seminary in Philadelphia; John Knox Bible Presbyterian College, Pasadena, Calififormia; and Shelton College, first at Ringwood, later at Cape May, New Jersey, and now in Florida. He accused the World Council of "radical pacificism . . . on the road of creating a super-church and desiring Rome in the family of the World Council."[25] To him the proceedings of the First Assembly of the World Council sounded more like Babel than Pentecost. Council leaders came under McIntire's attacks in the *Christian Beacon* with the main thrusts against such well-known Liberals as J. C. Bennett, E. T. Dahlberg, G. B. Oxnam, W. P. Pugh, J. R. Mott, C. P. Taft, H. P. Van Dusen, R. W. Sockman, and F. C. Fry. Of them all McIntire would write that their "blatant and blasphemous unbelief should be known in all the churches of the world."[26] Also on his list of leading apostates were H. S. Leiper, Douglas Horton, and S. M. Cavert.

Two more breaks brought McIntire's forces to a low ebb. One was the secession of the IFCA over many differences, one being the constant question as to the number of people for whom the ACCC and the *Christian Beacon* spoke. It was also evident that strong personalities were clashing. A second revolt came in 1968 when several leaders of the ACCC openly repudiated McIntire's domination, and control passed into the hands of such men as R. T. Ketcham, R. F. Hamilton, D. A. Waite, and John E. Milheim. In 1970 McIntire tried to wrest back the control of the Council at a meeting in Pasadena, Calififornia, but the entire meeting left the ACCC in a sordid shambles with a myriad of charges and countercharges and unresolved differences. Another break came in the summer of 1971

[25]Carl McIntire, *The Modern Tower of Babel* (Collingswood, N.J.: Christian Beacon, 1949), pp. 100, 112, 134.
[26]Ibid., p. 196.

when A. A. MacRae and most of the faculty of Faith Seminary left to organize Biblical Theological Seminary near Philadelphia, thus cutting student size to one-half and further splitting a weak voice.

But another side of the picture is the growing ministry of McIntire on the Twentieth Century Reformation Hour broadcast, particularly in the exposure of new evidences of apostasy and the spread of communistic influence and in open attacks on rioters, marchers, and the anti-War sentiment concerning the Vietnam situation. In this counteraction, McIntire has led marches and rallies in Washington, D. C., with some national recognition. In addition, he has led in the purchase of a large hotel complex at Cape May, New Jersey, the Christian Admiral, for conferences. He has moved his liberal arts college (Shelton College) to Cape Canaveral, Florida, where he has plans for a large Christian center. In July, 1972, McIntire ascended to the post of chancellor of Shelton, and at his suggestion, the board of the College named Hyland W. Shepherd as president. The latter had directed the music at McIntire's church in Collingswood, New Jersey, for twenty-four years. Thus his Fundamentalist empire expands, including his church, The Bible Presbyterian Church in Collingswood, New Jersey, the *Christian Beacon,* his large holdings at Cape May and Cape Canaveral, and his ever-widening radio ministry, which is a daily tonic to large audiences across the nation as he continues to expose and attack. His following numbers in the thousands—readers, students, and radio listeners, who are very faithful in their giving in order to keep abreast of the wrongdoings of politicians, educators, and religious leaders. The actual number of churches aligned with him is about one hundred in the Bible Presbyterian Synod, with a membership of approximately seventeen thousand—mostly small churches, with his own in Collingswood the only one of considerable size.

There is no listing of independent Presbyterian Churches in the country who have no affiliation with regular Presbyterian denominations. Therefore only an estimate can be made, and this would be, obviously, faulty. Upwards of 250 such congregations do exist, but no numbering of members has been attempted. It would be helpful to have them listed with their faithful pastors and members.

The Baptist Missionary Association (BMA)

Now twenty-three years old, this Fundamentalist Baptist group reports 1,425 churches with 194,000 members.[27] Formerly it was known as the North American Baptist Association, but a change in name was made so that it would not be confused with the liberal Northern Baptists. It was organized in May, 1950, by 822

[27]*The Baptist Missionary Association of America* (Jacksonville, Tex.: Baptist News Service, 1971).

messengers representing 465 churches from sixteen states. These had belonged to the American Baptist Association but broke away on the question of whether the churches were allowed proper voting privileges on the seating of messengers. The size of the movement deserves a full-length history. Only very brief booklets have yet appeared.[28]

In its two decades of growth, many worthy men have served in the BMA. A listing would include G. D. Kellar, E. T. Burgess, A. R. Reddin, O. D. Christian, Ralph Cottrell, John W. Duggar, D. O. Silvey, W. J. Burgess, W. R. Speer, T. O. Tollett, and James A. Henry, its president.

The doctrinal statements of the BMA follow closely the truths of Baptist Fundamentalism including the imminency of the Lord's coming, verbal inspiration, and separation from all heresies and human inventions that conflict with the Word of God. Great emphasis is put on the local visible church, rejecting "alien immersion" because it is not performed under the authority of a local New Testament Baptist church. In this respect, the Association follows the convictions of Pendleton and John R. Graves, and *Landmarkism* in its distinctives. The Association disdains any label as a denomination but claims to be only a fellowship of local churches. It prides itself in being in historic succession to apostolic principles and practices—a succession, however, based on principles, not popes.

From the 1971-1972 directory other statistics are available. Four bookstores are in operation; three Bible schools function, as do three junior colleges and one seminary. Some fifty periodicals are published. Over 107,000 are enrolled in Sunday Schools, and during the 1971-1972 year over thirteen million dollars was raised for all causes. Two million dollars was given to missions, education, and benevolences.

It might be noted that most churches in the BMA are small in comparison with many large independent churches in the nation. Latest reports show only six churches with over eight hundred members, while more than one thousand churches have two hundred or fewer members. The churches are found mainly in the Southwest with Texas leading with 502, followed by Arkansas with 359 and Mississippi with 159. Some cities and towns that have a concentration are shown in the following list:

Dallas, Texas	22 churches
Houston, Texas	14 churches
Gilmer, Texas	13 churches
Jonesboro, Arkansas	14 churches

[28]Namely, the one named above and one of the same title published by the Missions Office of the BMA, Little Rock, Ark., n.d.

Magnolia, Arkansas	11 churches
Little Rock, Arkansas	9 churches
Laurel, Mississippi	11 churches
Lucedale, Mississippi	10 churches
Jacksonville, Texas	10 churches
Livingston, Texas	12 churches
Lufkin, Texas	10 churches
Mineola, Texas	10 churches
Nacogdoches, Texas	14 churches

The Association operates the Baptist Missionary Association Theological Seminary at Jacksonville, Texas, where John W. Gregson was president until the summer of 1972, when he resigned to be full-time pastor of the First Baptist Church of Carthage, Texas. His successor is Eugene Murphy, who had been president of the Southeast Baptist College in Laurell, Mississippi. C. O. Strong is in charge of the BMA's Office of Publications in Texarkana, Texas. The missions work is directed by Craig Branham at 716 Main Street in Little Rock, Arkansas. One hundred and twelve missionaries are supported on sixteen fields, with thirty serving as home missionaries in the United States. In addition the fifteen state associations and eighty local and district associations have sixty-five missionaries locally. Mission fields include Latin America, Australia, Bolivia, Brazil, France, China, and Canada.

Southwide Baptist Fellowship (SBF)

This loosely connected fellowship of Fundamental Baptists in the Southeastern section of our nation owes its origin to a meeting of pastors in Highland Park Baptist Church in Chattanooga, Tennessee, on March 20, 1956. Its first name was the Southern Baptist Fellowship but was changed, lest it be mistakenly thought to be a part of the Southern Baptist Convention. There were 147 charter members of the new group with eight Southern states represented. Its purpose was to provide a fellowship for men of Fundamentalist Baptist convictions. This writer was asked to draw up a statement of faith and it is still the official doctrinal position; it affirms the common Fundamentalist truths with emphasis on the local church and the premillennial coming of the Lord. This statement was accepted at a large public rally held at Highland Park on November 28, 1956. Many of the charter members are still active in churches and schools, along with evangelistic ministries. Among the first members were such men as Lee Roberson, John R. Rice, Harold B. Sightler, J. R. Faulkner, Wayne Van Gelderen, Norman G. Lemmons, Gene Arnold, Bob Gray, Bob Bevington, and John R. Waters.

This fellowship has provided an annual assembly for Fundamental pastors and Christian workers, usually meeting for two days with stirring messages on soulwinning, the issues of the hour, building local churches, and points of separation. Several times it has met at Highland Park Baptist and other times at Winston-Salem, North Carolina; Greenville, South Carolina, at Bob Jones University; Garland, Texas; Lynchburg, Virginia; and Jacksonville, Florida. The arrangements for speakers and programs are left to host pastors.

By 1961 the membership was listed as 1,100. One can become a member by signing the doctrinal statement and paying an annual fee of two dollars. By 1971 the membership directory listed 1,195 members from the following states:

Alabama 72, Arkansas 11, California 8, Florida 109, Georgia 188, Illinois 14, Indiana 14, Kentucky 20, Louisiana 16, Maryland 16, Michigan 13, Missouri 26, North Carolina 180, Ohio 30, Oklahoma 19, Pennsylvania 14, South Carolina 129, Tennessee 132, Texas 69, Virginia 67, West Virginia 16, and others 32.

The Fellowship met in December, 1971, in Panama City, Florida, and elected officers for 1972: Jack Hudson of Charlotte, North Carolina, as moderator; Gary Coleman of Garland, Texas, and Ron Schaeffer of Tampa, Florida, as vice-moderators; and J. R. Waters of Laurens, South Carolina, as secretary-treasurer. Coleman is the moderator for 1972-1973. Its membership now stands at 1,500, with about half of that number being pastors of independent Baptist Churches. It estimates the total membership of churches represented as being 130,000—a figure used by the Associated Gospel Churches in representing it with the United States government for purposes of the chaplaincy. The Fellowship has passed resolutions condemning New Evangelicalism and the Ecumenical Movement and at several meetings has reaffirmed its loyalty to the Bible and its devotion to the country. Many men in it openly support the ministry of Carl McIntire and the International Council of Christian Churches.

Lee Roberson of Highland Park Baptist has held a commanding place of influence in the Southwide Fellowship because of the 33,000-member church he pastors and the growth of Tennessee Temple Schools. He has used this leadership wisely in encouraging small struggling churches and young pastors trying to build good works. He has freely provided the excellent facilities of Highland Park Baptist for meetings and allowed the inspiration of his large congregation and student body to inspire other Baptist pastors to continue their soulwinning efforts. This encouragement has been deeply appreciated and has drawn the pastors into a fellowship of men who support not only the work of the Fellowship but also the efforts of Tennessee Temple Schools, composed of a Bible college, a liberal arts college, and a seminary. This leadership, however, has raised some questions concerning the fact that Roberson has never, in his church or schools, provided outspoken leadership in leading churches out of the Southern Baptist Convention and by a continuing silence on issues of compromise, collaboration with New Evangelicals, and new forms of middle-of-the-roadism. This has been demonstrated by recognition and honors given such middle-of-the-roaders as George Sweeting, Merv Rosell, J. Vernon McGee, and Bill Bright of Campus Crusade.

The Fellowship has not had a phenomenal growth, but it has provided an annual opportunity for fellowship and inspiration for hundreds of pastors. At the present there is a slight trace of new-evangelical sympathy within its circle, but it is hoped that pastors will awaken to the leaven and prevent its spread. In this regard, constant alertness and sensitivity to compromise will be the price that pastors must pay if they are to avoid a softening of their stand by their opposition and an apathy aiding the enemies of the Faith. Eternal vigilance is a high price to pay, but without it the Southwide Fellowship can slip very easily into the middle road of empty profession and barren organization. Its future must be watched by those in the Southern states where the Lord has placed it.

Freewill Baptists

With over two thousand churches and three colleges, the Freewill Baptists have had a history of standing for evangelical truth with an Arminian emphasis and a touch-and-go attitude in the present conflict with compromise. Their men, east of the Mississippi, have been Fundamental in doctrine, even holding to the pretribulation rapture of the Church. West of the Mississippi, many of the pastors either believe or lean to an amillennial position. Thus the denomination as a whole must be listed as moderate Fundamentalist, although it has a strong core of militants. Until July, 1972, it was a member of the NAE, and it has suffered from this alliance, although the decision to withdraw does show a surer direction.

The group operates three schools: the Free Will Baptist Bible College, Nashville, Tennessee, under the leadership of L. C. Johnson; the Hillsdale Free Will Baptist Bible College, Moore, Oklahoma, whose president is Bill M. Jones; and the California Christian College, Fresno, California, under W. T. Jernigan. Among its other leaders are Rufus Coffey, Reford Wilson, R. E. Picirilli, Homer Willis, Lonnie Graves, Raymond Riggs, and Jack Paramore. Also working with the group in years past were Stanley Mooneyham, Jim Owen Jones, and Billy Melvin of NAE service, and Jerry Ballard, now working outside the group. Among the Freewill Baptists are strains of both militancy and moderation, caution being a quite common characteristic for the sake of denominational unity. More militant in their stand are such men as Graves, Ronald Creech, Dale Burden, Glenn Hill, James Pittman, C. R. Phillips, and Joseph Ange.

The Freewill Baptists have several publications, and a few representative ones bear mention. *Heartbeat* is aimed primarily at missions work, although it has published both Fundamental and new-evangelical articles; Reford Wilson is its editor. The official Freewill Baptist organ, *Contact,* is edited by Rufus Coffey and provides general news among the men and churches of the organization. Probably the most militant periodical is *The Evangel* (formerly *The Evangelistic Echoes*), edited by Van Dale Hudson. Another militant and outspoken one is the *Virginia Link*. A third is *The Witness* put out by the North Carolina Association, a state group militant above the rest. The latter is edited by Ronald Creech and has continued openly to oppose New Evangelicalism, as formerly represented in the denomination by Mooneyham. It played a large part in arousing pastors to the new-evangelical threat, as did alumni of Bob Jones University. These alumni were aroused to the danger by a censure motion against the leaders of the University in 1971, by the publication of a paper *The Contender,* and by this author's open attack on the steamroller tactics of the denomination.

In 1961 the National Association suffered a rupture when a number of churches in North Carolina broke away, the immediate cause being a controversy over the Edgemont Church in Durham, North Carolina. The National Association sided with the pastor, while several pastors in the state association supported the church; the national officers claimed the state officers were not congregational in their actions. The new group has used the word "Original" in its official title. It holds to Freewill Baptist truth and allows each congregation to be self-determining, except in case of a division in the congregation, when the Conference shall decide the outcome. The North Carolina group owns and operates Mount Olive Junior College with an enrollment of three hundred; in addition it has an Assembly at Black Mountain, North Carolina, and a Children's Home at Middlesex, North Carolina. The president of this group is F. B. Cherry of Daniels Chapel Bible Institute, Wilson, North Carolina; other leaders in this group include W. B. Raper, C. F. Bowen, and Walter Reynolds. The North Carolina group reports 225 churches with a combined membership of over 30,000.

How can a true and unbiased picture of Freewill Baptists be presented in relation to historic Fundamentalism? Its Arminian emphasis has isolated it from most Fundamentalists. Its inability to produce large churches has limited its influence. The large number of untrained pastors has tended to perpetuate a surface-type of evangelicalism. A strong segment has openly fought both Liberalism and New Evangelicalism. Many oppose anything liberal but ignore the dangers and drifts of New Evangelicalism as if they did not endanger either the schools or the churches. Others welcome open, unashamed entrance into new-evangelical work as spearheaded by the NAE.

Which group would win in a showdown was a question for some years prior to the decisive action taken at the annual meeting in Fort Worth in July of 1972, when the denomination voted to secede from the NAE. This did not end interest in the NAE, but it was a serious blow, producing a firmer Fundamentalist stance for the Freewill Baptists and putting them in the general camp of Bob Jones University, Maranatha Baptist College, the ABA, the BBF, and the BMA. How complete this victory has been will be a matter for careful observation and keen analysis.

The denomination now enlists some 375,000 members in its churches, with the largest being the Fellowship Free Will Baptist Church in Durham, North Carolina, pastored by Lonnie Graves. A great step forward would be the training of more men in sound Fundamentalist schools for future leadership in churches. It is sincerely hoped that the Freewill Baptists will heed this call and obey.

Orthodox Baptists

Some Fundamental Baptists have used the name "Orthodox" for some years to designate their doctrine and teaching. They owe their origin to the ministry of W. Lee Rector of the First Baptist Church in Ardmore, Oklahoma, who left Southern Baptist ranks in the early 1940's to organize the First Orthodox Baptist Church in Ardmore. In 1944 he opened the Orthodox Bible Institute at his church to help train young preachers. He was joined by several churches which left the Southern Convention because of the inroads of Liberalism. The Institute closed its doors in the late 1960's in order to assist in the start of a new school, the Orthodox Baptist College in Dallas, Texas, under James L. Higgs. Serving on its faculty was B. F. Dearmore, who had been dean at Norris' school. Other leaders in the Orthodox Baptist movement have been L. S. Ballard, J. Cullis Smith, Grady L. Higgs, W. L. Moser, Sr., and W. L. Moser, Jr. Supporting the movement at present are approximately three hundred churches, although most are independent Baptist Churches without the special designation of "Orthodox." The group is strictly Fundamental, maintaining a separation from apostasy, New Evangelicalism, and compromise. It is a solid group. The college in Dallas promises a bright future for pastors and churches.

Fundamental Methodists

Though there have been thousands of Methodists who have not agreed with the downward slide of Methodism to Liberalism and apostasy, they have found no way to stop it. These have desired that the grand old truths proclaimed by John Wesley be taught and practiced, but only a very few have had the courage to leave the denomination and separate for their faith. One group was the Southern Methodist Church, which was organized in January, 1940, in Columbia, South Carolina. It has been true to Wesley's doctrines and has separated from organized apostasy. Local churches own their property and call their own pastors rather than have them named by a bishop. Indeed, it has no bishops. It has four Annual Conferences with a total of 150 churches and approximately 20,000 members. It operates the Southern Methodist College in Orangeburg, South Carolina, which offers two years of liberal arts toward a B.A. in Bible. Among its leaders are Lynn Corbett, J. B. Gamble, and Glenn Comfort. In addition to Wesleyan doctrine it holds to the imminent coming of the Lord along with premillennial interpretations. It has remained segregated on the premise that integration would add to and not solve problems.

Another loosely connected fellowship of Fundamental Methodists is the American Association of Bible-Believing Methodists, Street, Maryland, with some 120 churches represented. Here some rather small but heroic groups may find fellowship and comfort and their names should be recognized. Among them would be the Francis Asbury Society of Ministers, Bible Methodist Missions, the Evangelical Methodist Church, the Bible Methodist Church, Independent Methodists, the Francis Asbury Evangel, the Fundamental Methodist Church, the John Wesley Fellowship, and Asbury Bible Churches. Leaders of these groups include such men as D. H. Knight, Jr., Amos Price, David Clark, and D. L. Gorham. A small group in addition to those listed is the Bible Protestant Church with 40 churches in New Jersey and Pennsylvania, but no listing of churches or memberships is available. The Francis Asbury Society, listed above, is an offshoot of the Southern Methodist Church, now four years old, and claims that new-evangelical moods have permeated Southern Methodists and that a soft attitude toward a strong separatist position has been developing. The Asbury Society speaks for about twenty-five churches.

Another worthy group of Fundamental Methodists is the Evangelical Methodist Church which began in Memphis, Tennessee, in 1946, led by J. H. Hamblen and E. B. Vargis. While small to begin with, this movement has grown to over two hundred churches in this country and an equal number in Mexico. There are three colleges operated by the Evangelical Methodists: Azusa Pacific, Azusa, California; John Wesley College, Greensboro, North Carolina; and Zennard College, Oskaloosa, Iowa. Ralph Vanderwood is the general superintendent, and Neal Anderson is superintendent of the Eastern Conference, with Gordon Johnson heading the Western Conference. Some of the leading pastors in this work are Frank Ray, William Ray Cloer, R. D. Driggers, Neal Anderson, and Frank Washburn. This group affirms the truths so precious to John Wesley, rejecting all forms of Liberalism and compromise, holding firmly to Bible holiness and a congregational form of church government. Many years ago the venerable H. C. Morrison of Asbury College prophesied that the day would come when an Evangelical Methodist Church would be needed. Truly he was a modern prophet in the best sense of the word.

The last of the dissenting groups to be recognized is the Association of Independent Methodists in the Deep South; it started seven years ago because of the deepening apostasy of the Methodist Church.

By this time some will ask how many independent churches of Baptist, Methodist, Bible, and Presbyterian persuasions there are. Only an estimate is permissible. A total of 13,000 Fundamental churches now exist in the nation, and of this number 1,500 are not listed with a national association or fellowship: the Baptists number 1,200; Bible or community churches, 150; Presbyterians, 125; and Methodists, 75. The total membership of the thirteen thousand churches would be near four million. Of these thirteen thousand less than one-third would qualify as militantly Fundamentalist because of the fact that pastors and congregations are not informed about issues, battles, dangers, and new types of compromise. Many hundreds could be indoctrinated into an out-and-out militant position if pastors and teachers would take the role of strong soldiers and not that of soft "sports."

New Testament Association of Independent Baptist Churches (NTAIBC)

One outcome of the hard-core Fundamentalism of the Conservative Baptist movement was the formation of the NTAIBC in the early 1960's. At first it was within the CB group, but it has now gone its independent way. In the fall of 1964 over 200 pastors and laymen met in Marquette Manor Baptist Church in Chicago to discuss plans for a new organization. In 1965, 335 messengers representing 100 churches met in Beth Eden Baptist Church in Denver to adopt a constitution and confession of faith. The next year the Association was formally organized at Eagledale Baptist in Indianapolis with 27 churches affiliating; it now has a total of 55 churches in its fellowship. Its office is located at 13030 North 47th Avenue, in Minneapolis, Minnesota.

The Association takes a firm stand on the Fundamentals with an emphasis on the local church, its complete autonomy, and adherence to the strict New Testament pattern. It provides an avenue of fellowship and service for Bible-centered independent Baptist churches. It is firmly committed to the pretribulational coming of the Lord and openly opposes not only Liberalism and conventionism but all forms of compromise, New Eangelicalism, and the ecumenical movements. The Association in its constitution forbids itself from legislating for the churches or attempting to interfere with the rights and complete autonomy of the churches.

Several men have given leadership to the group, and they include Richard C. Weeks, Allen Williams, Wayne C. Musson, Robert Terrey, and Richard Reynolds. Though small, the NTAIBC is a Fundamentalist Baptist fellowship in every sense of the word.

Interdenominational Fundamentalists

Sometimes historians labor at great length to exalt the various ministries of the Liberals and the Evangelicals, with a strong hint that Fundamentalists have not been involved in many things outside the local churches, where their pastors keep declaiming the Gospel. This is a one-sided picture at best, and too often grossly misleading. Even a casual look at the many ministries of Fundamentalists in the last two periods of its history would be proof of a very diverse and widespread outreach.

There have been untold numbers of radio broadcasts on both a national and a local scale. Bible conferences of great influence and vibrant ministry have mushroomed at many beautiful centers. Evangelists of outstanding stature and with lesser gifts have graced the scene. Dozens of rescue missions have been built and supported in order to bring the message of salvation to the derelicts of society, along with clothes and food. Tract societies have printed many millions of tracts to be distributed on street corners, in bus stations, in homes on house-to-house visitation, and in other places. Ministries geared to reach the very young and the teen-agers have soared in number and response (most of the worthwhile ones have been started and supported by Fundamentalists).

Christian day schools have sprung up in many centers and now enroll thousands in God-honoring training of children. Many Fundamental mission boards have arisen to ensure soundness of missionaries, appealing to sound churches for support. Mention

should be made of evening Bible schools set up in local churches to
help lay people study the Bible. Many noble Bible teachers and
preachers have had their sermons and commentaries published for
the benefit of thousands of readers. Christian magazines have filled
a void with information and inspiration. Christian education
departments have inspired new methods and techniques for the
communication of Scriptural truth. Summer camp programs especially adapted for the young have increased. Bible memorization programs have been widely used. These have all been a part
of a diverse and exciting array of Fundamentalist forces, no less
in number than those of Liberalism, Neo-Orthodoxy, or the denominational programs. We must not ignore the obvious fact, often
noted in our analysis, that a great majority of these have been taken
over by New Evangelicals or their collaborators. This we decry,
urging Fundamentalists to recover all they can and erect counter-
ministries and groups to offset the mighty tides of compromise.
We shall here examine some of these interdenominational Fundamentalist forces of this century.

A. Evangelism.   Three men stood out in the twentieth-
century field of evangelism: Billy Sunday, a Presbyterian, Bob
Jones, Sr., a Methodist, and Billy Graham, a Baptist. Sunday
provided a great boost to Fundamentalism through his converts;
Jones was the last of the old-time evangelists to have a solid Fundamentalist image; and Graham has been, and is, the spokesman for
New Evangelicalism. We shall look briefly at their ministries.

William A. (Billy) Sunday was born in Iowa in 1862. He played
major league baseball in Chicago, where he was saved at the old
Pacific Garden Mission. He worked for the YMCA for three years
before entering evangelism as an assistant to J. Wilbur Chapman,
who left the evangelistic field to become pastor of Bethany
Presbyterian Church in Philadelphia in 1895. Thereupon, Sunday
began his own ministry and in ten years was solidly established as
an evangelist. For the next twenty years he was the foremost of the
day. His greatest revivals came between 1914 and 1919, during
which time he had nine revivals in cities of over half a million
population. His unique style employed nerve-tingling dramatics; he
"skipped, ran, walked, bounced, slid, and gyrated on the platform."[29]
He would smash chairs as he fought the Devil. He would shed vest
and tie and roll up his sleeves; as no one before or since, he used the
sharpest kind of invective as he railed against the "hog-jowled,
weasel-eyed, sponge-columned, mushy-fisted, jelly-spined, pussy-

[29]Weisberger, p. 147.

footing, four-flushing, charlotte-russed Christian."[30] His attacks on booze consumers were sharp, for he called the drinker "a low-down, whiskey-soaked, beer-guzzling, foul-mouthed hypocrite."[31] He railed against liberal preachers, who were "fools . . . breaking their necks to please a lot of old society dames."[32] Tobacco was the "earmark of a damnable cigaret-smoking, cursing libertine."[33] Others sharing the spotlight with Billy were his wife, affectionately known by everyone as "Ma Sunday"; a singer, Fred Fisher; and, after 1909, Homer Rodeheaver with his famous trombone. It was noticeable in the 1920's that more and more of Sunday's meetings were held in small towns, for the greatest gatherings in the major cities were over. This downward slide continued until his death in 1935.

Billy Sunday died a legendary figure despite the fact that in the closing years of his lifetime, more and more Americans were turning from things religious to Hollywood, the radio, and the automobile and to the greatest of American specialities—the making of money. He was one of the greatest Fundamentalist figures in the first third of this century, although he was not trained as a minister nor did he understand the differences between Orthodoxy, conservative doctrine, and Fundamentalist distinctives. But his friends and followers were in those groups and not with the Modernists and the Liberals.

The second one, Robert R. (Bob) Jones, came from a family of twelve in southeast Alabama, in 1883. He thought Sunday was the greatest evangelist of all, and Sunday returned the compliment.[34] His big meetings started in 1916 and continued for half a century, with the biggest in Birmingham in 1921. Along with his many meetings, he started a school, Bob Jones College, at St. Andrews Bay, Florida, in 1926 with the announced intention that it be a "fundamentalist base for future evangelism."[35] He accepted the sage advice of H. C. Morrison of Asbury College that he "keep the platform hot."[36] No one has ever charged the University with a single departure from these basic convictions. In the Crash of 1929, assets of half a million were wiped out, and the school moved to Cleveland, Tennessee. The Cleveland property was sold in 1947, and the school moved to an 180-acre site in Greenville, South Carolina, where it now operates. Jones' son, Bob, Jr., added cultural aspects to

[30]Ibid., p. 249.
[31]Ibid., p. 251.
[32]Ibid., p. 250.
[33]Ibid.
[34]A most factual and appreciative study of this evangelist and his work has been done by a close associate, R. K. Johnson, in *Builder of Bridges* (Murfreesboro, Tenn.: Sword of the Lord, 1969).
[35]Ibid., p. 181.
[36]Ibid., p. 182.

the growing University with his gifts as a Shakespearean actor. He also developed an ability to analyze new types of compromise in the fields of evangelism and youth ministries. In addition, a film ministry was added (Unusual Films), and several widely acclaimed productions have been produced, including *Wine of Morning, Red Runs the River,* and *Flame in the Wind.* The campus also contains a world-famous art gallery.

A major issue to arise was that of Billy Graham's ecumenical evangelism, for Billy started his college training at Bob Jones College while it was still in Tennessee. Jones, Sr., contended that "Billy was selling our crowd down the river" by his yoke with non-Fundamentalists.[37] In 1968 Bob Jones, Sr., a rugged Fundamentalist, after a lifetime of ministry in soulwinning and education, went to his heavenly reward.

Little needs to be written of Billy Graham, for his name is a household word in the English-speaking world. Now in his middle fifties, this son of Presbyterian parents in Charlotte, North Carolina, has been in the spotlight for twenty years with his mammoth rallies and his friendships with the biggest names in politics, religion, and entertainment. He has been a catalyst, bringing together Liberals and Evangelicals to the embarrassment of Fundamentalists, who see such alliances and fellowships as essentially unscriptural and dishonoring to God. He has been a friend to such groups as the National Council of Churches and the Roman Catholic Church, accepting an honorary degree from a Catholic school, Belmont Abbey College in North Carolina.

But his mass rallies with thousands coming from all directions to giant stadiums, football fields, and amphitheaters, have drawn millions of Americans to hear the gospel he preaches, despite the most widely varied multitude of sponsors in the history of evangelism.[38] One of his friends and supporters, Robert O. Ferm, has published a defense of his inclusivism.[39]

By the time of the New York campaign of 1956 it was clear that Graham's sponsors would include all shades of Protestants represented in the Protestant Council of Churches in New York. Before that time Fundamentalists had worked with the Graham team in giant rallies; since that year they have separated from him because of his unscriptural fellowship and cooperation with liberal

[37]Ibid., p. 274.
[38]Among the men cooperating have been Norman Vincent Peale, John S. Bonnell, Gerald Kennedy, Louis Evans, Tom Skinner, James A. Pike, and liberal Anglican bishops.
[39]Robert O. Ferm, *Cooperative Evangelism* (Grand Rapids: Zondervan, 1958). Few published books have so many historical and theological errors and factual loopholes.

leaders and their groups. Added to his ministry have been the Hour of Decision on the radio and his hour-long telecasts in prime television time, costing millions of dollars. His type of evangelism has found its main support among new-evangelical churches and large Christian schools. Smaller schools and other Christian groups have been steamrollered to line up in his support or face a loss of prestige or almost certain splits in their constituencies.

Billy Graham has helped new-evangelical meetings such as the Berlin Congress, which welcomed Oral Roberts of Pentecostal fame and excluded Fundamentalist Carl McIntire. He has become the most famous ecumenical evangelist of history, and while Fundamentalist churches will reap a few converts from his meetings, the movement itself will continue to erode Fundamentalist strength and attract thousands of converts to new-evangelical and liberal schools and churches. Billy has drawn more to hear him than any of his contemporaries, but fewer remain as Fundamental believers. His ministry is not over; it bids fair to grow and spearhead protestant unity with the Roman Catholic Church in the building of the one-world church prophesied in Revelation 17-18, which is doomed for the judgment of God at the very end of the Great Tribulation. But few heed prophecies when they interfere with their programs. The sure erection of Babylon continues quickly before our very eyes, but few saints have their eyes open to see.

We should include the names of a few men who have preached the same Gospel to crowds and shared the evangelistic spotlight. One would be John R. Rice of Murfreesboro, Tennessee, who, now in his seventy-seventh year, is widely influential because of revival meetings and his paper, *The Sword of the Lord,* which has a circulation of 250,000. It has been the theological diet of hundreds of preachers for years. In addition, Rice has over 120 books in print with 36 million copies. The paper has reflected Rice's position as a soulwinner, revival promoter, and outspoken premillennial Bible preacher and defender. One feature of his ministry has caused widespread concern: his promotion of men who are openly aligned with such apostate groups as the Southern Baptists. Rice takes the position that men who love the Lord and get souls saved should be our friends, no matter what their affiliation, associations, or fellowship. On this basic issue a split has come in Fundamentalist ranks, and Rice has removed himself from the board of trustees of Bob Jones University.

The chancellor of the University, Bob Jones, Jr., disassociated himself from the Rice-sponsored International Conference on Biblical Evangelism, scheduled for August, 1972, but later cancelled. Jones charged that the conference, largely under Rice's influence, would not encourage the men now taking a fully separatist stand but would cater to the uncommitted pastors who should by now have made their commitment. Rice has openly defended his sympathies with W. A. Criswell of the Southern Baptists and John Walvoord, although both have cooperated with new-evangelical spokesmen and leaders. The Jones' position forced the scuttling of the International Conference, although Rice had published in *The Sword* a most impressive array of speakers, including the best-known names in the field of evangelism among Fundamentalists. That the Conference did not meet has pointed up a deep-seated split within Fundamentalist ranks over the sticky issue of separatism. This split has been widespread because of the open stand of Charles J. Woodbridge in his booklet *Biblical Separation* and the outspoken attack on Rice by Carl McIntire in his paper, *The Christian Beacon.* Both Woodbridge and McIntire underline the all-important issue now before Fundamentalists, that is, should Fundamentalists have anything at all to do with apostates, with those supporting apostasy, or with those who in any way aid or encourage a weak position toward New Evangelicalism in any form.

The ecumenical evangelism of Billy Graham has had a devastating effect on separatist union campaigns. By the 1940's, most of the evangelists that remained from the generation of Bob Jones, Sr., John E. Brown, Sr., and Mordecai Ham were nearing the close of their active ministries. However, new figures emerging on the national scene promised a bright for mass evangelism in America. At the time of Graham's rise, several other young professional evangelists—Jack Shuler, Charles B. Templeton, and Merv Rosell —as well as a Hebrew evangelist, Hyman Appelman; a blind evangelist, Walter Kallenbach; and a Baptist pastor, John Henry Hankins, had achieved national prominence with city-wide campaigns in large cities. Percy Crawford and Jack Wyrtzen had had evangelistic ministries among the youth associated with their radio broadcasts. The success of these evangelists had demonstrated that Fundamental believers and churches could still unite in large-scale evangelistic efforts without the assistance of liberal churches and religious groups. The advent of Graham's inclusivism left many professional evangelists in a quandary. Some notables from the pre-Graham era followed Graham into ecumenical evangelism. Others, including Appelman, J. Harold Smith, and Vance Havner, have sustained their ministries through Southern Baptist ties and affiliations. A few, like Clifford Lewis, have continued their separatist ministries, though on a smaller scale. Oliver Greene has been widely used in tent campaigns, as well as on radio.

But the main evangelistic effort among Fundamentalists in the

But the main evangelistic effort among Fundamentalists in the last decade has been in individual churches. Another generation of professional evangelists has arisen to stir up Fundamentalist congregations to soulwinning efforts. A list of those of national prominence who have been engaged exclusively or mainly in evangelism in recent years would include, among others, Fred Brown, Paul Levin, Monroe Parker, Bill Rice, Phil Shuler, Glen Schunk, and Hal Webb. A list of pastors and pastor-educators who maintain, in addition to their other responsibilities, evangelistic ministries of national scope and reputation would include, among others, Bob Gray, Jack Hyles, Tom Malone, John W. Rawlings, and Harold Sightler. One young evangelist, Jack Van Impe, is still having a considerable success with city-wide evangelistic campaigns, supported mainly by independent Baptist churches. The future of full-time separatist evangelistic ministries seems assured, and the recent emergence of such evangelists as Bill Hall, Ron Comfort, and Darrell Dunn indicates that the Lord will continue to provide gifted young men for this essential ministry.

B. Radio Broadcasting. Millions of dollars and millions of hours have been devoted to spreading the Word of God by means of the air waves. Several impressive personalities arose in this period to create radio empires for the Gospel. Best-known was the Old-Fashioned Revival Hour of Charles E. Fuller. His music and messages were consistently heartwarming. It is regrettable that in his last days he gave support to the Berlin Congress of new-evangelical sponsorship and allowed Fuller Seminary to slide into full-orbed New Evangelicalism. Under his son, Daniel, the Hour is now anemic in impact. His school, Fuller Seminary in Pasadena, California, under Harold Ockenga, Edward Carnell, and David Hubbard has become a center of theological training with high academic standards among New Evangelicals. Its scholarly faculty and accreditation have given it a vaunted place among evangelical training centers.

As widely known as Fuller's radio work was that of Walter A. Maier and his Lutheran Hour. Orthodox but not Fundamentalist, Maier belonged to the more conservative wing of the Missouri Synod and was a professor at Concordia Seminary in Old Testament, a Harvard-trained Ph.D. in Old Testament. He was a mighty radio preacher, and at one time his program was heard on over twelve hundred radio stations "carrying Christ to the nations." Fundamentalists appreciated his outspoken denunciations of sin and his exaltation of the Lamb of God as man's only Saviour. His work was indeed a monumental one during the 1940's.

Better known among young people was Percy Crawford and his Young People's Church of the Air, which reached its peak attraction about 1950. Crawford founded King's College, now located at Briarcliff Manor, New York. Starting as a Fundamentalist school, it has adopted, under the leadership of Robert A. Cook, a new-evangelical complexion. Crawford was a most effective evangelist among young people in rallies and summer conferences, but to the chagrin of many friends he turned against all separatists who would not support the Graham crusades. King's College now operates as a Christian liberal arts college, but, like so many in this class, it caters to Fundamentalists, New Evangelicals, and the generally Orthodox, thus taking a middle-of-the-road stance. Others in the same class are Gordon College, Barrington College, Biola College, Houghton College, and Wheaton College.

A third widely acclaimed radio ministry was the Radio Bible Class of Martin R. DeHaan, a medical doctor, Bible teacher, and pastor of Grand Rapids, Michigan. Unlike the others mentioned, DeHaan never departed from his tough Fundamentalism and so came to be the most outspokenly Fundamentalist of the large national broadcasters. He was dogmatic in expounding the truth, clear-cut in exposing the errors of the times, and constantly warning of the any-moment return of the Lord. All Fundamentalists should be grateful for DeHaan and his absolute fidelity to Bible truth and his boldness in applying it to every situation. The program is now carried on by his son, Richard.

Many churches and schools built radio stations and carried on good ministries over these outlets. It was also a period when city churches took to the airwaves with regular broadcasts of services or specially prepared programs. One was the Churchill Tabernacle of Buffalo, New York, using its own station, WKBW (Well-Known Bible Witness), under the name of its founder, Clinton H. Churchill. In the 1930's and 1940's it maintained outstanding radio ministries. On these programs appeared such men as Gipsy Smith and Oswald J. Smith. Others to preach on the radio from the Tabernacle were Bob Jones, Sr., and Bob Jones, Jr.

Another well-known broadcast was that of Calvary Baptist Church in New York City under the ministry of William Ward Ayer; it was carried over the powerful WHN in the nation's largest city. Anthony Zeoli conducted The Radio Bible Hour from 1940 onward. On the West Coast there was the radio program of the Church of the Open Door under the gifted ministries of L. T. Talbot, P. W. Philpott, and J. V. McGee. Christians in Southern California will remember the strong ministry of this center in days gone by and regret that under McGee it has drifted into a tolerant attitude toward New Evangelicalism of the Graham type, making its present pastorate a far cry from the great days of the past. In Los Angeles was the pungent radio ministry of R. P. "Fighting Bob" Shuler of Trinity Methodist Church.

A third center of power on the West Coast was the First Presbyterian Church of Seattle, Washington, under Mark Matthews. All gave great messages to the radio listeners. Schools with radio ministries included Moody Bible Institute with its radio voice, WMBI, and Bob Jones University with its WMUU; other schools and colleges followed suit.

C. Ministries to the Young. Children have not been neglected in this period. In addition to the thousands of Sunday School classes, Child Evangelism has drawn to its support a long list of lady Bible teachers and some consecrated laymen, who hold classes in neighborhood homes. The most widely known effort of this kind has been the Child Evangelism Fellowship, which was started in 1923 by J. Irvin Overholtzer with the purpose of winning children not attending any church. It was incorporated and greatly enlarged in 1937, with branches in all states and fifty foreign countries. It has a magazine, *Child Evangelism,* with an institute to train directors, but has no membership. It claims to be centered in the local church, but this position has greatly weakened as the organization has grown. It helps in summer camps, orphanages, radio programs, and vacation schools. It provides incentive for the memorization of Bible verses and has started "Good News Clubs" in homes. The leaders have shown a more than dangerous interest in new-evangelical movements, but in spite of this growing softness, it has continued a ministry for the young. Others working particularly with children include the Children's Gospel Hour with Harry Geiger of Chattanooga, Tennessee; the Children's Bible Mission, started in 1935 by Mr. and Mrs. Walter Jensen; the Rural Bible Crusade, started in 1937 by J. L. Hunter; the Bible Memory Association, started in 1944 by N. A. Woychuk; the Youth Gospel Crusade begun by R. W. Neale in 1943; Children for Christ, begun in 1945; the Christian Service Brigade, begun in 1937, and Pioneer Girls, dating back to 1939. We must add a warning that the listing of these does not imply that they are Fundamentalist at the time of this writing. Many Fundamentalists have been involved in their genesis and growth, but several now in places of leadership would disavow their support of the militant separatist Fundamentalist stand now needed in a most bewildering situation.

To reach young people for the Lord has been the object of a long list of youth organizations. One was Youth For Christ with such figures as Bev Shea, Billy Graham, Torrey Johnson, and Charles B. Templeton. It was an international movement by 1945 and was seen by many as the nearest thing to a national revival for both the youth and adults. Then, weakness in message and methods set in, and it is now a mere shadow of its former strength, with the present leadership in active cooperation with New Evangelicalism, having gone this way under the men named and more recently, under such leaders as Robert Cook and Ted Engstrom. One should not ignore two facts about YFC, namely, that it did reach thousands of young people with the Gospel in spite of its cheap theatrics, frothy programs, and a general Hollywood style of Gospel activity. Secondly, it paved the way for a wholesale sellout of many pastors and Christian leaders to a circus concept that anything goes, as long as people are reached with some truth of the Bible. Youth For Christ made stage performances so like Hollywood that others have adopted the same tawdry methods to work for the Lord. Highly emotional appeals were made on the basis of the identification of the speaker with football, backgrounds in crime, and previous addictions to more popular types of sinning. It accentuated "rally religion," and when the smoke passed, a large part of the younger generation of Christians was lost in frustration.

Also working with young people was Inter-Varsity Christian Fellowship with an aim of reaching the college campuses. It started in Cambridge, England. Led by Stacey Woods, it is now an international organization, which publishes the magazine *His*. Every third Christmas at Urbana, Illinois, on the University campus, it arranges a huge gathering of young people with headline speakers from evangelism, missions, and religious magazines. Fundamentalists are conspicuous by their absence from both the platforms and audiences. It is an all-out new-evangelical movement.

Sharing the spotlight on the campuses is Campus Crusade, which started in 1951 at the University of California at Los Angeles under Bill Bright. It has grown rapidly, with headquarters now at Arrowhead Springs, California, and has attracted leading figures in the business and theological world to its board and platforms. Under aggressive leadership, it has held clinics in large centers, using the cooperation of a wide range of Protestant churches, pastors, and laymen, to promote its well-known Four Spiritual Laws for soulwinning. Not as large as Campus Crusade is the ministry of Word of Life at Schroon Lake, New York, which attracts thousands of youth to its excellent facilities. It owes its ministry to the leadership of Jack Wyrtzen, who started with youth rallies in Times Square in New York in the 1940's. Since then he has drawn to his work such well-known figures as Carlton Booth, song leader; Charles J. Woodbridge, Bible teacher; and youth leaders C. C. Ryrie, H. G. Hendricks, and Lehman Strauss. Woodbridge has left the movement and in his recent booklet *Biblical Separation* named Jack as weak on separation. Its general ministry has been Fundamental, but its inclusivism has raised questions. It is hoped that Biblical stands will be taken by this strategic ministry. Also ministering to youth has been Young Life, organized in 1937 by James Rayburn.

Among the most promising movements for young people are the Christian-day-school movement and the camp ministry, which includes many summer programs. Both of these will have even larger parts to play in any planning for the future in reaching young people. There are approximately three thousand Fundamental Christian day schools in the country, and their number is growing at the rate of one hundred a year. Most of these are church related. The schools enroll approximately one million children each year. Outstanding leaders have been Henry Grube and Mark Fakkema, Sr., who started the National Union of Christian Schools in 1947 and later joined the National Association of Christian Schools. In 1960 Fakkema left that organization to form his own, Christian Schools Incorporated. He died in 1971.

Another leader, John Blanchard, is the present head of the National Association of Christian Schools. Still another active leader has been Paul Kienel, executive director of the California Association of Christian Schools, who has made a major contribution in promoting Christian schools on the West Coast. A graduate of Bob Jones University, Arlin Horton, has the largest Christian school in the country, the Pensacola Christian School, Pensacola, Florida, now twenty-eight years old with twenty-eight hundred students. Roy Lowrie has been a key figure in this work through writing and conferences for teachers. At present there are ten associations of Christian schools in our nation:

National Union of Christian Schools (Grand Rapids, Mich.)
California Association of Christian Schools (Whittier, Calif.)
National Association of Christian Schools (Wheaton, Ill.)
Arizona Association of Christian Schools (Phoenix, Ariz.)
Midwest Association of Christian Teachers (Indianapolis, Ind.)
Southeast Christian Educators Association (Pensacola, Fla.)
Mid-Atlantic Christian School Association (Brookhaven, Fla.)
Midwest Association of Evangelical Schools (Meno, Okla.)
New England Association of Christian Schools (Lexington, Mass.)
Northwest Fellowship of Christian Schools (Nampa, Idaho)

A continuing problem with these schools has been the procurement of qualified Christian teachers and administrative leaders. Two schools at present are leading the way in the training of personnel to fill the vacancies: Bob Jones University with its Department of Education under Walter G. Fremont, and Tennessee Temple Schools with its Christian Education Department under Roger Ellison. Many teachers have had Bible school training with additional courses at regular colleges with teacher training programs. Others have come from secular positions, while still others have received their preparation at Christian liberal arts colleges.

D.   Bible Teachers and Bible Conferences. It is a valuable part of the Fundamentalist heritage that many outstanding and gifted Bible teachers have appeared in the past century. We should do them homage and recommend that young preachers and missionaries stock their bookshelves with their many helpful commentaries and Bible studies. Perhaps some day a young research student in church history will render a great service by making a thorough study of this century's great Bible teachers in the United States. Another need is a worthwhile study of the Bible conference movement.

To list outstanding Bible teachers is both arbitrary and humbling, for many good men may be omitted from any list. A central figure would be Harry A. Ironside of Moody Church in Chicago, a writer and Bible conference speaker until his death in 1951. His many commentaries and Biblical addresses were always instructive and inspirational. In his class was Arno C. Gaebelein, a fine Hebrew Christian, whose works on prophecy earned him a reputation for rich scholarship. Another capable Bible student and teacher was Donald Grey Barnhouse of the Tenth Presbyterian Church in Philadelphia, whose many articles in *Revelation* and *Eternity* were of great help to careful students and scholars. It is a matter of deep regret that before his death, Barnhouse renounced his separatist stand and reaffiliated with denominational and compromise groups. William R. Newell of Plymouth Brethren circles was an excellent teacher and writer. His books on *Romans* and *The Revelation* are widely used in study. A gifted Bible teacher was L. S. Chafer, founder of Dallas Theological Seminary and author of a popular *Systematic Theology,* written from a dispensational interpretation. Another able teacher was William L. Pettingill of the Philadelphia School of the Bible and First Baptist Church in New York. Fundamentalism did not have a finer exponent and champion than Pettingill. The Moody Bible Institute faculty had such able Bible teachers as James M. Gray, P. B. Fitzwater, and Wilbur M. Smith.

The Bible conference circuits have had a galaxy of names such as A. T. Robertson, J. R. Sampey, R. G. Lee, H. M. Lintz, H. C. Thiessen, E. J. Young, H. W. Frost, James McGinlay, Vance Havner, Mel Trotter, J. Sidlow Baxter, G. Campbell Morgan, Alva McClain, J. Wilbur Chapman, M. R. DeHaan, Herbert Lockyer, Frank C. Torrey, C. L. Feinberg, J. Vernon McGee, J. D. Pentecost, R. T. Ketcham, William Evans, W. W. Ayer, J. J. Van Gorder, O. J. Smith, L. T.

Talbot, and W. H. Houghton. W. E. Biederwolf held a special place as a Bible teacher in the 1920's, as did R. A. Torrey. Many colleges and seminaries have had outstanding teachers of rare and enriching gifts.

The "grand old man" of the Bible conference movement was Winona Lake Bible Conference at Winona Lake, Indiana.[40] A new and complete study of this "the greatest of all Bible Conferences" needs to be done while many who knew it in its greatest days are still alive and can relive great moments of spiritual instruction and inspiration. The Conference was founded in 1895 by Sol C. Dickey, superintendent of Home Missions for the Presbyterians of Indiana. His purpose was to have a "religious chautauqua," that is, combine the best elements of Chautauqua in plays, musicals, and speeches with the Bible ministry that was the heart of D. L. Moody's conferences at Northfield, Massachusetts.

Winona Lake Conference was true to "the Fundamentals." The earliest spiritual leader of the Conference was J. Wilbur Chapman of Philadelphia. At first it was under Presbyterian control, but later it became interdenominational. William Jennings Bryan was one of the early leaders, and on the programs in its early years were Bishop E. H. Hughes, Paul and Lyell Rader, W. E. Biederwolf, J. C. Massee, W. B. Riley, and a noted hymn writer, E. O. Excell. In later years many noted Christian leaders graced the platforms such as R. G. LeTourneau, A. W. McKee, Melvin G. Kyle, L. S. Bauman, Gipsy Smith, and Billy Sunday. In fact, Sunday made his home at Winona Lake, and today it is a museum in his name. Homer Rodeheaver became a pillar in its programs with his trombone and song leading. A giant step in faith was the erection of the Billy Sunday Tabernacle to seat over seven thousand, which has been filled only a few times. Later, many church groups came to Winona; one was Youth For Christ International with its great crowds. J. P. Muntz served for years as director of Winona Lake Bible Conference.

Another expression of Fundamentalism is found in the complex of camps and summer conferences held in places of scenic beauty and vacation facilities. Many combined programs of varied activity with Bible study, prayer times, and devotional exercises for young people and adults. Much smaller than Winona Lake, they appealed to more provincial constituencies but sought to emulate Winona by using many men of national stature as Bible teachers. A complete list of these would be too long for this study, but we ought to include several of the better-known ones, both those of long standing and those of more recent beginning. Included would be Montrose, Maranatha,

[40]The only one to date has been *The Story of Winona Lake* by Vincent H. Gaddis and Jasper A. Huffman (Winona Lake, Ind.: Winona Lake Christian Assembly, 1960).

Word of Life, Pinebrook, The Firs, Gull Lake, Hume Lake, Ben Lippen, Lucerne, The Cedars, Rumney, Chetek, Bluewater, Keswick (both in New Jersey and Canada), The Bill Rice Ranch, The Wilds, Camp Joy, and Ontario Bible Conference. In addition, scores of churches have built their own conference camps and perform a worthwhile summer ministry.

14
The Face of Fundamentalism 1973

Its Dilemma

America faces a black hour, perhaps her last, as world crises mount and signs point to the imminent return of the Lord Jesus to rapture His Church, judge, make war, and pour out the thunderbolts of God's wrath on the entire earth. Spiritually bankrupt religions continue to drag millions into the empty caverns of lifeless ecclesiastical existence. Sects issue glowing promises but back them with frightening and insipid mockeries. Denominations engage in the unscriptural business of building kingdoms dominated by religious idealism but void of the power of the Holy Spirit. National demagogues clown their way through the maze of man-made programs, including some elements of truth along with false inducements to personal happiness. So-called statesmen paint rosy pictures of a great new world arising through staggering debts. Unprincipled leaders are wallowing in the slime-pits of dishonesty, corruption, vainglory, and self-exaltation; and evil is ever increasing as the nation races headlong toward the wrath of Almighty God.

Liberalism continues its vain history of Bible denials perfumed with more and more appeals to man's goodness and perfectability. New forms of compromise, Bible rejection, and outright disobedience to principles appear. A vast vacuum has been created, as far as truth, morality, and righteous purpose are concerned. And yet the modern pied pipers of the religious parade continue to play the sweet sounds that soothe millions into a false assurance—a terrible Satanic sleep—just before the greatest storm of all storms breaks, the storm of God's inescapable judgments on the nations because of sin. The clouds hang low as the Son is about to come and take His Church with Him; yet millions, standing on the brink, dance as if all were well and wickedness will go unjudged. A cosmic carnival is before our eyes, and none are so blind as the managers of the religious stage as they ignore the sure word of the prophecies of the Word of God.

In the midst of this terrible tragedy stands American Fundamentalism. It has spoken for the Lord and will continue to speak for Him and His Truth. Its message alone—of all messages being given to Americans—has been one of conformity to the Word, convictions based on the Word, and conflict because of the attacks on the Word. It has not denied, and cannot deny, the authority and infallibility of the Bible. Every demand is a divine one, and every command is deserving of complete obedience. For a century Fundamentalism has refused to bow its head or its heart to the vast capitulation of American Christianity to Liberalism, radicalism, and compromise in this spiritual Sahara. It has clung to the Gospel and done its best to teach the whole counsel of God. It has expounded the truths of the Book of God and tried, against terrifying odds and enemies, to expose the attacks on that Book and to label the thousands of well-educated attackers as enemies of the Word's truth. It has fought on in the greatest battle of the century, constantly aware that strong men were falling and that the young recruits for the war might not have the tenacity and the toughness of mind and lip to bear up in the titanic struggle.

Fundamentalism has lost the denominations, the old-line centers of learning, and the grand institutions of honor and religious accolade, which have been the pride and achievement of our long history. These were lost in the great battles, but the Faith has been preserved; the keeping of the Faith has been the one sure heritage of Fundamentalists for the past one hundred years in spite of the confusion, controversy, conflict, and corruption. It behooves us to take a good look at present-day Fundamentalism, assess its points of strength, and see very clearly its present dangers and weaknesses. Perhaps in this way we can take a look into the future, however short or long it may be.

Its Doctrines

These do not need to be listed, for they have been repeated over and over in our study. Historic Fundamentalism has given to the world a long list of Bible truths, indeed, all those found in the pages of the inspired Word. It has held without faltering to the verbal inspiration of the Bible in its original writings and to the reliability of the King James Version. It has shared this great conviction with the orthodox and conservative Bible believers the world over. It has affirmed the great doctrines of the Word, namely the depravity of man, the deity of the Lord Jesus Christ, the virgin birth, the sinless life of Christ, His vicarious atoning death, His bodily resurrection, and His ascension to the right hand of the Father. In addition, most Fundamental men made a doctrinal issue of His imminent coming to rapture the Church and take it to be with Him; the occurrence of the Rapture before the Great Tribulation of seven years; and the return of the Lord in power and great glory to reign from Jerusalem over the earth for one thousand years, commonly called the millennial reign. At the end of this reign, it has been believed, Satan will be judged forever, with all unbelievers cast into a lake of fire forever and forever. Then all the righteous will go with the Lord into the New Jerusalem, described in the last two chapters of the Book of the Revelation, to live forever and forever.

The historic Fundamentalist accepts literally the teachings of the Bible concerning the conduct of the church, the two ordinances of baptism and the Lord's Supper, the relationship of believers to the systems of the world, separation from worldly things, and the demands of the Bible for service and obedience on the part of every truly re-born believer. Briefly, in all things, the Bible is the sole and sufficient rule for that which is believed and practiced. One last point deserves special emphasis. The historic Fundamentalist not only holds to the exposition of the Bible in its every affirmation and attitude, but also sets himself to expose every affirmation and attitude not found in the Bible. His negatives, like his affirmations, are as many as those of the Bible. To expose is as vital to his faith as to expound the truths of the Scriptures. Truly he has no creed but the Bible.

Its Dangers

As Fundamentalists face the decade of the Seventies, there are on the horizon many unsuspected dangers and threats to their existence and certainly to their growth in this country. Any informed student of the decade ahead would do well to face these mounting threats. Should these continue, they augur the funeral of historic Fundamentalism. This chapter does not take the place of a full analysis, but it is hoped that it will serve as an introduction, so that pastors and other people will be alerted. The writer is fully aware of the chilly response warnings 'receive, even when documented and Biblically based. It is hoped that young men coming up within the ranks of Fundamentalism will take the warnings more seriously than those now in places of leadership who have accepted a compromise approach to many questions. We list a dozen dangers, recognizing this list to be incomplete.

1. The Dilemma and Drift of the Bible-School Movement. It is a thing of shame, a cause of spiritual nausea, to see so many Bible institutes and Bible colleges drift into an open-mindedness toward the men and movements of New Evangelicalism. The battles of the hour are blithely ignored or avoided. Students are not told of the perils and the pressures of the time. The Billy Graham successes have forced these small works to line up or lose supporters and friends. Few in the Bible school ranks have stood against the compromises, soft policies, and practices of the movement commonly called "cooperative evangelism." Several prominent names among Bible school leaders have taken an open stand for Graham and his new-evangelical crusades.

Few faculty members are informed on the battles and the victories of historic Fundamentalism, and even fewer are interested. Others on the teaching level are so devoted to their dispensational charts and trivia that the threats and poisons inherent in the present situation are either completely ignored or hushed up, lest their own compromises be exposed. These teachers point to Fuller Seminary, Dallas Seminary, and Wheaton College as institutions which have gained accreditation without clear-cut Fundamentalist attitudes. Worldliness has so infiltrated many of these Bible schools that standards are being lowered in matters of dress, appearance of students, and separation from amusements of known harm to Christian testimony. More and more concessions are made with each passing year. The Christian liberal arts colleges are leading them into open espousal of worldly pastimes and attitudes, and the consequence is a climate on campus that is half-hearted in its spiritual tone. Most alumni of the typical Bible school have been kept in the dark as to the questions and issues swirling within the confines of evangelicalism, mission boards, youth movements, and the worldwide forces supporting Billy Graham. They allow soulwinning figures to dazzle and blind them to new forms of compromise, soft attitudes, and middle-of-the-road methods. They assume the Bible schools are still sound in principle and practice because they teach some Bible courses. These alumni are utterly oblivious to the drift, delusion, and sellout of real Biblical principles in traditional centers of teaching, publishing, and missionary enterprise. Thus the young graduates are susceptible to new-evangelical moods and methods. Even in missionary circles, there is on the horizon the vast capitulation to Evangelism-In-Depth, another name for New Evangelicalism on the mission fields. Shall this blindness continue? Will the leaders of the Bible-school movement acquiesce in the great erosion of the Faith?

2. The Gimmicks Race. All Bible believers hold that the Gospel should be taken to as many as possible; because of this desire, revivals, evangelistic campaigns, all-night prayer meetings, and personal soulwinning have been used by Fundamental men. Until recently there has been one main way to attract people to the House of the Lord, and that has been the work of the Spirit through the preaching of the Word. A few have resorted to sensational exposés, discussion of burning current events, and pulpit blasts against social sins.

In the last five years a new item has made its appearance: the give-away programs of churches in order to attract greater numbers, especially children. To this has been coupled the performance of stage, radio, and television stars to interest pagans and fill church pews. Some have introduced such attractive gifts as bubble gum, hamburgers, goldfish, and silver half-dollars. Recently, one large church, in an effort to surpass existing Sunday School attendance records, advertised "special guests" Connie Smith of Grand Ole Opry, Colonel Sanders of Kentucky Fried Chicken fame, and Bob Harrington of Bourbon Street in New Orleans. All nineteen thousand attending were given some "finger-lickin' good" chicken to eat. Harrington's well-known extrovert evangelism, spiced with crude witticisms, was a sure way to attract the great crowd. Another pastor has had a man parachute out of a plane to boost Sunday School figures. Large sums are required to put on these evangelistic extravaganzas, and smaller churches must sit by and wonder how to get into the race or how to justify their inability to match these daring innovations.

More and more Fundamentalists are wondering how these new methods compare with New Testament practices. If some souls get saved, is a method therefore in order? Has Graham's new-evangelical approach so infiltrated the sacred halls of Fundamentalism that anything goes as long as people come? Should it be accepted that the New Testament is unclear on what methods to use; then every Fundamentalist church will be a law unto itself as to how far it can go in worldly ways to reach the world.

3. The Growth of the Keswick Movement. English Keswick, the mother of all Keswick groups, is a century old and arose for the purpose of analyzing the deep spiritual bankruptcy of believers and their churches; it sought to find Bible answers for the deepest needs of the saints. Most of the answers of the early leaders, such as Webb-Peploe and Hannah Pearsall Smith, arose out of a new devotion and obedience to the Word of God, serious Bible study, and a more genuine dedication to the ministry of the Holy Spirit. Steven Barabas of Wheaton College has made a careful study of the movement from a historical and devotional viewpoint.

The earlier Keswick did not make much of a dent on American Christians. But in the last two decades its teachings have become more widely known and accepted, mainly through the ministries of Alan Redpath, W. Ian Thomas, and Stephen Olford. Columbia Bible

College in Columbia, South Carolina, under the leadership of Robert
C. McQuilkin and G. Allen Fleece became a headquarters. The
movement has assimilated new attitudes, mostly from New
Evangelicalism, and this adds a new threat to Bible-believing
Fundamentalists; it has emphasized introspection and subjective
experiences above objective Bible truth. A common phrase used by
Keswick people is that "The Lord told me," or "This morning the
Lord showed me this," and all too often the ideas to follow have
never been found by the best of Bible students or exegetes. Somehow
the devotees of this movement have special access to the Lord's
ideas, many of them not found in the Bible at all. Biblical passages
and verses are openly tortured to fit the meanings of inner realities;
indeed, there is created an unrealistic spiritual world of special
insights not too far from Quaker "inner light" impressions.
Theology and careful Bible study are downgraded in the interest of a
devotional life and a "deeper" life. Soulwinning is decried as easy-
believism, and the local church largely ignored in the interest of
"Deeper Life Conferences." Its speakers of note are almost all posttribulational, and they are unanimous in assailing
Fundamentalists and their interest in eschatology. Extremes of
allegorizing of Old Testament stories are abundantly used in trying
to prove some special experience. The use of the prepositions "in"
and "out" must be seen in the light of an overcoming experience or
the loss of it. The Scofield Reference Bible is openly attacked as
almost an enemy of men's souls. Much of the Keswick mood has
infiltrated the Bible-school movement, because so many in the latter
are deficient in the tools of genuine Biblical exposition and
understanding. Two schools have been centers in promoting this
movement, Columbia Bible College, Columbia, South Carolina, and
Prairie Bible Institute in Three Hills, Alberta, Canada. Prairie,
though Canadian, has had its place of influence in American
evangelicalism because many American students have gone there to
study under the leadership of L. E. Maxwell.

   4. Counseling Christianity. Many are the tensions, fears,
and frustrations of Christians today. To help understand these and
provide answers, the ministry of counseling, especially of the type of
Henry Brandt and Clyde Narramore, has mushroomed. The
common arguments are that real believers have so many deep-
seated problems that pastors do not know and cannot recognize
them; only men with professional training and experience in
counseling can properly and factually analyze and cope with such
inner needs. Thus, a type of evangelical psychiatry has evolved, and
many are the testimonies in which much-sought-after and needed
help has been claimed to have been received. It is commonly
reasoned by many of evangelical persuasion that too many in

Christian service cannot recommend the proper Bible verses because they do not know the root of the problems of a Christian. Therefore, it is argued, a specialist must be called in, especially in the case of marital problems, where so many of the modern-day difficulties arise. If we admit these claims, then we obviously admit that the old-time pastor-preacher ministry of God's servants is not enough for the complications of modern society. Since so few men have had professional training in any counseling, it would seem that we have a host of God-called men in the ministry today who cannot meet the problems of their people.

If counseling is so vital as its proponents claim, will its new importance not ultimately affect the content of preaching? Should preaching become an analysis of emotional problems rather than the declaration of the Word of God? Does it mean that with the Bible and the Holy Spirit the believer cannot find the answers to his deepest needs without professional counseling? Has the entire Church Age till this generation been kept by the Lord under such ineffective ministry and darkness that such men as Narramore, and Brandt had to come to our rescue?

5. Vast Intellectual Wasteland. Since Fundamentalists have taken their places outside the denominational structures, they have separated themselves from the time-honored schools of higher learning and been forced to erect their own. Will they follow the accredited institutions in the academic depth of their faculties and the liberal-arts requirements of their students? In too many cases, almost any kind of academics has been defended on the ground of the Christian character of the teachers. Their gifts in the classroom and their broad exposure to the masters of their fields have been limited, while mature judgments based on proper research and graduate disciplines have, in too many cases, been non-existent. The picture at this point is extremely blurred. Bible institutes have resorted to rote memory as a sole classroom, exercise and many graduating from such backgrounds have assumed they had a respectable education. The Christian liberal arts colleges have done quite well in recruiting well-trained men for their faculties but have sadly neglected to examine their spiritual insights and Biblical knowledge. Thus they have been of little more Christian influence in the classroom than college teachers anywhere. They have pretended to have a Christian philosophy but have used very little of it in their work. Evangelical seminaries have made honest efforts to get men of good training, but their complete capitulation to New Evangelicalism has been a sad departure from Fundamentalism.

Bible schools set up the Accrediting Association of Bible Colleges (AABC) in 1947 to upgrade standards, but only a few schools have been accredited by this organization. Even many of those accredited fall short in requirements for entrance and the qualification of their faculty members—both in college degrees and in breadth of knowledge in the fields in which they offer courses. Actually, there are not enough properly trained men and women, fully qualified both academically and spiritually, to staff the total number of schools in existence. Inferior standards prevail on a national scale, while unsuspecting pastors and parents believe they are supporting and paying for a first-class education.

Fundamentalism does have three large schools that have attracted hundreds of young people preparing for the Lord's service. Here we ought to pay tribute to their leaders and faculties for their labors and sacrifices. Later we shall calssify them, along with other smaller institutions, according to the strictness and militancy of their separatist positions. The largest is Bob Jones University in Greenville, South Carolina.[1] Bob Jones, Sr., founded it in 1926 at St. Andrews Bay, Florida, with the firm purpose of "creating a fundamental base for future evangelism."[2] As already mentioned, from his close friend, H. C. Morrison of Asbury College, he took the fervent advice to "keep the platform hot."[3] Not a soul has ever charged that the school has violated its high principles.

In 1933 a move was made to Cleveland, Tennessee, upon the purchase of the old property of Centenary College. In 1947 the Cleveland campus was sold for a million and a half dollars, and a new campus built on a 180-acre property in Greenville. Fully accepting his father's doctrines and discipline was his son, Bob Jones, Jr., who succeeded as president and now holds the office of chancellor, which he assumed in June, 1971. To the founder has been attributed a "tumble bulldog tenacity" and a "sawdust aisle approach" and to the son "the polished well-educated approach with a voice that flows like ripples of water."[4]

The college has grown to be a university with approximately four thousand now enrolled in undergraduate and graduate programs and some 550 in its academy on the same campus. The value of the property is now close to forty million with a four-million-dollar "amphitorium" seating 7,200 now under construction. Bob Jones III was installed as the third president in June of 1971. The dedication of a long line of teachers and supporters has made its history a heroic one. Space allows the mention of only a few, but they represent a great host of dedicated teachers and workers at this mammoth

---

[1]Two factual accounts of the University have been written: by Melton Wright, *Fortress of Faith* (Grand Rapids: Eerdmans, 1960), and R. K. Johnson, *Builder of Bridges* (Murfreesboro, Tenn.: Sword of the Lord, 1969).

[2]Johnson, p. 181.

[3]Ibid., p. 182.

[4]Ibid., p. 29.

center of Fundamentalism. Among its best-known figures in faculty and administration have been R. K. Johnson, C. D. Brokenshire, Gilbert R. Stenholm, Grace Haight, Monroe Parker, James D. Edwards, Marshall Neal, and Walter Fremont. It has had, in addition, a host of supporters, both alumni and otherwise, well-known in Fundamentalist circles, and they would include Roland Rasmussen, E. J. Nelson, W. R. Rice, Tom Malone, Wayne Van Gelderen, William F. Schroeder, Glen Shunk, G. A. Weniger, B. R. Lakin, W. W. Ayer, Clifford Lewis, Jack Hyles, Arnold Hickok, J. W. Crumpton, J. B. Williams, Carl McIntire, Billy James Hargis, G. B. Vick, and B. Myron Cedarholm. In addition, hundreds of alumni in churches, business, missions, and teaching posts owe their training to it; its alumni now total eight thousand.

It has taken an openly Fundamentalist stand when utmost courage was needed, especially against the new-evangelical forces, causing a break with Billy Graham, who attended the school when it was in Tennessee. It continues to stress evangelism with special attention to its "preacher boys." It has enlarged its offerings to include teacher training, fine arts, and graduate studies in Bible; it has produced such full-length color films as *Wine of Morning, Red Runs the River,* and *Flame in the Wind.* In boldness of testimony and firmness of stand, it has become a weather vane of militant Fundamentalism, attracting both praise and scorn. One of the unique blessings on the campus is to see Mrs. Jones, Sr., now in her eighty-fifth year, alert in mind and body, with that winsome graciousness that has characterized her as the First Lady of the University since its founding, showing always a kindly interest in faculty and students.

The second school of the Fundamentalist trio is Tennessee Temple Schools in Chattanooga, Tennessee, now in its third decade of service. It was founded by Lee Roberson, pastor of Highland Park Baptist Church which now numbers thirty-three thousand members. The Schools include a Bible College, liberal arts college, and seminary. The three enroll over two thousand and show strong growth pattern. Roberson has continued to emphasize Baptist distinctives, the importance of the local church, and soulwinning. He has been ably assisted by such dedicated men as John Hermann, J. R. Faulkner, Douglas Cravens, Mark Cambron, John McCormick, Cliff Robinson, and A. A. Cierpke. Many Fundamentalist leaders have supported the work, including Jack Hudson, Bob Gray, John R. Rice, Jack Hyles, Lester Roloff, Tom Malone, Harold Sightler, Tom Freeny, Fred Brown, and Bill Rice. Roberson's strong ties with many independent Baptist pastors and the SBF have built a strong supporting constituency.

The third large Fundamentalist center is Baptist Bible College in

Springfield, Missouri, founded in 1950 by pastors who left the World Baptist Fellowship of J. Frank Norris to organize the BBF. We have met its leaders, Rawlings, Vick, Smith, Dowell, and Zimmerman. The single purpose of the school has been to train young men to build New Testament churches; certainly it is no reflection on its leaders to state that a Bible school to inspire young men to preach the Gospel and establish Baptist churches has been their sole aim and goal. They did not intend to erect a liberal arts school nor to duplicate existing Bible colleges. They knew and loved the Bible-centered evangelistic, church-building training they had heard about so many times from the pulpit of First Baptist in Fort Worth and in the classes of Norris and Entzminger. These emphases and methods have been the soul and secret of the Springfield school.

In connection with the Fellowship, we have noted its steady growth; today it is the largest Bible college in the world with 2,200 students, a testimony to the wise and energetic leadership of Vick and Rawlings and to the enthusiastic support of pastors and members of the two thousand Fellowship churches. Many large churches have helped the school, which does not charge tuition. Among the strong supporters are Temple Baptist in Detroit; Landmark in Cincinnati; Akron Baptist Temple, under Dallas and Charles Billington; the Canton Baptist Temple in Canton, Ohio, under Harold Henninger; High Street Baptist in Springfield, Missouri, under David Cavin; and Riverside Baptist, Fort Worth.

All three mammoth Fundamentalist centers face important tests in the immediate future as Fundamentalism is challenged. There is the test of aid to new-evangelical spokesmen and sympathizers. Another is the constant pressure of friends to lower standards on worldly amusements and worldly fashions. A further test is the appeal to lower standards of academics to suit the lazy-minded and indolent. Conversely, how to upgrade academic goals without intellectual stuffiness and sophistication will pose serious questions. A major test will be how to take a separatist stand and to keep on standing in the face of defections and soft attitudes.

6. Drifts and Cross-Currents in Missions Circles. New Evangelicalism has made deep inroads into the life and policies of most mission boards in the form of Evangelism-In-Depth. This new movement was born in the fertile brain of Kenneth Strachan of the Latin America Mission. It brings a broad inclusivism to activity on the fields similar to the broad inclusivism at home, with Protestants of all shades of doctrine invited to share in large ecumenical gatherings for soulwinning and strategic offensives. The success on the fields has paralleled that of the Graham steamroller at home. Some mission leaders such as A. F. Glasser and G. W. Peters have endorsed this new approach to missions, while others have supported it without openly saying so. Still others cooperate on a restricted basis. This new maze in missions has caused a great erosion in interdenominational boards within the Independent Foreign Missions Association (IFMA) and the Evangelical Foreign Missions Association (EFMA). Few missionaries have been told of these changes, and many good, sacrificing missionaries, unaware the missions are now in transition, slave under difficult conditions to carry on a faithful ministry. Many of the big names in missions circles have slipped into new-evangelical attitudes and methods but have not announced this—organizations such as Wycliffe Translators, Sudan Interior Mission, Africa Inland Mission, Greater Europe Mission, Overseas Missionary Fellowship, and Latin American Mission. This has faced pastors and missionary candidates with new problems of support and affiliation, and has caused many to wonder how groups in the mainstream of missionary enterprise could ever become entangled so in movements of compromise and inclusivism?

7. The Ebb Tide of Pulpit Oratory. This century has known men of commanding presence, knowledge, and gifted speech flavored with choice phrases and sentences long to be remembered. Among them have been such men as Norris, R. G. Lee, W. A. Maier, George Truett, Sam Morris, Courtland Myers, Bob Jones, Sr., Bob Shuler, W. A. Candler, R. H. Conwell, and J. R. Straton. These were more than pulpiteers; they were skilled artists in the use of Biblical knowledge and able at a moment's notice to stand and sway great crowds. When one looks at the American pulpits in 1973, the outlook is frightening. Very few aim at the grandeur of oratory and very few have the dedication of mind and thought to attain to great heights through speech. Few even reach their capacity for effective speech, and few that do have the knowledge will pay the price for a platform performance of liberty, powerful proclamation, and lasting impressions. Few have ever heard an orator and many would spurn this luxury if it were available. The pulpit has become more of a public-relations desk and a place to explain and educate. There is far too little Biblical exposition and even less exhortation

8. Continuing Pressures and Successes of New Evangelicalism. The leadership of Harold Ockenga, Billy Graham, Carl Henry, and William Bright has continued to engulf pastors, educators, mission leaders, and publishers to an unexpected degree. Under the large umbrella that is New Evangelicalism have come the middle-of-the-roaders, civil-rights spokesmen, Pentecostals, and leaders of ecumenical evangelism. The surprise has been the capitulation of the Bible schools to new-evangelical moods and activities, and this has taken place under the noses of trustees, administrators, and faculties, who have been in a Rip Van Winkle sleep. Teachers are hired without the slightest regard for their new-evangelical sympathies or collaboration. Others have felt the pressures to support the Graham Crusades or lose friends, and are afraid to raise issues lest they be called divisive. Others of even less conviction do not dare look at things as they are lest their future be jeopardized and their income be in doubt. The situation facing us nationally is in a jelly-on-the-wall chaos at present with little sign of change for the better.

A highlight of New Evangelicalism has been a series of congresses at Berlin, and Wheaton, and, most recently, the Spiritual Explosion, 1972, held June 12-17 in Dallas, Texas. Campus Crusade spearheaded the grand concourse of thousands of young and old, reportedly at a cost of four million dollars. Leaders in all the preparations have been Graham, Bright, Henry, and T. A. Raedeke. They have devised a grand blueprint for the years 1971-1973 with emphases on preparation, presentation, and penetration. The one outlined for 1973 goes under the name of Key '73, and to it have been invited both Roman Catholic and Greek Orthodox churches. Chairman of the main committee of Key '73 is Thomas Zimmerman, general superintendent of the Assemblies of God.

Explo '72 provided some interesting developments. Fifty-nine exhibitors were listed, including such schools as Asbury College, Calvin College, Grace Theological Seminary, Gordon Divinity School, Taylor University, and Westminster Seminary. Among the missions agencies were the American Board of Missions to the Jews, Sudan Interior Mission, Christian and Missionary Alliance Mission, Conservative Baptist Foreign Mission Society, World Vision, Gospel Missionary Union, Navigators, Wycliffe Translators, and Far Eastern Gospel Crusade.

The presence of some of these institutions and organizations surprised militant Fundamentalists, but even greater surprises came with the list of confirmed speakers. Practically all Protestant groups were represented. Representing Southern Baptists were Bob Harrington, W. A. Criswell, H. H. Hobbes, and John Bisagno—all men supporting the apostasy by promoting the Cooperative Program. From the Conservative Baptists came Earl Radmacher, Vernon Grounds, and Warren Webster. Representing the Northern Baptists were Lester Harnish and Carl Henry. Many were on the program from the Billy Graham organization, including Billy himself, Cliff Barrows, and Grady Wilson. From schools sound in doctrine were John Walvoord of Dallas Seminary, Armerding of Wheaton College, MacCorkle of Philadelphia College of Bible, Hoyt of Grace Seminary, Boon of Nyack, Kinlaw from Asbury, Wilbur Smith from Trinity, Bob Cook from King's College, and Rediger from Taylor University. Thomas Zimmerman and Charles Blair were of Pentecostal background and Harry Denman and Galloway came from the Methodist Church. Psychologists on the program included Clyde and Bruce Narramore of the Narramore Foundation. Allen Fleece of Keswick ties and persuasion also was on the program, along with Richard Halverson, a Presbyterian pastor in Washington, D. C., and Harold Lindsell, editor of *Christianity Today*. The American Bible Society contributed one speaker, as did the entertainment world, in the person of Dale Evans Rogers. Active new-evangelical spokesmen such as Tom Skinner and Leighton Ford were included. In fact, all shades of Protestant work were represented with the exception of the militant Fundamentalists.

A longer look at the program reveals this conglomeration: a professor from George Washington College, statesman Walter Judd, Oswald Smith of Toronto, Jack McAlister of World Literature, the head of Eastern Baptist Seminary, the head of Youth For Christ, Henry Brandt, Bill Glass, and a professor from Southern Baptist Seminary.

At least, for those participating, there can be now no facade. These men and organizations openly and unashamedly support New Evangelicalism in its evangelistic form. The unparalleled variety of speakers and denominational and non-denominational groups proved one strong contention made many times in this study, that New Evangelicalism has forged a union of evangelicals like that of the Liberals by the National Council, and the same tolerance toward all religious groups has surfaced and prevailed.Obviously, the injunction of Paul to reprove the works of darkness and to separate from those walking disorderly has been set aside in favor of massive efforts to reach people. An evangelical message has emerged with a new-evangelical method; Fundamentalists will find the message incomplete and the method unscriptural. At Dallas, Southern Baptists, Canadian Anglicans, Graham leaders, Bible-college voices, Bible teachers, psychologists, Methodist spokesmen, seminary figures, missions executives, and Bob Harrington all combined for Explo '72—more accurately, the New Evangelical National Council of '72 led by Graham.

Preparations have been under way for another mammoth evan-gelistic effort in 1973 under the title of Key '73, named after the Francis Scott Key Bridge in Virginia, near which planning meetings were held in 1967. An early listing of cooperating Christian organizations fortifies the case that more and more compromise marks the trail of new-evangelical evangelism. Among the groups already committed to this enterprise are Southern Baptists, Assemblies of God, Inter-Varsity, The National Council of Churches, The International Church of Foursquare Gospel, Evangelism-In-Depth, Friends United Meeting, Congregational

Christian Churches, *Christianity Today,* Associated Students of
Biola College, American Baptist Convention, and The United
Church of Canada. It is claimed that 130 groups will be working
together. Six periods of the year 1973 will be devoted to special
emphases such as Commitment and Lenten Bible Study. Mass
media will be employed, and two million dollars are to be used for
television and radio. On its executive committee are denominational
leaders from the Presbyterian Church, U. S.; Campus Crusade; the
Southern Baptist Convention; Assemblies of God; the Lutheran
Church, Missouri Synod; and the United Methodist Church. T. A.
Raedeke of the Lutheran Church, Missouri Synod, has been named
the executive director of the organization, whose offices are in St.
Louis, Missouri.

   9. Crusading Calvinism. In the last ten years a new threat
has emerged within Fundamentalism itself. This has been militant
and rigid Calvinism, usually expressed in its Five Points (TULIP),
total depravity, unconditional election, limited atonement,
irresistible grace, and perseverance of the saints. This system has
long been an integral part of such churches as the Presbyterian, the
colonial Congregational, and the Reformed, as well as a few Baptist
churches of the Spurgeon type. From its earliest history,
Fundamentalism has not taken any position on the Five Points or on
any of the points. The majority of Fundamentalists today follow
their fathers in refusing to make these five theological tenets a basis
of fellowship. On the other hand, a growing number within Baptist
circles have read the English Puritans and followed Spurgeon in the
persuasion that sovereign grace demands the acceptance of all of the
Five Points.

   One small Baptist paper, *The Baptist Examiner,* published by
John R. Gilpin at Ashland, Kentucky, keeps up a steady attack on all
who will not accept the Five Points, and publishes only articles by
those who do. Many Independents without any solid affiliation with
the national fellowships are promoters of hardline Calvinism. Most
Fundamentalists, had they been polled throughout their history,
would have accepted the tenets of total depravity and perseverance
of the saints, but the majority would have rejected limited atonement
and irresistible grace. On the point of unconditional election they
would have given the largest possible place to the work of grace, but
would have allowed a place for man's will in accepting that grace.
They would have refused to adopt any statement on the Five Points.
There does not seem to be, at the present time, any sure signs that
cresting Calvinism will sweep Fundamentalism from its moorings,
but it will continue to attract the more intellectual to its position,
confuse others, and cause its opponents to be disturbed and sensitive
over the issue.

10. Crisisitis. On the national scene, society is wracked by continual and seemingly insoluble problems and disorders. On the international scene the sky is even darker with the problems of Indochina, China, European defense and economic competition, Cuba, Northern Ireland, and the Middle East. The religious picture is disheartening with so many churches becoming stagmant, liberal, or radical. Many bustle with programs but offer little sound doctrine; some are caught up in highly financed efforts to corral millions of church members without much regard for spiritually affecting the masses involved. Dissensions abound, often from trivial causes. Each day, the American Christian must face disturbing crises, from both at home and abroad, which suggest to him that he is living on a cosmic powder keg. The travel in outer space excites his imagination and exalts man's great scientific abilities, but it has failed to help him as a confused individual in a confused society. Morals are openly attacked all around him. The chronically unemployed and the hippie are treated as American heroes. The schools are undisciplined academic department stores for untamed, lazy, sports-crazed youth. There they learn nothing of man's origin, purpose in life, nor destiny. This constant barrage of crises keeps him in a state of emotional agitation, sapping his emotional vitality. Crisisitis, aggravated by the sensationalist pulpit ministries of well-meaning preachers, has dulled the sharp edge of the Christian witness, adding to the sickness of mankind.

A particular manifestation of this crisis mentality has become common among Fundamentalist pastors, a kind of numbers neurosis that associates enormous size with significant service. In these desperate days, it is felt, something of great magnitude must be done and be done quickly. Certainly, all credit is due to the hardworking men who have built large centers of preaching and activity. Among them would be the largest, Highland Park Baptist in Chattanooga with 33,000 members, utilizing the main church and over forty chapels. Lee Roberson has built this mammoth Gospel-preaching center. Temple Baptist in Detroit lists some 15,000 members with a magnificent auditorium which can seat 4,500. First Baptist in Hammond, Indiana, reports about 14,000 members, as does Landmark Baptist in Cincinnati. Akron Baptist Temple in Akron, Ohio, led Sunday Schools for years, as it averaged some 6,000 in attendance in an ideal church plant and facilities. The Thomas Road Baptist in Lynchburg, Virginia, has reported over 19,000 present on a Sunday in 1972. First Baptist in Hammond, has helped set the pace in attendance with over 11,000 present at one Sunday School session. Landmark Baptist in Cincinnati has now one hundred buses traveling 350,000 miles a year to bring people to its

Sunday School, now close to 7,000 in average attendance. All of these are bustling empires and deserve to be held in awe and great respect. But does this not create a new problem? Should a young man feel it necessary to imitate one of these leaders, a Hyles, a Vick, a Rawlings, a Roberson, a Falwell, in order to serve the Lord faithfully? Will parrotism at this point bring blessing or frustration? There is real evidence that these empires will continue to grow and to be regarded as patterns for others to follow.

11. Involvement in Patriotic Movements. The participation of our country in overseas wars and problems has divided the country as nothing else has done. To millions of Americans it causes nothing less than nausea to see us so involved. That communistic influences have seriously affected our country none would deny. Should Red China be in the United Nations, and what should Fundamentalists do about it? Would the cause of the Lord be better served if more Christians gathered in public rallies either to support or to oppose government policies? Several men have been calling for more Christians to take an active part in political affairs in order to avert national disasters. Some have called for conferences to reaffirm our constitutional rights and guarantees and to alert the citizenry to impending doom. Some have called for Fundamentalists to march as often as possible to let their voices be heard. Among these have been Carl McIntire and Billy James Hargis. Both are effective speakers at rallies and on radio programs. Some Christians have found the John Birch Society the proper place for indoctrination about our liberties and our dangers.

There is no doubt that thousands have been awakened from their stupor and are reading widely for information on these evils and their history in our country. Conferences and rallies have been held at Tulsa at the Hargis center, and at Washington, led by McIntire. So far, most Fundamentalists have given their sympathy but little more to these operations. Several reasons have commonly been given: some are not sure there is much to be gained by these tactics; others do not want to be publicly embarrassed; others resent non-evangelicals on the Hargis programs; and others are merely timid. Many believe that we ought to be careful not to use carnal weapons in our warfare. Still others believe that the whole world scene is one of deterioration and will so continue till the rapture takes place, and that our main business should be to rescue people out of the mess and not try to improve it or preserve its good characteristics. The probability now exists that as more and more national issues come up, the pressure will increase on Fundamentalists to get into the fray and let their voices be heard, their lights shine, and their money help to stop the national erosion.

12. Separation. In what ways should a Christian separate from not only unbelievers but also believers who openly, by activities or associations, disobey the Word of God? How far should one carry separation in his relations with those Christians who differ with him in their understanding of what the Scriptures require? Fundamentalists have been unanimous in the belief that there is no Biblical justification for fellowship with, or support of, Modernists or Liberals, who deny the essential authority of the Word of God. And there has been a growing conviction that no truly born-again believer should remain inside any group or denomination which tolerates known critics of the Bible and apostates from the Faith.

Since 1950 this conviction has received a severe blow in that Graham and others in mass evangelism have welcomed Liberals, Modernists, and Catholics to large crusades. Notable among such men have been Norman Vincent Peale, Bishop Kennedy, and Bishop James A. Pike. This inclusivism has done much to break down the wall of separation between Liberals and Fundamentalists, since it was generally assumed that men like Graham were Fundamentalists. As the Graham crusades increased in numbers and support, more and more inclusivism seemed the order of the day, and Campus Crusade soon adopted the same broad base of operations as the Graham organization. Both gained in appeal, for great figures were quoted for the number of converts, and young men were swept up in the excitement of great movements and impressed with the importance of having "strategic ministries." Usually, all kinds of Protestants are found on sponsoring and planning committees , with some good Bible teachers willing to take part in order to have an opportunity to teach the truth.

Now a new ripple in Fundamentalism has been created by the pressure of the new-evangelical success. What should be the Fundamentalist attitude toward those who cooperate with Campus Crusade and the Graham movements? Should Fundamentalists cooperate with those who cooperate in inclusivist ministries and meetings? Should a Fundamentalist cooperate with a leader like John Walvoord of Dallas Seminary, who for ten years has brought non-Fundamentalists to speak at Dallas? Should Fundamentalists cooperate with a pastor like J. Vernon McGee, who cooperated with Bishop Kennedy in the Graham Los Angeles campaign? Should Fundamentalists endorse a man like W. A. Criswell of First Baptist Church in Dallas as long as he supports the Cooperative Program of the Southern Baptist Convention and cooperates with Harold Ockenga, a leader of New Evangelicals, in a conference in Jerusalem?

Should pastors and educators send young men to Dallas

Seminary for training, when such new-evangelical sympathizers as H. G. Hendricks, G. W. Peters, and H. W. Robinson are on the faculty? Should young men be recommended to Talbot Seminary when its dean, C. L. Feinberg, has taken part in a conference at Jerusalem along with Pat Boone and Tom Skinner? Should Fundamentalists continue to support Moody Bible Institute, whose president, George Sweeting, supported a Graham Crusade in Chicago? Should pastors and laymen continue to support mission boards which are involved in Evangelism-in-Depth? Should Fundamentalists support evangelical leaders and organizations because they are getting souls saved? Is soulwinning and preaching the Gospel enough to qualify a man for support in such days of apostasy, confusion, and compromise?

Are these men mentioned above not a part of an unorganized movement, which, for want of any official recognition or name, we may refer to as the SSS (Silence, Sympathy, or Support)? Since they will not take a militant stand against all forms of compromise and middle-of-the-roadism and assume a kindly attttitude toward Campus Crusade, Key '73, ecumenical evangelism, and increasing national activities based on expediency, the necessity of constituency support, and acquiescence in the popular drifts, are they not causing further erosion of historic Fundamentalism? Does not the moderate stance of Sweeting, Walvoord, Feinberg, Criswell, G. W. Peters, H.G. Hendricks, and McGee in the present razzle-dazzle of compromise activity demand that Fundamentalists face the situation honestly and declare wherever possible that these men are indeed of the SSS and are building more bridges of compromise and apostasy by their middle-of-the-roadism? Or shall we see softer and softer attitudes toward those who are soft in their approach? These are the questions, and others could be added. There are three answers, all coming from Fundamentalists themselves, and these we must note briefly.

One answer has come in a booklet written by Charles J. Woodbridge entitled *Biblical Separation* and published by the Peoples' Gospel Hour in Halifax, Nova Scotia, Canada.[5] Woodbridge is widely known for his outstanding gifts as a Bible teacher, having served in the pastorate and on the faculty of Fuller Seminary. To him, any connection, even remotely, with anything new-evangelical is a "sinister error," and he marks such men as Wilbur Smith, John Walvoord, and William Culbertson as "men in retreat." Proof of this is found in their association with Tom Skinner (who has spoken of

[5]The People's Gospel Hour was founded by Perry F. Rockwood, outspoken and knowledgeable Canadian Fundamentalist, who broadcasts daily over stations in the Canadian provinces and the United States. It is a Christ-honoring ministry, exposing the drifts and dangers of the day.

Jesus as a "gutsy revolutionary") in a conference in Jerusalem in June of 1971. Other leaders he criticizes are Jack Wyrtzen of Word of Life in New York, because he will not take a firm stand on "second degree" separation, and John R. Rice of the *Sword of the Lord,* well-known among Fundamentalists for his soulwinning conferences and revivals over a long period of time. To Woodbridge several Biblical passages endorse "second degree" separation, such as Jude 23; II Thessalonians 3:7-12; Nehemiah 13:1-3; Leviticus 15; Psalm 119:63, and II Corinthians 6:17. Others in places of evangelical leadership whom Woodbridge criticizes for lack of "second degree" separation are Charles W. Anderson, Robert A. Cook, and Samuel H. Sutherland. Woodbridge reminds them of the admonition of Spurgeon, who cut himself clear from those who err from the Faith and even from those who associate with them.

A second answer has come from veteran evangelist and writer, John R. Rice, who devoted part of the September 3, 1971 issue of the *Sword of the Lord* to answer the Woodbridge position. Rice contends that Woodbridge was neither scholarly nor reliable and holds that Christians should separate from unbelievers but not from good Christians. He does not believe that II Thessalonians 3:6 and Psalm 119:63 teach "second degree" separation. He rejects, in his dogmatic style, the Woodbridge call to "boycott" not only New Evangelicals but also their fellow-travelers, and upholds "good Christians" like W. A. Criswell, who joined in the June, 1971 conference in Jerusalem with Walvoord, Skinner, and Culbertson.

A third answer to this sticky question comes from Bob Jones, Jr., Chancellor of Bob Jones University. He has submitted his position in a booklet, *Scriptural Separation,* holding that there is no such thing as "first-degree" and "second-degree" separation, but only that taught by the Scriptures. To him it is clear that the Bible commands separation from those who aid and encourage any kind of compromise with infidelity. The positive teaching is that we should be helping men to take a Scriptural position, not the opposite. To illustrate, Jones would preach for a man in order to encourage him in his effort to bring his church out of an apostate denomination, but not to help him to get members to promote the apostasy of that denomination. The Bible demands opposition to apostasy, compromise, and infidelity.

Fundamentalists ought to study these three positions, for we cannot be ostriches and bury our heads. These issues are with us and must be faced and dealt with in a Biblical way.

Most assuredly, careful observers will be aware of other dangers which threaten us. One cannot ignore the pressure of the delusion artists of our generation—Oral Roberts, Rex Humbard, Garner Ted

Armstrong, and Katherine Kuhlman. Neither should we overlook the widely adopted heretical views of R. B. Thieme, Jr., of Houston, who spreads his poison into thousands of homes weekly through a tape ministry, dividing churches and uprooting pastors from old-fashioned doctrines and practices. A very close analysis will need to be made of the influence of Key '73, as it weakens evangelicals, sound schools, and mission boards in smashing down the high walls of separatism. It may well be the most successful move yet to promote the ecumenical movement and drive all churches, Protestant and Catholic, into union as a prelude to the erection of Babylon the Great. It is already evident that Protestant pastors are rushing into its waiting arms with a passion matched only by their involvement with Graham. One sad part of the story is the weakening of some independent pastors, who are promoting it because of a soulwinning emphasis on the surface. Another danger in many areas is that of the "Jesus People," who claim an allegiance to the Bible while acting the part of religious playboys and playgirls, and clutch constantly a religious image to justify their wild and weird antics and activities. They are receiving new support as more students and faculty members on so-called Christian campuses endorse, ape, and seek to "understand" them.

Its Divisions

After this long journey through a century of the history of American Fundamentalism, we ought to look closely at its present status, recognize its clearly defined divisions, and observe factually the dangers it faces. There is enough indifference toward it at the present time to raise serious questions as to whether it may long survive in such hostile surroundings. We do trust a sovereign God to preserve by His grace both His Word and His people on the earth, but we must also recognize the devices of the Devil, as he attempts to pull down the bulwarks of the Faith and to cause to crumble the very institutions that the Lord has raised up to preserve that Faith and to train others to do the same.

In assessing the strength of modern Fundamentalism, one must reckon with the existence of thirteen thousand churches in the nation that would call themselves Fundamentalist, which, at an average of 350 members, would yield an aggregate of four million members. Their ministries vary in scope from the bustling empires of such giants as the Highland Park Baptist Church in Chattanooga and the Temple Baptist Church of Detroit to the small, struggling country churches with only a few members and with limited potentiality for growth. The numbers are somewhat deceptive, however. Less than a third of these churches are militantly exposing the evils and dangers of the times, and most of their members are ignorant of the positions to which they have been committed by their identification of themselves with the Fundamentalist movement.

The schools and other organizations of modern professing Fundamentalism present an even more complex and confusing picture. To clarify this picture, we must introduce at this point a new classification. Too often the distinctives of historic Fundamentalism have been blurred, and the term is used loosely to denote dispensationalists, evangelicals, adherents of Orthodoxy, conservatives, holiness groups, and all varieties of religious enthusiasts. Of all the defining characteristics of historic Fundamentalism, the one most useful in distinguishing genuine modern Fundamentalism from the partial and spurious brands is militancy in the Biblical exposure of error and of all compromise with error. Accordingly, we may distinguish three kinds of modern *professing* Fundamentalists: the militant (the genuine, historic Fundamentalists), the moderate, and the modified.

A *militant* Fundamentalist of the historic type is one who interprets the Bible literally and also exposes all affirmations and attitudes not found in the Word of God. He must both expound and expose. Bible exposition is vital and essential, but alone it is not enough. It is at this point that many dispensationalists, such as Chafer, disqualify themselves from the circle of the militant. L. S. Chafer was a keen student of the truths of the Bible, but he did not expose the dangers and the drifts of his time. Most of his disciples have followed his weakness in this respect. In simple fact, these cannot be classified as militant Fundamentalists; they are able expositors of the Word but not militant in the exposure of non-Biblical concepts and activities. Most graduates of Dallas Seminary are of this kind. To be militant, one must tell the truth of the Bible and the truth about error and compromise. Exposure has been essential; now it is even more necessary because of new forms of middle-of-the-roadism, worldliness, and friendliness to apostate church activities.

At this point we desire to help American Christians, particularly pastors and young people by listing the *militant* Fundamentalist schools. This listing does not claim to be complete, but it is widely representative.

Arlington Baptist Schools
Baptist Bible College (Clarks Summit, Pa.)
Baptist Bible College (Denver)
Baptist Bible College (Springfield, Mo.)
Bob Jones University
Calvary College (Letcher, Ky.)
Central Baptist Seminary (Minneapolis)
Clearwater Christian College

Faith Theological Seminary
Florida Baptist Schools
Indiana Baptist College
Maranatha Baptist Bible College
Midwestern Baptist Bible College
Pillsbury Baptist Bible College
San Francisco Baptist Theological Seminary

There is a second class, that of the *moderate* Fundamentalist. He accepts all the affirmations or doctrines of the Bible but refuses to expose error, those who espouse error, wrong attitudes, questionable habits, and defections from Bible discipline. This results in indifference to hard-line Biblical separation. In this group are the dispensationalists who have worked faithfully to exegete and dig out Bible truth but who refuse to be as diligent—if, indeed, they show any interest—in exposing error and standing for Biblical attitudes and the application of Biblical standards to everyday situations. They avoid issues of personal separation from worldly things and are soft in their stand against friends engaged in compromise. They reject the role of the soldier and deny that there is a war on and that we are to fight and win in the battles. The moderates do not have a war psychology; in fact, they sweetly ignore the spiritual carnage caused by the subtle attacks and inroads of apostate movements and compromises in youth movements and missions boards. They disagree with some aspects of New Evangelicalism but refuse to identify it as a compromise movement. The moderates guard against alarm tactics and war nerves, communicating to people the idea that receiving truth is enough in the great war against the Word. They downgrade evangelistic preaching, soulwinning, and rigid personal separation.

Many honored schools are in the *moderate* camp today, and we name a few in order that pastors and young people may be alerted to the soft line of these educational institutions. Some representative moderate schools are:

Asbury College
Biola College
Cedarville College
Calvary Bible College (Kansas City)
Covenant College
Dallas Bible College
Dallas Seminary
Detroit Bible College
Florida Bible College
Grace College
Grace Seminary
Grand Rapids Baptist Seminary
Grand Rapids School of the Bible

John Brown University
Moody Bible Institute
Philadelphia College of Bible
Rockmont College
Talbot Seminary
Tennessee Temple Schools
Washington Bible College
Western Baptist Seminary
Westminster Seminary

There is a third class, the *modified* Fundamentalists. Most of them have a Fundamentalist background and affirm the inspiration of the Bible, the sinfulness of man, the deity of Christ, His atoning death, His bodily resurrection, and the return of the Lord. They are basically evangelical, but because of their surrender to New Evangelicalism they are outside the mainstream of historic Fundamentalism. This they have not announced, and they go on getting money and students from churches and groups because they have not announced their new-evangelical character. Their plea for love would be meaningful if they were honest in stating their departure from Fundamentalism. Most of their followers do not know of the differences which exist among evangelical people. They dismiss the doctrine of the imminent coming of the Lord as unimportant. They play down the importance of separation from all forms of apostasy and compromise. They affirm they are "fundamental" but use the term in reference to Reformation truths and not to the position of historic American Fundamentalism.

The schools in the *modified* or new-evangelical group may be represented by the following:

Barrington College
Columbia Bible College
Conservative Baptist Seminary
Fuller Seminary
Gordon College
Gordon Divinity School
Houghton College
King's College
LeTourneau College
Nyack College
Oral Roberts University
Taylor University
Trinity Seminary
Wheaton College

It should be noted that in both moderate and modified schools are some hard-line Fundamentalists who take good stands individually. Affiliated with schools with weak or blurred images, these men refuse to polarize themselves. They believe their ministry is honoring to the Lord in spite of the Biblical principle that a little leaven leavens the lump; their compromise reveals their unexpressed conviction that the lump will lumpen the leaven. In this, they are squarely set against the convictions of the Apostle Paul; moreover, they are party to compromise, erosion, and capitulation to the Satanic forces arrayed against historic Fundamentalism. In these schools the middle-of-the-roaders have taken charge of the administrations and faculty. While trustees of these schools ignore the pleas of knowledgeable Fundamentalists to clean house, the schools decline in spiritual perception, power, and the will to preserve Fundamentalism. Their graduates adopt the indifference of their teachers, and the churches follow suit.

The last area of Fundamentalist service to feel the attacks of the moderates and modified men has been the mission boards, but these have been so affected that a major transition is now in progress. Even mission leaders and publications hint at this great change, but factually little has been written. There is a small list of mission boards which have taken an out-and-out Fundamentalist stance in all the swirling issues. One major issue has been Evangelism-In-Depth as promoted by the Latin America Mission; in fact, it is New Evangelicalism on the mission fields. It is an unscriptural inclusivism in methods for the sake of larger attendance, involvements, and numbers responding. On this one issue the boards are dividing and will continue to do so. But there are still militant Fundamentalist boards, and some representative ones should be named for the help of earnest pastors and students, as well as the informed laymen who sincerely ask for information so that they may support the works of sound groups. Among the *militant* mission boards are the following:

Alaska Evangelization Mission
Association of Baptists for World Evangelism
Baptist Bible Fellowship Mission
Baptist International Missions
Baptist Mid-Missions
Bible Protestant Methodist Mission
Evangelical Baptist Missions
Gospel Fellowship Missions
Hebrew Christian Fellowship
Independent Board for Presbyterian Foreign Missions
International Missions
Maranatha Baptist Mission
Missions to Military
United Missionary Fellowship
World Baptist Fellowship Mission
World Baptist Mission
Worldwide Evangelical Fellowship

The second group of missions consists of those of *moderate* Fundamentalism, made up mostly of large faith missions, who have done sacrificial work for many decades. Now they are quite bewildered by the new methods and trends in missions in general and are equally unsettled as to their own direction in the days ahead. Most of the missionaries are Fundamentalists but remain associated with boards whose leaders are weakening in their separatist position and are willing to modify in order to work within the framework of modern missionary activities. A moratorium exists on discussion of the Graham issue, Evangelism-In-Depth, and the main facts of the worldwide ecumenical movement. In this fashion a tolerant attitude and *moderate* mood are gaining ground in these missions, and their direction is toward New Evangelicalism. The following missions are representative:

Africa Evangelical Fellowship
American Board of Missions to the Jews
Back to the Bible Mission
Central American Mission
Christian Missions in Many Lands
Gospel Missionary Union
North Africa Mission
Source of Light Mission
Trans-World Radio
Unevangelized Fields Mission
Word of Life Fellowship

The third group comprises the new-evangelical missions or *modified* Fundamentalists. Often this condition is not stated in the official literature, and pastors and people are not aware of the identification of the boards with either Evangelism-In-Depth or comparable compromise in missions. But in major part or in whole, these boards have adopted the thinking, the tolerant attitudes, the methods, and the techniques of the New Evangelicals. This group may be represented by the following:

Africa Inland Mission
Conservative Baptist Foreign Mission Society
Evangelical Alliance Mission (TEAM)
Evangelize China
Far Eastern Gospel Crusade
Greater Europe Mission
Jungle Aviation Fellowship
Latin America Mission
Missionary Internship
Northeastern Gospel Crusade
Overseas Missionary Fellowship
Pocket Testament League

Regions Beyond Mission
Sudan Interior Mission
World Vision
Worldwide Evangelization Crusade
Wycliffe Translators

To the despair and frustration of pastors, there is no list available which will reveal how mission leaders think, in what directions they are leading the boards, and how involved they are in the trends of compromise with and the actual espousal of new-evangelical attitudes. As the situation becomes more confused, more and more questions will have to be asked by supporters of these organizations. As of the present hour, militant Fundamentalists cannot recommend without question or reservation more than twenty mission boards of the over one hundred usually acknowledged to be sound and evangelical. To admit this is to recognize the tragic impasse to which we have come in schools, colleges, seminaries, and missionary enterprise.

The preceding lists of schools and mission boards have the shortcomings of all such attempts to impose a simple classification on a complex situation in flux. There is a continuing drift downward; many, perhaps most, organizations are in motion, some are hesitating, and a few seem firmly fixed. There is no stable position between militant, vigilant Fundamentalism and New Evangelicalism, which, indeed, may itself be a way station to the more overt forms of apostasy. The basis of this classification is militancy of opposition to all forms of compromise with apostasy, not primarily other identifying features of historic Fundamentalism; and, hence, the full endorsement of the author and publisher of all the schools and boards listed as *militant* should not be inferred. Some schools and boards have been included in the *moderate* group because, although suspicions have been raised, not enough evidence exists to place them definitely within the *modified* camp. Conversely, it should be acknowledged that within the *moderate*—and, to a lesser extent, within the *modified*—group are some individuals with militant convictions, especially in the case of the mission boards, which have missionaries serving faithfully in outlying areas who are not aware of what has been going on within their organizations. Especially, it should be emphasized that the lists are representative of the face of Fundamentalism in the fall of 1973, and readers should realize that such lists, unfortunately, will need to be amended continually as drifts and defections from the ranks of the faithful increase with the approach of the end of the age.

Nevertheless, despite their inevitable shortcomings, lists of organizations within professing Fundamentalism must be made and continue to be made so that genuine Fundamentalists will know where to direct their support. There is a general drowsiness among the saints at present, who have been so lulled into sleepy self-satisfaction that few are inclined to believe there is any danger at all. Most offer their support and blessing indiscriminately to the militant, the moderate, and the modified. How much compromise can be allowed before non-cooperation is a Biblical demand? To obey the Lord in the responsibility of separation will demand keenest discernment and a willingness to follow Biblical convictions wherever not only apostasy but also compromise has taken hold.

TOPICS FOR DISCUSSION AND RESEARCH

PERIOD ONE

1. How much did early Fundamentalism infiltrate such groups as Presbyterians, Anglicans, Methodists, and Holiness people?
2. Did Pentecostals, who arose late in this period, ever consider themselves a part of historic Fundamentalism?
3. List the leading liberal religious periodicals of that day which supported and promoted the Liberalism of the American type.
4. Can we trace the reaction of individual Methodists or Methodist groups during this period to increasing Liberalism?
5. How active a part did Fundamentalism take in social ministries such rescue missions, health care, and relief of the poor?
6. To what extent was this period a reaction and to what extent a restoration?
7. What early Fundamentalist was most knowledgeable on the details of the second coming?
8. How did early Fundamentalists come to embrace literalism in Bible interpretation?
9. Was it a weakness that Fundamentalism of this period was largely a preachers' movement? As such did it have precedents in church history?
10. List, college-by-college and seminary-by-seminary, the professors who led the institutions from Evangelicalism to Liberalism in this period.
11. In what specifics did Fundamentalism differ from Orthodoxy?

12. Were the early Fundamentalists concerned more with separation as a principle or with separation as a set of practices and habits?

13. Why was greatness of knowledge so largely characteristic of the first generation Fundamentalists and not of those of the third generation?

14. Why did Baptists not dominate in numbers in this period as they have more and more in succeeding generations?

15. Do the facts support the contention of the early Fundamentalists that the doctrine of imminency was a boon to missions?

16. Would the early Fundamentalists have accepted one holding to premillennialism but not to dispensationalism?

17. As A. H. Strong saw the effect of Liberalism on faculties of schools, why did he, an evangelical, name Liberals to his faculty at Rochester?

18. Would Fundamentalism have arisen had not Liberalism as a mighty flood forced a reaction?

19. Did Fundamentalism have a basic unity then, or was it simply an aggregate of islands of reaction? Was it mainly a joining of ranks to face a common foe?

20. Did early Fundamentalism count as heretics those who differed from it? How much did a man have to differ before being viewed as heretical?

21. Did Fundamentalists of that period see themselves as creating a new movement?

22. What general attitudes account for the fall of so many colleges and seminaries into liberal control?

23. Did Fundamentalism owe as much to English dispensationalism or to the Brethren movement as Sandeen maintains?

24. Did the Fundamentalists recognize their sharp differences with those of the Reformation backgrounds especially in the doctrines of millennialism and the local church?

25. What men living before the rise of American Fundamentalism contributed most to the understanding and appreciation of the doctrine of the imminent coming of the Lord?

26. Did the Fundamentalists see covenant theologians or amillennialists as being in error, and, if so, was the error regarded as of such seriousness as to force separation from them?

27. Can A. B. Simpson of the Christian and Missionary Alliance be counted among the Fundamentalists of this period?

28. Who would have been considered the ablest theologian among the Fundamentalists?

29. How many Fundamentalists were premillennial without having a dispensational interpretation?

30. Why did Fundamentalism arise in America and not in Europe where Liberalism had its earliest strongholds? Why has it been almost solely an American phenomenon?

31. Was the aftermath of the War Between the States congenial to the rise of the Fundamentalist Movement?

PERIOD TWO

1. How did it happen that whereas many Presbyterian figures were prominent in the First Period the number greatly decreased in the Second Period?

2. Was J. Frank Norris a typical Fundamentalist?

3. What mission boards were Fundamental in the Twenties?

4. Did the fellowship concept of Fundamentalists in this period contribute to the chaos and confusion of the third period?

5. To what factors can we attribute the obvious fact that Fundamentalism came to be a preachers' movement?

6. Did the eccentricities and questionable habits of Norris saddle Fundamentalism with a reputation for a behavior very unlike its beliefs?

7. What were the common traits of Norris, Riley, and Shields that pushed them to such heights of platform power and stature as preachers?

8. What were the attitudes of Riley, Norris, and Shields toward the evangelists of the period—Sunday, Biederwolf, and Bob Jones, Sr.?

9. Why did L. S. Chafer of Dallas Seminary stand so far aloof from such Fundamentalist leaders as Norris and Riley?

10. Why did the Fundamentalists accept Shields, who espoused amillennialism, as one of their leaders when Fundamentalism was a premillenial movement?

11. Did the start of "gap schools" with little regard for academics bring Fundamentalism within the shadow of ignorance and intellectual superficiality?

12. Why did W. B. Riley so denounce the Northern Baptists, inspire so many separatists, and yet remain within the Northern Baptist Convention till the year of his death?

13. What place did Wheaton College play in Fundamentalism under the leadership of Blanchard and Buswell?

14. Why has historic Fundamentalism produced so few church historians?

15. Was the "strong-man" practice within Fundamentalism a great weakness?

16. Is the influence of the Scofield Reference Bible in Fundamentalism a major factor in its history?

17. Would the BBU have been more greatly blessed if it had been separatist and not just non-cooperative?

18. Did the stalwarts of Fundamentalism regard the booklets on *The Fundamentals* as their platform of doctrine and belief?

19. Why did Fundamentalism of this period become dominated by Baptists?

20. How did the Fundamentalist-Modernist controversy affect mission boards, missionary work, and missionaries themselves?

21. Why did such leaders as R. A. Torrey and A. C. Dixon forsake the militant Fundamentalist movements?

22. Did the Fundamentalists of the second period vastly overestimate the Fundamental views of denominational leaders and writers?

23. Has the shallow preaching of many Fundamentalists been responsible for so many of their hearers' going off on tangents, into fanatical groups, and even into cults?

24. What papers and periodicals best represented the Fundamentalist position in the second period?

25. What parts were played by such schools as Westminster Seminary, Northern Baptist Seminary, and Eastern Baptist Seminary in the growth of Fundamentalism?

26. Could the WCFA have been rescued and caused to become a great national fellowship of Fundamentalism?

27. Were the empires of the Prima Donnas of Fundamentalism patterned after denominational structures and, therefore, foredoomed as manmade?

28. Why did Fundamentalism become so much weaker in the New England states than elsewhere?

29. Did Fundamentalists of this period see themselves as actively involved in social and political issues?

30. Was the invisible-visible church issue prominent in Fundamentalist controversy?

31. How many of the early Fundamentalists were strict Calvinists?

32. Who were the most effective Fundamentalist voices within the ranks of Methodism?

33. When orthodox Presbyterians split from the parent body in 1936, could they justly have been called Fundamentalists?

34. Why did T. T. Shields finally fade away from the scene of American Fundamentalism?

35. Has the Fundamentalist claim to preach the whole counsel of God been true in practice?

36. Was the influence of John Roach Straton on Fundamentalism a wholesome and positive one?

37. What part in the battles of Fundamentalism was played by James M. Gray of Moody Bible Institute?

38. Did the Bible schools prepare men adequately for the Gospel ministry?

39. What steps did administrators or trustees take to insure the Fundamentalist integrity of the Bible schools?

40. Did William Jennings Bryan play any significant part in the development of Fundamentalism?

41. Trace the influence of such schools as Wheaton College, Columbia Bible College, Moody Bible Institute, Dallas Seminary, Biola, Philadelphia College of the Bible, and Gordon College on the general trends of Fundamentalism.

42. How could so orthodox a denomination as the Northern Presbyterians fall into liberal thought?

43. Did the cooperation of Fundamental men in any way parallel that promoted by the ecumenical movement of the same period?

44. Were the primitive methods of the New Testament always regarded as guidelines in the work of missions and evangelism?

PERIOD THREE

1. Account for the great growth of the Baptist Bible Fellowship.

2. What has isolated the American Baptist Association from other Baptists?

3. How nonfundamental must an individual or organization be before separation from such is necessary?

4. Why have so many Fundamental preachers begun to emphasize Gospel preaching at the expense of exposition of the Scriptures?

5. Do any fellowships remain absolutely untainted by New Evangelicalism?

6. Why did this period not produce Fundamentalist prima donnas of the type of Norris, Shields, and Riley?

7. Did the Keswick movement make significant inroads into the Fundamentalism of this period?

8. How much Landmarkism has there been outside the American Baptist Association?

9. Why has Fundamentalism continued to exist as isolated islands of dissent and reaction instead of as a national movement?

10. Trace the gradual weakening of Fundamentalist groups by the constant pressure of New Evangelicalism.

11. Why has there not been a history of such movements as the WCFA, WBF, ABA, and other Fundamentalist groups? Does this lack indicate utter indifference to the historical significance of these groups and to the importance of their principles?

12. Would a union of Fundamentalist and Orthodox camps benefit both?

13. Should we regret the loss of the empires and emperors of the second period of Fundamentalism and desire such today?

14. Can strict Calvinism with its spiritualizing of prophetic scriptures be reconciled with Fundamentalism and its literalism?

15. Is the increasing use of gimmicks to promote church growth a manifestation of worldliness and a concomitant of other kinds of worldliness in the church?

16. Why do so many Fundamentalists discourage and discredit high academic standards in education?

17. Present the part played by such schools as Gordon, Kings College, Moody Bible Institute, Prairie Bible Institute, Philadelphia College of the Bible, Biola, and Wheaton in the advance or decline of Fundamentalism.

18. Have such publishers as Zondervan, Eerdmans, Moody, Scripture Press, and Union Gospel Press helped or hindered the growth of Fundamentalism?

19. Is Fundamentalism in any danger of carrying its separatism beyond essential matters to the point of smug, stagnant isolationism?

20. Should such groups as Free Will Baptists and Southern Methodists be considered within the mainstream of Fundamentalism?

21. Was Billy Graham's inclusivism the most divisive issue within Fundamentalism during the modern period?

22. Compare and contrast the respective roles of Dallas Seminary, Trinity Seminary, Grace Seminary, and Faith Seminary in the history of Fundamentalism.

23. What other mission boards besides those named can be listed as maintaining a militant Fundamentalist stand during this period? How many have changed from this stand and why?

24. Has the change of some Bible schools to liberal arts colleges weakened Fundamentalism?

25. What positive steps can be taken at the present to strengthen and repair a weakened Fundamentalism?

26. What attitudes are the first signs of a decline in Fundamental institutions?

27. Can we expect a renaissance of Fundamentalist scholarship?

28. When the General Assembly of the Presbyterian Church, USA, ruled in 1944 that dispensationalism was an error, was this a slap at Dallas Seminary, Bible schools, or Fundamentalism generally, which has espoused it?

29. Trace the history of the doctrine of Biblical separation.

30. In what ways has New Evangelicalism infiltrated such groups as the Conservative Baptists and the IFCA?

31. What new moves can be expected from New Evangelicals?

32. Since the BBF is growing rapidly despite the fact that its men are not trained in the traditional college-seminary plan, should this traditional plan be abandoned generally?

33. Why have the doctrines and churches of Liberalism been so much more effective in their self-perpetuation than those of Fundamentalism?

34. Could Fundamentalism have won any of the major denominations if it had shown a more charitable spirit?

35. Were many men persuaded to leave Fundamentalism because of the eccentricities, self-glory, and apparent hypocrisies of those in strategic places?

36. On what point or points must a historic Fundamentalist break fellowship with those who are not of this persuasion?

37. Can historic Fundamentalism survive within a denomination in which denominational survival has become paramount?

38. How many of the present splits within Fundamentalism are based on principle?

39. Has bigness become too important to some Fundamentalist leaders?

40. Can the American Council of Christian Churches ever again be a strong force in our generation when it is so badly scrambled?

41. Are Campus Crusade and the Graham crusades the main agencies in popularizing ecumenical evangelism? What others might be added to the list?

42. If New Evangelicalism be unbiblical leaven, how much of it can there be in a school before the leaven controls it?

43. Has Fundamentalism made a mistake by ignoring social issues and emphasizing too much the saving of souls?

44. Have Fundamentalists effectively informed the people in the pew about the titanic struggle now going on?

45. Could the different groups within Fundamentalism have been united for more effective attacks on Liberalism?

46. Determine the exact place of such men as A. C. Gaebelein, W. L. Pattingill, Bob Shuler, I. M. Haldeman, Paul Rader, and Courtland Myers within Fundamentalism.

47. Has the Fundamental Baptist Congress given a great boost to Fundamentalism?

48. Is there any genuine hope that the *moderate* schools and mission boards will ever take a militant stand?

49. What *moderate* schools are most likely to be the next to drift into out-and-out New Evangelicalism?

BIOGRAPHICAL INDEX

The Biographical Index has the twofold purpose of providing a convenient introduction to the persons whose names appear in the text—both the champions and faithful supporters of Fundamentalism and its enemies and deserters—and of honoring those who have shared in the sacrifices, agonies of soul, and solidarity of conviction that have characterized the movement since its inception. The brevity of the sketches is a regrettable but inevitable consequence of space limitations and, in certain cases, of the circumstance that complete biographical information was unattainable. Perhaps this index will serve as a stimulus and first step to the compilation of a much-needed Who's Who of American Fundamentalism.

The following legend explains the abbreviations used in the Index.

ABA	American Baptist Association
ABC	American Baptist Convention (formerly NBC)
ABFMS	American Baptist Foreign Mission Society
ACCC	American Council of Christian Churches
BBF	Baptist Bible Fellowship
BBU	Baptist Bible Union
BMA	Baptist Missionary Association
CBA of A	Conservative Baptist Association of America
CBF	Conservative Baptist Fellowship
CBFMS	Conservative Baptist Foreign Mission Society
FBF	Fundamental Baptist Fellowship
FCC	Federal Council of Churches

GARB	General Association of Regular Baptists
GARBC	General Association of Regular Baptist Churches
IFCA	Independent Fundamental Churches of America
MBA	Missionary Baptist Association
NABA	North American Baptist Association
NAE	National Association of Evangelicals
NBC	Northern Baptist Convention
SBC	Southern Baptist Convention
SIM	Sudan Interior Mission
WBF	World Baptist Fellowship
WBM	World Baptist Mission
WCC	World Council of Churches
WCFA	World's Christian Fundamentals Association

A

Adams, J. D. (?-1943). Prominent Philadelphia businessman. Executive secretary, Philadelphia Bible Conference 1917. Secretary, Philadelphia School of the Bible 1918-19; its general secretary 1919-33; its president 1933-36. 160

Akenson, Curtis B. (1913-). Baptist pastor in Groveland, Minn. Associated with First Baptist Church, Minneapolis, since 1942, first as assistant to W. B. Riley, then as pastor since 1944; affiliated with ABC; supports Graham ministry. 120, 199, 200

Alexander, Scotty (1915-). Pastor: Midway Baptist, Lubbock, Tex., 1942; Bible Baptist, Enid, Okla., 1943-63; Freeway Baptist, Houston, Tex., 1964-67; Castleberry Baptist, Fort Worth, Tex., since 1967. A founder of the BBF; its director for 18 years; its president in 1965; its vice-president for 2 years. 217

Alford, Henry (1810-71). English Bible scholar and writer. Dean of Canterbury in the Church of England. Outstanding student of the Greek N. T. An editor of *Expositor's Greek New Testament* (4 vols.). Sound in learning, but admired German Higher Criticism and radicalism. 32, 40

Allen, A. A. (1911-70). Pentecostal preacher, tent revivalist, radio personality. Headquarters at Miracle Valley, Ariz. Associated with the Assemblies of God, but his credentials terminated in 1956; died suddenly at Jack Tarr Motel, San Francisco. 196

Allen, John Henry (1820-98). Unitarian minister. Lecturer at Harvard Divinity School. Authority on the history of Unitarianism in New England. Pastor: Roxbury, Mass., 1843-47; Washington, D. C., 1847-50; Bangor, Me., 1850-57. Wrote for *The Christian Examiner* and *The Unitarian Review*. Wrote a 3-volume *Christian History*. 71

Allis, Oswald T. (1880-1973). Instructor, Princeton Seminary 1910-22. Asst. professor, Princeton Seminary 1922-29. Professor, Westminster Seminary 1930-36. Editor, *The Princeton Review* 1918-29. Contributing editor of *Christianity Today* 1938-73. 176, 237

Altizer, T. J. J. (1927-). Professor: Wabash College 1954-56; Emory U. 1956-68; State U. of N. Y. since 1968. Controversial atheist in 1960s who published *God Is Dead*. Solid proof of the extreme Modernism and unbelief taught inside Methodism. 102, 196

Anderson, Charles W. (1912-). Baptist pastor: National Park, N. J., 2 years; Wissinoming Baptist, Philadelphia, 5 years; Brookdale Baptist, Bloomfield, N. J., since 1939. Founder and president of Northeastern Collegiate Bible Institute, Essex Fells, N. J., since 1950. Has served on CBFMS, Pocket Testament League, SIM. 281

Anderson, Frederick L. (1862-1938). Northern Baptist pastor, St. Louis. Professor: Rochester Seminary 1888-1900; Newton Theological Institution, Newton Center, Mass., 1900-33. An evangelical, but blind and weak on the drift of Northern Baptists into apostasy. 150

Anderson, Herbert (1916-). Pastor: First Baptist, Gladstone, Ore., 1949-52; Calvary Baptist, The Dalles, Ore., 1952-58; First Baptist, Lebanon, Ore., 1958-62; Hinson Memorial, Portland, Ore., 1962-67. President, Conservative Baptist Association of America 1963-66. General director, CBFMS 1967-71. Pastor, Hinson Memorial since 1971. 225

Anderson, J. Neal (1920-). Evangelical Methodist pastor, Gibsonville, N. C., 1952-59. General supt., People's Methodist Church 1959-62. Dist. supt., Atlantic Evangelical Methodist Church 1962-66. Asst. general supt., Eastern Annual Conference since 1966. President, John Wesley College, Greensboro, N. C., 1960-67. Pastor: Mableton, Ga., 1967-71; Tobaccoville, N. C., since 1971. 248

Anderson, William M., Jr. (1889-1935). Presbyterian minister, East Dallas, 1914-15. Asst. secretary, Committee on Schools and Colleges 1915-17. Associate to his father, First Presbyterian, Dallas, Tex., 1917-24. Pastor, First Presbyterian, Dallas, Tex., 1924-35. Aided L. S. Chafer in founding Dallas Seminary.

Ange, Joseph G. (1922-). Pastor: Edgemont Free Will Baptist, Durham, N. C., 1952-57; Central Free Will Baptist, Royal Oak, Mich., 1957-66; Liberty Free Will Baptist, Durham, N. C., 1966-72. Director of religious activities, Free Will Baptist Bible College, Nashville, Tenn., since 1972. 245

Appelman, Hyman J. (1902-). Born a Jew in White Russia; came to the U. S. in 1914; practiced law in Chicago; served in U. S. Army medical division 1925-30. Baptist pastor in Okla. and Tex. 1930-34. State evangelist for Tex. 1934-42. International evangelist since 1942. 254

Armerding, Hudson T. (1918-). Professor and administrator, Gordon College. President of Wheaton College, Wheaton, Ill., since 1965. President, NAE. Talented new-evangelical leader, largely responsible for Wheaton College's drift into compromise and worldliness. 209, 235, 274

Armitage, Thomas (1819-96). Born in England; came to U. S. in 1838; served as a Methodist Episcopal pastor; became a Baptist in 1839. Pastor: Washington Avenue Baptist, Albany, N. Y., 1839-48; Norfolk Street Baptist, N. Y. C., later Fifth Avenue Baptist, 1848-96. Wrote a *History of Baptists*. 97

Armstrong, Herbert W. (1892-). Widely known broadcaster. Editor, *The Plain Truth*. Founder, Ambassador Colleges. Formerly with the Church of God, Stanberry, Mo. Started his own church in Ore. in 1933 after having discovered the "truths" of the Ten Lost Tribes, the True Sabbath, the Eternal Covenant; began his magazine in 1933, his radio program

The World Tomorrow in 1934; Garner Ted (1930-), his son, now associated with him. 196

Arnold, Gene (1920-). Founder, Fellowship Baptist Church, Roanoke, Va., 1952; its present pastor. Evangelist in the Virginias and Carolinas. Active in several independent Baptist fellowships. 242

Asbury, Francis (1745-1816). Pioneer Methodist circuit rider in U. S. Had little formal training; averaged over 6,000 miles a year on horseback in his evangelistic journeys. Asbury College named after him. A great servant and bishop of Methodism. 191

Ashbrook, William E. (1896-). Presbyterian pastor: Liberty United Presbyterian, Hubbard, Ohio, 1922-28; Neil Avenue, Columbus, Ohio, 1928-32; Glen Echo, Columbus, Ohio, 1932-40; Calvary Bible, Columbus, Ohio, 1940-71. Has openly opposed New Evangelicalism in his book *The New Neutralism.* 205, 211, 224, 227

Astruc, Jean (1684-1766). Scholarly Bible critic. Divided the first five books of the Bible (Pentateuch) according to the names for God (Jehovah and Elohim) and claimed there were many sources, editors, and writers in addition to Moses; attacked the authenticity and authority of the Bible. 152

Atkinson, William Elrie (1862-1935). A founder of Ouchita Baptist College, Okla. (SBC); chairman of its board for many years. Prominent legal figure in Ark., even serving as a judge. A leading Christian layman. 168

Aubrey, Edwin E. (1896-1956). Professor: Union Theological College, Chicago, 1920-22; Carleton College, Vassar, Miami U. 1922-29; U. of Chicago 1929-44, teaching Christian ethics 1929-35 and theology 1935-44. Thoroughgoing modernist educator. 100

Augsburger, Bryce B. (1922-). Pastor: First Baptist, Galveston, Mich., 1947-49; Livernois Avenue Baptist, Detroit, 1950-58; Marquette Manor Baptist, Chicago, 1958-66. President, Baptist Bible College, Denver, Colo., since 1966. Active in the FBF, WBM, CBF. 195

Augustine (Aurelius Augustinus) (354-430). Outstanding Church Father. Converted when 32; known for his *Confessions* and *The City of God;* wrote many theological works. Ardent churchman, sacramentarian. Helped prepare for the rise of Roman Catholicism in the Middle Ages. Bishop of Hippo, North Africa. 58, 63, 74, 117

Austin, Roy H. (1907-). Baptist pastor: Minnetonka, Little Falls, and Virginia in Minn., and Bend, Ore., for several years; Calvary Baptist, San Francisco, 1965-73. Active member and officer of the FBF, San Francisco Seminary board, WBF, and Lucerne Christian Conference Center. President, Association of Fundamental Baptist Churches of Northern California. 232

Ayer, William Ward (1892-). Baptist pastor: Central Baptist, Gary, Ind., 1927-32; Philpott Tabernacle, Hamilton, Canada, 1932-36; Calvary Baptist, N. Y. C., 1936-49. Widely known radio voice. Bible conference speaker. Writer. A consistent Fundamentalist in a 50-year ministry. Now retired and living in St. Petersburg, still continuing an active ministry of writing and speaking. 136, 157, 158, 256, 260, 271

B

Baillie, John (1886-1960). Presbyterian educator and writer. Professor, Edinburgh U., Scotland, 1909-12. Served in France in World War I 1915-19. Professor: Auburn Theological Seminary, Auburn, N. Y., 1919-27; Union Seminary, N. Y. C., 1930-34; Edinburgh 1934-56; Union, N. Y. C., 1956-57. Wrote several books; tried to unite Liberals and Conservatives. A president of the WCC. 39

Baldwin, Maurice (1836-1904). Church of England leader in Canada. Dean of Montreal 1872. Bishop of Huron, Canada, 1883-1904. Anglican in training and church life, but premillennial in prophecy. 28, 45

Ballard, Jerry (1935-). Director of Communications, National Association of Free Will Baptists. Editor, *Heartbeat* (Free Will Baptist paper). Editor, *World Vision* for 2 years. Now director of public relations, Columbia Bible College, Columbia, S. C. 244

Ballard, L. S. (1880-1961). Important leader, BMA and ABA. Instructor, Bible Institute, Ardmore, Okla. Organized and pastored Trinity Baptist Temple, Dallas, Tex., 1949-1960. Trinity Baptist Temple, now one of the largest Orthodox Baptist churches. 246

Balyo, John G. (1920-). Pastor: Christian Church, Three Oaks, Mich., 1942-45; Simonton Lake Baptist, Elkart, Ind., 1945-46; Bible Baptist, Kokomo, Ind., 1946-53; Cedar Hill Baptist, Cleveland, Ohio, 1953-72. Professor, Grand Rapids Bible Seminary since 1972. Has served on board of Baptist Mid-Missions and Council of Fourteen. 222

Barabas, Steven (1904-). Pastor, Ballston Center Presbyterian, Ballston Spa, N. Y., 1944-49. Professor, Wheaton College, Wheaton, Ill.; its chairman of the Department of Biblical Education since 1969. Associate editor, Zondervan *Pictorial Bible Dictionary* 1963. 21, 267

Barnes, Albert (1798-1870). Presbyterian pastor: Morristown, N. J., 1821-30; First Presbyterian, Philadelphia, 1830-67. Denied the limited atonement; accused of heresy, acquitted, but Northern Presbyterians split over this and other issues in 1830s. Active in abolition movement. 40, 74

Barnes, Marion (1913-). Professor, Wheaton College, Wheaton, Ill. Worked in chemical industries. President, Covenant College, Chattanooga, Tenn., since 1966. 239

Barnhouse, Donald Grey (1895-1960). Presbyterian minister. Graduate asst., U. of Pa. 1925-27. Pastor, Tenth Presbyterian, Philadelphia, 1927-60. Founder, *Revelation* magazine (later *Eternity*) which merged with *Christian Newsette* 1954, *Christian Digest* 1956, *Our Hope* 1958. Pungent, incisive Bible student and teacher. In last years, actively cooperated with Presbyterianism and Inter-Varsity. 205, 260

Barrows, Cliff (1923-). Song leader, Billy Graham Evangelistic Association. Gifted as a platform director of large crusade choirs. In the center of worldwide new-evangelical evangelism. 274

Barth, Karl (1886-1968). Swiss theologian. Giant in Protestant thought since 1920s. A founder of crisis theology or Neo-Orthodoxy which reaffirmed many Reformation doctrines with new meanings. Did not hold to verbal inspiration. Professor, Bonn until expelled by Nazis in 1935.

Professor, Basel 1935-68. Wrote *Romans,* a commentary, and *Church Dogmatics.* 98, 102

Bartlett, Billy Vick (1943-). Professor, Baptist Bible College, Springfield, Mo., teaching church history and Bible history. Wrote a book on the early days of the BBF, *A History of Baptist Separatism.* 133, 198

Bauman, L. S. (1875-1950). Brethren pastor: Morrill, Kan., 1894; Auburn and Cornell, Ill., 1895; Mexico, Kan., 1897; Philadelphia, 1900-10; Sunnyside, Wash., 1911-13; Long Beach, Calif., 1913-47. Good Bible student. Writer on prophecy. Many years on Foreign Missionary Society of the Brethren Church. 261

Baur, F. C. (1792-1860). Professor: U. of Blaubeurgen 1817-26; U. of Tübingen 1826-60. German historian and writer. Rejected the miracles of the Bible; dated many N. T. books as written in the second century. A gifted radical. 8, 9

Baxter, J. Sidlow (1903-). Born in Australia; came to England when 16 months old. Pastor: Northampton, England, for 4 years; Bethesda, England, for 4 years; Charlotte Chapel, Edinburgh, 1935-53. A Bible conference speaker since 1953. Wrote 20 books, including a 6-volume set, *Explore the Book.* 260

Beal, Richard S. (1887-). Baptist pastor: Forest City and Hume, Mo., 1909-11; Rich Hill, Mo., 1911-14; Victor, Colo., 1914-19; First Baptist, Tucson, Ariz., 1919-1959. Board of managers, NBC until leaving to work with Conservative Baptists. Solid Fundamentalist preacher and leader. 121

Beecher, Henry Ward (1813-87). Pastor: Lawrenceburg, Ind., 1838-39; Second Presbyterian, Indianapolis, Ind., 1839-47; Plymouth (Congregational), Brooklyn, N. Y., 1847-87. Widely known orator, lecturer, and liberal thinker. Editor, *The Christian Union.* 68

Bellamy, David (1906-64). First pastor of Hope Chapel Baptist, N. Y. C. (later renamed Calvary Baptist), 1847-50. 135

Bengel, Johann A. (1687-1752). German Lutheran theologian. Professor, U. of Denkendorf 1713-41. General supt., Herbrechtingen 1741-49. Prelate of Alpirspach 1749-52. Great expert on original texts of Bible. Pietistic and evangelical. Helped preserve sound doctrine in South Germany. 39

Bennett, Arthur (1864-?). Professor: Upper Iowa College; Highland Park College; Boston U. Dean, Des Moines U. 1925-29. Evangelical, but refused to take a Fundamentalist stand when the BBU controlled Des Moines U. 1927-29. 170

Bennett, John C. (1902-). Professor: Union Seminary, N. Y. C., 1930-31; Auburn Seminary 1931-35; Pacific School of Religion 1938-43; Union Seminary 1943-70. President, Union Seminary 1943-70. Leading Liberal and promoter of social gospel. 239

Berdyaev, Nicholas (1874-1948). Key figure among intellectuals in revival movements in Russian Orthodoxy. Mystic who doubted the value of doctrine. Taught at Moscow and an academy near Paris 1929-48; wrote 10 books. 102

Berntsen, William (1915-). Musician and a director in Christian education in churches in Tex., Ill., Iowa, Minn. A leader in Northwestern College since 1966, whose new campus at Roseville, Minn., opened in 1972. 121, 200

Bevington, Robert (Bob) (1927-). Baptist pastor, Newport, Tenn., 1958-52. Radio ministry since 1947. Active in Southwide Baptist Fellowship and International Fundamentalist Fellowship. Founder, 1952, and present pastor of Knoxville Baptist Tabernacle which has grown from 29 to 1,100 members. 242

Biederwolf, William E. (1867-1939). Ordained Presbyterian. Pastor, Broadway Church, Logansport, Ind., 1897-1900. Chaplain, Spanish-American War. Evangelist, 1900-39. Well-known Bible teacher and preacher. Head, Winona Lake Bible Conference 1922; Winona Lake School of Theology 1922-33. Pastor, Palm Beach, Fla., 1929-39. Solid, influential Fundamentalist. 88, 135, 261

Billington, Charles (1927-). Pastor, Akron Baptist Temple 1968, succeeding his father Dallas F. with whom he had worked. Akron Baptist Temple's membership on its 30th anniversary, 17,000. 220, 272

Billington, Dallas F. (1903-72). Wesleyan Methodist background in Ky. Founded Akron Baptist Temple, Akron, Ohio, 1934, which grew into one of the world's largest churches; it led all churches for years with a Sunday School of 6,000; its main work, soulwinning. 217, 219, 220, 272

Birch, John (1918-45). Student: Mercer U., Macon, Ga.; Bible Baptist Seminary, Fort Worth, Tex. Missionary to China under WBF, then led by J. Frank Norris. Captain, U. S. Army in China. Killed by Chinese communists. First Baptist Church in Fort Worth named a hall after him. John Birch Society has used his name. 131, 278

Bisagno, John (1934-). Pastor: First Southern Baptist, Del City, Okla.; now at First Baptist, Houston, Tex. Set a record for SBC of over 1,600 baptisms in 1 year. Former president of the Southern Baptist Pastors' Conference. 274

Bishop, George S. (1836-1914). Dutch Reformed pastor. A founder, Niagara Bible Conference. An author, *The Fundamentals* of 1909-12. Founder, Pisgah Conference 1878. Pastor, First Reformed, Orange, N. J., 1875-1906. Speaker, Seaside Bible Conference. 45, 50

Blackstone, W. E. (1841-1935). Methodist layman and Bible student. Supt., Chicago Jewish Mission. Interested in helping the Jewish people get back to Palestine. Best known for his book *Jesus Is Coming,* a compilation of Bible verses on the second coming. 29, 45

Blair, Charles (1917-). Pastor, Calvary Temple, Denver, Colo., since 1947, a 2-million-dollar Pentecostalist cathedral claiming 7,000 worshipers a week and telecasting its morning service over 25 stations. Member, board of directors of the National Sunday School Association. 274

Blanchard, Charles A. (1848-1926). Congregational pastor. President, Wheaton College, Wheaton, Ill., 1882-1926, succeeding his father Jonathan Blanchard. Fundamentalist of the first generation. Outspoken defender of the Bible. Led Wheaton to be outstanding in sound doctrine and high academics. 63, 75, 130

Blanchard, John (1916-). Headmaster, Ben Lippen School, Asheville,

N. C., 1946-49. Pastor, First Baptist, Plymouth, Mass., 1949-53. Director, Wheaton Academy 1962-65. Executive director, National Association of Christian Schools 1961-72. Board member, Council for American Private Education since 1971. Supt., Portland Oregon Christian Schools since 1972. 259

Blanchard, Jonathan (1811-92). Presbyterian minister. President, Wheaton College, Wheaton, Ill., 1862-82. Strong evangelical leader. Led Wheaton College to be an outstanding center of spiritual life and high academics, a "Fundamentalist island in a sea of unbelief." A founder of the North Central Association of Colleges. 75

Bliss, P. P. (1838-1935). Widely known and loved hymn writer. Baptist by convictions. Taught in public schools in Pa.; worked with D. L. Moody in evangelism; wrote "Man of Sorrows" and "Wonderful Words of Life." 72

Bogard, Ben M. (1868-1951). Baptist pastor with the ABA: Princeton, Ky.; Charleston, Mo.; Searcy, Ark.; Texarkana, Tex.; Antioch Baptist, Little Rock, Ark., 1920-45. A leader in forming the Arkansas State Association of Missionary Baptists and Sheridan Baptist College. A founder, ABA Sunday School Committee. Dean, Missionary Baptist Seminary at Little Rock 1943-45. Keen debater, author, speaker. 216

Bonar, Andrew A. (1810-92). Scottish Presbyterian minister. Premillennialist. Deeply devoted to the Lord; took the evangelical side when Presbyterianism in Scotland split in the 1840s. Friend of D. L. Moody. Wrote many books on the spiritual life. 59, 74

Bonnell, John S. (1893-). Presbyterian minister, St. John, Canada, 1923-29; Winnipeg, Canada, 1929-35; Fifth Avenue Presbyterian, N. Y., since 1935 as pastor and later as minister emeritus. Lecturer, Princeton Seminary since 1938. President, New York Theological Seminary since 1966. Wrote several books. 252

Boon, Harold W. (1910-). Christian Missionary Alliance pastor and educator. Registrar and academic dean, Nyack College 1940-68; its president since 1968, succeeding Thomas Mosely. The college's spiritual image has declined greatly under him. 71, 274

Boone, Charles (Pat) (1934-). Entertainer and singer. Church of Christ background; now actively identified with tongues movement. Participant in new-evangelical conferences. 207, 280

Booth, Carlton (1904-). Professor: Seattle Pacific College, in music; Providence Bible Institute 1930-55; Fuller Seminary since 1955. Gifted song leader and personal soulwinner. 258

Bowen, C. F. (1912-). Freewill Baptist pastor: N. C., 1937-45; East Nashville, Tenn., 1945-54. Professor, Free Will Baptist Bible College, Nashville, Tenn., 1953-58. Pastor: Shady Grove Church, Dunn, N. C., 1959-62; First Free Will Baptist, Wilson, N. C., since 1962. 245

Bowman, John W. (1894-). Presbyterian pastor and educator. Professor: a college in India 1927-36, its principal 1931-41; Western Seminary 1936-41; San Francisco Seminary 1944-61. In teaching ministry since 1961. Wrote 6 books. 100

Stanton, Mich., 1918-23. Professor of Biblical literature, Alma College 1915-43. Professor of O. T. languages and literature 1943-47, theology and modern languages 1947-54, dean of school of religion 1943-53 at Bob Jones U., Greenville, S. C. 271

Brooks, James H. (1830-97). Presbyterian pastor, Ohio and St. Louis, Mo. Ardent Fundamentalist. Editor, *The Truth*. Famed Bible teacher, C. I. Scofield was his student. Author, over 200 tracts and booklets. Pastor, Washington Avenue Presbyterian, St. Louis. Brookes Bible Institute in St. Louis named after him. One of main leaders in prophetic conferences of 1878 and 1886. 23, 24, 28, 36, 44, 45, 46, 47, 72, 76

Brooks, Keith L. (1887-1954). Baptist by convictions. Professor, Bible Institute of Los Angeles 1917-28, director of its correspondence school; Practical Bible Training Institute, Binghamton, N. Y. Editor, *The King's Business* for 7 years, *Prophecy Monthly*, and many booklets and charts on prophecy. 219

Brooks, Phillips (1835-93). Rector: Church of the Advent, Philadelphia, 1859-62; Holy Trinity, Philadelphia, 1862-69; Trinity, Boston, 1869-91. Bishop, the Church of England, Boston, 1891. Wrote "O Little Town of Bethlehem." An ardent, articulate Liberal. 68

Brooks, Samuel P. (1853-1931). Southern Baptist leader. President, Baylor U., Waco, Tex., 1902-31. Conservative, but defended his university when evolution and Liberalism crept in. A target of J. Frank Norris and outspoken Fundamentalists. 126

Brougher, J. Whitcomb (1870-1967). Pastor: First Baptist, Paterson, N. J., 1894-99; First Baptist, Chattanooga, Tenn., 1899-1904; White Temple, Portland, Ore., 1904-10; Temple Baptist, Los Angeles, Calif., 1910-26; First, Oakland, Calif., 1926-30; Tremont Temple, Boston, Mass., 1930-35; First, Glendale, Calif., 1935-45. President, NBC 1926. President, American Publication Society 1913-17. Fundamentalist who would not leave the NBC. 117, 150, 156, 163, 167, 174, 228

Brougher, J. Whitcomb, Jr. (1902-   ). West Coast Baptist pastor, First Baptist, Glendale, Calif., since 1927. Active in NBC (now American Baptist Convention). Like his father, sound in doctrine, but non-separating, though his denomination has gone into open apostasy. 117

Brougher, Russell M. (1896-   ). Fundamentalist Baptist pastor and evangelist inside the NBC and American Baptist Convention. Pastor: Salt Lake City 1922-24; Paterson, N. J., 1924-27; Baptist Temple, Brooklyn, N. Y., 1928-37. Member, Fundamentalist Fellowship for 15 years. Like his father and brother, sound in doctrine, but non-separating.

Brown, David (1803-97). Scottish Presbyterian minister. Professor, Free Church College, Edinburgh; its president in 1876. Sound in doctrine. Postmillennial. In later years, supported Liberalism and critical views of the Bible in his church. 36

Brown, Fred (1909-   ). Baptist evangelist. Has a long-established ministry in churches, which have seen many lasting results. Strong Bible preacher and teacher. Now lives in Chattanooga. 255, 271

Brown, John E. (1879-1957). Evangelist. Salvation Army convert. President,

Scarritt Collegiate Institute 1901-03. Editor, *Worldwide Revival.* Summer Bible conferences, Siloam Springs, Ark., 1913-40. Founder: John Brown College in 1919 (later University); schools at Sulphur Springs, Ark., Pacific Beach, Calif. Retired from the schools in 1948. 80, 162

Brown, Roy R. (1885-1964). Christian and Missionary Alliance pastor, Beaver Falls, Pa., 10 years. Started an Alliance work in Chicago. Dist. supt. under the Alliance. Started "The Radio Church of the Air" in 1922 at Omaha, Neb. Founder, Omaha Gospel Tabernacle in 1923. Widely known Bible conference speaker. 161

Brown, William Adams (1865-1943). Professor, Union Seminary, N. Y. C. in church history 1892-93, systematic theology 1893-95, theology 1895-1930, research 1930-36. A radical in doctrine. Author. Leader in ecumenical movement, in both the FCC and local church councils. 12, 99

Brown, W. Gordon (1904-). Canadian Baptist pastor and educator. Pastor: Orangeville Baptist, Orangeville, Ontario, 1922-30; Forward Baptist, Toronto, 1942-45; Runnymede Church, Toronto, 1946-71. Professor, Toronto Baptist Seminary 1927-48. Dean, Central Baptist Seminary, Toronto, since 1949. 112, 198

Brunner, Emil (1889-1966). Swiss theologian, teacher, and author. Professor, U. of Zurich, 20 years. Author, 25 books including *Dogmatics* and *The Mediator.* Lecturer, Princeton and Toyko. In early years, accepted Neo-Orthodoxy of Barth, but later broke from it. 98, 102

Brushwyler, Vincent (1903-). Pastor: Evangel Baptist, Newark, N. J., 1931-42; First Baptist, Muscatine, Iowa, 1942-44. A founder of CBFMS in 1943; its general director from 1944-64, under whose leadership it grew until it had over 400 missionaries. Pastor, First Baptist, Glen Ellyn, Ill., 1964-69. Now retired and living in Calif. 229

Bryan, William Jennings (1860-1925). Presbyterian elder. Three times candidate for President of the U. S. Secretary of State under Woodrow Wilson. "The great commoner." Defender of the Bible at Scopes trial in Dayton, Tenn., in 1925. Bryan College in Dayton, Tenn., built in his memory. 120, 132, 178, 261

Buckland, R. J. W. (1829-77). Baptist pastor, Ossining, N. Y., 1857-64; Calvary Baptist, N. Y. C., 1864-69. Lecturer on church history, Rochester Seminary 1869-77. 135

Bultmann, Rudolph (1884-). German theologian. Professor: Marburg 1912-16, 1921-51; Breslau 1916-20; Giessen 1920-21. Retired in 1951. Claimed the Bible contained many myths. A modern, radical liberal spokesman. 102

Burgess, W. J. (1897-). Baptist pastor in NABA churches. Pastor, Greenbrier Baptist, Greenbrier, Ark., for 16 years. Founder, Temple Baptist, Little Rock, Ark.; its pastor for 16 years. A leader in forming NABA in 1950; its secretary of missions 1951-69. 241

Burton, E. D. (1856-1925). Baptist liberal leader. Professor, in N. T.: Rochester Seminary 1882-83; U. of Chicago 1883-1923. Led hundreds of young men into religious doubts, substituting vague religious notions for the Word of God. 139, 153

Burtt, Edwin Arthur (1892-   ). Professor of philosophy: Columbia U. 1921-23; U. of Chicago 1924-31; Cornell U. 1932-60. Now retired and living in Utica, N. Y. Religious Liberal. 100

Bushnell, Horace (1802-76). Tutor, Yale U. 1829-31. Pastor, North Church, Hartford, Conn., 1833-59. Denied many essential doctrines of the Bible; taught the moral-influence theory of the death of Christ; taught that children should be brought up to become Christian through a process of learning; tried for heresy by Congregational pastors in 1850. 13

Bustard, William W. (1871-1935). Baptist pastor: Amesbury, Mass., 1898-1900; Dudley Street Baptist, Boston, Mass., 1900-09; Euclid Avenue Baptist, Cleveland, Ohio, 1909-25. Retired in 1925. 151

Buswell, J. Oliver, Jr. (1895-   ). Presbyterian pastor and educator. President, Wheaton College, Wheaton, Ill., 1926-39. President, National Bible Institute 1941-55 (later, Shelton College). Professor, Covenant Seminary, St. Louis, since 1955. 88, 181, 223, 237, 238, 239

Butler, Nicholas Murray (1862-1947). Leading figure in education. Professor, Columbia U. 1885-1901; its president and Barnard College's president from 1901-45. Made Barnard a center of progressive education. 94

C

Cadman, S. Parkes (1864-1936). Pastor: Metropolitan Temple, N. Y. C., 1895-1901; Central Congregational, Brooklyn, N. Y., 1901-36. Active in home missions. Many of his sermons published. Evangelical, but had no part in Fundamentalist work. Author, 13 books. 142

Calvin, John (1509-64). Great theologian. Reformer of Geneva 1536-64. Author, *The Institutes of the Christian Religion*. Unequaled influence on Reformed and Presbyterian churches. 39, 41, 51, 204

Cambron, Mark (1911-   ). Baptist pastor and teacher. Asst., W. B. Riley for 3 years. Pastor: Woodville, Wisc.; Nokomis, Minn.; Alton Park, Chattanooga, Tenn. Dean, Tennessee Temple Schools 1948-58. Founder, Seaside Mission for Jews, Miami, 1961. Director, Southwide Hebrew Mission, Miami, since 1969. Vice-president, Florida Bible College since 1966. 271

Cameron, Robert (?-1922). Canadian Baptist pastor in Ontario. Leader, Niagara Bible Conference. Took a posttribulational position. Editor, *Watchword* and *Truth*. Taught at Moody Bible Institute briefly in 1890s. 23, 72, 73

Canavan, Martin (1923-   ). Baptist pastor: First Missionary Baptist, Corcoran, Calif., 6 years; First Baptist, Dominguez, Calif., 18 years. Active in ABA; its president for 2 years. Registrar, California Missionary Bible Institute. Author, 3 books. 216

Candler, Warren A. (1857-1941). Methodist pastor 1875-86. A founder of Emory U., Atlanta, Ga., whose Candler School of Theology is named after him; its president, 1888-98. Editor, *The Christian Advocate*. Bishop, Methodist Episcopal Church, South 1898. Strong preacher. Conservative in theology. Opposed to union of northern and southern branches of Methodist Church. 174, 273

Carlson, George J. (1912-57). Baptist pastor; Tabernacle Baptist, Chicago,

Edgemont Church, Durham, N. C., 1949-68; Black Jack Church, Greenville, N. C., 1968-71; Daniels Chapel, Wilson, N. C., since 1971. Founder, Daniels Chapel Bible Institute, Wilson, N. C., 1972. 245

Christian, O. D. (1922-). Pastor: Post Oak Baptist, Fairfield, Tex., 1950-52; South Side Baptist, Dallas, Tex., 1952-64; First Baptist, Trinity Heights, Dallas, Tex., 1964-70; First Baptist, Rose Hill, Garland, Tex., since 1970. Recording secretary, MBA since 1965. 241

Churchill, Clinton H. (1888-). Businessman in Buffalo, N. Y. Converted under Billy Sunday 1917. Pastor, North Delaware Methodist, Buffalo, N. Y., 1917-21. Evangelist, 1921-22. Founder: Churchill Tabernacle on Main Street, Buffalo, N. Y., 1925; radio station WKBW (Well-Known Bible Witness) in Buffalo 1926. Both, centers of evangelism for 25 years. Church now closed and buildings used for radio and TV (WKBW). 189, 256

Cierpke, Alfred A. (1901-). Co-pastor: Tragheim Baptist, Königsberg, Prussia, Germany, 1931-34; Ortelsburg Baptist, Ortelsburg, East Prussia, 1935-38. Interim pastor, Erie Baptist, Cleveland, Ohio, 1950. Professor: Bob Jones U. 1943-47; Tennessee Temple Schools 1947-48 and dean of its seminary 1948-61. Retired in 1961. 271

Clark, David (1943-). Southern Methodist pastor: Prosperity, S. C., 1965-69; Bowman Southern Methodist, Bowman, S. C., 1969-70; Faith Independent Methodist, Union Springs, Ala., since 1970. A trustee and director of the Francis Asbury Society of Ministers. 247

Clarke, Adam (1762-1832). English Methodist theologian and writer. Devout scholar. Author, an 8-volume commentary on the Bible. 74

Clarke, William Newton (1840-1912). Baptist theologian and educator. Pastor: Keene, N. H., 1863-69; Newton Center, Mass., 1869-80; Montreal, 1880-83. Professor, Toronto Baptist College 1883-87 (now McMaster U.). Pastor, Hamilton, N. Y., 1887-90. Professor, Colgate U. 1890-1912. Author, 5 books. 12, 15-19, 94, 137

Clearwaters, Richard V. (1900-). Baptist pastor: Manhattan, Ill., 1926-29; Lawton, Mich., one year; Bethel Baptist, Kalamazoo, Mich., 1935-39; Fourth Baptist, Minneapolis, Minn., since 1940. Professor, Northwestern Schools and dean of the seminary for 5 years. Founder and president of Pillsbury Baptist Bible College. Founder and still president of Central Baptist Seminary, Minneapolis. Able preacher. Baptist Fundamentalist and knowledgeable pastor. 81, 120, 121, 195, 199, 200, 227, 231

Clement of Rome (c. 30-100). Church Father. One of the earliest church leaders we know about after N. T. times. Bishop of Rome (claimed to be fourth from Peter). His *Letter to the Corinthians,* one of the earliest Christian writings. 36

Cloer, William Ray (1913-). Nazarene pastor: Riverton, Wyo., 1939-53; Spartanburg, S. C., 1943-57. Evangelist 1947-53. Pastor, Taylor Evangelical Methodist, Columbia, S. C., since 1953. 248

Coe, George A. (1862-1951). Professor: U. of Southern California; Union Seminary, N. Y. C., 1909-22; Teachers' College, N. Y. C.; Northwestern U. Teacher of religious education. Led people away from the methods of the Bible. 99

Coffey, Rufus (1926-). Freewill Baptist pastor, S. C., and Tenn., for 13 years. Foreign missions work with Freewill Baptists for 5 years. Executive director of the National Association of Free Will Baptists, Nashville, Tenn., for 7 years. 244

Cole, Stewart G. (1892-). Professor: U. of Chicago 1918-19; U. of South Dakota 1922-23; Carleton College 1923-24; Crozer Seminary 1924-36. President, Kalamazoo College 1936-38. Visiting professor, U. of Chicago 1938-39. Founder and director, Bureau for Intercultural Education, N. Y., 1939-44. Director, Pacific Coast Council on Education, 1944-49. Author, 8 books. 2, 206

Coleman, Gary (1939-). Baptist pastor: Friendship Baptist, Horne County, Tex., 5 months; Bruton Road Baptist, Dallas, Tex., 5 years; Lavon Drive Baptist, Garland, Tex., since 1965. 243

Colgate, William (1783-1857). American manufacturer of soap. Contributed to religious and educational institutions, including Madison U., Hamilton, N. Y. (later, Hamilton Institute and Colgate Seminary). A founder, American Bible Society. At the end of his life, forsook all forms of organized religion. 68

Comfort, Glenn S. (1916-). Southern Methodist pastor, Richmond, Va., 1946-50; Memphis, Tenn., 1950-62; Baton Rouge, La., 1962-66. Vice-president, Mid-South Annual Conference (Southern Methodist). President, Southern Methodist Church with offices in Orangeburg, S. C., since 1966. 247

Comfort, Ronald G. (1938-). Baptist pastor for one year. In full-time evangelism for the last 11 years. Now lives in Clarksburg, W. Va. 255

Commager, Henry Steele (1902-). Outstanding American historian. Professor: New York U. 1926-29; Columbia U. 1929-56. Author, 33 books and now in progress a 50-volume set, *The Rise of the American Nation.* 4

Conrad, Arcturus Z. (1855-1937). Presbyterian minister. Pastor: Ainslie Street Church, Brooklyn, N. Y., 1885-90; Old South Congregational, Worcester, Mass., 1890-1902; Park Street, Boston, Mass., 1905-37. Strong evangelical pastor, writer, and leader, especially in his ministry in Boston. 90

Constantine (280-337). Roman emperor. Issued the Edict of Milan giving religious freedom 313; built first St. Peter's on the present site; set aside December 25 as the birthday of Christ (old Feast of Saturnalia); not baptized until old, as he believed all sins could be washed away at one time. 38, 39, 61, 74

Conwell, Russell H. (1843-1925). Baptist pastor and educator. Pastor, Grace Baptist Temple, Philadelphia, 1891-1925 (now Temple Baptist). Founder, Temple U. Famous for his lecture "Acres of Diamonds." Protested mildly when Northern Baptists headed into apostasy. 68, 107, 150, 156, 174, 273

Conybeare, William John (1815-57). English Bible scholar. Leader in the Church of England. Vicar for 6 years. Head, a school in Liverpool 1842-48. Famous for his excellent studies in the life and epistles of Paul. 41

Cook, Robert A. (1912-). Baptist evangelist, pastor, and educator. A leader in Youth for Christ 1948-57. Pastor, Midwest Bible, Chicago, 1958-63. President, King's College, Briarcliff, N. Y., since 1963. President, NAE. A leader among New Evangelicals. 208, 209, 256, 274, 281

Cooper, Jacob T. (1831-?). Presbyterian. Professor: Rutgers U.; U. of Michigan; Center College, Ky. Editor, *Bibliotheca Sacra.* Chaplain in the Civil War. 35

Corbett, Lynn (1921-). Southern Methodist pastor: Springfield, S. C., 1946-47; Hilda, S. C., 1946-47; Bishopville, S. C., 1947; Ridgeville, S. C., 1947-51; Bowman, S. C., 1951-56; Maple Street, Columbia, S. C., 1956-61. Vice-president. Southern Methodist Conference since 1966. 247

Cotton, John (1585-1652). Pastor, St. Botolph's, Boston, England. Eminent Puritan teacher, First Church, Boston, Mass., 1633-52. Keen in theology and church polity. A founder, "The New England Way" (the practices of the Puritan or Congregational churches). 25

Cottrell, Ralph (1921-). Baptist pastor. Part-time pastorates 1942-49. Pastor: Fifth Avenue Baptist, Pine Bluff, Ark., 1950-52; Immanuel Baptist, Nashville, Tenn., 1953-54; Ark. and La. 1954-68. Promotional director, Baptist Publications of the ABA since 1969. 241

Cox, Harvey (1929-). Professor, Oberlin College 1955-58. Served on the American Baptist Home Mission Society 1958-62; Gossner Mission, Berlin, 1962-63. Professor: Newton Theological Institution 1963-65; Harvard since 1965. Author and lecturer. 102

Cravens, Douglas (1920-). Baptist pastor and educator. Pastor: First Baptist, Roby, Tex., 1945-47; Reliance Baptist, Bryan, Tex., 1947-50; Lakewood Baptist, Harrison, Tenn., 1951-71. Professor, Tennessee Temple Schools since 1950; dean of the seminary; chaplain since 1972. 271

Crawford, Percy B. (1902-60). Youth leader and educator. Had large youth rallies in 1930s; started "The Young People's Church of the Air" in 1931. Founder, King's College in 1938. Evangelistic, but opposed to all those who would not cooperate with the New Evangelicals or Graham meetings. 195, 254, 256

Criswell, Wallie Amos (W. A.) (1909-). Powerful and eloquent Southern Baptist preacher. Pastor: First Baptist, Chickasha, Okla., 1937-41; First Baptist, Muskogee, Okla., 1941-44; First Baptist, Dallas, Tex., since 1944. President, SBC 1968-70. His strong preaching and his soulwinning emphasis have encouraged conservatives inside the denomination, attracted New Evangelicals, and influenced Fundamentalists to compromise. 158, 254, 274, 280, 281

Crittenden, George (1924-). Baptist pastor and figure in Tex. Fundamentalism. Pastor, Temple Baptist, Fort Worth, Tex., for the past 20 years. A close associate and admirer of J. Frank Norris. 217

Cross, George (1863-1929). Professor: McMaster U., Hamilton, Ontario, 1901-10; Rochester Seminary 1910-29. Lecturer: Yale; U. of Chicago. Spread Liberalism and radicalism; helped ruin hundreds of young men waiting to prepare for the ministry. 108, 139

Cross, I. K. (1917-). Baptist pastor and ABA leader. Pastor: Monticello, Ark.; Texarkana, Tex.; Somerset, Ky. Founder and first president, Eastern Bible Institute, Somerset, Ky., 1950-57. Now director of promotion and public relations for ABA, Texarkana, Tex. Pungent preacher and writer. 214, 215, 216

Crozer, John Price (1793-1866). Wealthy dealer in cotton goods. Gave generously to churches and colleges. Crozer Seminary started in 1866 because of his gifts, now closed and a part of Colgate-Rochester, N. Y. 68

Crumpton, James W. (1918-   ). Baptist pastor, Donelson, La.; Westside Baptist, Natchez, Miss., for the past 30 years. Founder and president, Maranatha Baptist Mission which for the past 11 years has been sending missionaries to South America. A dependable, gracious, hardworking Fundamentalist. 271

Culbertson, William (1905-71). Bishop of the Reformed Episcopal Church. President, Moody Bible Institute 1948. Began as a Fundamentalist, but became tolerant toward new-evangelical movements and allowed the Institute to become soft with biases against Fundamentalists and their works. 281

Cummings, Seldon W. (1864-1931). Pastor: Immanuel Baptist, Chester, Pa., 1898-1904; First Baptist, Amherst, Nova Scotia, Canada, 1904-08; First Baptist, Lowell, Mass., 1908-21; Ruggles Street Baptist, Boston, Mass., 1921-22, Professor, U. of Redlands, Calif., 1922-31. 151

Cummons, Bruce (1924-   ). Founder and pastor, Massillon Baptist Temple, Massillon, Ohio, started in 1950 in a rented store building with 22 people, now has 3,000 members and church property worth a million dollars. Publisher, *The Baptist Reporter*. A leader in the WBF. 226

Cushing, Richard (1895-1971). Roman Catholic priest, ordained in 1921. Pastor, Archdiocese of Boston 1921-39. Named Bishop of Boston in 1939, its archbishop in 1944; elevated to cardinal in 1954. Close friend of Joseph P. Kennedy family. A flamboyant Irish wit, way, and brogue. 210

Cyzicus, Gelasius of (?-?). Church historian in the second half of the fifth century, writing mostly in the 470s. Major work was on the Council of Nicea which was more of a compilation than a history. His writings, not considered too reliable. His work called "Syntagma." 37

D

Dahlberg, Edwin T. (1892-   ). Liberal Baptist pastor: First Baptist, Potsdam, N. Y., 1918-21; Maple Street, Buffalo, N. Y., 1921-31; First Baptist, St. Paul, Minn., 1931-39; First Baptist, Syracuse, N. Y., 1931-50; Delmar Baptist, St. Louis, since 1950. President, NBC 1946-48. On the central committee of the WCC 1948-54. 208, 239

Dailey, Parker (1928-   ). Pastor, Blue Ridge Baptist Temple, Kansas City, Mo., for many years. President, BBF 1970-72. 219

Darby, John N. (1800-82). Early teacher and Bible scholar of the Plymouth Brethren movement. Stressed prophecy and the imminent coming of the Lord; published many books on Bible studies. 57, 73, 235

Darrow, Clarence (1857-1938). Criminal lawyer and humanitarian. Famous cases: E. V. Debs, Loeb-Leopold, the Scopes trial in Dayton, Tenn., which debated the authority and reliability of the Bible (W. J. Bryan defended the Bible). 114, 115

Darwin, Charles (1809-82). English naturalist. Promoted the theory of evolution to explain the origin of all forms of organic life; wrote *The Origin of Species;* turned himself and others from a belief in the Bible to agnosticism. 11, 115, 117

Dautel, Hall (1910-). Baptist pastor: First Baptist, Henry, Ill., 1933-34; City Temple, Baltimore, Md., 1934-36; Faith Independent, Fawn Grove, Pa., 1937-40; First Baptist, Randolph, N. Y., 1940-42; Bethel Baptist, Erie, Pa., 1942-52; Temple Baptist, Portsmouth, Ohio, 1952-62; First Baptist, Harvey, Ill., 1962-72; North Chester Baptist, Chester, Pa., since 1972. Member, Baptist Mid-Missions board since 1948. Trustee, Baptist Bible College of Pa. since 1949. 222

Dean, John Marvin (1875-1935). Baptist pastor and educator. Pastor, Hinson Memorial, Portland, Ore., 1927-29. President, Western Baptist Seminary. Organizer, Northern Baptist Seminary 1913; its president 1913-18. 138, 151, 174

Dearmore, Ben F. (1898-1969). Baptist pastor for 45 years in Tex. Organized several churches. Professor: Bible Baptist Seminary, Fort Worth; its dean 1947-49 under J. Frank Norris; Independent Baptist College, Dallas, Tex. Pastor, Fort Worth. 134, 246

DeBlois, Austin K. (1866-1945). Baptist pastor and educator. Pastor: First Baptist, Elgin, Ill., 1899-1903; First Baptist, Chicago, 1903-11; First, Boston, Mass., 1911-26; President, Eastern Baptist Seminary, Philadelphia, 1926-36. Evangelical, but remained aloof from Fundamentalists who fought to keep Northern Baptists from apostasy. Did not protect his seminary from its present apostasy. 174

DeHaan, Martin R. (1891-1965). Widely known conference speaker. Founder, Radio Bible Class, Grand Rapids, Mich. Keen Bible expositor and Fundamentalist voice. 224, 256, 260

DeHaan, Richard (1923-). On the staff of Radio Bible Class for 30 years. Succeeded his father in 1965 as teacher of the class; added a TV program Day of Discovery in 1968 and is its speaker. 256

Delitzsch, Franz Julius (1813-90). O. T. scholar. Lutheran professor, Germany. Accepted Higher Criticism. Hebrew scholar whose O. T. writings are among the finest for understanding the original Hebrew text. 46, 62, 74

Delnay, Robert G. (1926-). Baptist educator. Professor: Central Baptist Seminary of Minneapolis; Baptist Bible College, Denver, Colo.; Piedmont Bible College, Winston-Salem, N. C., since 1968. Missionary, West Indies. Has made the most thorough study yet of BBU. 145, 150, 162, 167

Denman, Harry (1893-). Evangelical Methodist. Secretary, Sunday School Association, Birmingham, Ala., 1915-19. Church manager, First Methodist, Birmingham, Ala., 1919-38. General secretary, board of evangelism the Methodist Church 1938-65 (now United Methodist). Now retired. One of many evangelicals in apostate denominations. 275

De Wette, Wilheim (1740-1849). Renowned teacher and writer. Professor: Heidelberg; Berlin; Basel. Tried to harmonize revelation and reason. Disciple of Schleiermacher. 139

Dickey, Solomon C. (1858-1920). Presbyterian pastor, Neb. and Ind. 1882-94. Secretary of home missions for Ind. 1894-96. Founder, Winona Lake Bible Conference 1895; its general secretary for many years. 261

Diffenbach, Albert C. (1876-1963). Unitarian leader, writer, and editor, Pastor, Unitarian Church, Newton, Mass., 1927-40. Editor, *The Christian Register*. Named religious editor, *The Boston Transcript* in 1933. 180

Dillenberger, John (1918-). U. S. Army chaplain 1943-46. Professor: Union Seminary, N. Y., 1947-48; Princeton U. 1948-49; Columbia U. 1949-54; Harvard Divinity School 1954-58; Drew U. 1958-62; San Francisco Theological Seminary 1962-64; Graduate Theological Union, Berkeley, Calif., since 1964, and its president 1969-72. Author, 6 books. 91, 92

Dixon, Amri C. (1854-1925). Baptist pastor, Baltimore; Boston; Chicago; Metropolitan Tabernacle, London. Fundamentalist for many years, but deserted because of the stigmas and battles of separatism. 72, 126, 151, 163, 166

Dods, Marcus (1834-1909). Presbyterian minister and teacher. Pastor, Glasgow, Scotland. Teacher, New College, Edinburgh. Conservative in theology, but accepted the Higher Criticism. Helped prepare for the capitulation of Scottish Presbyterianism to Liberalism. 21

Donaldson, Fred S. (1897-). Baptist pastor: First Baptist, Lake Zurich, Ill., 1921; Messiah Baptist, Chicago, 1922-30; First Baptist, Plainfield, Ill., 1930-33. In missionary service 1933-41. Director of missions, BBF 1950-68. Retired in 1968; now living in San Diego, Calif. 198

Dowell, William E. (1914-). Baptist pastor, Merkel, Tex.; Corcoran, Calif.; La Habra and Lynwood, Calif.; High Street, Springfield, Mo., for 22 years; Jacksonville Baptist Temple, Jacksonville, Fla., for 5 years. Executive vice-president, Baptist Bible College, Springfield, Mo., for the past 6 years. President, BBF for 2 terms. 133, 195, 198, 217, 218, 272

Dowling, John (1807-78). Baptist pastor. Born in England; came to U. S. Pastor: Catskill, N. Y.; Newport, R. I.; Berean Baptist, N. Y. C., 1844-52; Philadelphia, 1852-56; Berean Baptist, N. Y. C., 1856-68; Newark; South Baptist, N. Y. C. 135

Driggers, Ronald D. (1924-). Methodist pastor: Kane, Ill., 1946-47; Worden, Ill., 1947-50; Dupont, Ind., 1950-51; Evangelical Methodist, Marshall, Tex., 1951-52; First Evangelical Methodist, Florence, Ala., 1952-54; First Evangelical Methodist, Macon, Ga., 1954-58; East Ridge Evangelical Methodist, Chattanooga, Tenn., 1958-60. Secretary, general conference, Evangelical Methodist Church 1954-60; its secretary, treasurer since 1960; its manager of publications since 1964. 248

Drummond, Henry (1851-97). Scottish lecturer of the Free Presbyterian Church. Believed in evolution; wrote *Natural Law in the Spiritual World;* had an impressive personality; was a friend of D. L. Moody for some years; moved thousands to religious enthusiasm; was an enemy of Fundamentalism. 80

Duffield, John T. (1823-1901). Early Fundamentalist. Professor of mathematics and Greek, Princeton U. 1847-98. Licensed to preach in 1866. Head, board of education, town of Princeton. Author, 6 books. 29, 40-41, 45, 75

Duggar, John W. (1912-). Pastor under BMA for 25 years; Sulphur Springs, Tex., 1941-42; Bogalusa, La., 1942-44; Port Arthur, Tex., 1944-49; Laurel, Miss., 1949-55; Central, Lubbock, Tex., 1955-60; First Baptist, Carthage, Tex., 1960-66. Secretary, Interstate Missions, 1966-70. Associate secretary of missions since 1970. Professor, Southeastern Baptist College; North American Baptist Theological Seminary. 241

E

Eddy, Sherwood (1871-1963). YMCA executive. National secretary, YMCA in India 1896-1911. Secretary, YMCA in America 1911. Main work among students. Early American Liberal in YMCA work. Active in social reform. 101

Edman, V. Raymond (1900-67). Missionary and pastor in the Christian Missionary Alliance. Professor, Nyack College, N. Y., 1921-22. Director, El Instituto Biblico del Ecuador, Ecuador, 1923-28. Pastor, Gospel Tabernacle, Worcester, Mass., 1929-35. Professor, Wheaton College, Wheaton, Ill., 1936-65; its president 1940-65. Editor, *The Alliance Weekly,* succeeding A. W. Tozer. Author, 19 books. Devotional and evangelical. Allowed his college to slip into New Evangelicalism and compromise. 233

Edwards, James D. (1914-). Professor, Bob Jones U. since 1936; its dean of men 1936-43; its dean of the school of commerce 1947-48; its dean of students 1947-53; its dean of administration since 1953. 271

Edwards, Jonathan (1703-58). Theologian, pastor, and writer. An outstanding figure in the Great Awakening. Pastor: Northampton, 1929-50; Stockbridge, 1950. Elected president of Princeton College in 1757, but died after 5 months in office. One of America's keenest theologians. 39

Eichhorn, Johann G. (1752-1827). German Higher Critic. Pioneer of Liberalism, particularly in the study of O. T. Professor, U. of Jena, Germany. 139, 152

Elgena, Carl E. (1917-). Baptist pastor: Cadosia, N. Y., 1942-44; Forestville, N. Y., 1944-47; Spruce Street, Philadelphia, 1947-52; First, Buffalo, N. Y., 1952-54; Grandview Park, Des Moines, Iowa, 1954-64. Vice-president, Baptist Bible College of Pa. 1964-66. Pastor: First Baptist, N. Y. C., 1966-69; Bethel Baptist, Cherry Hill, N. J., since 1969. 222

Ellison, Roger (1942-). Baptist pastor, Pine Hill Baptist Chapel, Chattanooga, Tenn., 1964-66. Youth director, Emmanuel Baptist, Liberty, S. C., 1966-68. Professor, Tennessee Temple Schools since 1968. Director of Christian education, Highland Park Baptist Church, Chattanooga, Tenn., since 1970. 259

Ely, Richard T. (1854-1943). Anglican social reformer. Professor of economics and politics: Johns Hopkins U. 1881-92; U. of Wisconsin 1892-25. Author, 15 books, many on economics. Guest lecturer, Northwestern U. 1925-33. 68

Engstrom Theodore (Ted) (1916-). Asst. to the president, Taylor U. 1939-40. Book editor, Zondervan Publishers 1941-51. Youth For Christ International 1951-63. Executive vice-president, World Vision since 1963. Author, 24 books. 208, 209

Entzminger, Louis (1878-1956). Baptist educator and Sunday School organizer. Worked with the Baptist state conventions of Fla. and Ky.; joined J. Frank Norris in Sunday School work in Fort Worth 1913; worked with Norris (except one year 1926-27) until he died; built large Sunday Schools in Fort Worth and at Temple Baptist, Detroit; built on principles of visitation, large classes, and the KJV of the Bible. 125, 127, 128, 133, 134, 166, 272

Epp, Theodore (1907-). Mennonite pastor, Goltry, Okla., and Kingman, Kan., 1922-39. Started "Back to the Bible" broadcast on May 1, 1939, which is now heard on 600 stations with 10 overseas offices; published 65 books and booklets; majored on sound doctrine, but in the last few years has been tolerant toward New Evangelicals. 162

Erdman, Albert (1838-1918). Strong premillennial Presbyterian pastor: Clinton, N. J., 1864-69; South Presbyterian, Norristown, N. J., 1869-1907; then its pastor emeritus 1907-18. 57

Erdman, William Jacob (W. J.) (1834-1923). Presbyterian pastor, St. Catharines, Ontario, 1859-60; St. Paul, Minn., 1860-61; Fayette, N. Y., 1861-67. Army chaplain 1864-65. Pastor: Ann Arbor, Mich., 1867-70; Fort Wayne, Ind., 1870-74; Jamestown, N. Y., 1874-75; Boston, Mass., 1886-88. Evangelist and Bible teacher 1888-1920. 28, 45, 50, 72

Evans, William (1870-1950). Presbyterian pastor: Goshen, Ind., 1895-97; Wheaton, Ill., 1897-1900. Director, Bible Course, Moody Bible Institute 1900-14. Dean and teacher, Bible Institute of Los Angeles 1915-18. Bible teacher 1918-50. Author, 12 books and 10 volumes on "Through the Bible." 260

Ewald, Heinrich (1803-75). German scholar, O. T. authority. Professor, U. of Göttingen. Rejected the conservative approach to the Bible; arrogantly promoted Liberalism; stressed liberal concept of progressive revelation. 139

Excell, E. O. (1851-1921). Methodist songwriter from Ohio. Strong prohibitionist. Song leader with evangelists such as Gipsy Smith, Sam Jones. Published several songbooks after 1881; wrote "Count Your Blessings," "Let Him In," "Since I Have Been Redeemed." 79, 261

F

Fairbairn, Andrew M. (1838-1912). Congregational pastor in England. Lecturer on religious subjects. Principal of a Congregational college. A Liberal in doctrine. A gifted teacher. 39

Fakkema, Mark, Sr. (1890-1971). Principal, Chicago Christian High School 1918. National Union of Christian Schools 1926-47. First education director, National Association of Christian Schools 1947-60. General manager, Christian Schools Service, Inc., 1960-70. 259

Falwell, Jerry (1933-). Founder and pastor, Thomas Road Baptist, Lynchburg, Va., which he started in 1960; its Sunday School attendance on

June 23, 1972, was 19,000; it telecasts over 400 stations; it has held several conferences for pastors; it has a large bus ministry; it opened Lynchburg Baptist College in 1972. 220, 278

Faulkner, J. R. (1914-). Baptist pastor, Rossville, Ga., 1945-49. Associate pastor, Highland Park Baptist, Chattanooga, Tenn., since 1949. Professor, Tennessee Temple Schools since 1946. 242, 271

Faunce, W. H. P. (1859-1930). Baptist Liberal and educator. Professor, Brown U. 1881-82. Pastor: Springfield, Mass., 1884-89; Fifth Avenue, N. Y. C., 1889-99. President, Brown U. 1899-1929. Lecturer: Yale; U. of Chicago. 97, 108, 138

Faussett, A. R. (1821-1910). Church of England minister in Ireland. Solid evangelical scholar. Author, 3 volumes of the 6-volume commentary of Jamieson, Faussett, and Brown on the entire Bible. 37, 57

Feinberg, Charles L. (1909-). Pastor, Cumberland Presbyterian, Dallas, Tex., 1936-41. Professor: Dallas Theological Seminary 1934-48; Talbot Theological Seminary since 1948 and now its dean. Excellent O. T. scholar and writer. 224, 260, 280

Ferm, Robert O. (1911-). Professor: U. of Buffalo; John Brown U.; Northwestern Schools. Dean of students, Houghton College 1952-59. Has worked closely with Billy Graham Association; tried to justify the Graham methods in Cooperative Evangelism. 210, 252

Fetler-Maloof, William A. (1883-1957). Born in Latvia; graduated from Spurgeons College; served in Christian work in St. Petersburg and Moscow; ordered out of Russia by the Czar; came to the U. S. where he started a Russian Bible Institute in Philadelphia; served with others as a missionary in the Ukraine and Poland; sent many copies of Russian Bibles from the U. S. after World War II; served most of his life without a mission board. 167, 168

Fiedler, C. G. (1890-1927). Baptist missionary under the ABFMS in Assam, India, 1921-27. 110, 227

Field, Thomas G. (1843-1926). Baptist pastor: Alton, Ill.; Winona, Minn.; Fourth Baptist, Minneapolis, 1881-87; W. Va., 1913. Secretary, ABFMS and American Baptist Home Mission Society in Ohio. 75

Fitzwater, Perry B. (1871-1957). Presbyterian pastor, teacher, and Bible student. Professor, Moody Bible Institute 1913-54; its dean; its director of the pastors' course. Author, The Preaching and Teaching of the New Testament. Strong Fundamentalist teacher with rugged, inflexible convictions. 260

Fleece, G. Allen (1909-). Presbyterian pastor, Bible teacher, and educator. Professor: Moody Bible Institute; Columbia Bible College; its president 1953-68. Pastor, Covington, Ga., and Chattanooga, Tenn. Now in Bible conference ministry, especially in Keswick conferences. 268, 275

Fleming, Gerald (1927-). Baptist pastor, Central Baptist, Euless, Tex., 1949-50. Founder and present pastor, Dayton Baptist Temple 1951. President, WBF 1961-62. 134, 198, 226

Fletcher, Joseph (1905-). Church of England minister. Dean, Graduate School of Applied Religion, Cincinnati, 1936-44. Professor, Episcopal

Theological Seminary, Cambridge, Mass., 1944-70. Visiting professor, U. of Va. since 1970. Known for his radical views in promoting "situation ethics," which justifies present changes in morals. 102, 158

Flower, Roswell (1888-1970). Leader, Assemblies of God. Editor, *The Christian Evangel.* First general secretary, Assemblies of God 1914-59. Organizer, NAE. Helped start World Pentecostal Fellowship 1949. 235

Ford, Leighton (1931-). Ordained Presbyterian minister. Brother-in-law of Billy Graham. Associate on the Graham team since 1955. 275

Forman, L. D. (1913-). ABA pastor: Taylor, Ark.; Cave City, Ark.; Sheridan, Ark.; Little Rock, Ark. President, Missionary Baptist Seminary 1946-66. Author and editor. 216

Fosdick, Harry Emerson (1878-1969). Pastor, Montclair Baptist, Montclair, N. J., 1904-15. Professor, Union Theological Seminary, N. Y. C., 1908-46. Pastor, Park Avenue Baptist, N. Y. C., 1924-30; Riverside Church, N. Y. C., 1930-48. Popular liberal preacher. Radio speaker, "National Vespers." Author, many books. 15, 85, 93, 94, 95, 96, 97, 98, 99, 100, 101, 110, 117, 118, 136, 137, 138, 149, 157, 176, 178, 180, 182

Foster, Frank H. (1851-1935). Strong conservative thinker. Professor, Naval Academy, Annapolis, Md., 1877; Congregational pastor, North Reading, Mass., 1877-79. Professor: Middlebury College, Vt. 1882-1884; Oberlin College, Ohio, 1884-92; Pacific Seminary, Berkeley, Calif., 1892-1902; Olivet College 1904-15; Oberlin 1925-35. Best books, *A Genetic History of New England Theology* and *Life of Edwards Amasa Park.* 2

Francke, August Hermann (1663-1727). German Pietist. Professor, U. of Halle. Excellent Hebrew scholar. Stressed the Christian life of fellowship and prayer; built the Halle Foundation, which consists of a school, printing press, orphanage, and missions work, on simple trust that the Lord would provide. 39

Frank, Walter (1914-). Pastor for 18 years. Youth for Christ International; its general director of the Greater Europe Mission since 1960. 225

Franklin, James H. (1872-1961). Secretary, American Baptist Foreign Mission Board 1912-34. Had pastorates in Colo. President, NBC 1933. President, Crozer Seminary, Chester, Pa., 1934-43. 180

Freeny, Tom (1918-). Baptist pastor for 15 years in Tenn., Ga., Ala. Professor, Tennessee Temple Schools. Head, Baptist International Missions for 12 years which presently has 400 missionaries and an annual budget of 2 million dollars. 271

Fremont, Walter G. (1924-). Leader, Christian-day-school movement. Professor, Bob Jones U.; its dean of education since 1953. Built an effective teacher-training program. Director, The Wilds camp in N. C.; Gospel Fellowship Association. 259, 271

Frost, Adoniram Judson (A. J.) (1837-?). Baptist pastor: Syracuse, N. Y.; Bay City, Mich., University Place, Chicago; San Jose, Calif., for 3 years; Sacramento 1879. Evangelist and Bible teacher. 45, 47, 64, 65, 75

Frothingham, O. B. (1822-95). New England writer and scholar in religious research. An authority on transcendentalism and the beliefs of Liberals. A careful student of the life of W. E. Channing. Staff, the *New York Tribune* for some years. 71

Fry, Franklin C. (1900-68). Lutheran pastor: Yonkers, N. Y., 1925-29; Akron, Ohio, 1929-44. Secretary of evangelism, United Lutheran Church 1930-38. President, Lutheran Church in America since 1962. Has promoted unscriptural ecumenism and aided Lutheranism into further apostasy. 196, 239

Fuller, Charles E. (1887-1968). Baptist pastor. Founder, Old-Fashioned Revival Hour in 1925 which grew to over 500 stations and was broadcast from Long Beach Auditorium, Calif. Founder, Fuller Theological Seminary, Pasadena, Calif., 1947, which, along with Fuller himself, joined the new-evangelical movement. 121, 162, 195, 203, 255

Fuller, Daniel P. (1925-). Son of Charles E. Fuller, Professor, Fuller Seminary since 1953; its dean of the faculty 1963-72. Director, The Joyful Sound, a new name for the Old-Fashioned Revival Hour. 255

Fuller, David Otis (1903-). Pastor: Chelsea Baptist, Atlantic City, N. J., 1924-34; Wealthy Street Baptist, Grand Rapids, Mich., since 1934. Strong Fundamentalist defender. Has served within the GARB; has served on the trustee board, Wheaton College. 145

Fulton, Howard C. (1891-1951). Baptist pastor: Franksville, Norwalk, Wisc.; Grand Rapids, Mich.; Belden Avenue Baptist, Chicago, 1931-51. Host pastor at the organization of the GARB in 1932. 171, 222

Furniss, Norman (1922-64). Professor in American history, Colorado State U. 1950-64; its chairman of the department of history for 3 years. Author, factual history of the controversy between Fundamentalists and Modernists in the NBC in the 1920s. 2, 115, 145

G

Gaebelein, Arne C. (1861-1945). Born in Germany; came to the U. S. in 1879. Methodist pastor, Baltimore and Hoboken, N. J., 1894-97. Director, a Jewish mission, N. Y. C., 1894-99. Editor, *Our Hope* 1894-1945. Keen student of prophecy. Sound Bible teacher and writer. Author, 41 books. 72, 73, 126, 161, 165, 260

Galloway, Paul V. (1904-). Methodist pastor, Ark., 1925-50; Okla., 1950-60. Made a bishop of the Methodist Church in 1960; has served on many councils to promote church unity. 275

Gamble, J. B. (1921-). Methodist pastor with Southern Methodist churches. Pastor, Hilda, S. C., and Williston, S. C., 1964-67. President, Southern Methodist College, Orangeburg, S. C., since 1967. 247

Gambrell, James Bruton (J. B.) (1841-1921). Baptist pastor, Miss. President, Mercer U. for 3 years. Professor, Southwestern Baptist Theological Seminary. An editor, *The Baptist Record*. Sound in doctrine, but silent when apostasy rushed into Baptist ranks in the South. 125

Gannett, Alden A. (1921-). Strong Bible teacher, preacher, and educator. President, London Bible College, London, Ontario, Canada, 1954-57. Professor, Dallas Seminary 1957-60. President, Southeastern Bible College, Birmingham, Ala., 1960-69. Missionary-at-large, Unevangelized Fields Mission 1969-72. President, Southeastern Bible College since 1972. 224

Garman, W. O. H. (1899-). Presbyterian minister and college teacher. Active in the International Council of Christian Churches. President, Associated Gospel Churches which has helped Fundamentalists to get into the chaplaincy. Pastor, Callender Memorial Church, Pittsburgh. 236

Garner, Albert (1920-). ABA leader, educator, and writer. Vice-president, ABA for 2 years. Dean, Texas Bible Institute. President, Florida Baptist Institute and Seminary, Lakeland, Fla., 1957-70. Now in the writing ministry and director, Blessed Hope Foundation. 216

Gasper, Louis (?-). Ordained Baptist. Professor of sociology and chairman of the department of philosophy, Pierce College, Los Angeles, since 1963. Author, 4 books. 2

Gates, I. E. (1874-1933). Baptist pastor in Tex. Baptist secretary in Ark. Founder and president, Wayland College 1910-16. Pastor, First Baptist, San Antonio; First Baptist, Amarillo, Tex. 129

Geiger, Henry C. (1899-). Baptist pastor and organizer of several Sunday Schools. Started a radio program for children 1945; started a TV program called The Children's Gospel Hour in 1945 which now is telecast over 260 stations. 257

Gilbert, Dan (1911-62). Baptist minister, talented speaker, and author. A secretary, WCFA. Wrote several books on the immoral and liberal influences on college campuses. Speaker, Prisoners' Bible Broadcast. 101, 161

Gilchrist, Paul (1932-). Presbyterian minister and educator. Professor, Covenant College, Chattanooga, Tenn.; its dean. Stated clerk of the Reformed Presbyterian Church, Evangelical Synod, since 1971. 239

Gillentine, E. C. (1884-1957). Pastor, evangelist, missionary, and editor with the ABA. President, ABA 1938-40. Editor, Sunday School materials 1941-54. Editor emeritus 1954-57. 214

Gillette, A. D. (1807-82). Baptist pastor: Syracuse; Fifth Baptist, Philadelphia, 1835-38; Eleventh Street Baptist, Philadelphia, 1838-52; Broadway Baptist (renamed Calvary Baptist in 1854), N. Y. C., 1852-63; First Baptist, Washington, D. C., from 1863 until ill health forced him to step down in 1869. 135

Gilmore, Joseph H. (1834-1918). Baptist pastor in N. H. Professor in Hebrew, U. of Rochester 1867-68; later, professor of rhetoric and English 1868-1908. Editor, *The Concord Monitor.* 75

Gilpin, John R. (1905-). Baptist pastor for 25 years in Independence, Ky.; Rossmoyne, Ohio; Russell, Ky. Pastor, Calvary Baptist, Ashland, Ky., for the past 20 years. Editor, *The Baptist Examiner.* 215, 276

Gladden, Washington (1836-1918). Congregational pastor: Brooklyn, N. Y., 1860-61; Morrisania, N. Y., 1861-66; North Adams, Mass., 1866-71; North Church, Springfield, Mass., 1874-82; First Congregational, Columbus, Ohio, 1882-1914. Author, 12 books. A leader in formulating and popularizing the social gospel. Called for Christians to build the Kingdom of God based on social justice. 13, 14, 68, 69

Glass, Bill (1935-). Former football star with the Cleveland Browns 1962-68. Full-time evangelist with an office in Dallas, Tex., working closely with Christian athletes since 1968. 275

Glasser, Arthur F. (1914-). U. S. Navy chaplain 1942-45. Missionary under China Inland Mission (now Overseas Fellowship) 1946-51. Professor, Columbia Bible College 1951-55. Served in the home office of China Inland Mission 1955-69. Professor, Fuller Seminary and one of the leaders in new-evangelical missions since 1969. 272

Glover, C. N. (1895-). Pastor with the ABA in Ark. Associate founder, Missionary Baptist Seminary, Little Rock, Ark., 1934. President, ABA 1941-46. Parliamentarian, ABA since 1950. 216

Godet, Frederick L. (1812-1900). Swiss theologian. Pastor for 22 years. Emphasized Reformed doctrine. A leading figure in evangelical circles. 45, 60

Godsoe, Frank (1891-). Baptist pastor: Tex.; Central Baptist, Oklahoma City; Crown Heights Baptist, Oklahoma City; Central Baptist, Amarillo, Tex. Chairman of the faculty, dean, and vice-president, Bible Baptist Seminary, Fort Worth. Now in semi-retirement in Del City, Okla. 217

Goodchild, Frank M. (1860-1928). Baptist Fundamentalist pastor in the NBC. Pastor: Armenia, N. Y., 1887-90; Spruce Street, Philadelphia, 1890-95; Central Baptist, N. Y. C., 1895-1924. Member, board of managers, American Baptist Home Mission Society. Member, Ministers and Missionaries Fund (NBC). 150, 154, 169

Goodwin, E. P. (1831-1901). Congregational pastor: Burke, Vt., 1859-60; First Congregational, Columbus, Ohio, 1860-67; First Congregational, Chicago, 1868-1900. 45

Gordon, Adoniram Judson (A. J.) (1836-95). Outstanding Baptist pastor and Fundamentalist. Pastor: Jamaica Plain, Mass., 1863-69; Clarendon Street Baptist, Boston, Mass., 1869-95. Founder Boston Missionary Training School (now Gordon College and Gordon Divinity School) 1889. Founder, Boston Industrial Home. Hymnwriter, "My Jesus, I Love Thee." Author, *Ecce Venit (Behold He Cometh)* and *The Ministry of the Spirit*. One of the founders of the early prophetic conferences. 19-26, 28, 29, 31, 45, 46, 47, 48, 50, 51, 52, 53, 70, 71, 72, 75, 76, 80, 116, 165

Gordon, Ernest (1867-1956). Excellent linguist and able student of the causes and nature of apostasy. Contributor, *Sunday School Times* for 30 years. Wrote the column "Religious Survey" 1922-56. Son of A. J. Gordon. Author, 22 books, best known of which was *The Leaven of the Sadducees*. 19, 25, 100

Gordon, George A. (1853-1929). Congregational pastor: Greenwich, Conn., 1881-84; Old South Church, Boston, 1884-1927. Learned Liberal. Wrote many books and articles. 71, 102

Gordon, Lynn Gray (1912-). Presbyterian missionary and educator. Chaplain in Korea 1952-54. President, Highland College, Calif., 1954-57. Pastor, Calvary Bible, Seattle, Wash., 1957-62. Worked with the Independent Board for Presbyterian Home Missions 1962-68. Professor, Faith Seminary, Elkins Park, Pa. General secretary, Independent Board for Presbyterian Foreign Missions since 1968; later, its acting president; its president since April, 1972, succeeding Dr. J. Gordon Holdcroft. 195

Gorham, Donald L. (1936-). Pastor with the Southern Methodist churches.

Professor, Southern Methodist College, Orangeburg, S. C., 1962-65 and pastor, Southern Methodist churches 1962-64. Now secretary of the ACCC with offices in Valley Forge, Pa. 195, 247

Graf, Karl H. (1815-69). German scholar and critic of the O. T. Professor, U. of Leipzig. Taught that the five books of Moses were written after the exile and with Wellhausen made this theory popular. 138

Graham, William Frank (Billy) (1918-). Baptist evangelist and world renowned speaker in public rallies, on radio, and on TV. President, Northwestern Schools 1947-51. Worldwide evangelist since 1951. Spokesman for New Evangelicalism. Author, several books. 120, 192, 194, 195 200, 204, 205, 208, 210, 211, 218, 225, 235, 252, 253, 254, 257, 271, 274, 275, 279, 280

Graves, John R. (1820-93). Pastor and Baptist editor, *The Tennessee Baptist*. Keen Bible student and debater. Held to Landmark views on John's baptism and the local church. One of his best books, *Landmarkism, What Is It?* At one time pastor, First Baptist, Nashville, Tenn. 56, 57, 214, 241

Graves, Lonnie (1925-). Pastor, Fellowship Free Will Baptist, Durham, N. C., the largest Free Will Baptist church in the world, having grown in 7 years from 8 people to 1,200 people. Broadcasts weekly on radio and TV. A converted gypsy. 244, 246

Gray, James M. (1851-1935). Protestant Episcopal minister. Rector, Church of England, Boston. Professor, Moody Bible Institute 1904; later, its president until he retired in 1934. An editor of the Scofield Reference Bible. Active, leading Fundamentalist. 26, 160, 170, 260

Gray, Robert C. (Bob) (1926-). Baptist pastor: Hampton, Fla.; Grand, Fla.; Trinity Baptist, Jacksonville, Fla., since 1954 where he has a large evangelistic ministry and Christian day school. 242, 255, 271

Gray, Robert L. (1927-). Pastor, Lawndale Bible (now Westchester Bible Church), Westchester, Ill., since 1954. Has served with Open Air Campaigners. Now serving as national president, IFCA 1972-75. 224

Greene, Oliver B. (1915-). Baptist evangelist and radio broadcaster. Now heard on a nationwide network The Gospel Hour on 150 stations. A tent preacher for 25 years. One of the best-known Fundamentalist evangelists in the Southeast. Has written many books and booklets. 254

Gregson, John W. (1923-). Pastor and educator with the BMA. Pastor, N. M. and Tex. Registrar and professor, Jacksonville Baptist College, Jacksonville, Tex. Professor, North American Baptist Theological Seminary 1957-71; its president 1967-71. Pastor, First Baptist, Carthage, Tex., since 1971. 242

Grounds, Vernon C. (1914-). Baptist pastor and educator. Pastor, The Gospel Tabernacle, Paterson, N. J., for 10 years. Dean, Baptist Bible Seminary, Johnson City, N. Y., 1945-51. Professor, Conservative Baptist Theological Seminary, Denver, Colo.; its president since 1956. Author, several books and articles. One of the more articulate of new-evangelical thinkers. 227, 231, 274

Grube, Henry, E. (1909-69). Founder and pastor, Mobile Gospel Tabernacle, Mobile, Ala., 1942-69. Organized Greystone Christian School, Mobile,

1947. Evangelist for years. Served in the Mel Trotter Mission, Grand Rapids, Mich., and the Gospel Center, St. Louis; helped to start 20 Christian day schools. 259

Guille, George W. (?-1931). Solid Bible student and teacher. Extension staff, Moody Bible Institute for 15 years. Helped L. S. Chafer in the founding of Dallas Seminary. President, Bryan College 1930-31. Pastor for some years: Mars Hill Presbyterian, Athens, Tenn., and Greene Street Presbyterian, Augusta, Ga. 160

Guinness, H. Grattan (1835-1910). English educator, missionary statesman, and co-founder of the Livingston Inland Mission, forerunner of Regions Beyond Mission. Outstanding prophecy student, devotional speaker, and missions leader. Started a missions school, London, 1873. 24, 70, 71

H

Haight, Grace (1863-1955). Independent missionary in China for 30 years. A boat missionary on the Nile River. Associate editor, *The Southern Missionary*. Professor in missions and hymnology, Bob Jones College 1930-55. Author, many poems and children's books. 271

Haldeman, Isaac Massey (I. M.) (1845-1933). Baptist pastor: Brandywine, Pa., 1871-75; Wilmington, Del., 1875-84; First Baptist, N. Y. C., 1884-1933, which, while he pastored, moved to its present site at Broadway and 79th Street and became eminent as a great national preaching center. A careful student and writer on prophecy. Author, several books and articles on the sins and influences of Liberalism. Given the title "the dispensational pastor" in the official history of the church. 160, 165

Hall, William W. (1933-). Baptist pastor in Tenn. Founder, Central Baptist, Greenville, Tenn. Has held several large meetings. Now lives in Memphis. 255

Halverson, Richard C. (1916-). Presbyterian minister, Fourth Presbyterian, Washington, D. C., since 1958. Actively connected with new-evangelical organizations, such as World Vision, Campus Crusade, and Navigators. 275

Ham, Mordecai (1877-1961). Baptist pastor, Bowling Green, Ky. 1900-01; First Baptist, Oklahoma City 1927-29. In full-time evangelism 1902-27 and 1929-61. Came from eight generations of Baptist preachers; traced his ancestry to Roger Williams. His converts, estimated at one million, include Billy Graham. His evangelism has included area-wide tent campaigns and radio work. 254

Hamilton, Harry G. (1886-). Baptist pastor: Wren, Ohio; Warsaw, Ind.; Austin, Minn., 1922-32; First Baptist, Buffalo, N. Y., 1932-40. Served at Akron Bible Institute; went to work with J. Frank Norris in the Bible Baptist Seminary, Fort Worth. Now retired and living in Fort Worth. 87, 221

Hamilton, Ray F. (1905-). Baptist pastor: Pa.; Quincy, Ill.; Belden Avenue, Chicago; Temple Baptist, Portsmouth, Ohio, since 1969. Secretary-treasurer, International Council of Christian Churches, 1963-68. Still actively associated with the ACCC. 195, 239

Hankins, Joe Henry (1889-1967). Baptist pastor. Fervent evangelist. Bible conference speaker. Pastored in Tex. 1925-35; Bells, 1925-26; White-wright, 1926-29; Childress, 1929-35. Pastored First Baptist, Little Rock, Ark., from which he retired in mid-1950's, continuing in Bible conference work. Well-known name in evangelism during the 1940's, holding some large campaigns. 254

Hargis, Billy James (1925-). Preacher, public speaker, and writer against anti-American activities such as communism. Radio campaigner. Founder, The American Christian College, Tulsa, Okla., 1970. Editor, *The Christian Crusader*. Author, several books. 157, 271, 278

Harnish, J. Lester (1913-). Baptist pastor: Brooklyn, N. Y., 1938-43; Philadelphia, 1943-48; Detroit, 1948-51; First Baptist, Portland, Ore., 1951-69. President, Eastern Baptist Seminary, Philadelphia, 1969-72. Pastor, Third Baptist, St. Louis, since 1972. Conservative denominationalist. 274

Harper, William Rainey (1856-1914). An expert in Hebrew and O. T. Principal, Masonic College, Macon, Tenn., 1875-76. Professor: Denison U. 1865-80; Baptist Union Theological Seminary, Chicago, 1879-86; Yale U. 1886-91. Founder and first president, U. of Chicago 1891-1906, the most radical Baptist school on the continent. An early American Liberal in religion. Author, 12 books. 12, 146, 206

Harrington, Bob (1928-). Southern Baptist evangelist with a clownish pulpit ministry. Has served as asst. pastor, First Baptist, New Orleans; publicized as "the chaplain of Bourbon Street"; gets large crowds to hear his bizarre remarks; has been used by some independent Baptists. 267, 274, 275

Harris, Elmore (1854-1910). Pastor, Walmer Road Baptist, Toronto, Canada. One of the first to detect trends of Liberalism in Canadian Baptist circles. Helped found Toronto Baptist College (now McMaster U.). Strong Bible teacher. 105

Harris, Laird (1911-). O. T. scholar. Professor: Faith Theological Seminary 1938-56; Covenant Seminary since 1956. Keen student and teacher of theology, O. T., and Barthianism. 86, 181, 237, 238, 239

Hart, Hornell (1888-1967). Sociologist. Strong promoter of the social gospel. Professor: Bryn Mawr College 1924-33; Hartford Seminary 1933-38; Duke Divinity School 1938-67. Author, 12 books. 98

Hartley, M. R. (?-?). Baptist missionary under ABFMS, Bengal-Orissa, India, 1917-25. Liberal in his views. Fundamentalists protested his appointment to foreign service. 228

Havner, Vance (1901-). Southern Baptist pastor, Salem Baptist, Weeksville, N. C., 1924-34, at 4 different times in these 10 years. Pastor, First Baptist, Charleston, S. C., 1934-40. Itinerant minister in churches, conferences, and revivals since 1940. Author, 26 books, including his autobiography. His own style is unique, witty, incisive, homespun, humorous, spiritual, and pointed. 254, 260

Heaton, Charles H. (1886-1946). Baptist pastor: Norville, Mich., 1912-14; Paw Paw, Mich., 1914-17. U. S. chaplain 1917-19. Pastor: South, Lansing, Mich., 1919-25; First, Elkhart, Ind., 1925-31; First, Newcastle, Pa., 1937-41; Covenant, Chicago, 1931-37; First, New Kensington, Pa., 1941-45;

Galilee, Chicago, 1945-46. Strong Fundamentalist, but unwilling to separate from his denomination when it went apostate. 154

Hebert, Arthur G. (1886-). English evangelical writer. Best-known work, *Fundamentalism and the Word of God,* which shows the sharp conflict between evangelical truth and Modernism. Has also written on the O. T. 21

Hegel, George William Frederick (1770-1831). German philosopher. Professor: U. of Jena; Heidelberg, 1816-18; Berlin 1818-31. Influential in the study of the philosophy of the tension between man and his world (thesis, antithesis, synthesis); identified God with the world process; provided background for both Marxism and German Liberalism. 7, 8

Heidegger, Martin (1889-). Jewish religious philosopher. Uses dialogue as the best means to teach. His main idea, "being." Wants us to concentrate on "is" not "that"; holds that God is dead and we are to think on "being itself." Active Zionist. Has tried to reconcile Jews and Arabs. 102

Hendricks, Howard G. (1924-). Professor: Southern Bible Institute, Fort Worth Bible Institute; Dallas Seminary, teaching in the field of Christian education, since 1945. Active with such new-evangelical groups as Scripture Press, NAE, and The Firs. Interesting speaker. Popular with middle-of-the-road groups. 209, 225, 258, 280

Henninger, Harold (1924-). A leader in the BBF. Founder and pastor for the past 26 years, Baptist Temple, Canton, Ohio, which has a beautiful Hall of Fame to honor great Christians. 219, 272

Henry, Carl F. H. (1913-). Baptist pastor, teacher, and writer. Professor: Northern Baptist Seminary 1940-47; Fuller Seminary 1947-56; now at Eastern Baptist Seminary. First editor, *Christianity Today* 1956-68. Open supporter of New Evangelicalism. Has helped plan Explo 72 and Key 73. 192, 203, 204, 206, 209, 210, 234, 273, 274

Henry, Jim (1934-). Baptist pastor: Canton, Tex., 1953-55; Fairfield, Tex., 1955-57; Calvary Baptist, Fairfield, Tex., 1957-61; Camden, Ark., 1961-64; Jacksonsville, Tex., 1964-66; Magnolia, Tex., since 1966. Active in MBA schools and committees. 241

Henshaw, John P. (1792-1852). Protestant Episcopal bishop. Very conservative. First bishop of R. I. 1843-52. Wrote a few books. 41

Hermann, John (1904-57). Pastor, Ainslie Baptist, Chicago, for 10 years. Professor, Bob Jones U. Academic vice-president, Tennessee Temple Schools from the founding, and dean of the college. 271

Hickok, Arnold (1927-). Pastor, First Baptist, Gunnison, Colo. Evangelist, 1966-67. Pastor, Heart to Heart Bible, Phoenix, Ariz., since 1967. Staunch knowledgeable Fundamentalist. 271

Higgs, Grady L. (1915-). Orthodox Baptist pastor: Dierks, Ark., 1946-47; Park Hill, Pueblo, Colo., 1947-61; Immanuel, Pueblo, Colo., 1961-64; Beacon Hill, Wichita Falls, Tex., 1964-68; Norman, Okla., 1968-72; College Heights Baptist, Temple, Tex., since 192. 246

Higgs, James L. (1936-). Pastor, Trinity Temple Baptist, Dallas, Tex., 1961-71. Founder and president, Orthodox Baptist College (now Independent Baptist College), Dallas, Tex., resigning in 1972. Professor, San Francisco Baptist Seminary 1973. 246

Hill, T. Wesley (1898-). Baptist pastor: Daisy, Lake City, Tracy City, and London, Tenn.; Central Baptist, Knoxville, Tenn., in 1931. Founder and pastor, Bible Baptist, Cincinnati, Ohio, after leaving the SBC (where all his previous churches had been), from 1932 until his retirement in 1972. 217

Hillard, B. H. (1889-1952). Baptist pastor: Broadhead, Ky., 1920-27; Monticello, Ky., 1927-30; Berea, Ky., 1930-33; Lockland Baptist, Cincinnati, Ohio, 1933-51; New Testament Baptist, Cincinnati, Ohio, 1951-52. 217

Hinson, Walter Benwell (W. B.) (1860-1926). Born in England; came to the U. S. in 1883. Pastor: Canada, 10 years; San Diego; White Temple, Portland, Ore., in 1910, which was renamed East Side in 1917 and renamed Hinson Memorial Baptist after his death. Solid Fundamentalist in swirling Baptist currents. 126, 154, 169, 228

Hobart, A. S. (1847-1930). Baptist pastor: Morris, N. Y.; Cincinnati, Ohio; Toledo, Ohio; Yonkers, N. Y. Professor, Crozer Seminary 1900-20. Pastor, Warburton Avenue Baptist, N. Y. C., 1920-23. A leader in education and missions. 153

Hobbs, Hershall H. (1907-). Baptist pastor: Ala.; First Baptist, Oklahoma City, Okla., since 1949. Preacher on the program of the SBC, The Baptist Hour. On many convention boards. Evangelical in preaching, but has poured thousands of dollars to promote the apostasy of the SBC. 274

Hodge, A. A. (1823-1886). Presbyterian theologian and educator. Professor: Western Seminary, Allegheny, Pa.; Princeton Seminary 1877-86. One of the strongest of orthodox men in the great tradition of Princeton. Sound Bible expositor. 176

Hodge, Charles (1797-1878). Presbyterian theologian. Author of a systematic theology. Professor, Princeton Seminary 1822-78. Learned and able defender of the Reformed faith. Many commentaries. 33, 40, 68, 176, 177

Holdcroft, J. Gordon (1878-1972). Long-time Presbyterian missionary in Korea. Executive secretary, Independent Board for Presbyterian Foreign Missions for 30 years. His book, *Into All the World* (published just after his death), sums up his lifetime research regarding world missions in the first centuries of the Christian era and sheds new light on early missionary work in the Far East in particular. A gifted and well-trained missions leader. 180

Hollowood, M. James (1916-). Pastor: First Baptist, Ashland, Pa., 1942-44; First Baptist, Dubois, Pa., 1944-52; First Baptist, Allentown, Pa., 1952-58. State secretary, Minnesota Baptist Convention 1958-66. Pastor, Prospect Avenue Baptist, Buffalo, N. Y., 1966-69. Professor: Central Baptist Seminary of Minneapolis 1958-65; Maranatha Baptist Bible College, Watertown, Wisc., since 1969. 155, 227, 232

Holmes, John Haynes (1879-). Unitarian minister and lecturer. Pastor: the Third Religious Society, Dorchester, Mass., 1904-07; Church of the Messiah (now the Community Church), N. Y., since 1907. Has served on several Unitarian boards, but officially left Unitarianism in 1919. Author, 13 books. Editor, *Unity.* 102

Horton, Arlin (1928-   ). Educator. Teacher, a mission school in Ky. 1951-52. Principal, Pensacola Christian Schools, Pensacola, Fla., since 1964. A leader in the Christian-day-school movement. 259

Horton, Douglas (1891-1968). Liberal Congregationalist. Head, Congregational Christian Churches 1938-55. Helped organize the National Council of Churches in 1950. Dean, Harvard Divinity School 1955-59. 239

Horton, Thomas C. (1848-1932). Associated with J. Wilbur Chapman, Bethany Presbyterian Church, Philadelphia, 1885-89. Secretary, St. Paul YMCA 1890. Pastor: Independent Church, St. Paul, 1894-1900; First Congregational (now Scofield Memorial), Dallas, Tex., 1904-06. Organized Bible Institute of Los Angeles in 1907. Associate pastor, Church of the Open Door, Los Angeles 1915-21. Editor, *The King's Business* 1910-25. 81, 161

Horton, Walter M. (1895-1966). Baptist leader (later Congregational). Professor: Union Seminary, N. Y. C., 1922-25; Oberlin Graduate School 1925-66. Author, 12 books. A Liberal, but fair to evangelicals. 101, 102

Houghton, George G. (1941-   ). Professor: Faith Bible Institute, St. Paul, 1965-66; Dallas Seminary; now Faith Baptist Bible College. His dissertation on A. J. Gordon is the most detailed study yet made of this early Fundamentalist. 19, 25

Houghton, Will H. (1887-1946). Baptist pastor and educator. Pastor: Canton, Pa., 1915-17; New Bethlehem, Pa., 1918-20; First Baptist, Norristown, Pa., 1920-24; Baptist Tabernacle, Atlanta, Ga., 1924-28; Calvary Baptist, N. Y. C., 1930-34. President, Moody Bible Institute, Chicago, 1934-46. 89, 136, 149, 233, 261

Hovey, Alvah (1820-1903). Baptist pastor and educator. Pastor, New Gloucester, N. H., 1848-49. Professor of Biblical literature, Newton Theological Institution 1849-99; its president 1868-98. 146, 150

Howard, Clinton (1868-1955). Temperance lecturer. Founder, Prohibition Union of Christian Men. Renowned Chautauqua speaker. Author. On the World Peace Commission 1920-24. 161

Howson, John S. (1816-85). English evangelical educator and minister of the Church of England. With Conybeare, he wrote the widely used work on the life and epistles of Paul. 41

Hoyt, Herman (1909-   ). Professor: Ashland College and Seminary; Grace Seminary, Winona Lake, when it was founded in 1937 to teach Greek and N. T.; its president since 1962. A leader in the Grace Brethren group. 274

Hubbard, David A. (1928-   ). Ordained Conservative Baptist pastor and educator. Professor, Westmont College 1957-63. Interim pastor, Montecito Community Church, Montecito, Calif., 1960-62. President and professor, Fuller Seminary since 1963. 255

Hudson, Van Dale (1943-   ). Freewill Baptist pastor, Nashville, Tenn.,

1964-66. Evangelist since 1966, averaging 43 revivals a year. Editor, *The Evangel.* Has served on committees of the National Association of Free Will Baptists. 245

Hudson, W. Jack (1922-). Called to preach in 1950. Pastor for the last 19 years, Northside Baptist, Charlotte, N. C., which is the largest Baptist congregation in the Carolinas, has a large Christian day school and radio ministry, and is now building a large beautiful complex. 243, 271

Hughes, Edwin Holt (1866-1950). Methodist pastor, Newton Center, Mass., 1892-96. President, DePauw U. 1903-08. Elected a bishop of the Methodist Church in 1908 and senior bishop in 1923. President, Boston U. 1923. Chancellor, American U. 1933. Author, 10 books. Sound in doctrine, but did not slow down the slide of his denomination into apostasy, nor leave it when apostate. 261

Hull, Merle R. (1921-). Baptist pastor: Fundamental Baptist, Marshalltown, Iowa, 1944-47; Walnut Street, Muscatine, Iowa, 1947-52; Grace, Flint, Mich., 1952-54. Joined Regular Baptist Press in 1954 where he is executive secretary and editor, *The Baptist Bulletin.* 222

Hunt, Emory William (1862-1938). Baptist pastor: Toledo, Ohio, 1887-1900; Boston, Mass., 1900-02. President, Denison U. 1902-13. General Secretary, ABFMS 1913-15. Pastor, First Baptist, Newton Center, Mass., 1915-19. President, Bucknell U. 1919-31. President, NBC 1910-12. 151

Huss, John (1369-1415). Reformer of Bohemia. Preacher. Professor, U. of Prague. Sought to be true to the Bible on salvation and the true Church, but the Roman Catholic Church had him burned at the stake in 1415. 38

Huston, Charles L. (1856-?). Manufacturer, Lukens Steel Company, Pa. Presbyterian elder, Chairman, WCFA 1918. President, Philadelphia School of the Bible 1921-28. Actively supported Westminster Seminary when it started in 1929. 160

Hyles, Jack (1926-). Baptist pastor: Miller Road Baptist, Garland, Tex., 1952-59; First Baptist, Hammond, Ind., since 1959. First Baptist has grown to 14,000 members. Opened Hyles-Anderson College in 1972. Holds many conferences for pastors in soulwinning and church building. 255, 271, 278

I

Ignatius (c. 35-107). Early Church Father. Bishop of Antioch. First to use the term "Catholic Church." Pupil of John the apostle. Was thrown to the wild beasts at Rome. Had a genuine devotion to the Lord. Wrote 15 letters. 36

Imbrie, Charles K. (1814-1892). Presbyterian pastor: Rahway, N. J., 1841-52; First, Jersey City, N. J., 1852-88; First, Bergen, N. J., 1888-1890; its pastor emeritus 1890-892. Served on the Presbyterian Board for Foreign Missions 1856-92. 32

Ingle, Robert D. (1904-67). Baptist pastor and leader in the WBF. Pastor, Berea Baptist, Jacksonville, Fla., 1929-67. His widow is the oldest living charter member this church has. A close associate of J. Frank Norris, who died while at Ingle's camp in 1952. President, WBF for 2 terms. Editor, *The Berean Banner.* 198, 217

Irenaeus (130-202). Bishop of Lyons in present-day France. Church Father. Strong apologist (defender) of Bible truth whose writings exposed the heresies of the Gnostics. Best-known work, *Against Heresies.* One of the earliest Fathers to try to build a theology using both the O. and N. T. 36

Ironside, Henry Allan (1876-1951). Outstanding Bible teacher, writer, and pastor. Served with the Salvation Army and then with the Brethren. Pastor, Moody Memorial Church 1930-48. Wrote 60 volumes. Warmhearted, knowledgeable Fundamentalist. 89, 165, 235, 260

J

Jackson, Paul R. (1903-69). Baptist pastor in rural churches: N. D., 1926-29; Strathmore, Calif., 1929-34; First Baptist, Ceres, Calif., 1934-45. Interim pastor, Wealthy Street Baptist, Grand Rapids, Mich., 1945-46. President, Baptist Bible Seminary 1946-60. National representative, GARBC 1960-69. 223

Jamieson, Robert (1802-80). Presbyterian minister in Scotland. Pastor, St. Paul's Free Church, Glasgow, 1844-80. Took the evangelical side when the Church of Scotland split in the famous Disruption of the 1840s. Wrote 2 volumes of the 6-volume commentary of Jamieson, Faussett, and Brown on the whole Bible. 37, 57

Janney, Al (1928-). Founder and pastor, New Testament Baptist, Miami, Fla., since 1954. Founder and president, Dade County Christian Schools. Leader, BBF. Opened the Shady Grove Camp and a college in 1971. 220

Jaspers, Karl (1883-1969). German philosopher. Professor, U. of Heidelberg. Dismissed by the Nazis in 1937. Professor, Basel 1937-69. Defended existentialism; wrote vaguely about the "being-object" and "being-I." 102

Jeremiah, James T. (1914-). Baptist pastor: Panama, N. Y., 1936-39; Emmanuel Baptist, Toledo, Ohio, 1939-50; Emmanuel Baptist, Dayton, Ohio, 1950-54. President, Cedarville College, Cedarville, Ohio, since 1954. On the board of Baptist Mid-Missions and Council of Fourteen. 222

Jernigan, W. T. (1927-). Freewill Baptist pastor and educator. Pastor: Tenn.; Okla.; Calif.; Cavanaugh Baptist, Fort Smith, Ark. President, California Christian College since 1969. Active in Freewill Baptist evangelism, church extension, and national missions. 244

Jessup, Morris K. (1830-1908). Banker, humanitarian, and supporter of the YMCA. Helped found the YMCA, N. Y.; gave a building (Jessup Hall) to Union Seminary, N. Y. C. Generous giver to missions and tract societies. 78

Johnson, Albert G. (1888-1971). Born in England; came to U. S. in 1913. Pastor: Albany Park Baptist, Chicago, 1918-24; Temple Baptist, Detroit, 1924-34; Hinson Memorial, Portland, Ore., 1934-55. President, Western Baptist Seminary 1955-64. Active in Conservative Baptist movement. President, CBFMS. 132, 150

Johnson, Gordon (1925-). Methodist pastor: Compton, Calif., 1949; Evangelical Methodist, Beaumont, Tex., 1952-53. Field representative, Upland College 1953-54. Pastor: Evangelical Methodist, Phoenix, Ariz.,

1955-60; Pacoima, Calif., 1960-65. Asst. general supt. for the West, Evangelical Methodist Church since 1966. 248

Johnson, L. C. (1914-). Freewill Baptist pastor and educator. Pastor: rural churches, Ga. and Tenn. 1934-36; Ashland, Tenn., 1937-39; Glennville, Ga., 1939-42; Tupelo, Miss., 1944-47. President, Free Will Baptist Bible College, Nashville, Tenn., 1942-44 and since 1947. A denominational leader. 244

Johnson, Robert Kirthwood (R. K.) (1910-72). Educator and Christian businessman. Supervised construction of the plant of Bob Jones U. in Greenville, S. C., 1947. Secretary and treasurer of the university and its business manager 1935-72. General manager, WMUU, the university radio station. Author, *Builder of Bridges* (biography of Bob Jones, Sr.). Secretary, Board of Trustees. Secretary, Executive Committee. 251, 270, 271

Johnson, S. Lewis (1915-). Pastor and educator. Professor, Dallas Seminary since 1945 and the head of its dept. of N. T. Has pastored in Dallas. 235

Johnson, Torrey M. (1909-). Baptist pastor, youth leader, evangelist. Pastor: Messiah Baptist, Chicago, 1930-31; Midwest Bible, Chicago, 1933-53. Youth For Christ leader 1944-48. In evangelism and Bible conferences 1953-67. Head, Bibletown, Boca Raton, Fla., since 1967. 257

Jones, Bill M. (1937-). Freewill Baptist pastor: Denison, Tex., 1957-58; Bowie, Tex., 1958-59. Missionary on the Ivory Coast 1959-69. Professor, Oklahoma Bible College 1959-70. Director of publications, Free Will Baptist Foreign Missions 1970-71. President, Hillsdale Free Will Baptist Bible College since 1971. 244

Jones, Bryan M. (1928-). Pastor, Entrican Community Bible Church, Entrican, Mich., 1952-54. Dean of men and instructor, Grand Rapids School of the Bible 1954-56. Pastor: Calvary Church, Wayland, Mich., 1956-64; Twin Branch Bible, Mishawaka, Ind., 1964-72. National executive director, IFCA since 1972. 224

Jones, E. Stanley (1884-1973). Ordained Methodist world statesman, missions leader, modernist writer. Ordained in the North Indiana Conference 1907. Pastor, The English Church, Lucknow, India, 1907-11. District missionary, The United Provinces 1911-17. Evangelist to the educated classes in India 1917-54. Elected bishop, but refused it. Best known for his liberal books, *The Christ of the Indian Road* and *The Christ of Every Road.* 102

Jones, Jim Owen (1942-). Mathematics teacher in the public schools, Nashville, Tenn. Asst. director of communications, Free Will Baptists in Foreign Missions 1968-69. Editor, *Contact.* Executive director, NAE 1968-70. Now editor of the official paper of NAE. 244

Jones, Robert R. (Bob) (1883-1968). From 1920 until his death, an evangelist of national and international stature. Founder, Bob Jones College (now university) at St. Andrews Bay, Fla. (now in Greenville, S. C.). Licensed by the Methodist Church to preach when 15. His life carefully portrayed in *Builder of Bridges* by R. K. Johnson. One of the most militant of old-time evangelists. Famous for his hard-hitting style, warmth of personal applications, incisive Christian philosophy and sayings. 80, 88, 90, 121, 134, 162, 174, 190, 193, 233, 250, 252, 254, 256, 270, 273

Jones, Robert R. (Bob), Jr. (1911-   ). Acting president, Bob Jones College 1932-47; president of the university 1947-71; its chancellor since 1971. Authority on Shakespeare. Author, 7 books. Pungent preacher. Editor, *Faith for the Family*. Radio speaker, evangelist, keen student of current events. A central figure in militant Fundamentalism. 77, 79, 195, 211, 219, 251, 252, 253, 256, 270, 281

Jones, Robert R. (Bob), III (1939-   ). Asst. dean of men, Bob Jones U. 1959-61. Professor in speech 1961-62. Asst. to the president 1962-63. Vice-president 1963-71. President of the university since 1971. Accomplished Shakespearean actor. Strong preacher. 195, 270

Jones, Rufus (1863-1948). One of best-known leaders of the Quakers. Principal, Oak Grove Seminary, Vassalboro, Me., 1889-93. Professor, Haverford College 1893-1934. Author, 40 books. Persuasive Liberal. Strong proponent of human goodness and the unity of all religious people. Denied all Bible doctrines. 93, 100

Jones, Rufus M. (1915-   ). Pastor: Westwood Baptist, Inkster, Mich., 1940-43; Livernois Avenue, Detroit, Mich., 1943-50. On administrative staff, Conservative Baptist Home Mission Society 1950-52; its general director since 1952. Active in starting new churches. Past president of NAE. 233, 235

Jones, Samuel Porter (Sam) (1847-1906). Methodist evangelist. Itinerant preacher of the Methodist Episcopal Church (South) in the North Georgia Conference 1872-80. Agent, North Georgia Orphans 1880-84. Full-time evangelist from 1884 until he died. A national figure. One of the foremost public speakers of his generation. Preached pungent, arresting sermons. 77, 79, 174

Judd, Walter (1898-   ). Missionary lecturer, conservative politician, member of Congress. An authority on China where he was born. Keen student on foreign affairs. Weak in theology. A Congregationalist. Served in the 78th to 87th congresses. 275

Judson, Adoniram (1788-1850). Pionéer American missionary to Burma. Inspired both Congregationalists and Baptists to organize boards to support missions. Lost two wives in a life of privation and suffering. Died and was buried at sea. 20

Justin Martyr (111-165). Early Church Father. A defender of the Faith. Wrote *The Apologies* and *A Dialogue with Trypho the Jew*. A student of philosophy. Beheaded in Rome. 36

K

Kallenbach, Walter D. (1905-46). Evangelist. Accomplished musician. Lost his sight in 1927 in a hunting accident. Afterward, graduated from college and seminary. Held many evangelistic meetings in churches. In 1941, preached the Easter sunrise service at Soldiers' Field in Chicago. Author, 5 books and many booklets. 254

Kant, Immanuel (1724-1804). German philosopher. Professor, U. of Königsberg, East Prussia. Based all ideas on reason and all knowledge on experience; rejected revelation. Major book, *The Critique of Pure Reason.* An open enemy of the Bible, though a great thinker. 7, 8, 9

Kellar, Gerald D. (1916-   ). Baptist pastor: Tex., 1937-40; First Baptist, Palmer, Tex., 1940-44. President, Jacksonville College, Tex., 1944-56. President, North American Baptist Theological Seminary 1956-67. President, Central Baptist College, Conway, Ark., 1967-70. Pastor, First Baptist, Galena, Kan., since 1970. First president of the BMA when it started in 1950. 241

Kellogg, Samuel Henry (S. H.) (1839-99). Presbyterian missionary in India 1865-71. Professor, Theological School in India 1873-76. Pastor, Third Presbyterian, Pittsburgh, 1877-86. Professor, Allegheny Seminary 1877-85. Pastor, St. James Presbyterian, Toronto, Canada, 1886-92. Author, 7 books. 30, 31, 47

Kemp, Joseph W. (1872-1933). Baptist pastor: Kelso, England, 1897-98; Hawick, England, 1898-1902; Charlotte Chapel, Edinburgh, 1905-15; Calvary Baptist, N. Y. C., 1915-17; Metropolitan Tabernacle, London, 1917-19. Spent the rest of his life in Australia and New Zealand and founded the New Zealand Bible Institute in 1930. 135

Kennedy, Gerald (1907-   ). Pastor: First Congregational, Collinsville, Conn., 1932-36; Calvary Methodist, San Jose, Calif., 1936-40; First Methodist, Palo Alto, Calif., 1940-42. Professor, Pacific School of Religion 1938-42. Pastor, St. Paul's, Lincoln, Neb., 1942-48. Elected a bishop of the Methodist Church in 1948. A bishop in the Los Angeles area since 1952. Author, 17 books. 252, 279

Kerfoot, Franklin H. (1847-1901). Baptist pastor: Midway and Forks, Elkhorn, Ky., 1875-77; Eutaw Place Baptist, Baltimore, Md., 1877-83; Strong Place Baptist, Brooklyn, N. Y., 1883-86. Professor, Southern Baptist Seminary 1886-99. Corresponding secretary, Home Mission Board of Southern Baptists 1899-1901. 112

Ketcham, Robert T. (1889-   ). Baptist pastor and GARB leader. Pastor: Roulette, Pa., 1912-15; Brookville, Pa., 1915-19; Butler, Pa., 1919-23; Niles, Ohio, 1923-27; Elyria, Ohio, 1927-32; Central Baptist, Gary, Ind., 1932-39; Walnut Street, Waterloo, Iowa, 1939-48. National representative, GARBC 1948-60. Consultant GARBC 1960-66. Active speaking and writing ministry since 1966. Author, several books and booklets. One of original founders of the GARBC. 89, 101, 166, 195, 211, 222, 239, 260

Kienel, Paul (1933-   ). Pastor with the Assemblies of God, editor, school principal. Executive director, California Association of Christian Schools since 1966 which under his leadership has grown 300%. 259

King, Martin Luther, Jr. (1929-68). Negro civil rights leader and pastor. Pastor, Dexter Avenue Baptist, Birmingham, 1954-60. Co-pastor (with his father), Ebenezer Baptist, Atlanta, 1960-68. Organized the Southern Christian Leadership Conference in 1957. Known for such phrases as "We shall overcome" and "I had a dream." A favorite with Liberals, do-gooders, and radicals. 102, 219

Kinlaw, Dennis (1922-   ). Methodist pastor: N. C., 1949-53; Loudinville Community Church, N. Y., 1955-61. Professor, Asbury College, Wilmore, Ky., 1963-66; its president since 1968. 274

Kirconnell, Watson (1895-   ). Canadian Baptist educator. Professor, Mc-Master U. 1940-48. President, Acadia U., Wolfville, Nova Scotia, 1948-64. A Liberal in theology. Helped Canadian Baptists to go farther down the road of apostasy. 107

Kirkland, A. J. (1902-72). An ABA pastor: Hillsboro, Ennis, White Oak, Corsicana, and Henderson, Tex. President and co-founder, Texas Bible Institute, Henderson, Tex., 1950-72. President ABA 1953-54. Editor. 216

Kirkland, Winfred (1872-1943). Author who used the pseudonym of James Priceman. Wrote such books as *The Living Church, Girls Who Became Artists, Portrait of a Carpenter,* and *Easter People.* One of her books *The Way of Discovery* was a part of the Machen controversy. Her works are both religious and humorous. 180

Knight, Durward H., Jr. (1919-   ). Methodist pastor: Weaverville, N. C., 1949-51; Maple Street Methodist, Columbia, S. C., 1951-54; pastorates in Jupiter and Salerno, Fla., 1954-59 (Southern Methodist); Salerno Southern Methodist 1959-64; Osceola Southern Methodist, Fla., 1964-66; First Southern Methodist, Atlanta, Ga., 1966-71; Center Independent Methodist, Atlanta, Ga., 1971-73. 247

Knox, John (1515-1572). Outstanding preacher and Reformer in Scotland. Led his country out of the control of the Roman Catholic Church. Opposed Mary, Queen of Scots. Dynamic and unique preacher. Founder of Presbyterianism in Scotland. Truly a great servant of the Lord. 41, 125, 204

Kurtz, Johann H. (1809-90). German church historian. Professor of O. T., U. of Dorpat 1849-69. Wrote full-time after 1870. A conservative Lutheran. Removed from the radicalism in scholars of his generation. 37

Kyle, Melvin G. (1858-1933). Presbyterian educator and editor. Professor, Xenia Theological Seminary 1908-30; its president 1922-30. Editor, *Bibliotheca Sacra.* One of the editors, *The Sunday School Times* 1911-33. Stalwart writer and teacher. 261

L

Ladd, George E. (1911-   ). Baptist pastor and educator. Pastor: Montpelier, Vt., and Boston, Mass. Professor, Gordon College 1946-50. Professor of N. T., Fuller Seminary, Pasadena, Calif., since 1950. Strong posttribulational teacher and writer. A leader in new-evangelical thought. 204

Laird, Harold S. (1891-   ). Presbyterian minister. Pastor: Arlington Church, Baltimore, Md., 1917-18; Henry Memorial, Philadelphia, 1919-25; First, Lewistown, N. J., 1925-29; Collingswood, N. J., 1929-32; Central Church, Wilmington, Del., 1933-36; First Independent, Wilmington, Del., 1936-46; First Independent, Wilmington, Del., 1946-52. In Bible conference and Bible teaching ministry since 1952. Helped organize Faith Theological Seminary which met for a time in his church; served on its trustee board for several years. Orthodox preacher and defender of the Faith. 239

Lakin, Baskin R. (B. R.) (1901-   ). Baptist evangelist and pastor. Pastor: Euclid Avenue Baptist, Bristol, Conn., 1937-39; Cadle Tabernacle, Indianapolis, Ind., 1939-52. While at Cadle Tabernacle, he conducted the Nation's Family Prayer Period. In full-time evangelism and Bible conference ministry since 1952. Several booklets and records. Has a radio broadcast. One of the old-time Gospel preachers. 271

Lange, Johann Peter (1802-84). German theologian, scholar, Reformed pastor. Professor: U. of Zurich 1869-70; U. of Marburg 1872-75. Major studies on the life of Christ, Christian doctrine, and a 25-volume commentary on the whole Bible. Careful student and one of the most learned Bible scholars of the last century. 39, 40, 41

Larkin, Clarence (1850-1924). Baptist pastor in Kennett Square, Pa., and Fox Chase, Pa., where he stayed 20 years. Ardent dispensationalist and Bible teacher by long and careful study. Made many studies of prophecies which led to his use of books such as *Rightly Dividing the Word* and corresponding charts. 150

Lawes, Curtis Lee (1868-1946). Baptist editor, *The Watchman Examiner*. Coined the word "Fundamentalist" in 1920 after attending a preconvention rally in Buffalo, N. Y. Editor, 1915-40. Sound in doctrine, but not a separatist. 150

Lee, Ivy (1877-1934). Newspaperman. On the personal staff of John D. Rockerfeller. Adviser to both railroad and steel companies. Lecturer several times, London School of Economics. Had Fosdick's sermon "Shall the Fundamentalists Win?" published. 95, 178

Lee, Robert G. (1886-   ). Southern Baptist pastor, orator, and writer. President, SBC 3 times. Pastor: Edgefield, S. C., 1920-21; First, New Orleans, La., 1921-25; Citadel Square, Charleston, S. C., 1925-27; Bellevue Baptist, Memphis, Tenn., 1927-59. Sound in doctrine and powerful speaker, but not a separatist. From the inside, has watched his denomination decline. 57, 121, 260, 273

Lehman, Glen (1907-   ). Pastor: Addison Heights Bible, Chicago, Ill., 1930-38; Lawndale Bible, Chicago, Ill., 1938-41; Dubuque Bible, Dubuque, Iowa, 1941-45; Union Gospel, Waterloo, Iowa, 1945-53; Pekin Bible, Pekin, Ill., 1953-59. National executive secretary, IFCA and editor, *The Voice* 1959-72. Full-time editor and speaker since 1972. 224, 225

Leiper, Henry S. (1891-   ). Presbyterian minister 1915-20. Joined the Congregationalists in 1920. Secretary, Student Volunteer Movement 1913-14. Pastor, N. Y. C., 1914-16. Missionary in Siberia 1918. Missionary in China 1918-22. Editor, *The Congregationalist*. On the staff of the FCC 1930-45. With the WCC 1945-48. Secretary of Congregational Missions 1952-59. With the American Bible Society since 1959. 102, 239

Lemmons, Norman Grady (1908-   ). Baptist evangelist and pastor. Founder and pastor, Davidson Memorial Baptist Church, Shelby, N. C., since 1941. Has held scores of tent meetings and church revivals; has helped in many Fundamentalist fellowships. 242

Lerrigo, P. J. (1875-1958). Baptist medical missionary under the Northern Baptist Foreign Mission Board in the Philippines 1902-14. In several administrative capacities with the ABFMS 1914-50. 227

LeTourneau, Robert G. (1888-1969). Christian businessman who built large earth-moving equipment. Founder, LeTourneau College, Longview, Tex. Gave generously to Christian works. Associated with the Christian and Missionary Alliance. As a layman, gave his testimony from coast to coast. 261

Levin, Paul (1914-). Baptist evangelist and writer of tracts. Started evangelistic meetings in 1934 with a blind gospel singer, Bob Finley; Heads Bible Tracts, Inc., which has published over 218 million copies of tracts in 75 languages and at present has requests for 50 million more. 255

Lewis, Clifford (1909-). Evangelist. ~~Professor: Baptist Bible Seminary, Johnson City, N. Y.; Dallas Seminary since 1968. Author, 2 books.~~ *and Educator* 254, ~~271~~ President: Kansas City Bible College, 1955-59; he has been an evangelist for 35 yrs.

Lindsell, Harold (1913-). Professor: Columbia Bible College 1942-44; Northern Baptist Seminary 1944-51; Fuller Seminary 1951-64. Editor, *Christianity Today* since 1964, a national voice of New Evangelicalism. 275

Linton, John (1888-1965). Born in Scotland. Baptist pastor: Reston, Manitoba, Canada, 1915-16; Parkdale Baptist, Toronto, 1916-20; Point St. Charles Baptist, Montreal, 1920-25; High Park, Toronto, 1925-34; New York Gospel Center, N. Y., 1936-38. Evangelist 1938-56. Pastor, Walkerville, Windsor, Ontario, 1957-60. Evangelist 1960-65. Died while preaching in Pontiac, Mich. 169

Lintz, Harry McCormick (1900-). Baptist pastor: Greenville, Tenn., for 8 years; First Baptist, Lake Charles, La. Extension staff, Moody Bible Institute 1928-37. Evangelist for 35 years. Now heads the Victory Crusade Evangelistic Association. 260

Lockyer, Herbert (1886-). Pastor in England and Scotland for 26 years. Came to the U. S. in 1935 to lecture under the auspices of Moody Bible Institute for 10 years. Since then, a free-lance Bible teacher and Bible expositor. Now retired and living in Bromley, England. Author, 50 books. 260

Loney, Clifford J. (1880-1966). Canadian Baptist pastor: Stouffville Baptist, Ontario, 1908-11; Immanuel Baptist, Brantford, Ontario, 1911-15; Stanley Avenue Baptist, Hamilton, Ontario, 1915-61. Joined T. T. Shields in protesting the spread of Modernism in Baptist circles and led his church to separate from the Ontario Convention. 112

Lorimer, George C. (1838-1904). Baptist pastor: Walnut Street, Louisville, Ky.; Paducah, Ky.; First Baptist, Albany, N. Y., in 1868; Tremont Temple, Boston, 1871-79 and 1891-1901; Madison Avenue, N. Y., 1901-04. Very active in Baptist circles. An open opponent of Liberalism. 29, 94, 113

Loveless, Wendell P. (1892-). Pastor: Wheaton Evangelical Free, Wheaton, Ill., 1952-57; Community Church, Boca Raton, Fla., 1957-61. First director of the radio dept. of Moody Bible Institute 1926-45. Professor, Moody Bible Institute 1945-47. Bible teaching ministry 1947-52. Director, religious activities, station KAIM, Honolulu, Ha., 1961-66. Associate pastor, First Chinese Church of Christ, Honolulu, Ha., since 1966. 223

Lowrie, Roy, Jr. (1927-). Director, a Christian camp for 25 summers. Headmaster and teacher, Delaware County Christian Day School, Newton Square, Pa., for the past 20 years. 259

Lummis, Henry (1825-1905). Methodist pastor and educator. Teacher in several schools in New England 1855-70. Pastor 1870-86. Professor, Lawrence U., Appleton, Wisc., 1886-1905. 33, 45, 50

Luther, Martin (1483-1546). German Reformer. Founder, the Lutheran branch of Protestantism. Attacked Romanism and its false teachings; stressed the N. T. truth, justification, by faith and the authority of the Bible over that of the Roman church. 41, 121, 204

M

Mabie, Henry Clay (H. C.) (1847-1918). Baptist pastor and missionary leader. Pastor: Rockford, Ill., 1869-73; Oak Park, Ill., 1873-75; Brookline, Mass., 1876-79; Indianapolis, 1879-83; Belvedere, Ill., 1883-85; St. Paul, 1885-88; Minneapolis, 1889-90. Corresponding secretary, American Baptist Missionary Union (now the ABFMS) 1890-1908. Editor, *The Christian Union* and *The Outlook*. 76

McAlister, Jack (1924-). Founder and president, World Literature Crusade since 1946, with offices in Studio City, Calif., and 35 offices around the world; it makes literature available to a million people a day; it has 800 full-time workers and broadcasts over 250 stations in Canada and this country. 275.

MacArthur, Robert Stuart (1841-1923). Pastor, Calvary Baptist, N. Y. C., 1870-1911. Strong Bible teacher, but did not involve himself in the Fundamentalist battles. Many of his books and sermons published. Increased the image of his church as a national preaching center on the East Coast. 135

Macartney, Clarence Edward (1879-1957). Presbyterian minister: Paterson, N. J., 1905-14; Arch Street, Philadelphia, 1914-27; First Presbyterian, Pittsburgh, 1927-53. Strong Orthodox preacher and defender of the Faith. Moderator of his denomination. Refused to leave when his church went apostate. 96, 137, 176, 178, 179, 180

McBurnie, Robert S. (1922-). Founder and pastor, First Southern Baptist, Overland Park, Kan., 1957-60. Fund director, A. B. Culbertson and Co. (church investments), Fort Worth, Tex., 1960-67. Professor: Lincoln U. 1967-71; Mid-America Nazarene College 1971-72; California Graduate School of Theology since 1972. 112, 113

McCarrell, William (1886-). Strong Fundamentalist leader in the Bible-church movement. Pastor, Norton Park Congregational Church (later, Cicero Bible Church), Cicero, Ill., 1913-60, for which he had built an auditorium to seat 1,500 by 1929. Trustee: Moody Bible Institute; Wheaton College; Pacific Garden Mission. A senior statesman, IFCA. 88, 223

McCaul, Robert (1886-). Baptist pastor: Olivet Baptist, Winnipeg, Canada, 1909-13; Center Baptist, Center, N. Y., 1913-14; Immanuel Baptist, Buffalo, N. Y., 1914-15; Churchille, N. Y., 1915-16; Rochester, N. Y., 1916-17; Washington Avenue Baptist, Brooklyn, 1917-27; Evangel Temple, Brooklyn, 1930-35; Manhattan Towers, N. Y., 1935-36; Brooklyn Baptist Tabernacle since 1936. Editor, *The Faith Press* and the *New York Christian*. 112

McClain, Alva (1888-1969). Brethren pastor, Philadelphia, 1918-23. Professor: Philadelphia School of the Bible 1909-23; Ashland College 1925-27; Bible Institute of Los Angeles 1927-29; Ashland Theological Seminary 1930-37. Founder and president, Grace Theological Seminary 1937-62. 260

MacCorkle, Douglas (1915-   ). Baptist pastor and educator. Pastor: Goffstown, N. H., 1941-44; Paris, Tex., 1944-47; Immanuel Baptist, Newton Center, Mass., 1947-54; Reinhardt Bible, Dallas, Tex., 1955-57. Dean, Washington Bible College 1957-63. President, Philadelphia College of Bible since 1963. 274

McCormick, Cyrus Gall (1809-84). American industrialist and inventor of farm machinery. Devout Presbyterian layman. Helped establish the Presbyterian Theological Seminary, Chicago (later, McCormick Seminary); helped other colleges with large sums of money. 271

McCormick, John (1922-   ). Baptist pastor: W. Va., 1943-55; Tenn., 1955-57; New Hope Baptist, Lafayette, Ga., 1957-58; Duncan Park Baptist, Chattanooga, Tenn., 1958-62; Chilhowie, Va., 1962-63. Professor: Tennessee Temple Schools 1956-62; Bible Institute of Texas 1963-67. Now in full-time Bible conference ministry. 271

McCullough, Chester J. (1918-   ). Baptist pastor: First, Richmond, Mich., 1952-54; First, Tipton, Ind., 1954-58; Joy Road, Detroit, 1958-66; First, Arvada, Colo., 1966-72; Grace Baptist, Decatur, Ala., since 1973. Treasurer, CBA of A for 5 years. Treasurer, CBF for 16 years. A leader in the WBM since its founding 8 years ago. 155

MacDormand, Thomas B. (1904-   ). Canadian Baptist educator and churchman. An executive officer with the Baptist Union of Western canada, Ontario-Quebec Convention and the Atlantic Baptist Convention. President, Eastern Baptist Seminary 1961-67. President, Baptist Federation of Canada since 1970. Liberal in theology and a keen participant in denominational affairs and policies. 109

McDowell, C. E. (1895-   ). Baptist pastor: Bloomfield, Iowa, 1932-37; Ottumwa, Iowa, 1937-43; Borger, Tex., 1943-51; Bible Baptist, Borger, Tex., 1951-59. Supply pastor, West Mineral, Kan., and Clayton, N. M., 1959-68. Went to assist M. O. Garner at Amarillo, Tex., in 1968; retired in 1972. 217

McGee, J. Vernon (1904-   ). Presbyterian pastor: Decatur, Ga.; Nashville, Tenn.; Cleburne, Tex.; The Church of the Open Door, Los Angeles, 1949-70. Bible conference speaker. Radio Bible teacher. Sound in doctrine, but openly supports new-evangelical movements. 244, 256, 260, 280

McGiffert, Arthur C. (1861-1933). Congregational scholar in church history. Professor: Lane Seminary 1888-93; Union Seminary, N. Y., 1893-26; its president 1917-26. His book, *History of Christian Doctrine,* widely used as a text. 94, 99, 100

McGinlay, James (1901-58). Founder and pastor, Central Baptist, London, Ontario for 13 years. A popular Bible conference speaker in U. S. and Canada. Pastor, Baptist Temple, Brooklyn, N. Y., in the 1950s. 171, 260

Machen, J. Gresham (1881-1937). Presbyterian minister, teacher, writer, defender of the Faith. Professor: Princeton Seminary 1906-29; Westminster Seminary 1929-37 which he helped found in 1929. A founder,

Independent Board of Presbyterian Foreign Missions. Great Greek N. T. scholar. Able writer in theology and the Reformed faith. Known widely for *The Virgin Birth, Christianity and Liberalism,* and *The Religion of Paul.* 88, 97, 170, 173, 174, 175, 176, 179, 180, 181, 182, 237, 239

McIntire, Carl (1906-). Presbyterian minister, Fundamentalist crusader, writer, and educator. Pastor: Chelsea Presbyterian, Atlantic City, N. J., 1931-33; Collingswood Presbyterian, Collingswood, N. J., 1933-38. Founder and pastor, Bible Presbyterian Church, Collingswood, N. J., since 1938. Editor, *The Christian Beacon.* Founder: The Twentieth Century Reformation Hour (radio); the ACCC; the International Council of Christian Churches. A leader of Shelton College and Faith Seminary. One of the best-known militant Fundamentalists of our time. 88, 171, 181, 190, 195, 199, 210, 223, 233, 237, 238, 239, 240, 243, 253, 254, 271, 278

Mackay, John A. (1889-). Presbyterian educator and ecumenical leader. Head of a college, Lima, Peru, 1925. On the staff, South America YMCA 1926-32. Secretary, Presbyterian Board of Foreign Missions 1932-36. President, Princeton Seminary 1936-59. Professor of Hispanic thought, American U. since 1960. 194

McKee, Arthur W. (1891-1953). Executive director, Winona Lake Bible Conference 1938-53. Composed gospel hymns and choruses; directed music at Moody Church for 5 years and later at the Church of the Open Door, Los Angeles. 261

McLaurin, John B. (1884-1952). Canadian missions leader. Pastor, Dufferin Street Baptist, Toronto, 1907-09. A missionary in India 1909-38. General secretary, Canadian Foreign Mission Board 1939-52. Conservative missionary cooperating with Liberals, Modernists, and Conservatives to extend the missionary work. 109

McMaster, William (1811-87). Canadian statesman. Baptist layman who left his estate to found a school which was first located at Toronto and later at Hamilton, Ontario, and which is the present McMaster U. It began on evangelical truth, but now has become a liberal college. 106, 107, 109

McNeeley, George (1878-1970). Baptist pastor and Bible teacher. Came to the U. S. in 1890 from Northern Ireland; ordained into the Church of England but left it in 1907 to become a Baptist. Pastor, Elizabeth Avenue Baptist, Newark, N. J., 1908-64, and during part of this time, he pastored City Temple, Newark. A widely known prophecy teacher. 160

McPherson, Aimee Semple (1890-1944). Founder, Foursquare Gospel Church (Angelus Temple) in Los Angeles. Flamboyant and gifted public speaker and actress. Pentecostal in doctrine, claiming such gifts as healing and tongues. Founder, LIFE College. 156

MacPherson, Merrill T. (1891-1960). Evangelistic singer 1916-18. Presbyterian pastor: Ashton and Franklin Grove, Ill., 1921-23; Spencer Memorial, Brooklyn, N. Y., 1924-26. Radio evangelist, Newark N. J. Pastor, North Broad Street Presbyterian, Philadelphia, 1930-36. Left the Presbyterian Church U. S. A. in 1936. Founder, Church of the Open Door, Philadelphia, 1936 (now located in Fort Washington, Pa.). President, lFCA 1944-46. On many sound mission boards and school boards. 223, 239

McQuilkin, Robert C. (1886-1952). Presbyterian minister and educator. Associated with the *Sunday School Times*. Founder and president, Columbia Bible College, Columbia, S. C., 1923-52. Founder, Ben Lippen School and Ben Lippen Conference, Asheville, N. C. Victorious life speaker and writer. 268

MacRae, Allan A. (1902-). Presbyterian minister, scholar, and educator. Professor: Westminster Seminary 1929-37; Faith Theological Seminary 1937-71. Helped found the Biblical Theological Seminary near Philadelphia in 1971 and has been its head since 1971. 88, 181, 190, 237, 240

Maier, Walter A. (1893-1950). Missouri Lutheran Synod professor and radio broadcaster. Professor, Concordia Seminary 1922-50. World renowned for his broadcast The Lutheran Hour, at one time heard on 1,200 stations. His preaching was Christ-centered, pungent, and Gospel-exalting; his field of teaching was O. T. Had 20 books (most were radio sermons). 195, 255, 273

Malone, Tom (1915-). Founder and pastor, Immanuel Baptist, Pontiac, Mich., for 30 years. Before that, an asst. to H. H. Savage. Widely known for his evangelistic preaching and soulwinning conferences. Founder and president, Midwestern Baptist College. 80, 195, 255, 271

Manly, Basil (1825-92). Baptist pastor: Providence, Ala., 1848-49; First Baptist, Richmond, Va., and president, Richmond Female Institution 1850-54. Professor, Southern Baptist Seminary 1859-61, 1865-71, 1877-92. President, Georgetown College 1871-77. 112

Manning, H. E. (1808-92). Church of England leader who became a Roman Catholic in 1851 and was made a cardinal in 1875. Very effective and persuasive defender of Romanism on the basis of the antiquity and glories of the Roman church. 52

Marcel, Gabriel (1889-). Philosopher and theologian. Belonged to the existentialist school, starting with human ego; stressed the truth of "He-Thou" relationship; claimed man shares the life of God. 102

Marling, A. E. (1858-1935). Presbyterian layman of N. Y. Built the YMCA on West 23rd Street. Elder, Brick Presbyterian Church, N. Y. C. Trustee, Columbia U. and Princeton Seminary 1911-26. On the Board of Foreign Missions for the Presbyterian Church, U. S. A. for 27 years. Tolerant of Liberals who pushed the missions work from the Bible. 180

Marquis, David C. (1834-1912). Presbyterian pastor: Decatur, Ill., 1863-66; Chicago, 1866-70; Baltimore, 1870-78; St. Louis, 1878-83. Professor, McCormick Seminary 1883-1909. Moderator, General Assembly 1886. 45, 54, 55, 56

Marshall, L. H. (1882-1953). Canadian Baptist educator. Professor in homiletics and pastoral care, McMaster U. 1925-30. A Liberal in theology. Led many young Canadian Baptists away from Fundamental truth. 108, 109, 167

Martin, T. T. (1862-1939). Southern Baptist evangelist, teacher, and writer. Professor, Baylor Female College, Belton, Tex., 1886-88. Pastor: Glenview Baptist, Glenview, Ky., 1890-91; Leadville, Colo., 1891-93; Canon

City, Colo., 1894-95; Glenview, Ky., 1895-96; Beattyville, Ky., 1896-97; Cripple Creek, Ky., 1897-1900. Full-time evangelist 1900-39. Organized the Blue Mountain Evangelists. Author, 5 books (one was *Hell in Our High Schools*). 90, 162, 165

Massee, Jasper Cornelius (J. C.) (1871-1965). Prominent Baptist pastor: Fla.; Brooklyn (Baptist Temple), N. Y.; Tremont Temple, Boston, Mass., 1922-29 which, under his evangelistic preaching, grew to 4,000 members. Fundamental leader in the NBC until 1924 when he cooperated with Liberals. A moderate in the battle. Author, 23 books. 89, 113, 117, 130, 150, 151, 152, 154, 155, 156, 160, 162, 167, 169, 228, 261

Masteller, Kenneth W. (1912-). Pastor: Evangelical Congregational, Trevorton, Pa., 1934-40; Haddon Heights Baptist, Haddon Heights, N. J., 1940-73. Secretary, Association of Baptists for World Evangelization 1951-72. On the Board of Trustees, Baptist Bible College of Pa. 1962-72. Active GARB leader. 222

Mather, Cotton (1668-1728). Son of the famous Increase Mather of Boston. His father's associate for most of his life at the Second Church (Congregational) in Boston, serving in this church for 45 years. Dogmatic Puritan. Wrote some 400 works. His library was reputed to be the largest on the continent. 74

Mather, Increase (1639-1723). Outstanding Puritan thinker and leader in Boston, Mass. Pastor for 59 years of the Second Church of Boston. President, Harvard College 1685-1701. First man in America to hold a D.D. degree. Great theologian, preacher, leader of men. 74

Matteson, Earle E. (1915-). Trained and served under W. B. Riley in Minneapolis. Youth pastor, Fourth Baptist, Minneapolis, 1935-45. Asst. pastor, First Baptist, Tucson, Ariz., 1945-52. Pastor: Palo Verde Baptist, Tucson, 1952-64; Beth Eden Baptist, Denver, Colo., since 1964. Active in the work of Conservative Baptists, FBF, WBM, Baptist Bible College in Denver. 227

Matthews, I. G. (?-?). Professor of Hebrew and O. T., McMaster U., Hamilton, Ontario, 1904-19. Outspoken Liberal. Helped the university to drift into apostasy. 107, 108

Matthews, Mark (1867-1959). Presbyterian minister in Ga. and Tenn. before going to First Presbyterian Church, Seattle, Washington, which became the largest Presbyterian church in the world, with 110 elders, 65 deacons, 13 assistants, and 26 branch churches. He pastored there for 38 years. Orthodox and evangelistic, but refused to support Machen and the Independent Board and stayed inside the denomination when it went into apostasy. 96, 174, 179, 180, 257

Matthews, Shailer (1863-1941). Professor: Colby College 1887-94; U. of Chicago 1894-1933, teaching N. T. and systematic theology. A leading Modernist of his generation. Great figure in the sellout of the NBC to apostasy. 85, 93, 102, 110, 145, 146

Maxwell, L. E. (1895-). Canadian educator and writer. Founder, Prairie Bible Institute, Three Hills, Alberta, 1922; now its principal emeritus. The institute now enrolls 1,000 in high school and institute. Author, several books. 268

Meacham, H. C. (?-?). Mayor of Fort Worth 1925-27. Open opponent of J. Frank Norris and his ministry. Operated a department store in the city. 132

Mekeel, Herbert (1904-). Presbyterian minister and educator. Pastor, First Presbyterian, Schenectady, N. Y., since 1937. At one time, dean of students, Fuller Seminary. President, NAE 1958-60. Resourceful scholar, speaker, minister of the Gospel. 233

Melito (?-c. 190). Bishop of Sardis in Asia Minor. Early Christian martyr. Most of his writings have disappeared. He wrote one defense of the Church and addressed it to Marcus Aurelius, the Roman emperor. 36

Melvin, Billy (1929-). Freewill Baptist pastor: Newport, Tenn., 1951-53; Richmond, Va., 1953-57; Norfolk, Va., 1951-59. Executive secretary, National Association of Free Will Baptists 1959-67. Executive director, NAE since 1967. 245

Milheim, John E. (1934-). Baptist pastor: Riverside, N. J., 1957-60; Calvary Baptist, Norwalk, Ohio, 1960-64. General secretary, ACCC. Editor, ACCent. Now, Professor, Baptist Bible College of Pa. 239

Miller, Andrew (1810-83). Started as a Baptist pastor, but left to become an interdenominational Bible teacher. Joined the Brethren and wrote a history of this group. A close friend of C. H. MacIntosh (CHM). Emphasized soulwinning rather than the details of dispensationalism. 235

Miller, William (1782-1849). Started as a Baptist preacher in N. Y., but turned to Adventist teaching. Held that the Lord would return in 1843 or 1844; denied the millennial reign of Christ but affirmed His soon return. His date-setting was a serious error. Later Seventh Day Adventists (such as Ellen G. White) took up his doctrine. 74, 75

Mills, B. Fay (1857-1916). Congregational evangelist 1885-95. Left evangelism to go into social service, even to fellowship with the Unitarians. Returned to the true faith in 1915 and served faithfully for the last year of his life. 75, 77, 79

Milner, Isaac (1750-1820). English historian. Professor, Oxford, Strong supporter of the Church of England. Wrote a history of the church, An Ecclesiastical History, a standard history text. 74

Milton, John (1608-74). World famous English poet and Puritan figure. Author of such works as Paradise Lost and Paradise Regained. Strong advocate of religious liberty. One of England's most gifted writers. 39

Montgomery, Mrs. Helen Barrett (1861-1934). Daughter of a Baptist pastor. Taught Bible classes in the Philadelphia area for 40 years. President, NBC 1910. A delegate to the Baptist World Alliance in 1923. Willed half a million dollars to 86 churches, colleges, hospitals, and missions. 147

Moody, Dwight Lyman (D. L.) (1837-99). Congregational evangelist in America and England. Founder, Moody Bible Institute and Northfield Schools. It is claimed that he traveled a million miles and preached to 100 million people. 24, 45, 59, 68, 71, 76, 77, 78, 79, 80, 93, 112, 119, 261

Moody, Paul (1879-1947). Son of D. L. Moody. Congregational pastor, St. Johnsbury, Vt., 1912-17. Associate pastor, Madison Presbyterian Church,

N. Y. C., 1919-21. President, Middlebury College, V., 1921-42. Associate pastor, First Presbyterian Church, N. Y., 1942-47. 78, 119

Mooneyham, W. Stanley (1926-). Freewill Baptist pastor: Tecumseh, Okla., 1948-49; Sulphur, Okla., 1949-53. Executive secretary, National Association of Free Will Baptists 1953-59. Editor, *Evangelical Action* 1959-64. Served the Billy Graham Association 1964-69. President, World Vision since 1969. 244

Moorehead, William G. (W. G.) (1836-1914). Presbyterian missionary, pastor, and educator. Professor, Xenia Seminary 1873-99; its president in 1899. Ardent premillennialist. One of the editors of the Scofield Reference Bible. 28, 45, 58

Morgan, G. Campbell (1863-1945). Congregational pastor, Westminster Chapel 1904-16 and 1935-43. Professor: Bible Institute of Los Angeles; Gordon College. Wrote 60 books. One of the best expositors of his generation. His daughter-in-law recently wrote his biography, *Man of the Word.* 260

Morris, Sam (1900-). Baptist evangelist and crusader against liquor. Learned premillennial truth from A. C. Gaebelein; started a broadcast in 1928 while a pastor in Weatherford, Tex.; went on radio XERF, Del Rio, Tex., in 1936. Now a leading temperance speaker on The Voice of Temperance from San Antonio. 273

Morrison, Charles Clayton (1874-1966). Disciples of Christ leader. Pastor in Iowa and Ill. 1892-1904. Editor, *The Christian Century* 1908-47, *The Pulpit,* and *Christendom.* 102

Morrison, Henry C. (1857-1942). Methodist pastor: Bedford, Ky.; Stanford, Ky.; Covington, Ky.; Highlands, Ky. A key figure in promotion of Methodist holiness and sanctification. President, Asbury College. A godly and gifted old-fashioned Methodist. 88, 90, 174, 190, 248, 251, 270

Moser, M. L., Sr. (1899-). U. S. Army 1917-19. Baptist pastor: Humphrey, Ark., 1923-24; Pine Bluff, Ark., 1924-27; Van Buren, Ark., 1927-31; Central Baptist, Little Rock, Ark., 1931-65. Author, several books. 246

Moser, M. L., Jr. (1925-). U. S. Marine Corps 1944-48. Missionary in Mexico 1952-65. Pastor, Central Baptist, Little Rock, Ark., since 1965, succeeding his father. Has written 5 books, one of which is *Good News for Modern Man—The Devil's Masterpiece.* 246

Mott, John R. (1865-1955). Student secretary, International YMCA 1888-1915. General secretary, YMCA 1915-31. Active in the Student Volunteer Movement. President, WCC 1948. A central figure in ecumenical missions. A conservative who promoted church unity at the expense of Bible truth. 149, 239

Moulds, G. H. (1915-). Professor, Kent State U., since 1948. Author, 4 books. 113

Moyer, Robert L. (1886-1944). Evangelist 1915-20. Pastor, First United Brethren Church, Minneapolis, 1920-27. Became an asst. to W. B. Riley at First Baptist, Minneapolis, in 1927 and was chosen pastor of First Baptist in 1943. Professor, Northwestern Schools. A fine teacher, Fundamentalist, and leader. 120, 199

Müller, George (1805-98). Pastor, evangelist, and orphanage leader in England. Started an orphanage in Bristol in 1836; cared for 10,000 orphans in his lifetime. Entire work based on faith in the Lord and His provisions. Wrote 5 books to show the answers to faith. 75

Mullins, Edgar Y. (1860-1928). Baptist pastor and theologian. Pastor: Harrodsburg, Ky.; Baltimore, Md.; Newton, Mass. President, Southern Baptist Seminary 1899-1928. Taught theology. Solid Bible scholar and teacher. Author, several books. 70, 130

Munhall, Leander W. (L. W.) (1843-1934). Methodist evangelist and writer. Preached over 50 years. Editor, *The Methodist*. Lived most of his life in Germantown, Pa. Solid, premillennial, old-fashioned Methodist. A clean witness to the Gospel and sanctification as taught by Wesley. 28, 45, 72 76, 88, 114, 160, 161

Muntz, J. Palmer (1897-). Baptist pastor: Chaffee, N. Y., 1923-24; Cazenovia Baptist, Buffalo, N. Y., 1924-62. Director, Winona Lake Bible Conference 1939-58, the largest of its kind in the world. Served in the Conservative Baptist Association of America, CBF, CBFMS. Now retired and lives in King of Prussia, Pa. 261

Murch, James Deforest (1892-). Ordained Disciples of Christ minister. Pastor, Disciples Church, Pittsburgh, Pa., 1915-16. Asst. editor, *The Standard* 1916-18. Professor, Cincinnati Bible Seminary 1925-37. Worked with the Standard Publishing Company 1934-45. Editor, *Evangelical Action* 1945-58. Author, 16 books. 233, 234

Murray, John (1898-). Professor: Princeton Seminary; Westminster Seminary 1930-66. Supported the Orthodox stand of Machen; taught in the field of systematic theology; retired in 1966; returned to his native Scotland. 181, 237

Musson, Wayne C. (1928-). Pastor: Central Baptist, Minneapolis, 1954-58; First Baptist, Lake Crystal, Minn., 1959-62; Oakdale Baptist, Oakdale, Minn., 1962-68; First Baptist, Rochelle, Ill., since 1969. Has served on boards of Minnesota Baptist Convention and Central Baptist Seminary. President and vice-president, New Testament Association of Independent Baptist Churches 1969-71. 249

Myers, Courtland (1864-1941). Baptist pastor: First, Syracuse, N. Y., 1890-93; First (later, Baptist Temple), Brooklyn, N. Y., 1893-1909; Tremont Temple, Boston, Mass., 1909-21; Immanuel Baptist, Pasadena, Calif., in 1921. One of the most stimulating hard-hitting Fundamentalists of his day. 89, 113, 147, 150, 152, 159, 273

N

Narramore, Bruce (1941-). Staff psychologist, Child Guidance Clinic, Lexington, Ky., 1965-67. Director of Counselling Services, Christian Counselling Center, Rosemead, Calif., 1967-69. Academic dean, Rosemead Graduate School of Psychology since 1969. Author, 2 books. 275

Narramore, Clyde M. (1916-). Consulting psychologist on the staff of the Los Angeles County Schools for 14 years. Founder and president, Narramore Christian Foundation, Rosemead, Calif. President, Rosemead Graduate School of Psychology. Author, several books. Has conducted many seminars. 269, 275

Neal, Marshall (1919-   ). Minister and educator. With Bob Jones U. as professor of N. T. since 1945, acting registrar 1957-58, registrar 1958-65, dean of the school of religion since 1965. Associate editor, *Biblical Viewpoint*. 271

Needham, George C. (1840-1902). Born in Ireland. Knew C. H. Spurgeon and H. Grattan Guinness. Came to the U. S. in 1867. Widely known for his role as secretary of the prophetic conferences in 1878 and 1886. Evangelist and Bible teacher. 28, 45, 46, 47, 62, 70, 75, 76, 165

Neighbour, Robert Edward (R. E.) (1872-1945). Missionary to Brazil under Southern Baptists. Pastor: East Macon Baptist, Macon, Ga., 1896-1901; Marue Baptist, Dublin, Ga., 1901-02; First Baptist, Americus, Ga., 1902-06; First, Salisbury, N. C., 1906-08; Southside Baptist, Spartanburg, S. C., 1908-11; Tabernacle Baptist, Augusta, Ga., 1914-16; First Baptist, Elyria, Ohio, 1919-25; Rader Tabernacle, Chicago, 1926-27; Mount Pleasant Baptist, Vancouver, Canada, 1930-31. After 1931, in Bible teaching. 89, 109, 163, 165, 166

Nelson, Edward J. (1923-   ). Evangelism 1949-60. Pastor, South Sheridan Baptist, Denver, Colo., since 1960, which had 140 in Sunday School in 1960 and in 1972 it averaged 1,700. President, Silver State High School. Aggressive Fundamentalist. 271

Newell, William R. (1868-1956). Once a pastor of a Congregational church, but for most of his adult life, he was identified with the Plymouth Brethren. A Bible teacher. R. A. Torrey sent him out to teach classes in St. Louis, Detroit, and Torqnto. In the 1920s he published *Romans*; in the 1930s, *Revelation*; and in the 1940s, *Hebrews*. All were great helps to Bible believers. 235, 260

Newman, A. H. (1852-1933). Baptist historian and educator. Professor: Southern Baptist Seminary 1877-81; McMaster U. 1881-1901; Baylor U. 1901-09; Southwestern Baptist Seminary 1909-13; Baylor U. 1913-20; Mercer U. 1921-29. Wrote a widely used text in church history. 116

Newman, John Henry (1801-90). English scholar and churchman who left the Church of England to join the Roman Catholic Church. Led 200 Anglican priests to follow him into Catholicism; wrote the famous hymn "Lead, Kindly Light"; elected a cardinal in the Roman church. 52

Newton, B. W. (1805-98). Early leader of the Plymouth Brethren in England. Opposed the "secret rapture" of J. N. Darby and later left the Brethren and pastored in London. Widely respected for his Bible knowledge. Author, several books. 73, 75, 235

Newton, John B. (1839-?). Church of England leader and bishop of Va. Rector: St. Luke's, Norfolk, Va.; Monument Church, Richmond, Va.; Essex County, Va. 30

Newton, Louie D. (1892-   ). Southern Baptist pastor. President, SBC 1940s. Professor, Mercer U. 1913-18. Editor, *The Christian Index* 1920-29. Pastor, Druid Hills Baptist Church, Atlanta, Ga., 1929-68. Not formally trained for pulpit ministry, but a gifted speaker with charm and congeniality. Helped Southern Baptists into further apostasy. 129, 182

Nicholson, William Rufus (W. R.) (1822-1901). Methodist pastor in New Orleans 1843-47. Left Methodism to join the Protestant Episcopal in which he served four churches: Grace Church Mission, New Orleans, 1847-49; St. John's Church, Cincinnati, Ohio, 1849-59; St. Paul's Church, Boston, Jass., 1859-72; Trinity Church, Newark, N. J., 1872-75. In 1875 he left the Episcopal Church to join the Reformed Episcopal Church where he served the Second Church (later, St. Paul's), Philadelphia, and in 1876 was ordained a bishop. Professor, Reformed Episcopal Seminary 1877-1901; its dean. 28, 34, 45, 47, 62, 70

Niebuhr, H. Richard (1894-1962). Evangelical Reformed scholar and writer. Joined the faculty, Yale Divinity School in 1931. His major field, social ethics and the work of building the "Kingdom" through Christian activities. 13, 102

Niebuhr, Reinhold (1892-1971). Minister of the Evangelical Synod of the Lutheran church. Pastor, Bethlehem Evangelical Church, Detroit, 1917-30. Professor, Union Seminary, N. Y. C., 1930-60. His field, applied Christianity. Author, many books. Acknowledged neo-orthodox scholar. 98, 120

Nietzsche, F. W. (1844-1900). German philosopher, heretic, and critic of Christian truth. Avid disciple of German radicalism. Taught that the German race was superior. Professor, Basel U. An atheist. Helped prepare for German socialism. 117, 152

Norris, George L. (1916-73). Son of J. Frank Norris. Asst., First Baptist Church, Fort Worth, Tex., 1942-44. Pastor, Gideon Baptist, Fort Worth, 1944-72. Professor, Bible Baptist Seminary (now Arlington Baptist Schools), Arlington, Tex., 1957-69. President, WBF 1953-57. Director of missions, WBF 1957-62. 132, 198

Norris, J. Frank (1877-1952). Pastor: Mt. Calm Baptist Church, Mt. Calm, Tex., while a student at Baylor U. 1898-1902; McKinney Avenue Baptist, Dallas, Tex., 1905-07. Editor, *The Baptist Standard* 1907-09. Pastor: First Baptist, Fort Worth, 1909-52; Temple Baptist, Detroit, 1934-48. Editor, *The Fundamentalist* (formerly, *The Fence Rail* and *The Searchlight*). The stormy and colorful Fundamentalist of Tex. with unusual gifts in preaching, Sunday School work, sensationalism, revivalism, and training preachers. 80, 85, 86, 87, 89, 105, 108, 109, 115, 122-134, 161, 163, 165, 166, 167, 168, 169, 170, 171, 172, 181, 182, 189, 197, 217, 220, 221, 226, 228, 272, 273

North, Frank M. (1850-1935). Methodist pastor: Florida, N. Y., 1873-74; Armenia, N. Y., 1874-76; Cold Spring-on-the-Hudson, N. Y., 1876-78; N. Y. C., 1879-87; Middleton, Conn., 1887-92. Secretary, New York City Extension 1892-1912. Editor, *The Christian City*. President, FCC 1916-20. 14

O

Ockenga, Harold John (1905-). Presbyterian minister, educator, New Evangelical leader. Pastor: Pittsburgh, 1930-36; Park Street Church, Boston, Mass., 1936-69. President, Gordon College and Gordon-Conwell Divinity School, Wenham, Mass., since 1969. Chairman of the trustees of Fuller Seminary when it opened in 1947. Coined the name "New Evangelicalism" and in 1957 clearly defined it. Strong supporter of new-evangelical movements and men. 162, 192, 203, 204, 205, 225, 234, 235, 255, 273, 279

O'Donnell, J. D. (1929-). Freewill Baptist pastor: Ragland, Ala., 1949-50; Columbus, Miss., 1950-55; Laurel, Miss., 1956-60; Richton, Miss., 1957-61; Grant Avenue Church, Springfield, Mo., 1971-73. Professor, Free Will Baptist Bible College, Nashville, Tenn., 1961-65. President, Hillsdale Baptist Bible College 1965-71. Editorial manager, Free Will Baptist Sunday School Department since 1973.

Oldham, Earl (1920-). Pastor, Calvary Baptist, Grand Prairie, Tex., since 1945. Dean and acting president, Bible Baptist Seminary 1952-53; its president (now Arlington Baptist Schools) since 1953. A leader in the WBF and key figure in the continuing ministry of J. Frank Norris. 134, 198, 226

Olford, Stephen F. (1918-). Baptist pastor: Richmond, England 1953-59; Calvary Baptist Church, N. Y. C., 1959-73. Very active in the Keswick movement and strong supporter of new-evangelical groups. On radio and TV. 191, 267

Olson, Arnold T. (1910-). Minister of Evangelical Free Church. Pastor: Houston, Minn., 1930-33; West Orange, N. J., 1933; Staten Island, N. Y., 1933-37; Minn., 1944-52. President of his denomination and a trustee of Trinity College since 1952. 209

Origen (Origenes Adamantius) (185-254). Church Father, teacher, and writer. Lived in Egypt and Caesarea. An ascetic. Wrote voluminously for his day, including the *Hexapla,* a 6-column Bible with various texts. Excellent student, but stressed allegorical interpretation of the Bible (always looking for hidden meanings). One of the founders of the amillennial view of the Bible. 30, 41, 63, 74

Overholtzer, J. Irwin (1877-1955). Church of the Brethren background. Encouraged by H. A. Ironside and Paul Rood to start a special ministry to reach children; founded Child Evangelism in 1936 in Rood's office at the Bible Institute of Los Angeles; gave his full time to it until he retired in 1952. 257

Oxnam, G. Bromley (1891-1963). Methodist pastor, Los Angeles, 1917-27. Secretary, Los Angeles Missionary and Church Extension. Professor of theology, Boston U. 1927-28. President, DePauw U. 1928-36. Leading Methodist Modernist. Elected a bishop in 1936. One of the promoters of Methodist apostasy. 196, 239

P

Papias (60-130). Bishop of Hierapolis. Tradition held that he was a student of the Apostle John and a friend of Polycarp. Devout Bible believer. Most of his writings have been lost. Held to the Lord's coming as a main truth. 36

Paramore, Jack (1936-). Freewill Baptist pastor: Kingston, N. C., 1955; Clarkesville, Tenn., 1957-58; Director of development, Free Will Baptist Bible College, Nashville, Tenn., since 1966. Evangelism 1958-66. 244

Parker, Monroe (1909-). Evangelist, educator, conference speaker, and missions leader. President, Pillsbury Baptist Bible College 1958-65. President, WBM. Constantly in revival meetings. Lives in Decatur, Ala. Fundamentalist leader. 200, 207, 227, 232, 255, 271

Parsons, Henry M. (1828-1913). Outstanding Presbyterian pastor, prophecy speaker, and Bible conference leader. Pastor: N. J.; Pa.; Buffalo, N. Y.; Knox Presbyterian, Toronto, Canada. Leader: prophetic conferences of 1878 and 1886; Sea Cliff Conference after 1900 when it broke from the Niagara Conference over the issue of the pretribulational rapture of the Church. 28, 33, 45, 54, 72

Patterson, A. L. (1903-). ABA pastor in DeKalb, Tex. Accountant with the Baptist Sunday School Committee of the ABA 1938-44; its business manager 1944-52. Secretary-treasurer of the missions of ABA since 1952. 214

Patterson, Frederic W. (1877-1965). Canadian Baptist pastor and educator. Pastor: Minnedosa, Manitoba, 1900-01; Winnipeg, 1901-04; Prince Albert 1904-05; Fir Baptist, Calgary, 1905-09; Edmonton, 1909-16; Winnipeg, 1916-19. Baptist secretary of the West 1919-23. President, Acadia U., Wolfville, Nova Scotia, Canada, 1923-48. A conservative Liberal who helped ruin Canadian Baptists. 109

Patton, Francis L. (1843-1932). Presbyterian pastor and educator. Pastor, N. Y. C. Professor, McCormick Seminary 1872-81. President and professor, Princeton Seminary 1881-1913. Moderator, General Assembly 1879. A champion of Orthodoxy. Last head of both the seminary and university at Princeton. 174, 176, 177

Peabody, Francis G. (1847-1936). Professor of theology, Harvard Divinity School 1881-86; its professor of Christian morals 1886-1913; its dean of the divinity school 1901-05. Liberal writer, promoting the building of the "Kingdom" as a social ideal. 68

Peale, Norman Vincent (1898-). Methodist minister and pastor, Marble Collegiate Church, N. Y. C., since 1932. Widely known for his books on positive thinking and self-rescue. Three characteristics of his writing: humor, humility, and humanity. 95, 102, 196, 210, 218, 252, 279

Pendleton, James M. (1811-91). Baptist pastor: Bethel, Hopkinsville, and Bowling Green, Ky.; Murfreesboro, Tenn.; Hamilton, Ohio; Upland, Pa. First theologian of Landmarkism. Editor, *The Tennessee Baptist*. Author, 9 books. The best-known writing, *An Old Landmark Reset* 1856. 214, 241

Pentecost, George F. (1841-1920). Presbyterian pastor: Ind.; N. Y.; Ky.; Boston, Mass. A Bible teacher. Served on the Board of Commissioners for Foreign Missions (Congregational). Wrote a 10-volume set on the Bible. 74

Pentecost, J. Dwight (1915-). Presbyterian pastor and educator. Pastor, St. John's Presbyterian, Devon, Pa., 1946-51. Professor: Philadelphia College of Bible 1948-55; Dallas Seminary since 1956. Pastor, Grace Bible, Dallas, Tex. 260

Percy, Jack O. (1908-). Missionary under SIM in Nigeria beginning in 1932. On the home staff, SIM. Resigned from SIM in 1959. Executive secretary, Interdenominational Foreign Missions Association 1959-62. Full-time Bible conference and missionary conference ministry since 1962. Has served with the Inter-Mission Orientation Program. 224

Peters, George N. H. (1825-1909). Lutheran pastor in Xenia and Springfield, Ohio. Wrote a 3-volume work on the millennial reign of Christ,

The Theocratic Kingdom. A contributing editor of *The Watchword.* 45, 50, 62, 63

Peters, George W. (1907-). Mennonite pastor, educator, and missions leader. Pastor: Fresno, Calif.; Buhler, Kan. Professor, Dallas Seminary since 1961. Articulate supporter of Evangelism-In-Depth, a form of New Evangelicalism on mission fields. 209, 225, 272, 280

Pettingill, William L. (1886-1950). Baptist Bible teacher, pastor, and writer. Helped found the Philadelphia School of the Bible in 1914 and served as its dean until 1928. Editor, *Serving and Waiting.* Excellent Bible expositor. Pastor: North Baptist, Wilmington, Del., 1903-13; First Baptist, N. Y., 1948-50. 97, 109, 120, 125, 150, 160, 161, 163, 165, 166, 169, 210, 223, 260

Pfleiderer, Otto (1839-1908). German religious leader. Professor, U. of Berlin. Tried to make Christianity relevant to his times; held Christianity included the truths of all other religions and philosophies. 41, 139

Phillips, Chester R. (1922)-). Pastor: Free Will Baptist Church, Smithfield, N. C., for 7 years; Nashville, Tenn., for 1 year; Greenville, N. C., since 1962. Has served on several Freewill Baptist boards in missions and education. 245

Philpott, Peter W. (1866-1957). Baptist pastor in Ind. Founder and pastor, Philpott Tabernacle, Hamilton, Ontario, 1892-1918. Pastor: Moody Memorial Church, Chicago, 1920-29; Church of the Open Door, Los Angeles, 1929-31. Noted Bible preacher and teacher. 88, 160, 256

Picirilli, Robert E. (1932-). Freewill Baptist pastor and educator. Professor: Free Will Baptist College, Nashville, Tenn., since 1955; its registrar since 1960. Pastor, Cofer's Chapel Church, Nashville, 1962-64. 244

Pickering, Ernest D. (1928-). Baptist pastor and educator. Pastor, Maranatha Bible Church, New Kensington, Pa., 1954-56. National executive secretary, IFCA 1954-59. Professor, Central Baptist Seminary of Minneapolis 1959-65. Pastor, Bible Baptist Church, Kokomo, Ind., 1965-69. Dean and president, Baptist Bible College of Pa. since 1970. 210, 227

Pierce, Earle V. (1869-1959). Baptist pastor: Ironton, Ohio, 1894-1900; First, Brookings, S. D. 1914-24; Lake Harriett, Minneapolis, 1924-39. Professor, Northwestern Schools 1911-21 and 1925-34. President, NBC 1937. 156

Pierson, Arthur T. (1837-1911). Presbyterian minister: Winstead, Conn., 1860; Binghamton, N. Y., 1860-62; Troy, N. Y., 1863; Waterford, N. Y., 1863-69; Second Church, Detroit, 1869-82; Second, Indianapolis, 1882-83; Bethany, Philadelphia, 1883-91. Became a Baptist in 1891. Pastor, Spurgeon's Tabernacle, London, 1891-93. Editor, *Missionary Review of the World.* Lecturer, Exeter Hall, London, 1904-07. Author, 14 books. 26, 45, 48, 49, 75, 76

Pietsch, W. E. (1886-1959). Missionary in the Orient. On the staff, Church of the Open Door, Los Angeles. An extensive Bible ministry. Pastor, Calvary Gospel Center, Grand Rapids, Mich. Had a daily radio program for 17 years. Founder and director, Alaska Evangelization Society in 1935. 223

Pike, James A. (1913-69). Modernist bishop of the Church of England with an office in San Francisco. A sarcastic critic of everything believed by Fundamentalists. Dean: St. John's, N. Y. C., 1952-58; Grace Cathedral, San Francisco, 1958-69. Founder, Foundation for Religious Transition. Influential apostate. 51-52, 102, 208, 252, 279

Pittman, James (1940-). Freewill Baptist pastor: Tenn., 1965-68; Ala., since 1968, now, Mt. Olive Free Will Baptist, Guin, Ala. A Fundamentalist voice. 245

Pius X (1835-1914). Italian leader of the Roman Catholic Church. Pope, 1902-14. Known as the Peasant Pope. Condemned Modernism. Vigorous opponent of all forms of Protestantism and of the separation of church and state. 67

Polycarp (69-155). Early Church Father. Disciple of the Apostle John. Burned at the stake as a Christian martyr. Probably bishop of Smyrna at an early age. A saintly figure. 36

Porter, Ford (1893-). Baptist pastor: Evansville, Ind.; First Baptist, Princeton, Ind.; Berean Missionary Baptist, Indianapolis, 1940-47; Lifegate Baptist, Indianapolis (formerly, Berean Gospel Temple), since 1947. Founder, Indiana Baptist College. Best known for his tract "God's Simple Plan of Salvation" of which 250 million copies have been sold. 211

Porter, J. W. (1863-1937). Baptist pastor and editor. Pastor: Germantown and Colliersville, Tenn.; Olive Branch Church, Miss.; Pee Wee Valley, Ky.; First, Newport News, Va.; First Baptist, Lexington, Ky., for 14 years; Third Avenue, Louisville, Ky., for 3 years; Immanuel Baptist, Lexington, Ky., for 14 years. Editor, *The Western Recorder* 1905-19. 88, 162

Poteat, Edwin M. (1861-1937). Baptist pastor: Chapel Hill, N. C., 1884-86; Lee Street, Baltimore, Md., 1886-88; Calvary, New Haven, Conn., 1888-98; Memorial, Philadelphia, 1898-1903; President, Furman U. 1903-18. On the board of promotion, SBC 1918-21. Professor, U. of Shanghai 1921-27. Interim pastor, First, Richmond, 1927-29. Pastor, Second Baptist, Atlanta, Ga., 1929-31. Professor, Furman U. 1931-37. Married a daughter of A. J. Gordon. Baptist Liberal. 25

Potter, Charles F. (1885-1962). Baptist pastor: Dover, N. H., 1908-10; Mattapan, Mass., 1910-14. Became a Unitarian; pastored Unitarian churches: Edmonton, Alberta, 1915-16; Marlborough, Mass., 1916-18; West Side Church, N. Y. C., 1919-25. Joined the Universalists in 1925. Pastor: The Church of Divine Paternity, N. Y. C., 1927-29; First Humanist Society, N. Y. C., 1929-62. 137

Powell, Adam Clayton (1908-71). Negro pastor, Abyssinia Baptist, N. Y. C. Congressman in the 79th to 87th congresses. Vigorous civil rights spokesman. Congress removed him from his seat. 219

Powers, A. T. (1896-). ABA pastor in Ark. and Tex. Secretary-treasurer of ABA missions 1948-52. Dean, Missionary Bible Institute, Minden, La., 1957-61. President, ABA 1957-58. 216

Powers, J. B. (1921-). ABA pastor in Tex. Recording secretary, ABA 1956-68. Moderator, Missionary Baptists of Ark. since 1972. Business manager, Sunday School Committee, ABA since 1968. 216

Price, Amos (1944-   ). Southern Methodist pastor: Denny Memorial, Sandy Run, S. C., 1965-68; Carolina Heights, North Augusta, S. C., 1968-71; Independent Methodist, Macon, Ga., since 1971. On the board of trustees, Francis Asbury Society; its secretary since 1972. 247

Pugh, William B. (1889-1950). Presbyterian church leader. Pastor: Beacon Street, Philadelphia, 1915-28; First Presbyterian, Chester, Pa., 1929-38. Asst. to the stated clerk, Presbyterian Church, U. S. A. 1922-38. Stated clerk 1938-50. On the executive committee, FCC. 239

Pusey, E. B. (1800-82). English Bible scholar, especially of the O. T. Belonged to the High Church which is much like the Roman Catholic. Open-minded when apostasy ruined the Church of England. 73

R

Rader, Daniel Paul (1879-1938). Pastor: a congregational church, Boston, Mass.; Congregational Church, Portland, 1906-08; Christian and Missionary Alliance Church, Pittsburgh, 1909-11; Christian and Missionary Alliance Tabernacle, Pittsburgh, 1912-15; Moody Church, Chicago, 1915-21; Chicago Gospel Tabernacle 1922-29; a tabernacle, Los Angeles, 1931-33; a tabernacle, Fort Wayne, Ind., 1933-35. President, Christian and Missionary Alliance, 1921-23. Left the Christian and Missionary Alliance in 1924 although he had been its president succeeding A. B. Simpson. Strong evangelist. 90, 261

Rader, Lyell M. (1876-1937). Christian Chemist. Widely used speaker to defend the scientific accuracy of the Bible. Brother of evangelists Paul and Luke Rader. Active in Salvation Army work. Said to have been a big witness with a big heart to go with his 350-pound body. 261

Radmacher, Earl (1931-   ). President and professor, Western Baptist Seminary, Portland, Ore. Openly cooperates with Campus Crusade. Open spokesman for New Evangelicalism. 274

Raedeke, T. A. (1914-   ). Lutheran minister of the Missouri Synod. Has served churches in Oklahoma City, and Deer River, Okla.; Duluth, and Wayzata, Minn. Director of evangelism for the synod for 14 years. Now, executive director of Key 73. 274, 276

Ragland, George (1876-1957). Professor: Baylor U. 1901-10; Georgetown College 1910-22. Pastor, First Baptist, Lexington, Ky., 1922-57. Editor, *The Sling and the Stone.* A strong contender for his convictions, but stayed inside the SBC. 130

Ramm, Bernard (1916-   ). Professor: Bethel Seminary; Baylor U. 1954-59; California Baptist Seminary in systematic theology since 1959. Author, 10 books, one of the best-known being *The Christian View of Science and the Scriptures.* Defender of new-evangelical concepts. 206

Raper, W. Burkette (1927-   ). Freewill Baptist educator and leader. Promotional director, Free Will Baptist State Convention of North Carolina 1953-54. President, Mt. Olive College, Mt. Olive, N. C., since 1954. A key figure in the Original Free Will Baptist (North Carolina). Has served on several state commissions and councils in his work with junior colleges. 245

Rasmussen, Roland (1920-   ). Evangelistic pastor of Canoga Park Baptist

Church, Canoga Park, Calif. Aggressive pulpit ministry in a growing area. 271

Rauschenbusch, Walter (1861-1918). Baptist pastor and educator. Pastor of a German Baptist church in N. Y. Professor, Rochester Seminary 1902-18. One of the leading figures in the social gospel. His book *The Theology of the Social Gospel* is a blueprint for reforming society to make it the Kingdom of God. An apostate Baptist. 85, 93, 94

Rawlings, John W. (1914-). Baptist pastor: Central Baptist, Tyler, Tex., 1940-51; Landmark Baptist Temple (formerly Lockland Baptist), Cincinnati, Ohio, since 1951. One of the founders of the BBF. Broadcasts his evening service over a network of stations as The Landmark Hour. Vice-president, Baptist Bible College, Springfield, Mo. Strong preacher and soulwinner. 133, 195, 198, 217, 218, 219, 255, 272, 278

Ray, Frank H. (1909-). Born and brought up in an old-fashioned Methodist church and family. A pastor in the Methodist Church (now the United Methodist) until 1953 when he resigned from his charge, the Holbrook Methodist, Atlanta, Ga. Founder and pastor since 1953, First Evangelical Church, Marietta, Ga. 248

Rayburn, James C., Jr. (1909-70). Presbyterian minister. Associated with his father in evangelism. A Sunday School missionary under the Presbyterian Board of Missions at Chama, N. M. Started the Young Life Campaign of U. S. A. in 1940; moved to Star Ranch, Colorado Springs, Colo., in 1947; retired from Young Life in 1964. 259

Rayburn, Robert (1915-). Presbyterian minister and educator. Pastor: Bellevue, Neb.; Gainesville, Tex.; Wheaton, Ill.; Hazelwood, Mo. President: Highland College, Pasadena, Calif., 1952-55; Covenant Seminary, St. Louis, since 1955. Now a member of the Reformed Presbyterian Church, Evangelical Synod. 238, 239

Rector, W. Lee (1883-1945). Professor: Baylor U.; Oklahoma Baptist U. Founder and president, Orthodox Baptist Institute, Ardmore, Okla., 1944-45. Editor, *The Orthodox Baptist.* Founder and pastor, First Orthodox Baptist Church, Ardmore, Okla., 1931-45. 246

Reddin, A. R. (1918-72). Director of the Harvest Gleaner Hour (radio) for the BMA 1971-72. Part-time pastorates in Ark. 1945-51. President, Central Baptist College, Conway, Ark., 1954-66; Southwestern Baptist College, Laurel, Miss., 1969-71. 241

Rediger, Milo A. (1913-). Friends pastor: Oak Ridge, Ind., 1936-38; Independent Evangelical Mennonite Church, Fort Wayne, 1938-40. Director, 146 Street Mission, N. Y. C., 1941-43. Professor, Taylor U. since 1943; its dean 1945-65; its president since 1965. 274

Redpath, Alan (1907-). Baptist pastor: Duke Street, Richmond, England, 1940-53; Moody Memorial Church, Chicago, 1953-62; Charlotte Chapel, Edinburgh, 1963-67. Well-known Keswick speaker and writer. Deeper life conferences. Now lives at Capernwray Fellowship in England. Director, Unevangelized Fields Missions. Evangelical; openly supports New Evangelicals. 21, 191, 267

Reed, Roy (1926-). ABA pastor in Ark., Kan., and Calif. Recording secretary, ABA since 1955. President: Oklahoma Missionary Baptist Institute 1957; California Baptist Institute since 1962. 216

Rees, Paul (1900-). Associate pastor, Pilgrim Tabernacle, Pasadena, Calif., 1920-23. Supt., Holiness Tabernacle, Detroit, 1928-32. Pastor, First Covenant Church, Minneapolis, 1938-58. On staff, World Vision since 1958. President, NAE 1952-54. Author, 18 books. 162, 205

Reuss, Edward G. E. (1804-91). Bible scholar and theologian from Alsace in Europe. Professor, U. of Strasburg for 60 years. A leading critic of the O. T. Prepared the way for the critical views of Graf and Wellhausen in that they denied the inspiration of the five books of Moses. 139

Revell, Fleming H. (1849-1931). Brother-in-law of D. L. Moody. Entered the publishing business in 1869. President, F. H. Revell Company 1890-1931. Trustee: N. Y. YMCA; Wheaton College; Mission to the Lepers. Also associated with New York Life Insurance Company. 72

Reynolds, Marion H., Jr. (1919-). Pastor, Grace Fundamental, Los Angeles. One of the founders (along with his father, M. H. Reynolds) of the Fundamental Bible Institute in 1936. Has helped found other Fundamental Bible churches. Active Fundamentalist spokesman and writer. Author, 70 booklets. A leader in the ACCC. 211

Reynolds, Walter (1926-). Freewill Baptist pastor: Nashville, Tenn., 1950-51; Goldsboro, N. C., 1951-53; Ahoskie, N. C., 1953-56; Ayden, N. C., 1956-59; Snow Hill, N. C., 1959-63; Dunn, N. C., 1963-66; General manager, Free Will Baptist Press, Ayden, N. C., since 1966. 245

Rhoades, Glen (1922-). Pastor, Manor Baptist Church, San Leandro, Calif., since 1945. Active Fundamentalist. A consistent supporter of San Francisco Baptist Seminary since its opening in 1958. 232

Rian, Edwin H. (1900-). Presbyterian minister, Westfield, N. J., 1928-30. Executive secretary, trustees, Westminster Seminary 1930-47. Vice-president: Trinity U., San Antonio, 1948-50; Beaver College 1950-54. President: Jamestown College 1954-60; Biblical Theological Seminary, N. Y., 1960-63. American Bible Society since 1963. Left the Orthodox Presbyterian to rejoin the Presbyterian Church, U. S. A. in 1947. Author, 5 books. His work, *The Presbyterian Conflict,* is a fine study of the Machen protest within Presbyterianism. 96, 137, 176

Rice, Bill (1912-). Baptist pastor: Gainesville, Tex., 1935-37; Dubuque Bible Church, Dubuque, Iowa, 1939-41. Full-time evangelist since 1941. Director, the Bill Rice Ranch, Murfreesboro, Tenn. Co-editor, *The Sword of the Lord.* Has a special ministry at his ranch to the deaf. 271

Rice, John R. (1896-). Baptist pastor, educator, writer, revivalist, and radio preacher. Launched *The Sword of the Lord* in 1934 which now has a circulation of 250,000; has written 124 books with a circulation of 36 million. An authority on soulwinning. Has led many conferences on soulwinning and revivalism. His headquarters is in Murfreesboro, Tenn. 120, 207, 242, 253, 271, 281

Rice, William R. (1920-). Pastor, Inter-City Baptist Church, Detroit, Mich., for several years. Has a large Christian day school and an impressive and magnificent senior citizens' home. A knowledgeable and gifted Fundamentalist with a keen awareness of present issues. 271

Riggs, Raymond (1915-). Founder, Central Free Will Baptist Church, Royal Oak, Mich., in 1938; its pastor 1938-53. Pastor, Bethany Free Will Baptist Church, Norfolk, Va., 1960-67. General director, Free Will Baptist Foreign Mission Board since 1967. Served 1 year as vice-moderator of the National Association of Free Will Baptists. 244

Riley, William Bell (1861-1947). Baptist pastor: Bloomington, Ill.; Calvary Baptist, Chicago; First Baptist, Minneapolis, Minn., 1897-1943. Ardent, knowledgeable Fundamentalist. Able debater. Founder and president, Northwestern Schools. A key figure in the WCFA and BBU. A gifted expositor of the popular style. Protested the drift of.the NBC into apostasy, but was unable to reverse the trend. 71, 80, 85, 86, 87, 105, 109, 112-121, 124, 130, 146, 147, 149, 150, 152, 153, 162, 163, 164, 165, 166 167, 169, 171, 172, 181, 189, 197, 199, 200, 208, 221, 228, 230, 231, 234, 261

Riley, Mrs. W. B. (1887-1971). Served at Northwestern Schools as dean of women and professor of English. Retired in 1958; married Dr. Riley in 1933, his first wife having died in 1931. Wrote a book on etiquette and a short biography of Dr. Riley. 113, 200

Rimmer, Harry (1890-1952). Pastor, First Friends Church, Los Angeles, 1916-19. Became a Presbyterian in 1919. Conference speaker, International Committee of YMCA 1920-25. Principal, Research Science Bureau 1920-55. Pastor, First Presbyterian, Duluth, Minn., 1934-40. Author, 41 books. Editor, *The Christian Faith and Life.* 90, 162

Ritchie, Homer (1926-). Pastor: Central Baptist, Athens, Tex., 1949-52; First Baptist, Fort Worth, Tex., since 1953, succeeding J. Frank Norris. Has led his congregation in building a beautiful new edifice. 122, 198

Ritschl, Albrecht (1822-89). Influential German Modernist. Scholar, writer, and teacher. Accepted critical views of the Bible, denying most sound doctrines and stressing the Kingdom of God as the religious community based on the love of God. In our response to that love, we form "value judgments." 7, 9, 10, 139

Roberson, Lee (1909-). Baptist pastor: Germantown, Memphis, and Greenbrier, Tenn.; now at Highland Park Baptist Church, Chattanooga, Tenn., since 1942. The church has grown to 33,000 members, including 40 branch chapels. Founder and president, Tennessee Temple Schools (starting in 1946). Hard working pastor, preacher, and soulwinner. 80, 195, 242, 243, 271, 278

Roberts, Oral (1918-). Pentecostal preacher with many large revival meetings. Founder and president, Oral Roberts U., Tulsa, Okla. Has a nationwide radio and TV ministry; has joined the United Methodist Church; has been accepted by the New Evangelicals. 196, 210, 234, 253, 281

Robertson, Archibald T. (A. T.) (1863-1934). Outstanding Baptist scholar, N. T. teacher, and writer. Professor of N. T. Greek, Southern Baptist Seminary 1888-1934. His Greek grammar of 1,400 pages was the greatest in the field. Author, 44 books. Conservative Baptist teacher. 174, 260

Robinson, Clifford E. (1928-). Baptist pastor: Theta, Tenn., 1949-50; Mt. Bethel, Cleveland, Tenn., 1951-52. Evangelism, 4 years. Professor, Tennessee Temple Schools since 1957. Also serves as asst. pastor, Highland Park Baptist Church, Chattanooga, Tenn. 271

Robinson, Haddow W. (1931-). Baptist pastor, Ore., 1956-58. Professor, Dallas Seminary since 1958. Active in evangelistic meetings. Involved in new-evangelical activities. 209, 280

Rockefeller, John D. (1839-1937). Capitalist and philanthropist. Went into the oil business in 1867; organized Standard Oil (later, Standard Oil of New Jersey) in 1870; retired in 1911. It is estimated that he gave 500 million dollars to schools and charities. Close friend of Harry Emerson Fosdick. 68, 97, 137, 138, 146, 149

Rockwood, Perry F. (1917-). Presbyterian minister, radio broadcaster, and Fundamentalist voice. Pastor: Little Harbour, Nova Scotia, Canada, 1941; Thorburn, Nova Scotia, 1942-44; Truro, Nova Scotia, 1945-47. Founder, the People's Gospel Hour, Halifax, Nova Scotia, Canada, in 1947 which he still directs. Now broadcasts 500 programs a week. Editor, *The Gospel Standard*. 280

Rodeheaver, Homer Allen (1880-1956). Song leader with Billy Sunday for most of his campaigns 1909-31. President, Rodeheaver Hall Mack Company. A Methodist. Founded a boys' ranch; toured the world with W. E. Biederwolf 1923-24; later in life, conducted song programs on NBC and CBS radio. His specialty was the trombone, which he played at large meetings. 261

Rogers, Dale (1912-). Singer, actress, and radio personality. A co-star in movies with her husband, Roy Rogers, whom she married in 1947. Both have been used by New Evangelicals. 275

Rogers, W. H. (1883-?). Baptist pastor in Ellendale, N. D., Vinton, Waterloo, and Muscatine, Iowa, and Wichita, Kan. Had a fine ministry at Hinson Memorial, Portland, Ore., and First Baptist, N. Y. C., 1934-40. Bible conference ministry after 1940. 166

Roloff, Lester (1914-). Baptist preacher and evangelist for 40 years. Has been a pastor in Tex. for 28 years; has started 2 missions and 5 homes for both children and adults; has a radio program The Family Altar Program now heard on 90 stations. Sound and appealing evangelistic preacher. 271

Rood, Paul W. (1889-1956). Pastor: First Covenant, Seattle, Wash., 1914-21; First Covenant, Turlock, Calif., 1922-33; Lake View Covenant, Chicago, 1933-35. President, Bible Institute of Los Angeles 1935-38. President, WCFA 1929-52. Also active in the Slavic Gospel Mission and Child Evangelism Fellowship. 90, 161, 162

Rosell, Marvin E. (Merv) (1912-). Evangelism, 40 years. Now in missions service under the name of American Crusade for Global Evangelism. Very active in youth rallies in the 1940s, city-wide meetings in the 1950s, and large meetings in Asian countries in the 1960s. 244

Ross, George A. J. (1865-1937). Presbyterian minister: Scotland 1890-97; England 1897-1902. Professor: Bryn Mawr College 1909-11; Presbyterian College 1911-12; Union Seminary, N. Y., 1912-26. Special lecturer, Union Seminary 1926-30. Influential Liberal. 97

Ryle, John Charles (1816-1900). Bishop of the Church of England, Norwich,

England. Sound in doctrine and evangelical in his views of the Bible. Author, several books. 29

Ryrie, Charles C. (1925-   ). Professor: Midwest Bible Institute 1947; Westmont College 1948-53; Dallas Seminary 1954-58 and since 1962. President, Philadelphia College of Bible 1958-62. Now, dean of graduate studies at Dallas Seminary. President, Central American Mission. Strong dispensationalist and mild separatist. 258

S

Sampey, John R. (1863-1946). Asst. to John A. Broadus, Southern Baptist Seminary 1885 and continued to serve at the seminary until 1942; its librarian in 1895; its president 1929-42. Served on the Sunday School Committee for 45 years; was a sound Southern Baptist, but did not fight the leaven of Southern Baptist apostasy. 70, 112, 122, 154, 260

Sandeen, Ernest R. (1908-   ). College professor and writer. Professor: Knox College; U. of Iowa; Notre Dame; now, U. of Minnesota. A research student of the early days of Fundamentalism. 2, 75, 206

Sankey, Ira (1840-1908). Gospel singer and Methodist hymn writer. Joined D. L. Moody in his evangelistic campaigns; sold 50 million copies of his *Gospel Hymns and Sacred Songs,* the proceeds from which went to Moody's schools. He was blind from 1903-08. 79

Sartre, Jean Paul (1905-   ). French existentialist. A follower of Hegel and Freud. Very mystical and vague in his thinking and writing. Believes God to be the Unapproachable Absolute; bases religion on our dealing with Being, Nothingness, and Becoming. 102

Savage, Henry H. (1887-1967). Baptist pastor: Barabee, Wisc.; First Baptist, Pontiac, Mich., 1924-61. Started broadcasting his Sunday morning service in 1926. A leader in Maranatha Bible Conference, Conservative Baptist groups and such boards as Africa Inland Mission, CBFMS, Greater Europe Mission, SIM, The Evangelical Alliance Mission, and Wycliffe. Was unwilling to fight New Evangelicalism when it infiltrated Conservative Baptist ranks. 120, 166

Savonarola, Girolamo Jerome (1452-98). Italian reformer in the Roman Catholic Church. Fiery preacher in Florence, Italy, against unrighteousness and the worldliness of the masses. Great crowds heard and partially repented of worldly things. But Pope Alexander VI turned against him, declared him a heretic, and had him burned. 121

Scarborough, Lee R. (1870-1945). Baptist pastor and educator. Pastor: First Baptist, Cameron, Tex., (1896-1901); First, Abilene, Tex., 1901-08. Professor, Southwestern Baptist Seminary 1908-45; its president 1914-45. Directed the Seventy-Five Million Dollar Campaign of SBC 1919-23 Opposed Fundamentalism while professor of evangelism at Southwestern; helped formulate the Cooperative Program; prepared the way for the sellout of SBC to apostasy. 126, 127, 130, 154, 165, 174

Schaeffer, Francis A. (1912-   ). Pastor: Grove City, Pa.; Chester, Pa.; St. Louis, Mo., 1938-48. A missionary in Europe 1948-53. Professor, Faith Seminary 1953-54. Organized L'Abri Fellowship, Huemoz, Switzerland, in 1955. Lectures and writes with a flair for the mystical, philosophical, and new-evangelical. 209.

Schaff, Philip (1819-93). Church historian of Swiss ancestry. Taught in Pa. Professor, Union Seminary, N. Y. C., 1870-93. Wrote an 8-volume church history; defended the Bible, but was unwilling to alert his hearers to the dangers of Modernism. His pattern has been followed by evangelical historians. 40

Schaffer, Ronald L. (1937-). Baptist pastor: Rogersville, Mo., 1 year; Bible Baptist, Plattsburg, N. Y., 4 years; Melbourne, Fla., 5 years; Temple Baptist, Tampa, Fla., for the past 5 years. Has a Christian day school and a radio ministry over 19 stations. 243

Schleiermacher, F. D. E. (1768-1834). Chaplain at a hospital, Berlin, 1796-1802. Pastor, Stolp 1802-04. Professor: Halle U. 1804-09; Berlin 1809-34. Theologian and philosopher. Religion was based on feelings and not the facts of the Bible. Based truth on emotions and the responses of the souls of men; said Jesus was an ideal man. 7, 9, 10

Schmidt, Robert O. (1918-). Baptist pastor in Kan. and Colo. 1947-53. A missionary in France 1954-62. Missions director since 1962, WBF, Arlington, Tex., on the grounds of the Arlington Baptist Schools. Solid Fundamentalist. 226

Schroader, William F. (1931-). Baptist pastor in Chicago and Milledgeville, Ill. Founder and pastor, Calvary Baptist, Oak Forest, Ill., since 1961. His church now has over 600 members and is one of the fastest growing churches in Ill. 271

Schunk, Glen (1918-). For several years an evangelist with large meetings in churches and schools. A Fundamentalist with a richly blessed ministry. 255, 271

Scofield, Cyris Ingram (C. I.) (1843-1921). Pastor, Bible teacher, and writer. Editor, *The Scofield Reference Bible.* Pastor: Moody Memorial, Chicago, 1895-1902; First Congregational, Dallas, Tex. (now, Scofield Memorial). Careful dispensational teacher, but never involved in the battles of Fundamentalism though he supplied preaching materials for militant Fundamentalists. 24, 36, 44, 54, 57, 111, 160, 164, 215, 231

Sears, Victor (1919-). Baptist pastor: Goshen and Mishawaka, Ind.; Castleberry Baptist, Fort Worth, Tex., 1964-69; First Baptist, Englewood, Colo., since 1969. Gifted evangelistic pastor. 211

Seiss, Joseph A. (1823-1904). Brought up a Moravian, but joined the Lutherans in 1839. Lutheran pastor: Martinsburg, 1844-47; Cumberland, Md., 1847-52; Baltimore, Md., 1852-58; St. John's, Philadelphia, 1858-74; Church of the Holy Communion, Philadelphia, 1874-1904. Best known for his well written volumes on Revelation. Strong premillennialist. Active in the early prophetic conferences. 29, 75

Seume, Richard H. (1915-). Pastor: Berachah Church, Houston, Tex., 1941-46; Madison Avenue Baptist, Paterson, N. J., 1946-53; Immanuel Baptist, Richmond, Va., 1953-67; Wheaton Bible Church, Wheaton, Ill., 1967-70. Chaplain, Dallas Seminary since 1970. Strong supporter of new-evangelical movement. 209

Shea, George Beverly (Bev) (1909-   ). On radio work in N. Y. 1929-38 while in the insurance business. On station WMBI (Moody Bible Institute), Chicago, 1938-44. Soloist for the Billy Graham crusades since 1947. Has 37 albums and 3 books. 257

Shedd, W. T. (1820-94). Presbyterian theologian, pastor, and writer. Professor: Auburn Seminary 1852-53; Andover Seminary 1855-62; Union Seminary, N. Y. C., 1863-74. Strong Calvinist. Opposed the Liberalism of his day. 74

Sheen, Fulton J. (1895-   ). Roman Catholic leader and bishop. Professor, Catholic U. of America 1926-50. National director, Society for Propagation of the Faith 1950-66. Bishop of Rochester, N. Y., since 1969. Author, 75 books. Editor, *Mission and World Missions.* 196

Sheldon, Charles M. (1857-1946). Congregational pastor: Waterbury, Vt., 1886-88; Central, Topeka, Kan., 1889-1912 and 1915-19. Editor, *The Christian Herald.* Author, 34 books including a fictional novel *In His Steps* which sold millions of copies. The book appealed for Christians to follow Jesus in every decision and activity, and many took it as a gospel of works. 14, 69

Shelley, Bruce (1927-   ). Baptist pastor and teacher. Pastor: Camden, S. C.; Coralsville and Windham, Iowa. Professor, Conservative Baptist Theological Seminary, Denver, Colo., since 1957. Has sanctioned the drift of Conservative Baptists into New Evangelicalism; has written a few books. 226

Shepherd, Hyland W. (1926-   ). Public school teacher in Pa. and N. J. 1949-69. Minister of music for 25 years at the Bible Presbyterian Church, Collingswood, N. J., under Carl McIntire. President, Shelton College, Cape Canaveral, Fla., since 1972. 240

Shields, Thomas Todhunter (T. T.) (1873-1955). Canadian Baptist pastor and crusader. Pastor: Florence, Ontario, 1894-95; Dutton, 1895-97; Delhi, 1897-1900; Wentworth Street, Hamilton, 1900-04; Adelaide Street, Toronto, Ontario, 1904-10; Jarvis Street, Toronto, Ontario, 1910-55. President, BBU 1923-30. Headed Des Moines U. 1927-28. President, Canadian Protestant League. Towering Bible pulpiteer. 80, 85, 86, 87, 88, 105, 106-112, 115, 124, 130, 131, 132, 154, 161, 163, 164, 165, 166, 167, 168, 169, 170, 171, 181, 182, 189, 197, 198, 199, 221, 228

Shimeall, R. C. (1803-74). Presbyterian pastor in N. Y. Presbytery. Had been in the Church of England and Dutch Reformed Church. A strong premillennialist. Wrote some books on the Lord's return. 74

Shuler, Jack (1918-62). Son of Robert P. "Fighting Bob" Shuler. In evangelism, with large area meetings and rallies. Gifted public speaker. 254

Shuler, Phil (1924-   ). Another son of R. P. Shuler. In evangelistic work for several years, especially among smaller churches. Now living in Calif. Strong preacher and Fundamentalist. His wife, a very talented musician. 255

Shuler, Robert P. (Fighting Bob) (1880-1966). Methodist pastor, writer, and defender of Wesleyan doctrines. Editor, *The Methodist Challenge.* Pastor: Va.; Tenn.; Tex.; Trinity Methodist, Los Angeles, 1920-1953. Gifted pulpiteer and a fighter against all forms of sin. Opposed Aimee

Semple McPherson; openly attacked drifts inside Methodism, but refused to leave his denomination. Once his church ministered to many thousands; now it is so weak that it has voted to join another United Methodist church. 88, 90, 126, 174, 190, 257, 273

Shurtleff, Ernest W. (1862-1941). Congregational pastor: Ventura, Calif., 1889-90; Plymouth, Mass., 1891-98; First Congregational, Minneapolis, Minn., 1898-1905. 14

Sightler, Harold B. (1914-). Baptist pastor and broadcaster. Pastor: Mauldin, S. C., 1943; Pelham Baptist, Pelham, S. C., 1943-52; Tabernacle Baptist, Greenville, S. C., 1952, which he organized and where he is still pastor with 2,500 members. Has conducted The Bright Spot Hour on radio since 1943. Solid Bible expositor among independent Baptists. 242, 255, 271

Silvey, D. O. (1904-). MBA pastor and editor. In several churches 1933-40. Pastor: Garrett Memorial, Hope, Ark., 1940-48; Central Baptist, Texarkana, Tex., 1948-52. Editor, *Baptist Publications* 1953-71. Retired in 1971. 241

Simpson, Albert B. (1844-1919). Presbyterian pastor: Hamilton, Ontario, 1865-74; Louisville, Ky., 1874-81; N. Y., 1881. Founder, the Christian Alliance 1887 which joined the Interdenominational Missionary Alliance in 1897 to create the Christian and Missionary Alliance. Editor, *The Alliance Weekly*. Wrote 16 volumes on the Bible. Leader in the founding of Nyack College. 70

Skinner, Tom (1942-). Radical left-wing Negro identified with civil rights movements and new-evangelical organizations. Poses as a second Martin Luther King, Jr. Engages in evangelistic work. 252, 275, 280, 281

Slade, Harold C. (?-). Baptist pastor, Timmins, Ontario, 1929-41. General secretary, Union of Regular Baptists (Canada) 1941-47. Asst. pastor, Jarvis Street Baptist, Toronto, 1947-55 and succeeded T. T. Shields as pastor in 1955 where he has remained. President, Toronto Baptist Seminary. Editor, *The Gospel Witness*. 106, 112, 199

Smith, Gerald Birney (1868-1929). Educator and liberal writer. Editor, *The Journal of Religion*. Professor: Oberlin College 1881-92; Wooster College 1892-95; U. of Chicago 1900-29. Helped to edit *A Dictionary of Religion*. Author, 5 books. 100

Smith, Hannah Pearsall (1832-1911). Quaker background. A woman of deep dedication and faith. Turned to Bible teaching. A pioneer in the English Keswick movement. Taught a devotional life. Best known for her book, *The Christian Secret of a Happy Life*. 267

Smith, J. Harold (1910-). Baptist pastor: Conestee, S. C.; Six Mile, S. C.; Northside Baptist, Anderson, S. C.; Woodland Park Baptist, Chattanooga, Tenn.; First Baptist, Fort Smith, Ark.; Windsor Park Baptist, Fort Smith, Ark., since 1964. Has been broadcasting since 1935. A strong evangelistic preacher. 162, 254

Smith, J. M. Powis (1866-1932). Professor: Des Moines U.; U. of Chicago 1902-32. A specialist in Semitic languages and Biblical literature. Had several books on the O. T. Gifted Liberal. Helped make the U. of Chicago a modernist center. 153

Smith, Kenneth I. (1915-). Chaplain, U. S. Navy 1944-46. Pastor: Wall Street Baptist, Jackson, Mich., 1946-54; Calvary Baptist, Fremont, Calif., since 1954. 232

Smith, Noel (1900-). Express manager between Nashville and Atlanta with the Southern Express Company for 15 years. Entered the Baptist ministry in 1934. Pastored churches in the SBC 1934-47. Editor, *The Fundamentalist* 1947-50. Helped found the BBF in 1950. Editor, *The Baptist Bible Tribune* since 1950. Keen student and writer of Baptist doctrine and our times. 198, 211, 217, 218, 219, 272

Smith, Oswald J. (1889-). Presbyterian minister: South Presbyterian, Chicago, 1914-15; Dale Presbyterian, Toronto, 1915-19. Worked with the Shantymen's Association 1919-20. Pastor: Parkdale Tabernacle, Toronto, 1920-21; The Alliance Tabernacle, Toronto, 1922-26; The Gospel Tabernacle, Los Angeles, 1927-28; Cosmopolitan Tabernacle, Toronto, 1928-30. Founder, The Peoples Church, Toronto, in 1930; its pastor, 1930-59. Wrote 35 books and 1,200 hymns. Missionary statesman. 256, 260, 275

Smith, Rodney (Gipsy) (1860-1947). British evangelist. Brought up in a real gipsy tent with very little formal education; worked for a while with the Salvation Army; made 50 trips to the U. S. to hold large evangelistic meetings; preached in largest churches and major halls. His singing was always a special treat to thousands. 77, 79, 80, 256, 261

Smith, Wilbur M. (1894-). Presbyterian pastor, author, and teacher. Pastor, Germantown, Pa. Professor: Moody Bible Institute 1938-47; Fuller Seminary 1947-63; Trinity Seminary since 1963. Now retired. Knowledgeable Bible student. Keen student of authors and books, but silent on the dangers facing Fundamentalists. 92, 93, 99, 101, 203, 219, 260, 274, 280

Smyth, Egbert C. (1829-1904). Baptist educator and liberal leader. Professor: Andover Seminary 1856-90. Most active in selling out his seminary under the guise of being a progressive (a common front for Liberals and compromisers); held that the seminary creed did not bind him in doctrine. 71

Smyth, Newman (1843-1925). Congregational pastor: Providence, R. I., 1867-70; Bangor, Me., 1870-75; Quincy, Ill., 1876-82; First Congregational, New Haven, Conn., 1882-1907. Author, 10 books. A leader in liberal apostasy. 71

Soares, T. G. (1869-?). Baptist pastor: Rockford, Ill.; Galesburg, Ill.; Oak Park, Ill. Professor, U. of Chicago 1919-25 and at the same time pastor of the nearby Hyde Park Congregational Church. 153

Sockman, Ralph (1889-). Secretary, N. Y. YMCA 1911-13. Associate minister, Madison Avenue Methodist Episcopal Church, N. Y. (now Christ Church), 1916; its minister 1917-61. Associate professor, Union Seminary, N. Y. C., 1947-62. President, FCC 1927-29. Author, several books. A modernist Methodist who helped ruin his church. 102, 239

Spener, Philip Jacob (1635-1705). German Pietist, preacher, and teacher. Professor, U. of Halle; while there, he founded the Halle Foundation, a complex including a school, printing press, orphanage, and medical dispensary—all based on faith. 39

Speer, W. R. (1915-). Pastor: 2 Baptist churchès in Okla. for 8 years; Potosi, Mo., 1952-67; Central, Conway, Ark., 1967-69; Megehee, Ark., 1969-72; Corinth, Miss., since 1972. Vice-president, NABA (now the MBA) 1951-53. President, BMA 1968-69. 241

Speers, J. M. (1862-1941). Merchant in linens in McCutcheon and Company, N. Y. Vice-president, Presbyterian Board of Foreign Missions. Treasurer, Student Volunteer Movement. A trustee of several colleges. 180

Spidle, Simeon (1867-1954). Baptist theologian and teacher in Canada. Professor, Acadia U., Wolfville, Nova Scotia, 1911-38. Conservative Liberal who led hundreds of young men into the abyss of liberal thought and helped ruin his college and convention. 109

Spurgeon, Charles Haddon (1834-92). Great English Baptist preacher. Built the world famous Metropolitan Tabernacle in 1862 and pastored it 30 years. Founder, Spurgeons College. Famous for his Bible-centered sermons. Editor, *The Sword and the Trowel.* Among his many good writings was *The Treasury of David.* 3, 17, 21, 70, 80, 106, 116, 175, 205, 276, 281

Stebbins, George C. (1846-1945). A Baptist. Gospel hymn writer. Led singing for A. J. Gordon; composed over 1,600 hymns; led the singing of large choirs in meetings for D. L. Moody; wrote such familiar hymns as "Ye Must Be Born Again" and "Jesus, I Come"; edited 6 editions of gospel hymns 1878-91. 79

Stenholm, Gilbert R. (1915-). With Bob Jones U. since 1934; its dean of the school of religion 1951-65; its director of religious activities 1951-54; its director of extension since 1950; its director of ministerial training and extension since 1965. 271

Stevenson, J. Ross (1866-1939). Presbyterian pastor and educator. Pastor, Sedalia, Mo., 1890-94. Professor, McCormick Seminary 1894-1902. Pastor: Fifth Avenue Presbyterian, N. Y. C., 1902-09; Brown Memorial Presbyterian, Baltimore, Md., 1909-14. President, Princeton Theological Seminary 1914-36. 177

Stewart, Lyman (1840-1923). A founder of Hardison and Stewart Oil Co. 1883, which merged with three other companies to form Union Oil Co. 1889-90. President and general manager of Union Oil 1894-1905; chairman of its board after 1905. A founder of Bible Institute of Los Angeles. With his brother, Milton, he financed the publication of *The Fundamentals* 1910-15. 175

Stidger, William L. (1885-1949). Methodist pastor and radio speaker. Pastor: Calvary Methodist, San Francisco, 1913-16; First Methodist, San Jose, 1916-19; St. Mark's, Detroit, 1920-26; Linwood Boulevard Methodist, Kansas City, Mo., 1925-29. Guest professor of preaching, Boston U. Radio broadcasting 1939-44. Author, 24 books. 102

Stifler, James M. (1839-1902). Baptist. Professor, Crozer Seminary, Chester, Pa., 1868-1902 (Crozer has now joined Colgate Rochester in Rochester, N. Y.). Author, 3 books. Several sermons published. 75

Stonehouse, Ned (1902-62). Professor, Westminster Seminary 1929-37. Named to succeed J. G. Machen as professor of N. T. at this seminary in 1937. Dean of the faculty 1955-62. Machen's biographer. 182

Stowell, Joseph M. (1911-). Baptist pastor: Calvary Baptist, Hancock, Mich., 1933-35; Gary, Ind., 1935-39; Tabernacle, Ithaca, N. Y., 1939-45; First, Bay City, Mich., 1945-49; First, Hackensack, N. J., 1949-69. National representative, GARBC since 1969. 116, 221, 222

Strachan, Kenneth (1910-65). Joined the Latin American Evangelization Campaign in 1936 (the name was changed to Latin America Mission). Dean, Bible Institute of the Mission in San Jose. Director of the mission 1950-65. Founder, Evangelism-In-Depth, which is New Evangelicalism on the mission field. 272

Strathern, Harold (?-1950). Director, LeTourneau Christian Camp Grounds, Canadaigua, N. Y. For many years, he worked with Interstate Evangelistic Association. 168

Straton, Hillyer H. (1905-70). Baptist pastor: Philadelphia; N. Y. C.; Muncie, Ind. Was associated with his father at Calvary Baptist in N. Y. C.; had a 20-year pastorate at Malden, Mass. 136, 142

Straton, John Roach (1876-1929). Baptist pastor: Second, Chicago, 1905-08; Immanuel, Baltimore, 1908-13; First, Norfolk, 1913-17; Calvary Baptist, N. Y. C., 1918-29. Outspoken Fundamentalist leader. Organized the Fundamentalist League of New York. Editor, *The Calvary Pulpit* and *Faith-Fundamentalist.* Colorful pulpiteer. Able debater. 85, 130, 135-143, 160, 166, 167, 171, 182, 227, 273

Strauss, David (1808-74). German philosopher and writer. Wrote a *Life of Jesus* in which he denied the deity of Christ, the virgin birth, and the miracles of the Bible.

Strauss, Lehman (1911-). Baptist pastor: Bristol, Pa., 1938-56; Highland Park, Detroit, 1956-63. In Bible conferences since 1963. Author, 14 books. Has a radio program broadcasting over 30 stations. 258

Strong, Augustus H. (1836-1921). Baptist pastor and educator. Pastor: First Baptist, Raverhill, Mass., 1861-65; First, Cleveland, Ohio, 1865-62. President, Rochester Seminary 1872-1912. A conservative theologian, but tolerant and thereby prepared the way for the downfall of his seminary. Author, 7 books including *Outline of Systematic Theology.* 146, 147

Strong, Charles O. (1925-). BMA pastor: Ark., 1949-67; Texarkana, Tex., 1969-71. Professor, Central Baptist College, Conway, Ark., 1956-67. Vice-president, BMA 1964-65. Editor, publications of the BMA since 1971. 242

Strong, Josiah (1847-1916). A Congregationalist. Pastor, Cheyenne, Wyo., 1871-73. Professor, Western Reserve College 1873-76. Pastor, Sandusky, Ohio, 1876-81. Secretary of Home Missions 1881-84. Pastor, Cincinnati, 1884-86. Director: Evangelical Alliance 1886-98; League of Social Service 1898-1902. Editor, *Social Progress.* 68

Sunday, William A. (Billy) (1862-1935). Presbyterian evangelist. Worked briefly with J. Wilbur Chapman in evangelistic meetings; then he went on his own and became a great crowd gatherer for 15 years before World War I and for 15 years after it. Dramatic, hard-hitting, acrobatic, and very stimulating in his preaching. It is estimated he had a third of a million converts. 79, 90, 250, 251, 261

Sutherland, Samuel H. (1900-). Presbyterian pastor and educator. Pastor: Grace Presbyterian, Hollywood, Calif., 1927-37; Calvary, Hollywood, 1938-41. Dean, Bible Institute of Los Angeles 1942-52; its president (it was later renamed Biola College) 1952-70. Active in the Accrediting Association of Bible Colleges and the IFCA. 224, 281

Sweet, William Warren (1881-1959). Methodist professor, writer, and outstanding historian in all fields of American Christianity. Professor: Ohio Wesleyan U. 1911-13; DePauw U. 1913-27; U. of Chicago 1927-46; Southern Methodist U. 1948-59. Author, 27 books. 219

Sweeting, George (1924-). Pastor, Grace Church, Clifton, N. J., 1948-50. Evangelism 1951-61. Pastor: Madison Avenue Baptist, Paterson, N. J., 1961-66; Moody Memorial, 1966-71. President, Moody Bible Institute since 1971. 244, 280

T

Taft, Charles P. (1897-). Prominent lawyer and religious figure. Since 1922, an attorney in Cincinnati where he was mayor 1955-57. President, FCC 1947-48. Son of President W. H. Taft. A member of the Church of England. On many boards and committees. 239

Talbot, Louis T. (1889-). Presbyterian pastor: Keokul, Iowa, 1921-25; Oliver Presbyterian, Minneapolis, 1925-29; Philpott Tabernacle, Hamilton, Ontario, 1929-31; Church of the Open Door, Los Angeles 1931-48. President, Biola College until 1952. Warmhearted evangelistic preacher and pastor and Fundamentalist. 90, 223, 256, 260, 261

Talmadge, T. DeWitt (1832-1902). Presbyterian minister and pulpiteer with many published sermons. Pastor: Reformed Dutch Church, Belleville, N. J., 1856-59; Syracuse, N. Y., 1859-62; Philadelphia, 1862-69; Central Church, Brooklyn, N. Y., 1869-94; Washington, D. C., 1894-1902. Editor, *The Christian at Work.* His sermons published weekly for 29 years. Editor, *The Christian Herald.* 68

Tassell, Paul (1934-). Baptist pastor and writer. Pastor: Second Baptist, Elberton, Ga., 1954-58; Bethany Baptist, Galesburg, Ill., 1958-65; Campus Baptist, Ames, Iowa, 1965-70. National youth representative, GARBC 1970-73. Pastor, Grandview Park Baptist, Des Moines, Iowa, since 1973. 222

Tatian (?-160). Early defender of the Christian church. Once he held to the Scriptures but turned to Gnosticism and believed the God of the O. T. was evil and opposed to the God of the N. T. Finally he turned to asceticism and celibacy. 36

Taylor, Clyde (1904-). Missionary to Peru 1925-27. In missions work, Columbia, South America, 1931-41. Pastor, Central Baptist, Quincy, Mass., 1942-44. Director of public affairs, NAE 1944-63. General director, NAE since 1963. New-evangelical spokesman. Author 5 books. 209, 234

Taylor, Hudson (1832-1905). English missionary statesman. Founder, the China Inland Mission (now Overseas Fellowship). Translator and traveler. By the time of his death, his mission had 205 stations with 800 missionaries, claiming 125,000 Chinese had been won. One of the most revered names in modern missions. 72

Templeton, Charles B. (1915-). Pastor, evangelist, and youth leader. Pastor: Avenue Road Church, Toronto, Ontario, 1941-48; Ewing Presbyterian, Trenton, N. J., 1951-52. Evangelism 1932-48. A featured speaker at Youth for Christ rallies. Now in TV work in Toronto. 254, 257

Terre-Blanche, Henry S. (1933-). Pastor: Truth Gospel Church, Hamilton, Ontario, 1965-69; Jennings Baptist, St. Louis, Mo., 1969-72; Tabernacle Baptist, Williamsport, Pa., since 1972. Has written a factual study of the life of J. Frank Norris in a master of theology thesis at Dallas Seminary. 122

Terrey, Robert J. (1920-). Pastor, Plymouth Baptist, Minneapolis, Minn., since 1961. Professor, Central Baptist Seminary of Minneapolis 1963-68. President, Plymouth Bible Institute since 1966. 249

Tertullian (160-220). Early Church Father, lawyer, and writer. Opposed to worldliness in the churches. Lived in North Africa. The first one to use the word "Trinity." Famous for his saying that "the blood of the martyrs is the seed of the Church." A man of strong convictions. Joined an independent group, the Montanists. 36

Thiessen, Henry C. (1885-1947). Baptist pastor and educator. Pastor, Pandora, Ohio, 1909-16. Professor: Fort Wayne Bible College 1916-23; Northern Baptist Seminary 1925-28; Evangelical U. 1929-31; Dallas Seminary 1931-35; Wheaton College 1936-46. Balanced Bible student and writer. 260

Thomas, Carey S. (1883-1956). Baptist pastor: Milburn, N. J., 1909-18; Belmont Avenue, Philadelphia, 1918-25; First, Altoona, Pa., 1925-50. Professor, Philadelphia School of the Bible. President, Conservative Baptist Theological Seminary, Denver, Colo., 1950-56. Strong Fundamental Baptist. 150

Thomas, W. H. Griffith (1861-1924). Ordained Church of England minister. Principal, Wycliffe Hall, Oxford U. 1905-10. A Church of England rector 1885-1905. Professor: Wycliffe College; U. of Toronto 1910-19. Author, 21 books. Helped L. S. Chafer in founding Dallas Seminary. 160

Thomas, W. Ian (1914-). English leader in the Keswick (Deeper Life) movement. Founded Capernwray Hall England, in 1947 as a holiday center for young people; organized the Torchbearers Fellowship in 1948; wrote several books. Conference speaker. 21, 191, 267

Tillich, Paul J. (1886-1965). Professor: 4 German universities; Union Seminary, N. Y. C., 1933-55; Harvard U. 1955-62; U. of Chicago 1962-65. Keen liberal thinker. American interpreter of Barth. Neo-orthodox writer. 102

Tischendorf, L. F. K. (1815-74). German scholar and student of the original languages and texts of the Bible. Discovered many very old manuscripts such as Codex Sinaiticus 1859; published many contributions to N. T. studies. 32

Tollett, T. O. (1922-). Before 1950, he served in the radio ministry of the BMA (Harvest Gleaner Hour) and as executive secretary of the NABA building corporation. Since 1950, he has been business manager of Baptist Publications Committee of the BMA. 241

Toplady, A. M. (1740-78). Minister of the Church of England. Rector, Broad

Hembury, England, 1768-88. Strong defender of Calvinism against Arminianism. Wrote the famous hymn "Rock of Ages." 74

Torrey, Frank C. (1894-). Asst. pastor, Baptist Temple, Brooklyn, N. Y., 1922-23. Professor, Philadelphia School of the Bible 1924-25. Pastor: First Baptist, Cherry Creek, N. Y., 1927; Merritt Park Gospel Church, Creeskill, Pa., 1927-31; Calvary Independent Baptist, Altoona, Pa., 1931-37; Calvary Independent, Lancaster, Pa., 1937-63. In Bible conference work 1963-70. 224, 260

Torrey, Reuben A. (1865-1928). Presbyterian evangelist, educator, and writer. Head, Moody Bible Institute 1899-1908. Dean, Bible Institute of Los Angeles in 1908. Helped organize the Church of the Open Door, Los Angeles, where he pastored. Evangelistic meetings around the world. Founder, Montrose Bible Conference. Sound in doctrine, but refused to fight for Fundamentalism. 78, 90, 126, 130, 160, 219, 261

Troelsch, Ernst (1865-1923). German philosopher and theologian. Professor: U. of Göttingen 1891-92; Bonn 1892-94; Heidelberg 1894-1915; Berlin 1915-23. Held that all religions were due to inner feelings with no outside revelation needed; taught that Christianity was only one of many good religions. 10

Trotter, Melvin E. (Mel) (1870-1940). Founder of 67 rescue missions throughout the U. S. One of the best-known men in his day in downtown mission halls. The best-known one he started was in Grand Rapids, Mich. He was converted at the Pacific Garden Mission in 1897. Author, 2 books. 260

Troup, Jock (1896-1954). Supt. of Gospel Union, Fifeshire, Scotland, 1928-30. Supt. of Tent Hall, Glasgow, 1932-45. Came to America under the auspices of Moody Bible Institute 1938-39. Evangelist in England and Ireland 1945-49. Served 6 months under J. Frank Norris in Fort Worth in 1950. Under Moody again in 1951. To Canada and the U. S. late in 1953. Died while preaching in Spokane, Wash. 197, 217

Truett, George W. (1867-1944). Pastor, First Baptist, Dallas, Tex., 1899-1944. Known for his pulpit gifts. Best-known Southern Baptist in his generation. A leader in the Baptist World Alliance. A conservative preacher, but fought Fundamentalism. Topical speaker, not a Bible expositor. Helped build the Cooperative Program and allowed Liberals to capture it to finance the apostasy of the Southern Convention. 124, 126, 128, 273

Trumbull, Charles G. (1872-1941). Editor, *The Sunday School Times* 1903-41. Learned Presbyterian. Wrote a biography of C. I. Scofield. A sound Bible expositor. Author, 8 books. 161

Tulga, Chester E. (1896-). Baptist pastor for 25 years: La Grange, Ohio; Galeton, Pa.; Miles, Ohio; North Platte, Neb.; Brookings, S. D.; Norwood Park, Chicago. Executive secretary, CBF for 12 years, and during this time, wrote the "Case" books. Professor, Eastern Baptist Institute, Somerset, Ky., for 2 years. 216, 227, 229, 230, 231

Tyng, Samuel H., Jr. (1839-98). Church of England minister: St. George's, N. Y., 1860-63; the Church of the Mediator, N. Y., 1864-65; the Church of the Holy Trinity 1865-81. Then he went into business for Mutual Life Insurance and became an officer in its European branch. President, American Chamber of Commerce at the time of his death. 24

U

Unger, Merrill F. (1909-). Pastor, educator, and writer. Pastor, Buffalo, N. Y. Professor: Dallas Seminary 1948-67; Gordon College. Outstanding Bible scholar with a widely used *Bible Dictionary* and several books on demon activity. Strong preacher. 224

V

Vanderwood, Ralph A. (1913-). Methodist pastor: Joseph, Ore., 1941; Ventura, Calif., 1941; Granada Park-Alhambra, Calif., 1941-47; Austin Tabernacle, Chicago, 1947-53; Woodland Community, Wichita, Kan., 1953-57; World Gospel Mission, Marion, Ind., 1957-62. General supt., Evangelical Methodist Church, Wichita, Kan., since 1962. 248

Van Dusen, Henry P. (1897-). Presbyterian minister and educator. Professor, Union Seminary, N. Y. C., 1926-63. Liberal spokesman. A favorite Modernist among intellectuals and churchmen. Strong promoter of the ecumenical movement. 100, 102, 239

Van Gelderen, Wayne (1924-). Pastor: Sylvania Heights Baptist, Miami, Fla., 1948-56; Joy Road Baptist, Detroit, 1956-60; Calvary Baptist, Durango, Colo., 1961-66; Marquette Manor Baptist, Chicago, since 1966. In the past pastorate, he has organized a church at Downer's Grove in the Greater Chicago area which he also pastors. Has served with the CBF, FBF and WBM. A consistent Fundamentalist pastor. 242, 271

Van Gilder, H. O. (1891-). Pastor: First Baptist, Perkesia, Pa., 1921-22; Lebanon, Ohio, 1922-23; Central Baptist, Columbus, Ohio, 1923-32; Temple Baptist, Portsmouth, Ohio, 1932-44. National representative, GARBC 1944-48. President, Western Baptist Bible College 1948-64. Pastor, First Baptist, Los Gatos, Calif., 1964-70. Now in Bible teaching ministry. 222

Van Gorder, John J. (1881-1961). Baptist pastor: Marysville, Ohio, for 4 years; Brookville, Pa., for 2 years; First Baptist, Butler, Pa., 1923-41. Went into full-time Bible conference ministry in 1941. A leader in the BBU. Author, several books. A close friend of W. L. Pettingill. 260

Vanhetloo, Warren (1924-). Baptist pastor: Eureka, Mich., 1947-49; Ashley, Mich., 1950-51; South Lyon, Mich., 1953-56. Professor, Central Baptist Seminary of Minneapolis since 1956; now its dean. 227

Van Impe, Jack (1931-). Full-time evangelist for the past 24 years. Has held meetings in all the states and 33 foreign countries. Headquarters in Royal Oak, Mich. Has several albums of records and sermons out. Accomplished musician. 255

Van Osdel, Oliver W. (1846-1935). Baptist pastor: Aledo, Ill.; Rock Island, Ill.; Ottawa, Kan.; Galesburg, Ill.; Spokane, Wash.; Wealthy Street Baptist, Grand Rapids, Mich., 1895 and 1909-34. Led his church out of the NBC in 1909; organized the Michigan Orthodox Baptist Association. A discerning Fundamentalist. Active in the WCFA, BBU, and GARB. 89, 146, 147, 163, 166, 169, 170, 171, 181, 221

Van Til, Cornelius (1895-). Educator, apologist, and writer. Pastor, Spring Lake Christian Reformed Church 1927-28. Professor: Princeton Seminary 1928-29; Westminster since 1929. Author, several books and articles, including *The New Modernism* in which he made a careful analysis of Barthianism. Sound Reformed scholar. 101, 181, 237

Vassar, John (Uncle John) (1813-78). A worker with the American Tract Society, the Duchess County Baptist Association (N. Y.), and a revivalist. Organized Sunday Schools among the troops in the Civil War. After 1872, many revivals in New England. 24

Vatke, Johann Karl W. (1806-82). Professor, U. of Berlin. A learned critic of the Bible. Believed most of Genesis was myth and that the five books of Moses were written after Moses' time. A keen modernist mind. 139

Veddar, Henry C. (1853-1935). Baptist historian and educator. Professor, Crozer Seminary 1894-1926. Helped the school go modernist. Wrote several books on the history of Baptists, but he always omitted any recognition of dangers facing believers, churches, and schools. Editor, *The Examiner* and *The Baptist Quarterly*. Author, 15 books. 100, 116, 139, 141, 153

Vick, G. Beauchamp (1901-). Baptist pastor and leader. Supt. under J. Frank Norris in Fort Worth and Detroit. Pastor, Temple Baptist, Detroit, since 1948. President: Bible Baptist Seminary, Fort Worth, 1948-50; Baptist Bible College, Springfield, Mo., since 1950. One of the founders and leaders of the BBF. 133, 195, 197, 198, 217, 218, 219, 220, 271, 272, 278

Vickery, Harry E. (1928-). Pastor, Baptist Temple, Springfield, Mo., since 1947. On the missions committee, BBF 1960-64. Founder and president of Springfield Baptist College since 1972. 220

Villers, Thomas J. (1861-1932). Baptist pastor: Gloucester, Mass., 1888-93; Syracuse, N. Y., 1893-13; First, Detroit, 1913-22; Portland, Ore., 1922-32. President, Foreign Mission Board, NBC 1918-22. 150

W

Waite. Donald A. (1927-). Baptist pastor: Newton, Mass., 1961; Newton Center, Mass., 1961-65. Associated with Carl McIntire in the Twentieth Century Reformation Hour. Prominent in the Radio and Television Commission of the ACCC. Wrote several exposés of liberal and compromising groups and meetings. Now teaching in the Philadelphia area. 211, 239

Walvoord, John F. (1910-). Presbyterian pastor and educator. Professor of theology, Dallas Seminary; its president since 1952. Scholarly dispensationalist. Active leader in the IFCA. Author, several books. On the committee of the New Scofield Reference Bible. 224, 254, 274, 280, 281

Wanamaker, John (1838-1922). Conservative generous Presbyterian. Founder, the firm of Wanamaker and Beacon (dept. store) in Philadelphia in 1861 and his own store in 1876 and one in N. Y. C. in 1896. Postmaster General of the U. S. 1889-93. Founder, Bethany Sunday School in Philadelphia in 1858 (the largest in the nation for years). First salaried secretary of the YMCA 1858. Very generous to churches and to Presbyterian Hospital. 29, 78, 79

Warfield, Benjamin Breckenridge (B. B.) (1851-1921). Brilliant mind in theology. Outstanding defender of the inspiration of the Bible and other

Reformed truths. Professor: Western Theological Seminary (1878-87); Princeton Theological Seminary 1887-1921. Editor, *The Presbyterian and Reformed Review.* Wrote many widely used books and articles. 22, 70, 174, 175, 176, 177, 181

Warren, William F. (1833-1929). Methodist theologian and educator. Professor of theology, Boston U. 1873-1923; its president until he retired from that office in 1920. Accepted and taught evolution and modern views of the Bible. A Liberal who helped Methodism to depart from the Faith. 33

Washburn, Frank E. (1920-). Methodist pastor. Served 6 years in the United Methodist denomination; left the denomination. Pastor, First Evangelical Methodist, Danville, Va., since 1955. Has held several revivals and has spoken at many camp meetings. 248

Waters, John R. (1923-). Baptist pastor: Banning, Calif.; Pacific Beach, Calif.; Faith Baptist Church, Laurens, S. C., since 1952. Active in several Fundamental fellowships. 243

Wayman, Harry C. (1881-1959). Baptist pastor and educator. Professor, Southern Baptist Seminary 1917-22. President: William Jewell College 1923-28; Des Moines U. 1928-29. After the closing of Des Moines in 1929, he went into Southern Baptist pastorates: First Baptist, Newport, Ky., 1929-43; First Baptist, Sarasota, Fla., 1943-49. 170, 171

Webb, Halvar C. (1926-). Successful evangelist with a widely-appreciated ministry among separatist Fundamental churches. Now lives in Ridley Park, Pa. 255

Webb-Peploe, Hanmer W. (1837-1923). Church of England minister. Sound in doctrine. One of the founders of Keswick movement, now often referred to as the Deeper Life or the Victorious Life movement. Spiritual experiences were put ahead of Bible exposition and objective doctrine. 267

Webster, Warren (1928-). Missionary under the CBFMS in Pakistan 1945-70. General director, CBFMS since 1971. As director, he has been party to the changes within the society as it accommodates to present missions' changes. 233, 275

Weeks, Richard C. (1919-). Baptist pastor and educator. Pastor, Donald Smith Memorial Baptist Church, Chicago, for 17 years. Professor: Pillsbury Baptist Bible College 1965-68; Maranatha Baptist Bible College, Watertown, Wisc., since 1968 where he serves as academic dean and teaches church history, Bible, and practical theology. A knowledgeable Baptist and keen student of Baptist history and Fundamentalism. 211, 232, 249

Welch, Claude (1922-). Professor: Princeton U. 1947-50; Yale U. 1951-54. Director, graduate studies and dean, graduate school of the Theological Union, Berkeley, Calif. 91, 92

Welch, W. Wilbert (1918-). Pastor: North Casanovia Baptist, Bailey, Mich., 1941-43; Calvary Baptist, Rome, Ga., 1944-50; Calvary Baptist, Muskegon, Mich., 1950-59. President, Grand Rapids Baptist College and Seminary since 1950. On the Council of Fourteen and Board of Baptist Mid-Missions and Hiawatha Mission. 222

power over a congregation. A central figure in the Great Awakening in the colonies. He was buried at Newburyport, Mass. 77, 101

Whitby, Daniel (1638-1726). English theologian and writer. Believed the millennium would come as a result of the effects of the Gospel. A pioneer in modern postmillennialism. Taught that Christ would come when the world was ready. 39

Whitcombe, W. S. (1905-). Canadian Baptist pastor and educator. Pastor: Westport, Ontario, 1924-25; Markham, Ontario, 1925-31. Professor, Toronto Baptist Seminary 1931-54. Pastor, Wishing Well Acres Baptist Church, Agincourt, Ontario, since 1954. Professor, Central Baptist Seminary, Toronto, Ontario. 112, 199

Whitsitt, William H. (1841-1911). A chaplain in the Civil War. A Baptist pastor, Albany, Ga., 1870-72. Professor, Southern Baptist Seminary 1872-99; its president 1877-99. He was asked to leave by the trustees because he wrote that believers' baptism had been "restored" in 1641 by English Baptists. Professor, Richmond College 1899-1911. 110

Whittle, D. W. (1840-1901). Evangelist and Bible teacher. Wrote over 200 hymns such as "Showers of Blessing" and "Moment by Moment." 28, 45

Wieman, Henry N. (1884-). Presbyterian pastor: St. Joseph, Mo., 1912-13; Davis, Calif., 1913-15. Professor: Occidental College 1917-27; U. of Chicago 1927-46. After retirement in 1946, he taught at the U. of Oregon and Southern Illinois U. A radical Modernist who ruined hundreds of young people in his classrooms. 101

Willard, Frances (1839-98). School teacher. Dean, Evanston College 1871-74. Worked full time in the temperance movement and women's suffrage. Headed the Women's Christian Temperance Union; averaged 400 lectures a year. Wrote some books. 69

Williams, Allen N. (1933-). Baptist pastor: Nashville, Minn., 1937-38; Luverne, Minn., 1938-49; Safford, Ariz., 1949-50; Lakewood, Colo., 1950-57; First, Rockford, Ill., 1957-63; First, Compton, Calif., 1963-65; Grace, Long Beach, Calif., 1965-66; New Testament, Long Beach, 1966-67; Faith, Grand Junction, Colo., since 1967. Active in Conservative Baptist Association of America, FBF, and WBM. 249

Williams, Arthur F. (1896-). Baptist pastor: Randall Memorial, Williamsville, N. Y., 1928-33; Park Avenue, Binghamton, N. Y., 1933-41; First, N. Y. C., 1941-47; First, Elyria, Ohio. Professor, Cedarville College 1953-67. Retired in 1967, but since then has supplied at churches in Dayton and Xenia, Ohio. 160, 222

Williams, David (1890-). Congregational pastor: Edgartown, Mass., 1914-16; Cleveland, 1916-24. Joined the Unitarians; pastored churches in Chicago 1924-28 and Rochester 1928. 36

Williams, J. B. (1916-). Baptist pastor in Tenn. before he went to Africa as a missionary under SIM. He was a deputation secretary under SIM before leaving it in protest over its drifts. Now he is actively engaged as deputation secretary for the South under Baptist Mid-Missions. Knowledgeable Fundamentalist and separatist. 271

Willis, Homer (1924-). Freewill Baptist pastor: Nashville, 1945-47; Hazel Park, Mich., 1947-52; Pikeville, Ky., 1952-56. Organized a church in Greensboro, N. C. Has been secretary-treasurer of National Home Missions. Now director of evangelism, Free Will Baptists. 244

Wilson, Art (1912-). Pastor, Calvary Baptist, Bellflower, Calif., 1961-62. Founder and pastor, Wichita Baptist Tabernacle, Wichita, Kan., 1938-69. President, BBF 1959-67. Now head of National Church Finance which helps churches secure mortgage financing. 198

Wilson, Grady (1919-). Baptist pastor in Bonneau, Berthers, Summerville, Friendship, and Charleston, S. C. Associate evangelist with the Billy Graham Evangelistic Association since 1947. 274

Wilson, Reford (1924-). Freewill Baptist pastor: Okla., 1948-51; Ark., 1951-56; Mich., 1956-57. Director of foreign missions, National Association of Free Will Baptists since 1962. 245

Wilson, Robert Dick (1856-1930). Presbyterian minister and O. T. scholar. Professor: Pittsburgh Seminary 1880-1900; Princeton Seminary 1900-29; Westminster Seminary 1929-30. Learned linguist. Sound Orthodox teacher and writer. Supported Machen in exposing the Liberalism of the Presbyterian Church, U. S. A. 88, 174, 176, 179, 181

Wilson, Walter L. (1881-1969). Medical doctor, preacher, and writer. Began his practice of medicine in Kansas City in 1904. Founder, Kansas City Bible College (now Calvary College) in 1932. Founder, Central Bible Hall (now Central Bible Church) in 1920. Started a radio broadcast in 1924. Industrious soulwinner. 109, 163

Winchester, A. B. (1858-1943). Canadian Presbyterian minister. Pastor: Kitchener, Ontario; and Knox Church, Toronto, 1901-21. Guest lecturer, Dallas Seminary 1924-31. Bible conference speaker after 1921. A leader in the WCFA. 160

Winrod, Gerald B. (1900-57). Preacher, writer, and lecturer. Founder, The Defenders of the Faith 1925, Salina, Kan. (later moved to Wichita, Kan.). Able debater. Fought evolution and Modernism. Editor, *The Defenders* which had a circulation of 110,000 in 1938. Ran for the U. S. Senate. 162

Wise, Stephen S. (1874-1949). Jewish scholar and rabbi. Born in Hungary. Rabbi of synagogues in N. Y. 1893-1900; Portland, Ore., 1900-06; and the Free Synagogue, N. Y., 1907-49. Editor, *Opinion*. Social reformer. 136

Wishart, Charles F. (1894-1960). Presbyterian minister, Eleventh Street Church, Pittsburgh, 1897-1910. Professor; Pittsburgh Seminary 1910-14; McCormick Seminary 1915-17. Pastor, Second Church, Chicago, 1914-19. President, Wooster College 1919-44. Moderator of the Presbyterian Church, U. S. A. 1923. 178

Witmer, Safari A. (1899-1962). Educator. Professor, Fort Wayne Bible College 1924-43; its dean 1935-42; its president 1945-57. Air Force chaplain 1943-45. Executive director, Accrediting Association of Bible Colleges 1957-62. 70, 71

Woelfkin, Cornelius (1859-1928). Baptist pastor: Bengell, N. Y., 1885-87; Hackensack, N. J., 1882-92; North Church, Jersey City, N. J., 1892-94; Greene Avenue, Brooklyn, N. Y., 1894-1905. Professor, Rochester Sem-

374

inary 1906-12. Pastor, Fifth Avenue Baptist, N. Y. C., 1912-22. In the last pastorate, the church moved to Park Avenue. He fought the Fundamentalists of the NBC and advanced the Modernism of the NBC. 97, 138, 154, 155

Wood, Nathan E. (1849-1937). Baptist pastor: Chicago; Brooklyn; Boston; Brookline, Mass. President, Newton Theological Institution 1899-1909. Pastor, First Baptist, Arlington, Mass., 1909-19 while teaching part-time at Gordon College. A solid Baptist pastor and teacher. 150

Wood, Nathan R. (1874-1961). Northern Baptist educator. President, Gordon College and Gordon Divinity School 1910-44. A conservative denominationalist, hoping that in his friendly understanding way he would keep the NBC more Christian. Instead, his toleration gave the Liberals more time to capture denominational machinery and force the Fundamentalists to leave. 77, 174

Woodbridge, Charles J. (1902-   ). Presbyterian minister, missionary, educator, and Fundamentalist voice. Born of missionary parents in China. Served in Africa. Elected the first secretary of the Independent Board of Presbyterian Foreign Missions. Pastor: Flushing, N. Y.; Savannah, Ga.; Salisbury, N. C. Professor, Fuller Seminary 1950-57. On the staff, Word of Life 1957-64. An open foe of New Evangelicalism. Keen Bible teacher and writer. 88, 180, 181, 190, 203, 204, 205, 237, 254, 258, 280, 281

Woods, Stacey (1909-). General secretary, Inter-Varsity Fellowship in Canada 1934-52. Inter-Varsity Fellowship in the U. S. 1940-60. In 1947, named the general secretary of the International Fellowship of Evangelical Students. His office has been in Lausanne, Switzerland, but his service with the last group ended in 1972. 258

Woychuk, N. A. (1915-). Cumberland Presbyterian pastor: Corsicana, Tex., 1935-38; Dawson, Tex., 1939-43; Shreveport, La., 1943-50. Head, Bible Memory Association and pastor, Cote Brilliante Presbyterian Church, St. Louis, since 1953. 257

Wright, J. Elwin (1896-1965). Evangelical in New England. In 1929 he founded the New England Fellowship with a ministry including a radio work, summer conference at Rumney, N. H., and a bookstore in Boston. Cofounder of the NAE. Secretary, World Evangelical Fellowship 1951-59. In his own quiet way, a New Evangelical. 233

Wycliffe, John (1320-84). English reformer and teacher at Oxford. Opposed transubstantiation and purgatory while still a Roman Catholic; sent out men to preach (Lollards). The Roman Church ordered his bones dug up and burned in 1428. 38

Wyrtzen, Jack (1913-). Youth leader, speaker, and soulwinner. Founder, Word of Life Camps, Schroon Lake, N. Y. Held large youth rallies in this country and abroad. Sound, fervent radio ministry. Strong ministry in South America. 254, 258, 281

Y

Young, Edward J. (1908-68). O. T. scholar and writer. Professor, Westminster Seminary 1937-68. Author, 12 books. Solid Orthodox scholar. 181, 260

Z

Zeoli, Anthony (1898-). Evangelism and Bible conference ministry since 1925. On the radio since 1940. Author, 15 books. Founder and director, The Radio Bible Hour in Philadelphia. 256

Zimmerman, Thomas (1917-). Assemblies of God pastor: Harrisburg, Ind., 1936-37; South Bend, Ind., 1937-40; Granite City, Ill., 1940-43; Springfield, Mo., 1943-46. Has held several offices in the Assemblies of God. General supt. since 1960. 274

Zimmerman, Wendell (1916-). Baptist pastor: Centertown, Ark.; Mo. Founder and pastor, Tabernacle Baptist Church, Joplin, Mo., 1940-43. Founder and pastor, Kansas City Baptist Temple for 25 years. Pastor since 1968, Jacksonville Baptist Temple, Jacksonville, Fla. Very active in the BBF. Has a growing Christian day school. 133, 272

GLOSSARY

A

Advent The first coming of Christ at His incarnation; His second coming; also the season of the year from Advent Sunday to Christmas as observed by liturgical groups.

agnostic Literally means "without absolute knowledge." Thus, one who does not deny the possibility of the existence and being of God but who says he does not have definite knowledge of God.

alien baptism In general, the view of baptism as practiced by groups of another doctrinal persuasion in contrast to that considered the proper mode. Landmark Baptists distinguish between pedo-baptism and alien baptism. Pedo-baptism refers to infant baptism and, therefore, to the modes of sprinkling and pouring. Alien baptism is immersion as practiced by those whose doctrinal persuasion differs from the Landmark position, whether they be Baptists or non-Baptists.

amillennial See **millennial.**

anathema An ecclesiastical term referring to that which is cursed or banned.

Anglican Of or pertaining to the Church of England or to the worldwide communion of episcopal churches patterned after and in fellowship with the Church of England. From a doctrinal perspective the Anglicans are modified Romanists in that they reject the supremacy of the Pope but retain the office of bishop; thus they are episcopal in government. Furthermore, they are modified Calvinists. They reject the Roman teaching that salvation is in and through the sacraments of the church. They also reject some of the teachings of Calvinism. Anglicans—or Episcopalians—have been divided into the high and the low groups. In the latter have

378

been many men of evangelical belief and spiritual depth. However, by now both groups have gone far astray in doctrinal error and ecumenism.

apostasy From the Greek *apostasia* meaning "to desert a post or responsibility." In the Authorized Version it is translated "falling away" (II Thess. 2:3). The context indicates that it means a departure from the correct doctrinal position and, thereupon, a readiness to receive and accept the person and teaching of the man of sin. Today the term refers to the worldwide departure from the authority of the Scriptures in matters of faith and practice.

association A group of churches which unite for collective advantage but which retain local autonomy in government.

atonement The work of our Lord Jesus Christ in the salvation of fallen mankind. The three key ideas embodied in the term are *redemption* (the price paid for man's salvation), *propitiation* (that work of Christ on the cross which satisfied the wrath of God toward sin and justly enables Him to deal in mercy and grace with the sinner), and *reconciliation* (that work of Christ on the cross directed manward whereby the sinner is restored to a place of fellowship with God from his former place as an alien and enemy of God).

Auburn Affirmation A statement of Liberalism and tolerance in the Presbyterian Church which led to a split of the Conservatives and the Liberals.

B

Bema Seat Translated in the Authorized Version "judgment seat." It is the judgment of the believer that will take place after the rapture of the Church but before the Lord's return to earth. Its purpose is to make manifest and deal with the sins of the believer that he has not dealt with in self-judgment. Its purpose is not condemnation but examination and the meting out of rewards.

blasphemy Speaking impiously or profanely of God, claiming or attributing to man that which belongs to God, or ascribing the works of God to Satan.

Buddhism A major Eastern religion following the teachings of Buddha. It teaches salvation by right living and believing and peace of mind through meditation.

C

Calvinism See **Reformed theology.**

charismatic From the Greek *charis* meaning "grace or favor." In the modern charismatic movement, the special gifts are usually restricted to speaking in tongues and healing. Whereas these gifts in the early church met a distinct need for furthering the testimony of the Gospel, today they are all too frequently sought after as an end in themselves. When these gifts are employed today by those who deny the Fundamentals of the Faith, it is evident that the spirit at work is not the Spirit of the Lord but rather an evil spirit. It is clear from Scripture that miracles can be performed through the power of the Evil One (Ex. 7:10-12; Rev. 13:11-15).

chiliasm Same as millennialism. See **millennial.**

Christocentric Bible teaching and preaching that emphasizes the Person and work of Christ. Often used in distinction from *Theocentric,* which emphasizes the Person and work of the Father.

confessions Used synonomously with **creeds.**

Confucianism A major Eastern religion following the teachings of Confucius. It emphasizes ancestor worship, devotion to family and friends, justice, and peace.

Congregational Of or relating to a body of churches formed early in the history of the American colonies which in doctrine essentially followed the Westminster Confession but in government remained autonomous rather than adopting a presbyterian or episcopal system. Congregationism very early in its history became liberal and unitarian in doctrine.

Conservative, Conservatism Individuals and churches professing belief in the Fundamental doctrines of the Faith. Conservatism contrasts with **Fundamentalism** in that it does not militantly contend for the Faith and denounce the errors of the apostasy. The term is often used synonomously with **orthodoxy.**

cooperative evangelism Formerly, an interdenominational union of churches, groups, and individuals of Fundamental, but otherwise divergent, doctrinal persuasion and practice in an evangelistic effort. Now, the inclusivistic evangelism of Billy Graham and others in which liberal churches and churchmen are invited to participate with Fundamental groups in evangelistic efforts. Frequently the message preached is sound enough, but the false impression is conveyed that the participating churches and individuals have the same Fundamental beliefs and purposes. Converts are referred to the cooperating churches irrespective of their soundness of belief.

covenant theology A system of Biblical interpretation which adheres to the following basic tenets: salvation is founded in the sovereign and elective decree of God; the promise of salvation is also for the children of elect parents, since they are in the covenant relationship; saints of the Old Testament, particularly Israel, are essentially one with the Church of the New Testament, which shares in their promises of blessing and their future; the promises to Israel are not meant to be fulfilled in an earthly millennium but rather have a spiritual fulfillment in Heaven.

creeds Doctrinal standards or statements formulated by men expressing their understanding of the major teachings of the Bible. For example, the Westminster Confession of Faith.

D

dispensationalism A system of Biblical interpretation adhering to literalism in interpretation and distinguishing a series of periods in God's dealings with man in which God introduced a succession of tests of responsibilities. In each of these tests of responsibilities man has proved an utter failure when left to himself and so has been thrust upon the grace of God for salvation. The commonly taught dividing points of the dispensations are the Fall, the flood, the call of Abraham, the giving of the Law at Sinai, the Cross, the rapture of the Church, and the return of Christ.

E

ecclesiastical separation See **separation.**

ecclesiasticism Of or relating to the church. Commonly denotes church doctrine and practice which may or may not be in agreement with the Scriptures.

ecumenical movement A movement worldwide in scope. In the religious sense it is the moving together of religious bodies. This is accomplished by dialogue (emphasizing the points of agreement and de-emphasizing the points of doctrinal divergence) and gradualism. The ultimate aim is for all religious groups to be one.

epiphany An appearance or manifestation, particularly of Deity. Expecially, the first appearing of our Lord in His birth and incarnation into this world.

eschatology From the Greek *eschatos,* "last," and *logos,* "word"; thus, last things. The declarations of Scripture concerning the future, especially the end time.

evangelical From the New Testament word *evangellion* which means "gospel" or "good news." Historically, the term describes those who hold that man is a lost sinner and must be saved by the grace of God through faith in the Son of God. As a designation, it has included all groups that have accepted the truths of the Bible as they support the Gospel.

Evangelism-In-Depth A cooperative evangelistic effort sponsored by the Latin America Mission primarily in Latin America but also in the Appalachian area in the United States. The plan is to saturate a country with evangelism for one year by a combination of missionary organizations and enterprises. Its weaknesses are its soliciting of cooperation without regard to purity of doctrine and practice and its removal of the trained leadership from a country, after the year has ended, to the next major area of thrust.

evolution The concept that within all matter and life is a principle which impels development from the simple and undefined to that which is ever more complex and sophisticated.

exegete An individual who studies the Bible by taking the individual words, phrases, and sentences, and drawing out from them their precise meanings.

F

Fatherhood of God The teaching that since God is the Father of all men and loves all men He would not send any of His children to Hell. The term used along with this is *the brotherhood of man.* In the sense that God is the Creator of mankind He is the Father of all. But sin brought alienation from God, and man can claim Him as Father only after the new birth. those who deny or minimize the doctrine of the new birth take comfort in this liberal teaching.

first- and second-degree separation See **separation.**

futurist In prophecy the term denotes the future fulfillment of portions of Scripture. For example, Revelation 4-21.

G

German rationalists German philosophers of the nineteenth century who contended that truth and knowledge are established by reason and not by empirical (experiential) means or by supernatural revelation such as the Scriptures.

Great Tribulation The seven-year period between the rapture of the Church and the visible return of the Lord to the earth (second coming). It corresponds to the seventieth week of Daniel's prophecy and to the events of Revelation 4-18. Its purpose in God's plan is by chastisement to turn the heart of Israel to Himself, judge the nations of the world, and destroy the apostate world church. Fundamentalism holds the pretribulational view that the rapture precedes the Tribulation, which is followed by the second coming. The midtribulational view teaches that the Church will go partway through the Tribulation, which will close with the second coming. The posttribulational view teaches that the Church will go through the Tribulation and be raptured at its close and that the rapture will be followed by the second coming of the Lord to establish His millennial reign.

H

heresy A teaching deviating from the clear expression of Scripture.

Higher Criticism An approach to the Bible taken by nineteenth-century German Biblical scholars and theologians who were strongly influenced by the German rationalism of the times. To a large degree it ruled out the supernatural elements in the Bible and denied the early authorship of the Pentateuch (first five books of the Bible) by Moses and of the prophetical books. It ascribed only human authorship to the Bible and rejected its divine inspiration. It provided the foundation of the Liberalism and Modernism of the twentieth century.

humanism In a religious context, an attitude that emphasizes the importance of human capabilities (especially, reason) and earthly values in opposition to the Christian view of man and the importance of the supernatural.

I

Immaculate Conception The teaching of Rome that the soul of Mary, in her conception, was preserved from original sin.

immanence of God Scripture teaches that God is present everywhere. Some philosophers who reject the God of the Scriptures identify God and nature as one and the same thing (pantheism). Others envisage a world-soul or a rational principle pervading all of the material world and directing it. The Scriptures, however, clearly teach that though God is present everywhere He is of a separate essence from the material world, which is His creation.

inclusivist policy In religion, the inclusion in a body or denomination of individuals who hold opposing convictions, yet maintain tolerant attitudes toward each other. Many Conservatives have remained within liberal denominations, hoping to rescue some that would otherwise be lost. However, this approach gives the appearance of an endorsement of a system of error.

inerrancy The infallibility of the Bible. That is, it is without error in its original manuscripts.

infidel From the Latin *in,* "not," and *fidelis,* "faithful." Thus, one who rejects religious belief, whether Christianity or any other religion.

interdenominationalism A spirit of willingness to overlook minor differences of doctrine or practice in order to achieve some Christian purpose.

internationalism The political thought advocating a central world government in order to bring peace, equity, and justice to all. The theory will be workable only when Christ Himself is the Ruler.

L

Laodicean Refers to the last of the seven churches described in Revelation 2-3, characterized by deadness; thus, "characterized by spiritual coldness and deadness."

Liberalism Religious Liberalism has varied somewhat from country to country. In America it is inseparably identified with the social gospel, which addresses itself to the social needs rather than the heart needs of man. It is derived from the **German rationalists** and **Higher Criticism.** It rejected miracles and the inspiration of the Bible. It sought to harmonize the Scriptures with science. Those who, at the turn of the century, actively contended for these ideas may be designated as Modernists, though in belief they would be classified as Liberals.

M

M and M Fund Ministers' and Missionaries' Fund, a pension fund in the Northern Baptist Convention. Used to discourage members from separating from the Convention.

Methodism The system of belief and practice originated by John and Charles Wesley. Because of their strict and methodical discipline in the Christian life they were dubbed Methodists.

Millennium From *mille* meaning "thousand" and *annus* meaning "year." Scripture teaches that there will be a one-thousand-year reign of Jesus Christ on the earth, characterized by peace, justice, and equity. There are several views of Christ's return in relation to the Millennium. Amillennialists say that there will not be a literal earthly reign of Christ on earth and that the promises of millennial blessing are to be realized in a spiritual sense in Heaven. Premillennialists say that Christ will come back to earth prior to establishing His reign of one thousand years. Post-millennialists say that through the preaching of the Gospel the world will be won to the Lord and that the one-thousand-year era will be consummated by the return of the Lord.

Millerism The teaching of Seventh Day Adventists in regard to future things as propounded by Miller, one of their early leaders.

Modernism See **Liberalism.**

mysticism The attempt to find truth in sources other than sensory perception and written revelation.

N

Nazarene A member of the Church of the Nazarene, whose distinctive doctrine is entire sanctification, specifically that a work of grace subsequent to regeneration cleanses the heart from original sin.

Neo-Orthodoxy A theological position halfway between Conservatism and Liberalism. Because it contains truth along with error, it is more insidious and dangerous than an open espousal of error. The following are its positions on major doctrines. (1) It regards Jesus as the revelation of God, being the Word of God. The written word is human and therefore to a greater or lesser degree contains error. Thus it cannot fully give the revelation of God. (2) It is existential in method. It contends that one must have an experience (divine-human encounter) with God that transcends rational explanation. (3) It does not take the fall of Adam literally; instead it holds that Adam is a figure of all men who fall. (4) It presents nebulous views of the atonement of Christ. (5) It strongly emphasizes the social welfare of man, insisting that the church must give itself to the needs of society rather than merely rescuing individuals out of the muck of society. (6) It considers matters of eschatology to be beyond human analysis; and, consequently, it does not consider the events of Daniel and Revelation to have a literal fulfillment.

New Evangelicalism An attitude or position which professes to adhere to the Fundamentals of the Faith but advocates a spirit of re-examination of the basic doctrines, an attitude of tolerance toward the Liberals and an entering into "dialogue" with them, and an emphasis on the love and mercy of God rather than on His holiness and righteousness.

O

orthodoxy From the Greek *orthos,* "right," and *doxa,* "opinion"; thus "right belief" as opposed to heresy. In this sense the term began to be used in the second century. In a more specific sense, the term refers to an adherence to the central doctrines affirmed by the churches descending from the Reformation and expressed in their **creeds.** For a detailed comparison with *Fundamentalism,* see chapter 10, especially pp. 174-75.

P

patriarchal Referring to the period of the great fathers of the nation of Israel, namely, Abraham, Isaac, and Jacob.

Pietism An unorganized movement beginning in the seventeenth century in Germany because of deadness in the state churches, particularly the Lutheran. Members of the state churches held informal meetings consisting of prayer, Bible study, hymn singing, testimonies, and expressions of a deepened spiritual life. Its influence continued into the eighteenth and nineteenth centuries through the Moravians and the Wesleys and the University of Halle.

positive thinking An approach to spiritual health, popularized by Norman Vincent Peale, which stresses the importance of mental attitudes to the achievement of proper and desirable modes of life.

posttribulational See **Great Tribulation.**

predestination A theological doctrine commonly associated with Calvinism which states that God has foreordained all things which come to pass, including the final salvation of certain men and also, according to some, the final reprobation of others.

presbytery The second level of governmental authority in the presbyterian system. The session is the first level over the local church, and the second level is the presbytery, which is over several sessions and their respective churches.

pretribulational See **Great Tribulation.**

prophecy The message of a prophet, foretelling that which God has revealed to the prophet shall come to pass or declaring the Word of God to His people. The minister of God today is a prophet in the second sense in that he is a proclaimer or preacher of that which God has declared, including things to come.

puritanism A movement originating in England within the established church in reaction to the Act of Uniformity of 1559. Its Calvinistic writers and leaders particularly advocated stricter discipline and better preaching. The pilgrims brought it to America, where it exercised an influence on seventeenth and eighteenth century life toward austere, holy living.

Q

Quaker "inner light" The prompting of the Holy Spirit in the heart of the person, directing him in what he should say or do. The danger is that the person may mistake his own inclinations or the moving of a false spirit for the leading of the Holy Spirit. Those stressing the "inner light" looked for leading beyond—and sometimes in disregard of—the explicit instructions of the written Word.

R

rapture The return of the Lord to take to Himself the Church. The event includes the resurrection of the bodies of the dead in Christ and the changing of the bodies of those who are alive. It is not to be confused with His *second coming*, which will be visible to all, when He returns to earth to set up His millennial reign. The rapture precedes the Tribulation, and the second coming is at its close and precedes the Millennium.

Reformed theology The system of theology developed by the Reformers, the most notable of whom was John Calvin. Calvinism adheres to the doctrines of total depravity, unconditional election, limited atonement, irresistible grace, and perseverance of the saints. Reformed theology also includes covenant teaching (see **covenant theology**). Evangelicals have appreciated Calvinism's insistence on the inspiration of the Bible and the doctrines of sin and grace. Many evangelicals have differed with the Reformed systems on the issues of election and the human will.

revelation The revelation of God to man is both natural (the witness of creation) and supernatural. Supernatural revelation includes God's revelation of Himself through the Incarnate Word (the Lord Jesus Christ) and the written Word (the Scriptures). The supernatural inspiration of the written revelation has been insistently attacked by Higher Criticism and liberal theology.

S

sectarian Of or relating to the teaching of a particular system of belief.

separation The Biblical principle that the believer is to keep himself unspotted from the world is called personal separation. Ecclesiastical separation refers either to an individual's separating himself from a church that endorses or condones apostasy or to a local church's separating itself from a denomination or association that endorses or condones apostasy. First-degree separation is the refusal of Christian fellowship to a person or group of persons who condone or practice wrongdoing. Second-degree separation is the refusal of Christian fellowship to a person or group of persons who, though standing for what is right, nevertheless continues fellowship with one who walks in error.

the sinner to secure his forgiveness and impute to him righteousness. Also, *vicarious.*

syncretism Literally "combination." In a religious context, the efforts of various bodies of Christendom to merge into ever larger bodies, with a one-world church as the ultimate goal. *Syncretism* also may refer to efforts to harmonize Christian and non-Christian thought.

T

theology From the Greek *theos,* "God," and *logos,* "word." The systematized body of truth dealing with God, His creation, and the relationship between God and His creation.

tribulational See **Great Tribulation.**

Trinity Literally, "three." In theology it is the teaching that God exists as three distinct persons—Father, Son, and Holy Spirit—yet one in essence. A paradox without any sufficient human analogy.

U

unitarianism The view which rejects the trinitarian view of God as being in three persons yet one in essence. It is characterized by freedom of thought and a humanistic view of man.

V

vicarious See **substitutionary.**

SELECTIVE BIBLIOGRAPHY

The following list is necessarily selective. It aims simply to include representative works by spokesmen for the major theological positions and attitudes discussed in the preceding chapters, as well as some of the more important accounts of aspects of the Fundamentalist movement. It is offered with the hope that an exhaustive listing and gathering of sources relevant to the history of Fundamentalism will be attempted soon. Much of the valuable material for a thorough study of Fundamentalism is in the form of tracts and pamphlets; articles in church papers and small religious periodicals; unpublished sermons, lectures, addresses, and reports; and accounts of debates on Bible themes. A concerted effort is long overdue to identify and collect these materials before they are irretrievably lost.

A list of dissertations and theses has been appended as an aid to further research.

Adair, James R. *The Life of M. R. DeHaan.* Grand Rapids: Zondervan, 1969.

Atkins, C. G. *Religion in Our Times.* New York: Round Table, 1932.

Allen, James H. *Our Liberal Movement in Theology.* 1892; rpt. New York: Arno, 1972.

Allen, L. K. *Bryan and Darrow at Dayton.* New York: Lee, 1925.

Ashbrook, William E. *The New Neutralism.* Columbus, Ohio: the author, 1969.

Atkins, C. G. *Religion in Our Times.* New York: Round Table, 1932

Ayer, William Ward. *God's Answers to Man's Doubts.* Grand Rapids: Zondervan, 1943.

Barabas, Steven. *So Great Salvation.* New York: Revell, 1957.

Bartlett, Billy Vick. *A History of Baptist Separatism.* Springfield, Mo.: Roark, 1972.

Biederwolf, William E. *The New Paganism.* Grand Rapids: Eerdmans, 1934.

B[lackstone], W. E. *Jesus Is Coming.* New York: Revell, 1908.

Boettner, Loraine. *Roman Catholicism.* Philadelphia: Presbyterian and Reformed, 1950.

Bridges, J. H. *"The God of Fundamentalism" and Other Studies.* Chicago: Pascal Covici, 1925.

Briggs, Charles A. *The Authority of Holy Scripture.* New York: Scribner's, 1891.

_____. *The Fundamental Christian Faith.* New York: Scribner's, 1913.

Brink, G. N. *Baptist Fundamentals.* Philadelphia: Judson, 1920.

Brown, William Adams. *The Essence of Christianity.* New York: Scribner's, 1902.

Bryan, William Jennings. *Orthodox Christianity Versus Modernism.* New York: Revell, 1902.

Carroll, B. H. *Ecclesia—The Church.* Ashland, Ky.: Baptist Examiner, n.d.

Cauthen, Kenneth. *The Impact of American Religious Liberalism.* New York: Harper, 1962.

Cavert, S. M. *Church Cooperation and Unity in America, 1900-1970.* New York: Association, 1970.

_____. *The American Churches in the Ecumenical Movement.* New York: Association, 1968.

Chafer, Lewis Sperry. *Systematic Theology.* Dallas: Dallas Theological Seminary, 1947.

Clarke, William Newton. *An Outline of Christian Theology.* New York: Scribner's, 1894.

Clearwaters, Richard V. *Forty Years of History Look Down on Conservative Baptists.* Minneapolis: Central Baptist, n.d.

Cole, Stewart. *A History of Fundamentalism.* New York: Smith, 1931.

Conrad, Arcturus Z. *Jesus Christ at the Crossroads.* New York: Revell, 1924.

Cross, I. K. *What Is the American Baptist Association?* Texarkana: Sunday School Committee, n.d.

_____. *The Church Local or Universal?* Texarkana: Sunday School Committee, n.d.

_____. *Who Are We?* Texarkana: Sunday School Committee, n.d.

Curtis, Richard V. *They Called Him Mr. Moody.* New York: Doubleday, 1962.

Darwin, Charles. *The Origin of Species.* New York: Dutton, 1948.

Diffenbach, Albert. *Religious Liberty: The Great American Illusion.* New York: Morrow, 1927.

Dillenberger, John, and Claude Welch. *Protestant Christianity.* New York: Scribner's, 1954.

Eddy, George Sherwood. *Religion and Social Justice.* New York: Doran, 1927.

English, E. Schuyler. *H. A. Ironside, Ordained of the Lord.* Grand Rapids: Zondervan, 1946.

Entzminger, Louis. *The J. Frank Norris I Have Known for 34 Years.* Fort Worth: The Fundamentalist, 1947.

Erdman, William J. *The Niagara Conference.* N.p., n.d.

Erickson, Millard. *New Evangelical Theology.* Westwood, N. J.: Revell, 1968.

Fairhurst, A. *Atheism in Our Universities.* Cincinnati: Standard, 1923.

Faulkner, J. A. *Modernism and the Christian Faith.* New York: Methodist Book Concern, 1921.

Feinberg, Charles L. *The Fundamentals for Today.* Grand Rapids: Kregel, 1958.

Ferm, Robert O. *Cooperative Evangelism.* Grand Rapids: Zondervan, 1958.

Fosdick, H. E. *A Guide to the Understanding of the Bible.* New York: Harper, 1938.

_____. *The Living of These Days.* New York: Harper, 1956.

_____. *The Modern Use of the Bible.* New York: Macmillan, 1924.

_____. *New Knowledge.* An abridgement of a sermon "Shall the Fundamentalists Win?" New York: Harper, 1922.

_____, ed. *Rufus Jones Speaks to Our Times: An Anthology.* New York: Macmillan, 1879.

Foster, Frank H. *A Genetic History of New England Theology.* New York: Russell and Russell, 1963.

Froom, Leroy. *The Prophetic Faith of Our Fathers.* Washington, D. C.: Review and Herald, 1954.

Frothingham, Octavius B. *Religion of Humanity.* 1875; rpt. Univ. of Pennsylvania Press, 1972.

The Fundamentals, 1900-1919. Ed. A. C. Dixon. Chicago: Testimony, 1912.

Fundamental Baptist Congress of North America. Des Plaines, Ill.: Regular Baptist Press, 1966.

Furniss, Norman. *The Fundamentalist-Modernist Controversy.* New Haven: Yale Univ. Press, 1954.

Gabriel, R. W. *Christianity and Modern Thought.* New Haven: Yale Univ. Press, 1924.

Gaddis, Vincent, and John A. Huffman. *The Winona Lake Story.* Winona Lake, Ind.: Winona Lake Assembly, 1960.

Garman, W. O. H. *Where Does Your Church Stand?* Pittsburgh: Associated Gospel Churches, n.d.

Gasper, Louis. *The Fundamentalist Movement.* Paris: Mouton, 1963.

Gatewood, Thomas. *Controversy in the Twenties.* Nashville: Vanderbilt Press, 1969.

Gaussen, L. *The Inspiration of the Holy Scriptures.* Trans. D. D. Scott. Chicago: Moody Press, 1949.

Giboney, E. P., and Agnes Potter. *The Life of Mark Matthews.* Grand Rapids: Eerdmans, 1948.

Gilbert, Dan. *Crucifying Christ in Our Colleges.* San Diego: Danielle, 1935.

_____. *Our Retreat from Modernism.* Findlay, Ohio: Fundamental Truth, 1948.

Gillentine, E. C. *What We Believe.* Texarkana: Sunday School Committee, n.d.

Gladden, Washington. *Applied Christianity.* Boston: Houghton Mifflin, 1893.

Glover, Robert H. *The Progress of World Wide Missions.* Rev. J. H. Kane. New York: Harper, 1924.

Gordon, Adoniram Judson. *Ecce Venit (Behold He Cometh).* London: Thynne, 1894.

_____. *If Christ Came to Church.* Philadelphia: American Publication Society, 1895.

_____. *The Ministry of the Spirit.* New York: Revell, 1894.

Gordon, Ernest B. *A. J. Gordon: A Biography.* New York: Revell, 1896.

_____. *An Ecclesiastical Octopus.* Boston: Fellowship Press, 1948.

_____. *The Leaven of the Sadducees.* Chicago: Moody Colportage, 1926.

Gordon, George A. *A New Epoch of Faith.* Boston: Houghton Mifflin, 1901.

Graves, John R. *Old Landmarkism: What Is It?* 1880; rpt. Ashland, Ky.: Baptist Examiner, n.d.

Grounds, Vernon C. *Seminary Studies.* Denver: Conservative Baptist Theological Seminary, n.d.

Haldeman, I. M. *Why I Am Opposed to Modernism.* New York: Fitch, 1929.

Harden, Margaret. *A Brief History of the Bible Presbyterian Church.* Collingswood, N. J.: Christian Beacon, 1966.

Harnack, Adolph. *What Is Christianity?* New York: Putnam, 1901.

Hebert, Gabriel. *Fundamentalism and the Church.* Philadelphia: Westminister Press, 1957.

Henry, Carl F. H. *Fifty Years of Protestant Theology.* Boston: Wilde, 1960.

_____. *The Uneasy Conscience of Modern Fundamentalism.* Grand Rapids: Eerdmans, 1947.

Henry, J. M. *A New Fundamentalism.* Chicago: Macmillan, 1924.

Hills, A. M. *Fundamental Christian Theology.* Pasadena: Kinne, 1931.

Hopkins, C. H. *The Rise of the Social Gospel in America.* New Haven: Yale Univ. Press, 1940.

Hersch, John. *Modern Religious Liberalism.* Chicago: Moody Press, 1925.

Ingwalson, K. W. *Your Church—Their Target: A Symposium by Thirteen Eminent Authorities.* Arlington, Va.: Better Books, 1966.

Ironside, Henry Allan. *A Historical Sketch of the Brethren Movement:* Grand Rapids: Zondervan, 1942.

_____. *The Lamp of Prophecy.* Grand Rapids: Zondervan, 1940.

Johnson, J. W. *Fundamentalism Versus Modernism.* New York: Century, 1925.

Johnson, R. K. *Builder of Bridges.* Murfreesboro, Tenn.: Sword of the Lord, 1969.

Jones, Bob. *Things I Have Learned.* New York: Loiseaux, 1944.

Jones, Bob, Jr. *Scriptural Separation.* Greenville, S. C.: Bob Jones Univ. Press, 1971.

Jorstad, Erling T. *Politics of Doomsday: The Fundamentalists of the Far Right.* Nashville: Abingdon, 1970.

Kane, J. Herbert. *A Global View of Christian Missions.* Grand Rapids: Baker, 1971.

Ketcham, Robert T. *The Answer.* 4th ed. Des Plaines, Ill.: Regular Baptist Press, 1965.

Keyser, L. S. *Contending for the Faith.* New York: Doran, 1920.

Lightner, Robert P. *New Evangelicalism.* Des Plaines, Ill.: Regular Baptist Press, 1954.

Loetscher, Lefferts A. *The Broadening Church.* Philadelphia: Univ. of Pennsylvania Press, 1954.

Macartney, Clarence E. *The Making of a Ministry.* Great Neck, N. Y.: Channel, 1961.

McCann, Alfred Watterson. *God or Gorilla.* New York: Devin-Adair, 1922.

McGiffert, Arthur Cushman. *The Rise of Modern Religious Ideas.* New York: Macmillan, 1915.

Machen, J. Gresham. *The Christian Faith in the Modern World.* New York: Macmillan, 1936.

——. *Christianity and Liberalism.* New York: Macmillan, 1926.

——. *The Origin of Paul's Religion.* 1925; rpt. Grand Rapids: Eerdmans, 1947.

——. *What Is Faith?* New York: Macmillan, 1926.

McIntire, Carl. *The Modern Tower of Babel.* Collingswood, N. J.: Christian Beacon, 1950.

——. *Servants of Apostasy.* Collingswood, N. J.: Christian Beacon, 1955.

——. *Twentieth Century Reformation.* Collingswood, N. J.: Christian Beacon, 1946.

McLoughlin, William G. *The American Evangelicals.* New York: Harper, 1968.

McPherson, G. W. *Crises in the Churches and Colleges.* Yonkers, N. Y.: the author, 1919.

Manning, W. T. *Fundamentalism or Modernism.* Washington, D. C.: National Cathedral, 1923.

Marty, Martin. *The New Shape of American Religion.* New York: Harper, 1959.

Massee, J. C. *The Second Coming.* Philadelphia: Philadelphia School of the Bible, 1923.

Matthews, Shailer. *The Faith of Modernism.* New York: Macmillan, 1924.

——. *New Faith for the Old.* New York: Doran, 1920.

Miller, Andrew. *The Brethren: Their Origin, Progress, and Testimony.* Hong Kong: Empire, 1963.

Morrison, H. C. *Crossing the Deadline.* Louisville, Ky.: Pentecostal Publishing Company, 1924.

Munhall, L. W. *The Lord's Return.* Germantown, Pa.: E. and E. Munhall, 1888.

Murch, James D. *Cooperation Without Compromise.* Grand Rapids: Eerdmans, 1956.

——. *The Growing Super Church.* Cincinnati: The National Association of Evangelicals, 1952.

Nash, A. S. *Protestant Thought in the Twentieth Century.* New York: Macmillan, 1951.

Nash, Ronald. *New Evangelicalism.* Grand Rapids: Zondervan, 1963.

Needham, George C., ed. *Prophetic Studies of the International Prophetic Conference.* New York: Revell, 1886.

Niebuhr, H. Richard. *The Kingdom of God in America.* Chicago: Wilmette Clark, 1937.

Niebuhr, Reinhold. *The Nature and Destiny of Man.* New York: Scribner's, 1964.

Norris, J. Frank. *The Inside Story of the First Baptist Church, Fort Worth, and Temple Baptist Church, Detroit.* Detroit: Temple Baptist Church, 1938.

——. *A Tale of Two Churches, or Inside the Cup.* Fort Worth: The Fundamentalist, n.d.

The Norris-Wallace Debate. Fort Worth: Fundamental Publishing Company, 1935

Packer, J. I. *Fundamentalism and the Word of God.* Grand Rapids: Eerdmans, 1959.

Parks, Leighton. *What Is Modernism?* New York: Scribner's, 1924.

Patterson, A. L. *The American Baptist Association.* Texarkana: Sunday School Committee, n.d.

Patton, F. L. *Fundamental Christianity.* New York: Macmillan, 1926.

Peale, Norman Vincent. *The Power of Positive Thinking.* New York: Prentice-Hall, 1954.

Pentecost, J. Dwight. *Things To Come.* Findlay, Ohio: Dunham, 1958.

Peters, George N. H. *The Theocratic Kingdom.* New York: Funk and Wagnalls, 1884.

Premillennial Studies of the International Prophetic Conference. New York: Revell, 1878.

Ramm, Bernard. *The Christian View of Science and the Scriptures.* Grand Rapids: Eerdmans, 1954.

Rauschenbusch, Walter. *Christianity and the Social Crisis.* New York: Macmillan, 1906.

_____. *The Theology of the Social Gospel.* New York: Macmillan, 1917.

Rian, Edwin H. *The Presbyterian Conflict.* Grand Rapids: Eerdmans, 1940.

Rice, John R. *Our God-Breathed Book—The Bible.* Murfreesboro, Tenn.: Sword of the Lord, 1969.

Riley, Marie. *The Dynamic of a Dream.* Grand Rapids: Eerdmans, 1938.

Riley, William B. *The Conflict of Christianity with Counterfeits.* Minneapolis: I. Woods, 1940.

_____. *The Crisis of the Church.* New York: Cook, 1914.

_____. *The Menace of Modernism.* New York: Christian Alliance, 1917.

Rimmer, Harry. *The Harmony of Science and Scripture.* Grand Rapids: Eerdmans, 1940.

Roy, Ralph L. *The Apostles of Discord.* Boston: Beacon Press, 1953.

Runyan, William Marion. *The Life of Dr. Gray at Moody Bible Institute.* New York: Oxford Press, 1935.

Sandeen, Ernest. *The Roots of Fundamentalism: British and American Millenarianism, 1800-1930.* Chicago: Univ. of Chicago Press, 1970.

Schleiermacher, F. D. E. *Discourses on Religion.* Trans. John Oman. New York: Harper, 1958.

Seiss, Joseph A. *The Apocalypse.* Philadelphia: Philadelphia School of the Bible, 1865.

Sheldon, Charles M. *In His Steps.* New York: Revell, 1921.

Shelley, Bruce. *A History of Conservative Baptists.* Denver: Conservative Baptist Seminary, 1960.

Shields, T. T. *Other Little Ships.* Toronto: Hunter, 1935.

_____. *The Plot That Failed.* Toronto: Gospel Witness, 1937.

Shimeall, R. C. *The Second Coming of Christ.* New York: Goodspeed, 1873.

Shipley, Maynard. *The War on Modern Science: A Short History of the Fundamentalist Attack on Evolution and Modernism.* New York: Knopf, 1927.

Smith, Gipsy [Rodney]. *As Jesus Passed By.* New York: Revell, 1905.

Smith, H. Shelton, R. H. Handy, and L. A. Loetscher. *American Christianity.* 2 vols. New York: Scribner's, 1963.

Smith, Wilbur M. *Therefore Stand.* Boston: Wilde, 1945.

Smyth, Egbert C. *Progressive Orthodoxy.* Boston: *Andover Review* editors, 1886.

Smyth, Newman. *Old Faith in New Light*. New York: Scribner's, 1879.
Sodergren, C. J. *Fundamentalism and Modernism*. Rock Island, Ill.: Augustana Book Concern, 1925.
Sterrett, J. M. *Modernism in Religion*. New York: Macmillan, 1922.
Stevick, D. B. *Beyond Fundamentalism*. Richmond, Va.: John Knox, 1964.
Stonehouse, Ned B. *J. Gresham Machen: A Biographical Memoir*. Grand Rapids: Eerdmans, 1955.
Stott, J. R. W. *Fundamentalism and Evangelicalism*. Grand Rapids: Eerdmans, 1959.
Stowell, Joseph M. *A History of the General Association of Regular Baptist Churches*. Hayward, Calif.: Gospel Tracts, 1949.
Straton, John Roach. *The Battle over the Bible*. New York: Doran, 1924.
———. *The Famous New York Fundamentalist-Modernist Debates*. New York: Doran, 1925.
———. *Fighting the Devil in Modern Babylon*. Boston: Stratford, 1929.
Strauss, David. *A Life of Jesus*. Trans. George Eliot. 1835; rpt. New York: Fortress, 1972.
Strong, Josiah. *Our Country*. New York: American Home Missionary Society, 1885.
Sumner, Robert L. *A Man Sent from God*. Grand Rapids: Eerdmans, 1959.
Sweet, William Warren. *The Story of Religion in America*. New York: Harper, 1939.
Talbot, Louis T. *God's Plan of the Ages*. Grand Rapids: Eerdmans, 1946.
Tarr, Leslie K. *Shields of Canada*. Toronto: Gospel Witness, 1967.
Tatum, Ray. *Conquest or Failure: A Biography of J. Frank Norris*. Dallas: Baptist Historical Foundation, 1966.
Torrey, R. A. *Higher Criticism and the New Theology*. New York: Gospel Publishing House, 1920.
Tulga, Chester A. *The Case Against Modernism*. Chicago: Conservative Baptist Fellowship, 1949.
———. *The Foreign Missions Controversy in the Northern Baptist Convention*. Chicago: Conservative Baptist Fellowship, 1950.
Van Til, Cornelius. *The New Modernism*. Philadelphia: Presbyterian and Reformed Publishing Company, 1947.
Vanderlaan, E. C. *Fundamentalism Versus Modernism*. New York: Wilson, 1925.
Walvoord, John F. *The Revelation*. Chicago: Moody Press, 1966.
Warfield, Benjamin Breckenridge. *The Inspiration of the Holy Scriptures*. 1927; rpt. Philadelphia: Presbyterian and Reformed Publishing Company, 1948.
———. *Miracles, Yesterday and Today*. Grand Rapids: Eerdmans, 1965.
Weisberger, Bernard A. *They Gathered at the River*. Boston: Little Brown, 1958.
West, Nathaniel. *Premillennial Studies of the International Prophetic Conference*. New York: Revell, 1879.
———. *The Thousand Years*. Chicago: Revell, 1880.
Williams, D. D. *The Andover Liberals: A Study in American Theology*. New York: Octagon, 1970.
Wilson, Talmadge. *Freeway to Babylon*. Seattle: the author, 1966.
Winrod, Gerald B. *Christ Within*. Wichita: Defenders, 1928.
Witmer, Safari A. *Education with Dimension*. New York: Channel, 1962.
Wood, Nathan R. *A School of Christ*. Boston: Gordon College, 1953.

Woodbridge, Charles J. *Biblical Separation*. Halifax, Canada: People's Gospel Hour, 1971.

_____. *Campus Crusade*. Greenville, S. C.: Bob Jones Univ. Press, 1970.

_____. *The New Evangelicalism*. Greenville, S. C.: Bob Jones Univ. Press, 1969.

Wooley, D. C. *The Baptist Advance*. Nashville: Broadman, 1964.

Wright, Melton. *Fortress of Faith*. Grand Rapids: Eerdmans, 1960.

Young, Edward J. *Thy Word Is Truth*. Grand Rapids: Eerdmans, 1957.

Unpublished Dissertations and Theses

Behney, J. B. "Conservatism and Liberalism in the Late Nineteenth Century." Ph.D., Yale Univ., 1941.

Bevier, W. A. "A History of the Independent Fundamental Churches of America." Th.D., Dallas Theological Seminary, 1957.

Bindschedler, Ernest. "Revelation and Faith: A Comparison Between the Fundamentals of Machen and the Theology of Crisis of Brunner." Th.D., Union Theological Seminary, 1927.

Boon, Harold. "A History of the Bible Colleges and Institutes." Ph.D., New York Univ., 1950.

Carlberg, R. L. "The Development of the Centralization Trend in the Northern Baptist Convention." Th.M., Eastern Baptist Seminary.

Cockran, Bernard. "W. N. Clarke, Exponent of the New Theology." Ph.D., Duke Univ., 1961.

Delnay, Robert G. "A History of the Baptist Bible Union." Th.D., Dallas Theological Seminary, 1963.

Harrington, C. E. "The Fundamentalist Movement in America." Ph.D., Univ. of California, 1959.

Houghton, George G. "The Contributions of A. J. Gordon to American Christianity." Th.D., Dallas Theological Seminary, 1970.

Hull, Lloyd. "A Rhetorical Study of the Preaching of W. B. Riley." Ph.D., Wayne State Univ., 1960.

James, Edgar C. "The Theological Distinctives of New Evangelicalism." Th.M., Dallas Theological Seminary, 1959.

Jones, Bob, Jr. "American Evangelism." M.A., Univ. of Pittsburgh, 1933.

Livingstone, William D. "The Princeton Apologetic as Exemplified in the Work of Benjamin B. Warfield and J. Gresham Machen." Ph.D., Yale Univ., 1948.

McBirnie, R. S. "Basic Issues in the Fundamentalism of W. B. Riley." Ph.D., Univ. of Iowa, 1952.

Moulds, George H. "The Conflict Between the Fundamentalists and the Modernists in the Northern Baptist Convention." M.A., Univ. of Iowa, 1940.

Nelson, Roland. "Fundamentalism and the Northern Baptist Convention." Ph.D., Univ. of Chicago, 1964.

Patterson, T. A. "The Theology of John R. Graves." Th.D., Southwestern Baptist Theological Seminary, 1944.

Ritchie, Homer G. "The Life and Career of J. Frank Norris." M.A., Texas Christian Univ., 1967.

Terre-Blanche, Henry S. "The Life of J. Frank Norris." Th.M., Dallas Theological Seminary, 1966.

Tinder, Donald George. "Fundamentalist Baptists in the Northern and Western United States." Ph.D., Yale Univ., 1972.

Weaver, Donald A. "The Theological Deviations of the New Evangelicalism." Th.M., Dallas Theological Seminary, 1962.

GENERAL INDEX

L

Landmark Baptist Temple (Cincinnati), 218, 219, 220, 272, 277
Landmarkers, 57, 214, 215, 241
Landmarkism, What Is It?, 214
Latin American Mission, 272, 273, 287
Lawrence University, 45, 50
Leaven of the Sadducees, The, 19, 25, 100
LeTourneau College, 285
Liberalism, 2, 3, 4, 10, 12, 21, 85, 87, 91, 93, 97, 98, 105, 156, 174, 178, 190, 222, 236, 249, 264
Liberals, 141, 145, 146, 149, 167, 251, 275, 279
Life of Jesus, 8
Life of Mark Matthews, 179
"Light on Prophecy," 159
Los Angeles Baptist Bible College, 222
Los Angeles Baptist Seminary, 209, 222
Los Angeles Fellowship, 79
Lucerne Christian Conference Center, 211, 232, 262
Lutheran Churches, 47, 276
Lutheran Hour, 195, 255

M

McCormick Theological Seminary, 45, 55, 68, 179
McKinney Avenue Baptist Church (Dallas), 122
McMaster University, 87, 106, 107, 108, 109, 167
Madison Avenue Baptist Church (New York), 94
Madison Square Presbyterian Church (New York), 95
Making of a Minister, The, 176
M and M Fund, 148
Maranatha Baptist Bible College, 155, 195, 232, 246, 284
Maranatha Baptist Mission, 286
Maranatha Bible Conference, 261
Mariners' Temple, (New York), 94
Marquette Manor Baptist Church (Chicago), 155, 229
Massachusetts Baptist Convention, 26

Massillon Baptist Temple (Massillon, Ohio), 226
Menace of Modernism, The, 111, 113, 114, 115, 117, 119
Mercer University, 131, 135
Methodist Challenge, The, 190
Methodist Churches, 47, 174, 191, 248, 275
Methodists, 174, 179, 190, 191, 213, 247-48, 249
Metropolitan Baptist Church (Washington, D. C.), 167
Metropolitan Tabernacle (London), 205
Michigan Orthodox Baptist Association, 144
Mid-Atlantic Christian School Association, 259
Midwest Association of Christian Teachers, 259
Midwest Association of Evangelical Schools, 259
Midwestern Baptist College, 195, 232, 284
Millerism, 74
Ministry of Healing, The, 22
Ministry of the Holy Spirit, The, 20, 21
Minneapolis Congress, 209
Minnesota Baptist Convention, 116, 155, 232
Miracles, Yesterday and Today, 22
Missionary Aviation, 226
Missionary Internship, 287
Missionary Letter Service, 236
Missionary Review of the World, The, 20
Missionary Union of Baptist Churches, 171
Missions to the Military, 286
Missouri Synod (Lutheran), 255, 276
Modern Use of the Bible, The, 95, 96
Modernism, 19, 108, 113, 114, 115, 117, 118, 119, 121, 129, 139, 147, 152, 164, 166, 218, 222, 236, 251
Modernists, 161, 163
Modern Tower of Babel, The, 239
Montanists, 215

DATE DUE

MAR 3 '76	APR 0 2 2003	
MAR 15 '77	SEP 0 8 2005	
APR 11 '77	MAR 13 2006	
JUN 29 '77	OCT 2 2 2007	
NOV 3 '77	OCT 2 6 2007	
NOV 15 '77	APR 0 4 2012	
AUG 7 '78		
AUG 8 '78		
NOV 14 '80		
FEB 18 1985		
MAR 04 1985		
MAR 20 1985		
APR 04 1985		
APR 30 1985		
I.L.L. # 4/198748		
APR 1 0		
OCT 2 5		

30 505 JOSTEN'S